LabVIEW®
Graphical
Programming

Practical Applications in Instrumentation and Control

Gary W. Johnson
Electronics Engineering Department
Lawrence Livermore National Laboratories

McGraw-Hill, Inc.
New York   San Francisco   Washington, D.C.   Auckland   Bogotá
Caracas   Lisbon   London   Madrid   Mexico City   Milan
Montreal   New Delhi   San Juan   Singapore
Sydney   Tokyo   Toronto

Library of Congress Cataloging-in-Publication Data

Johnson, Gary W.
    LabVIEW graphical programming : practical applications in
  instrumentation and control / Gary W. Johnson.
      p.   cm. — (Visual technology series)
    Includes index.
    ISBN 0-07-032692-4
    1. LabVIEW.   2. Scientific apparatus and instruments—Computer
  simulation.   3. Computer graphics.   I. Title.   II. Series.
  Q185.J64   1994
  006—dc20   94-11516
                                                         CIP

LabVIEW and National Instruments are registered trademarks of National
Instruments Corporation. All other product and company names are
trademarks or trade names of their respective companies.

    3 4 5 6 7 8 9 0   DOC/DOC   9 0 9 8 7 6 5

ISBN 0-07-032719-X
PART OF
ISBN 0-07-032692-4

*The sponsoring editor for this book was Daniel Gonneau, the editing supervisor
was Fred Bernardi, and the production supervisor was Donald Schmidt.*

Printed and bound by R. R. Donnelley & Sons Company.

Table of Contents

Chapter One
Roots

Chapter Two
Inputs and Outputs

Chapter Three
LabVIEW Programming Techniques

Chapter Four
Building an Application

Chapter Five
Instrument Drivers

Chapter Six
Using the DAQ Library

Chapter Seven
Writing a Data Acquisition Program

Chapter Eight
Process Control Applications

Chapter Nine
Physics Applications

Chapter Ten
Data Visualization and Image Processing

Chapter Eleven
Automated Test Applications

Appendix A
Guide to Platform Dependency

Appendix B
Index to VIs on the Accompanying Diskette

Appendix C
Sources

Foreword

I have known Gary since the dawn of the LabVIEW era. He was one of the early pioneer users of LabVIEW 1 (the Jurassic version), all of whom deserve Purple Hearts for their efforts. For years Gary has participated in the evolution of LabVIEW by providing valuable feedback on his experiences using it in numerous applications, and by offering many thoughtful suggestions and an occasional stinging critique. He has built and rebuilt uncountable VIs, always striving for the most lucid diagram. I can't think of anyone more qualified to write a LabVIEW book.

The LabVIEW developers always wanted a book, but none of us wanted to write one. We were too busy designing and implementing the next version of the software to write a book. Also, most of us enjoy writing about as much as we enjoy public speaking, toothaches, and migraines. I suspect that any user who considered writing a book probably figured he would be spending most of the time apologizing for LabVIEW shortcomings rather than expounding on productivity enhancements ("of course wires should stretch when you move something, but until that's implemented..."; or, "while you wait for the VI to load..."; and so on). When we released LabVIEW 2, the time was ripe for a book, and when we released the PC version, the urgency peaked. Gary took on the challenge, all the more difficult because LabVIEW was (and still is) a moving target, and he no doubt lost sleep in the process.

LabVIEW 1 was a revolutionary product, but it only hinted at what might be possible. It was underpowered and underfeatured, yet it truly inspired people. And that inspiration led them to attempt applications that we never thought possible. It was a strange experience to be congratulated for our creativity and innovation but then pummeled for not having done this or that, not being fast enough, requiring too much memory, and so on. Users dismissed our protests that we never intended LabVIEW to be used that way as irrelevant. How could we argue? After all, we had had the same visions internally within the LabVIEW development team. We just didn't expect such a sudden and overwhelming response from our customers.

Thanks to Gary, and to many users like him, we have made numerous enhancements and refinements to LabVIEW since its introduction. The suggestions and complaints of users, and perhaps most importantly, their unbounded patience and enthusiasm, were all invaluable. But even with the release of LabVIEW 3, there are still aspects of the original vision not yet implemented. Even though the code has tripled in size, and the feature set has grown dramatically, the list of user requests seems to be just as large as ever, maybe even larger. So much code to write, so little time.

I can't conclude without mentioning that the Macintosh was a key inspiration for the invention of LabVIEW and that it continues to exert a profound influence on the development team. As I sit here editing on my Quadra 610 while it plays a Chopin CD in the background, I have to chuckle at the naïveté and enthusiasm we embraced as we developed LabVIEW 1 on the Macintosh 512K. It was a formidable task—daunting for those of us with a UNIX background - but we knew the Mac was the only machine that could produce the result we envisioned. And we were absolutely convinced that the Mac philosophy is right—simply stated, the user's time is much more valuable than the developer's. A decade later, with the broad availability of Microsoft Windows 3 and machines to run it, this philosophy has become conventional wisdom. There is a great opportunity to apply it more broadly.

Gary has done a superb job in describing LabVIEW and a variety of applications that can be built upon it. His relaxed style is a pleasure to read, tricking you into learning something without really making an effort. I hope you will enjoy reading this as much as I did.

Jeff Kodosky, Vice President Research and Development
National Instruments
Austin, TX, January 1994

Introduction

Almost 10 years have passed since the inception of LabVIEW. In that time it has become an enabling technology for the world of instrumentation, data acquisition, control, and data analysis. A product of National Instruments Corporation (Austin, Texas), it is a purely graphical, general-purpose programming language with extensive libraries of functions, an integral compiler and debugger, and an application builder for stand-alone applications. LabVIEW version 3, released in October 1993, runs on Apple Macintosh computers, IBM PC compatibles with Microsoft Windows, and Sun SPARCstations. Programs are portable among the various platforms. The concept of virtual instruments (VIs), pioneered by LabVIEW, permits you to transform a real instrument (such as a voltmeter) into another, software-based instrument (such as a chart recorder), thus increasing the versatility of available hardware. Control panels mimic real panels, right down to the switches and lights. And all programming is done via a block diagram, consisting of icons and wires, which is directly compiled to executable code; there is no underlying procedural language or menu-driven system.

As an instrumentation engineer, I find LabVIEW indispensable—a flexible, timesaving package without all the frustrating aspects of ordinary programming languages. The one thing LabVIEW has been missing all these years is a useful application-oriented book. The manuals are fine, once you know what you want to accomplish. And the classes offered by National Instruments are highly recommended if you are just starting out. But how do you get past that first, blank screen? What are the methods for designing an efficient LabVIEW application? And what about interface hardware and real-world signal conditioning problems? In this book, I describe practical problem-solving techniques that aren't in the manual, nor in the introductory classes—methods you learn only by experience.

So far as possible, this book is platform independent, as is LabVIEW itself. Occasional topics arise where functionality is available only on one or two of the computers. Dynamic Data Exchange (DDE), for example, is only available under Microsoft Windows. Appendix A is a portability guide that you can consult when developing applications that you intend to propagate among various platforms.

A diskette is included with this book. On it you will find many useful utility VIs and working examples (such as a simple data acquisition system). Each example is discussed in detail in the text. The diskette is in MS-DOS format, readable on the PC, the Macintosh (using Apple File Exchange), and on the Sun, under SunOS 4.1.2 and later, using the option mount command as described in Appendix B.

Chapter 1, *Roots*, starts off with an entertaining history of the development of LabVIEW. The rest of the chapter is devoted to basic advice—choosing equipment for a system and sources for help with your LabVIEW-related problems.

The basics of interface hardware, signal conditioning, and analog/digital conversion are discussed in Chapter 2, *Inputs and Outputs*. Notably, this chapter contains no LabVIEW programming examples whatsoever. The reason is simple—more than half the "LabVIEW" questions that coworkers ask me turn out to be hardware and signal-related. Information in this chapter is vital and will be useful no matter what software you may use for measurement and control.

In Chapter 3, *LabVIEW Programming Techniques*, we get down to basic programming techniques. After a discussion of the principles of dataflow programming, we look at the available data types and programming structures in LabVIEW, and finish off with the subtleties of timing and file I/O. This is by no means a rewrite of the manuals, nor is it a substitute for an introductory LabVIEW course. You are encouraged to consult those sources, as well, in the process of becoming a skilled LabVIEW user.

Chapter 4, *Building an Application*, shows you how to design a LabVIEW application. Here, I assume that you are not a formally trained software engineer, but rather a technically skilled person with a job to do (that certainly describes me!). We'll walk through the development of a real application that I wrote, starting with the selection of hardware, and going on to prototyping, designing, testing, and documenting the program.

If you connect your computer to any external instruments, you will want to read Chapter 5, *Instrument Drivers*. It begins with the basics of communications and I/O hardware (GPIB, RS-232, and VXI), then covers recommended driver development techniques and programming practices. Instrument drivers can be fairly challenging to write. Since it's one of my specialties, I hope to pass along a few tricks.

Chapter 6, *Using the DAQ Library*, is a practical view of the data acquisition (DAQ) library, which is the set of LabVIEW VIs that support plug-in data acquisition boards. All aspects of high- and low-speed analog, digital, and counter/timer operations are discussed in detail with useful applications.

Some topics may seem at first to be presented backwards—but for good reasons. In Chapter 7, *Designing a Data Acquisition System*, the first topic is data analysis. Why not talk about sampling rates and throughput first? Because the only reason for doing data acquisition is to collect data for analysis. And if you are out of touch with the data analysis needs, you will probably write the wrong data acquisition program. Other topics in this chapter are sampling speed and throughput optimization and configuration management. We finish with some real applications that you can actually use.

Chapter 8, *Process Control Applications*, is a large, generalized chapter because it covers not just industrial control, but all types of measurement and control situations. We'll look at man-machine interfaces, sequential and continuous control, trending, alarm handling, and interfacing to industrial controllers, particularly programmable logic controllers (PLCs). LabVIEW is just now making inroads in industrial control; consider this chapter the tip of the iceberg.

LabVIEW has a large following in physics research, so Chapter 9, *Physics Applications*, is devoted to such applications. Particular situations and solutions in this chapter are electromagnetic field and plasma diagnostics, measuring fast pulses with transient recorders, and handling very large data sets. This last topic, in particular, is of interest to almost all users because it discusses techniques for optimizing memory usage. (There are tidbits like this all through the book; by all means, read it cover to cover!)

My favorite is Chapter 10, *Data Visualization and Image Processing*, because it shows off some of the data presentation capabilities of LabVIEW. Many third-party products are featured—those that enable you to acquire video signals, process and display images, and make three-dimensional plots.

ATE (automated test equipment) is a specialized, but popular, LabVIEW application area that is discussed in Chapter 11, *Automated Test Applications*. Important topics include test sequencing with a Test Executive and reporting of results.

While writing this book, I found that user-supplied example VIs were hard to obtain, owing to the fact that so many of us work for government laboratories and places that just don't like to give away their software. Where it was not possible to obtain the actual code, I attempted to reconstruct the important aspects of real applications to give you an idea of how you might solve similar problems. Third-party LabVIEW products, such as driver and analysis packages, are described where appropriate. They satisfy important niche requirements in the user community at a reasonable cost, thus expanding the wide applicability of LabVIEW.

If nothing else, I hope that my enthusiasm for LabVIEW rubs off on you.

Acknowledgments

I would like to thank the following persons and organizations who contributed valuable material, advice, and review services to this book:

Audrey Harvey (National Instruments)
Kevin Schmeisser (National Instruments)
Michael Santori (National Instruments)
Andrew Agoos (Software Engineering Group)
Scott Hamilton (Pyxis Corporation)
Neil Insdorf (Graftek)
Dennis Erickson (Bonneville Power Administration)
Corrie Karlsen (Lawrence Livermore National Laboratory)
Mark Scrivener (Lawrence Livermore National Laboratory)
Dr. Paul Daley (Lawrence Livermore National Laboratory)
Dr. Edmund Ng (Lawrence Livermore National Laboratory)
John Baker (Lawrence Livermore National Laboratory)
Lynda Gruggett (G Systems)
Jeff Parker (Metric Systems)
Horacio Zambrana (Eloret Institute)
Mark Newfield (NASA-Ames)
Amy Regan (Los Alamos National Laboratory)

John Leehey (nuLogic, Inc.)
Dr. Dana Redington (Redwolf Enterprises)
Biopac Systems, Inc.
Marty Vasey (LabVIEW consultant)
Ann Menendez (GTFS)
Bill Jenkins (Stellar Solutions)
Dr. Jim Henry (University of Tennessee at Chatanooga)
Dan Snider (Snider Consultants)

I would also like to thank the developers at National Instruments who supplied vital information without which this book would not be possible, particularly Jeff Kodosky, Meg Kay, Rob Dye, Gregg Fowler, Steve Rogers, Brian Powell, Crystal Doubrava, Jack Barber, and especially Monnie Anderson for his critical technical review. Particular credit is given to the fine support staff in the National Instruments Technical Publications and Graphic Arts departments for the editing and desktop publication services: Tom Chamberlain, chief editor, Katharine Decker, technical illustrator *par excellence* (she was so talented, I married her!), and Trish Hill, desktop publishing.

And finally, thanks to the people who *really* made it all happen: Jack MacCrisken (for proposing the project and then making me "swallow the elephant"), Roxanne Green and Sandy Bartnett for managing the overall project.

Roots

LabVIEW has certainly made life easier for this engineer. I remember how much work it was in the early 1980s to write hideously long programs to do even simple measurement and control tasks. Scientists and engineers only automated their operations when it was absolutely necessary, and the casual users and operators wouldn't dare tamper with the software because of its complexity. This computer-based instrumentation business was definitely more work than fun. But everything changed when, in mid-1987, I went to a National Instruments product demonstration. They were showing off a new program that ran on a Macintosh. It was supposed to do something with instrumentation, and that sounded interesting. When I saw what those programmers had done—and what LabVIEW could do—I was stunned! Wiring up *icons* to write a program? *Graphical* controls? Amazing! I had to get a hold of this thing and try it out for myself.

By the end of the year, I had taken the LabVIEW class and started on my first project, a simple data acquisition system. It was like watching the sun rise. There were so many possibilities now with this easy and fun-to-use programming language. I actually started looking for things to do with it around the lab (and believe me, I found them). Such a complete turnaround from the old days. Within a year, LabVIEW became an indispensable tool for my work in instrumentation and control. Now, my laboratories are not just *computerized*; they are *automated*. A computerized experiment or process relies heavily on the human operators. The computer makes things easier by taking some measurements and simple things like that, but it's far from being a hands-off process. An automated experiment, on the other hand, is one in which you set up the equipment, press the *start* button on the LabVIEW screen, and watch as the computer orchestrates a sequence of events, takes measurements, and presents the results. That's how you want your system to work, and that's where LabVIEW can save the day. Let's start out by taking a look at the world of automation.

LabVIEW and Automation

Computers are supposed to make things easier, faster, or more automatic, i.e., less work for the human host. LabVIEW is a unique programming system that makes computer automation a breeze for the scientist or engineer working in many areas of laboratory research, industrial control, and data analysis. You have a job to do—someone is probably paying you to make things happen—and LabVIEW can be a real help in getting that job done, provided that you apply it properly. But debates are now raging over this whole business of computers and their influence over our productivity. For instance, an article I read recently reported that we now tend to write longer proposals and reports (and certainly prettier ones) than we used to when only a typewriter was available. The modern word processor makes it easy to be thorough and communicate our ideas effectively. But does this modern approach always result in an improvement in productivity or quality? Sometimes we actually spend *more* time to do the same old thing.

You must avoid this trap. The key is to analyze your problems and see where LabVIEW and specialized computer hardware can be used to their greatest advantage. Then, make efficient use of existing LabVIEW solutions. As you will see, many laboratory automation problems have already been solved for you and the programs and equipment are readily available. There are no great mysteries here, just some straightforward engineering decisions you have to make regarding the advantages and disadvantages of computer automation. Let's take a pragmatic view of the situation. There are many operations that beg for automation. Among them:

- Long-term, low-speed operations such as environmental monitoring and control.

- High-speed operations, such as pulsed power diagnostics, where a great deal of data is collected in a short time.

- Repetitive operations such as automated testing and calibration, and experiments that run many times.

- Remote or hazardous operations where it is impractical, impossible, or dangerous to have a human operator present.

- High-precision operations that are beyond human capability, such as the star-tracking activity required for telescopes.

- Complex operations with many inputs and outputs.

In all of these cases, please observe that a computer-automated system makes practical an operation or experiment that you might not otherwise attempt. And automation may offer additional advantages:

- Reduces data transcription errors. The old "graphite data acquisition system" (a pencil) is prone to many error sources not present in a computer data acquisition system. Indeed, more reliable data often leads to better quality control of products and new discoveries in experimental situations.

- Eliminates operator-induced variations in the process or data collection methods. Repeatability is dramatically improved because the computer never gets tired and it always does things the same way.

- Increases data throughput because you can operate a system at computer speed rather than human speed.

There are some disadvantages hiding in the process of computer automation, however:

- May introduce new sources of error through improper use of sensors, signal conditioning, and data conversion equipment, and occasionally, through computational (e.g., roundoff) errors.

- Misapplication of any hardware or software system is a ticket for trouble. For instance, attempting to collect data at excessively high rates results in data recording errors.

- Reliability is always a question with computer systems. System failures (crashes) and software bugs plague every high-tech installation known, and they will plague your system as well.

Always consider the cost-effectiveness of a potential automation solution. It seems like everything these days is driven by money. If you can do it cheaper-better-faster, it is likely to be accepted by the owner, the shareholders, or whoever pays the bills. But is a computer guaranteed to save you money or time? If I have a one-time experiment where I can adequately record the data on a single stripchart recorder, an oscilloscope, or with my pencil, then taking two days to write a special program makes no sense whatsoever.

One way to automate (or at least computerize) simple, one-time experiments is to build what I call a LabVIEW "crash cart" much like the doctor's crash cart in an emergency room. When someone has a short-term measurement problem, I can roll in my portable rack of equipment. It contains a Macintosh with LabVIEW, analog interface hardware, and some programmable instruments. I can quickly configure the general-purpose data acquisition program, record data, and analyze it, all within a few hours. This is a concept you might want to consider if you work in an area that has a need for versatile data acquisition. Use whatever spare equipment you may have, recycle some tried-and-true LabVIEW programs, and pile them on a cart. The crash cart concept is simple and marvelously effective.

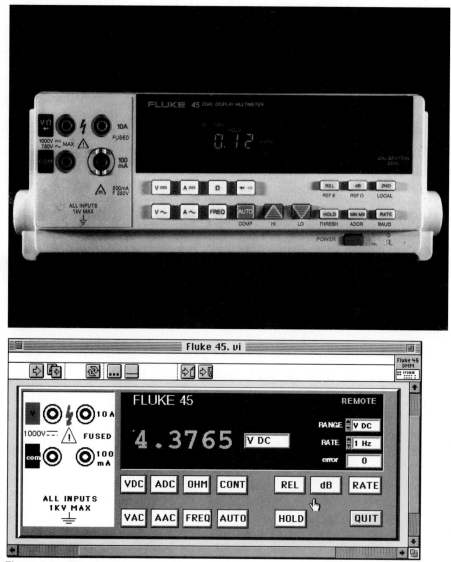

Figure 1-1. This virtual instrument is a customized version of the real instrument, having only the features that you need.

Automation is expensive: the cost of sensors, computers, software, and the programmer's effort quickly add up. But in the end, a marvelous new capability can arise. The researcher is suddenly freed from the labor of logging and interpreting data. The operator no longer has to orchestrate so many critical adjustments. And data quality and product quality rise. If your situation fits the basic requirements where automation is appropriate, then by all means consider LabVIEW as a solution.

Virtual Instruments–LabVIEW's Foundation

LabVIEW made the concept of the **virtual instrument (VI)** a practical reality. The objective in virtual instrumentation is to use a general-purpose computer to mimic real instruments with their dedicated controls and displays, but with the added versatility that comes with software. Instead of buying a stripchart recorder, an oscilloscope, and a spectrum analyzer, you can buy one high-performance analog-to-digital converter and use a computer running LabVIEW to simulate all of these instruments and more. The VI concept is so fundamental to the way that LabVIEW works that the programs you write in LabVIEW are in fact called **VIs**. You use simple instruments (**subVIs**) to build more complex instruments just as you use subprograms to build a more complex main program in a conventional programming language.

Virtual Versus Real Instrumentation

Virtual instrumentation systems like LabVIEW inevitably invite comparison to real physical instrumentation. The major drawback in using a personal computer for implementing virtual instruments is that the computer has only one central microprocessor. An application that uses multiple instruments can easily overburden the processor. A stand-alone instrument, however, may contain any number of processors, each dedicated to specific processing tasks. In addition, these multiple processors can operate in parallel, providing a great increase in overall performance. But this increase in performance results in the expensive price tag accompanying many dedicated instruments.

The technology in plug-in boards is advancing to address these issues, however. Many boards now contain their own processors and are available at a more reasonable price. Digital signal processors are a good example of special-purpose processors that find their way onto plug-in boards. Many plug-in data acquisition boards also have sophisticated direct memory access (DMA), timing, and triggering capabilities that can span multiple boards, resulting in improved synchronization and signal coupling between boards. These developments have brought parallel processing capabilities to personal computers, making them more sophisticated platforms for instrumentation and data acquisition applications. Sophistication breeds complexity, however, because you must have greater knowledge of these hardware components and their interconnection than is required to use a stand-alone instrument with similar capabilities. Virtual instrumentation software is essential for turning these sophisticated hardware combinations into usable instrumentation systems.

Virtual instrumentation offers the greatest benefit over real instruments in the areas of price/performance, flexibility, and customization. For the price of a dedicated high-performance instrument, you can assemble a personal computer-based system with the fundamental hardware and software components to design virtual instruments targeted for specific applications. The hardware may be plug-in boards, stand-alone instruments, or a combination of both. In either case, a software interface can be as complicated or as simple as necessary to serve the application. You can simplify the operation of a complex stand-alone instrument with virtual instruments that focus on controlling only subsets of the instrument's full capabilities. I, for one, get lost in the buttons and menus on the panels of many modern instruments.

Although LabVIEW has existed since 1986, the virtual instrumentation and block diagram concepts embodied in its design are still at the leading edge of instrumentation and computer science technology today. The cost of developing test program software continues to rise with the increasing complexity of the devices being tested and the instruments needed to test them. Software modularity, maintainability, and reusability, key benefits of LabVIEW's hierarchical and homogeneous structure, are critically important to reducing the development burden of individual software developers. Reusing routines that you have written and sharing them with others can save a great deal of time and make programs more reliable.

Virtual instrumentation is becoming increasingly important in the instrument control world. **VXI** (VMEbus Extensions for Instrumentation), a major development in instrumentation, is a standard that defines physical and electrical parameters, as well as software protocols, for implementing instrument-on-a-card test systems. A VXI instrument is a card that plugs into a chassis containing several cards. Because they are plug-in cards and not stand-alone boxes, individual VXI instruments do not have front panel user interfaces. Users cannot interact with a VXI instrument simply by pressing a few buttons or reading displays on a front panel. VXI systems must be controlled by a computer, or some other processor-based device, placing new demands on computer software for controlling instrumentation.

VXI instruments are natural candidates for virtual instrumentation implementations. In the area of user interaction, software front panels offer a visual means of controlling a "faceless" VXI instrument. In addition, the combination of plug-in modules and the high-performance timing and communications capabilities of the VXIbus makes the configuration of a VXI test system much more complex than a GPIB test system. LabVIEW's method of graphically connecting virtual instruments into a block diagram accelerates the configuring and programming of VXI test systems.

Why Does Gary Use LabVIEW?

I use LabVIEW because it has significant advantages over conventional languages and other control and data acquisition packages.

* My productivity is simply better in LabVIEW than with conventional programming languages. I've measured a factor of five (compared with C on a small project). Others have reported improvements of 15 times. You can now routinely deliver quick prototypes as well as finished systems in what used to be record time.

* The graphical user interface is built in, intuitive in operation, simple to apply, and as a bonus, nice to look at.

* LabVIEW is a real programming language, not a specialized application. It has few intrinsic limitations.

- There is only a minimal performance penalty when compared with conventional programming languages. No other graphical programming system can make this claim.

- Programmer frustration is reduced because hideous syntax errors are eliminated. Ever got yourself into an argument with a C compiler over what is considered "legal"? Made an seemingly minor error with a pointer and had your machine crash?

- Many important high-level operations have been encapsulated in convenient VI libraries for quick application. Most of them are included with the program or are otherwise available free or at reasonable prices from third parties.

- Programming in LabVIEW is fun. I would *never* say that about programming in C (challenging, yes, but fun, no).

Like any other tool, LabVIEW is only useful if you know how to use it. The more skilled you are in the use of that tool, the more you will use it. After six years of practice, let's just say that I'm *really comfortable* with LabVIEW. It's gotten to the point where it is at least as important as a word processor, a multimeter, or a desktop calculator in my daily work as an engineer.

The Origin of LabVIEW

A computer scientist friend of mine relates this pseudo-biblical history of the computer programming world:

> In the beginning, there was only machine language, and all was darkness. But soon, assembly language was invented, and there was a glimmer of light in the Programming World. Then came FORTRAN, *and the light went out.*

This verse conveys the feeling that traditional computer languages, even high-level languages, leave much to be desired. You spend a lot of time learning all kinds of syntactical subtleties, metaphors, compiler and linker commands, and so forth, just to say "Hello, world." And heaven forbid that you should want to draw a graph or make something move across the screen or send a message to another computer. We're talking about many days or weeks of work here. It's no wonder that it took so many years to make the computer a useful servant of the common person. Indeed, even now it requires at least a moderate education and plenty of experience to do anything significant in computer programming. For the working scientist or engineer, these classical battles with programming languages have been most counterproductive. All you wanted to do is make the darned thing display a temperature measurement from your experiment, and what did you get?

(beep)SYNTAX ERROR AT LINE 1326

Thanks a lot, oh mighty compiler. Well, times have changed in a big way because LabVIEW has arrived. At last, working troops like us have a programming language that eliminates that arcane syntax, hides the compiler, and builds the graphical user interface right in. No fooling around, just wire up some icons and run. And yet, the thought of actually *programming with pictures* is so incredible when contrasted with ordinary computer languages. How did they do it? Who came up with this idea?

Here is a most enlightening story of the origins of LabVIEW. It's a saga of vision; of fear and loathing in the cruel world of computer programming; of hard work and long hours; and of breakthroughs, invention, and ultimate success. The original story, *An Instrument That Isn't Really*, was written by Michael Santori of National Instruments and has been updated for this book.[*]

Introduction

Prior to the introduction of personal computers in the early 1980s, nearly all laboratories using programmable instrumentation controlled their test systems using dedicated instrument controllers. These expensive, single-purpose controllers had integral communication ports for controlling instrumentation using the *IEEE 488* bus, also known as the *General Purpose Interface Bus (GPIB)*. With the arrival of personal computers, however, engineers and scientists began looking for a way to use these cost-effective, general-purpose computers to control benchtop instruments. This development fueled the growth of National Instruments, which by 1983 was the dominant supplier of GPIB hardware interfaces for personal computers (as well as for minicomputers and other machines not dedicated solely to controlling instruments.)

So, by 1983, GPIB was firmly established as the practical mechanism for electrically connecting instruments to computers. Except for dealing with some differing interpretations of the IEEE 488 specification by instrument manufacturers, users had few problems physically configuring their systems. The software to control the instruments, however, was not in such a good state. Almost 100% of all instrument control programs developed at this time were written with the BASIC programming language because BASIC was the language used on the large installed base of dedicated instrument controllers. Although BASIC had advantages (including a simple and readable command set and interactive capabilities), it had one fundamental problem: like any other text-based programming language, it required engineers, scientists, and technicians who used the instruments to become programmers. These users had to translate knowledge of their applications and their instruments into the lines of text to produce a test program. This process, more often than not, proved to be a cumbersome and tedious chore, especially for those with little or no prior programming experience.

---

[*]   ©1990 IEEE. Reprinted, with permission, from IEEE Spectrum, Vol. 27, No. 8, pages 36-39, August 1990.

A Vision Emerges

National Instruments, which had its own team of programmers who had to struggle to develop BASIC programs to control instrumentation, was sensitive to the burden that instrumentation programming placed on engineers and scientists. A new tool for developing instrumentation software programs was clearly needed. But what form would it take? Dr. James Truchard and Jeff Kodosky, two of the founders of National Instruments, along with Jack MacCrisken, who was then a consultant, began the task of inventing this tool. Truchard was in search of a software tool that would markedly change the way engineers and scientists approached their test development needs. The model for this search was the electronic spreadsheet. The spreadsheet addressed the same general problem Truchard, Kodosky, and MacCrisken faced—making the computer accessible to non-programming computer users. Whereas the spreadsheet addressed the needs of financial planners, this entrepreneurial trio wanted to help engineers and scientists. They had their rallying cry—they would invent a software tool that had the same impact for scientists and engineers that the spreadsheet had on the financial community.

In 1983, the company, still relatively small in terms of revenue, decided to embark on a journey that would ultimately take several years. Truchard committed research and development funding to this phantom product and named Kodosky as the person to make it materialize. MacCrisken proved to be the catalyst—an amplifier for Kodosky's innovation while Truchard served as the facilitator and primary user. Dr. T, as he is affectionately known at National Instruments, has a knack for knowing when the product is "right."

Kodosky wanted to move to an office away from the rest of the company, so he could get away from the day-to-day distractions of the office and create an environment ripe for inspiration and innovation. He also wanted a site close to the University of Texas at Austin, so he could access the many resources available at UT, including libraries for research purposes, and later, student programmers to staff his project. There were two offices available in the desired vicinity. One office was on the ground floor with floor-to-ceiling windows overlooking the pool at an apartment complex. The other office was on the second floor of the building and had no windows at all. He chose the latter. It would prove to be a fortuitous decision.

All the World's an Instrument

The fundamental concept behind LabVIEW was rooted in a large test system that Truchard and Kodosky had worked on at the Applied Research Laboratory in the late 1970s. Shipyard technicians used this system to test Navy transducers. However, engineers and researchers also had access to the system for conducting underwater acoustics experiments. The system was flexible because Kodosky had incorporated several levels of user interaction into its design. A technician could operate the system and run specific test procedures with predefined limits on parameters while an acoustics engineer had access to the lower-level facilities for actually designing the test procedures. The most flexibility was given to the researcher, who had access to all the programmable hardware in the system to configure as he desired (he could also blow up the equipment if he wasn't careful). Two major drawbacks to the system were that it was an incredible investment in programming time—over 18 man-years—and that users had to understand the complicated mnemonics in menus to change anything.

Over several years, Kodosky refined the concept of this test system to the notion of instrumentation software as a hierarchy of *virtual instruments*. A virtual instrument (VI) would be composed of lower-level virtual instruments, much like a real instrument was composed of printed circuit boards, and boards composed of integrated circuits (ICs). The bottom-level VIs represented the most fundamental software building blocks: computational and input/output (I/O) operations. Kodosky gave particular attention to the interconnection and nesting of multiple software layers. Specifically, he envisioned VIs having the same type of construction at all levels. In the hardware domain, the techniques for assembling ICs into boards are dramatically different than for assembling boards into chassis. In the software domain, assembling statements into subroutines differs from assembling subroutines into programs and these activities differ greatly from assembling concurrent programs into systems. The VI model of homogeneous structure and interface at all levels greatly simplifies the construction of software—a necessary achievement for improving design productivity. From a practical point of view, it was essential that VIs have a superset of the properties of the analogous software components they were replacing. Thus, LabVIEW had to have the computational ability of a programming language and the parallelism of concurrent programs.

Another major design characteristic of the virtual instrument model was that each VI had a user interface component. Using traditional programming approaches, even a simple command line user interface for a typical test program was a complex maze of input and output statements often added after the core of the program was written. With a VI, the user interface was an integral part of the software model. An engineer could interact with any VI at any level in the system simply by opening the VI user interface. The user interface made it easy to test software modules incrementally and interactively during system development. In addition, because the user interface was an integral part of every VI, it was always available for troubleshooting a system when a fault occurred. (The virtual instrument concept was so central to LabVIEW's incarnation that it eventually became embodied in the name of the product. Although Kodosky's initial concerns did not extend to the naming of the product, much thought would ultimately go into the name LabVIEW, which is an acronym for Laboratory Virtual Instrument Engineering Workbench.)

A Hard-Core UNIX Guy Won Over by the Macintosh

The next fundamental concept of LabVIEW was more of a breakthrough than a slow evolution over time. Kodosky had never been interested in "personal computers" because they didn't have megabytes of memory and disk storage, and they didn't run UNIX. About the time Kodosky started his research on LabVIEW, however, his brother-in-law introduced him to the new Apple Macintosh personal computer. Kodosky's recollection of the incident was that "after playing with MacPaint for over three hours, I realized it was time to leave and I hadn't even said 'hello' to my sister." He promptly bought his own Macintosh. After playing with the Macintosh, Kodosky came to the conclusion that the most intuitive user interface for a VI had to be a facsimile of a real instrument front panel. Most engineers learn about an instrument by studying its front panel and experimenting with it. With its mouse, menus, scroll bars, and icons, the Macintosh proved that the right interface would also allow someone to learn software by experimentation. VIs with graphical front panels that could be operated with a mouse would be simple to operate. A user could discover how they work, minimizing documentation requirements (although people rarely documented their BASIC programs anyway).

Putting It All Together With Pictures

The final conceptual piece of LabVIEW was the programming technique. A VI with an easy-to-use graphical front panel programmed in BASIC or C would simplify operation, but would make the development of a VI more difficult. The code necessary to construct and operate a graphical panel is considerably more difficult than that required to communicate with an instrument.

To begin addressing the programming problem, Kodosky went back to his model software product, the spreadsheet. Spreadsheet programs are so successful because they display data and programs as rows and columns of numbers and formulas. The presentation is simple and familiar to business people. What do engineers do when they design a system? They draw a block diagram. Block diagrams help an engineer visualize his problem but only suggest a design. Translation of a block diagram to a schematic or computer program, however, requires a great deal of skill. What Kodosky wanted was a software diagramming technique that would be easy to use for conceptualizing a system, yet flexible and powerful enough to actually serve as a programming language for developing instrumentation software.

Two visual tools Kodosky considered were flow charts and state diagrams. It was obvious that flow charts could not help. These charts offered a visualization of a process, but to really understand them, you have to read the fine print in the boxes on the chart. Thus, the chart occupies too much space relative to the fine print yet adds very little information to a well-formatted program. The other option, a state diagram, is flexible and powerful but the perspective is much different than that of a block diagram. Representing a system as a collection of state diagrams requires a great deal of skill. Even after completion, the diagrams must be augmented with textual descriptions of the transitions and actions before they can be understood.

Another approach Kodosky considered was **dataflow diagrams**. Dataflow diagrams, long recommended as a top-level software design tool, have much in common with engineering block diagrams. Their one major weakness is the difficulty involved in making them powerful enough to represent iterative and conditional computations. Special nodes and feedback cycles have to be introduced into the diagram to represent these

Figure 1-2.   Jack MacCrisken, Jeff Kodosky, and Jim Truchard, LabVIEW inventors.

computations, making it extremely difficult to design or even understand a dataflow diagram for anything but the simplest computations. Kodosky felt strongly, however, that dataflow had some potential for his new software system.

By the end of 1984, Kodosky had experimented with most of the diagramming techniques, but they were all lacking in some way. Dataflow diagrams were the easiest to work with up until the point where loops were needed. Considering a typical test scenario, however, such as "take 10 measurements and average them," it's obvious that loops and iteration are at the heart of most instrumentation applications. In desperation, Kodosky began to make ad hoc sketches to depict loops specifically for these types of operations. Loops are basic building blocks of modern structured programming languages but it was not clear how or if they could be drawn in a dataflow concept. The answer that emerged was a box; a box in a dataflow diagram could represent a loop. From the outside, the box would behave as any other node in the diagram, but inside it would contain another

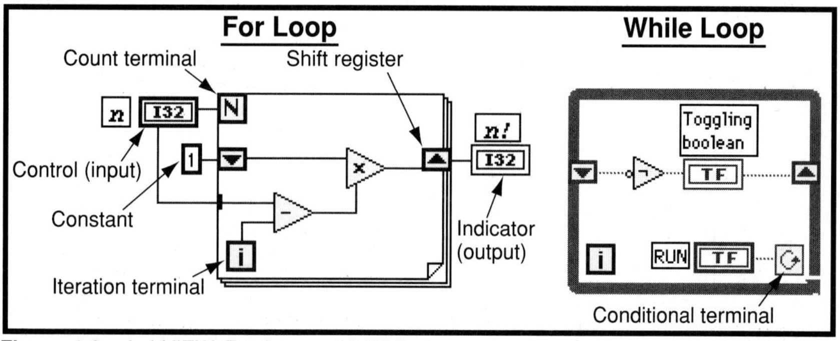

Figure 1-3. LabVIEW For Loop and While Loop programming structures with Shift Registers to recirculate data from previous iterations.

diagram, a "subdiagram," containing the contents of the loop. All the semantics of the loop behavior could be encapsulated in the border of the box. In fact, all the common structures of structured programming languages could be represented by different types of boxes. Kodosky was convinced he had achieved a major breakthrough but he was still troubled by a nagging point. His "structured dataflow" diagrams were inherently parallel because they were based on data flow.

There are times when it is important to force operations to take place sequentially—even when there is no data flow requiring it. For example, a signal generator must provide a stimulus before a voltmeter can measure a response, even though there isn't an explicit data dependency between the instruments. A special box to represent sequential operations, however, would be cumbersome and take up extra space. During one of their design discussions, Truchard suggested that steps in a sequence were like frames in a movie. This comment led to the notion of having several sequential subdiagrams share the same screen space. It also led to the distinctive graphic style of the **Sequence Structure**, as shown in Figure 1-4.

After inventing the fundamentals of LabVIEW block diagramming (two U.S. patents were issued in 1990), it was a simple matter of using MacPaint to produce pictures of VI panels and diagrams for several common applications. When Kodosky showed them to some engineers at NI, the impact was dramatic. The engineers understood the meaning of the diagrams and correctly guessed how to operate the front panel. Of equal importance, the reviewers expressed great confidence that they would be able to construct such diagrams easily to create applications. Now the only remaining task was to write the software, facetiously known as SMOP: Small Matter of Programming.

Favoring the Underdog Platform for System Design

Although Kodosky felt that the graphics tools on the Macintosh made it the computer of choice for developing LabVIEW, the clearer marketing choice was the DOS-based IBM PC. The Macintosh could never be the final platform for the product because it wasn't an

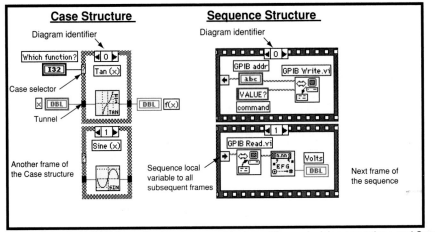

Figure 1-4. LabVIEW Case structures are used for branching or decision operations and Sequence Structures are used for explicit flow control.

open machine, and sales people would never be able to sell it because the Macintosh was considered a toy by many scientists and engineers. Politics and marketing aside, it wasn't at all clear that you could build a system in which a user draws a picture and the system *runs* it. Even if such a system could be built, would it be fast enough to be useful? Putting marketing concerns aside momentarily, Kodosky decided to build a prototype on the Macintosh prior to building the *real* system on a PC.

Kodosky's affinity to the Macintosh was not for aesthetic reasons alone. The Macintosh system ROM contains high performance graphics routines collectively known as QuickDraw™ functions. The Macintosh's most significant graphics capability is its ability to manipulate arbitrarily shaped regions quickly. This capability makes animated, interactive graphics possible. The graphics region *algebra* performed by the Macintosh is fast because of the unique coordinate system built into QuickDraw: the pixels are between, not on, the gridlines. In addition, the graphics display of the Macintosh uses square pixels, which simplifies drawing in general and rotations of bitmaps in particular. This latter capability proves useful for displaying rotating knobs and indicators on a VI front panel.

The operating system of the Macintosh is well integrated. It contains graphics, event management, input/output, memory management, resource and file management, and more—all tuned to the hardware environment for fast and efficient operation. Also, the Macintosh uses Motorola's 68000 family of microprocessors. These processors are an excellent base for large applications because they have a large uniform address space (handling large arrays of data is easy) and a uniform instruction set (compiler generated code is efficient). Remember that this is 1985: the IBM PC compatibles were still battling to break the 640 kilobyte barrier and had no intrinsic graphics support. It wasn't until Microsoft released Windows 3.0 in 1991 that a version of LabVIEW for the IBM PC became feasible.

Ramping Up Development

Kodosky hired several people just out of school (and some part-time people still in school) to staff the development team. Without much experience, the team members were not daunted by the size and complexity of the software project they were undertaking and instead they jumped into it with enthusiasm.

The team bought ten Macintoshes equipped with 512 kilobytes of memory and internal hard-disk drives called "HyperDrives." They connected all of the computers to a large, temperamental disk server. The team took up residence in the same office near campus that Kodosky had used for his brain-storming. Eleven people crammed into 800 square feet. As it turned out, the working conditions were almost ideal for the project. There were occasional distractions with that many people in one room but the level of communication was tremendous. When a discussion began between two team members, it would invariably have some impact on another aspect of the system they were inventing. The other members working on aspects of the project affected by the proposed change would enter the discussion and quickly resolve the issue. The lack of windows and clocks also helped the team stay focused. (As it turned out, the developers were so impressed with the productivity of the one-room team concept that the LabVIEW group is still located in one large room, although it now has windows with a great view.)

They worked long hours and couldn't afford to worry about the time. All-nighters were the rule rather than the exception and the lunch break often didn't happen until 3:00 p.m. There was a refrigerator and a microwave in the room so the team could eat and work at the same time. The main nutritional staples during development were double-stuff Oreo cookies and popcorn, and an occasional mass-exodus to Armin's for Middle-Eastern food.

The early development proceeded at an incredible pace. In four months time, Kodosky had put together a team and the team had learned how to program the Macintosh. MacCrisken contributed his project management skills, and devised crucial data structure and software entity relationship diagrams that served as an overall road map for software development. They soon produced a proof-of-concept prototype that could control a GPIB instrument (through a serial port adapter), take multiple measurements and display the average of the measurement. In proving the concept, however, it also became clear that there was a severe problem with the software performance. It would take two more development iterations and a year before the team would produce a viable product.

Stretching the Limits of Tools and Machine

After finishing the first prototype, Kodosky decided to continue working on the Macintosh because he felt the team still had much to learn before they were ready to begin the "real" product. It was at this time that the team began encountering the realities of developing such a large software system. The first problems they encountered were in the development tools. The software overflowed some of the internal tables, first in the C compiler and then in the linker. The team worked with the vendor to remedy the problem. Each time it occurred, the vendor expanded the tables. These fixes would last for a couple of months

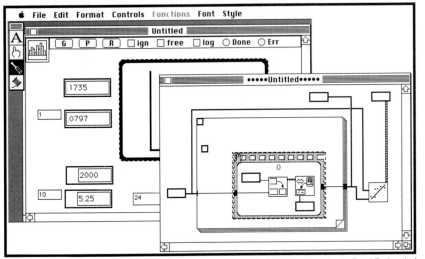

Figure 1-5. Screenshots from a very early prototype of LabVIEW. Thanks to Paul Daley (a Lawrence Livermore colleague) who discovered these old LabVIEW versions deep in his diskette archive.

until the project grew to overflow them again. The project continued to challenge the capabilities of the development tools for the duration of the project.

The next obstacle encountered was the Macintosh jump table. The project made heavy use of object-oriented techniques, which meant many function calls, causing the jump tables to overflow. The only solution was to compromise on design principles and work within the limits imposed by the platform. As it turned out, such compromises would become more commonplace in the pursuit of acceptable performance.

The last major obstacle was memory. The project was already getting too large for the 512 kilobyte capacity of the Macintosh and the team still hadn't implemented all the required functions, let alone the desirable ones they had been hoping to include. The prospects looked dim for implementing the complete system on a DOS-based PC, even with extensive use of overlaying techniques. This situation almost proved fatal to the project. The team was at a dead end and morale was at an all-time low. Apple came to the rescue by introducing the Macintosh Plus in January 1986. The Macintosh Plus was essentially identical to the existing Macintosh except that it had a memory capacity of one megabyte. Suddenly there was enough memory to implement and run the product with most of the features the team wanted.

Once again, the issue of the Macintosh marketability arose. A quick perusal of the DOS-based PC market showed that the software and hardware technology had not advanced very much. Kodosky decided (with approval by Dr. Truchard after some persuasion) that having come this far on the Macintosh, they would go ahead and build the first version of LabVIEW on the Macintosh. By the time the first version of LabVIEW was complete, there would surely, they thought, be a new PC that could run large programs.

Facing Reality on Estimated Development Times

The initial estimates of the remaining development effort were grossly inaccurate. The April 1986 introduction date passed without a formal software release. In May, in anticipation of an imminent shipping date, the team moved from their campus work room to the main office, where they could be close to the application engineers who did customer support. This event created much excitement but still no product.

It was at this point that the company became overanxious and tried to force the issue by prematurely starting beta testing. The testing was a fiasco. The software was far from complete. There were many bugs encountered in doing even the most simple and common operations. Development nearly ground to a halt as the developers spent their time listening to beta-testers calling in the same problems.

As the overall design neared completion, the team began focusing more on details, especially performance. One of the original design goals was to match the performance of interpreted BASIC. It was not at all clear how much invention or redesign it would require to achieve this performance target, making it impossible to predict when the team would achieve this goal. On most computational benchmarks, the software was competitive with BASIC. There was one particular benchmark, the Sieve of Eratosthenes, that posed, by nature of its algorithm and design, particular problems for dataflow implementations. The performance numbers the team measured for the sieve benchmark were particularly horrendous and discouraging—a fraction of a second for a compiled C program, two minutes for interpreted BASIC, and over eight hours for LabVIEW.

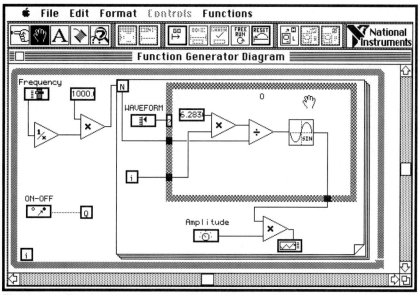

Figure 1-6. This diagram screenshot is from LabVIEW beta 0.36 in June 1986. Some of the familiar structures (While and For Loops, and a Case structure) had appeared by this time.

Kodosky did his best to predict when the software would be complete based on the number of bugs but was not sure how the major bugs would be found, much less fixed. Efficient testing of such a complex interactive program was a vexing and complex problem. The team finally settled on the *bug day* approach. They picked a day when the entire team would stop working on the source code and simply use LabVIEW. They would try all types of editing operations, build as many and as varied VIs as they could, and write down all the problems they encountered until the white boards on every wall were full. The first bug day lasted only three hours. The team sorted the list and for the next five weeks fixed all the fatal flaws and as many minor flaws as possible. Then they had another bug day. They repeated this process until they couldn't generate even one fatal flaw during an entire day. The product wasn't perfect, but at least it would not be an embarrassment.

Shipping the First Version

In October 1986, the team figured out how to bypass some of the overhead in calling a subVI, producing some improvement in performance (for all but the sieve benchmark, which was better but still 20 times slower than in BASIC). The decision was made to ship the product. The team personally duplicated and packaged the first fifty disks and hand-carried them to shipping. Version 1.0 was on the streets.

The reaction to LabVIEW was, in a word, startling. The product received worldwide acclaim as the first viable "visual," or graphical, language. There were many compliments for a well-designed product, especially from research and development groups who had their Macintosh-based projects canceled by less adventurous CEOs and marketing departments. Interestingly enough, the anticipated demand of the targeted BASIC users did not materialize. These people were apparently content to continue programming as they had been doing. Instead, LabVIEW was attracting and eliciting demands from customers who had never programmed at all but who were trying to develop systems considered extremely difficult by experienced programmers in any language. Yet these customers believed they could successfully accomplish their application goals with LabVIEW.

Apple Catches Up With The Potential LabVIEW Offers

Shortly after shipment of LabVIEW began, the company received its first prototype of the Macintosh II. This new version of the Macintosh had many design features that promised to legitimize the Macintosh in the scientific and engineering community. The most important of these features was that the new machine had an open architecture. Previous Macintosh versions could not accommodate plug-in expansion boards. The only mechanisms available for I/O were RS-422 and SCSI (Small Computer Systems Interface) ports. National Instruments sold stand-alone interface box products that converted these ports to IEEE 488 control ports but performance suffered greatly.

The Macintosh II's open architecture made it possible to add not only IEEE 488 support but also other much-needed I/O capabilities, such as analog-to-digital conversion and digital I/O. The Macintosh II used the NuBus architecture, an IEEE standard bus that gave the new machine high-performance 32-bit capabilities for instrumentation and data acquisition that were unmatched by any computer short of a minicomputer (the PC's bus was 16 bit). With the flexibility and performance afforded by the new Macintosh, users now had access to the hardware capabilities needed to take full advantage of LabVIEW's virtual instrumentation capabilities. Audrey Harvey (now a system architect at National Instruments) led the hardware development team that produced the first Macintosh II NuBus interface boards, and Lynda Gruggett (now a LabVIEW consultant) wrote the original *LabDriver* VIs that supported this new, high-performance I/O. With such impressive new capabilities and little news from the PC world, National Instruments found itself embarking on another iteration of LabVIEW development, still on the Macintosh.

Effective memory management turned out to be the key to making this graphical language competitive with ordinary interpreted languages. The development team had used a literal interpretation of dataflow programming. Each time data (a wire) leaves a source (a node), the Macintosh Memory Manager was called to allocate space for the new data, adding tremendous overhead. Other performance factors involved effective interpretation of the VI and diagram hierarchy and the scheduling of execution among nodes on the diagram. It became obvious that memory reuse was vital but a suitable algorithm was far from obvious. Kodosky and MacCrisken spent about four intensive weekend brainstorming sessions juggling the various factors, eventually arriving at a vague algorithm that appeared to address everything. The whiteboard was covered with all sorts of instantiation diagrams with "little yellow arrows and blue dots" showing the

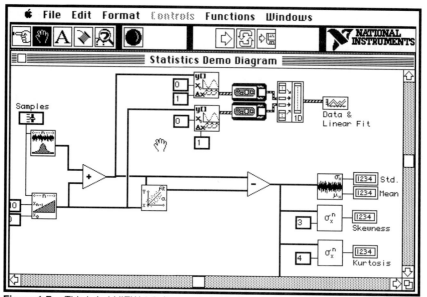

Figure 1-7. This is LabVIEW 1.2. It ran only in black and white and you couldn't move an object once it was wired. Somehow, we early users managed to get a *lot* accomplished, and enjoyed ourselves, at that.

Figure 1-8. This is how we got to know the LabVIEW 1 development team: the *About LabVIEW* dialog had these way-cool portraits.

prescribed flow of data. Then, one Monday morning, they called in Jeff Parker (now a LabVIEW consultant) and Steve Rogers (still a LabVIEW developer at National Instruments) and introduced them to this magnificent algorithm. The two of them proceeded to implement the algorithm (to the point that Kodosky and MacCrisken admittedly don't understand it anymore!) They kept the famous whiteboard around for about a year, occasionally referring to it to make sure everything was right. LabVIEW 1.1 included these concepts, known collectively as *inplaceness.*

While the development team was working with the new Macintosh, they were also scrambling to meet some of the demands made by customers. They were simultaneously making incremental improvements in performance, fixing flaws that came to light after shipment began, and trying to plan future developments. As a result of this process, LabVIEW progressed from version 1.0 to version 1.2 (and the Sieve slimmed down to 23 seconds). LabVIEW 1.2 was a very reliable and robust product. I, for one, wrote a lot of useful programs in version 1.2 and I can't recall crashing.

The Macintosh II gave LabVIEW a much-needed and significant boost in performance. The improvement, however, was short-lived. The internal architecture of LabVIEW 1.2 was showing signs of distress and the software was apparently abusing the Macintosh resource manager as well as its memory manager. It was becoming clear that the only real way to enhance capabilities was with a complete redesign. At the least, a redesign could incorporate new diagram analysis algorithms and a fast, built-in compiler that would eliminate performance problems once and for all. The major objective of the redesign was to achieve execution performance within a factor of two of compiled C.

LabVIEW 2–A First-Rate Instrument Control Product Becomes A World-Class Programming System

Even as the plans for the next-generation LabVIEW were becoming firm, customers were fast approaching, and exceeding, the limits of LabVIEW 1.2. Some users were building systems of VIs using up to eight megabytes of memory (the current limit on a Macintosh II). The *mega-applications* took up to 30 minutes to load into memory. Users reeled at the infamous "Too many objects" error message. And members of the development team often shuddered when they thought of the huge number of allocated structures and the complexity of their interconnection needed to make such a system work.

The decision to redesign LabVIEW brought with it a new set of pressures. In responding to some of the customer demands, the company had to admit that version 1.2 was at its design limits. As a result, work began on a new version, already becoming known as LabVIEW 2. Once the word was out, the development team was pressured into predicting a release date. Despite Kodosky's best intentions, the scope of the redesign resulted in several missed shipping deadlines. Realize that the design of a hierarchical dataflow compiler with polymorphic functions and sophisticated memory management was new science—and it took awhile.

LabVIEW 2 was designed with formalized object-oriented programming (OOP) techniques, on the insistence of Jeff Parker. OOP has many advantages over common procedural languages, and in fact it was an enabling technology in this case. Unfortunately, OOP tools for C language development were in a rather primitive state in 1988, so the team wrote their own spreadsheet-based development tools to automatically generate source code files. These tools remain in use because they remain more efficient than C++, though Kodosky reports that C++ is under serious consideration now for reasons of future support and portability.

The development team released an alpha version of the software in late 1988. Cosmetically, this version appeared to be in excellent shape. The compiler was working well and showed great increases in performance. There were also many enhancements in the editing capabilities of the product. All these positive signs resulted in an air of excitement and of imminent release. Unfortunately, the team had a long list of items they knew had to be fixed to produce a technically sound product. Over a year elapsed before the team released the final product. In January 1990, LabVIEW 2 was shipped to the first eager customers. I have to say that being a beta tester was a real thrill: the improvement in speed and flexibility was astounding.

LabVIEW 2's compiler is especially notable not only for its performance but for its integration into the development system. Developing in a standard programming language normally requires separate compilation and linking steps to produce an executable program. The LabVIEW 2 compiler is an integral, and invisible, part of the LabVIEW system, compiling diagrams in a fraction of the time required by standard compilers. From a user's point of view, the compiler is so fast and invisible that LabVIEW 2 is every bit as interactive as the previous interpreted versions.

The Port to Windows and Sun

The next major quest in the development of LabVIEW was the portable, or platform-independent version. Dr. Truchard (and thousands of users) had always wanted LabVIEW to run on the PC, but until Windows 3.0 came along, there was little hope of doing so because of the lack of 32-bit addressing support that is vital to the operation of such a large, sophisticated application. UNIX workstations, on the other hand, are well-suited to such development, but the workstation market alone was not big enough to warrant the effort required. These reasons made Kodosky somewhat resistant to the whole idea of programming on the PC, but MacCrisken finally convinced him that *portability* itself—the isolation of the machine-dependent layer—is the real challenge. So *The Port* was on.

Microsoft Windows turns out to be an impediment to 32-bit applications (Windows itself, and DOS, are 16-bit applications). Only in Appendix E of the Windows programming guide was there any mention whatsoever of 32-bit programming techniques. And, most of the information contained in that appendix referred to the storage of data, not application program writing. Finally, only one C compiler—Watcom C—was suited to LabVIEW development. But before Watcom C became available, Steve Rogers created a set of glue routines that translate 32-bit information back and forth to the 16-bit system function calls (in accordance with Appendix E). He managed to successfully debug these low-level routines without so much as a symbolic debugger, working instead with

Figure 1-9.   The team that delivered LabVIEW 2 into the hands of engineers and scientists, clockwise left to right: Jack Barber, Karen Austin, Henry Velick, Jeff Kodosky, Tom Chamberlain, Deborah Batto, Paul Austin, Wei Tian, Steve Chall, Meg Fletcher, Rob Dye, Steve Rogers, and Brian Powell. Not shown: Jeff Parker, Jack MacCrisken, and Monnie Anderson.

hexadecimal dumps. This gave the development team a six-month head start. Rogers sums up the entire situation: "It's ugly."

Development on the Sun SPARCstation, in contrast, was a relative breeze. Like all good workstations, the Sun supports a full range of professional development tools with few compromises—a programmer's dream. However, the X Windows environment that was selected for the LabVIEW graphical interface was totally different from the Macintosh or Windows toolbox environments. A great deal of effort was expended on the low-level graphics routines, but the long-term payoff is in the portability of X Windows-based programs. Development on the Sun was so convenient, in fact, that when a bug was encountered on the Windows version, the programmer would often do his or her debugging on the Sun rather than suffering along on the PC. Kodosky reports, "The Sun port made the PC port much easier and faster."

LabVIEW 2.5, which was released in August, 1992, required rewriting about 80% of LabVIEW 2 to break out the machine-dependent, or *manager*, layer. Creating this manager layer required some compromises with regard to the look and operation of the particular platforms. For instance, creating *floating windows* (like the LabVIEW Help window) is trivial on the Macintosh, difficult on the PC, and impossible under X Windows. The result is some degree of least-common-denominator programming, but the situation is expected to improve in future versions.

Figure 1-10.   *"Some new features are so brilliant that eye protection is recommended when viewing."* The team that delivered LabVIEW 2.5 and 3.0 includes (left to right, rear) Steve Rogers, Thad Engeling, Duncan Hudson, Kevin Woram, Greg Richardson, Greg McKaskle. Middle: Dean Luick, Meg Kay, Deborah Batto-Bryant, Paul Austin, Darshan Shah, Apostolos Karmirantzos. Seated: Brian Powell, Bruce Mihura. Not pictured: Gregg Fowler, Don Stuart, Rob Dye, Jeff Kodosky, Jack MacCrisken, Stepan Riha.

LabVIEW 3 and Beyond

The LabVIEW 2.5 development effort established a new and flexible architecture that made the unification of all three versions in LabVIEW 3 relatively easy. LabVIEW 3 includes a number of new features beyond those introduced in version 2.5. Many of these important features came from suggestions of users like you, accumulated over several years. Kodosky and his team, after the long and painful port, finally had the time to do some really creative programming. For instance, there had long been requests for a method by which the characteristics of controls and indicators could be changed programmatically. The *Attribute Node* addressed this need. Similarly, *Local Variables* now make it possible to both read from and write to controls and indicators. This is an extension of strict dataflow programming, but it is a convenient way to solve many tricky problems.

Many new features are still in the planning stages. Here are a few teasers to keep you interested in future versions of LabVIEW:

- **Undo** (at last!) The seemingly trivial act of undoing a mistaken action while editing a LabVIEW diagram is a programmer's nightmare. But, Kodosky reports he thinks he has a solution.

- **Improved support for large projects.** LabVIEW has moved into the world of serious program development, where teams of programmers use strict software quality assurance and software engineering techniques. New tools to manage large projects are under development.

- **More ports**. Plenty of other machines, particularly workstations, will be able to run LabVIEW in the future.

- **Generation of intermediate code**. Rather than having the compiler generate an executable program directly, it will generate an intermediate language. This will ease the process of porting LabVIEW, speed compiling, and make it easier to download code to other processors.

- **Distributed LabVIEW**. In the future, you will be able to compile and download parts of your LabVIEW programs to other processors. For instance, you could have several processors on plug-in boards, at remote locations on a network, or running in outboard I/O interface boxes. This will dramatically improve real-time performance and free you from having to use several languages to build a distributed processing system.

LabVIEW Influences Other Software Products

The concepts found in LabVIEW have already influenced the design of many other instrumentation products, especially in the areas of software front panels and iconic programming. Such products exist for Macintosh, DOS, Windows, and UNIX-based computers. Although at first glance these products are easily confused with LabVIEW, the differences are many.

Like LabVIEW, most instrumentation software products now offer some form of front panel-oriented user interface. The role of a LabVIEW front panel is unique, however, in comparison to other products. A graphical front panel in most instrumentation software products is simply a display/user interface mechanism introduced into an otherwise conventional, or textual language-based, programming system. The sole purpose of the panel in such a system is to serve as a top-level interface to an instrument or plug-in board. Users typically do not have the flexibility to customize their own front panel; it is merely a user-friendly tool supplied by the vendor. These panels are either not applicable to or not available as an interface for use within an application program.

In LabVIEW, a front panel is a integral component of every software module (or VI). A LabVIEW front panel can serve as the interface to any type of program, whether it is a GPIB instrument driver program, a data acquisition program, or simply a VI that performs computations and displays graphs. The methodology of using and building front panels is fundamental to the design and operation of LabVIEW; for every front panel there is an associated block diagram program and vice versa. Front panels can appear at any level in a LabVIEW VI and are not restricted to the highest level.

Another aspect of LabVIEW that finds its way into other software products is **iconic programming**. As with front panels, the iconic programming systems found in other products are largely add-on shells used to hide some of the details of systems based on conventional programming methodologies. Such products offer a predefined, set number of operations that can be used in iconic form. While generally quite simple to use because of their turnkey nature, these systems are not easily expanded because adding new functions is either impossible or requires a user to revert back to a standard programming language to create new icons. These iconic programming systems address organization of the high-level aspects of a test but do not have graphical constructs for specifying programming operations such as execution order, iteration, or branching. In addition, these systems typically do not support building a module that can be used in iconic form at a higher level.

LabVIEW's iconic programming language is not simply an organizational tool. It is a true programming language complete with multiple data types, programming structures, and a sophisticated compiler. LabVIEW is unique for its hierarchy and expandability. VIs have the same construction at all levels so the creation of a new high-level VI is simply a matter of combining several lower-level VIs and putting a front panel on the new combination. Because LabVIEW's graphical programming system offers the functionality and performance of conventional programming languages, users can add new functions to the system without having to resort to the use of another programming language.

Product History

Many of the original development team members continue to maintain the product while researching future extensions and directions. Several of them, including Lynda Gruggett and Jeff Parker, have gone on to start successful businesses of their own, specializing in LabVIEW programming. As you might expect with a project of such a large scope,

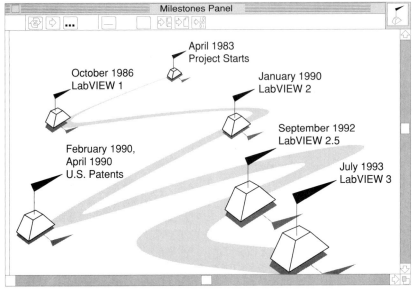

Figure 1-11.   The LabVIEW Development milestones.

LabVIEW continues to introduce National Instruments to many new applications and markets. Meanwhile, meeting the demanding needs of engineers and scientists will continue to make LabVIEW significant both as a product and as a standard for measuring software innovation.

How to Assemble a System

So you have a job to do, something to automate, and you wonder where to begin. I call this the blank canvas syndrome, where you have an infinite set of possibilities, and probably more than one that will do the job. What you need to do is list all the requirements and constraints of your project, discuss the situation with your colleagues, and choose a logical system configuration.

Having a list of requirements or objectives is such a fundamental first step, and yet we skip this step more often than not. I like to spend an appropriate amount of time with the project managers, designers, and prospective users to find out what they *really* need. For most projects, you can just scribble down notes, making sure that you completely understand the problem. Then, go back to your office (or garage, or whatever), and try to write a *requirements document*. This may or may not be a formal exercise with strict format specifications, depending on your company's policies. I like to draw pictures of the physical plant, floor plans, and a good overall block diagram of the system, along with some words that describe what the whole thing does. Then, make a list of the proposed sensors and signals, required performance specifications, and other features. You can never have too much information this early in a project. Hopefully, there is a project manager involved who understands the scope of work. It is vital that your project doesn't fall prey to underestimation of the instrumentation and control efforts. Do you need more help? Get it. Is the schedule realistic? If not, then either the cost, the performance specifications, or the schedule will have to change.

Use Equipment That's Familiar

Using hardware and software with which you are familiar gives you a quicker start and shorter learning curve. I hate seeing someone forced to use a Brand X computer when he or she is already an expert with Brand Y because so much time will be spent fiddling with the system instead of getting useful work accomplished. Of course, there are many reasons for choosing a particular computer or I/O system. You must consider the big picture.

The deciding factor in choosing a computer or I/O system is often a matter of complying with standards within your company or work area. If yours is a Sun world, you probably will stay with Sun, unless there is some overriding reason to look elsewhere. On the other hand, if nobody is there to force the decision, then you are a kid in a candy store, with many choices to make.

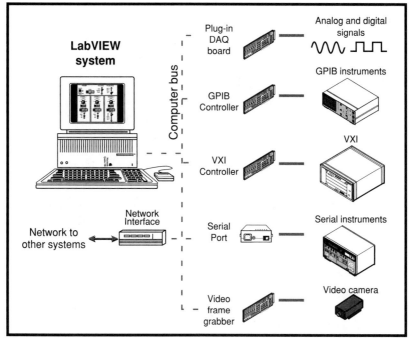

Figure 1-12. Choices, choices. Your system will consist of one or more computers running LabVIEW, one or more types of I/O hardware, and perhaps some network connections.

Picking an I/O System

LabVIEW is amenable to most any I/O interface known to the world of instrumentation so you are generally free to shop around. Figure 1-12 shows the most common interfaces: plug-in data acquisition boards, video frame grabbers, GPIB, VXI, and serial instruments. Using network connections, it is also possible to communicate with remote, intelligent devices or computers, running LabVIEW and other programs, that add another dimension to data acquisition and control. I've found that the biggest determining factors in choosing an I/O system are:

- Previous (positive) experience with the equipment or recommendations from someone you trust.

- Immediate availability of hardware. I'm more likely to use something that is left over from another project, or something that I can order and have delivered in short order.

- Suitability for the purpose. It doesn't do much good to have lots of the *wrong* hardware available. Compare specifications and requirements carefully before committing to any hardware solution.

- Drivers—the low-level interface software for an instrument—are important. If there is a LabVIEW driver available for a given instrument, you will save time and effort because writing a driver is sometimes as complex as writing a major application.

- Reliability and safety. Requirements for very high reliability or personnel safety should strongly influence your choice of hardware (and software).

- Cost per channel.

Plug-In Boards

Plug-in data acquisition boards have made a major impact on the instrumentation world because they turn a general-purpose computer into an instrument that connects directly to signals in the outside world. They are versatile and cost-effective. For instance, the MIO-16-series board from National Instruments gives you 16 analog inputs, two analog outputs, and 16 digital input/output bits. The MIO-16 is, by the way, the most popular multifunction board in the world and is very well supported by LabVIEW. Chapter 7, *Writing a Data Acquisition Program*, is devoted to using the LabVIEW data acquisition (DAQ) library, and much of that information applies directly to the MIO-16. With the addition of appropriate signal conditioning and external multiplexers, you can handle hundreds of inputs and outputs while using only one slot in your computer. You can choose among boards that offer maximum sampling rates from 25 kHz to 1 MHz with 12 to 16 bits of resolution. Most support direct memory access (DMA) data transfers to improve performance. Boards with more advanced features are being introduced constantly.

A wide range of data acquisition boards are available for IBM PC and Macintosh, but you won't find near the same selection for the Sun. National Instruments will help rectify this situation with the release of its first plug-in data acquisition board for the Sbus, the

SB-A2200. It offers 25 MFLOPS of processing power and high accuracy analog input-output via two 16-bit analog input channels and two 16-bit analog output channels. The company also has a Sun version of that popular multifunction MIO-16 board under development. While the Sun may not be as ripe a platform for data acquisition, it continues to be an ideal host for GPIB and VXI instrument control applications.

You can use modern programmable instruments to augment the performance of your LabVIEW system. While plug-in boards accommodate a wide variety of signals, they don't solve every problem. As an example, a digital oscilloscope can acquire very high frequency waveforms (well beyond the capability of any plug-in board) that you can upload, analyze, display, and store. Similarly, the plethora of functions available in the modular VXI format makes it possible to build a custom high-performance test and measurement system with LabVIEW orchestrating the operation. And serial instruments represent the lowest-cost solution to remote-control interfacing.

GPIB, VXI, and Serial Instruments

VXI interface boards, using the MXIbus, are available from National Instruments with full LabVIEW driver support at all levels for the Sun, IBM PC, and Macintosh. You can program everything from the lowest register-level operations on up—whatever the job requires. MXIbus offers very high throughput. You can also control VXI via GPIB.

GPIB interfaces are particularly versatile and easy to use, thanks to the thoughtful design of the hardware standards and boards, and to the built-in support in the LabVIEW GPIB library. For the Sun, IBM PC, and Macintosh, National Instruments makes plug-in boards that offer high-performance DMA transfers and IEEE 488.2 compliance. You can also use external GPIB interfaces. For instance, on a Sun or Macintosh that does not have a free slot for a plug-in interface, you can use the GPIB-SCSI-A box, which plugs into the SCSI port. For a longer reach, consider the GPIB-ENET, a GPIB interface that permits the control of instruments over a TCP/IP Ethernet link. The regular LabVIEW drivers work transparently with both of these special interfaces.

Serial port communications are supported by the serial port functions built into LabVIEW, though the protocols are so poorly standardized in the serial world that you generally end up putting more effort into writing serial drivers than you would with GPIB or VXI.

By the way, all of the DAQ, GPIB, and serial functions are portable over all of the platforms, so long as the appropriate interface hardware is installed. It's pretty amazing to write a GPIB driver on a Mac then email it to a Sun user who proceeds to run it unmodified.

Special-Purpose I/O Systems

For every industry or environment, there are specialized instruments, interface standards, and communications protocols. Regardless of the situation, you should have no fear of using LabVIEW to accommodate those unusual standards. In fact, if you ask around, you will probably find a reasonable combination of hardware and LabVIEW drivers to do the job. Here are a few examples.

In the commercial aircraft industry, modern flight control systems often use the Digital Information Transfer System (DITS), a specialized local area network (LAN) that uses the ARINC protocol. Another LAN, used mostly on military aircraft, is MIL-STD-1553A/B. If you wanted to test something that was connected to one of these systems, you would find that several manufacturers make VXI modules that transmit or receive data using the appropriate protocols. The modules plug into a standard VXI mainframe and connect to the LAN using the required connectors. Onboard intelligence handles all the low-level timing and protocol generation, so your program can easily exchange messages with other nodes on the network. LabVIEW drivers are available for several of these modules.

Biomedical applications have some different requirements. Notably, it is very dangerous to connect anything electrical to a living specimen, because leakage currents can be lethal. For this reason, federal laws state that you may only use hardware designated for the application when connecting to human subjects (and it pays to be careful with our other animal friends, as well!). One company that makes a line of affordable analog interface equipment for life science research is Biopac System, Inc. Their data acquisition and stimulus-response units are modular, multichannel devices with a high-speed serial interface for use with PCs and Macintoshes. Dedicated software is provided, and LabVIEW support is available as well.

Industrial process control applications call for robust and reliable low-speed analog and digital I/O interfaces and controllers, often in the form of Programmable logic controllers (PLCs). The physical plant is usually spread out over a large area and is filled with equipment that induces noise in analog signals. For this reason, a LAN or other communications scheme is desirable. PLCs use proprietary serial protocols, many of which are supported by LabVIEW drivers available from third-party developers. Another type of I/O hardware in wide use is made by Opto-22. This is a low-cost, modular interface that supports a wide range of analog and digital input and output signal types, from millivolt inputs to 220 VAC outputs. A local *brain board* scans the I/O modules and communicates with the remote host computer over a serial line. LabVIEW drivers are available for Opto-22, as well. (I know—I wrote the package.)

Sometimes you need to go mobile with your measurements. Laptop PCs and Macintosh PowerBooks, when combined with battery-operated I/O hardware, make LabVIEW a mobile solution. The aforementioned Biopac equipment has a battery-power option to support their MP100-series modules in the field. Dana Redington, a MacArthur Foundation fellow at the University of California, took such a system to India to study the effects of meditation on the nervous systems of highly trained yoga masters. He collected electrocardiogram, skin temperature, respiration, and hand sweating data while the subjects underwent their behavioral maneuvers. I suspect that's about as far afield as LabVIEW can get! You can also build your own battery power source for some kinds of the I/O hardware that may not already offer the option. I did it with Opto-22 by connecting a gel-cell battery to a DC-to-DC converter that supplied the required voltages. With LabVIEW running on a PowerBook, we were able to record electrochemical measurements while sitting in a small boat in the Pacific Ocean.

Limitations to Consider

It's important that you learn the limitations of a LabVIEW-based system and its associated hardware. Throughout this book you will find discussions of performance issues. But in the final analysis, there are few hard limits that will absolutely rule out a particular system configuration. I find it wise to obtain benchmarks, recommendations, and examples from others who have tackled similar projects. Learn from other people's experiences and mistakes. See Appendix C, *Sources*, for help and answers and below for tips on making contact with the Outside World.

Perhaps the biggest concern with the general-purpose platforms that LabVIEW runs on is their real-time response limitations. Realize that Windows, UNIX, and the Macintosh operating system are quite complex and are not really optimized for real-time applications. By the way, we need to set some guidelines for *real-time* here and now. The precise definition of real-time depends on your application's temporal response. This includes both the cycle time or sampling rate and the computer system's latency–the time it takes to respond to an external occurrence. Real-time control of your home heating system requires a response time of about one minute. High-pressure regulators often need to respond in something less than one second. Real-time flight controls in an F-16 fighter are sampled at 45 Hz. And real-time sequencers in an inertial confinement fusion experiment at Lawrence Livermore National Laboratories have to respond in something under a nanosecond. Now that's quite a range. Which *real-time* applies to your situation, and which requirements do you think that LabVIEW has a chance of meeting?

With the internal timing functions available in LabVIEW, I generally draw the line at about 0.1 second. Faster than that, you will generally see excessive timing uncertainty. At one-second cycle rates, you will rarely encounter any significant problems. However, there are other activities that take place on your computer that can upset even a one-second operation. On a Sun SPARCstation, it has been noted that incoming mail stops everything for a moment. On a Macintosh, inserting a floppy disk will noticeably interrupt the system. And under Windows and on the Macintosh, mouse activity, especially holding the mouse button down while the cursor is in a scroll bar, effectively freezes the machine. These and other nondeterministic effects can be obtrusive in many real-time systems and you must learn how to deal with them.

One thing you can do is network several LabVIEW systems to divide the workload between real-time activity and user interface activity. With the networking support in LabVIEW, you can have one machine that polls the I/O hardware, collects and preprocesses raw data, and does any real-time control. Another machine can periodically communicate with the real-time machine to upload and download information. Then the operator is free to use that computer without fear of interrupting a time-critical task.

Using an external "smart" controller is the best choice when fast, repeatable, real-time response is important. PLCs, discussed in Chapter 8, *Process Control Applications*, are widely used for industrial process control because they are fast, reliable, and easy to use. With a PLC and LabVIEW as the man-machine interface, you can build an excellent control system with true millisecond response. Similarly, packaged data acquisition units make it possible to gather data at high speeds (perhaps in a remote or hazardous location), reduce the data, and transmit it to the LabVIEW host for display. Plug-in digital signal processing (DSP) boards can be programmed to do high-speed control algorithms without interruption from the host computer. Almost any device can be integrated nicely into your overall strategy to improve real-time performance. Your job is to choose the *right* devices.

Picking a Computer

At the time of this writing, LabVIEW runs on the Macintosh with System 6.0.5 or System 7, on IBM PC compatibles running Windows 3.1 or Windows NT, and on the Sun SPARCstation running Solaris 1 or Solaris 2. If you're expecting me to recommend particular models, you're out of luck. New versions of CPUs and operating systems come out so quickly these days that almost anything I say here is born obsolete. Therefore, I'll just give you some general guidance.

Performance

LabVIEW is graphics-intensive. For those of you who grew up with simple command-line operating systems, the burden of all those graphics on the CPU seems immense. Fortunately, the latest generation of computers rises to the task without undue expense. For most applications, I recommend the fastest Macintosh or PC that you can afford. An adequate LabVIEW machine might look like this:

- Macintosh: 68030–25 MHz with floating-point unit (FPU), 8 MB RAM, 120 MB hard disk, 13" color monitor

- PC with Windows 3.x: 80486DX–50 MHz, 8 MB RAM, 120 MB hard disk, SVGA monitor, 3.5" floppy

- Sun: SPARCstation 1 with 24 MB of main memory, 32 MB of disk swap space, and 100 MB hard disk space

Serious LabVIEW applications demand serious hardware. If you expect to handle large data sets (megasamples of data), do image processing, or display data at high speeds, then a faster system is mandatory. Developing a large LabVIEW application is faster and more enjoyable when the system responds quickly, so there is a productivity factor here, as well: buying a more expensive system pays off in the long run. A high-performance machine might look like this:

- Macintosh: 68040-33 MHz, 20 MB RAM, 500 MB hard drive, 19" color monitor

- PC with Windows 3.x: 80486–66 MHz, 20 MB RAM, 500 MB hard drive, 19" SVGA color monitor and graphics accelerator

- Sun: SPARCstation 10, 32 MB of main memory, 64 MB of swap space, 19" color monitor, 200 MB hard disk space

The PowerPC is another option just coming on the market at this writing and will be supported by the Macintosh operating system, Windows NT, and PowerOpen. This new RISC machine looks really promising as a LabVIEW platform, assuming that suitable I/O interface hardware is available. Other UNIX workstations, such as those from Hewlett-Packard and Digital Equipment Corp., are also logical targets for LabVIEW. Stay tuned.

Memory and Disk Capacity

Your LabVIEW system will need plenty of memory. While UNIX workstations are almost always configured with large memories, you will have to upgrade your Macintosh or PC to make it really useful. The recommended 8 MB of RAM is really a bare minimum; 16 MB is much more practical, and you can *never* have too much. Applications which demand large amounts of memory include image processing, multidimensional data visualization (graphing), and some waveform acquisition situations. It's fairly hard to calculate the exact amount of memory you will need because of the way that LabVIEW allocates data structures, and the ever-increasing complexity (feature creep) of your program as it develops. For signals like waveforms, you can count on using at least four bytes per sample and sometimes as many as 16 depending on the processing that you do. Think about this: one million data points may require 16 million bytes of memory! Images, which are generally one byte per pixel, actually end up consuming at least twice that much when displayed and several times more if they are converted to other data types for computations. Virtual memory, where the disk drive augments physical RAM memory, is available on all of LabVIEW's platforms but it won't solve all of your problems. Real-time performance of virtual memory is poor, and large, contiguous data structures typically cannot be broken up for swapping out to disk.

Disk capacity is also important. LabVIEW itself requires between 20 and 50 MB of disk space (64 MB on the Sun) and the applications you write will occupy even more. Acquired data is often the determining factor when choosing the capacity of your disk drive. Capacity is fairly easy to calculate, assuming that you know what kind of data you are saving and how many samples are to be stored. For instance, ordinary single-precision floating point numbers, when stored in binary format, require four bytes per sample. If those numbers are converted to text format, they may require as many as 12 bytes per sample—a good reason for saving data in binary format. Most images occupy one byte per pixel, assuming 256 gray levels or colors. Thus, a typical 640 by 480 pixel image requires 307 KB of disk space. If you expect to store lots of data, plan to buy high-capacity removable media, such as magneto-optical disks. Most facilities that I've seen use them.

Expansion Slots

One of the best ways to add I/O interface capability to your computer is to install a plug-in board. GPIB interfaces, multifunction analog and digital I/O interfaces, and DSP accelerators are in widespread use on Macs and PCs. By planning ahead, you can determine how many and what type of expansion slots you might need.

A typical configuration on a Macintosh is to install an MIO-series multifunction board and a GPIB board with DMA support such as the NB-DMA-2800 (both from National Instruments). This setup will support the world of GPIB instruments and provide some analog and digital I/O connections as well. On new Macs, video and networking support is built in, so these may be the only boards you need to install. I've always considered the 3-slot Macs to be the minimum for serious LabVIEW systems, and the big 5- or 6-slot Macs desirable where you are unsure what the future may hold.

In the PC world, most desktop machines come with many expansion slots, though many of those slots may be consumed by disk, video, sound, serial, printer, and network interfaces. Newer PCs build in some of this functionality, which opens up some slots for data acquisition boards, GPIB interface boards, or whatever. Just beware of *pizza-box* configurations with few slots. The *type* of bus your PC has can make a big difference in performance and availability of plug-in boards. By far the most common bus is the PC/AT, or Industry Standard Architecture (ISA), bus. Sadly, it offers about the lowest performance available, being only 16 bits wide and operating no faster than 8 MHz. (Realistically, this turns out to be a fairly minor limitation; the speed of the CPU when number-crunching is more likely to limit your system's overall performance.) Much better is the Extended ISA (EISA) bus, which offers a 32-bit data path and much higher transfer rates. The Microchannel bus, which is also 16 bits, falls somewhere in between. Look carefully in the catalogs to determine which bus structure best fits your application. National Instruments Application Note 011, *DMA Fundamentals on Various PC Platforms* may help.

National Instruments now offers SBus versions of its popular data acquisition plug-in boards for Sun SPARCstations. You can use an SBus plug-in board or a SCSI port GPIB adapter to obtain a GPIB interface on the Sun SPARCstation. Another alternative is an Ethernet GPIB interface, such as National Instruments' GPIB-ENET/Sun. This permits you to control GPIB devices anywhere on an Ethernet network. For data acquisition, you can use National Instruments SBus boards, including the SB-A2200 or SB-MIO-16 series.

Networking

In this well-connected era, no computer should be an island. With network hardware and software, most computers today can share printers, access file servers and electronic mail systems. With a LabVIEW system, this opens the possibility of sharing data between two or more computers. By using the TCP/IP networking protocol support in LabVIEW, you can (in theory) exchange data with other computers over wide areas and even those not necessarily running LabVIEW. Having access to file servers is a big plus because you can easily archive data remotely. You can even talk to a GPIB instrument on Ethernet by using an interface such as the GPIB-ENET/Sun. Beware, though, of real-time data logging via Ethernet and similar networks. They are notorious for adding nondeterministic delays that are unacceptable in real-time applications.

All Macintoshes and Suns have built-in networking support, while the PC can support a variety of network types through the use of plug-in boards. Ethernet connections are probably the most versatile because nearly all computers can access Ethernet and it offers reasonable performance. On all platforms, you can use LabVIEW's built-in TCP/IP functions to establish connections and transfer data. LabVIEW also has drivers for higher-level protocols that are useful for controlling other programs and/or transferring data. LabVIEW on the Macintosh supports AppleEvents (which will also be available under Windows and on the Sun in the future). Under Windows, LabVIEW has Dynamic Data Exchange (DDE) capability, which may be extended transnetwork by using NetDDE. So far, LabVIEW for the Sun only supports TCP/IP. What is important is to decide what your goals are, seek out some of the third-party LabVIEW networking support packages, and work with a network manager. These things get complicated in a hurry!

Other Software to Consider

In addition to LabVIEW and all the usual applications you probably have on your computer, here are a few items worth considering.

Compiler for CINs: Many advanced LabVIEW users eventually want to write Code Interface Nodes (CINs). CINs must be written in C. The preferred compilers are:

- Macintosh: Think C (Symantec Corp.) and MPW C (Apple Computer)

- Windows: Watcom C (Watcom Corp.)

- Sun Solaris: Unbundled ANSI C compiler

Drawing: Sometimes you will want to add custom graphics to your LabVIEW panels. This requires the use of a graphics application, which may be as simple as a shareware paint or draw application or as complex as a professional CAD package.

Analysis and graphing applications: There are many, many applications available for data analysis and graphing, assuming that you don't do these operations in LabVIEW. Such applications as Igor and the Spyglass products (Mac only), PVWave, IDL, Matlab, Mathematica, and National Instruments HiQ (all platforms) are extremely powerful and produce publication-quality graphs. Sometimes, all you need is an ordinary spreadsheet, and that's fine. Special LabVIEW drivers are available for Igor, Matlab, Mathematica, and HiQ that support each application's proprietary file formats and/or allow the application to be connected to LabVIEW.

Sources for Help and Answers

LabVIEW is a complex product and nobody expects you to puzzle through everything on your own. Lots of people come to me with questions about getting started with and using LabVIEW, so here are some of my shrink-wrapped answers.

Get Trained

The first thing I suggest is that you take the courses offered by National Instruments. The introductory course is three days time well-spent. You learn how to navigate LabVIEW and use the tools, how to build simple applications and drivers, and how to debug and document your work. Many users (including me) took this course with essentially no prior knowledge of LabVIEW, or even the particular computer it runs on, and immediately set to work on an actual application. In fact, it's important that you start your first application soon after the course to reinforce what you have learned. You can also take the advanced courses, but I usually recommend that you do so only after using LabVIEW for a while—maybe a couple of months or so. National Instruments also sells the workbooks that go with their classes. That might be an option if you can't make it to a class.

This book is not intended as a tutorial, but the LabVIEW tutorial manual, included with every new copy of LabVIEW, is an excellent starting-out guide that walks you through the basics of creating VIs. Also, those of you who work for larger companies may even have in house training facilities or consultants who can help you get started.

Use the Example VIs

LabVIEW comes with many, many example VIs. National Instruments also has additional examples, utilities, and libraries available via mail or electronic communications (see the *Bulletin Boards* section below). It is important for you to spend time browsing the examples because they demonstrate many common programming techniques. Some of the examples are real, working systems. For instance, in the data acquisition examples, you will find programs that use National Instruments' plug-in boards to acquire data at high speeds, store it on disk, and read it for display. All of this is free, and you are free to copy these programs and modify them for your own applications. Major example topics include:

* Analysis—DSP, statistics, signal generation, measurements

* Applications—ATE, simple data acquisition and control techniques

* CIN—basics of Code Interface Nodes

* Data acquisition (DAQ)—analog and digital I/O and counter/timer examples

* Files—basic text and binary file I/O, data logging, spreadsheet formats

* General—tips, programming structures, graphs, attributes, VI setup options

* GPIB—using GPIB instruments; basic drivers

* Networking—TCP/IP, DDE, AppleEvents

* Picture—using the Picture VI package

* Serial—communicating via the serial port

When All Else Fails, Read the Directions

Better yet, read the directions *first*. Do you have any idea how many phone calls to software companies are simple-minded questions that are easily solved by perusing the index of the user manual? The LabVIEW manuals are written by the developers and some major in-house users at National Instruments, then edited by a Tech Pubs team led by an eminently-qualified guy (who just happens to be the same guy who edited this book). They really know what they're talking about, the writing is clear, and the indexes have improved dramatically over the years. I've found the user manual to be one of the keys to becoming a proficient LabVIEW user because it contains all the details you could ever want to know. An effective way to learn something is to read, practice, then read again. Throw in some formal training, and you too can become a high-paid consultant.

In addition to the user manual, there are of course all the specialty manuals that come with LabVIEW—the function reference manual, the data acquisition VI reference manual, and so forth. These are truly indispensable because they help to explain the *big picture*. For instance, what is the difference between a datalog file and a byte stream file? You can find that in the function reference manual under file I/O functions. And the data acquisition library is sufficiently complex that you need to read the background information in the first few chapters before doing anything serious.

A great deal of supplementary information is available (free!) from National Instruments in the form of application notes and technical notes. Application notes describe major topics pertaining to LabVIEW and the related use of various National Instruments products. Some of my favorites are Application Note 006, *Developing a LabVIEW Instrument Driver*, and Application Note 043, *Measuring Temperature with Thermocouples*. Technical notes are more limited in scope and are intended to explain subtle details of LabVIEW operation. They go out of date quickly because every time there is a new version of the program, the details change. Technical notes are of particular interest to advanced users who want to make fullest use of LabVIEW capabilities. All of the application notes and technical notes can be obtained by contacting National Instruments or via the bulletin boards.

Bulletin Boards

Speaking of bulletin boards, if you have a modem, you can call up the National Instruments user bulletin board at any time to download a variety of files, from instrument drivers to example programs. You may also upload your own files to the BBS so that the applications engineers can help solve your problems quickly and efficiently.

Using the National Instruments BBS

You will need a modem, preferably a fast one if you plan to transfer many VIs, and you will need a communications program that supports x modem, y modem, or z modem. The telephone numbers are (512) 794-5484 and 794-5422. Communications settings are: 8 data bits, 1 stop bit, no parity, and any speed up to 9600 baud (V.32 compatible). You will find information on GPIB and DAQ hardware products, LabVIEW (all platforms), LabWindows, and other products, in various directories. Contact National Instruments for complete instructions. Those of you who are familiar with bulletin board operations can probably figure it out after a brief hacking session.

FTP File Servers for LabVIEW Users

In addition to the dial-in bulletin board, those of you who have access to the Internet with an application that supports **File Transfer Protocol (FTP)** can access two LabVIEW-related servers. National Instruments has one, with the Internet alias **ftp.natinst.com** (IP number 130.164.1.2). On it you will find much of the same information that is available on the regular bulletin board. The advantage, of course, is that FTP transfers are generally faster—effectively 50K baud or greater—depending on the physical connection that you have and the amount of traffic on the network. You log in with user name *anonymous* and enter your Internet address for the password.

Another server is **ftp.pica.army.mil**, which is sponsored by the U.S. Army's Picatinny Arsenal and is used in conjunction with the info-labview mail group described below. The regular anonymous login applies. Several hundred LabVIEW users regularly access this server and most of the contributions are left by users. Utility VIs, small applications, relevant documents, and demo versions of commercial LabVIEW add-on packages are available on this server.

FTP services are built right into UNIX machines, so you Sun users are all set, once you have an Ethernet connection that is routed to the outside world and the Internet; just use the FTP command. Mac users need MacTCP, which is available from Apple, and a communications package that supports FTP transfers. Examples are Fetch, TurboGopher, NCSA Telnet, and VersaTerm Pro. PC users will need a Telnet application, included with most commercial networking packages.

The Internet is a world of its own with thousands of users and FTP sites. I've enjoyed (and sometimes wasted) plenty of time prowling among the servers of the world. For more information, check out *The Whole Internet Users Guide and Catalog*.

The Internet Mailgroup

Most of you probably have electronic mail (email) access through one method or another. If your mail service, like most, is linked to the Internet, then you can join in the fun of the LabVIEW mailgroup. Mailgroups use ordinary email to automatically distribute contributed messages to all subscribers. You send a message, and everyone on the list (now over 300 users) will see it and have a chance to respond. Several application engineers at National Instruments monitor the traffic, and sometimes join in the free-for-all. There are all kinds of requests posted. Many messages are from users in search of special instrument drivers; there are lots of people who have written incomplete drivers that aren't necessarily suited to widespread distribution, but are useful just the same. Another popular area is application-specific questions. For instance, if you are planning to write a LabVIEW program to do some specialized measurements or analysis, just post a message describing your problem, and see who is doing similar work. There is a great deal of information sharing going on in the mail group. I've made many friends in the mail group, some of whom contributed to this book. The mail group is also a forum for, "Gee, I wish LabVIEW could do so-and-so." I've seen some rather lively discussions ensue when someone's hot-button gets pressed.

To join, send a message to: info-labview-request@pica.army.mil and tell the list maintainer (Tom Corradeschi) that you would like to sign up. If you have a preferred email address, give that to him; otherwise he'll use the return path from your message. To post a message for all to see, send it to info-labview@pica.army.mil. Remember to be considerate to others. Don't send a message intended for a particular person to the whole group; use that person's email address, not info-labview's. For the same reason, be careful when using the *reply* command in your email program because that routes your reply back through the whole system. Also, remember that others can't see your facial expressions or hear your tone of voice. The best advice I've heard is that, what you type into an email message should be suitable for viewing by your mother. For more insight on this subject, read *Email Etiquette* by Guy Kawasaki in the November 1991 issue of MacUser.

LabVIEW Technical Resource (LTR)

LabVIEW Technical Resource is a quarterly newsletter that is a gold mine of information for LabVIEW system developers. It's written by Lynda Gruggett and Jeff Parker who were both on the original LabVIEW development team and now run their own consulting businesses. Feature articles in each issue explain LabVIEW programming methodology, tips and techniques, and include in-depth technical case studies of user applications. Each issue also includes a diskette with the latest nifty example VIs. In the future, they're likely to come up with even more interesting tidbits to accompany the newsletter. Like this book, it's full of practical hands-on information, and I highly recommend that you subscribe if you can. It is published by LTR Publishing and currently costs $95 per year. See Appendix C, *Sources*, for ordering information.

User Groups

There is no substitute for direct, human contact in any endeavor. Ever take any music lessons? You learn more in the first hour with a teacher than you will in two months of fooling around on your own. LabVIEW is the same way. Learning this complex, visual language is much easier with live teachers and demonstrations. That's why I recommend taking the LabVIEW class. But you can also benefit from working with other users at all experience levels.

Because LabVIEW is so popular, National Instruments has helped form user groups all over the world. In the San Francisco area, for instance, we have two user groups that meet every two months. The meetings are based on user presentations, which are most enlightening. It's fun to see how others solve their automation problems, and compare their techniques with your own. At most meetings, there is also a presentation by a National Instruments representative, showing LabVIEW techniques and applications or new products. It's also a good place to meet other users with common interests. (Actually, I just go because there's usually free food.) And remember that user group meetings of a sort can take place in your area, your plant, and even in your office on a smaller scale. All you need is two or more people with a common interest and good things will surely happen. Show one another what you are working on and ask questions. Learn not to be afraid to show your work and accept positive criticism. Sharing and synergy are two of the most valuable assets that any project can have.

The Alliance Program—Consultants

If you get involved with an application where you think you may need outside help, call National Instruments and ask for National Instruments *Solutions*, a guide to third-party products and consultants. This guide, which is updated periodically, contains information about developers whose products are based on National Instrument's products (both hardware and software), as well as consultants who recommend National Instrument's products. In it you will find descriptions of many useful products, some of which are mentioned in this book. It's worth reading through the guide because you may discover that someone has already written a package that solves a major part of your current problem. Consultants (like me) are also listed with descriptions of their areas of expertise. We can help with everything from writing drivers, to system configuration, to the production of complete turn-key systems.

If you are an experienced LabVIEW user or developer who has a product or service that you would like to offer to the rest of the world, call National Instruments and talk to the Alliance Program manager for more information.

Educational Applications

For those of you in the realm of education, National Instruments has a literature kit available entitled *National Instruments In Education*, an information resource for professors and researchers. It gives lists of contact names, article reprints, data sheets, and other related information.

(800) IEEE 488

For information or assistance with any National Instruments product, including LabVIEW, call (800) 433-3488 or (512) 794-0100. They wrote the program and they designed the interface hardware, so by golly they had better have all the answers. Also remember to find out who your district sales manager is; he or she can answer lots of questions regarding system configurations, pricing, delivery, local user groups, and so forth.

REFERENCES

1. *An Instrument that isn't Really*, IEEE Spectrum, Vol. 27, No. 8, August 1990.

2. E. Krol, *The Whole Internet Users Guide and Catalog*, Sebastopol, CA: O'Reilly and Associates, 1992.

3. National Instruments Application Note 011, *DMA Fundamentals on Various PC Platforms* (part number 320358-01).

4. National Instruments Application Note 006, *Developing a LabVIEW Instrument Driver* (part number 320344-01).

5. National Instruments Application Note 043, *Measuring Temperature with Thermocouples* (part number 340524-01).

If you would like to read more about the theory behind LabVIEW, there are many technical articles available:

*   "Objects and Messages in the LabVIEW Graphical Programming System," by Jeff Kodosky, *Proceedings of SEAM '93* (Scientific and Engineering Applications of the Macintosh), August 2, 1993.

*   "Visual Programming Using Structured Data Flow," by Jeffrey Kodosky, Jack MacCrisken, and Gary Rymar, *Proceedings of the 1991 IEEE Workshop on Visual Languages*, Kobe, Japan, October 8-11, 1991.

*   "Visual Object-Oriented Programming," by Rob Dye, *Dr. Dobb's Macintosh Journal*, Fall 1989.

*   "Visual Programming in LabVIEW," by Jeff Kodosky and Jack MacCrisken, *1989 IEEE Workshop on Visual Languages*, October 4-6, 1989, Rome, Italy.

*   "Using an API as a Developer Platform," by Jeffrey M. Parker, *Dr. Dobb's Software Engineering Sourcebook*, Winter 1988.

*   "Where Graphical User Interfaces Fit," by Jeffrey Kodosky, *EDN Special Supplement*, November 3, 1988, pages S46-S47.

*   "Graphical Programming," by Jeff Kodosky and Robert Dye, *Computer Graphics World*, December 1987.

*   "Block Diagrams and Icons Alleviate the Customary Pain of Programming GPIB Systems," by Ron Wolfe, *Electronic Design*, April 17, 1986.

Inputs and Outputs

To automate your lab, one of the first things you will have to tackle is *data acquisition—* the process of making measurements of physical phenomena and storing them in some coherent fashion. It's a vast technical field with thousands of practitioners, most of whom are hackers like us. How did I learn about data acquisition? By *doing it*, plain and simple. Having a formal background in engineering or some kind of science is awfully helpful, but schools rarely teach the practical aspects of sensors and signals and so on. I think that it's most important that you get the big picture—learn the pitfalls and common solutions to data acquisition problems—and then see where your situation fits into the Grand Scheme.

This chapter should be of some help because the information presented here is hard-won, practical advice, for the most part. The most unusual feature of this chapter is that it contains no LabVIEW programming information. There is much more to a LabVIEW system than LabVIEW programming! If you plan to write applications that support any kind of input/output (I/O) interface hardware, read on.

Origin of Signals

Data acquisition deals with the elements shown in Figure 2-1. The physical phenomenon may be electrical, optical, mechanical, or something else that you need to measure. The sensor changes that phenomenon into a signal that is easier to transmit, record, and analyze–usually a voltage or current. Signal conditioning amplifies and filters the raw

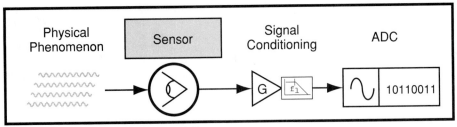

Figure 2-1.   Elements of the data acquisition process.

signal to prepare it for analog-to-digital (A/D) conversion, which transforms the signal into a digital pattern suitable for use by your computer.

Transducers and Sensors

The **transducer** converts one physical phenomenon into another; in our case, we're mostly interested in an electrical signal as the output. For instance, a thermocouple produces a voltage that is related to temperature. An example of a transducer with a nonelectrical output is a liquid-in-glass thermometer. It converts temperature changes to visible changes in the volume of fluid. An elaboration on a transducer is called a **sensor**. It starts with a transducer as the front end, but then adds signal conditioning (such as amplifiers), computation (such as linearization), and a means of transmitting the signal over some distance without degradation—a great advantage in practical terms, because you don't have to worry about noise pickup when dealing with small signals. Of course, this added capability costs money and may add weight and bulk.

Figure 2-2 is a general model of all the world's sensors. If your instrument seems to have only the first couple of blocks, then it's probably a transducer. Table 2-1 contains examples of some sensors. The first example, a temperature transmitter, uses a thermocouple with some built-in signal conditioning. Many times you can use thermocouples without a transmitter, but as we'll see later, you always need some form of signal conditioning. The second example, a pressure transmitter, is a slightly more complex instrument. I came across the third example, a magnetic field sensor, while doing

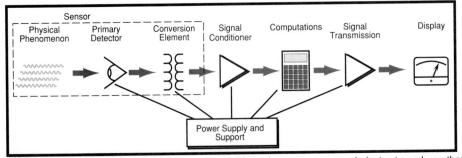

Figure 2-2.   A completely general sensor model. Many times, your sensor is just a transducer that quits after the conversion element.

some research. It uses an optical principle called Faraday rotation in which the polarization of light is affected by magnetic fields. If your data acquisition system interprets light intensity as an input signal, this technology is definitely for you.

Table 2-1. Three Practical Examples of Sensor Systems

Block	Example A	Example B	Example C
Phenomenon	Temperature	Pressure	Magnetic field
Detector	—	Diaphragm displace-ment	Faraday rotation
Transducer	Thermocouple	LVDT	Laser and photo-diode
Signal conditioner	Cold junction; amplifier	Demodulator	ADC
Computations	Linearize	Linearize; scale	Ratio; log; scale
Transmission	0–10 VDC	4–20 mA	RS-232 serial
Display	Analog meter	Analog meter	Computer system
Support	DC	DC (2-wire current loop)	DC; cooling

Example A: Temperature measurement using a thermocouple with cold-junction compensation, linearization, and analog output.

Example B: A pressure sensor using a linear variable differential transformer (LVDT) to detect diaphragm displacement, with analog output.

Example C: Magnetic field measurement using an optical technique with direct digital transmission to a computer. This represents a sophisticated state-of-the-art sensor system.

A detailed discussion of sensor technology is beyond the scope of this book. The references cover all aspects of the physics of transducers and the practical matters of selecting the right sensor. For the purposes of data acquisition, there are several important things you need to know about each of your sensors:

- The nature of the signal it produces—voltage, frequency, impedance, and so on—determines what kind of signal conditioning, A/D converter (ADC), or other hardware you might need.

- Susceptiblity to noise pickup or loading effects from data acquisition hardware.

- How the sensor is calibrated with respect to the physical phenomenon. In particular, you need to know if it's nonlinear, or if it has problems with repeatability, overload, or other aberrant behavior.

- What kind of power or other utilities the sensor might require. This is often overlooked, and sometimes becomes a show-stopper for complex instruments!

When you start to set up your system, try to pick sensors and design the data acquisition system in tandem. They are highly interdependent. The world's greatest sensor, when monitored by the wrong ADC, is of little value. It is important that you understand the details of how your sensors work. Try them under known conditions if you have doubts. If something doesn't seem right, investigate. When you call the manufacturer for help, it may well turn out that you know more about the equipment than the designers, at least in your particular application.

Modern trends are toward *smart sensors* containing onboard microprocessors that compensate for many of the errors that plague transducers, like nonlinearity and drift. Such instruments are well worth the extra cost because they tend to be more accurate and remove much of the burden of error correction from you, the user. For low-frequency measurements of pressure, temperature, flow, and level, the process control industry is rapidly moving in this direction. Companies such as Rosemount, Foxboro, and Honeywell make complete lines of smart sensors.

More complex instruments can also be considered *sensors* in a broader sense. For instance, a digital oscilloscope is a sensor of voltages that vary over time. Your LabVIEW program can interpret this voltage waveform in many different ways, depending upon what the 'scope is connected to. Note that the interface to a sensor like this is probably GPIB or RS-232 communications rather than an analog voltage. That is the beauty of using a computer to acquire data: once you get the hardware hooked up properly, all that is important is the signal itself.

Actuators

The opposite of a sensor, an **actuator** converts a signal (perhaps created by your LabVIEW program) into a physical phenomenon. Examples of actuators include electrically actuated valves, heating elements, power supplies, and motion control devices like servomotors. Actuators are required any time you wish to **control** something like temperature, pressure, or position. It turns out that we spend most of our time measuring things (the data acquisition phase) rather than controlling them, at least in the world of research. But control does come up from time to time, and you need to know how to use those analog and digital outputs so conveniently available on your interface boards.

Almost invariably, you will see actuators associated with **feedback control loops**. The reason is simple. Most actuators produce changes in the physical system that are more than just a little bit nonlinear, and are sometimes unpredictable. For example, a valve with an electropneumatic actuator is often used to control fluid flow. A common problem with valves is that the flow varies in some nonlinear way with respect to the valve's position. Valves stick and slide when they open or close but don't always stick and slide in the same places. These are real-world problems that simply can't be ignored. Putting feedback around such actuators helps the situation greatly. The principle is simple. Add a sensor that measures the quantity that you need to control. Compare this measurement with the desired value (the difference is called the error) and adjust the actuator in such a way as to minimize the error. The chapter on process control delves more deeply into this subject.

The combination of LabVIEW and external loop controllers makes this whole situation easy to manage.

An important consideration for actuators is what sort of voltage or power they require. There are some industrial standards that are fairly easy to meet, like 0–10 VDC or 4-20 mA—modest voltages and currents. But even these simple ranges can have added requirements, like isolated grounds, in which the signal ground is not the chassis of your computer. If you want to turn on a big heater, you may need large relays or contactors to handle the required current; the same is true for most high-voltage AC loads. Your computer doesn't have that kind of output, nor should it. Running lots of high power or high voltage into the back of your computer is not a pleasant thought! Try to think about these requirements ahead of time.

Categories of Signals

You measure a signal because it contains some type of useful information. Therefore, the first questions you should ask are what information does the signal contain and how is it conveyed? Generally, information is conveyed by a signal through one or more of the following parameters: state, rate, level, shape, or frequency content. These parameters determine what kind of I/O interface equipment and analysis techniques you will need.

Any signal can generally be classified as analog or digital (Figure 2-3). A digital, or binary, signal has only two possible discrete levels of interest—a high (on) level and a low (off) level (Figure 2-4). An analog signal, on the other hand, contains information in the continuous variation of the signal with time (Figure 2-5).

There are two types of digital signals and two types of analog signals. The two digital signal types are the **on-off** signals and the **pulse train** signal. The two analog signal types are the **DC** signal and the **AC** signal.

The first type of digital signal is the **on-off** signal. An on-off signal conveys information concerning the digital state of the signal, either on (high voltage) or off (low voltage). Therefore, the instrument needed for this type of signal is a simple digital state detector, which determines whether the signal is high (above some threshold) or low (below some threshold). For example, the output of a transistor-transistor logic (TTL) switch is an example of a digital on-off signal.

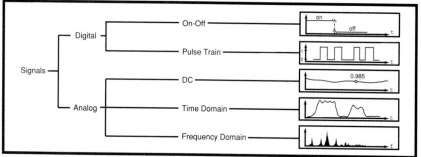

Figure 2-3. Classifications of signals.

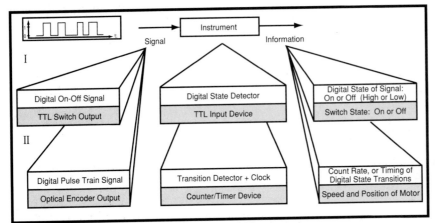

Figure 2-4. Types of digital signals: (I) on-off and (II) pulse trains.

The second type of digital signal is the **pulse train** signal, which is a series of state transitions. Information is contained in the number of state transitions occurring, the rate at which the transitions occur, or the time between one or more state transitions. To measure a pulse train signal, an instrument must be able to detect and count digital transitions. In addition, a timer device is also required to time the state transitions. An example of a digital pulse train signal is the output of an incremental optical encoder mounted on the shaft of a motor.

Whereas the pulse train is a form of serial data, some sensors provide several bits simultaneously in parallel fashion. An example is an absolute optical encoder with 16 optical tracks and 16 detectors that produces a 16-bit digital word, corresponding to 65,536 distinct positions per revolution. Such an instrument requires a parallel digital input device (a register) so that you can read all of the bits simultaneously.

Both on-off and pulse train signals are also used for a variety of control purposes. An instrument that can generate digital on-off signals can be used to turn devices on and off.

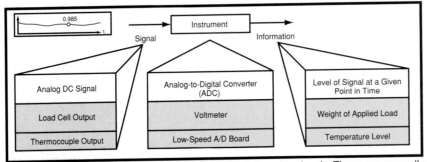

Figure 2-5. Here is an example of low-frequency or DC analog signals. These are generally easy to acquire since there is no tricky timing or high sampling rates. Watch out for DC stability and resolution requirements, however.

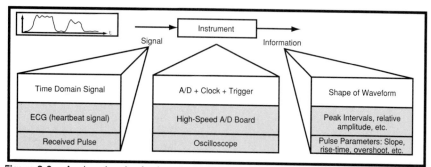

Figure 2-6. Analog signals of a time-domain nature. The manner in which the signal varies with time s very important, so your acquisition system has to attend to matters of timing and triggering.

An instrument capable of generating digital pulse train signals can be used for applications that require timing signals, such as controlling the position and speed of a stepper motor.

Analog **DC** signals are static or slowly varying analog signals. The most important characteristic of the DC signal is that information of interest is conveyed in the level, or amplitude, of the signal at a given instant.

When measuring a DC signal, you need an instrument that can detect the level of the signal. The measurement is not critical as long as the signal varies slowly in comparison. Therefore, the fundamental component of the instrument is an ADC, which converts the analog electrical signal into a digital number that the computer interprets.

Common examples of DC signals include temperature, pressure, battery voltage testing, strain gauge outputs, flow rate, and level measurements. In each case, the instrument monitors the signal and returns a single value indicating the magnitude of the signal at a given time. Therefore, DC instruments often report the information through devices such as meters, gauges, strip charts, and numerical readouts.

Analog **time domain** signals are distinguished by the fact that they convey useful information not only in the level of the signal, but also in how this level varies with time. When measuring an AC signal, often referred to as a **waveform**, you are interested in some characteristics of the shape of the waveform, such as slope, locations and shapes of peaks, and so on. You may also be interested in its frequency content.

To measure the shape of an AC signal, you must take a precisely timed sequence of individual amplitude measurements, or *samples*. These measurements must be taken close enough together to adequately reproduce those characteristics of the waveform shape you want to measure. Also, the series of measurements should start and stop at the proper time to guarantee that the useful part of the waveform is acquired. Therefore, the instrument used to measure time domain signals consists of an ADC, a sample clock, and a trigger. A sample clock accurately times the occurrence of each A/D conversion.

Figure 2-7 illustrates the timing relationship between an analog waveform, a sampling clock, and a trigger pulse. Each dot on the waveform represents an acquired value. To ensure that the desired portion of the waveform is acquired, you can use the trigger to start and/or stop the waveform measurement at the proper time according to some external

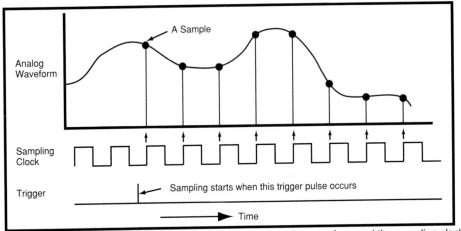

Figure 2-7. An illustration of the relationship between an analog waveform and the sampling clock and trigger that synchronize an ADC.

condition. For instance, you may want to start acquisition when the signal voltage is moving in a positive direction through 0 V. A/D boards and oscilloscopes generally have trigger circuits that respond to such conditions.

Another way that you can look at an AC signal is to convert the waveform data to the **frequency domain**. Information extracted from frequency domain analysis is based on the frequency content of the signal, as opposed to the shape, or time-based characteristics, of the waveform. Conversion from the time domain to the frequency domain on a digital computer is carried out through the use of a **Fast Fourier Transform** (FFT), a standard function in the LabVIEW digital signal processing (DSP) function library. The Inverse Fast Fourier Transform (IFFT) converts frequency domain information back to the time domain. In the frequency domain, you can use DSP functions to observe the frequencies that make up a signal, the distribution of noise, and many other useful parameters that are otherwise not apparent in the time domain waveform. Digital signal processing can be performed by LabVIEW software routines or by special DSP hardware designed to do the analysis quickly and efficiently.

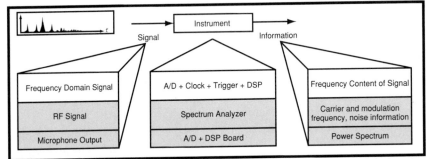

Figure 2-8. Here is an example of observing the frequency domain aspect of analog signals. This adds another dimension: the frequency content conveys much of the information. Significant processing of the signal is often required.

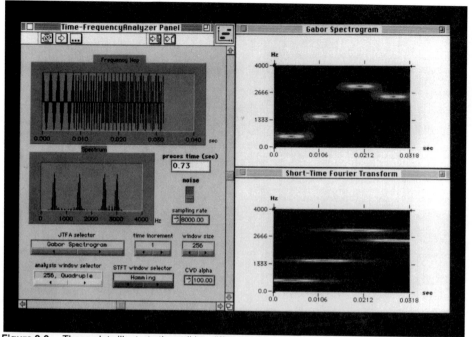

Figure 2-9. These plots illustrate the striking differences between a JTF analysis plot of a chirp signal analyzed with the short-time FFT spectrogram and the same chirp signal analyzed with the new Gabor Spectrogram algorithm.

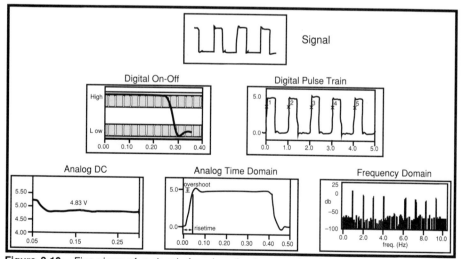

Figure 2-10. Five views of a signal. A series of pulses can be classified several different ways depending on the significance of its time, amplitude, and frequency characteristics.

There is one more way to look at analog signals, and that is in the **joint time-frequency (JTF) domain**. This is a combination of the two preceding techniques. JTF signals have an interesting frequency spectrum that varies with time. Examples are speech, sonar, and advanced modulation techniques for communication systems. The classic display technique for JTF analysis is the **spectrogram**, a plot of frequency versus time, for which LabVIEW has one of the very best, the Gabor Spectrogram algorithm (Figure 2-9).

As Figure 2-10 shows, the signal classifications described in this section are not mutually exclusive. A single signal may convey more than one type of information. In fact, the digital on-off, pulse train, and DC signals are just simpler cases of the analog time domain signals that allow simpler measuring techniques.

The example below demonstrates how one signal can belong to many classes. The same signal can be measured with different types of instruments, ranging from a simple digital state detector to a complex frequency analysis instrument. This greatly affects how you choose signal conditioning equipment.

Signal Conditioning

Professor John Frisbee is hard at work in his lab, trying to make a pressure measurement with his brand-new computer:

> Let's see here ... This pressure transducer says it has a 0–10 VDC output, positive on the red wire, minus on the black. The manual for my data acquisition board says it can handle 0–10 VDC. No sweat. Just hook the input up to channel 1 on terminals 5 and 6. Twist a couple of wires together ... tighten the screws ... run the data acquisition demo program, and ... Voila! But what's this? My signal looks like ... *garbage!* My voltmeter says the input is DC, 1.23 V, and LabVIEW seems to be working OK, but the display is *really noisy*. What's going on here?

Poor John. He obviously didn't read this chapter. If he had, he would have said, "Aha! I need to put a lowpass filter on this signal and then make sure that everything is properly grounded and shielded." John did not realize that his A/D plug-in board is doing no averaging or filtering. What John needs is **signal conditioning**, and believe me, so do you. This world is chock-full of noise sources and complex signals–all of them guaranteed to corrupt your data if you don't take care to separate the good from the bad.

There are several steps in designing the right signal conditioning approach for your application. First, remember that you need to know all about your sensors and what kind

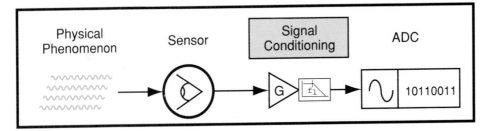

of signals they are supposed to produce. Then, you need to consider grounding and shielding. You may also need to use amplifiers and filters. Finally, you can list your specifications and go shopping for the right data acquisition hardware.

Grounding and Shielding

Noise sources are lurking everywhere, but by following some simple principles of grounding and shielding, you can eliminate most noise-related problems right at the source–the wiring. In fact, how you connect a sensor to its associated data acquisition hardware greatly affects the overall performance of the system. Another point on the subject: measurements are inherently inaccurate. A good system design minimizes the distortion of the signal that takes place trying to measure it: noise, nonlinear components, distortion, and so on. The wire between sensor and data acquisition can never improve the signal quality. You can only minimize the negatives with good technique. Without getting too involved with electromagnetic theory, I'll show you some of the recommended practices that instrumentation engineers everywhere use. Let's start with some definitions.

Ground. Absolutely the most overused, misapplied, and misunderstood term in all of electronics. First of all, there is the most hallowed *earth ground* that is represented by the electrical potential of the soil underneath your feet. The green wire on every power cord, along with any metal framework or chassis with 120 VAC main power applied, is required by the *National Electrical Code* to be connected through a low-resistance path to the aforementioned dirt. There is exactly one reason for its existence—*SAFETY.* Sadly, we somehow come to believe that *grounding* our equipment will magically siphon away all sources of noise, as well as evil spirits. Baloney! Electricity flows only in closed circuits, or loops. You and your equipment sit upon earth ground like a bird sits upon a high-voltage wire. Does the bird know he's living at 34,000 V? Of course not. There is no complete circuit. This is not to say that connections to earth ground (which I will refer to as **safety ground** from here on) are unnecessary. You should always make sure that there is a reliable path from all of your equipment to safety ground as required by code. This prevents accidental connections between power sources and metallic objects from becoming hazards. Such fault currents are shunted away by the safety ground system.

What we really need to know about is a reference potential referred to as signal **common**, or sometimes as a **return** path. Every time you see a signal or measure a voltage, always ask the question, "Voltage ... with respect to what reference?" That reference is the signal common, which in most situations is *not* the same as safety ground. A good example is the negative side of the battery in your car. Everything electrical in the vehicle has a return connection to this common, which is also connected to the chassis. Note that there is no connection whatsoever to earth ground—the car has rubber tires that make fair insulators—and yet, the electrical system works just fine (except if it's very old, or British).

In my labs, we run heavy copper braid, welding cable, or copper sheet between all the racks and experimental apparatus according to a grounding plan. A well-designed signal common can even be effective at higher frequencies where second-order effects like **skin**

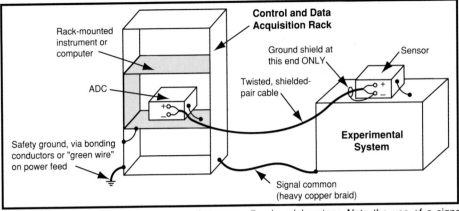

Figure 2-11. Taking the system approach to grounding in a laboratory. Note the use of a signal common (in the form of heavy copper braid or cable to tie everything together). All items are connected to this signal common.

effect become important. See the references for instructions on designing a quality grounding system—it's worth its weight in Excedrin.

Single-ended connections are the simplest and most obvious way to connect a signal source to an amplifier or other measurement device (Figure 2-12). The significant hazard of this connection is that it is highly susceptible to noise pickup. Noise induced on any of the input wires, including the signal common, is added to the desired signal. Shielding the signal cable and being careful where you make connections to the signal common can help the situation. Single-ended connections are most often used in wide-bandwidth systems like oscilloscopes, video, radio frequency (RF), and fast pulse measurements where low-impedance coaxial cables are the preferred means of transmission.

Differential connections depend on a pair of conductors where the voltage you want to measure (called the **normal-mode signal**) is the difference between the voltages on the individual conductors. The reason you use differential connections is that noise pickup usually occurs equally on any two conductors that are closely spaced, like a twisted pair of wires. That way, when you take the difference between the two voltages, the noise cancels

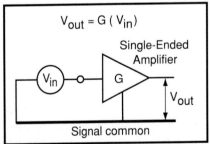

Figure 2-12. A single-ended amplifier has no intrinsic noise rejection properties. You need to carefully shield signal cables and make sure that the signal common is noise-free as well.

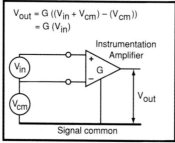

Figure 2-13. Instrumentation amplifiers effectively reject common-mode (V_{cm}) signals, such as noise pickup, through cancellation. The normal-mode (differential) signal is amplified.

but the difference signal remains. An **instrumentation amplifier** is optimized for use with differential signals, as shown in Figure 2-13. The output is equal to the gain of the amplifier times the difference between the inputs. If you add another voltage in series with both inputs (called the **common-mode signal**), it cancels just like the noise pickup. The common mode voltage can't be infinitely large, though, since every amplifier has some kind of maximum input voltage limit—watch out for overloads. Differential inputs are available on most low-frequency instrumentation such as voltmeters, chart recorders, and computer I/O boards such as those made by National Instruments. **RULE:** *Always use differential connections*, except when you can't:

Electromagnetic Fields

Noise is injected into your measurement system by interaction with **electromagnetic fields**, which are all around us. Without delving into Maxwell's equations, here are a few simple principles of electromagnetism that you can use when connecting your data acquisition system.

- Two conductors that are separated by an insulator form a **capacitor**. An electric field exists between the conductors. If the potential (voltage) of one conductor changes with time, a proportional change in potential will appear in the other. This is called capacitive coupling. Moving things farther apart reduces the coupling.

- An electric field cannot enter a closed, conductive surface. That's why sitting in your car during a thunderstorm is better than sitting outside. The lightning's field cannot get inside. This kind of enclosure is also called a Faraday cage or **electrostatic shield.**

- A time-varying magnetic field will induce an electrical current only when a closed, conductive loop is present. Furthermore, the magnitude of the induced current is proportional to the intensity of the magnetic field and the area of the loop. This property is called inductive coupling, or **inductance**. Open the loop, and the current goes away.

- Sadly, **magnetic shielding** is not so easy to design, for most situations. This is because the magnetic fields that we are most concerned about (low frequency, 50/60 Hz) are very penetrating, and require very thick shields of iron or even better magnetic materials, like expensive mu-metal.

Here are the basic practices you need to follow to block the effects of these electromagnetic noise sources:

- Put sensitive, high-impedance circuitry and connections inside a metallic shield that is connected to the common-mode voltage (usually the *low side*, or common) of the signal source. This will block capacitive coupling to the circuit (source 1), as well as the entry of any stray electric fields (source 2).

- Avoid closed, conductive loops—intentional or unintentional—often known as **ground loops**. Such loops act as pickups for stray magnetic fields (source 3).

- Avoid placing sensitive circuits near sources of intense magnetic fields, like transformers, motors, and power supplies. This will reduce the likelihood of magnetic pickup that you would otherwise have trouble shielding against (source 4).

Another unsuspected source of interference is the lovely color monitor on your PC. It is among the greatest sources of electrical interference known. Near the screen itself, there are intense electric fields due to the high voltages that accelerate the electron beam. Near the back, there are intense magnetic fields caused by the flyback transformer that generates high voltage. Even the interface cards in your computer, for example the video adapter, and the computer's digital logic circuits are sources of high-frequency noise. And *never* trust a fluorescent light fixture.

Radio-frequency interference (RFI) is possible when there is a moderately intense RF source nearby. Common sources of RFI are transmitting devices like walkie-talkies, cellular phones, commercial broadcast transmitters of all kinds, and RF induction heating equipment. Radio frequencies radiate for great distances through most nonmetallic structures, and really high (microwave) frequencies can even sneak in and out through cracks in metal enclosures. You might not think that a 75 MHz signal would be relevant to a 1 kHz-bandwidth data acquisition system, but there is a phenomenon known as parasitic detection or demodulation that occurs in many places. Any time an RF signal passes through a diode (a rectifying device), it turns into DC plus any low frequencies that may be riding on (modulating) the RF carrier. Likely parasitic detectors include all of the solid-state devices in your system, plus any metal oxide interfaces (such as dirty connections). As a licensed radio amateur, I know that parasitic detection can occur in metal rain gutter joints, TV antenna connections, and stereo amplifier output stages. This results in neighbors screaming at me about how I cut up their TV or stereo.

When RFI strikes your data acquisition system, it results in unexplained noise of varying amplitude and frequency. The solutions to RFI are:

- Shield all the cables into and out of your equipment.

- Add RF-rejection filters on all signal and power leads.

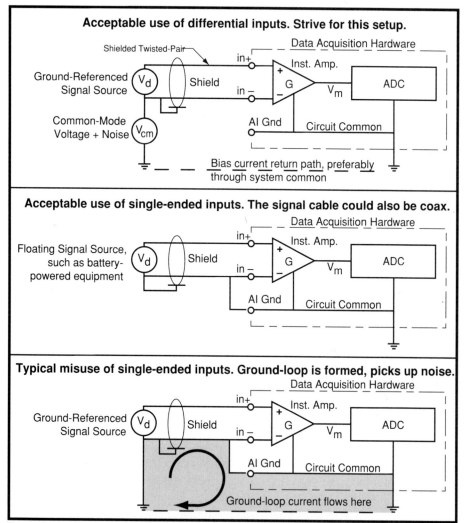

Figure 2-14. Proper use of differential and single-ended signal connections is shown in the top two drawings. The bottom one is that all-too-common case where a ground-loop is formed, enhancing the pickup of noise borne by magnetic fields.

- Put equipment in well-shielded enclosures and racks.

- Keep known RF sources and cables far away from sensitive equipment.

- Keep the guy with the walkie-talkie OUT OF YOUR LAB.

Thermojunction voltages are generated any time two dissimilar metals come in contact with one another in the presence of a temperature gradient. This principle, known as the Seebeck effect, is the way a thermocouple generates its tiny signal. Problems occur in data acquisition when you attempt to measure DC signals that are in the microvolt to millivolt range, such as those from thermocouples and strain gauges. If you connect your instruments with wires, connectors, and terminal screws made of different metals or alloys, then you run the risk of adding uncontrolled thermojunction voltages to the signals— possibly to the tune of hundreds of microvolts. The most common case of thermojunction error that I see occurs when operators hook up thermocouples inside an experimental chamber and bring the wires out through a connector with pins made of copper or stainless steel. The thermocouple alloy wire meets the connector pin and forms a junction. Then, the operators turn on a big heater inside the chamber, creating a huge temperature gradient across the connector. Soon afterwards, they notice that their temperature readouts are *way off*. Those parasitic thermojunction voltages inside the connector are appearing in the data. Here are some ways to kill the thermojunction bugs:

- Make all connections with the same metallic alloy.

- Keep all connections at the same temperature.

- Minimize the number of connections in all low-level signal situations.

In Figure 2-14, you can see some typical signal connection schemes. Shielded cable is always recommended to reduce capacitive coupling and electric field pickup. Twisted, shielded pairs are best, but coaxial cable will do in situations where you are careful not to create the dreaded ground loop that appears in the bottom segment of Figure 2-14.

Why Use Amplifiers or Other Signal Conditioning?

As you can see, even the way you hook up your sensors can affect the overall performance of your data acquisition system. But even if the grounding and shielding are properly done, you should consider using **signal conditioning**, which includes **amplifiers** and **filters**, among other things.

Amplifiers improve the quality of the input signal in several ways. They boost the amplitude of smaller signals, improving the resolution of the measurements. They offer increased driving power (lower output impedance), which keeps components like ADCs from loading the sensor. They have differential inputs, a technique well known to help reject noise. An improvement on differential inputs, an **isolation amplifier**, requires no signal common at the input whatsoever. Isolation amplifiers are available with common-mode voltage ranges up to thousands of volts. Amplifiers are vital for microvolt signals like those from thermocouples and strain gauges. In general, you should try to amplify your low-level signal as close to the physical phenomena itself as possible. Doing this will help you increase the *signal-to-noise ratio* (SNR).

Filters are needed to reject undesired signals, such as high-frequency noise, and to provide **anti-aliasing** (see the next section). Most of the time, you need lowpass filters, which reject high frequencies while passing low frequencies including DC. The best filters are made from resistors and capacitors (and sometimes, inductors). **Switched capacitor**

filters are a modern alternative to these ordinary analog filters. They use arrays of small capacitors that are switched rapidly in and out of the circuit, simulating large resistors on a much smaller (integrated circuit) scale.

Using a signal conditioning system outside of your computer also enhances safety. If a large overload should appear, the signal conditioner will *take the hit* rather than passing it directly to the backplane of your computer (and maybe all the way to the mouse or keyboard!) A robust amplifier package can easily be protected against severe overloads through the use of transient absorption components (such as varistors, zener diodes, and spark gaps), limiting resistors, and fuses. Medical systems are covered by Federal regulations regarding isolation from stray currents. *Never connect electronic instruments to a live subject (human or otherwise) without a properly-certified isolation amplifier and correct grounding.*

Certain transducers require **excitation**. Examples are resistive temperature detectors (RTDs), thermistors, potentiometers, and strain gauges (Figure 2-15). All of these devices produce an output that is proportional to an excitation voltage or current as well as to the physical phenomenon they are intended to measure. Thus, the excitation source can be a source of noise and drift and must be carefully designed. Modular signal conditioners, like the Analog Devices 5B series products and SCXI hardware from National Instruments, include high-quality voltage or current references for this purpose.

Some signal conditioning equipment may also have built-in **multiplexing**, which is an array of switching elements (relays or solid-state analog switches) that route many input signals to one common output. For instance, using the National Instruments SCXI equipment, you can have hundreds of analog inputs connected to one multiplexer at a location near the experiment. Then, only one cable needs to be connected to your computer. This dramatically reduces the number and length of cables.

To drive actuators of one type or another, you need signal conditioning. As with input signals, isolation is one of the major considerations, along with requirements for extra drive capability that many simple output devices can't handle directly.

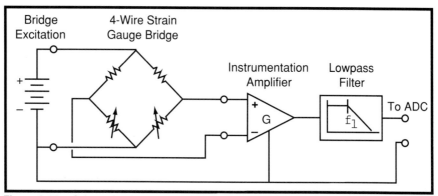

Figure 2-15.   Schematic of a signal conditioner for a strain gauge, a bridge-based transducer that requires excitation. This signal conditioner has an instrumentation amplifier with high gain, followed by a lowpass filter to reject noise.

For digital outputs, most I/O boards offer simple TTL logic drivers, which swing from zero to about +3 V, depending on the load (you need to consult the specifications for your hardware to make sure). If you want to drive a solenoid valve, for instance, much more current is needed—perhaps several amperes at 24 VDC or even 120 VAC. In such cases, you need a relay of some type. Electromechanical relays are simple and cheap with good contact ratings, but sometimes they require more coil current than a TTL output can supply. Sensitive relays, such as reed relays, are acceptable. Solid-state relays use silicon controlled rectifiers (SCRs) or triacs to control heavier loads with minimal control current requirements. Their main limitation is that most units are only usable for AC circuits. Many types of modular I/O systems have options for these higher voltages and currents. If you need to drive other types of logic, or require large output voltages and/or currents at high speed, a special interface circuit may have to be custom designed.

Most of the analog world gets by with voltage outputs in the range of ±10 V or less, and current outputs of 20 mA or less. These outputs are commonly available from most I/O boards and modular signal conditioners. If you need more current and/or voltage, you can use a power amplifier. Audio amplifiers are a quick and easy solution to some of these problems, though most of them have a highpass filter that rolls off the DC response. To control big heaters, motors, and other heavy loads, look to triac-based power controllers. They permit an ordinary analog voltage or current input to control tens or even hundreds of kilowatts with reasonable cost and efficiency. One thing to watch out for is the need for isolation when you get near high-power equipment. An isolation amplifier could save your equipment if a fault occurs; it may also eliminate grounding problems, which are so prevalent around high-power systems.

Choosing the Right I/O Subsystem

As soon as your project gets underway, try to make a list of the sensors you need to monitor along with any actuators you need to drive. Exact specifications on sensors and actuators will make your job much easier. As an instrumentation engineer, I spend a large part of my time on any project collecting data sheets, calling manufacturers, and peering into little black boxes trying to figure out the important details I need for interfacing. Understanding the application is important, too. Just because a pressure transducer will respond in 1 µs doesn't mean that your system will actually have microsecond dynamic conditions to measure. On the other hand, that super-fast transducer may surprise you by putting out all kinds of fast pulses because of little bubbles whizzing by in the soup. Using the wrong signal conditioner in either case can result in a phenomenon known as *bogus data*.

Since you are a computer expert, fire up your favorite spreadsheet or database application and make up an instrument list. The process control industry goes so far as to standardize on a format known as instrument data sheets, which are used to specify, procure, install, and finally document all aspects of each sensor and actuator. Others working on your project will be very happy to see this kind of documentation.

For the purposes of designing an I/O subsystem, your database sometimes might include the following items:

- Instrument name or identifier

- Location, purpose, and references to other drawings such as wiring and installation

- Calibration information: Engineering units (like psig) and full-scale range

- Accuracy, resolution, linearity, and noise, if significant

- Signal current, voltage, or frequency range

- Signal bandwidth

- Isolation requirements

- Excitation or power requirements: Current and voltage

To choose your I/O subsystem, begin by sorting the instrument list according to the types of signals and other basic requirements. Remember to add plenty of spare channels! Consider the relative importance of each instrument. If you have 99 thermocouples and one pressure gauge, your I/O design choice will certainly lean toward accommodating thermocouples. But that pressure signal may be the single most important measurement in the whole system; don't try to *adapt* its 0-10 V output to work with an input channel that is optimized for microvolt thermocouple signals. For each signal, determine the minimum specifications for its associated signal conditioner. Important specs are:

- Adjustability of zero offset and gain

- Bandwidth—minimum and maximum frequencies to pass

- Filtering—usually anti-aliasing lowpass filters

- Settling time—time required to arrive at the final value

- Phase shift characteristics—important for pulse and high-frequency measurements

- Accuracy

- Gain and zero offset drift with time and temperature (very important)

- Excitation: Built in or external?

- For thermocouples, cold-junction compensation and linearization

Next, consider the physical requirements. Exposure to weather, high temperatures, moisture and other contamination, or intense electromagnetic interference may cause damage to unprotected equipment. Will the equipment have to work in a hostile environment? If so, it must be in a suitable enclosure. If the channel count is very high, having many channels per module could save both space and money. Convenience should not be overlooked: ever work on a tiny module with small terminal screws that are deeply recessed into an overstuffed terminal box? These are practical matters; if you have lots of signals to hook up, talk this over with the people who will do the installation.

If your company already has many installations of a certain type of I/O, that may be an overriding factor, so long as the specifications are met. The bottom line is always cost. Using excess or borrowed equipment should always be considered when money is tight. You can do a cost-per-channel analysis, if that makes sense. For instance, using a multifunction board in your computer with just a few channels hooked up through Analog Devices 5B series signal conditioners is very cost-effective. But if you need more than 16 channels, SCXI would certainly save money over the 5Bs. You might even consider a multipurpose data acquisition and control unit, such as Hewlett-Packard's HP3852A, which is competitive for larger channel counts and offers stand-alone programmability.

Careful analysis of your system's needs in the beginning will result in money and aggravation saved in the end. Trust me; I've been there.

Sources for Signal Conditioning Hardware

I have had good luck with the following manufacturers of signal conditioning hardware (see Appendix C, *Sources*, for addresses and phone numbers).

Figure 2-16. EG&G Automotive Research (San Antonio, TX) has the type of industrial environment that makes effective use of SCXI signal conditioning products. (Photo Courtesy of National Instruments and EG &G Automotive Research.)

National Instruments	SCXI
Analog Devices	Modular signal conditioning modules, low and high-frequency; packaged data acquisition systems.
Action Instruments, Inc.	Low-frequency industrial signal conditioning modules and transmitters.
Moore Industries	Low-frequency industrial signal conditioning modules and transmitters.
Frequency Devices, Inc.	Anti-aliasing filters, individual modules or many channels in a chassis; digitally programmed frequency.

Acquiring the Signal

Until now, we've been discussing the real (analog) world of signals. Now it's time to digitize those signals for use in LabVIEW. By definition, **analog** signals are **continuous-time**, **continuous-value** functions. That means they can take on any possible value and are defined over all possible time resolutions. (By the way, don't think that *digital* pulses are special; they're just analog signals that happen to be square waves. If you look closely, they have all kinds of ringing, noise, and slew rate limits—all the characteristics of analog signals.)

An ADC samples your analog signals on a regular basis and converts the amplitude at each sample time to a digital value with finite resolution. These are termed **discrete-time**, **discrete-value** functions. Unlike their analog counterparts, discrete functions are defined only at times specified by the sample rate and may only have values determined by the resolution of the ADC. In other words, when you digitize an analog signal, you have to *approximate*. How *much* you can throw out depends on your signal and your specifications for data analysis. Is 1% resolution acceptable? Or is 0.0001% required? And how fine does the temporal resolution need to be? One second? Or one nanosecond? Please be realistic. Additional amplitude and temporal resolution can be EXPENSIVE. To answer the questions, we need to look at this business of sampling more closely.

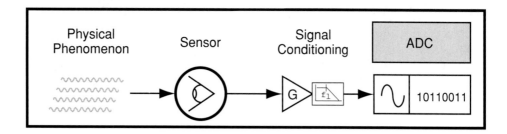

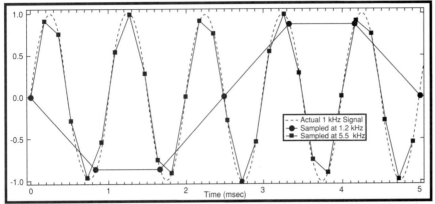

Figure 2-17. This figure shows a graphical display of the effects of sampling rates. When the original 1 kHz sine wave is sampled at 1.2 kHz (too slow), it is totally unrecognizable in the data samples. Sampling at 5.5 kHz yields a much better representation. What would happen if there was a lot of really high-frequency noise?

Sampling Theorem

A fundamental rule of sampled data systems is that the input signal must be sampled at a rate greater than twice the highest frequency component in the signal. This is known as the **Nyquist** criterion. Stated as a formula, it requires that $f_s/2 > f_a$, where f_s is the sampling frequency and f_a is the signal being sampled. Violating the Nyquist criteria is called **undersampling**, and results in **aliasing**. Look at Figure 2-17, which illustrates a sampled data system.

I started out with a simple 1 kHz sine wave (dotted lines), and then sampled it at two different frequencies, 1.2 kHz and 5.5 kHz. At 5.5 kHz, we're above the minimum required sampling rate, which would be 2.0 kHz, and the data points look something like the original (with a little bit of information thrown out, of course). But the 1.2 kHz data is aliased: it looks as if the signal frequency is 200 Hz, not 1 kHz. This effect is also called **frequency fold back**: everything above $f_s/2$ is folded back into the sub-$f_s/2$ range. If you undersample your data and get stuck with aliasing in your data, can you *undo* the aliasing? *No!* Not even the Great Wizard can get the misplaced information back. You must *never* undersample if you hope to make sense of waveform data.

Let's go a step further and consider a nice 1 kHz sine wave, but this time add some high-frequency noise to it. We already know that a 5.5 kHz sample rate will represent the sine wave all right, but any noise that is beyond $f_s/2$ (2.75 kHz) will alias. Is this a disaster? That depends on the **power spectrum** (amplitude squared versus frequency) of the noise or interfering signal. Say that the noise is very, very small in amplitude—much less than the resolution of your ADC. In that case it will be undetectable, even though it violates the Nyquist criteria. The real problems are medium-amplitude noise and spurious signals. In Figure 2-18, I simulated a 1 kHz sine wave with lowpass-filtered white noise added to it. If we use a16-bit ADC, the specs say its noise floor is about -115 dB. Assuming that the signal is sampled at 5.5 kHz as before, the Nyquist limit is 2.75 kHz.

Filtering and Averaging

To get rid of aliasing, you need to use a type of **lowpass filter**, known in this case as an **anti-aliasing filter**. Analog filters are absolutely mandatory, regardless of the sampling rate, unless you know the signal's frequency characteristics and can live with the aliased noise. There has to be *something* to limit the bandwidth of the raw signal to $f_s/2$. The analog filter can be in the transducer, the signal conditioner, on the A/D board, or in all three places. The filter is usually made up of resistors, capacitors, and sometimes operational amplifiers, in which case it's called an **active filter**. You can build active filters yourself with simple components, or buy them in modular form from a variety of suppliers. One problem with analog filters is that they can become very complex and expensive. If the desired signal is fairly close to the Nyquist limit, the filter needs to cut off very quickly, which requires lots of stages (this is more formally known as the **order** of the filter's **transfer function**).

Digital filters can augment, but not replace, analog filters. Digital filter VIs are included with the LabVIEW analysis VIs, and they are functionally equivalent to analog filters. The simplest type of digital filter is a **moving averager** (examples of which are available with LabVIEW), which has the advantage of being usable in real-time on a sample-by-sample basis. One way to simplify the anti-aliasing filter problem is to **oversample** the input. If your A/D hardware is fast enough, just turn the sampling rate way up and then use a digital filter to eliminate the higher frequencies that are of no interest. This makes the analog filtering design problem simpler because the Nyquist frequency has been raised much higher, so the analog filter doesn't have to be so sharp. A compromise is always necessary. You need to sample at a rate high enough to avoid significant aliasing with a modest analog filter, but sampling at too high a rate may not be practical because the hardware is too expensive and/or the flood of extra data may overload your poor CPU.

A potential problem with averaging comes up when you handle nonlinear data. The process of averaging is defined to be the summation of several values, divided by the

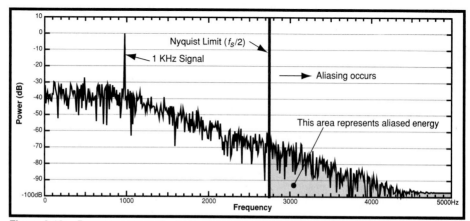

Figure 2-18. Power spectrum of a 1 kHz sine wave with lowpass-filtered noise added.

number of values. If your data is, for instance, exponential in nature, then averaging values (a linear operation) will tend to bias the data. (Consider the fact that $\exp(x) + \exp(y)$ is not equal to $\exp(x + y)$). One solution is to linearize the data before averaging. In the case of exponential data, you should take the logarithm first. You may also be able to ignore this problem if the values are closely spaced—small pieces of a curve are effectively linear. It's vital that you understand your signals qualitatively and quantitatively before applying *any* numerical processing, no matter how innocuous it may seem.

If your main concern is rejecting 60 Hz line frequency interference, an old trick is to grab an array of samples over one line period (16.66 ms). You should do this for every channel. Using plug-in boards with LabVIEW's data acquisition drivers, you can adjust the sampling interval with high precision, making this a reasonable option. Set up a simple experiment to acquire and average data from a noisy input. Vary the sampling period and see if there isn't a null in the noise level at each 16.66 ms multiple.

If you are attempting to average recurrent waveforms to reduce noise, remember that the arrays of data that you acquire must be perfectly in-phase. If a phase shift occurs during acquisition, then your waveforms will partially cancel each other or distort in some other dismal way. Triggered data acquisition (discussed later) is the normal solution because it helps to guarantee that each buffer of data is acquired at the same part of the signal's cycle.

Some other aspects of filtering that may be important to some of your applications are **impulse response** and **phase response**. For ordinary data logging, these factors are generally ignored. But if you are doing dynamic testing like vibration analysis, acoustics, or seismology, impulse and phase response can be very important. As a rule of thumb, when filters become very complex (high-order), they cut off more sharply, have more radical phase shifts around the cutoff frequency, and (depending on the filter type) exhibit more ringing on transients. Overall, filtering is a rather complex topic that is best left to other books. *The Active Filter Cookbook* is one of my favorites. Even with an electrical engineering degree and lots of experience with filters, I still use it to get a quick answer to practical filtering problems.

The best way to analyze your filtering needs is to use a spectrum analyzer. That way, you know exactly what signals are present and what has to be filtered out. You can use a dedicated spectrum analyzer instrument (*very* expensive), a digital oscilloscope with FFT capability (or let LabVIEW compute the power spectrum), or even a multifunction I/O board running as fast as possible with LabVIEW doing the power spectrum.

Looking at the power spectrum, you can see that some of the noise power is above the floor for the ADC and is also at frequencies above 2.75 kHz. This little triangle represents aliased energy and gives you a qualitative feel for how much contamination you can expect. Exactly what the contamination will look like is anybody's guess. It depends on the nature of the out-of-band noise. In this case, you can be pretty sure that none of the aliased energy will be above -65 dB. The good news is that this is plain old uncorrelated noise, so its aliased version will also be uncorrelated. Not a disaster, just another noise source.

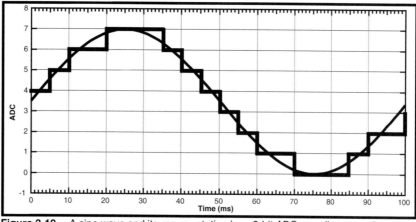

Figure 2-19. A sine wave and its representation by a 3-bit ADC sampling every 5 ms.

About ADC, DAC, and Multiplexers

Important characteristics of an ADC or a D/A converter (DAC) are resolution, range, speed, and sources of error. (For a detailed look at all of these parameters, consult the *Analog-Digital Conversion Handbook*, available from Analog Devices.)

Resolution is the number of bits that the converter uses to represent the analog signal. The greater the number of bits, the finer the resolution of the converter. Figure 2-19 demonstrates the resolution of a hypothetical 3-bit converter, which can resolve 2^3, or 8 different levels. The sine wave in this figure is not well represented because of the rather coarse **quantization** levels available. Common ADCs have resolutions of 8, 12, and 16 bits, corresponding to 256, 4,096, and 65,536 quantization levels. Using high-resolution converters is generally desirable, although they tend to be somewhat slower.

Range refers to the maximum and minimum voltage levels that the ADC can quantize. Exceeding the input range results in what is variously termed clipping, saturation, or overflow/underflow, where the ADC gets stuck at its largest or smallest output code. The **code width** of an ADC is defined as the change of voltage between two adjacent quantization levels or, as a formula,

$$\text{Code width} = \frac{\text{range}}{2^N}$$

where N is the number of bits, and code width and range are measured in volts. A high-resolution converter (lots of bits) has a small code width. The intrinsic range, resolution, and code width of an ADC can be modified by preceding it with an amplifier that adds gain. The code width expression then becomes

$$\text{Code width} = \frac{\text{range}}{\text{gain} \cdot 2^N}$$

High gain narrows the code width and enhances the resolution while reducing effective range. For instance, a common 12-bit ADC with a range of 0-10 V has a code width of 2.44 mV. With a gain of 100, the code width becomes 24.4 µV, but the effective range becomes 10/100 = 0.1 V. It is important to note the tradeoff between resolution and range when you change the gain. High gain means that overflow occurs at a much lower voltage.

Conversion speed is determined by the technology used in designing the ADC and associated components, particularly the **sample-and-hold** amplifier that *freezes* the analog signal just long enough to do the conversion. Speed is measured as the interval between conversions or samples per second. Figure 2-20 compares some common ADC technologies, typical resolutions, and conversion speeds. A very common tradeoff is resolution versus speed; it simply takes more time or is more costly to precisely determine the exact voltage. In fact, high-speed ADCs, like flash converters that are often used in digital oscilloscopes, decrease in effective resolution as the conversion rate is increased. Your application determines what conversion speed is required.

There are many sources of **error** in ADCs, some of which are a little hard to quantify; in fact, if you look at the spec sheets for ADCs from different manufacturers, you may not be able to directly compare the error magnitudes because of the varying techniques the manufacturers may have used.

Simple errors are **gain** and **offset** errors. An ideal ADC follows the equation for a straight line, $y = mx + b$, where y is the input voltage, x is the output code, and m is the code width. Gain errors change the slope (m) of this equation, which is a change in the code width. Offset errors change the intercept (b), which means that zero volts input doesn't give you zero at the output. These errors are easily corrected through calibration. Either you can adjust some trimmer potentiometers so that zero and full-scale match a calibration standard, or you can make measurements of calibration voltages and fix the data through a simple straight-line expression in software. Some fancy ADC systems include self-calibration right on the board.

Linearity is another problem. Ideally, all the code widths are the same. Real ADCs have some linearity errors that make them deviate from the ideal. One of the measures of this error is **differential nonlinearity**, which tells you the worst-case deviation in code width. **Integral nonlinearity** is a measure of the A/D transfer function. It is measured as the worst-case deviation from a straight line drawn through the center of the first and last code widths. An ideal converter would have zero integral nonlinearity. Nonlinearity errors are much more difficult to calibrate out of your system. To do so would mean taking a calibration measurement at each and every quantization level and using that data to correct each value. In practice, you just make sure that the ADC is tightly specified and that the manufacturer delivers the goods, as promised.

If a **multiplexer** is used before an ADC to scan many channels, **timing skew** will occur (Figure 2-21). Since the ADC is being switched between several inputs, it is impossible for it to make all the measurements simultaneously. A delay between the conversion of each channel occurs, and this is called skew. If your measurements depend on critical timing

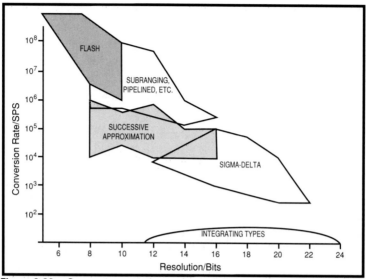

Figure 2-20. Some representative analog to digital converter performance characteristics. (*Courtesy of Analog Devices, Inc.*)

(phase matching) between channels, you need to know exactly how much skew there is in your A/D system.

Multiplexers are used as a cost-saving device, since ADCs tend to be among the most expensive parts in the system, but the skew problem can be intolerable in some applications. Then, multiple ADCs or multiple sample-and-hold amplifiers (one per channel) are required to sample the signals simultaneously. These are the approaches taken by the National Instruments SCXI-1140 and A2000-series boards, respectively.

You can remove the data skew in software, as long as you know exactly what the skew is. If the skew is a multiple of the sample period, you can just shift an array of data over by the appropriate number of elements. If this simple shifting procedure is insufficient, you will have to implement an elaborate interpolation scheme. Chances are, this won't be quite as accurate as the multiple ADC approach, and that's the reason we prefer to use an optimum hardware solution.

One misconception about ADCs is that they always do some averaging of the input signal between conversions. For instance, if you are sampling every millisecond, you might expect the converted value to represent the average value over the last millisecond of time. This is true only for certain classes of ADCs, namely dual-slope integrators and voltage-to-frequency converters. Ubiquitous high-speed ADCs, as found on most multifunction boards, are always preceded by a **sample-and-hold (S/H)** amplifier.

The S/H amplifier samples the incoming signal for an extremely brief period of time (the **aperture time**) and stores the voltage on a capacitor for measurement by the ADC. The aperture time depends on the resolution of the ADC, and is in the nanosecond range for 16-bit converters. Therefore, if a noise spike should occur during the aperture time, you will get an accurate measurement of the *spike*, not the real waveform. This is one more reason for using a lowpass filter.

When a multiplexer changes from one channel to another, there is a period of time during which the output is in transition; this is known as the **settling time**. Because of the complex nature of the circuitry in these systems, the transition may not be as clean as you might expect. There will be overshoot and several cycles of damped sinusoidal ringing. Since your objective is to obtain an accurate representation of the input signal, you must wait for these aberrations to decay away. Settling time is the amount of time required for the output voltage to begin tracking the input voltage within a specified error band after a change of channels has occurred. It is clearly specified on all ADC system data sheets. You should not attempt to acquire data faster than the rate determined by settling time plus ADC conversion time.

Many A/D systems precede the ADC with a **programmable gain amplifier (PGA)**. Under software control, you can change the gain to suit the amplitude of the signal on each channel. A true instrumentation amplifier with its inherent differential connections is the predominant type. You may have options, through software registers or hardware jumpers, to defeat the differential mode or use various signal grounding schemes, as on the National Instruments MIO-16 series multifunction boards. Study the available configurations and find the one best suited to your application. The one downside to having a PGA in the signal chain is that it invariably adds some error to the acquisition process in the form of offset voltage drift, gain inaccuracy, noise, and bandwidth. These errors are at their worst

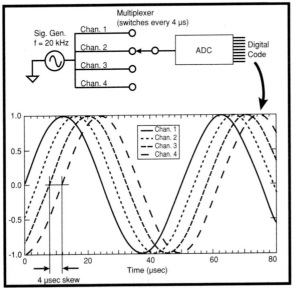

Figure 2-21. Demonstration of skew in an ADC with a multiplexer. Ideally, there would be zero switching time between channels on the multiplexer; this one has 4 µs. Since the inputs are all the same signal, the plotted data shows an apparent phase shift.

at high gain settings, so study the specifications carefully. An old axiom of analog design is that high gain and high speed are difficult to obtain simultaneously.)

Digital-to-Analog Converters

Digital-to-analog converters (DACs) perform the reverse action of ADCs—a digital code is converted to a proportional analog voltage. We use DACs to generate analog stimuli, such as test waveforms and actuator control signals. By and large, they have the same general performance characteristics as ADCs. Their main limitations, besides the issues we've already discussed, are **settling time** and **slew rate**. When you make a change in the digital code, the output is expected to change instantaneously to the desired voltage. How fast the change actually occurs (measured in volts per second) is the slew rate. Hopefully, a clean, crisp step will be produced. In actuality, the output may overshoot and ring for awhile, or may take a more leisurely, underdamped approach to the final value. This represents settling time. If you are generating high-frequency signals (audio or above), you need faster settling times and slew rates. If you are controlling the current delivered to a heating element, these specs probably aren't much of a concern.

Table 2-2. Straight Binary Coding Scheme for a Unipolar, 3-Bit Converter

Number	Decimal Fraction		Straight Binary
	Positive	Negative	
7	7/8	-7/8	111
6	6/8	-6/8	110
5	5/8	-5/8	101
4	4/8	-4/8	100
3	3/8	-3/8	011
2	2/8	-2/8	010
1	1/8	-1/8	001
0	0/8	-0/8	000

When a DAC is used for waveform generation, it must be followed by a lowpass filter, called a **reconstruction filter**, which performs an anti-aliasing function in reverse. Each time the DAC output is updated (at an interval determined by the timebase) a step in output voltage is produced. This step contains a theoretically infinite number of harmonic frequencies. For high-quality waveforms, this out-of-band energy must be filtered out by the reconstruction filter. DACs for audio applications, like National Instruments A2100 series audio boards, include such filters and have a spectrally pure output.

Digital Codes

The pattern of bits—the digital *word*—used to exchange information with an ADC or DAC may have one of several coding schemes, some of which aren't intuitive. If you ever have to deal directly with the I/O hardware (especially in lower-level driver programs), you will need to study these schemes. If the converter is set up for **unipolar** inputs (all-positive or all-negative analog voltages) the binary coding is straightforward, as in Table 2-2. But to represent both polarities of numbers for a **bipolar** converter, a *sign bit* is needed to indicate the signal's polarity. The bipolar coding schemes shown in Table 2-3 are widely used. Each has advantages, depending on the application.

Table 2-3. Some Commonly Used Coding Schemes for Bipolar Converters (in this case a 4-bit example). Note that the sign and magnitude scheme has two representations for zero.

Number	Decimal Fraction	Sign + Magnitude	Two's Complement	Offset Binary
7	7/8	0111	0111	1111
6	6/8	0110	0110	1110
5	5/8	0101	0101	1101
4	4/8	0100	0100	1100
3	3/8	0011	0011	1011
2	2/8	0010	0010	1010
1	1/8	0001	0001	1001
0	0+	0000	0000	1000
0	0-	1000	0000	1000
-1	-1/8	1001	1111	0111
-2	-2/8	1010	1110	0110
-3	-3/8	1011	1101	0101
-4	-4/8	1100	1100	0100
-5	-5/8	1101	1011	0011
-6	-6/8	1110	1010	0010
-7	-7/8	1111	1001	0001
-8	-8/8		1000	0000

Triggering and Timing

Triggering refers to any method by which you synchronize an ADC or DAC to some event. If there is a regular event that causes each individual A/D conversion, it's called the **timebase**, and is usually generated by a crystal-controlled clock oscillator. For this discussion, we'll define triggering as an event that starts or stops a *series* of conversions that are individually paced by a timebase.

When should you bother with triggering? One situation is when you are waiting for a transient event to occur—a single pulse. It would be wasteful (or maybe impossible) to run your ADC for a long period of time, filling up memory and/or disk space, when all you are interested in is a short burst of data before and/or after the trigger event. Another use of triggering is to force your data acquisition to be in-phase with the signal. Signal analysis may be simplified if the waveform always starts with the same polarity and voltage. Or, you may want to acquire many buffers of data from a recurrent waveform (like a sine wave) to average them, thus reducing the noise. Trigger sources come in three varieties: external, internal, or software-generated.

External triggers are digital pulses, usually produced by specialized hardware or a signal coming from the equipment that you are interfacing with. An example is a function generator that has a connector on it called *sync* that produces a TTL pulse every time the output waveform crosses 0 V in the positive direction. Sometimes you have to build your own trigger generator. When dealing with pulsed light sources (like some lasers), an optical detector such as a photodiode can be used to trigger a short but high-speed burst of data acquisition. Signal conditioning is generally required for external triggers because most data acquisition hardware demands a clean pulse with a limited amplitude range.

Internal triggering is built into many data acquisition devices, including oscilloscopes, transient recorders, and multifunction boards. It is basically an analog function where a device called a **comparator** detects the signal's crossing of a specified level. The slope of the signal may also be part of the triggering criteria. Really sophisticated instruments permit triggering on specified patterns—especially useful in digital logic and communications signal analysis. The on-board triggering features of the National Instruments boards are easy to use in LabVIEW, courtesy of the data acquisition VIs.

Software-generated triggers require a program that evaluates an incoming signal or some other status information and decides when to begin saving data or generating an output. A trivial example is the Run button in LabVIEW that starts up a simple data acquisition program. On-the-fly signal analysis is a bit more complex and quickly runs into performance problems if you need to look at fast signals. For instance, you may want to save data from a special analyzer only when the process temperature gets above a certain limit. That should be no problem, since the temperature probably doesn't change very quickly. A difficult problem would be to evaluate the distortion of an incoming audio signal and save only the waveforms that are defective. That might require DSP hardware. It might not be practical at all, at least in real-time.

Throughput

A final consideration in your choice of converters is the **throughput** of the system, a yardstick for overall performance, usually measured in samples per second. Major factors determining throughput are:

- A/D or D/A conversion speed

- Use of multiplexers and amplifiers, which may add delays between channels

- Disk system performance, if streaming data to or from disk

- Use of DMA, which speeds data transfer

- CPU speed, especially if a lot of data processing is required

- Operating system overhead

The glossy brochure or data sheet you get with your I/O hardware rarely addresses these very real system-oriented limitations. Maximum performance is achieved when the controlling program is written in assembly language, one channel is being sampled with the amplifier gain at minimum, and data is being stored in memory with no analysis or display of any kind. Your application will always be somewhat removed from this particular benchmark.

Practical disk systems have many throughput limitations. The disk itself takes a while to move the recording heads around and can only transfer so many bytes per second. The file system, and any data conversion you have to do in LabVIEW, are added as overhead. For really fast I/O, you simply have to live within the limits of available memory. But memory is cheap these days, and the performance is much better than that of any disk system. If you really need 256 MB of RAM to perform your experiment, then don't fool around, *just buy it*. Tell the purchasing manager that Gary said so.

Buffered DMA for acquisition, waveform generation, and digital input or output is built into the LabVIEW support for many I/O boards, and offers many advantages in speed because the hardware does all the real-time work of transferring data from the I/O to main memory. Your program can perform analysis, display data, and perform archiving tasks while the I/O is in progress (you can't do *too* much processing though...). Refer to your LabVIEW data acquisition VI library reference manual for details on this technique.

If you need to do much on-the-fly analysis, adding a **DSP board** can augment the power of your computer's CPU by off-loading tasks like FFT computations. Using a DSP board as a general-purpose computer is another story; actually another *book!* Programming such a machine to orchestrate data transfers, do control algorithms, etc., requires programming in C or assembly language using the support tools for your particular DSP board. If you are an experienced programmer, this is a high-performance alternative. The rest of us have to stick to post-run analysis, or simply get more and/or faster computers.

REFERENCES

1. Thomas G. Beckwith and R. D. Marangoni, *Mechanical Measurements,* Reading, MA: Addison-Wesley, 1990, ISBN 0-201-17866-4.

2. Harry R. Norton, *Electronic Analysis Instruments,* Englewood Cliffs, N.J.: Prentice Hall, 1992, ISBN 0-13-249426-4.

3. Ramon Pallas-Areny and J.G. Webster, *Sensors and Signal Conditioning*, New York: Wiley, 1991, ISBN 0-471-54565-1.

4. Donald R. J. White, *EMI Control Methodology and Procedures*. Available from Don White Consultants, Gainesville, VA (703)347-0030.

5. Ron Gunn, Designing System Grounds and Signal Returns, *Control Engineering*, May 1987.

6. Ralph Morrison, *Grounding and Shielding Techniques in Instrumentation*, New York: Wiley-Interscience, 1986.

7. Henry W. Ott, *Noise Reduction Techniques in Electronic Systems*, New York: Wiley, 1988, ISBN 0-471-85068-3.

8. Data acquisition VI reference manual, part of the LabVIEW manual set.

9. Don Lancaster, *Active Filter Cookbook*, Indianapolis: Howard W. Sams & Co., 1975, ISBN 0-672-21168-8.

10. Robert W. Steer Jr., Anti-aliasing Filters Reduce Errors in A/D Converters, *EDN*, March 30, 1989.

11. Daniel H. Sheingold, *Analog-Digital Conversion Handbook*, Englewood Cliffs, N.J.: Prentice Hall, 1986, ISBN 0-13-032848-0.

12. Donald R. J. White, *Shielding Design Methodology and Procedures*, Gainesville, VA: Interference Control Technologies, 1986, ISBN 0-932263-26-7.

3

LabVIEW Programming Techniques

This chapter is devoted to the nuts and bolts of LabVIEW programming. Make no mistake about it: LabVIEW is a programming language and a sophisticated one at that. It takes time to learn how to use it effectively. When I went to that first LabVIEW test-drive, I was certainly impressed with the ease with which we made a spectrum analyzer out of an oscilloscope. After I bought the program, I went through the getting started part of the manual, and that helped. But soon, I started asking questions like, "How do you get data into a spreadsheet, and format a command string for GPIB, and run my test every 3.7 seconds, and..." and all kinds of things. It became apparent that I needed help getting started, so I took the LabVIEW class, and later, the advanced LabVIEW class.

And you should, too, even though it costs money and takes time. It's *worth* it. Ask any of the MBAs in the front office; they know the value of training in terms of dollars and cents as well as worker productivity. The new LabVIEW tutorial that comes with the package is very helpful for beginners. It's a combination of a getting started manual and a training manual. I highly recommend that you go through the LabVIEW tutorial before reading this chapter. It introduces you to the terms and concepts that this chapter expands upon. Don't rush through it too quickly. There is a great deal of information to absorb. I like to read, experiment, then read some more, when I'm learning a new application like this.

Another thing you should do is spend plenty of time looking at the example VIs that come with the LabVIEW package. Collectively, the examples contain about 80% of the basic concepts that you really need to do an effective job, plus a lot of ready-to-use drivers and special functions. The rest you can get right here. Remember that this book is not a replacement for the user manual. Yeah, I know, you don't read user manuals either, but it might be a good idea to crack the manuals next time you get stuck. I think they are pretty well-written. What I want to cover here are some important concepts that should make your programming more effective. My examples are based on the analysis of real applications.

Sequencing and Dataflow

Regular programming languages (and most computers) are based on a concept called **control flow**, which is geared toward making things happen one step at a time with explicit ordering. The LabVIEW language (**G**), on the other hand, is a **dataflow** language. All it cares about is that each **node** (an object that takes inputs and processes them into outputs) has all its inputs available before executing. This is a new way of programming—one that you have to get used to before declaring yourself a Qualified LabVIEW Programmer. The dataflow concept should be used to its best advantage at all times. This section discusses some of the concepts of dataflow programming with which you should be familiar.

Figure 3-1 compares ordinary procedural programming (like Basic or C) with dataflow programming. In all cases, the PROCESS A and B step can execute only after GET A and GET B are completed. In the procedural language we have forced GET A to happen before GET B. What if the source of data for B was actually ready to go before A? Then you would

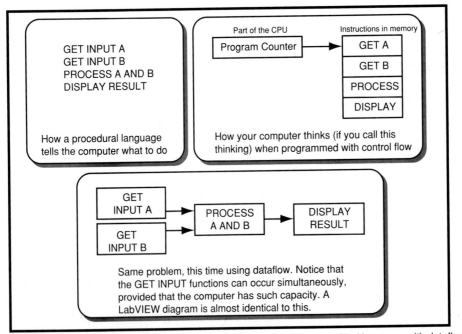

Figure 3-1.   Compare and contrast control flow programming in a procedural language with dataflow programming in LabVIEW.

end up wasting time waiting for A. The dataflow version says nothing about whether GET A or GET B must go first. If the underlying code (courtesy of the LabVIEW compiler) is intelligent enough, the two GET tasks will overlap in time as required, enhancing throughput for this imaginary system.

LabVIEW permits you to have any number of different nodes on a diagram all executing in parallel. Furthermore, the LabVIEW environment supports parallel execution, or multitasking, between multiple VIs, regardless of the capability of the operating system or computer. These capabilities give you great freedom to run various tasks asynchronously with one another without doing any special programming yourself. On the other hand, you sometimes need to force the sequence of execution to guarantee that operations occur in the proper order. For that, LabVIEW has several methods.

Sequence Structures

The simplest way to force the order of execution is to use a Sequence structure as in the upper example of Figure 3-2. Data from one frame is passed to succeeding frames through **Sequence local variables**, which you create through a pop-up menu on the border of the Sequence structure. In a sense, this method avoids the use of (and advantages of) dataflow programming. You should try to avoid the overuse of Sequence structures. LabVIEW has a great deal of inherent parallelism, like our example above where GET A and GET B could be processed simultaneously. (Future computers with multiprocessor architectures could make good use of this feature.) Using a Sequence structure guarantees the order of execution but prohibits parallel operations. For instance, asynchronous tasks that use I/O devices (like GPIB and serial communications and plug-in boards) can run concurrently with CPU-bound number crunching tasks. Your program may actually execute faster if you can enhance parallelism by reducing the use of Sequence structures. Note that Sequence structures add *no code or execution overhead* of their own. Perhaps the worst features of Sequence structures are that they tend to hide parts of the program and that they interrupt the natural left-to-right program flow. The lower example in Figure 3-2 is much easier to understand and permits parallel execution of GET A and GET B.

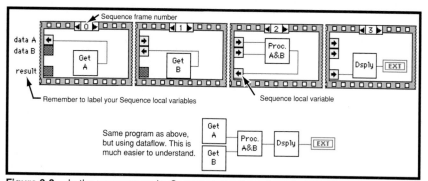

Figure 3-2. In the upper example, Sequence structures force LabVIEW to *not* use dataflow. Do this only when you have a good reason. The lower example shows the preferred method.

Zealots may consider the Sequence structure something to avoid at all costs. Not so. Sequencing is mandatory in some problems and can clarify the program structure by grouping logically-connected operations into neat frames. You can also use them to conserve screen space. Don't get carried away with the *avoidance* of Sequence structures. A contrived "pure dataflow" diagram that uses no Sequence structures may obscure the intentions of your code as badly as the overuse of Sequence structures. Good use of dataflow results in a clear, single-page main program that is easy to understand. Similarly, you can encapsulate major parts of your main program in frames of a Sequence structure to enhance its readability. Try not to use too many local variables in the Sequence structure, because they can make it difficult to follow the flow of data.

Data Dependency

A fundamental concept of dataflow programming is **data dependency**, which dictates that a given node can't execute until *all* of its inputs are available. So in fact, you can write a program using dataflow or not. Let's look at an example that is very easy to do with a Sequence structure, but is better done without. Consider Figure 3-3, which shows four possible solutions to the problem where you need to open a file, read from it, then close it.

Solution A uses a Sequence structure. Almost everybody does it this way the first time. Its main disadvantage is that you have to flip through the frames to see what's going on. Now let's do it with dataflow. A problem arises in solution B that may not be obvious, especially in a more complicated program: Will the file be read before it is closed? Which function executes first? Don't assume top-to-bottom or left-to-right execution when no data dependency exists! Make sure that the sequence of events is explicitly defined when

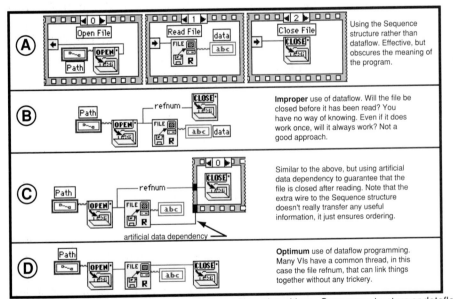

Figure 3-3. Four ways to open, read, and close a file, using either a Sequence structure or dataflow programming methods.

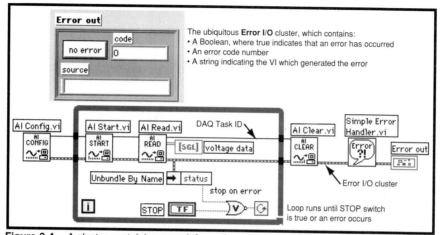

Figure 3-4. A cluster containing error information is passed through all the important subVIs in this program that uses the DAQ library. The While Loop stops if an error is detected, and the user ultimately sees the source of the error displayed by the Simple Error Handler VI. Note the clean appearance of this style of programming.

necessary. A solution is to create **artificial data dependency** between the Read File and the Close File functions, as shown in example C. I just connected one of the outputs of the Read File function (any output will do) to the border of the Sequence structure. That single-frame sequence could also have been a Case structure or a While Loop—no matter: it's just a container for the next event. The advantage to this style of programming is clarity: the entire program is visible at first glance. Once you get good at it, you can write many of your programs this way.

Adding Common Threads

Going further with the idea of data dependency, you can build flow control right into your subVIs as demonstrated in example D. If you make a collection of subVIs that are frequently used together, give them all a common input/output terminal pair so that they can be "chained" together without requiring Sequence structures. In the case of LabVIEW's file I/O functions, it turns out that the file refnum is duplicated by the Read File function and it can be passed along to the Close File function. Thus, the read operation has to be completed before it permits the file to be closed. Problem solved, and very neatly.

A good common thread is an error code, since just about every operation that you devise probably has some kind of error checking built into it. Each VI should test the incoming error and not execute if there is an existing error, then pass that error (or its own error) to the output. You can assemble this error information into a cluster containing a numeric error code, a string containing the name of the function that generated the error, and an error Boolean for quick testing. This technique, which is a relatively new standard first promoted by Monnie Anderson at National Instruments, is called **Error I/O** and appears frequently in the LabVIEW VI libraries. Particular examples are the data acquisition

(DAQ) library VIs (Figure 3-4) and drivers for VXI instruments. Error I/O is discussed in detail in Chapter 5, *Instrument Drivers*.

Looping

Most of your VIs will contain one or more of the two available loop structures, the **For Loop** and the **While Loop**. Besides the most obvious use—repeating an operation many times— there are many less obvious ways to use a loop (particularly the While Loop) that are helpful to know about. We'll start with some useful details about looping that are very often overlooked.

Subtleties of the For Loop

Use the For Loop when you definitely know how many times a subdiagram needs to execute. Examples are building and processing arrays and repeating an operation a fixed number of times. Most of the time, you process arrays with a For Loop because LabVIEW already knows how many elements there are, and the **auto indexing** feature takes care of the iteration count for you automatically: all you have to do is wire the array into the loop, and the count will be equal to the number of elements in the array. But what happens when you hook up more than one array to the For Loop, each with a different number of elements? What if the count terminal, [N], is given a different value? Figure 3-5 should help clear up some of these questions. The smaller count always wins. If an empty array is hooked up to a For Loop, that loop will *never* execute.

Also, note that there is no way to abort a For Loop. In most programming languages, there is a GOTO or an EXIT command that can force the program to jump out of the loop. Such a mechanism was never included in LabVIEW because it destroys dataflow continuity. Suppose you just bailed out of a For Loop from inside a nested Case structure. To what values should the outputs of the Case, let alone the loop, be set? Every situation would have a different answer; it is wiser to simply enforce good programming habits. If you need to escape from a loop, use a While Loop! By the way, try popping up (see your tutorial manual for instructions on popping up on your platform) on the border of a For Loop, and use the Replace option of the pop-up menu to change the loop to a While Loop with no rewiring. Besides swapping loops, you can use the Replace option to swap between Sequence and Case structures while LabVIEW preserves the frame numbers. See the LabVIEW documentation for more information about the Replace command.

Wonderful Whiles

The **While Loop** is one of the most versatile structures in LabVIEW. With it, you can iterate an unlimited number of times and then suddenly quit when the Boolean **conditional terminal**, [↻], becomes false.

If the conditional terminal is left unwired, the loop executes exactly *one time*. If you put uninitialized shift registers on one of these one-trip loops and then construct your entire subVI inside it, the shift registers become a memory element between calls to the VI. You

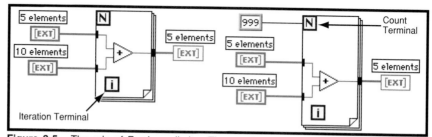

Figure 3-5. The rule of For Loop limits: *The smallest count always wins*, whether it's the count terminal, or one of several arrays.

can retain all sorts of status information this way, like knowing how long it's been since this subVI was last called (see the section on shift registers, below).

Pretest While Loop

What if you need a While Loop that does not execute *at all* if some condition is false? We call this a pretest While Loop, and it's really easy to do (Figure 3-6.) Just use a Case structure to contain the code that you might not want to execute.

Graceful Stops

It's considered bad form to write an infinite loop in LabVIEW (or any other language, for that matter). An infinite loops run, forever, generally because the programmer told it to stop only when 2+2=5, or something like that. I remember running FORTRAN programs on the old Cyber 175 back at school, where an infinite loop was rather hard to detect from a timesharing terminal—there was always an unpredictable delay before the friendly '\' prompt came back, regardless of how long your program took to execute. Trouble was, some folks had to pay real money for computer time, and that computer cost about $1000 per hour to run! The hazard in LabVIEW is that the only way to stop an infinite loop is to click the Stop button in the toolbar (run mode palette). I/O hardware could be left in an indeterminate state. As a minimum, you need to put a switch on the front panel, name it RUN, and wire it to 🔄 . There's a really cool stop sign I've been using that's pasted into

Figure 3-6. A pretest While Loop. If the pretest condition is false, the False frame of the Case is executed, skipping the actual work to be done that resides in the True case.

This loop may cycle once more after the RUN switch is set to false...

...whereas this loop will stop as soon as the sequence is finished.

Figure 3-7.   The left example may run an extra cycle after the RUN switch is turned off. Forcing the switch to be evaluated as the last item (right example) guarantees that the loop will exit promptly.

a Boolean; the Boolean palette even has buttons pre-labeled STOP. Use whatever is appropriate for your experiment.

A funny thing happens when you have a whole bunch of stuff going on in a While Loop: it sometimes takes a long time to stop when you turn off that RUN Boolean you so thoughtfully included. The problem (and its solution) are shown in Figure 3-7. What happens in the left frame is that there is no data dependency between the "guts" of the loop and the RUN switch, so the switch may be read before the rest of the diagram executes. If that happens, the loop will go around one more time before actually stopping. If one cycle of the loop takes ten minutes, the user is going to wonder why the RUN switch doesn't seem to do anything. Forcing the RUN Boolean to be evaluated as the last thing in the While Loop cures this extra-cycle problem.

Shift Registers

Shift registers are special local variables available in For and While Loops that transfer values from the completion of one iteration to the beginning of the next. Any kind of data can be stored in a shift register. Also, you can add as many terminals as you like to the left side, thus returning not only the (n-1)th value, but (n-2), (n-3), etc. This gives you the ability to do digital filtering, modeling of discrete systems, and other algorithms. Figure 3-8 is an implementation of a very simple infinite impulse response (IIR) filter which operates as a moving averager. You can see from the strip charts how the random numbers have been smoothed over time in the filtered case. National Instruments Application Note 008, *Linear Systems in LabVIEW*, discusses difference equations, Z transforms, and signal flow diagrams in detail.

Besides purely mathematical applications like this one, there are many other things you can do with shift registers. Figure 3-9 is a very common construct where an array is assembled based on some conditional test of the incoming data. In this case, it's weeding out empty strings from an incoming array. This program is frequently seen in configuration management programs (see the data acquisition applications in Chapter 7, *Writing a Data*

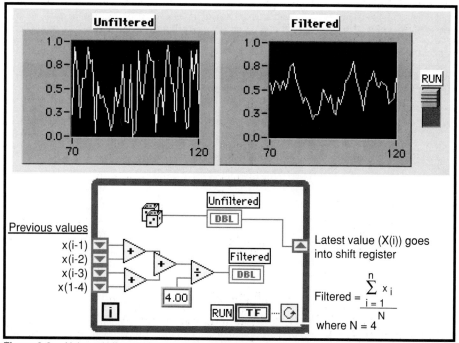

Figure 3-8. Using a shift register to perform a simple running average on random numbers. Note the difference in the graphs of filtered and unfiltered data. This is a very simple case of an infinite impulse response filter.

Acquisition Program). In that case, a user is filling out a big cluster array that contains information about the various channels in the system. Leaving a channel name empty implies that the channel is unused, and should be deleted from the output array. The Build Array function is located inside a Case structure that checks to see if the current string array element is empty. To initialize the shift register, I created a two dimensional (2D) string array, left it empty, and hid the control.

Uninitialized Shift Registers

Notice the use of an empty 2D string array control as the shift register initialization in Figure 3-9. What would happen if that empty array already had something in it? That data would appear in the output array ahead of the desired data. That's why we want an *empty* array for initialization. What happens if it is left out altogether? The answer is that the first time the program runs after being loaded, the shift register is in fact empty and works as expected. But it then *retains its previous contents until the next execution.* Every time you run this modified VI, the output string would get bigger and bigger. All shift registers are initialized at compile time as well: arrays and strings are empty, numerics are zero, and Booleans are false. There are some important uses for uninitialized shift registers that you need to know about.

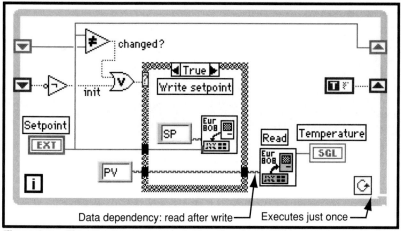

Figure 3-9. This VI writes a new setpoint to a Eurotherm 808 temperature controller only when the user has changed the value. It then reads the current temperature. The upper shift register saves the previous setpoint value for comparison. The lower shift register is used for initialization. A setpoint will always be written when the VI is first run.

First, you can use uninitialized shift registers to keep track of state information between calls to a subVI. In Figure 3-10, a shift register saves the previous value of the Setpoint front-panel control and compares it to the current setting. If a change of value has occurred, the new setting is sent to a temperature controller via the serial port. By transmitting only when the value has changed, you can reduce the communications traffic. This technique can make a VI act more intelligently toward operator inputs. Use a second shift register (Boolean) to force the transmission of the setpoint the first time this VI is run. Since the Boolean shift register is false when loaded, you can test for that condition as shown here. Then, write True to the shift register to keep the VI from performing the initialization operation again.

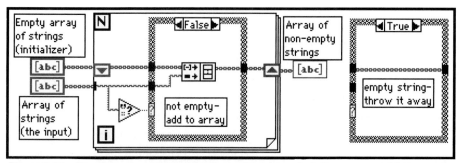

Figure 3-10. Weeding out empty strings with a shift register. A similar program might be used to select special numeric values. Notice that we had to use the function, Build Array, a relatively slow construct, but also unavoidable.

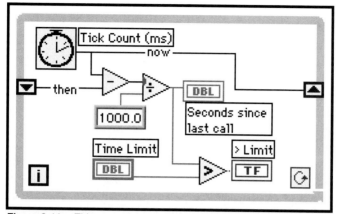

Figure 3-11. This example shows how to use an uninitialized shift register to determine how long it's been since this VI was last called. This makes the VI time aware: useful for data logging, watchdog timing, or time-dependent calculations.

The shift register in Figure 3-11 keeps track of the elapsed time since the subVI was last called. If you compare the elapsed time with a desired value, you could use this to trigger a periodic function like data logging, or watchdog timing. This technique is also used in the PID control VI library for the PID (Proportional Integral Derivative) control blocks whose algorithms are time-dependent.

Global and Local Variables

Another, very important use for uninitialized shift registers is the creation of **global variable VIs**. In G, a variable is a wire connecting two objects on a diagram. Since it exists on one diagram, it is by definition a local variable. By using an uninitialized shift register in a subVI, two or more calling VIs can share information by reading from and writing to the shift register in the subVI. This is a kind of global variable and it's a very powerful construct. Figure 3-12 shows what the basic model looks like.

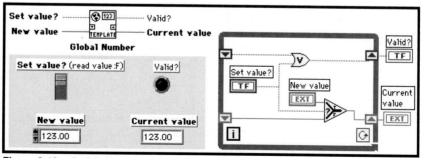

Figure 3-12. A global variable VI that stores a single numeric value. You could easily change the input and output data type to an array, a cluster, or anything else.

If *Set Value* is true (write mode), the input value is loaded into the shift register and copied to the output. If Set Value is false (read mode), the old value is read out and recycled in the shift register. The *valid* indicator tells you that something has been written; it would be a bad idea to read from this global and get nothing when you expect a number. Important note: For each global variable, you must create a VI with a *unique name*.

There are several really nice features of global variables. First, they can be read or written any time, any place, and all callers will access the same data. This includes multiple copies on the same diagram (see the Flashing Lights section later in this chapter) and, of course, communications between top-level VIs. This permits asynchronous tasks to share information. For instance, you could have one top-level VI that just scans your input hardware to collect readings at some rate. It writes the data to a global array. Independently, you could have another top-level VI that displays those readings from the global at another rate, and yet another VI that stores the values. This is like having a global database or a client-server relationship among VIs.

Because these global variables are VIs, they are more than just memory locations. They can process the data and they can keep track of time like the Interval Timer VI in Figure 3-13. Each channel of this interval timer compares the present time with the time stored in the shift register the last time that the channel's Event output was true. When the Iteration input is equal to zero, all of the timers are synchronized and forced to trigger. This technique of initialization is another common trick. It is convenient because you can wire the Iteration input to the iteration terminal, ⬛, in the calling VI, which then initializes the

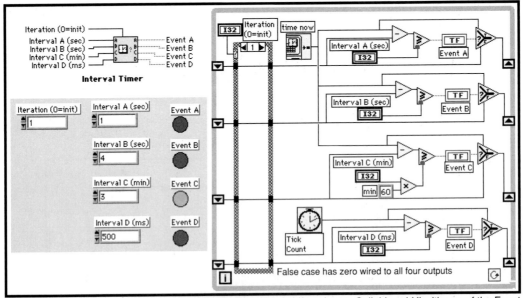

Figure 3-13. A time interval generator based on uninitialized shift registers. Call this subVI with one of the Event Booleans connected to a case statement that contains a function you wish to perform every *Interval* seconds. For instance, you could place a strip chart or file storage function in the true frame of the case structure.

subVI on the first iteration. I use this timer in many applications throughout this book, and it is available on this book's diskette.

As you can see, one global variable can store multiple elements of different types. Just add more shift registers and input/output terminals. Using clusters or arrays, the storage capacity is virtually unlimited.

LabVIEW has built-in global variables, as well (discussed in the next section). They are faster and more efficient than these shift register-based globals, and should be used preferentially. However, you can't embed any intelligence in them since they have no diagram; they are merely data storage devices.

There is one more issue with these global variables: performance. Simple types like numerics and Booleans are very fast, limited only by LabVIEW's subVI calling overhead. Arrays or clusters of numerics and Booleans are a little slower, but the number of elements is what is most important. The real killer is when your global carries clusters or arrays that contain strings. This requires the services of the memory manager every time it is called, and thus the performance is relatively poor (almost 100 times slower than a comparably sized collection of numerics.)

Built-In Global Variables

With LabVIEW 3, global variables are built in. To create a global variable, you place it on the diagram by selecting it from the Structs and Constants function menu. Then double-click on it to open and edit its front panel, exactly like any subVI. You can place any number of controls on the panel, name them, and then save the global with a name—again, just like any subVI. Back on your main diagram, pop up on the global, and select one of the controls that you put in the global, then choose whether you wish to read or write data. Finally, wire it to the appropriate source or destination. At any time, you can open the panel of the global variable to view or change its contents. That can be very helpful during a debugging session.

The difference between built-in globals and the kind you make yourself with a subVI is that the built-in ones are not VIs and as such cannot be programmed to do anything besides simple data storage. However, built-in globals are about ten times faster for most data types. Another advantage of the built-in globals is that you can have all the global data for your entire program present in just one global variable but access them separately with no penalty in performance. With subVI-based globals, you can combine many variables into one global, but you must read and write them all at once, which increases execution time and memory management overhead. Thus, built-in globals are preferred for most applications for performance reasons.

A hazard you need to be aware of when using either type of global variable is the potential for **race conditions**. A race condition exists when two or more events can occur in any order, but you rely on them occurring in a *particular* order. While you're developing your VI, or under normal conditions, the order may be as expected and all is well. But under different conditions the order may vary, causing the program to misbehave. Sequence structures and data dependency prevent this from being a general problem in

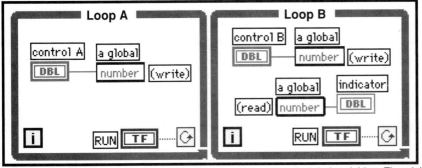

Figure 3-14. Race conditions are a hazard associated with all global variables. The global gets written in two places. Which value will it contain when it's read?

LabVIEW, but global variables can violate strict dataflow programming. Therefore, it's up to you to understand the pitfalls of race conditions.

In Figure 3-14, two While Loops are executing at the same time (they don't necessarily have to be on the same diagram). Both loops write a value to a global number, and one of the loops reads the value. The trouble is, which value will the global contain when it's time to read it? The value from Loop A or the value from Loop B? Note that there can be any number of data writers out there, adding to the uncertainty. You might try to add an elaborate handshaking, timing, or sequencing scheme to this simple example to force things to occur in a predictable fashion.

An all-around safe approach to avoiding race conditions is to write your overall hierarchy in such a way that a global can be written from only one location. Furthermore, you must make sure that you never read from a global before it is initialized. This is one of the first rules taught for traditional languages: initialize the variables, then start running the main program.

If your application has a global array, there is a risk of excessive data duplication. When an array is passed along wires on a single diagram, LabVIEW does an admirable job of avoiding array duplication, thus saving memory. This is particularly important when you want to access a single element, by indexing, adding, or replacing an element. But if the data comes from a global variable, your program has to read the data, make a local copy, index or modify the array, then write it back. If you do this process at many different locations, you end up making many copies of the data. This wastes memory and adds execution overhead. The solution is to create a subVI that encapsulates the global, providing whatever access the rest of your program requires. It might have single-element inputs and outputs, addressing the array by element number. In this way, the subVI has the only direct access to the global, guaranteeing that there is only one copy of the data.

Global variables, while handy, can quickly become a programmer's nightmare because they hide the flow of data. For instance, you could write a LabVIEW program where there are several subVIs sitting on a diagram with no wires interconnecting them and no flow control structures. Global variables make this possible: the subVIs all run until a global Boolean is set to false, and all of the data is passed among the subVIs in global variables.

The problem is, nobody can understand what is happening since all data transfers are hidden. Similar things happen in regular programming languages when most of the data is passed in global variables rather than being part of the subroutine calls. This data hiding is not only confusing, it is dangerous. All you have to do is access the wrong item in a global at the wrong time, and things will go nuts. How do you troubleshoot your program when you can't even figure out where the data is coming from or going to?

The answer is to use global variables only where there is *no other dataflow alternative*. Using global variables to carry configuration information from one top-level VI to another is perfectly reasonable. Using globals to carry data from one side of a diagram to the other "because the wires would be too long" is asking for trouble. One more helpful tip with any global variable: use the Show... Label pop-up item (whether it's a built-in or VI-based global) to display its name. When there are many global variables in a program, it's difficult to keep track of which is which, so labeling helps.

Multiple, Asynchronous Loops in One Diagram

Here is a classic application for global variables. Recall that objects on a LabVIEW diagram run in parallel, within the constraints of dataflow. (Technically, this is referred to as "arbitrary interleaving" on a single-processor system.) A diagram can therefore have more than one loop running at a time, at totally unrelated speeds or intervals. This has some interesting applications that are most useful.

Figure 3-15 pictures two While Loops that perform independent functions. The upper one, which might be called the master, runs at a fixed 100 ms cycle time and uses the AI Single Channel VI (from the DAQ library) to read an analog input and display it on a waveform chart. The master loop runs until the user turns off the RUN Boolean control. Note that the state of the RUN control (false) is written to a global Boolean when the loop is finished.

The lower loop, the slave, runs until the global Boolean becomes False. Note that there are no timing functions in this loop; it runs as fast as LabVIEW will permit—a rate significantly faster than the master loop. Inside the slave loop, there is a Case structure connected to a Boolean control called Open the SubVI. When it is true, a subVI inside the True frame of the Case is called. The subVI has been set to **Show front panel when called**. This is a setup item available through a pop-up menu option on the subVI called **SubVI Node Setup**. Thus, when the user clicks the Open button, the subVI appears, then continues to run until some condition internal to that subVI is satisfied, at which time control returns to the slave loop, which is free to run once again. Note that while the subVI is running the slave loop is suspended. LabVIEW demands that *all* nodes inside a loop structure must be finished before the loop can cycle again.

What would happen if the contents of the slave loop were placed inside the master loop? When the subVI opens, the main loop would be suspended and it could not collect any data until the subVI is through. In our master-slave example, the main loop continues to run at its nominal rate at all times.

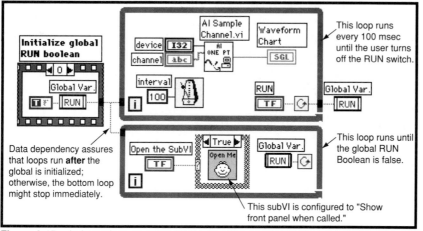

Figure 3-15. Independent, asynchronous While Loops. The RUN global Boolean terminates both loops from one RUN switch. You can expand this technique to control as many independent loops as you need.

There is one more required initialization action. At the left side of the diagram, the RUN global variable is initialized to True (run), and wires to both loops force the loops to wait until the global has been initialized. If this were not done, the slave loop might stop immediately if the global Boolean was initially False. The Boolean constant and the global variable must be encased in a structure of some kind to guarantee that the initialization is completed before the loops start.

Flashing Lights

Another really cool use of global variables and asynchronous While Loops is to flash a Boolean indicator. (This bit of programming is necessary because, at this date, LabVIEW does not have a blink attribute for its indicators.) An application for this is a WAIT sign that blinks while some input hardware is waiting for a trigger. It gives the user a warm-fuzzy feeling to know that the VI has not died. Figure 3-16 shows how you do it. A global RUN Boolean is used once again so that the upper loop, which waits for a GPIB service request, can stop the lower loop, which blinks the light. Some extra logic is included in the lower loop in the form of a Selector function that makes sure that the light is off when exiting.

The slick way to make the *WAIT* sign is to use a Boolean indicator with a suitable message in its true state. Color the false state to totally transparent by using the Coloring tool with All set to T (transparent). This way, when it's true, the message appears out of nowhere, even if it's on top of some other object on the panel, then disappears again when it's false.

Local Variables

Another way to manipulate data within the scope of a LabVIEW diagram is with **local variables**. A local variable allows you to read data from or write data to controls and

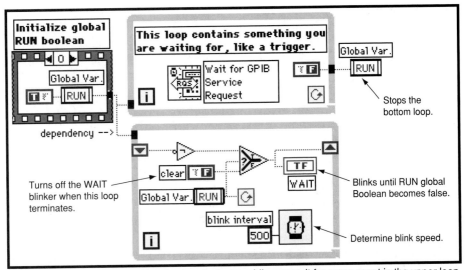

Figure 3-16.   Flashing a waiting Boolean indicator while you wait for some event in the upper loop. The global RUN Boolean ties everything together. A subtle improvement included here in the lower loop makes sure that the indicator is set to False when everything is done.

indicators without directly wiring to the usual control or indicator terminal. This means you have unlimited read/write access from multiple locations on the diagram. To create a local variable, select a Local Variable from the Structs & Constants palette. Pop up on the local variable node and select the item you wish to access. The list contains the names of every control and indicator defined. (If you change the name of a control or indicator that is accessed by a local variable, you will have to reselect it from the local.) Then, choose whether you want to read or write data. The local variable then behaves exactly the same as the control or indicator's terminal, other than the fact that you are free to read *or* write. Here are some important facts about local variables.

- Local variables act only on the controls and indicators that reside on the same diagram. You can't use a local variable to access a control that resides in another VI. Use global variables, or better, regular wired connections to subVIs to transfer data outside of the current diagram.

- You can have as many local variables as you want for each control or indicator. Note how confusing this can become: imagine your controls changing state mysteriously because you accidentally selected the wrong item in one or more local variables.

- Like global variables, you should use local variables only when there is no other reasonable dataflow alternative. They bypass the explicit flow of data, obscuring the relationships between data sources (controls) and data sinks (indicators).

Figure 3-17 demonstrates a simple and safe use for a local variable. When you start up a top-level VI, it is important that the controls be preset to their required states. In this example, a Boolean control opens and closes a valve via a digital output line on a plug-in

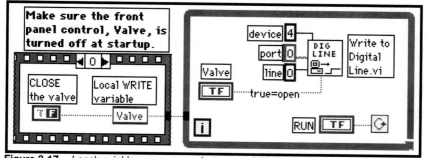

Figure 3-17.   Local variables are a convenient way to initialize front panel controls.

board. At startup, a local variable sets the Boolean control to False before starting the While Loop. If you have many controls to initialize in this manner, you will need just as many local variables. Note the Sequence structure surrounding the initialization part of the program. This guarantees that the local variable has done its work before the While Loop starts. Otherwise, a race condition might arise.

The same technique is useful at all levels in a hierarchy, but please note that you can initialize the controls in a subVI by assigning them to terminals on the subVI's icon, then wiring in the desired values from the calling VI. This is a case where there is a better dataflow alternative. However, if you intend to use a VI at the top level, there is no such alternative and you can use local variables with my blessing.

Another problem solved by local variables is one we have visited before: stopping a parallel While Loop. In Figure 3-15, we used a global variable to stop the slave loop. You can also use a local variable in a similar manner, as shown in Figure 3-18. There is one catch: you can't use a local variable with a Boolean control that has its mechanical action set to one of the *latch* modes. Those are the modes you would normally use for a "stop" switch, where the switch resets to its off position after it is read by the program. Why this limitation? Because there is an ambiguous situation: If the user throws a Boolean into its temporary (latched) position, should it reset after being read directly from its regular terminal, or when it is read by a local variable, or both? There is no universal answer to this situation, so it is not allowed. Figure 3-18 has a solution, though. After the two loops stop, another local variable resets the switch for you.

You will surely dream up many uses for local variables. But a word of caution is in order regarding race conditions. It is very easy to write a program that acts in an unpredictable or undesirable manner because there is more than one source for the data displayed in a control or indicator. What you must do is explicitly define the order of execution in such a way that the action of a local variable cannot interfere with other data sources, whether they are user inputs, control terminals, or other local variables on the same diagram. It's difficult to give you a more precise description of the potential problems because there are so many situations. Just be sure to think carefully before using local variables, and always test your program thoroughly.

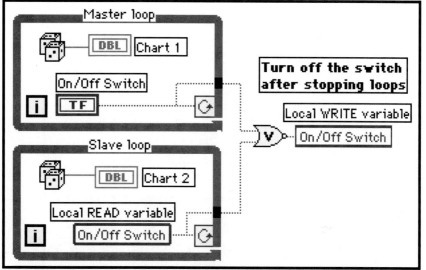

Figure 3-18. This example shows how to use local variables to stop a parallel While Loop. The switch is programmatically reset because latching modes are not permitted for Boolean controls that are also accessed by local variables.

Strings

Every programmer spends a lot of time putting **strings** of characters together and taking them apart. Strings are useful for indicators where you need to say something to the operator, for communications with GPIB and serial instruments, and for reading and writing data files that other applications will access. If you've had the displeasure of using *old* FORTRAN (say, the 1966 vintage), you know what it's like to deal with strings in a language that didn't even have a string or character *type*, let alone string functions. We LabVIEW users are in much better shape, with a nice set of string-wrangling functions built right in. If you know anything about the C language, some of these functions will be familiar. Let's look at some common string problems and their solutions.

Building Strings

Instrument drivers are the classic case study for string building. The problem is to assemble a command for an instrument (usually GPIB) based on several control settings. Figure 3-19 was taken from the Tektronix 370A instrument driver which uses most of the tricks you need to know. Here's how it works.

1. The Pick Line & Append function is driven by a ring control named **Pulse** that supplies a number (0, 1, or 2) that is mapped into the words OFF, SHORT, or LONG. These key words are appended to the initial command string, STPGEN PUL:.

2. The Concatenate Strings function tacks on a substring, CUR:. If you need to concatenate several strings, you can resize Concatenate Strings to obtain more inputs.

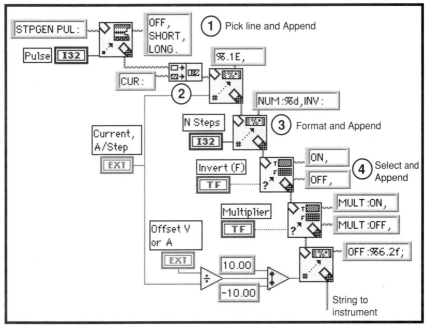

Figure 3-19. String building in a driver VI. This one uses most of the major string building functions in a classic diagonal layout common to many drivers.

3. The Format & Append function is the most versatile function for appending numeric values. You need to learn a little about C-style formatting commands (see the LabVIEW manual for details) to use this function. The percent sign tells it that the next few characters are a formatting instruction. What is nice about this function is that it not only formats the number in a predictable way, but you can also tack on other characters before or after the value. This saves space and gets rid of many Concatenate Strings functions. In this example, the format string `NUM:%d,INV:` translates to a prefix, `NUM:`, a decimal value specified by `%d`, and finally a suffix, `INV:`.

4. The Select & Append function uses a Boolean control to pick one of two choices, like ON or OFF, which is then appended to the string. This string building process may continue as needed to build an elaborate instrument command.

One function missing from this example is Index & Append. It's much like Pick Line & Append, but it chooses from an array of strings. It's very handy if there are a large number of choices; just fill up an array control with the desired settings and pick from them.

Taking 'em Apart

The other half of the instrument driver world involves interpreting response messages. The message may contain all sorts of headers, delimiters, flags, and who-knows-what, plus a few numbers or important letters that you actually want. Breaking down such a string is known as parsing. It's a classic exercise in computer science, and linguistics as well. Remember how challenging it was to study our own language back in fifth grade—parsing sentences into nouns, verbs, and all that? I thought that was tough; then I tackled the reply messages that some instrument manufacturers come up with! Figure 3-20 comes from one of the easier instruments, again the Tektronix 370A driver.

A typical response message would look like this:

```
STPGENNUMBER:18;PULSE:SHORT;OFFSET:1.37;INVERT:OFF;MULT:ON;
```

Let's examine the diagram that parses this message.

1. The top row is based on the versatile Match Pattern function. Nothing fancy is being done with it here, other than searching for a desired keyword. The user manual fully describes the functions of the many special characters you can type into the **regular expression** input that controls Match Pattern. One other thing I did is pass the incoming string through To Upper Case. Otherwise, the pattern keys would have to contain both upper and lower case letters. The output from each pattern match is known as **after substring**. It contains the remainder of the original string immediately following the pattern, assuming that the pattern was found. If there is any chance that your pattern might not be found, test the **offset past match** output; if it's less than zero, there was no match, and you can handle things at that point with a Case structure.

2. Each of the **after substrings** in this example is then passed to another level of parsing. The first one uses the From Decimal function, one of several number extractors; others handle octal, hexadecimal, and fraction/scientific notation. These are very robust functions. If the incoming string starts with a valid numeric character, the expected value is returned. The only problem you can run into is cases where several values are run together such as [123.E3-.567.89]. Then you need to use the Format & Strip function to break it down, provided that the format is fixed. That is, you know exactly where to split it up. You could also use Match Pattern again if there are any other known, embedded flags, even if the flag is only a space character.

3. After locating the keyword PULSE we expect one of three possible strings: OFF, SHORT, or LONG. Index & Strip searches a string array containing these words, and returns the index of the one that matches (0, 1, or 2). The index is wired to a ring indicator named **Pulse** that displays the status.

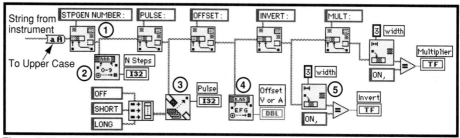

Figure 3-20. Using string functions to parse the response message from a GPIB instrument. This is typical of many instruments you may actually encounter.

4. Keyword OFFSET is located, and the substring is passed to the From Exponential/ Fract/Sci function to extract the number, which in this case is in fractional form.

5. INVERT is located next, followed by one of two possible strings, ON or OFF. When I wrote this VI, I first used Index & Strip again, with its search array containing ON and OFF. But a bug cropped up! It turned out that another keyword farther along in the string (MULT) also used ON and OFF. Since Match Pattern passes us the *entire remainder* of the string, Index and Strip happily went out and found the *wrong* ON word—the one which belonged to MULT. Things were okay if the INVERT state was ON , since we found that right away. The solution I chose was to use the String Subset function, split off the first three characters, and test only those. You could also look for the entire command, INVERT:ON or INVERT:OFF. Moral of story: Test thoroughly before shipping.

Other difficult parsing problems arise when you attempt to extract information from text files. If the person who designed the file format is kind and thoughtful, all you will have to do is search for a key word then read a number. I've seen other situations that border on the intractable; you need to be a computer science whiz to write a reliable parser in the worst cases. These are very challenging problems, so don't feel ashamed if it takes you a long time to write a successful LabVIEW string parsing VI.

Dealing with Unprintables

Sometimes you need to create or display a string that contains some of the unprintable ASCII characters, like control-x or the escape character. The trick is to use the pop-up menu item, **Enable '\' Codes**, which works on front panel control and indicators as well as diagram string constants. LabVIEW will interpret one or two-character codes following the backslash character as shown in Table 3-1. You can also enter unprintables by simply typing them into the string. Control characters, carriage returns, etc., all work fine... except for the Tab (control-i)—LabVIEW uses the Tab key to switch tools, so you have to type '\t'. Note that the hexadecimal codes require upper-case letters.

Table 3-1.   Escape Sequences ('\' codes) for Strings.

Escape Codes	Interpreted As
\00-\FF	hexadecimal value of an 8-bit character
\b	backspace (ASCII BS or equivalent to \08)
\f	formfeed (ASCII FF or equivalent to \0C)
\n	newline (ASCII LF or equivalent to \0A)
\r	return (ASCII CR or equivalent to \0D)
\t	tab (ASCII HT or equivalent to \09)
\s	space (equivalent to \20)
\\	backslash (ASCII \ or equivalent to \5C)

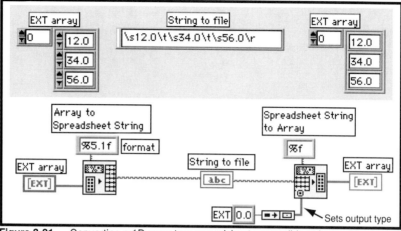

Figure 3-21.   Converting a 1D array to a spreadsheet-compatible string and back.

Spreadsheets, Strings, and Arrays

Frequently you will need to write your data to disk for later use by spreadsheet programs and other applications that prefer tab-delimited text. Such a string looks like this:

```
value <tab> value <tab> value <cr>
```

A very important portability note is in order here. All three platforms are different with respect to their end-of-line character. A platform-independent constant, End Of Line, is available from the Structures and Constants palette that automatically generates the proper character when ported. The proper characters are:

Macintosh: carriage return (\r)
PC: carriage return, then line feed (\r\n)
Sun: line feed (\n)

A really interesting problem crops up with string controls when the user types a carriage return into the string: LabVIEW always inserts a *linefeed*. For the examples in this book, I generally use a carriage return, since I'm a Mac user. But remember this portability issue if you plan to carry your VIs from one machine to another.

To convert arrays of numerics to strings, the easiest technique is to use the Array to Spreadsheet String function. Just wire your array into it along with a format specifier, and out pops a tab-delimited string, ready to write to a file. For a one-dimensional (1D) array (Figure 3-21), tab characters are inserted between each value, and a carriage return at the end. This looks like one horizontal row of numbers in a spreadsheet. You can read the data back in from a file (simulated here) and convert it back into an array by using the Spreadsheet String to Array function. It has the additional requirement that you supply a *type specifier* (such as a 1D array) to give it a hint as to what layout the data might have. The format specifier doesn't have to show the exact field width and decimal precision; plain "%e" or "%d" generally does the job for floating point or integer values, respectively.

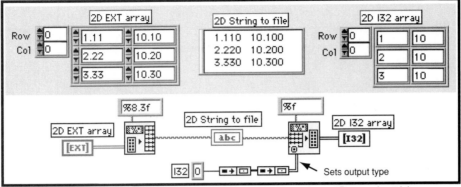

Figure 3-22.   Converting an array to a table and back, this time using a 2D array (matrix).

In Figure 3-22, a two-dimensional (2D) array, also known as a matrix, is easily converted to and from a spreadsheet string. In this case, you get a tab between values in a row and a carriage return at the end of each row. Notice that I hooked up Spreadsheet String to Array to a different type specifier, this time a long integer (I32). Resolution was lost because integers don't have a fractional part; this is to demonstrate that you need to be careful when mixing data types.

A more general solution to converting arrays to strings is to use a For Loop with a shift register containing one of the string conversion functions and the Concatenate Strings function. Sometimes, this is needed for more complicated situations where you need to intermingle data from several arrays, when you need many columns, or when you need other information within rows. Figure 3-23 uses these techniques in a situation where you have a 2D data array (several channels and many samples per channel), another array with timestamps, and a string array with channel names.

The names are used to build a header in the upper For Loop, which is then concatenated to a large string that contains the data. This business can be a real memory burner (and *slow*, as well) if your arrays are large. The strings compound the problem. If you're doing a data acquisition system, try writing out the data as you collect it, processing and writing out one row at a time, rather than saving it all up until the end. On the other hand, file I/O operations are pretty slow, too, so some optimization is in order. See Chapter 7, *Writing a Data Acquisition Program*, for in-depth coverage. Film at eleven.

Arrays

Any time you have a series of numbers that need to be handled as a unit, they probably belong in an **array**. Most arrays are 1D (a column or vector), a few are 2D (a **matrix**), and hardly any are 3D or greater. LabVIEW permits you to create arrays of numerics, strings, Booleans, and pretty much any other data type other than arrays. Arrays are often created by loops as shown in Figure 3-24. For Loops are the best for this application because they preallocate the required memory when they start. While Loops can't; LabVIEW has no

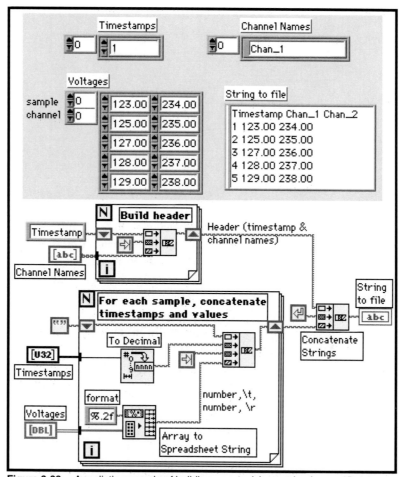

Figure 3-23. A realistic example of building a spreadsheet string from a 2D data array, a timestamp array, and a string array containing channel names for the file's header. If this solution is still too slow for your application, you have to implement it in C code through a Code Interface Node.

way of knowing how many times a While Loop will cycle, so the Memory Manager may have to be called many times, slowing execution.

You can also create an array by using the Build Array function (Figure 3-25). Notice the versatility of Build Array. It lets you concatenate entire arrays to other arrays, or just tack on single elements. There's a pop-up menu on each input terminal that lets you set the type to Array Input or Element Input. If the input type is Element, the output will be an array of those elements. If the input type is Array, the output will be a similar array. To handle more than one input, you can resize the function by dragging at a corner.

Figure 3-26 shows how to find out how many elements are in an array by using the Array Size function. An empty array has zero elements. You can use the Index Array function to extract a single element. Like most LabVIEW functions, Index Array is polymorphic and will return a scalar of the same type as the array.

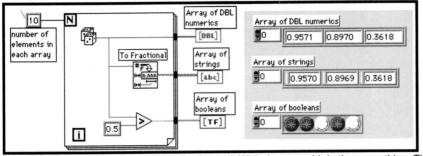

Figure 3-24.   Creating arrays using a For Loop. A While Loop would do the same thing. This is an efficient way to build arrays with many elements.

If you have a multidimensional array, these same functions still work, but you have more dimensions to keep track of (Figure 3-27). Array Size returns an array of values, one per dimension. Index Array can be resized by dragging at a corner to accommodate more dimensions. You have to supply an indexing value for each dimension. An exception is when you wish to slice the array, extracting a column or row of data, as in the bottom example in Figure 3-27. You use a pop-up menu item on the indexing terminal called Disable Indexing to change to this mode of operation. Supply one indexing value and the output is an array with one less dimension than the input array.

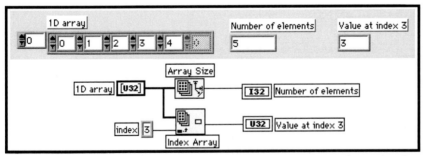

Figure 3-25.   How to get the size of an array and fetch a single value. Remember that all array indexing is based on zero, not one.

Initializing Arrays

Sometimes you need an array that is initialized when your program starts, say, for a lookup table. There are several ways to do this:

- If all the values are the same, use a For Loop with a constant inside. Disadvantage: it takes a certain amount of time to create the array.

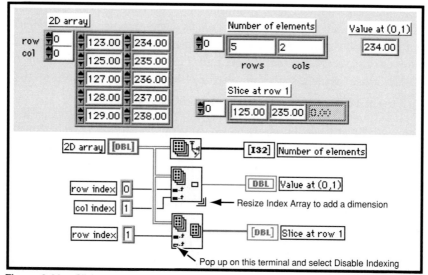

Figure 3-26. Slicing and indexing 2D arrays is a little different, since you have two indices to manipulate at all steps.

- Use the Initialize Array function with the **dimension size** input connected to a constant numeric set to the number of elements. This is equivalent to the previous method, but more compact.

- Similarly, if the values can be calculated in some straightforward way, put the formula in a For Loop and generate it that way.

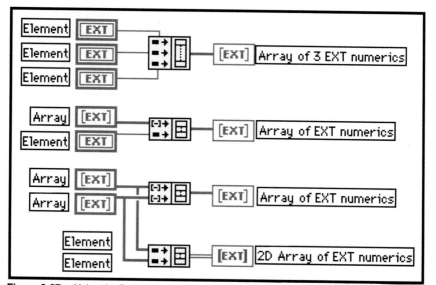

Figure 3-27. Using the Build Array function. Use the pop-up menu on its input terminals to determine whether the input is an element or an array. Note the various results.

- Create a front-panel array control and manually type in the values. Select **Make Current Value Default** from the control's Data Operations pop-up menu. From then on, that array will always have those values (unless you change them). From the diagram, you can select **Hide Front Panel Control** to keep anyone from modifying the data. Disadvantage: data takes up extra space on disk when you save the VI.

- If there is much data, you could save it in a file and load it at startup.

A special case of initialization is that of an **empty array**. This is *not* an array with one or more values set to zero, false, empty string, or the like! It contains *zero* elements. In C or Pascal, this corresponds to creating a new pointer to an array. The most frequent use of an empty array is to initialize a shift register that is used to hold an array (as described in the next section). Here are three ways to create an empty array (Figure 3-28):

1. Create a front-panel array control. Select **Empty Array**, and then **Make Current Value Default** from the control's pop-up menu. This is, by definition, an empty array.

2. Create a For Loop with the loop count, **N**, wired to zero. Place a diagram constant of an appropriate type inside the loop and wire outside the loop. The loop will execute zero times (i.e., not at all), but the array that is created at the loop border tunnel will have the proper type.

3. Use the **Initialize Array** function with the **dimension size** input unconnected. This is functionally equivalent to the For Loop with N=0.

Array Memory Usage and Performance

Perhaps more than any other structure in LabVIEW, arrays are responsible for a great deal of memory usage (see Chapter 9, *Physics Applications*, for some examples). It's not unusual to collect thousands or even millions of data points from an experiment and then try to analyze or display it all at once. Ultimately, you may see a little bulldozer cursor

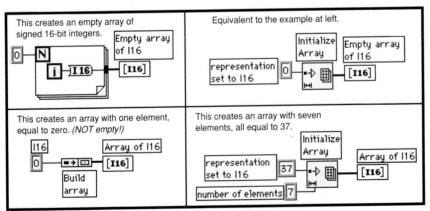

Figure 3-28. Several ways of programmatically initializing arrays.

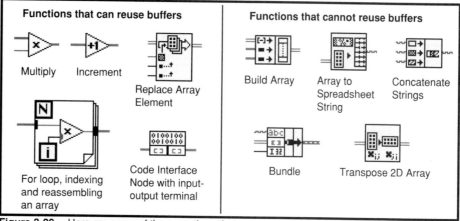

Figure 3-29. Here are some of the operations that you can count on for predictable reuse or non-reuse of memory. If you deal with large arrays or strings, think about these differences.

and/or a cheerful dialog box informing you that LabVIEW has run out of memory. There are some things you can do to prevent this occurrence.

First, read National Instruments LabVIEW Technical Note 012, *Minimizing the Number of Data Buffers*; I'll summarize it here. LabVIEW does its best to conserve memory. When an array is created, LabVIEW has to allocate a contiguous area of memory to store the array. (By the way, every data type is subject to the same rules for memory allocation; arrays and strings, in particular, just take up more space.) If you do a simple operation like multiplying a scalar by an array, no extra memory management is required (Figure 3-29). An array that is indexed on the boundary of a For Loop, processed, and then rebuilt also requires no memory management. The Build Array function, on the other hand, always creates a new data buffer. It's better to use the Replace Array Element function on an existing array as shown in Figure 3-30.

One confusing issue about multidimensional arrays is keeping track of the indices. Which one is the row and which one is the column? Which one does a nested loop structure act upon first? I keep track of this by looking at the indicator on the panel, like the one in Figure 3-30. The top index (called channel, in this example) is also the top index on the Replace Array Element function; this is also true on the Index Array function. So, at least you can keep track of *that* much. When you access a multidimensional array with nested loops as in the previous example, the outer loop accesses the top index, and the inner loop accesses the bottom index. By the way, it is good form to label your array controls and wires on the diagram as I did in this example. To summarize:

Loop	1D array	2D array	3D array
Outer	column	row	page
Middle		column	row
Inner			column

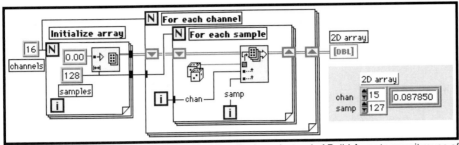

Figure 3-30.   Use Replace Array Element inside a For Loop instead of Build Array to permit reuse of an existing data buffer. This is much faster.

All this memory reuse business also adds overhead at execution time because the **memory manager** has to be called. Talk about an overworked manager. The poor guy has to go searching around in RAM looking for whatever-sized chunk the program happens to need. If a space can't be found directly, the manager has to shuffle other blocks around until a suitable hole opens up. This can take time, especially when memory is getting tight. This is also the reason your VIs sometimes execute faster the *second* time you run them: most of the allocation phase of memory management is done on the first iteration or run. Similarly, when an array is created in a For Loop, LabVIEW can usually predict how much space is needed and call the memory manager just once. Not so in a While Loop, since there is no way to know in advance how many times you're going to loop. Also not so when array building or string concatenation occurs inside a loop—two more situations to avoid when performance is paramount.

Clusters

You can gather several different data types into a single, more manageable unit, called a **cluster**. It is conceptually the same as a *record* in Pascal or a *struct* in C. Clusters are normally used to group related data elements that are used in multiple places on a diagram. This reduces wiring clutter: many items are carried along in a single wire. They also reduce the number of terminals required on a subVI. Using clusters is good programming practice, but it does require a little insight as to when and where they are best employed. If you're a novice programmer, look at the LabVIEW examples and the figures in this book to see how clusters are used in real life.

An important fact about a cluster is it can contain only controls or indicators but not a mixture of both. This precludes the use of a cluster to group a set of controls and indicators on a panel. The reason is simple: a cluster has only one terminal on the diagram, and a given terminal can be either a control or an indicator, but not both. Use graphical elements from the **Decorations** palette to group controls and indicators. (See the section on global and local variables for techniques on how to make input/output controls.)

Clusters are assembled on the diagram by using either the Bundle function (Figure 3-31) or the Bundle by Name function (Figure 3-32). The data types that you connect to these functions must match the data types in the destination cluster (numeric

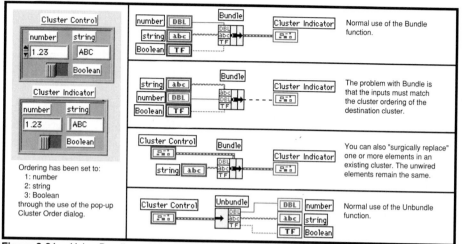

Figure 3-31. Using Bundle and Unbundle functions on clusters.

types are polymorphic; you can safely connect an integer type to a floating point type). Using Bundle has one further restriction: the elements must be connected in the proper order. There is a pop-up menu option on the cluster border called **Cluster Order** that you use to set the ordering of elements. You must carefully watch cluster ordering. Two otherwise identical clusters with different element orderings can't be connected. An exception to this rule, one which causes bugs that are difficult to trace, is where the misordered elements are of similar data type (for instance, all are numerics). You can connect the misordered clusters, but element A of one cluster may actually be passed to element B of the other. This blunder is far too common, and is one of the reasons for using Bundle by Name. To disassemble a cluster, you can use the Unbundle or Unbundle by Name functions. When you create a cluster control, give each element a reasonably short name. Then, when you use Bundle by Name or Unbundle by Name, the name doesn't take up too much space on the diagram. There is a pop-up menu option on each of these functions (**Select Item**) with which you select the items to access. Named access has the additional advantage that adding an item to the related cluster control or indicator doesn't break any wires like it does with the unnamed method. Always use named access except when there is some compelling reason not to.

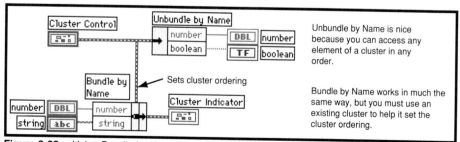

Figure 3-32. Using Bundle by Name and Unbundle by Name.

When you use Bundle by Name, its middle terminal *must* be wired. The functions of the middle terminal on Bundle by Name are to determine the data types and to set the item names. Even if you have wired all input elements, you must wire the middle terminal because the input elements only determine the data types. The Bundle function does not have this limitation; you need only wire to its middle terminal when you wish to access a limited set of a cluster's elements.

Clusters are often incorporated into arrays. It's a convenient way to package large collections of data such as I/O configurations where you have many different pieces of data to describe a channel in a cluster, and many channels (clusters) in an array. Cluster arrays are also used to define many of the graph and chart types in LabVIEW, a subject discussed in detail in Chapter 10, *Data Visualization and Image Processing*. Figure 3-33 shows the LabVIEW equivalent of an "array of arrays": as an array of clusters of arrays. Note the difference between this construct and a simple 2D array, or matrix. Use these arrays of cluster arrays when you want to combine arrays with different sizes. Multidimensional LabVIEW arrays are always rectangular.

Timing

Depending on your needs, LabVIEW's timing functions can be simple and effective, or totally inadequate. And the problems are not all the fault of LabVIEW itself; there are fundamental limitations on all general-purpose computer systems with regard to real-time response, whatever *that* means (one second? .01 second? 1 nanosecond?). Most applications I've seen work comfortably with the available LabVIEW time measurements that resolve milliseconds, and many more operate with one second resolution. A few applications demand sub-millisecond resolution and response time, which is problematic due primarily to operating system issues. Those cases require special attention. So what's with all this timing stuff, anyway?

Where Do Little Timers Come From?

When LabVIEW was born on the Macintosh, the only timer available was based on the 60 Hz line frequency. Interrupts to the CPU occur every 1/60th of a second and are counted as long as the Mac is powered on. This timer, still emulated on all Macs, is called the **tick**

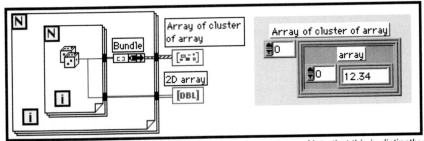

Figure 3-33. Building an array of clusters that contains an array. Note that this is distinctly different from a 2D array.

count, though it is no longer directly accessible in LabVIEW 3. The modern emulation actually uses a 1 ms resolution counter that is based on a crystal-controlled oscillator inside the Versatile Interface Adapter (VIA) chip. However, LabVIEW calls a Macintosh toolbox routine that emulates the old 60 Hz ticker, so even though the timing icons *say* 1 ms, you only *get* 16.66 ms resolution on the Macintosh.

On IBM PC compatibles, the hardware that keeps track of time is not well standardized and in fact the resolution is operating system dependent. Under Windows 3.x, resolution is normally limited to 55 ms. There is an option, however, that you can access through the `LABVIEW.INI` file that sets the resolution to a genuine 1 ms (see the LabVIEW manual for configuration instructions). There is one problem with the high-resolution mode that you need to be aware of. Under Windows, the processor receives an interrupt at each tick of the clock—1000 times every second, with 1 ms resolution selected. That's a *lot* of interrupts, though it doesn't normally cause any problems... except (sometimes) when you are using the DAQ library. Most DAQ operations that access plug-in boards generate some interrupts. (If you don't have DMA support, an interrupt is generated for every A/D conversion.) Sometimes, a DAQ interrupt occurs while the processor is servicing a clock interrupt, and disaster strikes: you may miss data, find yourself at the DOS prompt, or simply crash. But in fact these failures are rare. You just need to be aware of the problem, do lots of testing, and switch back to the default 55 ms mode if you have a case of nerves.

On the SPARCstation, time is derived from a hardware clock that resolves 100 µs, and LabVIEW obtains an accurate 1 ms. No funny business there. As you can imagine, these platform-dependent differences in resolution are important in any application that requires timing information much better than about 1 s.

Another timer that is available in LabVIEW is the system clock/calendar which is maintained by a battery-backed crystal oscillator and counter chip. This timer has a resolution of one second. Most computers have a clock/calendar timer of this kind. The timing functions that get the system time are Get Date/Time In Seconds, Get Date/Time String, and Seconds To Date/Time. These functions are as accurate as your system clock. You can verify this by observing the drift in the clock/calendar displayed on your screen. It's probably within a minute per month. The bad news is, you can only resolve one second.

Three fine-resolution timer VIs are available in LabVIEW: Wait (ms), Wait Until Next ms Multiple, and Tick Count (ms). These functions attempt to resolve milliseconds with the aforementioned limitations of the operating systems.

All timers are asynchronous; that is, they do not tie up the entire machine while waiting for time to pass. Any time you insert a call to Wait (ms) into a VI, it pretty well guarantees that any other VIs not dependent on this one that might need to run will get their chance at that point. Other applications running in the background on the Macintosh or under Windows 3.x will also be more likely to get a chance to run as well. UNIX users don't have this concern since that operating system automatically gives each task a time slice. (Note that UNIX does not change the behavior of LabVIEW timers themselves; it only affects the distribution of time slices between LabVIEW and other programs.)

Using the Built-In Timing Functions

There are two things you probably want to do with timers. First, you want to make things happen at regular intervals. Second, you want to record when events occur.

Intervals

If you want a loop to run at a nice, regular interval, the function to use is Wait Until Next ms Multiple. Just place it inside the loop structure and wire it to a number that's scaled in milliseconds. It waits until the tick count in milliseconds becomes an exact multiple of the value that you supply. If several VIs need to be synchronized, this function will help there, as well. For instance, two independent VIs can be forced to run with harmonically related periods like 100 ms and 200 ms as shown in Figure 3-34. In this case, every 200 ms, you would find that both VIs are in sync. The effect is exactly like the action of a metronome and a group of musicians—it's their heart beat. This is not the case if you use the simpler Wait (ms) function; it just guarantees that a certain amount of time has passed, without regard to *absolute* time. Note that all of these timers work by *adding* activity to the loop. That is, the loop can't go on to the next cycle until everything in the loop has finished, and that includes the timer. Since LabVIEW executes everything inside the loop in parallel, the timer is presumably started at the same time as everything else. Note that "everything else" must be completed in *less* time than the desired interval. The timer does not have a magic ability to speed up or abort other functions. Wait Till Next ms Multiple will add on extra delay as necessary to make the tick count come out even, but not if the other tasks overrun the desired interval. When to use each of the timers:

- Highly regular loop timing—use Wait Till Next ms Multiple

- Many parallel loops with regular timing—use Wait Till Next ms Multiple

- Arbitrary, asynchronous time delay to give other unrelated tasks some time to execute—use Wait (ms)

- Single-shot delays (as opposed to cyclic operations, like loops)—use Wait (ms)

Figure 3-34.   Wait Until Next ms Multiple (the two left loops) keeps things in sync. The right loop runs every 100 ms, but may be out of phase with the others.

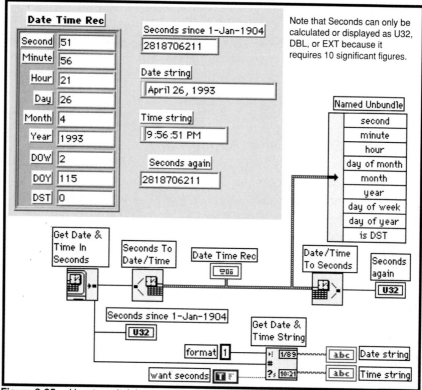

Figure 3-35. How to switch between the various formats for system time, particularly getting in and out of the **date time rec** cluster.

What Time Is It?

To find out what time it is with one-second resolution, use one of the system time functions with whatever format you need.

• Get Date/Time In Seconds returns the number of seconds since midnight, January 1, 1904. This epoch time standard is used on many computer systems because you can easily scale it to hours, days, or whatever. It conveniently carries date and time in one unsigned 32-bit (U32) value.

• Get Date/Time String returns formatted strings containing time and date. Nice for screen displays or printing in reports. It has several formatting options.

• Seconds To Date/Time returns a **date time rec** cluster that's useful for extracting individual time and date values, like finding the current month. I use this function when I want to build a specially formatted time and date string.

• Date/Time to Seconds converts the date time rec back to seconds. It's useful when you want to combine individual time and date items, like letting the user sift through data by the day of the week.

Figure 3-35 shows how all of these functions can be connected together. An important fact you must know about is that time in seconds requires 10 significant figures. That resolution can be carried by only three of LabVIEW's data types: U32 integer and DBL or EXT floating point. If it ever gets converted to any other type, or if it gets printed out as a string with less than 10 decimal digits, resolution will be lost. This is also a problem when importing these time values into other applications that accept single-precision floating point data.

Sending Timing Data to Other Applications

Many graphing programs do a lousy job of importing time stamps of the form, "23-Jun-1990 10:03:17." Epoch seconds are OK, but then the other program has to know how to compute the date and time, which requires a big algorithm. Most spreadsheet programs can handle epoch seconds if you give them a little help. In Microsoft Excel, for instance, you must divide the epoch seconds value by 86,400, which is the number of seconds in a day. The result is what Excel calls a Serial Number, where the integer part is the number of days since the zero year, and the fractional part is a fraction of a day. Then, you just format the number as date and time.

Something I found very useful in data logging is to save the time in **decimal hours**. For instance, if it's 3:30 PM, decimal hours equal 15.50. Thus, you know what time of day things were started, and you can easily plot your data versus this simple number. The VI shown in Figure 3-36 does the trick. It uses two uninitialized shift registers to keep track of the starting time (in hours and seconds), which are saved when the VI is first run. From then on, the time reads out in decimal hours. If the VI gets called after midnight, the hours keep incrementing. After a week, for instance, it will return 168.00 hours. Resolution is limited by your operating system.

High-Resolution and High-Accuracy Timing

If your application requires higher accuracy or resolution than the built-in timing functions can supply, then you will have to use some additional hardware. I know of at least two solutions. First, you can use one of the National Instruments data acquisition (DAQ) boards as a timekeeper. DAQ boards include a stable timebase with microsecond resolution that is used to time A/D conversions and drive various counter-timers. Through the DAQ VI library, you can use these timers to regulate the cycle time of loops, or as a high-resolution clock for timing short-term events. Chapter 6, *Using the DAQ Library*, discusses these techniques in detail.

You can also read the time from an external clock if your lab has a suitable timing source. For instance, timebase generators for use with analog tape instrumentation recorders are based on a standard called IRIG (InterRange Instrumentation Group) that uses a serial interface with up to 100 nsec resolution. Another source of absolute timing information is the National Institute of Standards and Technology (NIST) time services which offer encoded time and date via radio. And the new Global Positioning System (GPS) receivers can resolve absolute time to 100 nsec anywhere on Earth. The key to using one of these timing sources is to obtain a suitable interface to your computer and a LabVIEW driver. Keep in mind the ultimate limitation for precision timing applications: software latency. It takes a finite amount of time to call the Code Interface Node (CIN) that fetches the time measurement or that triggers the timing hardware. If you can set up the hardware in such a way that there is no software "in the loop," high precision is feasible.

One maker of such interfaces is Bancomm. They make VME, VXI, and ISA-bus time code processors and clocks, as well as GPS satellite receivers, displays, and an Ethernet-based time server. One board of particular interest to PC users is the bc630AT Real-Time Clock. It decodes IRIG-A and IRIG-B time code formats and has an access latency of less than 150 μsec. You can synchronize multiple computers via an RS422 link between bc630AT boards. A LabVIEW driver for Windows is available from Bancomm. Contact the company for more information about any of these products.

Dennis Erickson, Senior Electronics Engineer at Bonneville Power Administration, designed a Macintosh-based LabVIEW system called the Portable Power System Monitor (PPSM) that measures disturbances in the electrical distribution system over the Western half of the U.S. and Canada[*]. Many PPSMs are networked together via modems and other network connections to provide the ability to trace disturbance origins through the use of time correlation. One challenge he had to overcome is the fact that these widely separated machines had to maintain absolute time synchronization to a fraction of a second over very long periods of time. The Macintosh system clock is insufficiently stable for this application, so he turned to a hardware solution. TrueTime Corporation makes a NuBus board, the Model 560-5701 MAC II-SG Generator/Synchronizer board, which reads IRIG-B time code. Dennis already has access to IRIG sources at most of his locations, but if required, it's also available from GPS or WWV receivers. He has a LabVIEW driver that reads the time from the board and adjusts it to local or universal (UTC) time. TrueTime also supplies a utility program that sets the Macintosh clock.

Another requirement that Dennis has is that the sampling clock for his MIO-16 A/D board must be very stable. An option on the MAC II-SG board is a 1 MHz clock output that can be connected to the sample clock input of the A/D. This avoids any long-term drift in synchronization between analog samples and the master clock. With this method, he can now time tag his data to 1 μs with excellent accuracy.

Files

Sooner, not later, you're going to be saving data in disk files for future analysis. Perhaps the files will be read by LabVIEW, or another application on your computer, or on another machine of different manufacture. In any case, that data is (hopefully) important to someone, so you need to study the techniques available in LabVIEW for getting the data on disk reliably and without too much grief.

---

[*]   Erickson, Dennis C. and Robert J. Albright, *Design of a LabVIEW-Based Portable Power System Disturbance Monitor*, paper presented at the 1993 National Instruments User Symposium. Available from National Instruments.

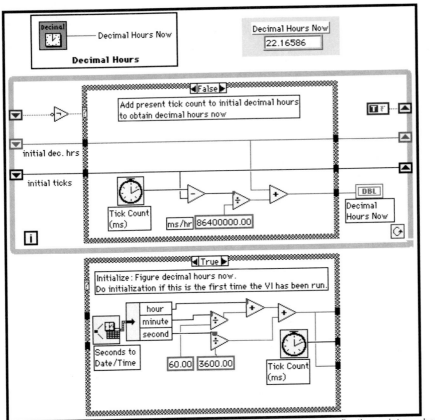

Figure 3-36. The Decimal Hours VI returns the time in hours, but as a floating point number, with millisecond resolution. It doesn't roll over to zero when you go through midnight.

Before you start shoveling data into files, make sure that you understand the requirements of the application(s) that will be reading your files. Every application has preferred formats that are described in the appropriate manuals. If all else fails, it's usually a safe bet to write out numbers as **ASCII text** files, but even that simple format can cause problems at import time—things like strange header information, incorrect combinations of carriage returns and/or line feeds, unequal column lengths, too many columns, or wrong numeric formats. **Binary** files are even worse, requiring tight specifications for both the writer and the reader. They are much faster to write or read and more compact than text files though, so learn to handle them as well. This section includes discussions of some common formats and techniques that you can use to handle them.

Study and understand your computer's file system. In the LabVIEW Function Reference Manual there is a nice discussion of some important details like **path** names and file reference numbers (**refnums**). If things really get gritty, you can also refer to the system reference manuals, like *Inside Macintosh*, or one of the many UNIX, DOS, or Windows programming guides you can pick up at the bookstore.

Accessing Files

File operations are a three-step process. First, you create or open a file. Then you write data to the file and/or read data from the file. Finally, you close the file. When creating or opening a file, you must specify its location. Modern computing systems employ a hierarchical file system, which imposes a directory structure on the storage medium. You store files inside directories, which you can store in other directories. To locate a file within the file system, LabVIEW uses a path naming scheme that works consistently across all operating systems. On the Macintosh and DOS/Windows, you can have multiple drives attached to your machine and each drive is explicitly referenced. On the Sun, UNIX hides the physical implementation from you. Here are some examples of absolute path names:

```
Macintosh
HD80:My Data Folder:Data 123
Windows
C:JOE\PROGS\DATA\DATA123.DAT
Sun
usr/johnny/labview/examples/data_123.dat
```

LabVIEW's path control (from the Path & Refnum menu) automatically checks the format of the path name that you enter and attempts to coerce it into something valid for your operating system. Paths can be built and parsed, just like strings. In fact, you can convert strings to paths and back using the conversion functions, String to Path and Path to String. There are also several functions in the File I/O function palette to assist you in this. Figure 3-37 shows how the Build Path function can append a string to an existing path. You might use this if you had a predefined directory where a file should be created and a file name determined by your program. Given a valid path, you can also parse off the last item in the path by using the Strip Path function. In the example in Figure 3-37, the path is parsed until you get an empty path. Constants, such as Empty Path and Not A Path, are useful for evaluating the contents of a path name. The **Default Directory** constant leads you to a location in the file system specified through the LabVIEW preferences. You can also obtain a path name from the user by calling the File Dialog function. This function prompts the user for a file and determines whether the chosen file exists.

Once you have selected a valid path name, you can use either the New File function to create a file or the Open File function to gain access to an existing one. Both of these functions return a **file refnum**, a magic number that LabVIEW uses internally to keep track of the file's status. This refnum is then passed to the other file I/O functions rather than the path name. When the file is finally closed, the refnum no longer has any meaning and any further attempt at using it will result in an error.

File Types

LabVIEW's file I/O functions can read and write virtually any file format. The three most common formats are:

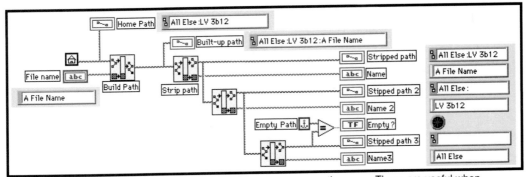

Figure 3-37. LabVIEW has functions to build, parse, and compare path names. These are useful when programmatically manipulating file names.

- ASCII text-format byte stream files.
- Binary-format byte stream files.
- LabVIEW datalog-format files.

ASCII text files are readable in almost any application and are the closest thing to a universal interchange format available at this time. Your data must be formatted into strings before writing. The resulting file can be viewed with a word processor and printed, so it makes sense for report generation problems as well. A parsing process, as described in the strings section, must be used to recover data values after reading a text file. The disadvantage of a text file is that all this conversion takes extra time and the files tend to be somewhat bulky when used to store numeric data.

Binary-format byte stream files typically contain a bit-for-bit image of the data that resides in your computer's memory. They cannot be viewed by word processors, nor can they be read by any program without detailed knowledge of the file's format. The advantage of a binary file is that little or no data conversion is required during read and write operations, so you get maximum performance. Binary files are usually much smaller than text files. For instance, a 1000-value record of data from a data acquisition board may be stored in a 16-bit binary file, occupying 2,000 bytes on disk. Converted to text, it may take up to 10,000 bytes, or five times as much. The disadvantage of binary files is their lack of portability—always a serious concern.

LabVIEW offers another option, the **datalog-format file**, which is a special binary format. This format stores data as a sequence of records of a single arbitrary data type that you specify when you create the file. LabVIEW indexes data in a datalog file in terms of these records. Notice that these records can be a complex type, such as a cluster, which contains many types of data. LabVIEW permits random read access to data log files, and time stamps are included with each record. Datalog format is discussed in detail in Appendix A of the LabVIEW user manual in case you need to read datalogs with other applications or cluster-written programs.

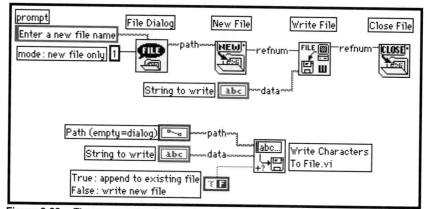

Figure 3-38. The upper example uses the built-in file I/O functions to create, open, and write text data to a file. The lower example uses one of the utility functions, which includes error handling to boot.

Writing Text Files

Here's the basic procedure for most situations that write data to text files:

1. Determine the path name.

2. Open or create the file.

3. Convert the data to a string if it's not already in string format.

4. Write the string to the file.

5. Close the file.

The upper example in Figure 3-38 uses several of the built-in file I/O functions to perform these steps. First, the user sees a dialog box requesting the name and location of a new file. The File Dialog function has a **select mode** input that restricts the possible selections to existing files, non-existing files, or both. In this example, I wanted to create a new data file, so I set the mode to 2 which forces the user to choose a new name. Next, the New File function creates the desired file on the specified path. It returns a refnum for use by Write File which does the real work in this program. Assume that the string to write is already formatted as desired. Finally, the Close File function flushes the data to disk and closes the file. Note the clean appearance of this example, thanks to the use of the flow-through refnum parameter.

Each of the file I/O functions returns an error code. In this simple example, no error checking was performed–a risky proposition for file I/O activity. Lots of things can go wrong. For instance, the user might click the CANCEL button in the file dialog box or the disk might be full. You should enclose each of the file I/O functions in a Case structure so that it runs only when the preceding function returns zero for its error code. Better yet, just use one of the file utility VIs, located in the Utilities function menu. They have error checking built in.

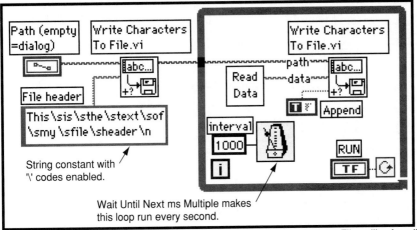

Figure 3-39. A simple data logger that uses the Write Characters to File utility for all the file management. In the loop, data is acquired, formatted into a suitable string, and saved by Write Characters to File. Simple, eh?

Your VIs need not be cluttered with lots of file management functions. Furthermore, you should not have to write much code to do 90% of all file I/O. The utilities and examples supplied with LabVIEW are quite helpful in this regard. In the bottom half of Figure 3-38, the utility VI, Write Characters To File, replaces the collection of functions in the upper example, and it includes error checking. You should open that VI and see how it's built from lower-level file I/O utility functions. If the incoming pathname is empty, the File Dialog function asks you for a file name then creates the file to be written. If the pathname is not empty, the VI attempts to create the file using that pathname. A Boolean input lets you select between append mode (for preexisting files) or file creation. If no errors are detected, the data string is written to the file, then the file is closed. If the operation of this utility isn't exactly what you need, you can modify the original and save it under a different name.

A practical example that uses this file utility, a simple data logger, is shown in Figure 3-39. When Write Characters To File is first called, it creates a data file and writes some header information. Since the VI has an output containing the path of the file chosen, the path is available for use in later operations on that file without reprompting the user. Inside the While Loop, a subVI reads data from some source and returns it in text format. Again, Write Characters To File is called, but with the mode set to append. The loop executes once per second, regulated by Wait Until Next ms Multiple. The result is a file containing a header followed by records of data at one-second intervals.

This text-based scheme has some performance limitations. If you need to save data at really high rates (like thousands of samples per second), the first thing to consider is binary-format files, which are very fast. If you must use text files, one way to speed things up is to avoid closing the file after writing each record. The file system maintains a memory-based file buffer, called a **disk cache** that increases disk performance. Closing the file flushes the file buffer to disk. This forces the disk to move the heads around (called

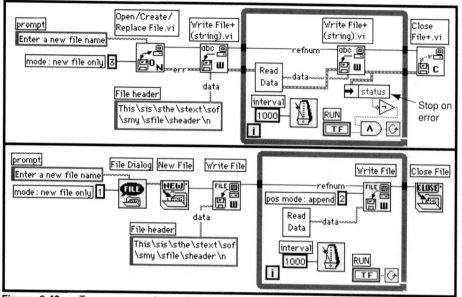

Figure 3-40.   Two more versions of the simple data logger. The upper example uses the intermediate file utility VIs with error I/O. The lower one uses the low-level file I/O services for minimum overhead, but with no error checking.

seeking), then write the data, a time-consuming process that limits throughput. If you avoid closing the file until you are done, the disk cache can keep a moderate amount of data in memory, flushing to disk only when it becomes full. The disadvantage to using the disk cache is that if your computer crashes during data collection, data in the disk cache will be lost. For this reason, LabVIEW has a file I/O function, Flush File, that intentionally writes the output buffer to disk. You call Flush File occasionally to limit the amount of data in the buffer. This whole subject is treated in detail in National Instruments Technical Note 004, *Protecting File Data from System Failures*.

Figure 3-40 shows two rewrites of the simple data logging example. The upper example uses the intermediate level file utilities with error I/O. This is the preferred level at which you should work because errors are so common with file access. Furthermore, the intermediate library has many handy features such as file replacement dialog boxes, and VIs that directly accept numeric arrays as well as strings. The only thing these functions don't support is LabVIEW datalog files. For this example, a new file is created and a header is written outside the loop. Inside the loop, I added error I/O to the Read Data VI so that it can abort the While Loop as can the Write File+ VI. This is a robust program.

The lower example uses the low-level file I/O functions to achieve slightly better performance, but at a cost of having no error handling. Write File is called inside the While Loop with its **pos mode** input set to write data starting at the current file mark: data will be appended at each call. If the Read Data VI requires little execution time, this VI can log data at rates as high as thousands of records per second.

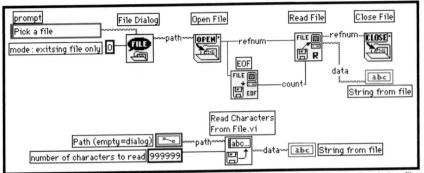

Figure 3-41.   The upper example uses the built-in file I/O functions to open an existing file and read text data from it. The lower example uses one of the utility functions.

Reading Text Files

Reading data from a text file is similar to writing it:

1.   Determine the path name.

2.   Open the file.

3.   Read the string from the file.

4.   Close the file.

5.   Convert the string to a suitable format, if necessary.

Figure 3-41 shows two examples that are symmetrical with the previous ones. The main difference is that the Read File function can read any number of bytes (the **count** input) starting at any location in the file (the **pos offset** input). By default, Read File starts reading at the beginning of the file (which is what you would normally do) and **count** is zero (it reads no data). For the simplest case, just wire a constant to **count** and set it to a number larger than the expected amount of data. The example in Figure 3-41 shows another method where the EOF (end of file) function returns the number of bytes in the file which is then wired to Count. I normally use the constant.

As before, you can use a utility VI, Read Characters From File, to save much programming effort. It has two inputs of particular interest: **number of characters** and **start of read offset** that function similarly to the Read File inputs **count** and **pos offset.** To read the whole file, you should again wire **number of characters** to a large constant value. Looking further through the file utility VIs, you will find other useful VIs like Read From Spreadsheet File, shown in Figure 3-42. This VI loads one or more lines of text data from a file and interprets it as a 2D array of numbers. You can call it with **number of rows** set to one to read just one line of data at a time, in which case you can use the **first row** output (a 1D array). If the rows and columns need to be exchanged, set **transpose** to true. Like many of the utilities, this one is based on another utility subVI, Read Lines From File, that understands the concept of a line of text. On various systems, the end-of-line character may be a carriage return (Macintosh), a line feed (newline) character (Sun), or a carriage return

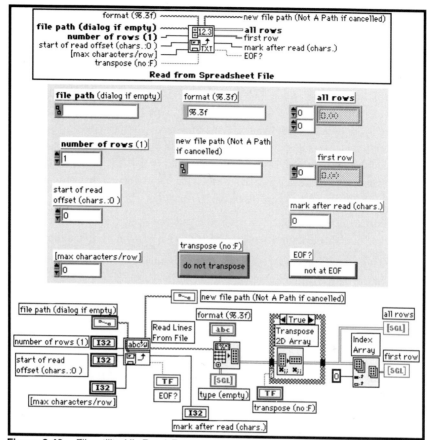

Figure 3-42. File utility VI, Read From Spreadsheet File, interprets a text file containing lines of numbers as a matrix (2D array).

followed by a line feed (PC). This functionality is built into the Read File VI. Read Lines From File goes on to read multiple lines until the end of the file is encountered.

Binary Files

The main reasons for using **binary files** as opposed to ASCII text is that they are faster for both reading and writing operations and they are generally smaller in size. They are faster because they are smaller and require no data conversion (see the section on conversions). Instead, an image of the data in memory is copied byte for byte out to the disk, and then back in again when it's read. Converting to ASCII also requires more bytes to maintain numerical precision. For example, a single-precision floating-point number (SGL; four bytes) has seven significant figures. Add to that the exponent field and some ± signs, and you need about 13 characters, plus a delimiter, to represent it in ASCII. In binary you need only store the four bytes, a savings of more than three to one. Byte stream binary files (as opposed to datalog files) are also **randomly accessible**. That means you can tell the disk drive to read or write particular areas or individual bytes in the file.

One small problem: the program that reads the data must know every little detail about how the file was written. Data types, byte counts, headers, and so forth have to be specified. You can't view it like an ASCII text string, so there's little hope of deciphering such a file without plenty of information. Even LabVIEW datalog files are not immune to this problem. If you can't tell the file I/O functions what data type the datalog file contains, it can't be accessed. (The development team tells me they have a solution to this quandary: a command that will create a front panel to display the data in a datalog file. Watch for it.) On the other hand, consider the fact that parsing an arbitrary ASCII text file is also nontrivial, as we discussed in the section on strings. That's why there aren't any universal text file interpreter VIs. You should consider using binary files when:

- Real-time performance is crucial. Avoiding the numeric-to-text conversion and the extra amount of data that accompanies an ASCII file will definitely speed things up.

- You already have a requirement for a certain binary format. For instance, you may be writing files in the native format of another application.

- Random read/write access is required.

To make a binary file readable, you have several options. First, you can plan to read the file back in with LabVIEW because the person who wrote it should darned well be able to read it. Within LabVIEW, the data could then be translated and written to another file format, or just analyzed right there. Second, you can write the file in a format specified by another application. Third, you can work closely with the programmer on another application, or use an application with the ability to import arbitrary binary formatted files. Applications such as Igor, S, IDL, and Spyglass Transform do a credible job of importing arbitrary binary files. They still require full information about the file format, however. Here are several common data organization techniques I've seen used with binary files:

1. One file, with a header block at the start that contains indexing information such as: number of channels, data offsets, and data lengths. An example of this is the Continuous Acquisition to File (Binary) examples in the Data Acquisition Examples library. It is also used by many commercial graphing and analysis programs, such as Igor (Wavemetrics Corp.).

2. One file, organized as a linked list. Each record (say, a channel of data) is written with its own header that tells the reader where this record begins and ends, and also tells it where to find the next record in the file (this is called a link.) This technique is used by some database programs.

3. Two files, one containing only the actual binary data, and another containing an index to the data, perhaps in ASCII format. My HIST trending package uses this technique with an index file that is also binary. I worked on another binary file set (the format came from VAX-land) that used an ASCII index file. That was nice because you could figure out what was in the binary file just by printing out the index.

In all of these formats, the index or header information is likely to include things like channel names, calibration information, and other items you need to make sense of the data. Binary files are much more than a big bag of bytes.

Writing Binary Files

LabVIEW's file I/O functions make it easy to access binary files. The effort, as with text files, is all in the data formatting. You have to figure out how to deal with your particular header or index format, and of course the data itself. Sorry, but that's *your* problem, since no two formats are the same. The best I can do is show you the basic features of random access files.

Figure 3-43 is a simple driver VI for a binary file format that I just made up. This format has a header containing one I32 (4 bytes) that is the number of data samples to follow. The data follows immediately afterward, and is in SGL floating-point format. Each time this driver is called, the data array is appended to the file and the header is updated to reflect the total sample count.

An important concept in file access is the **file mark**, which is a pointer to the current location in the file, measured in bytes. It is maintained invisibly by the file system. With the **pos mode** and **pos offset** inputs on the Write File, Read File, and Seek functions you can place the mark anywhere you wish. This is how you achieve random access: figure out where you are, then move to where you need to be. If the mark is at the end of the file and you call Write File, data is appended. If the mark is in the middle of the file, then Write File will overwrite existing data at that point in the file.

In this example, the calling VI opens and closes the data file and passes the file's refnum via a **Byte Stream refnum** control. (If you ever need to pass the refnum for a datalog-

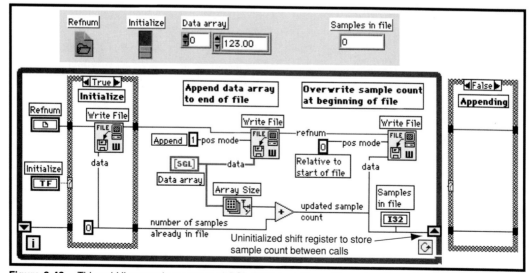

Figure 3-43. This subVI appends an array of SGL floats to a binary file and updates the sample count, an I32 integer, located at the beginning of the file.

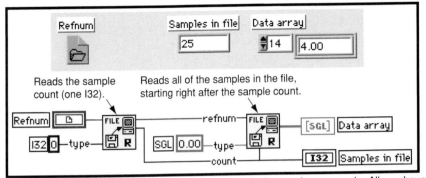

Figure 3-44. Reading the simple binary file created in the previous example. All you have to do is read the first four bytes, which represent the number of samples to follow, then read that number of data points.

format file, you have to use a **Data Log refnum** control.) On the first call to this VI, Initialize should be set to true, which results in the sample count being set to zero and written to the file. An uninitialized shift register stores the sample count for use on subsequent calls.

After initialization, Write File is called with **pos mode** set to 1, which means append data to the end of the file. Since Write File is polymorphic, I just wired the incoming data array to the **data** input. The size of the array is added to the previous sample count. Then, Write File is called again but this time with **pos mode** set to 0, which forces it to begin writing at the start of the file. The data in this case is our updated sample count, an I32 integer, which overwrites the previous value without bothering data elsewhere in the file.

Reading Binary Files

Reading the data is even easier, at least for this simple example, as shown in Figure 3-44. Read File is called with the **type** input wired to an I32 constant so that it returns the sample count with the appropriate interpretation. Then, Read File is called again to read the data, which is in SGL format. Because **count** is wired, Read File returns an array of the specified type. No special positioning of the file marker was required in this example because everything was in order. Things are more complex when you have multiple data arrays and/or headers in one file.

Figure 3-45 is a more robust version of the previous example, this time using two of the high-level file I/O utilities. Read Characters From File opens the file and reads four bytes representing the sample count. The From Decimal function interprets the four-character string as a number. The Read From SGL File VI begins reading at the current file mark, which was returned by Read Characters From File. Read From SGL File can return either a 1D or 2D array of SGL values. In this case, I wired the sample count to the input **ID count** to tell the VI to return data as a 1D array. Unlike the previous example, this one will generate a dialog box if a file error occurs. You could also write an equivalent program with the intermediate level file I/O utilities.

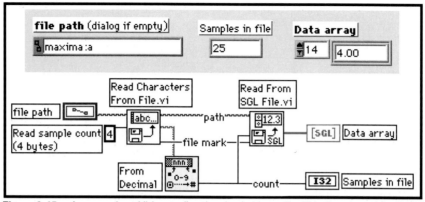

Figure 3-45. A more robust VI for reading the simple binary file. This time, I used the file I/O utilities that add error handling.

Writing Datalog Files

LabVIEW datalog files conveniently store data in binary format one record at a time. A record can be any LabVIEW data type, though you will usually use a cluster containing several data types. To access datalog files, you make use of the fact that the file I/O functions are polymorphic. Whenever you make a connection to the **type** input of a New File or Open File function, it assumes that you intend to access a datalog file containing records of the type you just connected. When the file is opened, the refnum (properly called a **datalog refnum**) carries information that describes the type of data in the file. The Read File and Write File functions then adapt to the appropriate type. You get a broken wire if you attempt to wire the **data** terminal to a source or destination of the wrong type.

Figure 3-46 is a rework of our simple data logger using LabVIEW datalog files. At the lower left, the data type is specified as a cluster containing a string and an SGL numeric array. By wiring it to the **type** input of the File Dialog function, you limit the user's choice of file types to those with this particular type. Similarly, New File responds by creating a

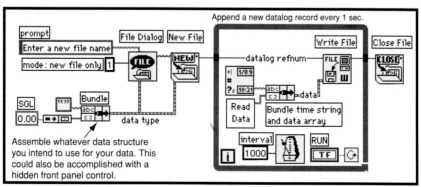

Figure 3-46. Writing data to a datalog file. The data type in this case is a cluster containing a string and a numeric array. Records are appended every second.

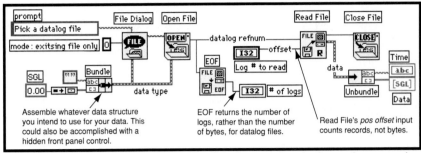

Figure 3-47.   This VI reads a single datalog of the format written by the previous example.

file with a datalog refnum that corresponds to this type. In the While Loop, Write File appends one record per iteration, containing a string with the current time and an array of values. The datalog refnum tells Write File what data type to expect. Note that datalog files are effectively append only; you cannot overwrite selected logs in an existing file. To edit the contents of a datalog file, you must open the file and copy the desired records to another, similar datalog file.

You can also create datalog files by using the built-in data logging functions under the File menu. When you select the Log function for the first time, LabVIEW will prompt you for a new or existing datalog file, then the data presently displayed on the front panel will be appended to that file. Similarly, if you turn on the Log to Disk icon, ![icon], in the execution palette, the front panel will be logged automatically each time the VI finishes execution. A datalog record is a cluster containing each item on the panel. To determine or change the order of the items, select Panel Order from the File menu. These are standard datalog files, readable by the methods described below. You can also view the contents of each record right on the panel by choosing Retrieve from the File menu. This is a convenient way of storing and retrieving VI setups.

Reading Datalog Files

You can read one or more records at a time from a datalog file. Figure 3-47 shows the basic method by which you read a single record. The EOF function reports the number of logs in the file, rather than the number of bytes, as it did with a byte stream text file. Similarly, Read File responds to its **pos offset** input by seeking the desired record number rather than a byte number. In this example, one record containing the expected bundle of data, is returned as a cluster.

If you want to read more than one record at a time, just connect a numeric value to the **count** terminal of Read File as shown in Figure 3-48. Its output will then be an array of the data type previously defined. You can also wire the **pos offset** input to select which record is the first to be read. With these two controls, you can read any number of records (in sequence) from any location in the file. For more on reading and writing datalog files, see the examples that come with LabVIEW.

Data Types and Conversions

One thing that proves that LabVIEW is a complete programming language is its support for all data types. Numbers can be floating point or integer, with various degrees of precision. Booleans, bytes, strings, and numerics can be combined freely into various structures, giving you total freedom to make the data type suit the problem. **Polymorphism** makes this potentially complicated world of data types into something that even the novice can manage without much study. Polymorphism is the ability to adjust to input data of different types. Most built-in LabVIEW functions are polymorphic. VIs that you write are not truly polymorphic—they can adapt between numeric types, but not between other data types such as string to numerics. Most of the time, you can just wire from source to destination without much care since the functions adapt to the kind of data that you supply. For instance, in Figure 3-49, a constant is added to each value in an array. Amazing! Most other languages would require you to write a loop to do that. How does LabVIEW know what to do? The key is object-oriented programming, where polymorphism is but one of the novel concepts that make this new programming technology so desirable. There are of course limits to polymorphism, as the bottom example in the figure shows. The result of adding a Boolean to string is a little hard to define, so the natural polymorphism in LabVIEW doesn't permit these operations. But what if you actually *needed* to perform such an operation? That's where conversions and type casting come in.

Conversions and Coercion

Data in LabVIEW has two components, the **data** itself and its **type descriptor**. You can't see the type descriptor; it is used internally to give LabVIEW directions on how to handle the associated data—that's how polymorphic functions know what kind of data is connected. A type descriptor identifies the type of the data (such as a DBL floating point array) and the number of bytes in the data. When data is **converted** from one type to another, both the data component and the type descriptor are modified in some fashion. For example: `I32`—`DBL`—`DBL` , where an I32 (signed integer with 32 bits, or 4 bytes) is converted to an DBL (64-bit, or 8-byte floating point), the value contained in the I32 is changed into a mantissa and an exponent. The type descriptor is changed accordingly, and this new data type takes up a bit more memory. For conversion between scalar numeric types, the process is very simple, generally requiring only one CPU instruction. But if aggregate types are involved (strings, clusters, etc.), this conversion process takes some

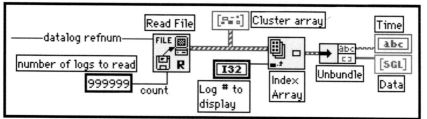

Figure 3-48.   This code fragment reads all of the records from a datalog file.

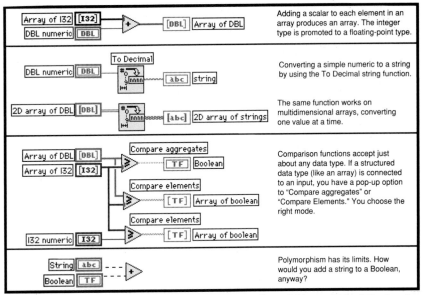

Figure 3-49. Polymorphism in action. Think how complicated this would be if the functions did not adapt automatically. The lower example shows the limits of polymorphism. How in the world could you add a Boolean or a string? If there was a way, it would be included in LabVIEW.

time. First, the value has to be interpreted in some way, requiring that a special conversion program be run. Second, the new data type may require more or less memory, so the system's memory manager may need to be called. By now you should be getting the idea that conversion is something you may want to avoid, if only for performance reasons.

Conversion is explicitly performed by using one of the functions from the Conversion menu. They are polymorphic, so you can feed them scalars (simple numbers or Booleans), arrays, clusters, etc., as long as the input makes some sense. There is another place that conversions occur, sometimes without your being aware. When you make a connection, sometimes a little gray dot appears at the destination's terminal: I32 DBL DBL . This is called a **coercion** dot and performs exactly the same operation as an explicit conversion function. One other warning about conversion and coercion: *be wary of lost precision.* A DBL or EXT floating point can take on values up to $10^{\pm 237}$ or thereabouts. If you converted such a big number to an unsigned byte (U8), with a range of only 0-255, then clearly the original value could be lost. It is generally good practice to modify numeric data types to eliminate coercion because it increases efficiency. Use the **Representation** pop-up menu item on controls, indicators, and diagram constants to adjust the representation.

Intricate Conversions and Type Casting

Besides simple numeric type conversions, there are some more advanced ones that you might use in special situations. This is an advanced topic, so I've saved it for last.

Figure 3-50 uses intertype conversion to make a cluster of Booleans an array. Cluster to Array works on any cluster that contains only controls of the same type (you can't mix in

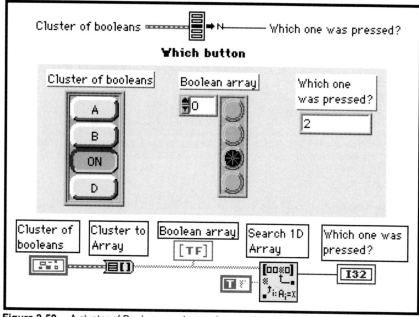

Figure 3-50. A cluster of Booleans makes a nice user interface item, but it is hard to interpret. Using a conversion function (Cluster to Array), the cluster is converted to an array that the **Search 1D Array** function can search through to find the true bit.

strings, numerics, etc.). Once you have an array of Booleans, Boolean Array to Number uses Search 1D Array to find the first element that is true. Search 1D Array returns the element number, which is what we want. This number could then be passed to the selection terminal in a Case structure to take some action based on which switch was pressed.

Figure 3-51 shows a way to use a nice-looking set of ring indicators in a cluster as a status indicator. An array of I32 numerics is converted to a cluster by using the Array to

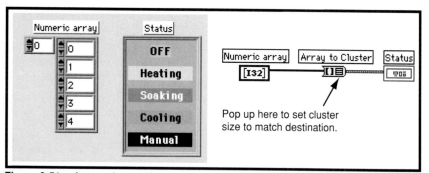

Figure 3-51. A numeric array is converted to a cluster of ring indicators (which are of type I32) by using Array to Cluster. Remember to use the pop-up item on this conversion function, called Set Cluster Size, for the number of cluster elements. In this case, the size is five.

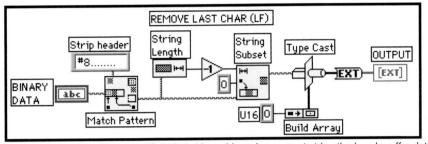

Figure 3-52. Lifted from the HP 54510 driver, this code segment strips the header off a data string, removes a trailing line feed character, then type casts the data to a U16 integer array, which is finally converted to an EXT array.

Cluster function. A funny thing happens with this function: how does LabVIEW know how many elements belong in the output cluster (the array can have any number of elements)? For this reason, they added a pop-up menu item on Array to Cluster called Set Cluster Size. You have to set the number to match the number of elements in the indicator (five, in this case) or you'll get a broken wire.

One of the most powerful ways to change one data type to another is **type casting**. As opposed to conversions, type casting only changes the type descriptor. *The data component is unchanged.* The data is in no way rescaled or rearranged; it is merely interpreted in a different way. The good news is that this process is very fast, though a new copy of the incoming data has to be made, requiring a call to the Memory Manager. The bad news is that you have to know what you're doing! Type casting is a specialized operation that you will very rarely need. LabVIEW has enough polymorphism and conversion functions built-in so that you rarely need the Type Cast function.

The most common use for the Type Cast function is shown in Figure 3-52, where the data string returned from an oscilloscope is type cast to an array of integers. Notice that some header information and a trailing character had to be removed from the string before casting. Failure to do so would leave extra garbage values in the resultant array. Worse yet, what would happen if the incoming string were off by plus or minus one byte at the beginning? Byte pairs, used to make up I16 integers, would then be incorrectly paired. Results would be very strange.

Warning: The Type Cast function expects a certain byte ordering, most-significant byte first in the case of the Macintosh. But not so on the PC! Intel and Motorola have opposing schemes for byte ordering. This is an example where your code, or the data you save in a binary file, may not be machine-independent.

If you get into serious data conversion and type casting exercises, be careful and be patient. Sometimes the bytes are out of order. In that case, try the Swap Bytes or Swap Words functions, both from the Conversion palette of the Functions menu. Some instruments go so far as to send the data backwards, that is, the first value arrives last. You can use the Reverse Array or Reverse String functions to cure that nasty situation. Split Number and Join Number are two other functions that allow you to directly manipulate the

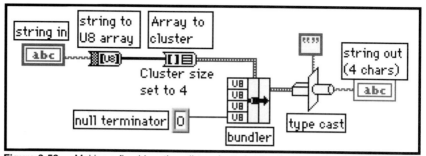

Figure 3-53. Making a fixed-length, null-terminated string for compatibility with the C language. The key is the Array to Cluster conversion that produces a fixed number of elements. This is a really obscure example.

ordering of bytes in a machine-independent manner. Such are the adventures of writing instrument drivers, a topic covered in detail in Chapter 5, *Instrument Drivers.*

Get Carried Away Dept.

Here's a grand finale for our conversion and type casting discussion. Say that you need to fix the length of a string at three characters and add on a *null* (zero) terminator. I actually had to do this for autocompatibility with another application that expected a C-style string, which requires the addition of a null terminator. Let's use everything we know about the conversion functions and do it like Figure 3-53.

This trick (courtesy of Rob Dye, a member of the LabVIEW development team) makes use of the cluster size setting in an Array to Cluster conversion function. The bundler allows parallel access to the whole string, so it's easy to change one character, in this case the last one. It turns out that this program is very fast because all of the "conversions" performed here are actually type casting operations underneath. The disadvantage of this technique, as compared to using a couple of string functions, is that it is hard to understand. I know; it took me a few minutes to figure out.

REFERENCES

1. Erickson, Dennis C. and Robert J. Albright, *Design of a LabVIEW-Based Portable Power System Disturbance Monitor*, paper presented at the 1993 National Instruments User Symposium. Available from National Instruments.

2. National Instruments Technical Note 001, *Array Handling: Making Multicolumn Tables* (part number 340001-01).

3. National Instruments Technical Note 002, *How to Create Array Constants* (part number 340002-01).

4. National Instruments Technical Note 003, *Using Output Tunnels to Build Arrays* (part number 340003-01).

5. National Instruments Technical Note 004, *Protecting File Data from System Failures* (part number 340004-01).

6. National Instruments Technical Note 012, *Minimizing the Number of Data Buffers* (part number 340202-01).

7. National Instruments Application Note 008, *Linear Systems in LabVIEW* (part number 340020-01).

Building an Application

Most of the real programming applications I've looked at over the years seemed as though they had just "happened." Be it FORTRAN 77, Pascal, or LabVIEW, it was as if the programmer had no real goals in mind—no sense of mission or understanding of the Big Picture. No planning. I actually had to use an old data acquisition system that started life as a hardware test program. One of the techs sat down to test some new I/O interface hardware one day, so he wrote a simple program to collect measurements. Someone saw what was going on and asked him if he could store the data on disk. He hammered away for a few days, and, by golly, it worked. The same scenario was repeated over and over for several years, culminating in a full-featured... *mess*. It collected data, but nobody could understand the program, let alone modify or maintain it. By default, this contrivance became a standard data acquisition system for a whole bunch of small labs. It took years to finally replace it, mainly because it was a daunting task. But LabVIEW made it easy.

Haphazard programming need not be the rule. Computer scientists have come up with an arsenal of program design and analysis techniques over the years, all of them based on common sense, and all of them applicable to LabVIEW. If you happen to be familiar with these formalisms, like structured design, by all means use those methods. But you don't need to be a computer scientist to design a quality application. Rather, you need to think ahead, analyze the problem, and generally be methodical. This chapter should help you see the big picture and design a better application. Here are the primary steps I use to build a LabVIEW application:

1. Define and understand the problem.

2. Specify the type of I/O hardware you will need.

3. Prototype the user interface.

4. Design, then write the program.

5. Test and debug the program.

6. Write the documentation (*please!*).

To make this whole process clearer, I'm going to go through a real example: a LabVIEW-based control and data logging system for Larry's Vacuum Brazing Lab (call it **VBL**, for short). At each step, I'll outline the general approach then illustrate my particular tactics and the problems I discovered in the VBL project.

Define the Problem

If you, the system designer, can't understand the problem, all is lost! You will stumble about in the dark, hoping to accidentally solve your customer's problem through blind luck or divine intervention. Sorry, but that's not going to happen. What you need to do is spend a significant amount of time just understanding the problem. At this point, you don't need a computer at all, just a pencil and maybe a voltmeter or an oscilloscope, and the desire to find out what is really going on.

Analyze the User's Needs

I like to interview the end users in several sessions. Talk to everyone involved, with particular attention to the operators—the ones who actually have to interact with the VIs you write. Even if *you* are the customer, you still have to go through this step to make sure that you have all the important specifications on paper. How else will you know when you're done?

Tell your customers about LabVIEW. Show them what it can do in a live demonstration. That way, you can speak a common language—talk of controls, indicators, files, and subVIs. In return, your customer should show you the system that needs to be monitored or controlled. Learn the proper terminology. Maybe you need to read up on the technology if it's something you've never worked with before. I didn't know what vacuum brazing was until I spent a couple of hours with Larry. Here's what I learned:

> The principle of vacuum brazing is simple. Brazing involves joining two materials (usually, but not always, metal) by melting a filler metal (such as brass) and allowing it to wet the materials to be joined. Soldering (like we do in electronics) is similar. The idea is not to melt the materials being joined, and that means carefully controlling the temperature. Another complication is that the base metals sometimes react with the air or other contaminants at high temperatures, forming an impervious oxide layer that inhibits joining. Larry's solution is to put everything in

a vacuum chamber where there is no oxygen, or anything else for that matter. Thus, we call it vacuum brazing. The VBL has five similar electric furnaces, each with its own vacuum bell jar. The heater is controlled by a Eurotherm model 847 digital controller, which measures the temperature with a thermocouple and adjusts the power applied to the big electric heater until the measured temperature matches the setpoint that Larry has entered.

Gather Specifications

As you interview the customers, start making a list of basic **functional requirements and specifications**. Watch out for the old standoff where the user keeps asking what your proposed system can provide. You don't even *have* a proposed system yet! Just concentrate on getting the real needs on paper. You can negotiate practical limitations later. Ask probing questions that take into consideration his or her actual understanding of the problem, his or her knowledge of instrumentation, and LabVIEW's capabilities. If there is an existing computer system (not necessarily in the same lab, but one with a similar purpose), use that as a starting point. As the project progresses, keep referring to this original list to make sure that everything has been addressed. Review the specifications with the user when you think you understand the problem. Here are some important requirements to consider:

- What are the basic operations, steps, event sequences, and procedures that the software needs to perform? This determines much of the overall structure of the program.

- What displays and controls are required? Break down displays by type, such as charts, graphs, numerics, strings, and Booleans. Consider which screen object controls or displays which signals.

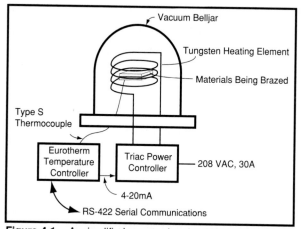

Figure 4-1. A simplified vacuum brazing furnace. The temperature controller adjusts power to the heating element until the measured temperature matches the desired setpoint. Not shown is the vacuum pump and other support equipment. Serial communications makes it possible for LabVIEW to run this furnace.

- Determine the signal analysis needs such as statistics, linearization, peak detection, frequency transforms, filtering, etc. If unusual algorithms are required, seek details early in the project. What needs to be done in real-time versus post-run analysis? This may drastically affect your choice of computer and the system's overall performance.

- What will be done with the data that will be collected? Compatibility with other applications (sometimes on other computers) is an important issue. You must always save the data in a suitable format, and you should be involved with the development of analysis tools. Various options for real-time exchange with other programs also may be considered (Dynamic Data Exchange, Interapplication Communication).

- What other information needs to be recorded besides acquired data? Often, users like to save run setup information or comments in a running log format with time stamps.

- How much of this is *really* necessary? Separate needs from wants. Prioritize the tasks. Realize that there are *always* constraints on budget and/or time and you have to work within these constraints.

The major requirements for the VBL project I divided into *must-haves*, and *future additions*, which prioritized the jobs nicely. Larry was really short of funding on this job, so the future additions are low priority.

Must-Haves

1. All five systems may operate simultaneously.

2. Procedure is: ramp up to a soak setpoint, then go to manual control so user can "tweak" temperature up to melting point. Resume ramp on command.

3. LabVIEW will generate the temperature ramp profiles. User needs a nice way to enter parameters and maintain recipes.

4. Strip chart indicators for real-time temperature trends.

5. Notify user (beep and/or dialog) when the soak temp is reached.

6. Alarm (beep and dialog) when temperature exceeds upper limit in controller.

7. Make post-run trend plots to paste into Microsoft Word report document.

Future Additions

1. Control vacuum pumpdown controller. This will require many RS-232 ports.

2. Trend vacuum measurement. This will require even more RS-232 ports.

Draw a Block Diagram

Draw a preliminary **block diagram** of the system. Think in terms of **signal flow** all the way from I/O hardware to computer screen and back out again. What are the inputs and outputs? This will define the signals, and the signals will define the kind of I/O hardware and data presentation that you will need. List the characteristics of each signal. Some of the items to consider are:

- Sensor and actuator types, manufacturers, model numbers, etc.

- Number of channels, categorized by signal type.

- Signal characteristics: voltage, current, pulse rate, etc.

- Frequency content—determines sampling rates and filtering requirements.

- Isolation and grounding requirements.

- Type of analysis to be performed—influences acquisition and storage techniques.

Get as much detail as possible right now. This information is vital if you hope to design a really successful automation package. It would be a shame to misspecify I/O hardware or write a program that simply doesn't account for the needs of all the instruments you plan to support.

For VBL, I learned that there would only be two basic signals running between the computer and each furnace–the measured temperature from the controller and the setpoint going to the controller (Figure 4-2). In their raw forms, both are DC analog signals. The Eurotherm controller converts the signals to and from digital commands that are transmitted over an RS-422 serial communications line. RS-422 permits multidrop connections, meaning that multiple controllers can share a single communications line. Therefore, I knew that no signal conditioning of the usual type was needed, but a driver for this particular Eurotherm controller would have to be written. As a bonus, the communications hardware uses differential connections to enhance noise rejection—very thoughtful, these engineers.

Collect details on any special equipment proposed for use in the system. Read the technical manuals to figure out how to hook up the signal lines and for signal specifications. For all but the simplest instruments there may be a significant driver development effort required (especially for GPIB or serial communications), so you will need to get a copy of the programming manual as well. Sometimes one major instrument *is* the I/O system, as I discovered with VBL.

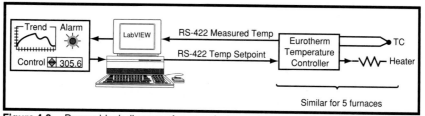

Figure 4-2. Draw a block diagram of your project to make sure you know how the pieces fit together. This one was really simple, with only one input and one output for each of five furnaces.

Specify the I/O Hardware

Now that you know what instruments will be used on your project, follow the steps outlined in Chapter 2, *Inputs and Outputs*, to determine what kind of I/O hardware to use. The signals your instruments produce will define the hardware. There are many factors to consider, so choose wisely.

Since you have to write a LabVIEW program to support the I/O, having examples of completed **drivers** available will save you much time and effort. The LabVIEW instrument library contains hundreds of ready-to-use drivers, all available free. Even if your instrument isn't in the library, there may be something very close—a different model by the same manufacturer—that is easily modified. If you plan to use any of the National Instruments multifunction boards, prowl through the example VIs to find relevant demonstration programs that you can use as starting points. For simple projects, it's surprising how quickly you can modify the examples to become the final application.

Availability and performance of drivers is one more consideration in your choice of I/O hardware. You may need to do some preliminary testing with the actual instruments and data acquisition equipment before you commit to a final list of specifications. Be absolutely sure that you can meet the user's needs for overall throughput–the rate at which data can be acquired, processed, displayed, and stored. Write some simple test VIs at this point and rest better at night. The Speed Tester VI in Figure 4-3 is useful when you have a subVI that you want to exercise at top speed. You can put anything inside the For Loop and get a fairly accurate measure of its execution time. Make sure that the VI does plenty of iterations so that you get enough timing resolution. As you learned in Chapter 3, *LabVIEW Programming Techniques*, there are limitations on the timing precision of some computers.

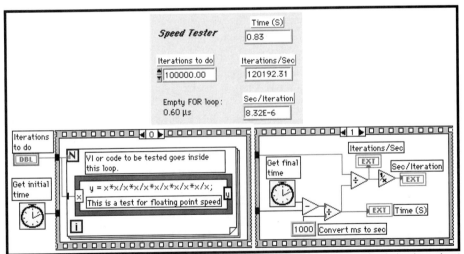

Figure 4-3.   A general-purpose speed tester VI that is used when you need to check the throughput or iteration rate of a subVI or segment of code. In this example, I did 10 floating-point operations. The speed of my Macintosh Quadra 950 was 1.3 megaflops, after subtracting LabVIEW's overhead for the For Loop.

If you want to benchmark events with microsecond precision, use the timing example VI, **Timer Template (us)**, which makes use of the timing hardware on an MIO-16 board.

In most cases you can't write the application unless you know what hardware will be used. For instance, in a high-throughput data acquisition application where many thousands of samples per second of data are streamed to disk, you probably can't do much on-the-fly analysis, graphics, or changing of windows because of the extreme performance demands on the CPU. On the other hand, programming a low-speed temperature recorder has no such demands and permits a substantial amount of real-time processing and display.

The Eurotherm controllers use the serial port for communications. Even though Larry was only asking for one sample per second top speed, I suspected that there could be an upper limit to the total throughput lurking close by. Serial instruments are notorious for adding lots of preamble and postamble information to otherwise simple messages, which compounds the problem of an already-slow communications link. The bad news was that there was no driver available, so I had to write one from scratch before any testing was possible. The good news was that it only took 30 ms to exchange a message with a controller. That means I could move about 33 messages per second, distributed among the five controllers, or about 6 messages per controller per second. Not a problem, unless he ever wants to triple the number of furnaces.

Prototype the User Interface

An effective and fun way to start designing your application is to create prototype front panels that you can show to the users. The panels don't have to work at all, or maybe you can just hook up random number generators to animate the graphs and other indicators. Don't spend much time programming; concentrate on designing panels that meet the specifications. Consider the best types of controls and indicators for each signal. Make a list of inputs and outputs, grouped in some logical categories, and pair them up with the most sensible control and indicator types. If you have to write a formal software requirements document, you can paste images of your mock front panels into the document. That makes your intentions clearer.

Remember that you have an arsenal of graphical controls available. Don't just use simple numerics where a slide or ring control would be more intuitive. Import pictures from a drawing application and paste them into **Pict Ring controls** or as states in Boolean controls, and so forth, as shown in Figure 4-4. Color is fully supported in LabVIEW (except in this book). Deal with indicators the same way. Use the **Control Editor** to do detailed customization. The Control Editor is accessed by first placing a control on the panel then choosing **Edit Control** from the Edit menu. You can resize and color all of the parts of any control and paste in pictures for any part, then save the control under a chosen name for later reuse. Be creative!

Booleans with pictures pasted in are especially useful as indicators. For instance, if the True state contains a warning message and the False state contains a rectangle of similar size, but filled with nothing and having the foreground color set to transparent (an invisible pen pattern), then the warning message will appear as if by magic when the state is set to

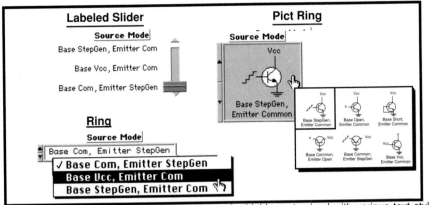

Figure 4-4. Numeric and Boolean controls can be highly customized with various text styles and imported pictures. Here are three sensible numeric controls that could be used for the same function. Pick your favorite.

True. Similarly, an item can appear to move, change color, or change size based on its state through the use of these pasted-in pictures. Note that the built-in LabVIEW controls and indicators can't be made to move or change size programmatically, at least not yet.

Real-time trending is best handled by the various charts, while single-shot arrays of data are best displayed on the graph. Note that these, too, have many features that you can customize, such as axis labels, grids, colors, and so forth. Chapter 10, *Data Visualization and Image Processing*, discusses graphs in detail.

Experiment, but please be consistent. Try not to get too carried away with colors, fonts, and pictures. They quickly become distracting to the operator when overused. Instead, stick to some common themes. Pick a few text styles and assign them to certain purposes. Similarly, use a standard background color (like gray or a really light pastel), a standard highlight color, and a couple of "status" colors like bright green and red. Human factors specialists tell us that **consistency** really is the key to designing quality man-machine interfaces. Operators will be less likely to make mistakes if the layouts among various panels are similar. The *LabVIEW Style Guide* contains many tips on designing panels, if you want to pursue this matter further. An informal document, the style guide was written by Meg Kay and me. In it, we discuss the basic elements of LabVIEW programming style. It is currently available from the National Instruments FTP server (ftp.natinst.com), the info-labview mailgroup server (ftp.pica.army.mil), or from the authors. A formal, revised edition should be available in 1994.

Simple applications may be handled with a single panel, but more complex situations call for multiple VIs to avoid overcrowding the screen. Subdivide the controls and indicators according to function or mode of operation. See if there is a way to group them such that the user can press a button that activates a subVI that is set to **Show front panel when called** (part of the VI Setup menu, available by popping up on the icon). The subVI opens and presents the user with some logically related information and controls, and stays around until an Exit button is pressed, after which its window closes—like a dialog box,

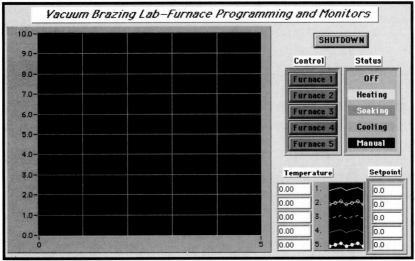

Figure 4-5. "Can you make that graph a little taller?" he asked. "No sweat," I replied, while calmly resizing the graph.

but much more versatile. Look at the Window options in the VI Setup menu. It contains many useful options for customizing the look of the VI window. Functions for configuration management, special control modes, alarm reporting, and alternative data presentations are all candidates for these dynamic windows. Examples of dynamic windows and programming tricks illustrating their use are discussed in Chapter 8, *Process Control Applications.*

Your next step is to show your mockup panels to the users and collect their comments. If there are only one or two people who need to see the demonstration, just gather them around your computer and do it live. Animation really helps the users visualize the end result. Also, you can edit the panels while they watch (Figure 4-5).

If the audience is bigger than your office can handle, try using a projection screen for your computer down in the conference room. LCD panels and RGB projectors are widely available now and offer reasonable quality. That way, you can still do the live demonstration. As a backup, take screen shots of the LabVIEW panels that you can edit in a draw/paint application and add descriptive notes. Besides making a nice handout, hard copies are especially useful for projects that require quality assurance plans and formal design reviews. Gotta have things in print, you know.

> The Vacuum Brazing Lab had only a few things to display during normal operation: the five furnace temperatures, their setpoints, and their status (heating, soaking, cooling, etc.). That suggested one nice front panel with a big stripchart and a few other indicators. Next, I needed a panel through which Larry could edit the ramp-and-soak temperature recipe for each furnace—an ideal application for a dynamic window. Finally, there had to be a panel for manual control of the furnace. That panel needed controls like auto/manual, recipe start/stop,

and manual setpoint entry. It, too, was to be a dynamic window that appeared whenever a button on the main panel was pressed. I created rough versions of the three panels, made some dummy connections that animated it all, and showed it to Larry.

Iterate on your preliminary design. Big projects may require several demonstrations to satisfy the more critical users. This is especially true if you have collected additional requirements because of the impact of your presentation. People start seeing alternatives they previously had not imagined. Take notes during the demonstrations and add to your requirements list. Discuss the new ideas and requirements with your cohorts and try to come up with likely programming solutions to the more difficult problems. Remember to keep the users in the communications loop during all phases of the review process. They will be the ultimate judges of your work and you certainly don't want to surprise them on the day of final delivery.

Design, Then Write Your Program

Don't be stymied by the Blank Screen Syndrome. The same effect occurs in many fields when it's time to create something: the writer with a blank sheet of paper or the painter with an empty canvas. Prototyping the user interface takes care of the panel, but the diagram starts as a big collection of unconnected controls and indicators. Where to start?

Modern software engineering starts a project in the same way as any other engineering discipline: with a **design**—a plan of attack. You must do the same. The alternative is to sit in front of your computer hoping for divine inspiration to somehow guide you toward the optimum program. Most likely, you'll end up with another of those *little test programs* that balloon into full-featured, unmaintainable disasters. Instead, let's try using some design practices that work well in the LabVIEW environment.

In case you're wondering why designing and writing the program are wrapped into this one section instead of being separated, I have a good reason: Most LabVIEW VIs run nicely on their own, with no main program. This is an important LabVIEW advantage that is often overlooked. Once you get past the most general stages of design, you start writing subVIs that beg to be run, tested, and optimized as you go. No need to write elaborate test programs. No need to wait until the entire application is assembled, complete with a bunch of buried bugs.

The ability to do **rapid prototyping** in LabVIEW is one of the major reasons for the product's success. You can quickly throw together a test program that improves your understanding of the underlying hardware and the ways in which LabVIEW behaves in your particular situation. These prototype programs are extremely valuable in the overall development process because they allow you to test important hypotheses and assumptions before committing yourself to a certain approach. Your first try at solving a problem may be ugly, but functional; it's the *later iterations* of this initial program that you actually deliver. This concept of **iterative design** is often the only practical approach to solving laboratory problems where the requirements change as fast as you can modify the program.

If you can't seem to arrive at a concrete list of requirements, just do the best you can to design a flexible application that you can update and extend on short notice.

If you're an experienced programmer, be sure to use your hard-learned experience. After all, LabVIEW is a programming language. All the sophisticated tools of structured analysis can be applied (if you're comfortable with that sort of thing), or you can just draw pictures and block diagrams until the functional requirements seem to match. This world is too full of overly rigid people and theorists producing more heat than light. Let's get the job done!

Top-Down or Bottom-Up?

There are two classic ways to attack a programming problem: from the top down, and from the bottom up.

Top-down structured design begins with the big picture: "I'm going to control this airplane; I'll start with the cockpit layout." When you have a big project to tackle, top-down works most naturally. LabVIEW has a big advantage over other languages when it comes to top-down design: it's easy to start with the final user interface and then animate it. A top-down LabVIEW design implies creation of dummy subVIs, each with a definite purpose and interrelationship to adjacent subVIs, callers, and callees, but at first without any programming. When the hierarchy is complete, then you start filling in the code.

Bottom-up structured design begins by solving those difficult low-level bit manipulation, number crunching, and timing problems right from the start. Writing an instrument driver tends to be this way. You can't do anything until you know how to pass messages back and forth to the instrument, and that implies programming at the lowest level as Step One. Each of these lower-level subVIs can be written in complete and final form and tested as a standalone program. Your only other concern is that the right kind of inputs and outputs are available to link with the calling VIs.

Don't be afraid to use both techniques at once, thus ending up "in the middle," if that seems to feel right. Indeed, you need to know *something* about the I/O hardware and how the drivers work before you can possibly link the raw data to the final data display.

> That Eurotherm controller had to be attacked before I could proceed with the main program design for VBL; I had to know what kind of information would be exchanged with it. The Eurotherm driver was definitely bottom-up design because it required the formatting of some pretty cryptic string commands plus the handling of serial port timeouts and other errors. When the driver was done, I could attack the main programming task from the top down by animating my dummy panels. The driver just acted as a data *source* or *sink*.

Modularity

Break the problem into modular pieces that you can understand. I call this the Divide and Conquer technique and it works in every imaginable situation from designing a computer to planning a party. The **modules** in this case are **subVIs**. Each subVI handles a specific

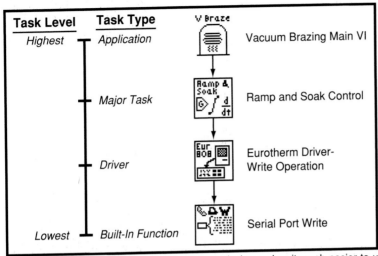

Figure 4-6. Using modularity in your program design makes it much easier to understand. This is one slice through the VI hierarchy of my VBL project.

task—a function or operation that needs to be performed. Link all the tasks together, and an **application** is born.

One of the tricks is to know *when* to create a subVI. Don't just lasso a big chunk of a diagram and stick it in a subVI because you ran out of space; that only proves a lack of forethought. Instead, always think in terms of tasks. Design and develop each task as if it were a standalone application. That makes it easier to test and promotes reuse in other problems. Each task, in turn, is made up of smaller tasks... the essence of top-down design.

Any properly-designed task has a clear purpose. Think of a one-sentence thesis statement that clearly summarizes the purpose of the subVI: "This VI loads data from a series of transient recorders and places the data in an output array." If you can't write a simple statement like that, you may be creating a catchall subVI. (A good place to put this thesis statement is in the VI Description dialog box.) Also consider the reusability of the subVIs you create. Can the function be used in several locations in your program? If so, you definitely have a reusable module. On the other hand, excessive modularity can lead to inefficiency because each subVI adds calling overhead at execution time (a few microseconds per VI), and takes up more space on disk.

There are additional advantages to writing a modular program. First, a simple diagram is easier to understand. Other programmers will be able to figure out a diagram that has a few subVIs much more readily than a complex diagram with level upon level of nested loops and Sequence structures. Second, it is generally easier to modify a modular program. For instance, you might want to change from one brand of digital voltmeter to another. By incorporating well-written, modular drivers, you would just substitute Brand X for Brand Y and be running again in minutes. Finally, a simpler diagram compiles faster (and I *hate* to wait). One goal in LabVIEW programming is to make your diagrams fit on a standard screen (whatever size is most common for computers like yours). This forces you to design and lay out diagrams in a thoughtful manner. It's not a strict rule, however.

Choose a Strategy

Your initial objective is to decide on an overall **strategy**—how you want your application to work in the broadest sense. Here are some models, which I call **canonical VIs**, that represent many of the fundamental structures of LabVIEW applications that I've seen.

Initialize, Then Loop

The simplest applications initialize, then loop. You perform some initialization, like setting up files and starting the hardware, and then drop into a loop that does the main task. The main loop usually consists of four steps that are repeated at a rate that matches the requirements of your signals:

1. Acquire

2. Analyze

3. Display

4. Store

In a well-written program, these steps would be encapsulated in subVIs. After the main loop has terminated, there may also be a shutdown or cleanup task that closes files or turns off something in the hardware. This strategy is a classic for ordinary data acquisition. The first two canonical VIs, shown below, work this way.

Canonical VI No. 1 (Figure 4-7) is by far the most commonly used program structure in all of LabVIEW, primarily because it is an obvious solution. An overall Sequence structure forces the order of initialize, main operation, and shut down. The main While Loop runs at a regular interval until the user stops the operation or some other event occurs. Frequently found inside the main loop is another Sequence structure that contains the operations to be performed: acquire, analyze, display, and then store.

An improvement on the previous example, shown in Figure 4-8, makes effective use of dataflow programming and can be somewhat easier to understand. Connections between

Figure 4-7. Canonical VI No. 1: a sequence containing frames for starting up, doing the work and shutting down. A classic for data acquisition programs. The While Loop runs until the operation is finished. The Sequence inside contains the real work to be accomplished.

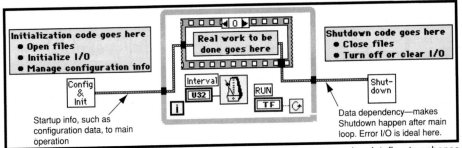

Figure 4-8. Canonical VI No. 2: same functionality as No. 1, but this time using dataflow to enhance readability, which is desirable. Note that the connections between the three main operations are not optional: they force the order of execution.

the three major operations (initialize, main operation, and shut down) force the order of execution in the same way that an overall Sequence structure does, only the overall program is not obscured. The same methodology can and should be applied inside the main While Loop by using common threads between the functions employed there. The net result is a clearer program, explainable with just one page. This concept is used by most advanced LabVIEW users.

Independent Loops

Any time you have two tasks that you need to do at different speeds, consider using multiple independent While Loops that operate in parallel on one diagram (Figure 4-9). I also use independent loops when there is a main task that needs to run regularly and one or more secondary tasks that run only when the operator throws a switch. If data needs to be exchanged between the loops, as it often does, use global variables. In this example, a global Boolean stops the loops at the appropriate time, and another global carries a cluster of settings between the two loops.

Remember to initialize the RUN global Boolean before it is to be read anywhere else. If you are using a loop like the one shown in this example, put a time delay inside the loop to keep it from hogging time when nothing is happening. I usually pick a time like 100 or 200 ms because that's about the threshold of human perception.

Global variables tend to hide the flow of data if they are buried inside subVIs. To make your programs easier to understand, a good policy is to place all global variables out on the diagram where they are easily spotted. In this example, the Manual Control subVI reads settings information from a global, changes that information, then writes it back to the global. I could have hidden the global operations inside the subVI, but then you wouldn't have a clue as to how that subVI acts on the settings information, which is also used by the Ramp & Soak Controller subVI. It also helps to show the name of the global variable so that the reader knows where the data is being stored.

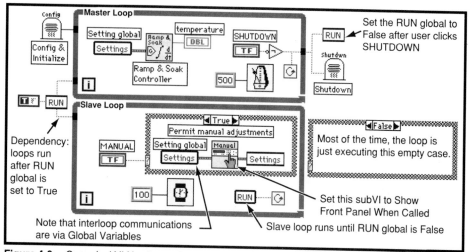

Figure 4-9. Canonical VI No. 3: parallel loops. For VBL, I used two independent loops: the upper one for the actual control, and the lower one to handle manual operation (shown simplified here). This way, the main control loop always runs at a constant interval regardless of the state of the manual loop. A global Boolean stops the bottom loop and status information is passed between the loops in another global variable.

Client-Server

I stole the term **client-server** from the world of distributed computing where a central host has all the disk drives and shared resources (the **server**), and a number of users out on the network access those resources as required (the **clients**). Here is how it works in a LabVIEW application: You write a server VI that is solely responsible for, say, acquiring data from the hardware. Acquired data is prepared and written to one or more global variables that act like a database. Then, you design one or more client VIs that read the data in the global variable(s). This is a very powerful concept, one that you will see throughout this book and in many advanced examples.

A good use for this might be process control (Chapter 8, *Process Control Applications*) in which the client tasks are things like alarm generation, real-time trending, historical trending to disk, and several different operator interface VIs. The beauty of the client-server concept is that the clients can be completely independent top-level VIs, running at different rates, in different windows, even on different machines if you use a network. You can also set the **priority** of execution for each VI through the **VI Setup** dialog box. Typically, the server would have higher priority to guarantee fresh data and good response to the I/O systems while the clients would run at lower priority. If you want one button to shut down everything, add a RUN Boolean control to a global variable and wire that into all the clients.

Menu-Driven

Sometimes you want a single panel that the operator uses as a main menu to access various modes of operation. A good example is automatic test applications where the operator

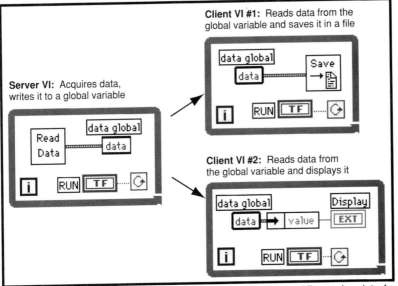

Figure 4-10. Canonical VI No. 4: Client-server systems. Client VIs receive data from a server VI through a global variable. This permits time-independence between several VIs or loops.

decides which test to perform by clicking a button. That button starts a subVI that does the work. When it's done, control returns to the main menu.

Back in Figure 4-9, the lower While Loop (the slave) contains a Case structure that is controlled by a button on the panel. When the button is pressed (True state), a VI inside the case is called. That VI is set to **Show front panel when called**, so its panel appears and remains visible until this VI's execution terminates, at which time it closes again, providing that you set it to **Close afterwards if previously closed**. Both of these options are available in the VI Setup pop-up menu. Several Case structures could be placed inside one While Loop to permit the user to call various subVIs. The structure of a typical subVI called by this method is shown in Figure 4-11. Advanced versions of these schemes are discussed

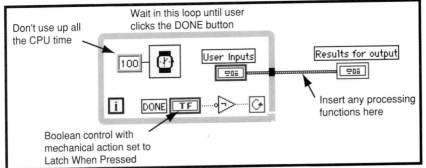

Figure 4-11. Canonical VI No. 5: used in Show Front Panel When Called subVIs. Sits around in the While Loop until the user clicks the DONE button, then sends the output back to the calling VI. An enhancement is to put data validation inside the loop.

in greater detail in Chapter 7, *Writing a Data Acquisition Program*, and Chapter 8, *Process Control Applications*.

State Machines

There is a very powerful and versatile alternative to the Sequence structure, called a **state machine**, as described in the Advanced LabVIEW Training course. It uses a Case structure wired to a counter that's maintained in a shift register in a While Loop. This technique allows you to jump around in the sequence by manipulating the counter. For instance, any frame can jump directly to an error handling frame. This technique is widely used in driver VIs and is most applicable to situations that require extensive error checking. Any time you

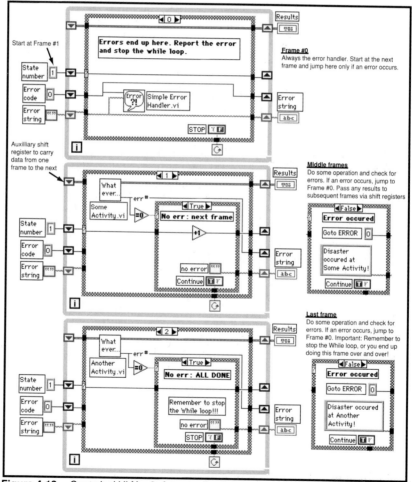

Figure 4-12. Canonical VI No. 6: A generalized state machine. Any frame of the Case structure can "jump" to any other by manipulating the State Number shift register. Error codes and messages are passed to an error handler in frame zero. Normal execution proceeds from frame 1 through frame 2. Frame 0 or frame 2 can stop execution. An exceptionally versatile concept, well worth studying.

have a chain of events where one operation depends on the status of a previous operation, a state machine is a good way to do the job.

Figure 4-12 is a generalized example of the structure of a state machine. If anything goes wrong at any step, it jumps to frame zero where an error handler will report what went wrong. The State Number is maintained in a shift register, so any frame can jump to any other frame. Error messages and error codes are also passed in shift registers, if they are needed. Shift registers must also be used for any data (like the Results of the two activity subVIs in this example) that needs to be passed between frames. One of the configuration tricks you will want to remember is to use frame zero for errors. That way, if you add a frame later on, the error frame number doesn't change; otherwise you would have to edit every frame to update the error frame's new address.

Each frame that contains an activity also has a Case structure that checks for errors (or other conditions) to see where the program should go next. In driver VIs, you commonly have to respond to a variety of error conditions in which you may want to retry communications, abort, or do something else depending on the condition detected. The state machine lets you handle these complex situations. One more tip: I always forget to stop the While Loop after the final frame. The program executes the last frame over and over, often with very strange results. Remember to put the little False Boolean constant where it belongs: in the error handler frame *and* in the last frame of the sequence.

The VI Hierarchy as a Design Tool

A good way to start mapping out your application is to sketch a preliminary **VI hierarchy**. To see what this might look like, open a LabVIEW example VI and select Show Hierarchy from the Windows menu. You don't need to start off with lots of detail. Just scribble out a map showing the way you would like things to flow, and the likely interactions between various subVIs, as in Figure 4-13. Modular decomposition in many languages looks like this figure. There's a main program at the top, several major tasks in the middle level, and system support or I/O drivers at the lowest level. You could also draw this as a nested list, much the way file systems are often diagrammed.

Each **node** or item in the hierarchy represents a task, which then becomes a subVI. Use your list of functional requirements as a checklist to see that each feature has a home

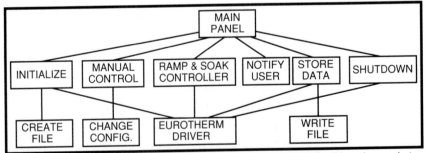

Figure 4-13. A preliminary VI hierarchy for VBL. At this point, I really did not know what was going to happen inside each subVI, but at least I had an idea about the division of labor.

somewhere in the hierarchy. As you add features, you can keep adding nodes to this main sketch, or make separate sketches for each major task. Modularity again! No need to worry about the programming details inside a low-level task; just make sure you know what it needs to do in a general way. Remember that the hierarchy is a design tool that should be referred to and updated continuously as you write your programs.

> The ramp-and-soak controller (one of the major subVIs in VBL) looked simple enough at first, but turned out to be one of the trickiest routines I've ever written. Without a healthy respect for modularity, I would have had a much more difficult time. The problems stemmed from interactions between various modes of operation, such as manual control, ramping, and soaking. My hierarchy sketch was a real mess by the time I was through, but it was the only way to track those modes and interactions with ease.

If you have experience with formal software engineering techniques, including Computer Aided Software Engineering (CASE) tools, by all means use them. The methods recommended by software engineers are all applicable to LabVIEW. In particular, entity diagrams and state diagrams map nicely into the VI hierarchy, while data flow diagrams can map directly into LabVIEW block diagrams.

Programming by Plagiarizing

A secret weapon for LabVIEW programming is making use of available example VIs. Many of your problems have already been solved by someone else, but the trick is to get hold of that code. The examples and driver libraries that come with LabVIEW are a goldmine, especially for the beginner. Start prowling these directories, looking for tidbits that may be useful. If you have access to a LabVIEW user group, be sure to make some contacts and discuss your more difficult problems.

You can start with some of the canonical VIs we have discussed. These structures are found in just about every application, sometimes in combination. The simplest VIs don't require any fancy structures or programming tricks. Instead, you just plop down some built-in functions, wire them up, and that's it. This book contains many programming constructs that you will see over and over. Some of them are included on the diskette that accompanies this book.

The examples, utilities, and drivers can often be linked together to form a usable application in no time at all. Data acquisition using multifunction boards is one area where I rarely have to write my own code. Using the examples and utilities pays off for file I/O as well. I mention this because everyone writes their own file handlers for their first application. It's rarely necessary, because 90% of your needs are probably met by a pair of file utility VIs that are already on your hard disk: Write Characters to File and Read Characters From File. The other 10% you can get by modifying an example or utility to meet your requirements. Little effort on your part, and lots of bang for the buck for the customer. That's the way it's supposed to work.

Pay Attention to Your Data

Consider the information that has to be passed from one part of the program to another. Any time you write a subVI that performs some task, make a list of the inputs and outputs. How do these inputs and outputs relate to other VIs in the hierarchy that have to access these items? Do the best you can to think of everything ahead of time. At least, try not to miss the obvious like a channel number or error flag that needs to be passed to most of the VIs in the hierarchy.

Think about the number of terminals available on the connector pane and how you would like the connections to be laid out. Is there enough room for all your items? If not, use clusters to group related items together. Always leave a few uncommitted terminals on the connector pane in case you need to add an item later. That way, you don't have to rewire everything. Clusters make sense for other reasons. For instance, passing the name and calibration information for a signal along with its data in one cluster makes a nice unit that clarifies the program. Clustered data minimizes the number of wires on the diagram, too.

Data structures such as clusters and arrays also make handling data more efficient when closely coupled to the **algorithms** that you choose. An algorithm is a stepwise procedure that acts upon some associated data. Conversely, a well-chosen data structure reflects the organization of its associated algorithm. Getting them to work in harmony results in a clear LabVIEW diagram that runs at top speed.

A sample of this idea is shown in Figure 4-14. If there are many channels to process, keep them in an array. Having an array implies using a For or While Loop to process that array. After processing inside a loop, the logical output structure is another array. If the array needs to carry more information than simple numerics, make it a cluster array, as in the figure. The snippet of code shown here could readily stand on its own as a subVI, doing a task of data acquisition. Furthermore, it could easily be enhanced by adding more items to the clusters, such as channel calibration information. Thinking ahead to relate algorithms and data structures can certainly make your program easier to understand and easier to modify.

An important feature of LabVIEW that can help you manage complicated data structures is the **Type Definition** which performs the same function as a typedef in C and a Type statement in Pascal. You edit a control using the LabVIEW **Control Editor**, in which you can make detailed changes to the built-in controls. Add all of the items that you need in the data structure. Then, you can save your new control with a custom name. An option in the Save dialog is **Save Control as Type Definition**. If you select this item, the control can't be edited from the panel of any VI in which it appears; it can only be modified through the Control Editor. The beauty of this scheme is that the control itself now defines a data type and changing it in one place (the Control Editor) automatically changes it in every location where it is used. If you don't use a Type Definition and you decide to change one item in the control, then you must manually edit every VI in which that control appears. Otherwise, broken wires would result throughout the hierarchy. As you can see, Type Definitions can save you much work and raise the quality of the final product.

Since VBL had five similar furnaces to control, it was obvious that they should be processed in a For Loop with N set to 5. The data I had to act on was basically the status of each temperature controller and its associated recipe for ramping and soaking. Since my program had several ways to access the data (manual control, recipe editor, automatic controller, etc.), the best solution was to create a global variable, as shown in Figure 4-15. This is actually a **global named set** where the "name" is the furnace number to access. It's a kind of database with the furnace number as the key. Because there is just one cluster to keep track of, each subVI that accesses this global is similar in form.

Sketching Program Structure

I use a really powerful, visual tool to design my LabVIEW programs. It's called **LabVIEW sketching** and it requires sophisticated hardware: *a pencil and paper.* The idea is to "think in LabVIEW" and put your conceptual program design on paper. You can work at any level of detail. At first, you'll be attacking the main VI, trying to make the major steps happen in the right order. Later on, you will need to figure out exactly where the data comes from, how it needs to be processed, and where it needs to go. Representing this

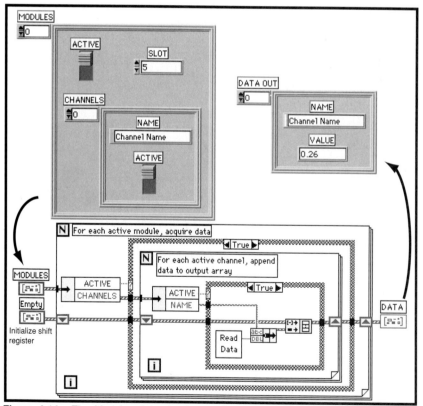

Figure 4-14. The Modules data structure at the upper left implies the algorithm at the bottom because the way that the cluster arrays are nested is related to the way the For Loops are nested.

information graphically is a powerful notion. What's even better is that you can implement these sketches directly as LabVIEW diagrams without an intermediate translation step.

You can also do sketching on your computer with LabVIEW. This has the advantage of permitting you to try out programming techniques that might simplify the problem. Then, your test diagram can be pasted right into the real VI. I do this a lot when I'm not sure how a built-in function works. I hook it into a simple test VI and fiddle with it until I really understand. It's a much better approach than to bury a mysterious function deep inside an important VI, then have to figure out why things aren't working later on.

Show your sketches to other LabVIEW users. Exchange ideas as you do the design. It's a vastly underused resource, this synergy thing. Everyone has something to contribute—a new way of looking at the problem, a trick they heard about, or sometimes a ready-to-use VI that fills the bill.

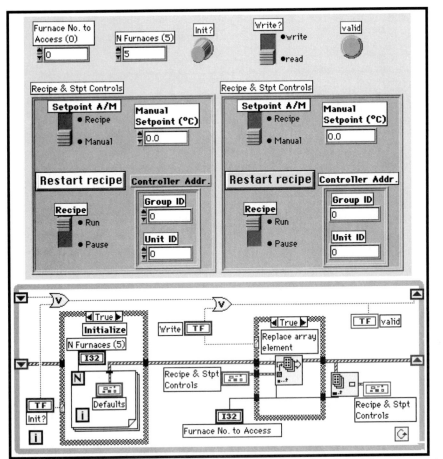

Figure 4-15. The Controller Settings Global contains a cluster with all the information needed to keep track of each furnace's status in VBL. The left one is a control for writing to the global, and the right one is an indicator for readout from the selected furnace.

Pseudo-Coding and Language Translation

If you are an experienced programmer, you may find that it's easier to write some parts of your program in a procedural language or **pseudo-code**. Of course, you should only do this if it comes naturally. Translating Pascalese to LabVIEW may or may not be obvious or efficient, but I sometimes use this technique instead of LabVIEW sketching when I have a really tough numerical algorithm to hammer out.

Figures 4-17 and 4-18 show a likely mapping between some example pseudo-code and a LabVIEW data structure, and the associated LabVIEW diagram that is a translation of the same code.

There's something that bothers me about this translation process. The folks who thought up LabVIEW in the first place were trying to free us from the necessity of writing procedural code with all its unforgiving syntactical rules. Normally, LabVIEW makes complicated things simple, but sometimes it also make simple things complicated. Making an oscilloscope into a spectrum analyzer using virtual instruments is really easy, but making a character-by-character string parser is a real mess. In such cases, we choose the best tool for the job at hand, and be happy.

To design the difficult ramp-and-soak control logic in VBL, I found that a pseudo-code approach was easier. I didn't have to look far to recover this example; it was pasted into a diagram string constant in the subVI called "Recipe Control Logic," as you can see in

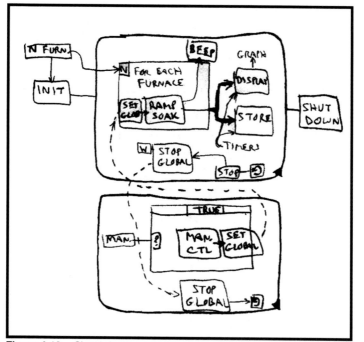

Figure 4-16.   Sketch for the main VI used in VBL. Not very detailed at this point, but it sure gets the point across.

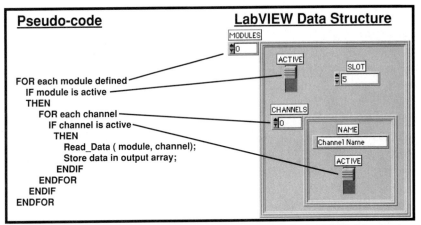

Figure 4-17. A mapping between a pseudo-code segment and a LabVIEW data structure.

Figure 4-19. I won't bother to reproduce the entire VI diagram here because it has too many nested Case structures to print in a reasonable space.

You also have the choice of using **Code Interface Nodes (CINs),** which are written in C and link nicely into LabVIEW. They are ideal in cases where you want to import existing code because you can do so almost directly. CINs are also needed for direct access to your computer's system routines, graphics toolbox, and the like. The problem with CINs is that the average user can't maintain them because they require a compiler for, and knowledge of, another language. Furthermore, CINs must be recompiled before they can run on a different computer. That's why I call them *sins*. They do make a great escape hatch for situations where you have no other choice.

Ranges, Coercion, and Default Values

Expect users to supply ridiculous inputs at every possible opportunity. A program that does not self-destruct under such abuse is said to be **robust**. Quick-and-dirty test programs are rarely robust. Commercial applications like word processors are highly robust, lest the

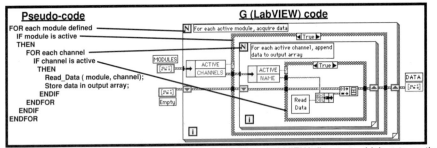

Figure 4-18. The same pseudo-code, translated into a LabVIEW diagram, which acts on the data structure from the previous figure. If this is your cup of tea, by all means use this approach.

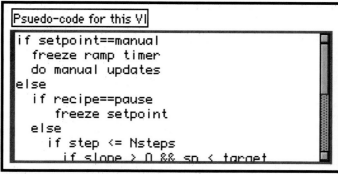

```
Psuedo-code for this VI
if setpoint==manual
   freeze ramp timer
   do manual updates
else
   if recipe==pause
      freeze setpoint
   else
      if step <= Nsteps
         if slope > 0 && sp < target
```

Figure 4-19. If you do decide to use pseudo-code to design your program, include it right on the diagram by pasting it into a string constant like this.

publisher go out of business. You may need to put appreciable effort into bullet-proofing your LabVIEW application.

On numeric controls, set the **Data Range...** item to *coerce* values into the desired range (minimum, maximum, and increment). If the values are not evenly spaced (such as a 1-2-5 sequence) use a function similar to Find Range from String, described in the National Instruments Application Note 006, *Developing a LabVIEW 2 Instrument Driver,* or the Range Finder VI shown in Figure 4-20. Don't, as a rule, choose Suspend in the Data Range dialog box, because the front panel of the VI then has to be memory-resident all the time in case it needs to be opened.

More complex situations must be handled programmatically. For instance, many GPIB instruments limit the permissible settings of one control based upon the settings of another: a voltmeter might permit a range setting of 2,000 V for DC, but only 1,000 V for AC. If the affected controls (for example, Range and Mode) reside in the same VI, put the interlock logic there. If one or more of the controls are not readily available, you can request the present settings from the instrument to make sure that you don't ask for an invalid combination.

String controls and tables are particularly obnoxious because the user can (and will) type just about anything into one. Think about the consequences of this for every string in your program. You may need to apply a filter of some type to remove or replace unacceptable characters. For instance, other applications may not like a data file where the name of a signal has embedded blanks or nonalphanumeric characters. String length may need adjustment. On the disk that accompanies this book, there is a VI called Fix String Length that truncates long strings and pads short ones.

One nefarious character is the carriage return. Users sometimes hit the carriage return key to "enter" text into a LabVIEW string control, thus appending \r to the string. Do you care? If it's a problem, you need to search for it and kill it. Note that training users will not solve the problem!

Controls should have reasonable default values. It's nice to have a VI that does not fail when run *as-opened* with default values. After entering the values you desire, select **Make Current Value Default** from the control's pop-up menu or from the Operate menu.

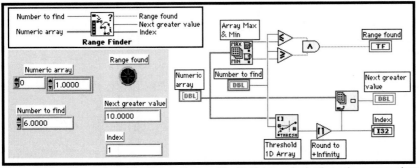

Figure 4-20. My version of the Range Finder utility VI. This one looks through an array of permissible values and finds the one that is greater than or equal to the value you wish to find. It returns that value and the index into the number to find array. (Available on the accompanying disk.)

Remember to show the default in parentheses in the control's label so that it appears in the Help window. But don't make the data in graphs and arrays into default values (unless it's really required); that just wastes disk space when the VI is saved.

Make intelligent use of default values. In the utility VI Write Characters to File, the default path is empty, which forces a file dialog box to appear when there is no path supplied to the VI. This can save the use of a Boolean switch in many cases.

Handling Errors

Another aspect of robust programs is the way they handle run-time errors. Commercial software contains an incredible amount of code devoted to error handling, so don't feel silly when half your diagram is devoted to testing values and generating dialog boxes. Most problems occur during the initial setup of a system, but may rarely occur thereafter. It may seem wasteful to have so much code lying around that is used only 0.01% of the time. But it's the startup phase where users need the most information about what is going wrong. Put in the error routines and *leave them there*. If you want, add a Boolean control to turn off dialog generation. Realize that dialog boxes tie up the VI from which they are called until the user responds. This is not a good mode of operation for an unattended system, but you may still want to see dialogs during a trouble shooting session.

Every call to an I/O driver or file service VI should be followed by an **error handler** of some kind. You should expect such I/O activities to fail at any time because of several major reasons:

- A system configuration error has been made. For instance, some equipment has not been properly installed or connected. Also, with plug-in boards, you must install the correct I/O handler in your operating system.

- Improper parameters have been supplied, such as channel numbers or file path names.

- A programming error has occurred on the diagram. Typically, you forgot to wire a required parameter.

- LabVIEW bugs crop up (incredible, but true).

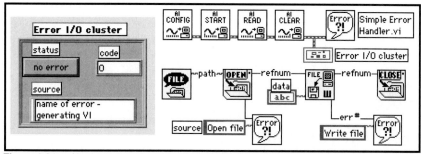

Figure 4-21.   Always use an error handler with file I/O and hardware I/O operations. The Simple Error Handler VI makes it easy. It accepts the standard Error I/O cluster or error codes and messages.

A good error handler tells the user:

•   Where the error came from

•   What might have caused the error

•   What actions he or she might take to fix and/or avoid recurrence

•   One or more appropriate options for escape (continue, stop, abort, etc.)

Errors should always be reported in plain language, though an error code number is usually displayed in addition in case a system guru wants to dig deeper.

Dialog boxes are a logical choice when the error is severe enough that user intervention is required. A string indicator on the panel of a VI will suffice when the message is more of an informative nature.

Error handler VIs are included with LabVIEW in the Utilities palette of the Functions menu. My favorite is called **Simple Error Handler** and it works for just about any purpose. You can feed it an error code number or a standard **Error I/O cluster** and it will generate a formatted message and an optional dialog. Error I/O has become very popular in LabVIEW programming because it solves one of those universal needs, and as such, it works as a common dataflow thread between many VIs, as you can see in Figure 4-21. The data acquisition library and many of the newer driver VIs use it. If the error handlers supplied don't suit your needs, use them as a foundation for your own customized version.

If an error condition is severe enough that execution of the VI cannot or must not continue, you can call the **Stop** function (the one in the Miscellaneous functions that looks like a stop sign). However, calling it can be risky if any I/O activity is pending. Realize that the Stop function causes the entire hierarchy of VIs to abort immediately. If a buffered data acquisition operation is in progress, it keeps going. Analog and digital outputs retain their last values. It may be difficult to clear up these conditions. Therefore, use the Stop function with caution.

> VBL had to run reliably when unattended. Therefore, I had to avoid any error dialogs that would "lock up" the system. When you call one of the dialog subVIs, the calling VI must wait for the user to dismiss the dialog before it can continue execution. My solution was to add a switch to

enable dialog generation only for test purposes. If a communications error occurred during normal operation, the main program would simply go on as if nothing had happened. This was a judgment call based on how critical the operation was. I decided that no harm would come to any of the furnaces because even the worst-case error (total communications failure) would only result in a *really long* constant temperature soak.

Putting It All Together

Keep hammering away at your application, one VI at a time. Use all the tools we have discussed for each step of the process. Remember that each VI can and should be treated as a stand-alone program. Break it down into pieces you understand (more subVIs) and tackle those one at a time. Then, build up the hierarchy, testing as you go. It's a reliable path to success. Never write your program as one, huge VI—the LabVIEW equivalent of a 40,000-line main program—because it will be very difficult to troubleshoot, and difficult for others to understand.

LabVIEW inventor Jack MacCrisken is a firm believer in iterative design after watching many users go through the development process over the years. His rule of thumb is that every application should be written twice. The first time, it's ugly, but it gets the job done and establishes a viable hierarchical approach. The second time, you sweep through and optimize, clean up, and document each VI, along with redesigning any parts of your program that no longer suit the overall requirements.

Check your user requirements document from time to time to make sure that everything has been addressed. Keep the users in the loop by demonstrating parts of your application as they are completed. It's amazing what an operator will say when shown a LabVIEW panel that mimics real laboratory equipment. You need this feedback at all stages of development as a form of *reality check.* In the real world of science, requirements change. If the experiment succeeds, the requirements grow. If it produces unexpected results, requirements change. And users change, too! You and your programs need to be flexible and ready to accept change.

Testing and Debugging Your Program

If you have designed your program in a modular fashion, testing will *almost* take care of itself: you are able to test each subVI independently, greatly increasing your chances of success. It's comforting to know that each module has been thoroughly thrashed and shows no signs of aberrant behavior. Nonmodular programming will come back to haunt you because a big, complicated diagram is much harder to debug than a collection of smaller, simpler ones.

Debugging is a part of life for all programmers (hopefully not *too* big a part). LabVIEW has some tools and techniques that can speed up the debugging process. Read over Chapter 3 of the LabVIEW user manual on Executing VIs. It has a whole list of debugging techniques. Here are a few of the important ones.

See What the SubVIs Are Up To

The first debugging technique is to open any subVIs that might be of interest in finding your problem. While a top-level VI executes, open and observe the lower-level VIs. Their panels will update each time they are called, allowing you to see any intermediate results. This is a good way to find errors like swapped cluster elements. If the value on one panel doesn't agree with the value on another panel, you have your wires crossed somewhere. It's another reason for using Type Definitions on all your clusters.

There is one special trick to viewing the panels while running: If a subVI is set up to be **reentrant**, then you must double-click that subVI node on the diagram it is called from *while the caller is running*. Otherwise, you will just be looking at another copy of the reentrant code. Reentrant VIs have independent data storage areas allocated for each instance in which the VI is used. Examples of reentrant VIs are the GPIB library and some of the data acquisition VIs.

You will also note that execution slows way down when panels are open. This is caused by extra graphic updates. On a panel that is not displayed, the graphics don't have to be drawn and that saves much execution time. There is also a saving in memory on VIs that are not displayed because LabVIEW must duplicate all data that is displayed in an indicator. If you are running a fast application where timing is critical, having extra panels open may murder your real-time response, so this debugging technique may not be feasible. I've actually used this very fact as a debugging tool in driver development. Sometimes, an instrument doesn't respond to commands as fast as you think and your VI can get out of sync. Having a lower-level VI's panel open can add just enough delay that the system starts working. Then you have a clue as to where to add some additional delay or logic.

Setting Breakpoints

A **breakpoint** is a marker you set in a computer program to pause execution when the program reaches it. You can set breakpoints in any subVI by clicking on the Breakpoint button ![...], which then changes to ![ ]. When that VI is called, it opens, execution of the calling VI is suspended, and the subVI will not proceed until you click one of the following buttons on the control bar:

![->] Runs the subVI as if it were a top-level VI being run on its own. You can run it over and over again, changing the input values and observing the results. A really cool thing you can do while in this state is to edit the values of *indicators*. If the VI runs for a long time and you need to abort it, you can click the Stop button ![STOP], and it will return to the suspended state once again. This is the one time when the Stop button does not stop the entire hierarchy.

![->] is the Resume button. Click this after you are finished fiddling with any values on the panel. The subVI closes and control returns to the calling VI.

Another way to set breakpoints is with the VI Setup... option, Suspend When Called. If a subVI's panel is not open when the breakpoint occurs, it will open automatically. The same thing happens when you have a numeric control or indicator set to suspend on a range error—a kind of conditional breakpoint. You might use this feature when something disastrous would happen if somebody entered an illegal value.

One Step at a Time

Sometimes you just can't figure out what's happening when the VI runs at full speed. In that case, try **single stepping** the execution of your program. Single-stepping mode is entered by clicking on the Step Mode button ⬜, which then changes to 〰 (Figure 4-22). While the VI is running, the Step button ⌐ appears. Click this button each time you want to execute the next node on the diagram. You can have several panels open at one time to examine the state of all the various inputs and outputs as you step through the main VI. Or, you can enable single stepping in an open subVI. That way, the main VI will run at full speed except when that subVI is called, at which time you can examine the subVI's activity in detail.

Execution Highlighting

Another way to see exactly what is happening in a diagram is to enable **execution highlighting**. Click on the execution highlighting button 💡, and notice that it changes to 💡. Run the VI while viewing the diagram. When execution starts, you can watch little bubbles run along the wires, representing the flow of data. Each time the output of a node generates a value, that value is displayed in a little box. This mode is most useful in conjunction with single stepping: you can carefully compare your expectations of how the VI works against what actually occurs.

My favorite use for execution highlighting is to find an infinite loop or a loop that doesn't terminate after the expected number of iterations. While Loops are especially prone to execute forever. All you have to do is accidentally invert the Boolean condition that terminates the loop, and you're stuck.

Sometimes a VI tries to run forever even though it contains no loops. One cause may be a subVI that contains an infinite loop. Reading from a serial port is another way to get stuck because that operation has no timeout feature. If no characters are present at the port, the VI will wait forever. (The solution to that problem is to call the Bytes at Serial Port function to see how many characters to read, then read that many. If nothing shows up after a period of time, you can quit without attempting to read.) That is why you must always design low-

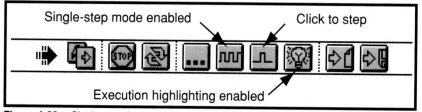

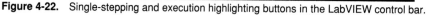

Figure 4-22. Single-stepping and execution highlighting buttons in the LabVIEW control bar.

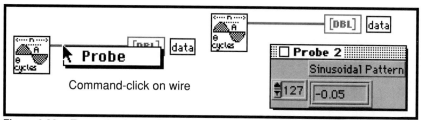

Figure 4-23. To use the data probe, pop up on any wire while the VI is executing. Select Probe from the pop-up. The little window that appears contains live data.

level I/O routines and drivers with timeouts. In any case, execution highlighting will let you know which node is "hung."

> Since VBL used the serial port to communicate with the Eurotherm temperature controllers, I had to write a robust serial port driver with timeouts. Chapter 5, *Instrument Drivers*, discusses this exact problem and solves it with a state machine and the Bytes at Serial Port function.

Be warned that highlighting greatly reduces performance because of all the graphical activity. I don't know how many times I've gone through a debugging session, accidentally leaving highlighting turned on. Then I wonder why the machine is so slow. To keep users from accidentally turning on execution highlighting or the other debugging features, you can disable these features. To do this, use the **VI Setup...** dialog and deselect the Debugging option.

Peeking at Data

It is often helpful to look inside a VI at intermediate values that are not otherwise displayed. Even if no problems are evident, this can be valuable—one of those lessons that you can only learn the hard way, by having a VI that appears to be working, but only for the particular test cases that you have been using. I like to connect extra, temporary indicators at various points around the diagram as a sanity check. Look at things like the iteration counter in a loop, or the intermediate results of a complicated string search. If the values you see don't make sense, find out why not. Otherwise, the problem will come back to haunt you.

Versions of LabVIEW starting with 2.5 also have a **Probe** tool. While a VI is executing, pop up on any wire and select Probe from the pop-up menu. A little window appears that displays the value flowing through that wire. It works for all data types—even clusters and arrays—and you can even pop up on data in the probe window to prowl through arrays. You can have as many probe windows as you like, floating all over the diagram. If the VI executes too fast, the values may become a blur; you may need to single-step the VI in that case. I like the probe because I don't have to create, wire, and then later delete all kinds of temporary indicators.

Debugging Global Variables

If your program uses many global variables or VIs that use uninitialized shift registers for internal state memory, you have an extra layer of complexity and many more opportunities for bugs to crop up. Here's a brief list of common mistakes associated with global variables and state memory:

- Accidentally writing data to the wrong global variable. It's easy to do; just select the wrong item on one of LabVIEW's built-in globals, and you're in trouble.

- Forgetting to initialize shift-register based memory. Most of the examples in this book that use uninitialized shift registers have a Case structure inside the loop that writes appropriate data into the shift register at initialization time.

- Calling a subVI with state memory from multiple locations without making the subVI reentrant when required. You need to use reentrancy whenever you want the independent calls *not* to share data, for instance when computing a running average.

- Conversely, setting up a subVI with state memory as reentrant when you *do* want multiple calls to share data. Remember that calls to reentrant VIs from different locations don't share data.

- Race conditions. You must be absolutely certain that every global variable is accessed in the proper order by its various calling VIs. The worst case is where you attempt to write and read a global variable on the same diagram without forcing the execution sequence. Race conditions are absolutely the most difficult bugs to find and are the main reason you should avoid using globals haphazardly.

How do you debug these global variables? The first thing you must do is locate all of the global variable's callers. Open the global variable's panel and select This VI's Callers from the Windows menu. Write down every location where the global is accessed, then audit the list and see if it makes sense. Keep the panel of the global open while you run the main VI. Observe changes in the displayed data if you can. You may want to single step one or more calling VIs to more carefully observe data. One trick I've used is to add a new string control called *info* to the global variable. At every location where the global is called to read or write data, I add another call that writes a message to the *info* string. It might say, "SubVI abc writing xyz array from inner Case structure." That makes it abundantly clear who is accessing what.

> The bugs I found in the VBL project were mostly due to unforeseen conditions. Changing operating modes in midstream created misbehavior because I did not plan for situations where the system was not initialized or used in the normal sequence. Another insidious bug was a couple of swapped cluster elements. The pop-up menu item on clusters called **cluster order** is really important. I managed to exchange a setpoint with a measured value in one location, and I could not detect this error until the whole application was wired up. I found that error by having several subVI panels open at once. Since VBL was developed in

LabVIEW 2.2, type definitions and Unbundle By Name were unavailable; they would have saved me some time.

Documentation

Most programmers hold documentation in the same regard as root canal surgery. Meanwhile, users hold documentation dear to their hearts. The only resolution is for you, the LabVIEW programmer, to make a concerted effort to get that vital documentation on disk and perhaps on paper. This section describes some of the documentation tools and formats that have been accepted in commercial LabVIEW software.

The key to good documentation is to generate it as you go. For instance, when you finish constructing a new subVI, fill in the **Get Info...** VI description item as described below. Then, when you want to put together a software maintenance document, you can just copy and paste that information into your word processor. It's much easier to explain the function of a VI or control when you have just finished working on it. Come back in a month, and you won't remember any of the details.

If you want to write commercial-grade LabVIEW applications, you will find that documentation is at least as important as having a well-designed program. As a benchmark, I spend at least 25% of my time on a given contract entering information into various parts of VIs and in the production of the final document.

VI Descriptions

The VI description in the **Get Info...** dialog box available from the File menu is often a user's only source of information about a VI. Think about the way that you find out how someone else's VIs work, or even how the ones in the LabVIEW libraries work. Isn't it nice when there's online help, rather than having to dig out the manual? Important items to include in the description are:

- An overview of the VI's function (followed by as much detail about the operation of the VI as you can supply)
- Instructions for use
- Description of inputs and outputs
- Author's name and date
- Modification history

Information can be cut and pasted into and out of this window. If you need to create a formal document, you can copy the contents of this description into your document. This is how I manage to deliver a really nice looking document with each driver that I write without doing lots of extra work. I just write the description as if I were writing that formal document. You can also use the **VI List** application as described below in the section on formal documents to extract these comments automatically.

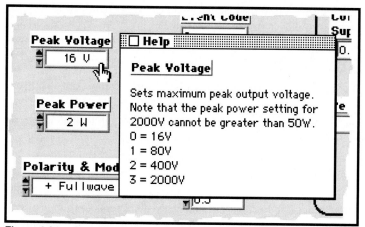

Figure 4-24.   Control descriptions are really helpful, but only if you remember to type them in!

You can also display the VI description by:

- Selecting the *Connector Pane and Description* option when printing.

- Showing the Help window and placing the wiring tool on a subVI's icon on the block diagram. (Due to space limitations, only part of the description can be displayed in the Help window.)

Control Descriptions

Every control and indicator should have a description entered through the **Description** pop-up menu, which is part of the Data Operations pop-up menu. You can display this information by showing the Help window and placing the cursor on the control. You can also display it by placing the wiring tool on the control's terminal on the block diagram. This is very handy when you are starting to wire up a very complex VI with many front panel items. The control description should contain the following general information, where applicable:

- Purpose or function of the control or indicator

- Limits on numeric values (I usually write, *Range: 0-128.*)

- Default values

- Special interactions with other control settings

   This is the most underused feature of LabVIEW. When confronted with a new VI, a user typically has no alternative but to guess the function of each control and indicator. It is a welcome sight to have a brief message show up in the LabVIEW Help window just by pointing at the object. Get in the habit of entering a description as soon as you create the object. Then, if you copy the object to other VIs, the description follows along. Much easier than saving the documentation for *later.* Remember to tell users about this feature.

Documenting the Diagram

While the overall VI description provides adequate coverage of the purpose and function of a VI, it leaves something to be desired when it comes to explaining the diagram. There are many helpful items that you can add to a diagram to make it easier to understand (assuming that you have laid it out in a neat and orderly fashion). Many of these techniques appear in the examples in this book.

- Label every loop and every frame of Case and Sequence structures. Place a free label (using the labeling tool) inside each frame that states the objective of that frame, e.g., "Read data from all configured channels." Sometimes it helps to use a larger font or set the style to bold to make the label stand out.

- Label important wires, especially when the wire is very long or its source is somehow obscured. I like to make the foreground color transparent (T) and the background color white, then place the label right on the wire.

- Use large, bold, key numbers located near important parts of the diagram, then use a scrolling diagram string constant (located off to the side or bottom of the diagram) to explain each key item. This technique reduces clutter within the diagram but provides much information nearby. (Monnie Anderson, analyst at National Instruments, promotes this one; I've started to use it more and more.)

- Add an index to Sequence structures. If you have a Sequence structure with more than two or three frames, create a list outside the structure that helps the user quickly locate the desired frame.

Other Ways to Document

One foolproof way of getting important instructions to the user is to place a block of text right on the front panel where it can't be missed. Like a pilot's checklist, a concise enumerated list of important steps can be invaluable. You might even put a suggestion there that says, "Select Get Info from the File menu for instructions."

If a front panel has a large string indicator, have it do double duty by putting instructions in it, then Make Current Value Default. Note that you can type into an indicator as long as the VI is in Edit mode.

Writing Formal Documents

If you need to prepare a formal document describing your LabVIEW project, try to follow the conventions described here. The final product should end up looking much like the LabVIEW data acquisition VI reference manual. My objective here is to help propagate a consistent style of documentation so users can more quickly understand what you have written. If you work for a big company, they may have a style guide for technical writers that should be consulted as well. General document style is beyond the scope of this book; only the specifics of content and format as they pertain to VI descriptions are discussed.

Document Outline

For an instrument driver or similar package, a document might consist of the basic elements listed below:

1. Cover page

2. Table of contents

3. Introduction—"About this Package"

4. Programming notes—help the user apply the lower-level function VIs

5. Using the demonstration VI

6. Detailed description of each lower-level function VI

The first five items are general in nature. Use your best judgement as to what they should contain. The last item, the detailed description of a particular VI, is the subject of the rest of this section.

Connector Pane Picture

Using a screen capture utility, take a screen shot of the LabVIEW Help window while it contains the connector pane of the VI being documented. Then, paste the captured information into a painting or drawing application. Surround the connector pane and its title with a rectangle. Select these items and import them into your word processor as shown below. This gives the reader a handy key to the VI's connections, just like you find in the LabVIEW manuals.

VI Description

If you have already entered a description of the VI in the **Get Info...** box with the VI, open it, select all the text, and copy it to the clipboard to import it into a document in your word processor. There is a utility VI called **VI List** (available on the diskette that accompanies this book) that is able to copy all of the VI description strings from directories and libraries of VIs into a new text document. This automates the process for you. Just run the top-level VI (VI List) and follow the directions. Since it's a LabVIEW program, you can modify it to reformat the text as you like.

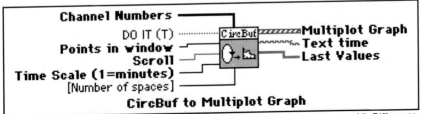

Figure 4-25.　The connector pane is an important part of the document for any VI. Different text styles can indicate relative importance of each terminal.

Names of input and output terminals should be in bold face. If your word processor can do page layouts, the description can flow around the connector pane picture. Here is the text that goes with the connector pane shown in Figure 4-25:

> A handy multichannel plotter for use with the Circular Buffer trending VI. Calls the Circular Buffer driver to return the desired quantity of data for one or more channels. Displays data as a multigraph plot and returns the last values for the specified channels. All channels share a common time base. Supports all the features of the Circular Buffer VI. To see this VI in action, run the Circ Buf Example VI, then run this VI. Since the Circular Buffer is a kind of global variable, its data can be shared between these independent, top-level VIs.

Terminal Descriptions

Every input and output needs a description that includes the information below.

- The data type
- What it does
- Valid range (for inputs)
- Default value (for inputs)

A new standard for terminal labeling has appeared recently, one that makes use of text style to indicate how frequently you need to change each item. When you create the VI, modify the font for each front panel item as follows: Use boldface for items that you will have to change often, use the normal font for items that you plan to use less often, and put square brackets [label] around the labels of items where the default value usually suffices. Figure 4-25 is one such VI that has all three label types. When you write the terminal descriptions into a document, put them in this prioritized order so the user will see the most-used items first. I like to start each line with a picture of the appropriate LabVIEW terminal data type, followed by the terminal's name, then its description, range, and default value:

> **I32** **Peak Voltage** sets the maximum peak output voltage. Note that the peak power setting for 2000V cannot be greater than 50W. The possible values are as follows:
>
> 0: 16 V (Default)
> 1: 80 V
> 2: 400 V
> 3: 2,000 V

Make a complete set of terminal icons that can be kept in a separate document. Open them at the same time as your project document. Just copy and paste the icons. I made such a document in Microsoft Word that I call *LabVIEW Helpers*. It also includes preformatted document sections and styles that speed up and standardize my work. If you can't handle all this graphical stuff, at least show the data type in text format. Examples:

I32	I32 integer
[DBL]	array of DBL numerics
[[DBL]]	2D array of DBL numerics
cluster	cluster
ABC	string

Programming examples include simple examples using your VI. For example, show how the VI is used in a loop or in conjunction with graphs or an analysis operation. Put completed examples on disk where the interested user can find them and try them out.

Final Touches

If you follow the directions discussed here, you will end up with a well-designed LabVIEW application that meets the specifications determined early in the process. A few final chores may remain.

Test and verify your program. First, compare your application with the original specifications one more time. Make sure that all the needs are fulfilled—controls and indicators are all in place, data files contain the correct formats, throughput is acceptable, etc. Second, you should abuse your program in a big way. Try pressing buttons in the wrong order and entering ridiculous values in all controls. Where data files are involved, I like to go out and modify, delete, or otherwise mangle the files without LabVIEW's knowledge, just to see what happens. Remember that error handling is the name of the game in robust programming. If you are operating under the auspices of formal software quality assurance, you will have to write a detailed validation and verification plan, followed by a report of the test results. A phenomenal amount of paperwork will be generated.

Train your users. Depending on the complexity of the application, this may require anything from a few minutes to several hours. I once developed a big general-purpose data acquisition package and I had about 15 people to train to use it. The package had lots of features and most of the users were unfamiliar with LabVIEW. My strategy was to personally train two people at a time in front of a live workstation. The user's manual that I wrote was the only other teaching aid. After going through the basic operations section of the manual in order during the training session, the students could see that the manual was a good reference when they had questions later. It took about two hours for each training session, much of which consisted of demonstration by me, with hands-on practice by the users at each major step. Simple reinforcement exercises really help the students to retain what you have taught them. I learned very soon afterwards that everyone really appreciated these training sessions because they helped them get a jump start in the use of the new system.

Last, but not least, make several **backup** copies of all of your VIs and associated documents. Hopefully, you have been making some kind of backups for safety's sake all along. It's an important habit to get into because system failures and foul-ups on your part should never become major setbacks. I like to keep the working copy on my hard disk, a daily backup on another (removable) hard disk, and a safety copy on floppies or some other media, perhaps a file server. When you make up a deliverable package, you can put a set of master floppies in one of those clear plastic diskette holders in the back of the user's manual. Looks really "pro."

VBL Epilogue

It turns out that it took longer to get the equipment fabricated and installed in Larry's lab than it did for me to write the application. I did all the testing in my office with a Eurotherm controller next to my Mac, including all the demonstrations. Since there was plenty of time, I finished off the documentation and delivered a copy in advance—Larry was pleasantly surprised. Training was spread out over several sessions, giving him plenty of time to try out all the features. We tested the package thoroughly without power applied to the furnaces for safety's sake. Only a few final modifications and debugging sessions were needed before the package was ready for real brazing runs. It's been running constantly since late 1992 with excellent results. Larry is another happy LabVIEW customer.

REFERENCES

1. *LabVIEW Style Guide.* An informal document, written by Gary Johnson and Meg Kay, that discusses the basic elements of LabVIEW programming style. Currently available from the National Instruments FTP server (ftp.natinst.com), the info-labview mail group server (ftp.pica.army.mil), or from the author.

Instrument Drivers

A LabVIEW **instrument driver** is a collection of VIs that control a programmable instrument. Each routine handles a specific operation such as reading data, writing data, or configuring the instrument. A well-written driver makes it easy to access an instrument because it encapsulates the complex, low-level hardware setup and communications protocols. You are presented with a set of driver VIs that are easy to understand, modify, and apply to the problem at hand.

The main reference that you need to read is Application Note 006, *Developing a LabVIEW Instrument Driver*, available free from National Instruments [Ref. 1]. It's one of my all-time favorite programming guides. (For a long time, it was the only programming guide to LabVIEW; Kevin Schmeisser of National Instruments deserves a lot of credit for forging ahead and writing it in the first place.) I won't duplicate here what it already says so well. Instead, I'll concentrate on design techniques and some of the tricks I've learned by writing a dozen or so major drivers.

About the Instrument Library

One of the reasons that LabVIEW has been so widely accepted is because of the way it incorporates instrument drivers. Unlike many competing applications, LabVIEW drivers are written in LabVIEW—complete with the usual panels and diagrams—instead of arriving as precompiled black boxes that only the manufacturer can modify. That means you can start with an existing driver and adapt it to your needs as you see fit. Another important asset is the National Instruments **instrument library**. It contains drivers for hundreds of instruments using a variety of hardware standards such as GPIB, RS-232/422, VXI, and CAMAC. Each driver comes with documentation and is fully supported by National Instruments. They are also *free*. Obtaining drivers from the library is easy:

- Call National Instruments at (800) 433-3488 and they will mail you diskettes.

- Call your local National Instruments representative. They often have copies of the drivers locally.

- Use the dial-up **bulletin board** if you have a modem. All the GPIB, serial, and CAMAC drivers are available for downloading.

- Use the **Internet FTP server** if you have access to Internet services. It offers the same files as the bulletin board.

Many of the drivers are commercial-grade software, meaning that they are thoroughly tested, fairly robust, documented, and supported. They are also one of your best resources for instrument programming examples (particularly the more recent ones). Whenever you need to write a new driver, always look at an existing driver that is related to your new project. Programming by plagiarizing is very productive and promotes standardization among drivers. Ideally, every instrument should be a drop-in replacement for every other instrument of its genre. No need to reinvent the wheel!

National Instruments welcomes contributions to the instrument library. If you have written a new driver that others might be interested in using, consider submitting it. Instrument vendors can also join the **Instrument Library Developer's Program (ILDP)**, which formalizes this process. Consultants who are skilled in writing instrument drivers can join the Alliance Program and become Certified Instrument Driver Developers. If you have that entrepreneurial spirit, you could even sell your driver package, providing there's a market. Software Engineering Group (Cambridge, MA) was probably the first to do this with their Highway View™ package that supports Allen-Bradley programmable logic controllers (PLCs). It's been a successful venture. Many other manufacturers of programmable instruments also *sell* their drivers rather than placing them in the library. If you can't find the driver you need in the library, give the manufacturer a call.

Driver Basics

Writing a driver can be trivial or traumatic; it depends on your programming experience, the complexity of the instrument, and the approach you take. Start by reading the application note, *Developing a LabVIEW Instrument Driver*, which will give you an overview of the preferred way to write a driver. Then, spend time with your instrument and the programming manual. Figure out how everything is supposed to work. Then decide what your objectives are. Do you just need to read a single data value, or do you need to implement every command? This has implications with respect to the complexity of the overall project.

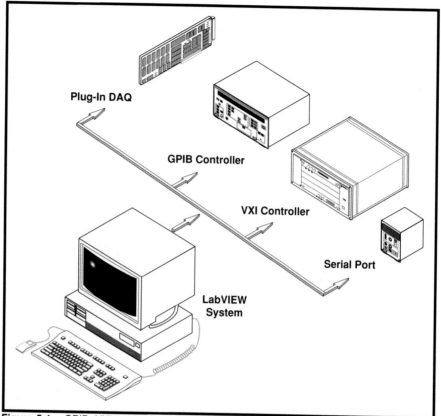

Figure 5-1. GPIB, VXI, and serial communications are very common, and are simplified by using instrument drivers. Plug-in data acquisition cards require special, low-level drivers. Drivers for National Instruments' boards are supplied with LabVIEW.

Communication Standards

The kinds of instruments you are most likely to use are "smart," stand-alone devices that use one of several communication standards, notably **serial**, **GPIB**, and **VXI**. These are the ones we'll tackle. Plug-in data acquisition boards are also extremely common. If you are using boards made by National Instruments, the drivers are already written and are supplied with LabVIEW in the form of example VIs and the DAQ VI library; they are discussed in Chapter 6, *Using the DAQ Library.* Programming for other manufacturer's plug-in boards and special hardware I/O subsystems is best accomplished in a procedural language like C, and implemented as Code Interface Nodes (CINs) in LabVIEW. Though CIN programming is beyond the scope of this book, the general principles discussed in this chapter are still relevant. A very good overview of GPIB and serial interfaces is available in the *Instrument Communication Handbook* [Ref. 2].

Serial Instruments

Popular serial communication standards include RS-232C and RS-422A. These standards are defined by the Electronics Industries Association (EIA) and include specifications for cabling, connector pinouts, signal levels, and timing. The advantages of serial communication are simplicity and low cost. RS-232 has been around for a long time, so there is plenty of cheap hardware available. The disadvantage is that serial systems tend to be slow (you can only move one bit of data at a time), and the protocols are sometimes burdensome in terms of programming.

RS-232C is the most common standard, supported by virtually all computer systems and most serial instruments. It uses the familiar 25-pin D-style connector for most equipment, or a 9-pin version on IBM PC systems. The standard defines functions for all the pins, though you will most often see just a few of the lines used: transmit data, receive data, and ground. The other pins are used for handshaking, with functions like Clear to Send and Ready to Send. These functions are supported by the LabVIEW serial port functions, if your instrument requires their use. The main limitation of RS-232 is that it is electrically single-ended, which results in poor noise rejection. The standard also limits the maximum distance to 100 meters, though this is frequently violated in practice. The top data rate is normally 19200 baud (bits per second), but some systems support higher speeds. It's also the most abused and ignored standard in the industry. Manufacturers take many liberties regarding signal levels, baud rate, connectors, and so forth. Not all "RS-232 compliant" devices are actually compatible. Beware!

RS-422A is similar to RS-232, but uses differential drivers and receivers, thus requiring two pairs of wires plus a ground as the minimum connection. Because of its superior noise rejection and drive capability, RS-422 is usable to 1200 meters at speeds below 9600 baud, and up to 1 Mbaud at shorter distances. Macintosh serial ports are RS-422A compliant.

Other standards in this series are RS-423A and RS-485A. RS-423A is identical to RS-232C, except that the electrical characteristics are improved to support higher transmission rates over longer distances. RS-485A is an extension of RS-422A that supports multidrop systems (multiple talkers and listeners on one set of wires). Generally, your computer will need an adapter box to properly support these standards. You can buy adapter boxes that provide electrical compatibility between all of these standards from companies such as Black Box.

The most common problems you will encounter when setting up RS-232-style serial communications systems are:

- Swapped transmit and receive lines. Though the standards clearly define which is which, manufacturers seem to take liberties. I always manage to hook things up backwards the first time, and the whole system is dead. The answer is to use a *null modem* cable that swaps these critical lines.

- Failure to properly connect the hardware handshaking lines. For instance, some instruments won't transmit until the **Clear to Send (CTS)** line is asserted. Study your instrument's manual and try to find out which lines need to be connected.

- Wrong speed, parity, or stop bits settings. Obviously, all parties must agree on these low-level protocol settings.

- Multiple applications trying to access the serial port. If the **Serial Port Init** function returns an error, make sure that there are no other programs running on your computer that might be using the same serial port. For instance, AppleTalk on a Macintosh seizes the printer port and you must disable it if you wish to use that port.

GPIB Instruments

Hewlett-Packard Corporation gets credit for inventing this popular communications and control technique back in 1965, calling it the HP Interface Bus (HP-IB), a name they use to this day. The Institute of Electrical and Electronics Engineers (IEEE) formalized it as **IEEE 488** in 1978, after which its common name, **General-Purpose Interface Bus (GPIB)** was adopted. It's a powerful, flexible, and popular communications standard supported by thousands of commercial instruments and computer systems. Right now, LabVIEW has more GPIB drivers than any other type. The most important characteristics of GPIB are:

- It is a parallel, or bus-based, standard capable of transferring one byte (eight bits) per bus cycle.

- It is fairly fast, transferring up to about 800,000 bytes per second.

- Hardware takes care of timing and handshaking.

- It requires significantly more expensive and complex hardware than serial interfaces.

- Distance is limited to 20 meters unless special bus extender units are added.

- Up to 15 devices can coexist on one bus; up to 31 with a bus expander unit.

There is also a newer version of this standard, **IEEE 488.2**, established in 1987. The original standard didn't address data formats, status reporting, error handling, etc. The new standard does. It standardizes many of these lower-level protocol issues, simplifying your programming task. Of course, only the most recently designed instruments are 488.2 compliant and there aren't very many as yet; the GPIB interface installed in your computer must also be up-to-date. The newer National Instruments GPIB boards support 488.2, and the LabVIEW GPIB library is based on it.

Even after the 488.2 standard was implemented, chaos reigned in the area of instrument command languages. A consortium of instrumentation companies convened in 1990 to define the **Standard Commands for Programmable Instrumentation (SCPI)** and programmers' lives became much easier. SCPI defines:

- Commands required by IEEE 488.2. Example: *IDN? (send instrument identification).

- Commands required by SCPI. Example: ERR? (send the next entry from the instrument's error queue).

- Optional commands. Example: DISP (controls presentation of display information).

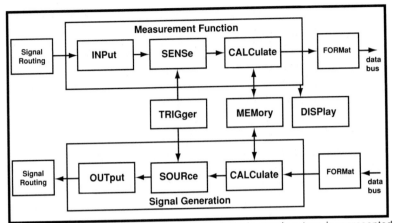

Figure 5-2. The SCPI instrument model. Each block, or subsystem, is represented by a consistent command hierarchy.

Commands are structured as a hierarchical command tree. You specify a function, a sub-function, a sub-subfunction, etc., separated by a colon (:) character. For instance, the SCPI message for an autoranging voltage measurement would be:

```
SENSE:VOLTAGE:RANGE:AUTO
```

The first time I programmed a SCPI-compliant instrument (the HP 54510A Digitizing Oscilloscope), it was a pleasant surprise because the command set... *made sense*! Also, the SCPI model (Figure 5-2) covers instruments of all kinds with a general model, so the programs you write tend to be reusable. By all means, feel welcome to borrow code directly from drivers for other SCPI instruments and save yourself some time.

The bad news is, GPIB is a fairly complex communications standard. The good news is, 95% of the time all you need to do is write a simple command string and read back a reply string. However, there are times when you need to use some of the more sophisticated aspects of GPIB, like the device and controller functions. To really be successful in applying advanced functions, you will probably want to read up on the GPIB standard, or maybe even take an IEEE 488 course, such as the one that National Instruments offers.

VXI Instruments

One of the newer industry-standard computer buses, VME, has been extended to support an instrument-on-a-card architecture. **VME Extensions for Instrumentation (VXI)** is a standard that was first established in 1987 by the *VXI Consortium*, and has been formalized as IEEE standard 1155-1993. The goals of the consortium are to bring the following benefits to test and measurement scientists and engineers: increased test throughput, smaller instrument and system size, reduced cost, more precise timing and synchronization, and a standardized hardware system for programming and configuration. This standard is intended to take instrument systems into the next generation. Dozens of manufacturers are producing VXI instruments, interface equipment, and software, including Tektronix, Hewlett-Packard, Racal-Dana, Wavetek, and National Instruments.

VXI (quaintly pronounced *vixie*) modules plug into a mainframe with up to 13 slots. The leftmost slot, called Slot 0, has special hardware features. The module that goes there is responsible for certain **system resources**: backplane clocks, trigger signals, and configuration signals. Typically, the Slot 0 module is either the system controller, or is directly connected to an external system controller. However, since VXI is a modern computer architecture that fully supports multiple processors and shared main memory— up to 4 gigabytes, thanks to its 32-bit bus—Slot 0 may or may not be the *only* controller. In fact, any instrument can talk to (and control) any other instrument. For instance, a digitizer module can control a trigger generator, then directly store the acquired data in the main, shared memory for use by the controller. With these specifications, VXI has tremendous versatility and a great deal of potential.

An important feature of VXI systems is that most modules have no front panel controls, just I/O connectors and (sometimes) indicator lamps. A decade ago this would have been impractical because the complete burden of control is shifted to the software. But now, we have LabVIEW and the concept of virtual instruments where, as the National Instruments banner says, *The Software is the Instrument*. Instead of buying expensive specialty instruments, you combine a number of generic instruments. VXI was designed from the ground up to offer high performance in this software-dominated architecture. All you have to do is readjust your thinking with regard to solving instrumentation problems from real instrument to virtual instrument.

The majority of VXI devices can be classified as either **register-based** or **message-based**. Register-based and message-based devices differ in their control interfaces. Some VXI devices are capable of both modes of control.

Register-based devices are programmed at a low level using binary information. You read and write directly to and from hardware registers on the device. The obvious advantage of this is speed: there is essentially no overhead at the destination as there would be for parsing command strings. The disadvantage is that each device requires customized manipulation of its registers and the programming is quite tedious.

Message-based devices, in contrast, communicate at a high level using ASCII characters—just like GPIB. The strings you send to message-based devices must be in the device's specific language, but you don't have to be concerned with module-specific registers, binary transfers, and so on. Many VXI message-based instruments are SCPI compliant, which means you can use parts of drivers that were written for other SCPI instruments, most likely GPIB. The disadvantage of message-based instruments is that the data transfers are somewhat slower due to the overhead of creating, parsing, and sending ASCII messages.

There are several ways to configure the intelligence in a VXI system (Figure 5-3). One way is to use a **GPIB-to-VXI interface module** in Slot 0. The interface module effectively puts a GPIB front end on a VXI chassis so that each VXI module appears to be a separate GPIB instrument. This is an advantage if you already understand GPIB and have

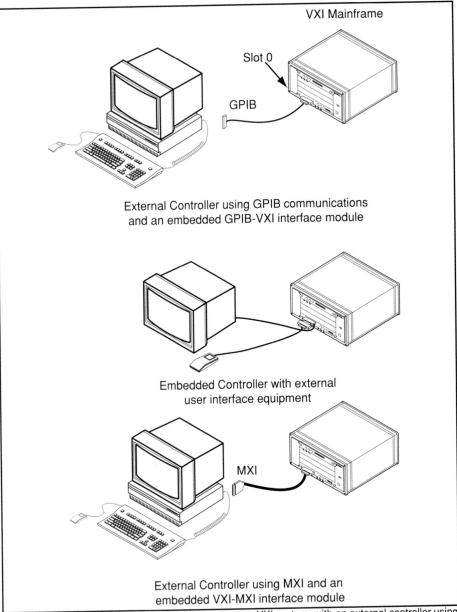

VXI Mainframe

Slot 0

GPIB

External Controller using GPIB communications
and an embedded GPIB-VXI interface module

Embedded Controller with external
user interface equipment

MXI

External Controller using MXI and an
embedded VXI-MXI interface module

Figure 5-3.   This figure shows three valid ways to run a VXI system: with an external controller using GPIB communications, with MXI communications, or with an embedded controller (which might be running LabVIEW).

a GPIB interface in your computer. The module takes care of all the resource manager duties to configure and initialize the instruments. Each instrument is assigned a unique GPIB address. Then, the GPIB-to-VXI interface translates GPIB messages to VXI message-based commands and passes them to the appropriate module. Your GPIB-based host computer simply communicates using standard GPIB protocol (read, write, poll, etc.). Additional functionality (such as access to register-based control and high-speed memory transfers) is available by addressing the GPIB-to-VXI interface module itself.

The second way to configure a VXI system is to use an **embedded controller**. An embedded controller is a custom computer designed specifically for VXI and packaged in a VXI module. Embedded computers offer the smallest physical size and the highest performance because they communicate directly with the VXI backplane. Many types of embedded controllers are available, most notably the 80386/486 family. These are complete computers, including memory, disks, video display interfaces, network connections, and so on. Therefore, you can run LabVIEW on one of these machines, right in the VXI mainframe—a tidy, high-performance package. Naturally, you could also write your programs using other languages, but who would ever want to do *that*?

National Instruments invented a third configuration: **Multisystem Extension Interface (MXIbus)**, a high-performance communication link that interconnects devices using multiconductor cables. MXI (pronounced *mixie*) works like a regular computer bus, but is cabled for high-speed communication between physically separate devices. It minimizes software protocol overhead by providing direct control and shared memory between devices, and matches the data transfer rates of high-performance computers and peripherals. You plug an MXI interface board into your computer's backplane, plug an MXI controller into Slot 0 of a VXI mainframe, and connect them with a ribbon cable. Performance is nearly as good as that of an embedded controller.

From the user's perspective, a desktop PC connected to the VXIbus via the VXI-MXI interface is identical to using a dedicated VXI embedded controller. The National Instruments NI-VXI bus interface software is a comprehensive software package for configuring, communicating with, and troubleshooting a VXI system. The NI-VXI bus interface software includes a Resource Manager program (RM) for initializing your system, a library of software routines for programming your system, a Resource Editor program (VXIedit) for configuring your VXI system resources, and a VXI Interactive Control program (VIC) for interacting with and troubleshooting the VXIbus. To use LabVIEW to program a VXI system with either an embedded controller or a VXI-MXI interface, you will also need the LabVIEW VXI VIs found exclusively with the LabVIEW VXI Development System. Registered LabVIEW users can order an upgrade to obtain these VIs. GPIB-VXI based systems do not require this additional software; only your existing GPIB software tools are required.

Learn About Your Instrument

You can't program it if you don't understand it. When I receive a new instrument for a driver project, I'm not always familiar with its purpose or its modes of operation. I fully expect that it will take several hours of experimenting with the controls and reading the user manual before I'm comfortable with the fundamentals. It's also a good idea to connect the instrument to some kind of signal source or output monitor. That way, you can stimulate inputs and observe outputs. I have a function generator, a voltmeter, and an oscilloscope, plus test leads and accessories to accommodate most instruments. Sometimes, I need to borrow more exotic equipment.

VXI instruments are a little more challenging to learn to use because they don't have front panels. Regular GPIB rack-and-stack instruments let you fiddle with the knobs, which helps a lot during the get-acquainted phase. VXI requires you to hook up the communications link, get it working, then use some kind of software tool to poke commands at the instrument and read the returned values.

Obtain and study the programming manual. Some companies write programming manuals that border on works of art, as you will find with the newer HP and Tektronix instruments. Other manuals are little more than lists of commands with terse explanations (I'll be a nice guy and let those companies remain anonymous). Pray that you don't end up with one of the latter. By the way, programming manuals are notorious for errors and omissions. I think it's because so few people actually *do* any low-level programming; they rely on people like us to do the dirty chore of writing a driver. If you find mistakes in a manual, by all means tell the manufacturer so they can fix it in the next revision.

Even the best manuals can be kind of scary—some complex instruments have really big manuals. What you have to do is skim through a couple of times to get a feel for the overall structure of the command set. Pay attention to the basic communications protocol, which is especially important for instruments that use the serial port. Also, figure out how the instrument responds to and reports errors. Take notes, draw pictures, and make lists of important discoveries.

Interactions between settings need special attention. For instance, changing from volts to amps on a DMM probably implies that the Range control takes on a different set of legal values. Sending an illegal range command may cause the meter to go to the nearest range, do nothing, or simply *lock up*! (Newer instruments are getting better about these sorts of things; in the old days, rebooting an instrument was sometimes required.) Your driver will need to arbitrate these control interactions, so note them as soon as they're discovered.

Determine Which Functions to Program

Nothing is quite so overwhelming as opening the programming manual and finding out that your instrument has *4,378 commands*! Obviously, you're not going to implement them all; you need to decide which commands are needed for your project.

If you are hired specifically to write an instrument driver, like those of us in the consulting world, the customer will probably supply a list of commands that you are required to support. If the list is long, you simply take more time, charge more money, and become rich. But if you are writing a driver for your own specific application, you probably don't have the time to develop a comprehensive driver package. Instead, you must determine the scope of the job and decide exactly which functions you need to implement. Here are some functions that most simple driver packages should support:

- **Basic communications**—the ability to write to and read from the instrument, with some form of error handling. Easy with GPIB or VXI, somewhat more complicated with serial devices.

- **Sending commands**—the ability to tell the instrument to perform a function or change a setting.

- **Transferring data**—if the instrument is a measurement device like a voltmeter or oscilloscope, you probably need to fetch data, scale it, and present it in some useful fashion. If the instrument generates outputs like a waveform generator, you need to write blocks of data representing waveforms.

- **Configuration management**—the ability to load and store the settings of many of the instrument's important controls all at once. Some instruments have internal setup memory, while others let you read and write long strings of setup commands with ease. Others offer no help whatsoever, making this task really difficult.

- **Important controls**—there are always a few basic controls that you simply *must* support, like the mode and range on a DMM. More extensive drivers generally support more controls.

The basic question to ask is, will the user do most of the setup manually through the instrument's front panel, or will LabVIEW have to do most of the work? With VXI, the answer is easy: there are *no* front panels controls, so your LabVIEW driver has to implement most, if not all, of the available control functions. If I'm using LabVIEW on the test bench next to an oscilloscope, I manually adjust the 'scope until the waveform looks OK, then just have LabVIEW grab the data for later analysis. No software control functions are required in this case. If the application is in the area of automated test equipment (ATE), instrument setups have to be controlled to guarantee that the setups are identical from test to test. In that case, configuration management will be very important and your driver will have to access many control functions.

Think about the intended application; then look through the programming manual again and pick out the important functions. Make a checklist and get ready to begin communicating with your instrument.

Establish Communications

After studying the problem, your next step is to establish communications with the instrument. You may need to install communications hardware (like a GPIB interface board); then you need to assemble the proper cables and try a few simple test commands to see that the instrument hears you. If you are setting up your computer or interface hardware for the first time, consider borrowing an instrument with an available LabVIEW driver to try out. It's nice to know that there are no problems in your development system.

Hardware and Wiring

Serial: Problematic because the standards are so often violated (nonstandard standards?), serial hardware is more challenging to hook up than the other types. Figures 5-4A and 5-4B show the wiring diagrams for the Macintosh and the IBM PC/AT versions. Your instrument's manual has to supply information about connector pinouts and the

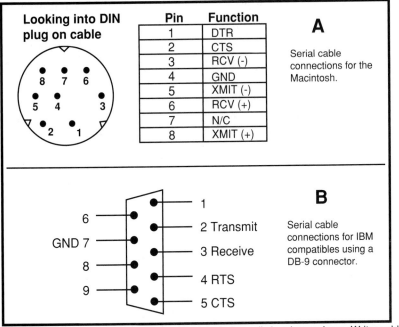

Looking into DIN plug on cable	Pin	Function	A
	1	DTR	
	2	CTS	Serial cable connections for the Macintosh.
	3	RCV (-)	
	4	GND	
	5	XMIT (-)	
	6	RCV (+)	
	7	N/C	
	8	XMIT (+)	

Figure 5-4. Serial port wiring. For the Macintosh, I usually butcher an ImageWriter cable because it has the DIN8 connector with all eight wires ready to go. For IBM PCs using a DB-9 connector, you can get cables and connectors like this at your local electronics emporium.

requirements for connections to hardware handshaking lines (like CTS and RTS). The usual wiring error is to swap transmit and receive lines on RS-232. RS-422 adds to the problem by permitting you to swap the positive and negative lines as well. One trick I use to sort out the wires is to test each pin with a voltmeter. The negative lead of the meter should go to the ground pin. Transmit lines will be driven to a nice, solid voltage (like +3 V), while receive lines will be zero, or floating randomly. You can also use an oscilloscope to look for bursts of data if you can force the instrument to go into *talk* mode. A **null modem** cable or adapter usually does the trick for RS-232 signal mix-ups. It effectively swaps the transmit and receive lines and provides jumpers for CTS and RTS. Be sure to have one handy, along with some gender changers (male-to-male and female-to-female connectors), when you start plugging together serial equipment.

GPIB: You need some kind of IEEE 488 interface in your computer. Plug-in boards from National Instruments are the logical choice since they are all supported by LabVIEW and they offer high performance. External interface boxes (SCSI, RS-232, or Ethernet to GPIB) are also usable. Cabling is generally easy with GPIB because the connectors are all standard. Just make sure that you don't violate the 20-meter maximum length; otherwise, you may see unexplained errors and/or outright communication failures. Incredibly, people have trouble hooking up GPIB instruments. Their main problem is making sure that the connector is pushed all the way in at both ends. Always start your testing with just one instrument on the bus to avoid unexpected addressing clashes.

VXI: If you are using a GPIB interface to your VXI equipment, refer to the GPIB setup information above. If you are using MXI-VXI, you need to make sure your MXI card is properly installed in your PC, and that your VXI-MXI interface is in Slot 0 of your chassis. If you are using an embedded controller, you need only plug it into Slot 0 and you are ready to boot.

Because there are no cables associated with the VXIbus (exception: MXI cable), connecting your instruments is generally a simple matter of setting unique logical addresses on each instrument and plugging them into your VXI chassis. Depending on your chassis, however, you may have to configure some jumpers. Some models (particularly older ones) require you to physically install or remove Bus Grant, Interrupt Acknowledge, and ACFAIL jumpers on the VXIbus backplane depending on whether or not you will be installing an instrument in a particular slot. The BG* and IACK* daisy-chain jumpers propagate the Bus Grant and Interrupt Acknowledge signals across unused slots, or for slots with installed modules that do not propagate these signals.. These signals are normally propagated by each installed module from the appropriate input pin BGxIN* or IACKIN* on its P1 connector to the appropriate output pin (BGxOUT* or IACKOUT*). The continuity of BG0*-BG3* and IACK* from Slot 0 must be maintained for proper system operation. Normally, then, these jumpers should be removed for each slot in which a module is installed, and replaced when the module is removed. Newer VXI chassis models have jumperless backplanes and automatically connect and disconnect these signals as you install and remove modules. Check your mainframe's user manual to see if you need to configure jumpers in your mainframe.

Protocols and Basic Message Passing

GPIB: Figure out how to set the GPIB address of your instrument, or at least find out what the address is. From the instrument's manual, determine what the command terminator is (carriage return, linefeed, EOI asserted, or a combination), and pick out a simple command to try out. The GPIB Read and GPIB Write VIs both have an input called **Mode** that controls EOI, carriage return, and linefeed actions. Make sure that this mode setting is appropriate to your instrument. The default (**Mode**=0) works for most instruments, in my experience. The GPIB Test VI shown in Figure 5-5 is an interactive general purpose GPIB instrument controller that you can use to test commands one at a time. For convenience, there are four write messages so you can quickly send a sequence of messages. Type in your commands, and move the big selector switch to the first command you wish to send. With the function switches, choose **W** (write), **R** (read only), or **B** (both; write then read) and run the VI. See how the instrument reacts. Look at the *error out* window and see if there are any unexpected errors reported.

On the first try, you may get a timeout because the GPIB address is incorrect. If all else fails, go through all the addresses from 1 to 31 (zero is the controller) until you get a response. You can use the FindLstn VI (in the 488.2 library) to find all listeners on the bus; it returns an array of addresses. In really tough cases, you may have to use a GPIB bus analyzer (HP, Tektronix, National Instruments, and IOTech all make them) to examine the

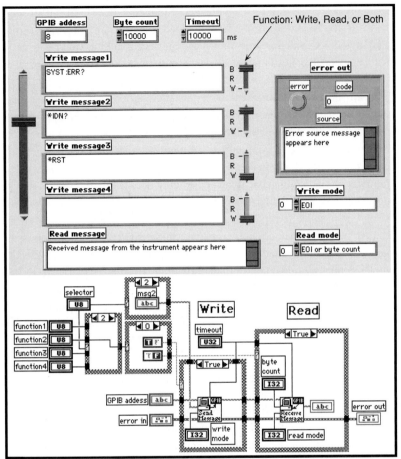

Figure 5-5. An interactive GPIB communicator, GPIB Test is useful for testing commands. You can write, and/or read as desired. It's easy to switch among the four messages for transmission.

bus traffic. Always verify the command terminator. If the instrument expects EOI and you don't send it, nothing will happen.

Another classic hang-up with GPIB involves the issue of **repeat addressing**. When the controller (your computer) talks to another device on the bus (an instrument), the first thing the controller has to do is *address* the instrument. If the controller wishes to communicate with the same device again, it may take advantage of the fact that many (but not all) instruments remember that they are still addressed. If the instrument doesn't remember that it is still addressed, then you need to enable the repeat addressing action in your system's GPIB driver. On the Macintosh, this is a checkbox called Repeat Addressing in the NB Handler INIT Control Panel. Under Windows, you set it from ibconf. On the Sun, it can't be set directly. On all platforms, you can use the GPIB Initialize VI to set repeat addressing. I get calls all the time regarding drivers I've written that don't work reliably, and this is the

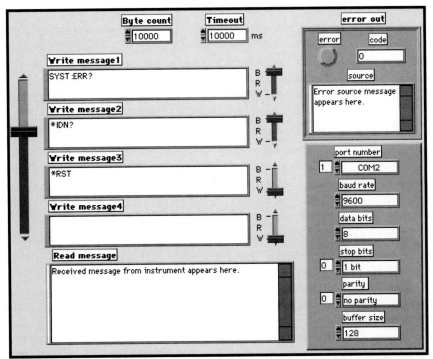

Figure 5-6. Serial Test is helpful for testing serial port instruments. It lets you read and/or write any number of characters, supports timeouts, and reports errors. Note the similarity with GPIB Test; it's more than just the front panel, the diagrams are almost clones as well.

first thing I tell the user to check (after seeing that the cable is plugged in and the address is properly set).

Serial: Unlike GPIB, serial instruments have little in common with each other since there are essentially no standards in use. Some instruments are individually addressed so that they can be used in multidrop networks like RS-423A. Others have no addressing and are designed for use on a dedicated link. Protocols vary from a GPIB-like ASCII message exchange to pure binary with complex handshaking. Study your instrument's programming manual and figure out what protocol it uses. If it's a simple ASCII-based scheme, you can use a terminal emulator application (the same one you use with a modem) to test out commands. Or, you can use the Serial Test VI, shown in Figure 5-6. Like its GPIB cousin, you can write and read strings to and from the instrument. The VI includes timeouts and error reports in case something is amiss.

Be sure to set the basic serial parameters: speed (baud rate), bits per character, stop bits, parity, and XON/XOFF action. LabVIEW's Serial Port Init function sets these parameters and more. If you use a terminal emulator, you will have to do the same thing in that program. Check these parameters very carefully. Next to swapped transmit and receive lines, setting one of these items improperly is the easiest way to fail to establish communication with a serial instrument.

Instruments that use those nasty binary protocols with lots of handshaking are nearly impossible to test by hand. The problem is that they require you to type lots of escape codes ('\' codes in LabVIEW strings) because most of the characters are non-ASCII, unsigned bytes. Also, there may be two or more message exchange phases for just one command, which is rather tedious. For these instruments, I try to muddle through at least one command just to find out if the link is properly connected, then plunge right in and write the LabVIEW code to handle the protocol. Hopefully, I'm 90% successful on the first try because debugging is difficult. Modifying the Serial Test VI is also a good way to get started. Add frames to the Sequence structure that do the operations your instrument needs.

As with GPIB, you can use a serial line analyzer (made by HP, Tektronix, and others) to eavesdrop on the communications process. The analyzer stores lots of characters and decodes them to whatever format you like (ASCII, hex, octal, etc.). This really helps when your driver *almost* works but still has reliability problems.

VXI: Setting up a VXI system is quite similar to setting up a GPIB system; in fact, GPIB is the most frequently used communications interface for VXI. Again, like a pure GPIB system, start by making sure that you know your system configuration and that everything is properly connected. The utility VI, VXI Test, is just like GPIB Test, sharing most of the basic controls. The one difference is that you must select the communications *platform*, either GPIB or MXI.

In starting up the VXI system when using either an embedded controller or VXI-MXI, you must first run VXIinit. This program, included in the NI-VXI software, initializes the registers on your hardware. You may wish to make this program run automatically at system startup time. Next, you need to run the Resource Manager (RM), whose responsibilities include identifying all devices in the system, managing the system self-tests and diagnostics, configuring address maps, configuring the system's commander/servant hierarchy, allocating interrupt lines, and initiating normal system operation. In LabVIEW, you should call the InitVXIlibrary VI at the start of your application. This VI is the application startup initialization routine and performs all necessary installation and initialization procedures to make the NI-VXI interface functional. This includes copying all of the RM device information into the data structures in the NI-VXI library. The Open VXI Instrument VI, found on the VXI Instrument Driver Support disk, calls the InitVXIlibrary VI when you initialize an instrument driver. You should use the Open VXI Instrument VI in all VXI instrument driver initialization VIs.

When using the GPIB-VXI interface, you do not need to perform any of these steps. You do, however, need to identify the GPIB secondary address that the GPIB-VXI assigns to your particular VXI instrument. The Open VXI Instrument VI performs this secondary address query, storing the full GPIB address (primary+secondary) of your instrument in a global VI which returns an instrument ID. Using the VXI Instrument Driver Support VIs, you will pass in the instrument ID to communicate with your instrument. If you are not using the VXI Instrument Driver Support VIs and wish to communicate using the GPIB Write/Read primitives, you will still need to know the secondary address. You can obtain this by issuing the `LaSaddr?` `<la>` query to the National Instruments GPIB-VXI. For more information, consult your GPIB-VXI user manual.

Driver Design Techniques

Building instrument drivers is no different from any other LabVIEW project. All the techniques discussed in Chapter 4, *Building an Application*, are fully applicable. You still need to define the problem, do some preliminary testing and prototyping, then follow good design and programming practices. Iterate on your design until you have something clean and reliable. Follow up with thorough testing and documentation, and you will have a versatile product that is easy to use and easy to maintain. To help you get started in the right direction, I've assembled some recommendations and working examples that represent good driver design techniques.

Modularity by Grouping of Functions

I've seen two extremes of **modularity** applied to LabVIEW instrument drivers: *infinite* and *none*. Naturally, I'm going to preach for something in between. Infinite modularity is where there is one subVI for every individual command. Okay, it's not really infinite, but you get my point. There are several problems with this approach. One, the interaction between control settings is really hard to arbitrate because each function has to query the instrument to see what state it's in, rather than just comparing a few control settings on the VI's panel. Two, the user has to plow through the directories and libraries, searching for the desired command. And three, there are just too darned many VIs, which becomes a nightmare for the poor guy who has to maintain the library. Guess what happens when you find a mistake that is common to all 352 VIs? *You get to edit every single one of 'em.*

Having no modularity is the other extreme. You may find it in *trivial* drivers where there are only a couple of commands and hence, just one VI. In that case, it's probably okay. You may also find a lack of modularity in complex drivers written by a novice, in which case it's a disaster. There is nothing quite like a diagram with sequences inside of sequences inside of sequences that won't even fit on a 19-inch monitor. In fact, these aren't really drivers at all. They are actually dedicated applications that happen to implement the commands of a particular instrument. This kind of "driver" is of little use to anyone else.

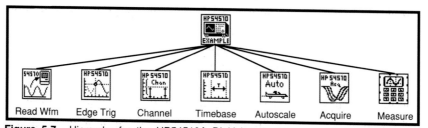

Figure 5-7. Hierarchy for the HP54510A Digitizing Oscilloscope driver. Commands are nicely grouped by function, making them easy to access.

A better way to modularize a driver in LabVIEW is to build VIs that group the various commands by function. Like the SCPI model, you might have a VI for triggering functions, a VI for input channel selection, one for timebase setup, and so forth. Another model is the front panel of a modern oscilloscope. It has dozens of knobs and switches, but they are logically grouped, both by physical layout and (usually) by artwork on the panel. These intuitive control groupings make an instrument easier to learn and increase the operator's efficiency. That's how we want our LabVIEW drivers to work, too.

The top-level hierarchy for the HP54510A Digitizing Oscilloscope driver shown in Figure 5-7 is representative of a moderately complex driver package. Of the hundred or so commands available, I selected the ones that seemed most useful and grouped them according to function. One of the function VIs, HP54510A Timebase, is shown in Figure 5-8. It concisely implements the basic capabilities of the instrument's timebase

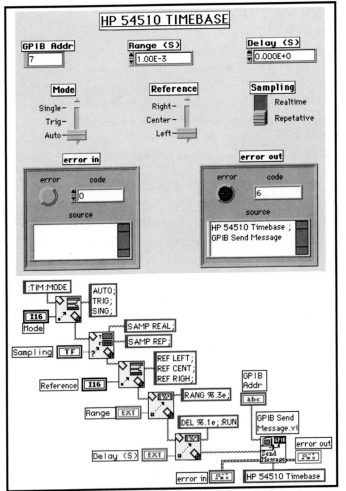

Figure 5-8. Front panel and diagram for the HP54510A Timebase VI.

section. If a user needs to add a more advanced command, there is plenty of panel and diagram space to do so.

Moderate modularity yields to infinite modularity when you have to implement "miscellaneous" commands. For instance, the HP54510A Autoscale VI consists of just one switch: **autoscale on/off.** This command doesn't fit with anything else, and it is normally used by itself. It would be illogical to throw this switch in with other unrelated functions.

Read and Write In the Same SubVI

On most instruments, commands have both a read and a write mode. That allows you to remotely set a control (like the operator turning a knob) or to read the current setting of a control (like the operator looking at a knob). Which action(s) should a driver VI support? Like so many other design questions, the answer to this read/write problem depends on the application. (Note that we're talking about controls only; you almost always have to read data from the instrument.)

Many drivers are designed to write control settings (command) but not to read back the settings. It's simpler to write such a program—it takes only about half the amount of

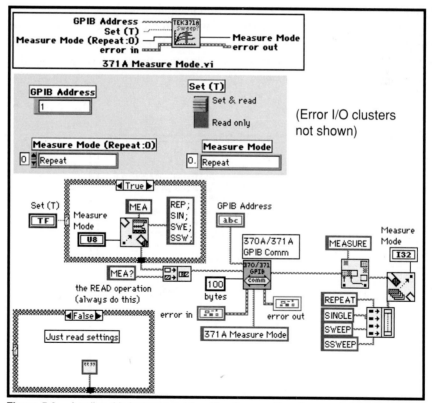

Figure 5-9. A call to this instrument driver VI writes a setting, then reads it back, or only reads the current setting. The 370A/371A GPIB Comm subVI handles all the communications.

programming—and it's generally sufficient for most applications. But there are some situations where you will want to read the settings. Occasionally, a setting needs to be read back because settings on some controls interact in a complex or ill-defined manner. It may be difficult to keep track of *all* control settings inside your program, in which case it's reasonable to go out and fetch the actual state of the instrument. Or, you may want to do a control readback as a safety measure to confirm that an important setting was accepted.

A truly complete driver package includes full read/write capability. This comes at the expense of time and effort in writing the package plus the extra code that has to be carried along. It is, however, the most versatile scheme. If you wish to implement both read and write modes in a single VI, here is a scheme that I recommend.

The driver VI in Figure 5-9 has a switch called **Set** by which you write a setting then read it back, or only read the current setting of the instrument's **Measure Mode** control. For this instrument, the command for the measure mode setting is MEA followed by a keyword, such as REP (repetitive). If you put a question mark after the command, the present setting is returned. In the diagram, you can see a Case structure controlled by the **Set** switch. If the switch is True (the *set*, or write mode), a GPIB command is generated that sets the instrument's measure mode. Then, the query command (MEA?) is appended to read the current state of the control, regardless of whether or not a new state was sent. The 370A/371A GPIB Comm subVI writes the command, then reads the response, which is decoded and displayed in a Ring indicator, **Measure Mode**. If the **Set** switch is False, new settings are not sent; only the MEA? command is sent, then the response is decoded as before. This VI only handles a single command, but the scheme is readily extended to support an arbitrary number of commands.

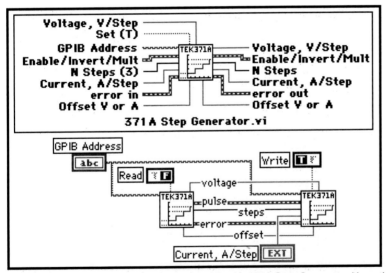

Figure 5-10. Applying one of the read/write VIs, the 370A Step Generator. Here, the user wishes to adjust a single control (current) while maintaining the values of all the others.

An application showing the versatility of the read/write technique, the 370A Step Generator, appears in Figure 5-10. When a single function VI sets many controls, you normally have to keep track of, and send, all of the commands at once even though you only intend to change one of them. By using a read-only call to the subVI followed by a write-then-read call, you can avoid this problem. Because the outputs of the VI are an exact image of the inputs, you can wire them straight across, with the insertion of the particular control(s) that need to be updated.

The alternative is to keep track of all the settings within your main program. You might use global variables as a storage location, or perhaps a set of shift registers in a While Loop.

Error I/O Flow Control

Another characteristic of a robust driver is that it handles error conditions well. Any time you connect your computer to the outside world, unexpected conditions are sure to generate errors, and the instrument driver software is the place to trap those errors. Your response depends on the nature and severity of the error, the state of the overall system, and options for recovery.

The most straightforward error response is a **dialog box**. Assuming that an operator is always available to respond, the dialog box can present a clear statement about the error: who, what, when, where, and why. Dialogs are always appropriate for fundamental errors such as basic setup conflicts ("No GPIB board in slot 3"), and for catastrophic errors where the program simply cannot continue without operator intervention ("The power supply reported a self-test failure and has shut down"). It's also helpful to receive informative dialogs when you are setting up an instrument for the first time. For complicated instrument systems, you might consider adding extra dialog boxes that can be disabled with a switch once the system is up and running. A new concept in driver development uses an *Error Query* global variable that stores a Boolean value for each instrument that determines whether or not errors should be checked and displayed. Each driver subVI reads this global variable and acts accordingly. By turning off error checking, you save some execution time. Using a global variable saves you from having to wire a **dialog error** Boolean to every driver subVI.

Automatic error recovery is used often in serial communications systems, particularly those that span great distances and/or run at high speeds. Local area networks typically have sophisticated means of error detection and automatic message retransmission. For a serial instrument, you may be able to attempt retransmission of data if a timeout occurs or if a message is garbled. Retransmission can be added to a state machine-based driver without too much trouble. If a message is invalid, or if a timeout occurs, you could jump back to the first frame of the sequence and send the command again, hoping for success on the second try. An important feature to include there would be a limit on the number of retransmissions; otherwise, you would end up in an infinite loop if the instrument never responds. Such automatic actions should be limited to the lowest levels of a driver package, as in the example of a serial interface. Serious measurement and control applications are designed to report *any* error that is detected to guarantee data quality and system reliability.

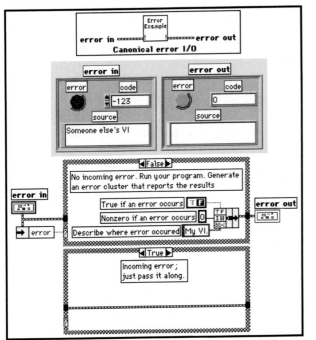

Figure 5-11. The canonical error I/O VI. You can encapsulate any program inside the False case.

Therefore, you should think carefully before making your program so smart that it *fixes* or ignores potentially dangerous error conditions.

You can use error handling to promote dataflow programming and simplify applications of a driver package. As described in Chapter 4, *Building an Application*, under *Handling Errors*, you create an error I/O cluster containing error information and pass it from one VI to the next. If an error is generated by one VI, the next one will *know* about the error and be able to take appropriate action. For instance, if a function that initializes the instrument fails, it probably makes no sense to continue sending commands. The error I/O scheme can manage this decision at the driver level, rather than forcing the user to add Case structures to the top-level VI. Most VIs respond to an incoming error by skipping all activity and simply pass the incoming error through.

A canonical VI with error I/O is shown in Figure 5-11. The error in and out clusters always appear in the connector pane as shown. Doing so permits all users of error I/O to line up their VIs in an even row. The cluster contents are always the same:

Item No. 1: **Error** (Boolean). True means an error occurred.

Item No. 2: **Code** (I32). An error code number used for message generation.

Item No. 3: **Source** (string). Contains the name of the VI that generated the error.

On the diagram, the **error in** Boolean is tested, and if it's true, you may run a special error response program, or simply pass the error along to the **error out** indicator and do

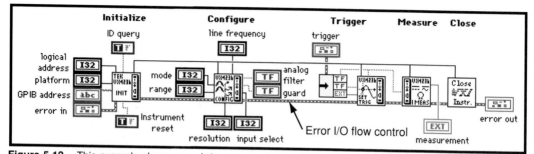

Figure 5-12. This example shows error in/error out using the Tektronix VX4236 DVM, a VXI instrument. Note how clear and simple this application is, with no need for flow control structures. Error I/O is built into the VXI driver support and you can build on it as shown here.

nothing else. If no incoming error is detected, then it's up to your program to generate an error cluster of its own, depending on the outcome of the operation that it performs.

Figure 5-12 is an example of error I/O in action. Error I/O is a part of the VXI Communication VIs that do the basic VXI read and write operations (they're available from the instrument library). This technique makes it easy to do your error handling in a consistent fashion all the way from the bottom to the top of the hierarchy. As you can see from the diagram, applying the Tektronix VX4236 DVM driver is very easy because of the use of error I/O.

Table 5-1. Predefined LabVIEW Error Codes for Driver VIs

1210	Instr. Driver: Parameter out of range.
1220	Instr. Driver: Unable to open instrument.
1221	Instr. Driver: Unable to close instrument.
1223	Instr. Driver: Instrument identification query failed.
1225	Instr. Driver: Error triggering instrument.
1226	Instr. Driver: Error polling instrument.
1228	Instr. Driver: Error writing to instrument from file
1229	Instr. Driver: Error reading from instrument to file.
1230	Instr. Driver: Error writing to instrument.
1231	Instr. Driver: Error reading from instrument.
1232	Instr. Driver: Instrument not initialized.
1234	Instr. Driver: Error placing instrument in local mode.
1236	Instr. Driver: Error interpreting instrument response.
1239	Instr. Driver: Error in configuring timeout.
1240	Instr. Driver: Instrument timed out.
1300	Instr. Driver: Instrument-specific error.

At some point in your application, usually at the end of a chain of I/O operations, the error cluster is submitted to an error handler. The error handler decodes the **code** number into plain language and appends the **source** string. That way, the user will understand what the error is and where it came from without resorting to an error message table or a lot of debugging. The message is often displayed in a dialog box.

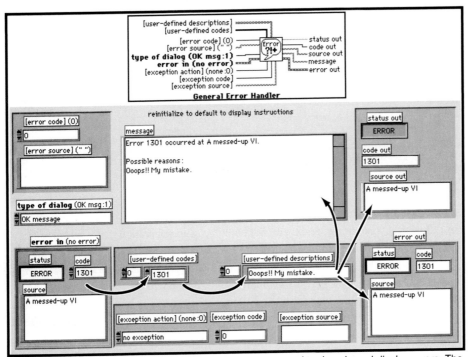

Figure 5-13. The General Error Handler utility VI is all you need to decode and display errors. The arrows indicate how the VI can decode user-defined error codes and messages, in addition to predefined error codes.

Error codes are somewhat standardized. Zero generally means no error. Many error codes that are generated by LabVIEW are available from the **Error Ring diagram constant**. You drop it on the diagram and choose one of the many available error codes by name. Its output is an I32 integer. For instance, selecting **Bad path** returns 71. Table 5-1 lists the error codes that are reserved for use with instrument driver VIs. If you use one of these codes in your own drivers, the error handlers that come with LabVIEW will be able to interpret them. (Codes from 5000 to 9999 are reserved for miscellaneous user-defined errors; they are not automatically interpreted by the error handlers.)

The General Error Handler utility VI (Figure 5-13) accepts the standard error cluster or the individual items from an error cluster and decodes the code numbers into a message that it can display in an error dialog and in an output string. A useful feature of this handler is its ability to decode user-defined error codes. You supply two arrays: **user-defined codes** and **user-defined descriptions**. The arrays have a one-to-one correspondence between code numbers and messages. With this handler, you can automatically decode both predefined errors (such as GPIB and VXI), plus your own special cases. I would suggest using the codes starting at 1301 because those are reserved for instrument-specific errors.

Error I/O is becoming popular because it simplifies diagrams by eliminating the need for many flow control structures. By all means, use it in all of your drivers and other LabVIEW projects.

Using a Communications SubVI

The simple act of exchanging messages with an instrument is not always so simple. Serial instruments are the most complex, often requiring that special headers, checksums, and end-of-message flags be added to the basic message. Many GPIB instruments require you to perform a Serial Poll to check for errors, then fetch the error code if one is detected. The list goes on and on. If you duplicate this programming in each of your driver's function VIs, it will be much harder to understand and maintain, not to mention that it will take up more disk space. Instead, create a *communications subVI* that encapsulates this low-level programming. Below are some examples of *comm* VIs for GPIB, serial, and VXI instruments that you can use in your drivers.

In the future, LabVIEW will probably incorporate more and more communications functionality into high-level VIs. For instance, all forms of serial, GPIB, and VXI communications may be handled by just a few functions that are built into LabVIEW—in much the same way that all file I/O operations are currently handled. The intent is to help you avoid having to work at the lowest levels of communications interfacing whenever possible. This is consistent with the high-level nature of LabVIEW. The current VXI interface library is probably the closest, conceptually, to this future scheme and you should consider using it as a model for any major driver development efforts.

GPIB Communications SubVI

Typical steps that need to be performed when communicating with a GPIB instrument are:

1. Send a command using the GPIB Write VI or the GPIB Send Message VI and check for GPIB bus errors.

2. If a response is expected, call the GPIB Read VI or the GPIB Receive Message VI with the expected number of bytes, and check for GPIB bus errors.

3. If the instrument is capable of reporting command execution errors, see if the last command generated an error.

The GPIB Send Message VI is shown in Figure 5-14. It encapsulates GPIB Write and GPIB Status in a more useful subVI that uses error I/O. The main inputs are the **GPIB address**, and the **write buffer** (message to send). Errors are detected by GPIB Status. If it returns True in element 15 of the status array, an error has occurred and the GPIB error number is returned in the **error out** cluster. The **Write Mode** input is identical to that of the GPIB Write VI and determines how the message should be terminated.

Figure 5-15 shows the connector pane for the GPIB Receive Message VI. Its internal structure is quite similar to GPIB Send Message and the error checking is identical.

You can start with these two communications utilities, then add features or combine them into one, unified, comm VI, as I usually name it. The typical comm VI sends a command, then, if the number of bytes to read is greater than zero, it reads a reply message. Some instruments, especially older ones, require extra characters in every command message and/or they include extra characters in reply messages. In such cases, you can

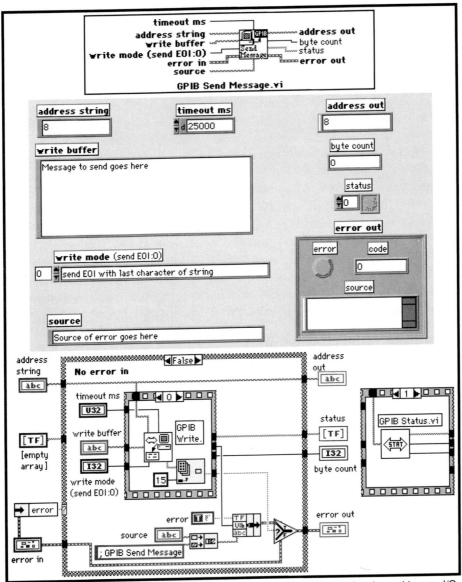

Figure 5-14. GPIB Send Message VI starts with the basic GPIB Write function then adds error I/O.

incorporate any extra string handling functions in the comm VI. This technique cleans up the diagrams of all higher-level driver VIs and prevents duplication of code.

If you are programming a SCPI-compliant instrument, you can read errors from the standardized SCPI error queue. A driver support VI, SCPI Error Report, polls the instrument and returns a string containing any error messages via the regular **error out** cluster. You could add this function to your comm VI, as well. Events are stored in a queue—oldest events are read out first—so you need to read events out after every

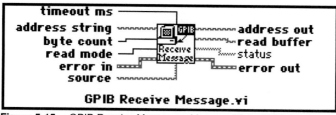

Figure 5-15. GPIB Receive Message adds error I/O to GPIB Read.

command to keep from filling the queue with old, uninteresting events. The disadvantage of this technique is that it adds additional communications overhead. The Read SCPI Error Queue VI checks the state of the Error Query global variable at each call, enabling you to turn off error checking dynamically. The National Instruments Application Note 006, *Developing a LabVIEW Instrument Driver*, discusses SCPI error handling in detail.

Serial Communications SubVI

Just about every instrument that uses serial communications has its own unique protocol. As a result, it's hard to write a truly general-purpose communication subVI. What I *have* managed to do is put together a reasonably versatile model that you can use as a starting point for other serial instruments. This one is from the Eurotherm 808 Digital Controller driver, which you can get from the driver library. The instrument is a single-loop PID (proportional-integral-derivative) controller used to regulate feedback loops in industrial processes. It has an option for RS-232 or RS-422 communications, permitting read/write access to almost all of its settings. After fumbling around with separate VIs for reading data and writing commands, I finally decided that a single comm VI was the right thing to use. It turned out to be useful in other serial port projects as well. Its panel is shown in Figure 5-16. I wrote it before the era of error I/O, but it is easily adapted; all you have to do is bundle the error indicators and assign error code numbers from the 1200 series.

The Eurotherm 808 protocol is fairly complicated, allowing you to do things like avoid readdressing an instrument if you just finished talking to it. While this saves a few bytes in the message, it also complicates the heck out of the programming, so I decided not to bother with that feature. You will probably have to make similar decisions. This VI handles the lowest level of message exchange in a straightforward manner. Higher-level VIs take care of things like formatting the command, tacking on a header, and adding a checksum. You could easily add those other tasks to this VI. The steps performed are:

1. Write the command string. If a serial port error occurs, go to Frame 0 and report the error in plain English.

2. If the **Read** switch is set to True, a reply message containing data is expected. Read one character at a time, appending the characters to a string, until an end-of-message character is encountered.

3. If the **Read** switch is set to False, just one character is expected, indicating acknowledgment of the command.

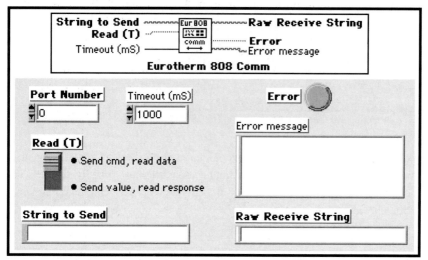

Figure 5-16. The Eurotherm 808 Comm VI is typical of serial port communications handlers. It uses a state machine to arbitrate message passing and error response.

4. To close out the message exchange, send an end-of-transmission character. Flush the receive buffer in case extraneous characters are present.

5. Report any errors.

The programming structure used here is a state machine, a technique described in Chapter 4, *Building an Application*. It permits you to jump around between steps in the program depending on the conditions at the end of each step. Frame 0 of the Case structure

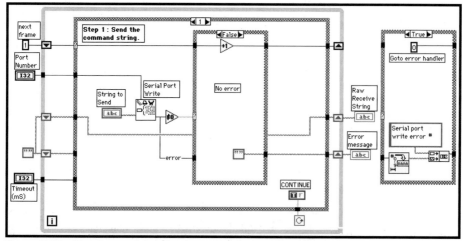

Figure 5-17. First frame of the Eurotherm 808 Comm VI, a robust serial port communications handler, designed as a state machine. A serial port write operation is performed. If an error occurs, the serial port error number is appended to an error message, and execution jumps to Frame 0, the error handler. Normal execution proceeds to Frame 2 (shown in Figure 5-18).

is an error handler. Naturally, you start the program in some other frame—in this case, Frame 1. If an error occurs, jump to Frame 0, which formats an error message, flushes the receive buffer, and stops the While Loop. The other frames normally execute in order, but it would be reasonable to build in logic to, say, attempt retransmission of a message if an error occurs. The state machine technique is powerful and flexible—just the ticket for these difficult serial port drivers.

Figures 5-17 to 5-19 dissect the Eurotherm 808 Comm VI. Learn from it, copy it, and adapt it as you see fit. Messages are formatted by higher-level VIs, though it might be possible to include the formatting in this VI. Typical of serial instruments, Eurotherm uses a binary message format with start and end-of-message characters and a data checksum for

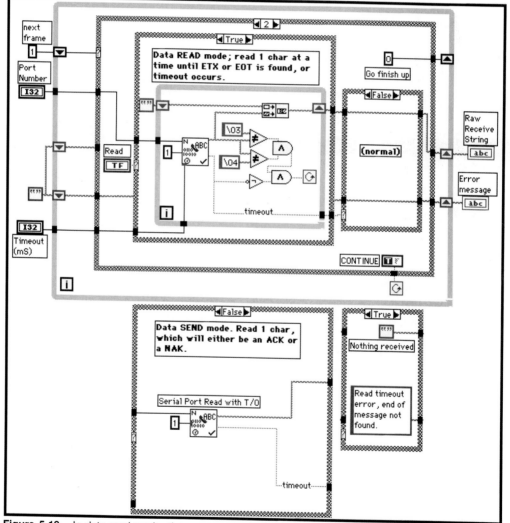

Figure 5-18. In data read mode, the program reads data until one of the end-of-message characters is detected. The string is built in a shift register. If the command only sends data, then just one character is expected, so the False case reads just one. Frame 0, the error handler, is always executed next.

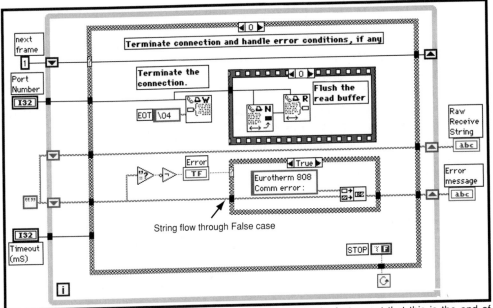

Figure 5-19. The final act is to send a single character that tells the instrument that this is the end of transmission and the receive buffer is cleared out. If an error occurred anywhere in the previous frames, the Error Boolean is set to true and the error message is shipped out to the indicator.

error detection. I should also mention that there is a parallel to the GPIB send/receive message VI pair for the serial port: Serial Port Send Message and Serial Port Receive Message. They are almost drop-in replacements for their GPIB cousins, except for the fact that serial ports have some different setup parameters than GPIB. Error handling, including timeouts, is included.

Figure 5-18 shows the frame where messages are received. Unlike GPIB Read, there is no timeout on Serial Port Read. Instead, you should use the example VI, Serial Read with Timeout. Otherwise, any communications failure will cause your VI to hang.

Flushing the Receive Buffer

A problem that often occurs with serial drivers is that the incoming data buffer may fill with characters that you don't expect. Then, when you send a command to the instrument and sit around waiting for a special response character, what you will actually be reading is old data. A solution is to begin the sequence of events with the simple piece of code shown in Figure 5-20. This is a flush buffer procedure that reads all the bytes that are present in the serial port receive buffer. After flushing, go ahead and send a command, and you will have more confidence that the data you receive is in response to that command. In the Eurotherm driver, the flush is done in Frame 0. This empties the buffer after every message exchange, guaranteeing a clear buffer for the next message exchange.

VXI Communications SubVIs

The VXI standard came along later in the life of LabVIEW, and as a result the VXI driver library is highly standardized with a well-designed hierarchy. (Older GPIB instrument drivers could benefit from insertion of these new standards, but it would be rather costly to rewrite all those old drivers.)

Given the complexity caused by the number of controller options, VXI functions, and instrument types available to VXI users, National Instruments has developed a set of high-level VIs for use in VXI instrument drivers to help simplify development. The VXI Instrument Driver Support Library is controller-independent and works with both message-based and register-based VXI instruments. Instrument drivers built from the VXI Support Library work with National Instruments PC-based VXIpc embedded controllers, MXI interfaces for the PC AT, EISA, PS/2, Sbus, and Macintosh computers, and the GPIB-VXI Slot 0 controller. The LabVIEW VXI Instrument Driver Support VIs are distributed with the LabVIEW VXI Instrument Driver Library. You must have these VIs to use the LabVIEW VXI instrument drivers.

For an instrument driver to communicate with a particular VXI instrument, it must know the logical address of the instrument, and also the type of controller that is serving as its master. In the case of MXI-VXI or embedded controllers, VXI word serial communication is required, while in the case of GPIB-VXI controller, GPIB reads/writes are needed. Generally, the type of I/O operation required does not affect the contents of the actual message sent to the instrument; therefore, the same instrument driver message building routines can be used with either Word Serial or GPIB communications. With that in mind, to make an instrument driver work with either type of controller, at least three controls are required on the front panel to specify the information needed to address the instrument: a control that identifies the controller as one requiring either NI-VXI or NI-488 calls; a control for the unique logical address of that particular instrument, and a control for the GPIB primary address of the GPIB-VXI and the secondary GPIB address it assigns to the instrument (in the case of GPIB-VXI controlled instruments). Not only would these controls take up a significant amount of front panel space, but users would be required to remember a great deal of information to communicate with their VXI instruments.

VXI Instrument Global

Using the concept of instrument identifiers, you must first run the Open VXI Instrument VI to open the instrument and generate an instrument ID. For subsequent operations with the instrument, only this instrument ID is needed. In other words, one addressing control

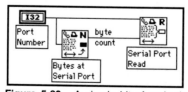

Figure 5-20. A simple bit of code that flushes the serial port buffer. Use it before sending any commands, or any time that you want to make sure the buffer has been emptied.

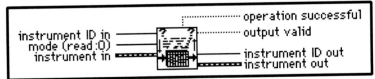

Figure 5-21. VXI Instrument Global stores information about each VXI instrument in the system and assigns instrument IDs.

(instrument ID) replaces the three controls previously needed for addressing. This is much the same as using a refnum for file I/O or a **Task ID** for DAQ operations. Information about each instrument is stored in a global storage VI, VXI Instrument Global, which is called by the VXI Receive Message, VXI Send Message, VXI Read Register, and VXI Write Register VIs. One additional step is required: you must call the Close VXI Instrument VI to take an instrument out of VXI Instrument Global when you are finished. The VIs included in the VXI Instrument Driver Support Library are described below.

The VXI Instrument Global VI stores information about each VXI instrument in the system and assigns instrument IDs. The use of instrument IDs simplifies the task of addressing the correct instrument in an instrument driver because information such as controller platform (embedded, GPIB-VXI, or MXI-VXI), logical address, and GPIB address is stored during instrument initialization and replaced with a simple numeric identifier for subsequent I/O operations.

There are several modes of operation for this VI. Mode 0 (read) returns information about an instrument with the specified instrument ID. If no instrument is currently using that ID, the output valid Boolean will be False. Mode 1 (add) takes the information entered in the instrument in cluster and stores it, returning the instrument ID assigned to that instrument. Mode 2 (change) replaces the stored information for the entered instrument ID with the information currently in the instrument in cluster. If no instrument is using that ID, the operation successful Boolean will be False. Mode 3 (delete) removes the information stored at the entered instrument ID and also places that ID on a list of available ID numbers. Again, if no instrument is using that ID, the operation successful Boolean will be False. Finally, mode 4 (clear all) removes all stored information and makes all instrument IDs available for use.

Open VXI Instrument

The Open VXI Instrument VI loads information about an instrument into the VXI Instrument Global VI and assigns an instrument ID to that instrument. Before assigning the

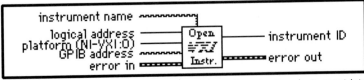

Figure 5-22. Open VXI Instrument loads information about an instrument into the VXI Instrument Global VI and assigns an instrument ID to that instrument.

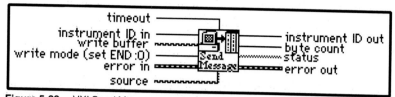

Figure 5-23.   VXI Send Message sends a string to a message-based VXI instrument, much like GPIB Send Message does for GPIB instruments.

ID, the VI searches the VXI Instrument Global to see if that instrument already exists (one with the same LA, platform, and GPIB address). If so, the existing instrument ID is returned, otherwise a new instrument ID is generated. The instrument ID is used in subsequent instrument driver VIs or I/O functions to communicate with the instrument.

VXI Send Message

The VXI Send Message VI sends a string to a message-based VXI instrument. To communicate with an instrument, you must first open the instrument by running the Open VXI Instrument VI or running the initialize VI for the instrument (initialize VIs call the Open VXI Instrument in their block diagrams). Use the instrument ID generated by the Open VXI Instrument to address the specific instrument; then set the write mode and enter the string to send.

VXI Receive Message

The VXI Receive Message VI reads a string from a message-based VXI instrument. To communicate with an instrument, you must first open the instrument by running the Open VXI Instrument VI or the initialize VI for the instrument (initialize VIs call the Open VXI Instrument in their block diagram.) Use the instrument ID generated by the Open VXI Instrument to address the specific instrument; then set the read mode and enter the byte count for the expected message.

Close VXI Instrument

The Close VXI Instrument VI searches the VXI Instrument Global VI for the entered instrument ID. If the ID is valid, the instrument at that ID is removed from the VXI Instrument Global VI and the instrument ID is made available for reuse.

As you can see, this VXI communications library is highly ordered. To build a driver VI hierarchy, you build driver subVIs that call VXI Send Message and VXI Receive Message.

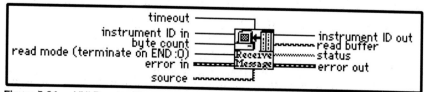

Figure 5-24.   VXI Receive Message reads a string from a message-based VXI instrument, much like GPIB Receive Message does for GPIB instruments.

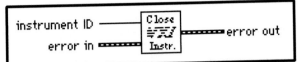

Figure 5-25. Close VXI Instrument removes the instrument from the VXI Instrument Global VI.

Figure 5-26 is one such example. At the highest level of the hierarchy, you call Open VXI Instrument, then call your individual driver subVIs, and finally call Close VXI Instrument. (It makes no sense to open and close instruments at each driver call.) Since error I/O is used throughout the hierarchy, you can pass the error cluster to the General Error Handler at the end of the chain to report any errors that might have occurred.

Timing and Handshaking

What happens when your 300 MHz, 986ZX computer sends a bunch of commands in rapid-fire mode to a poor, unsuspecting instrument? Will the commands be buffered in high speed memory for later processing? Or will the instrument simply halt and catch fire? What if there is a communications error? Instruments are *not* infinitely fast—they require some time to respond to commands—and your driver must synchronize itself to the needs of the instrument. Timing and handshaking techniques, both hardware and software, are available and necessary to manage these situations.

GPIB

An important feature of the IEEE 488 standard is that the exchange of individual bytes is arbitrated by hardware **handshaking** signals. The talker makes sure that the listener is

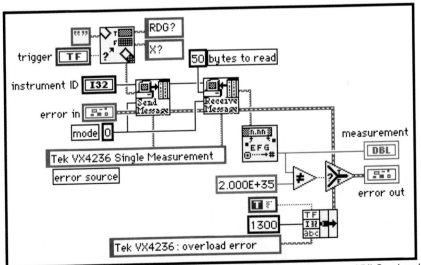

Figure 5-26. One of the driver VIs for the Tektronix VX4236 DMM. It uses VXI Send and Receive Message VIs to read a single measurement from the instrument.

ready to receive the next byte. The talker then places the data on the bus, tells the listener that the data is ready, then waits for an acknowledgment—and all of this is done by hardware. Therefore, no matter how fast or how slow the various devices on the bus may be, you have reasonable assurance that the individual bytes will be successfully transmitted. Only in cases where there is an electrical problem with the bus will you see low-level communications errors. Using cables that are too long or poorly shielded may corrupt the signals. Nevertheless, low-level timing is not your problem, unless you happen to be designing GPIB interface hardware.

As an aside, this issue of data integrity on GPIB raises some interesting questions. Please note that there is no hardware verification for data integrity in the GPIB standard. Thus, there is a potential for data corruption, and your run-of-the-mill driver software will never know it, particularly if the corrupted data is inside of a waveform or binary data stream. (Invalid commands are another story: instruments reject them.) You can cause such errors to occur—I have—by using defective cables and improperly installed GPIB extenders. If the error rate is fairly low (say, one bad bit in 10,000), *most* information will be transferred intact. But occasionally, there will be an (undetected?) error. How can you fix this problem? The only way I know is adding error detection or correction bytes to the data stream. A checksum or an exotic cyclic redundancy check (CRC) code is a likely candidate. Note, however, that the code must be generated and decoded by all devices on the bus. Seen any oscilloscopes with a CRC byte in the waveform data? I haven't. Apparently, this problem will not soon be solved, at least for older communication standards like GPIB. Just be aware that it exists, and if you are working on a *really* critical system, be prepared to justify your choice of communication technique.

Even though the individual bytes make it through, low-level communications problems can still occur. The culprit is usually the **end of information (EOI)** signal and some special characters that may be required to terminate each message. The GPIB Write VI has a **mode** control that optionally appends a carriage return (CR) and/or a line feed (LF) character to the string. This saves you from having to concatenate a final character to each command string. Additionally, the mode control lets you specify whether or not EOI will be asserted with the last character. Most instruments use mode=0, which does not append anything to the string, but does assert EOI with the last character of the string. Similarly, GPIB Read has a **mode** control that specifies conditions for terminating a read operation. You should check your instrument's manual to find the correct mode setting. Sometimes a bit of experimentation with the GPIB Test utility VI can clear up any uncertainties.

Another catch is that some instruments require repeat addressing as described earlier in this chapter. Make sure you clearly specify in your driver documentation what the proper setting is for repeat addressing and/or unaddressing.

Sending commands at the wrong time can be a problem. Any command that initiates a time-consuming operation has the potential for putting the instrument offline for awhile. For instance, if you tell your instrument to perform an extensive self-diagnostic test, it may ignore all GPIB activity until the test is completed, or it might buffer the commands for later execution. Also, the *rate* at which commands are sent can be important. Most instruments permit you to send many commands in one string. The question is, will all the commands in the string be received before the first one is executed? Most times, the answer is yes, but there may be dire implications if the instrument ignores half the commands you just sent.

There are two ways to solve these timing problems. First, you can add delays between commands by sending them one at a time in a Sequence structure where every other frame of the sequence contains a LabVIEW timer. The second method is to find out if the previous operation is complete. If you enable **service requests (SRQ)** for your instrument, you can use the Wait for GPIB Service Request VI to tell you when the operation is complete. This technique is often used with digital oscilloscopes; a simplified example is shown in Figure 5-27. For VXI instruments, use the Wait for Interrupt VI from the VXI library. If your instrument is SCPI compliant, the Operation Complete (*OPC?) command gives you a status report.

Serial Handshaking

Serial instruments use various combinations of software and hardware techniques to perform handshaking. As usual, it's important to find out exactly what methods your instrument understands.

Hardware handshaking uses the extra control lines that are part of the RS-232C standard. Using the Serial Port Init VI, you can configure LabVIEW to support **Clear to Send (CTS)** and/or **Data Terminal Ready (DTR)** handshaking. If CTS handshaking is enabled, the remote device asserts CTS whenever it is ready to receive data. This is also

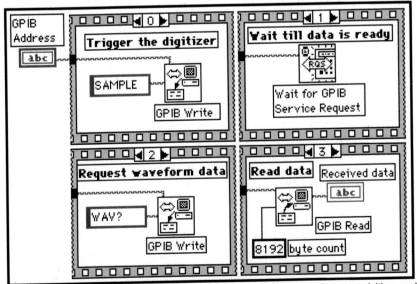

Figure 5-27. Wait for GPIB Service Request synchronizes waveform acquisition and readout. Frame 0 triggers a digitizer. Frame 1 waits for an SRQ, indicating that the data is ready. Frames 2 and 3 request and then read the data.

known as input handshaking. If DTR handshaking is enabled, the computer asserts the DTR line when it is ready to receive data. This is also known as output handshaking. Wiring for a typical CTS/DTR arrangement is shown in Figure 5-28. I've found very few commercial instruments that use this protocol. By and large, the manufacturer just tells you to connect only the data lines (transmit and receive data, and ground), and ignore the other handshaking connections.

The most common technique for software handshaking is called *XON/XOFF protocol*. If you have ever used a standard ASCII terminal connected to a modem or mainframe computer, you probably have used this protocol to pause screen scrolling. When the receiver can no longer accept data, it sends XOFF (usually control-s) to tell the sender to stop sending data. When the receiver is again ready, it sends XON (usually control-q) to indicate that transmission can begin again. The XON and XOFF characters can be independently enabled through the Serial Port Init VI. An important thing to remember about this protocol is that the XON and XOFF characters are *always* interpreted as XON and XOFF. Therefore, you should not send binary data with this protocol because the data may contain bytes with values equal to XON and XOFF. Another hazard of this protocol crops up when a receiving device *forgets* to send XON, in which case the sender ends up waiting forever to transmit data. Keep this in mind when you write a driver; make sure that the VI times out if this deadlock condition should arise.

Other forms of software handshaking have been devised by various manufacturers. Some use characters other than XON/XOFF, so LabVIEW's built-in functionality can't help you. Instead, your driver has to watch for the magic character and respond accordingly. Another technique uses multiple exchanges of special characters to force the sender and receiver to agree that they are both ready for an upcoming data transfer. Needless to say, there is a large amount of overhead and complexity associated with such a driver. The state machine architecture, while tricky to implement, is about the only way to arbitrate such complex protocols.

Range Checking

An important part of making your driver robust is expecting the user to enter unexpected values into every control. One way to handle these situations is by setting the limits on

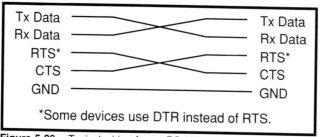

Figure 5-28. Typical wiring for an RS-232 serial device using null-modem hardware handshaking. Just to make things interesting, some devices use RTS and some use DTR for a similar function. Hopefully, your manual sorts this out.

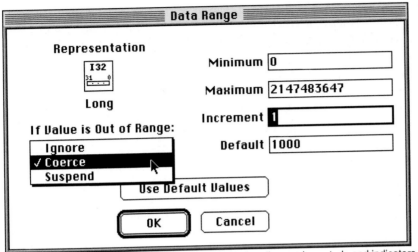

Figure 5-29. The Data Range dialog box, available for all numeric controls and indicators through a pop-up menu. Use this to limit unexpected input values to a more reasonable range.

numeric controls through the use of the **Data Range** dialog from the control's pop-up menu (Figure 5-29). Enter minimum, maximum, and increment limits; then select **Coerce** from the menu to force the user's input into range. If you choose **Suspend** for the range error action, the VI's front panel is loaded from disk and opens up if a range error occurs. This takes a moment for the disk access, but may be the best way to respond to some situations. Selecting **Ignore** (the default) turns off range checking. The disadvantage of using the Data Range dialog items is you get no feedback to tell you that coercion is occurring. Also, if you copy the control, the Data Range setup goes with it. If you forget to change the setup for the new control, it may behave improperly.

Changing the **representation** of a numeric control or indicator may also limit the range of the input, particularly for integer types. For instance, a U8 control can only represent integers between zero and 255. Anything greater than 255 is coerced to 255 and anything less than zero is coerced to zero. If the values are not evenly spaced (such as a 1-2-5 sequence) use a function similar to the Range Finder VI described in Chapter 4, *Building an Application* (Figure 4-19).

Other difficult situations must be handled programmatically. Many instruments limit the permissible settings of one control based upon the settings of another. For example, a voltmeter might permit a range setting of 2000 V for DC, but only 1000 V for AC. If the affected controls (e.g., **Range** and **Mode**) reside in the same VI, put the interlock logic there. If one or more of the controls are not readily available, you can request the present settings from the instrument to make sure that you don't ask for an invalid combination. This may seem like a lot of work, but I've seen too many instruments that go *stark, raving bonkers* when a bad value is sent.

String controls don't have a feature analogous to the Data Range dialog; all the checking has to be done by your program. LabVIEW has several string comparison functions that are helpful. You can use the Empty String/Path? function to test for empty strings and path names, which are probably the most common out-of-range string entries. The other string comparison functions (Decimal Digit?, Hex Digit?, Octal Digit?, Printable?, and White Space?) tell you the *lexical class* of the first character in a string. They also act on the ASCII equivalent of a number. Figure 5-30 shows how you might check to see that all characters of a string are decimal digits.

There is one other method of range checking, instrument error queries, that relies on the instrument to detect and correct error conditions and report them back to LabVIEW. Only possible with instruments featuring this capability, the error query method simplifies both VI development and VI use when properly implemented. The Read SCPI Error Queue VI provides this service when used with SCPI-compliant instruments. Each time you send a series of commands to the instrument, call Read SCPI Error Queue to report any problems. A well-designed instrument will respond with an informative message ("Timebase out of range for this mode") if a clash occurs among settings.

Boundary conditions—values like zero, infinity (Inf), and empty string—cause lots of trouble in instrument drivers. Use the Data Range setup, comparison functions, and error queries to prevent defective values from finding their way to the instrument, and always test your drivers to make sure that ridiculous inputs don't stop the show.

Setup Management

An important part of software that supports smart instruments is **setup management**. A good driver package allows you to save and recall collections of control settings, which are usually called instrument setups. This saves much time, considering how many controls are present on the front panels of some instruments.

Historical note: Digital storage oscilloscopes (DSOs) gradually became so complex and feature-laden that it was considered a badge of honor for a technician to obtain a usable trace in less than five minutes. All those buttons and lights and menus and submenus were really boggling! The solution was to provide an *auto-setup* button that got something visible on the display. Manufacturers also added some means by which to store and recall setups. All the good DSOs have these features, nowadays.

Sophisticated instruments usually have built-in, nonvolatile storage for several settings, and your driver should have a feature that accesses those setup memories. If the instrument

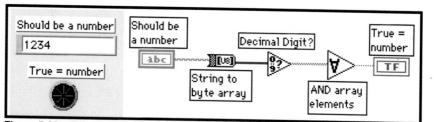

Figure 5-30. This VI checks to see that all characters in a string are decimal digits. The comparison function Decimal Digit? tests one character at a time, building a Boolean output array. The logical AND of all these values is True if all the characters are okay.

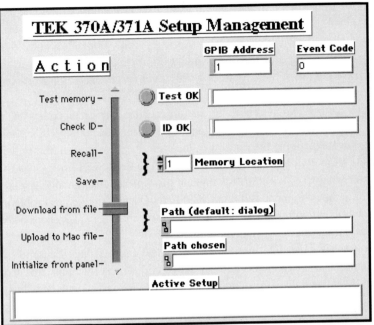

Figure 5-31. Panel for the Tektronix 370A/371A Setup Management VI. It allows you to load and save complete instrument setups, to check the instrument's ID, and to test its memory. Figures 5-32 through 5-35 show the parts of the diagram that manage setups. Error I/O clusters are not shown.

has no such memory, then write a program to upload and save setups on disk for cataloging and later downloading. You may want to provide this local storage even if the instrument *has* setup memory; what if the memory fails, or is accidentally overwritten? Also, you may want to carry setups around on a diskette for use with similar instruments in other locations.

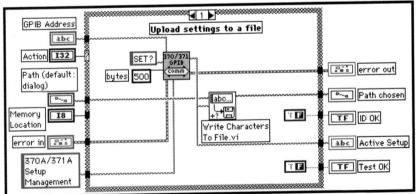

Figure 5-32. Frame 1 requests the present setup then writes it to a file. Since the setup is just a long ASCII string containing GPIB commands, you can read it back from the file and send it to the instrument to restore all of the settings.

Figures 5-31 through 5-35 show how I managed setups for the Tektronix 370A/371A curve tracers, which are fairly complicated GPIB instruments. This setup management VI has a total of seven functions, as you can see by the **Action** control. It supports uploading and downloading of setups to files on your LabVIEW system, and local storage and recall of settings on the instrument's internal disk drive. Other functions are: initialize, check instrument ID, and test memory. To save space, I'll just show the setup management functions here. You can get this driver from the instrument library if you want to copy from it. The figure captions explain the function of each frame of the Case structure that is connected to the **Action** control.

It was really nice of Tektronix to include the **SET?** command, which responds with a long ASCII string that contains a series of valid setup commands. You can look at the string (it's displayed in the **Active Settings** string indicator), edit it (if you're careful!), and save it to a file as I did in this driver. Then, it's a simple matter of writing the whole string back to the instrument to restore all the settings. Having built-in setup memory in the instrument is even easier to use; just tell it to store and recall setups from the desired memory location, or file number, in the case of the 370A/371A.

Other instruments are not so nicely equipped. If it won't send you one long string of commands, you may be stuck with the task of requesting each individual control setting, saving the settings, then building valid commands to send the setup back again. This can be pretty involved; I've only done it once, and I think that's the last time. Instead, you probably will want to use the instrument's built-in setup storage. If it doesn't even have *that*, tell the manufacturer what you think of their interface software.

If your function VIs support reading and writing in the same VIs, you have another option. The values returned by each VI can be saved in binary format for later recall, at which time the values are sent to the instrument by the same VI that read them. LabVIEW can read and write the image of a cluster in binary format by using a datalog file; all you have to do is combine all the important settings into a big cluster (Figure 5-36). After

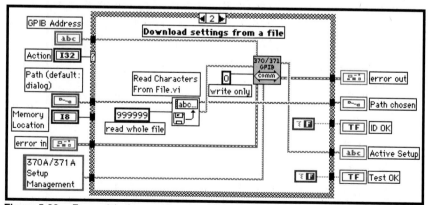

Figure 5-33. Frame 2 is the complement of Frame 1: the long setting string is read from a file and written to the instrument. Since the instrument created all the commands, one would expect them to all be valid.

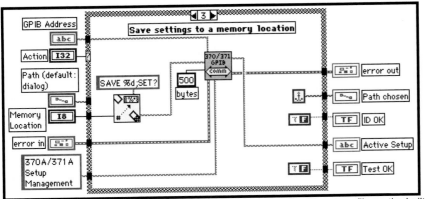

Figure 5-34. Frame 3 tells the instrument to save the present settings to a file on the built-in disk drive. Many instruments use nonvolatile RAM or EEPROM memory instead of magnetic media.

reading the data from the file, unbundle the values and send them to the instrument using the reverse procedure.

Documentation

The real measure of quality in instrument driver software is the documentation. Drivers tend to have many obscure functions and special application requirements, all of which need some explanation. A driver that implements more than a few commands may even need a function index so that the user can find out which VI performs a desired operation. And establishing communications may not be trivial, especially for serial instruments. Good documentation is the key to happy users. Review the documentation section near the end of Chapter 3, *LabVIEW Programming Techniques*. It describes most of the techniques and recommended practices that you should try to use.

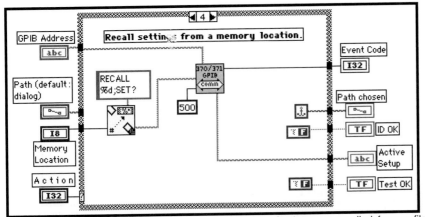

Figure 5-35. Frame 4 is the complement to Frame 3. Settings are recalled from a file on the instrument's built-in disk drive.

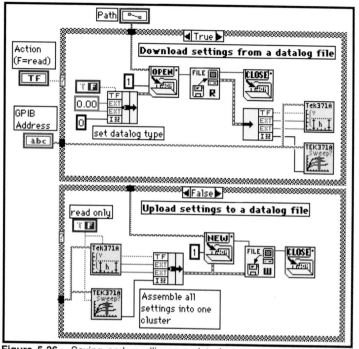

Figure 5-36. Saving and recalling complete instrument setups from datalog-format files. If your function VIs support both read and write modes, and they read and write all the same data types, this is easy to do.

When you start writing the first subVI for a driver, type in control and indicator descriptions through the **Description** pop-up menu. This information can be displayed by showing the Help window and is the easiest way for a user to learn about the function of each control. If you enter this information right at the start, then any time you copy the control or indicator, the description goes with it. Besides, when you're writing the VI, you probably know everything there is to know about the function, so the description is really easy to write. I like to copy text right out of the programming manual, if it's appropriate. It pays to document as you go.

The VI description in the **Get Info...** dialog box from the File menu is often a user's only source of information about a VI. Try to explain the purpose of the VI, how it works and how it should be used. This text can also be copied and pasted into the final document.

Always include some kind of document on disk with your driver. Drivers that are part of the instrument library should have a really complete writeup, with illustrations. If you're just doing an in-house driver, think about your coworkers who will one day need to use or modify your driver when you are not available. Also, remember that the stranger who looks at your program six months from now may well be *you*. Include things like: how to connect the instrument, how to get it to *talk*, problems you have discovered (and their resolutions), and of course a description of each function VI. Such information is not only useful, but it may make you *famous* rather than *infamous*.

REFERENCES

1. National Instruments Application Note 006, *Developing a LabVIEW Instrument Driver* (part number 320344-01).

2. *Instrument Communication Handbook*, IOTech, Inc., 1991. Available from IOTech, 25971 Cannon Road, Cleveland, OH 44146.

3. *NI-VXI C Software Reference Manual*, available from National Instruments.

4. *GPIB-VXI User Manual*, available from National Instruments.

5. *VXI-1000 User Manual*, available from National Instruments.

6. *VXI Course Manual*, available from National Instruments.

7. *GPIB Course Manual*, available from National Instruments.

8. *Black Box Catalog*, available from Black Box Corporation, P.O. Box 12800, Pittsburgh, PA 15241 (800-552-6816).

Using the DAQ Library

One reason for the success of LabVIEW is the **data acquisition (DAQ) library** for programming plug-in boards made by National Instruments. Analog, digital, and timing I/O boards are available for the PC with ISA, EISA, and Micro channel buses, for most models of the Macintosh, and the Sun SBus. You can add external signal conditioning and multiplexers, particularly SCXI (Signal Conditioning eXtensions for Instrumentation), to improve signal quality and expand the number of channels. Multiple boards can be interconnected by the RTSI (Real-Time System Integration) bus, using a ribbon cable that routes timing and trigger signals between boards to synchronize various operations. Direct memory access (DMA) is available to improve data transfer speeds. And all of these features are directly accessible through the DAQ library, which is distributed with every copy of LabVIEW. It's a popular and cost-effective combination for modern instrumentation systems.

The LabVIEW data acquisition VI reference manual, part of the LabVIEW manual set, is the primary source for information about the DAQ library. It contains details about every DAQ function, information on basic applications, and the board-specific details that affect some operations. You should spend time becoming familiar with this important manual. This chapter is by no means a replacement for the manual; it merely amplifies the basic concepts. The good news about the DAQ library is, it's really easy once you understand the general idea.

A word about boards made by other manufacturers: none are supported by the DAQ library, unless someone happens to build an exact clone of a National Instrument product. Other boards are certainly usable with LabVIEW; you just need a suitable driver. Unfortunately, you have to give up the tight integration among boards that the RTSI bus supplies, and of course you probably won't have the consistent interface offered by the DAQ library. By all means, if you choose to use a foreign board, encourage those who write the drivers to emulate the DAQ library to make your life as a programmer somewhat easier. When should you *not* use the DAQ library and plug-in boards?

- When the signals are very far from your computer. Remote scanners or other smart I/O systems with a communications link will save much signal wiring and reduce the chances of noise pickup. Opto-22 Optomux modules, for instance, are cheap and simple, and use a simple RS-422 serial link that you can run for long distances; with a modem, the distance is unlimited.

- When sampling rates are very high—beyond the basic capabilities of plug-in boards which are currently limited to 1 MHz. Modular digitizers, such as VXI or CAMAC, or digitizing oscilloscopes serve these high-frequency needs effectively.

Almost any other situation can be handled with plug-in boards, as long as you have the right signal conditioning and/or multiplexers, like SCXI, available.

Hardware Options

National Instruments offers many products that you can assemble into a full-featured instrumentation system in conjunction with LabVIEW—their catalog lists dozens of plug-in boards and different kinds of signal conditioning hardware. Let's take a quick look at some of your options.

Multifunction I/O Boards

The quickest way to get a LabVIEW system into operation in a laboratory situation is to buy a multifunction I/O board. National Instruments has two lines of multifunction boards: the low-cost **Lab** series, and the full-featured **MIO** series. Every board has the following general features:

- Several analog inputs, with a multiplexer and programmable-gain amplifier
- A 12- or 16-bit ADC with available sampling rates to 200 kHz
- Two analog outputs with separate DACs
- One or more 8-bit bidirectional digital I/O ports
- Several programmable counter/timers

Connections to the outside world are made with a ribbon cable, which you plug into a terminal block (like the model CB-50 connector), or a cable adapter that connects to a variety of signal conditioning devices like the Analog Devices 5B series modules for analog signals. These simple hardware setups pretty well cover the basic requirements of routine, low-speed, data acquisition and control with low channel counts.

If you need more channels, you can add an analog multiplexer, like the AMUX-64T, or connect your multifunction board to SCXI modules (described below), which offer a very large channel count. For low-level signals like thermocouples, you need to choose a board with high gain and/or use an external amplifier or signal conditioner. The DAQ library knows all about the multifunction boards, the AMUX-64T, and SCXI modules, making them very easy to use. Using external signal conditioning means that you may have to keep track of some additional scale factors when you write your LabVIEW program.

Analog I/O Boards

For specialized analog applications, you can buy a dedicated analog I/O board. The first board in this series, the A2000, has four channels with 12-bit, 1 MHz simultaneous sampling. You would choose this board in preference to an MIO-series board when any delay or timing skew between channels caused by a multiplexer is undesirable. The A2000 also has true analog triggering, much like that of an oscilloscope.

For high-accuracy, dynamic signal acquisition, like audio and vibration analysis, the A2100 and A2150 boards are recommended. They use 16-bit sigma-delta ADCs originally intended for digital audio applications, with some enhancements to optimize their absolute accuracy and DC performance. Maximum sampling rates are 48 kHz for the A2100 and 51.2 kHz for the A2150. The A2100 has two inputs and two outputs; the output specifications are similar to those of the inputs. The A2150 has four inputs.

If you need more analog outputs, the AO-6 and AO-10 series offer six or 10 12-bit DACs with the ability to directly drive either voltage (±10 V) or current (4-20 mA) loads.

Digital and Timing I/O Boards

For purely digital I/O applications, you can buy the DIO series boards which offer up to 96 TTL-compatible input/output bits. You can use each line individually to sense contact closures or to drive relays, for instance, or you can use an entire 8- or 16-bit port as a parallel interface to other computer-based equipment. The DAQ library supports everything from single-bit operations to block mode DMA parallel transfers. Note that you will usually need some kind of signal conditioning to interface the relatively sensitive TTL I/O ports to real-world loads that require higher voltage or current. National Instruments offers the SSR series signal conditioning modules for AC and DC loads, complete with optical isolation or SCXI modules with relays or optically isolated I/O. Or, you can build your own interface circuits as required.

A unique interface, the TIO series, features 10 general-purpose counter/timers plus 16 digital I/O bits. With a TIO board, you can set up fairly complex arrangements of event counters, delays, and timers to control various time-dependent events. Again, these boards have TTL-level signals, requiring some form of signal conditioning for most applications.

SCXI

A cost-effective way to add lots of I/O channels to your computer is to use SCXI hardware with a multifunction board. The SCXI line encompasses an array of analog and digital input and output modules with built-in multiplexing so that one plug-in board can access hundreds of channels. You install one or more modules in an SCXI chassis, and connect one of the modules directly to the plug-in board via a ribbon cable or to the parallel port of a PC if you use the SCXI-1200 multifunction module. The chassis has a power supply and a backplane with analog and digital busses that permit communication and synchronization among modules. Up to eight SCXI-1001 chassis with a total of 96 modules can be combined into one system. And, like the plug-in boards, the DAQ library handles SCXI channels transparently. Just specify the chassis, module, and channel numbers that you want to access.

The SCXI line is very popular and more options are becoming available. Analog modules include low-cost multiplexers, and isolated inputs with optional excitation for transducers like RTDs and strain gauges. All analog inputs are differential and have available lowpass filtering and programmable gain amplifiers. Digital I/O modules are available for optically isolated inputs and outputs, and various relay outputs that handle higher voltages and currents.

Most SCXI hardware is limited to a maximum 10 m cable run from the chassis to the computer. Newer modules, like the SCXI-1200, incorporate the functionality of a plug-in board right on the module. The SCXI-1200 uses a PC-compatible parallel port for all communication, so no plug-in boards are required. You can also add third-party port

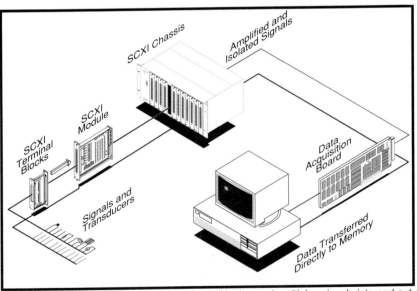

Figure 6-1. SCXI modules provide signal conditioning and multiplex signals into and out of plug-in data acquisition boards.

extenders to extend the link up to 100 ft while providing good throughput. Future modules may feature local intelligence and high-performance communications links for remote operation, while maintaining the consistent software interface of the DAQ VI library.

Portable DAQ

For portable DAQ applications using notebook or laptop computers, you can use one of the newer products that require no plug-in slots at all. The DAQCard series are Personal Computer Memory Card International Association (PCMCIA) cards with I/O capabilities similar to the traditional plug-in boards. For example, the credit card-sized DAQCard-700 features 16 single-ended or 8 differential analog inputs, a 100 kHz sampling rate, two 8-bit digital I/O ports, and two counter/timers.

An alternative port for DAQ is the parallel printer port, found on almost every desktop and notebook PC. For example, the DAQPad-1200 incorporates the functionality of a plug-in multifunction I/O board in a self-contained box that connects directly to the parallel port.

Direct Memory Access (DMA)

Here are a few notes regarding DMA and the DAQ library.

- DMA is highly desirable because it improves the rate of data transfer from the plug-in board to your computer's main memory. In fact, high-speed operations are often impossible without it. The alternative is interrupt-driven transfers, where the CPU has to laboriously move each and every word of data. Most PCs can handle several thousand interrupts per second, and no more.

- A DMA controller is built into the mother board of every IBM-compatible PC, and all but the lowest-cost plug-in boards (like the PC-LPM-16) include a DMA interface.

- At this writing, no Macintosh model has built-in DMA. Instead, you can buy another interface board with a DMA controller, such as an NB-DMA-2800, and attach a RTSI cable between it and the I/O board. Otherwise, you're stuck with (very slow) interrupt-driven transfers.

- On the Macintosh, the DAQ library will *automatically* use DMA any time the required hardware is available (remember to connect the RTSI cable or all I/O operations will fail). On the PC, you have control over whether DMA is employed.

Basics of the DAQ Library

Two words describe the LabVIEW DAQ library: *consistent* and *integrated*. Every DAQ function uses a consistent set of input and output parameters, and the functions work consistently among the various I/O boards, even across LabVIEW's platforms. You can write a program for an NB-MIO-16 multifunction board on a Macintosh, carry a floppy disk over to a Windows machine with an AT-MIO-16, and the program will work there without modification. Because the DAQ library has been an important part of LabVIEW

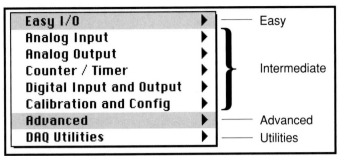

Figure 6-2.   Hierarchy of the DAQ library.

for many years, you can be assured that the two are tightly integrated. For instance, you can wire a data array from an analog acquisition DAQ operation directly to a Waveform Graph, and you can intermix the DAQ error I/O chain with the error I/O chain for the file utilities. These facts make the library relatively easy to apply, once you understand the organization, conventions, and terminology.

DAQ Library Hierarchy

The function menu for the DAQ library in Figure 6-2 shows the overall hierarchy. **Easy I/O** is great for getting started, but is rather limited in its functionality. The **intermediate** level is where you will do most of your work once you get to know the library. **Advanced** VIs are only used when you need to access certain less-frequently used features of the library. Easy I/O VIs are built from intermediate VIs, and intermediate VIs are built from advanced VIs. Utilities are special functions that help you perform operations like thermocouple linearization. From top to bottom, the library is consistent in its use of common input and output terminal names.

Easy I/O

The eight easy I/O VIs were created with the express purpose of simplifying your life as a developer. You need to know very little about the operation of the DAQ library or your particular I/O board to acquire analog data or drive analog outputs with the easy I/O functions. They are written at the same high level as many of the example VIs, using the intermediate VIs and a built-in call to the error handler to notify you should anything go wrong. You are encouraged to use the easy I/O VIs or examples as a starting point for your applications, modifying them as required. Just remember to save your modified VI with a new name! Being an intrinsically lazy person, I use the easy I/O library whenever I can. The major capabilities missing from easy I/O are buffered I/O operations, triggering, and counter/timer operations. For these, you must use the intermediate VIs.

Intermediate

Serious DAQ applications typically require you to use the intermediate library. They offer much more functionality than the easy I/O library, but you will have to do more wiring and

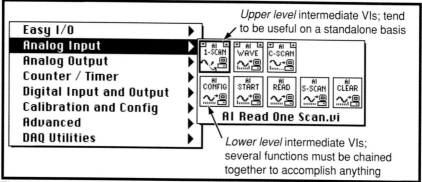

Figure 6-3. Within the intermediate library, there is a further subdivision of capability. *Upper level* intermediate VIs can often be used on their own.

have a deeper understanding of the data acquisition hardware. Important features of the intermediate library that the easy I/O library lacks are:

- Advanced buffer management, such as circular buffering
- External timing and triggering options
- Counter/timer operations
- Timeout limits
- Calibration and hardware configuration control
- Access to the RTSI bus interconnection functions
- Direct access to status information

Error handling is more flexible than that of the easy I/O VIs, too, because you have direct access to the error I/O clusters. Of all the functions in this library, the ones that you will use most are digital I/O, buffer management, and calibration and configuration. This is a very flexible library and, like all the DAQ functions, is well documented in the reference manual. If you look at the intermediate VI palettes, you will see that the VIs appear in rows. This is intentional. VIs in the upper rows actually operate at a somewhat higher level, and often can be used without any other DAQ VIs, a bit like the easy I/O library. Figure 6-3 shows a sample.

Advanced

The advanced VIs provide access to the lowest level of programming in the DAQ library. They make direct calls to the NI-DAQ driver through the use of Code Interface Nodes, so there is no lower-level programming for you to study or modify. Very few applications require that you use the advanced VIs; the intermediate VIs are the ones you should concentrate on for most applications. Here are a few of the capabilities of the advanced VIs that the intermediate VIs lack.

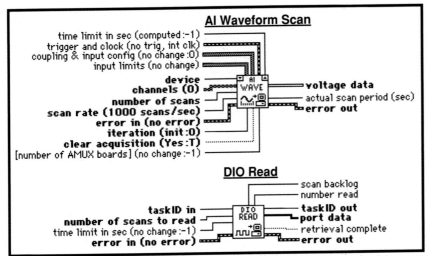

Figure 6-4.   Connector panes for a couple of intermediate VIs, showing some of the most common signal names.

- Multiple buffering

- Full access to all status information

- Direct control of polarity and gain

- Sampling rate specifications in terms of sampling clock period and clock divisor

- Unscaled output data specification

We won't spend much time on the advanced library. You can see how it's applied by examining the diagrams of the intermediate VIs, or by reading the manual.

Conventions Used in the DAQ Library

Signal names, parameter formats, and connector pane layouts are well standardized in the DAQ library. Figure 6-4 shows two intermediate VIs that are good examples. The first thing you should notice is the style of the control and indicator names. A boldface label means that the control or indicator is one that you need to investigate and understand first. Furthermore, boldface terminals usually need to be wired; their default inputs are very often invalid.

Labels appearing in plain text indicate terminals that are generally useful, but you don't always have to understand them or wire to them. Square brackets ([]) highlight terminals that you rarely need to use. Control labels also contain default input values where appropriate. For instance, the input label, **channels (0)**, means that the **channel** control will be set to channel zero if you leave it unwired. These labeling conventions are a really good idea and I highly recommend that you follow them when creating your own VIs.

Defaults

The DAQ library uses several methods for the management of default values, all of which are intended to save you wiring. First is the notion of a **default input**: the default value of a front panel control, like the zero value for **channels (0)**. If the default input suits your needs, you don't have to wire that control. Second, there is the **default setting**. Default settings are recorded by the driver. For instance, the trigger and clock settings for analog acquisition, once set, are retained until you cause them to change. On many inputs, you will see the notation, **(no change:0)**. The default value for such a control is zero, and it forces the driver to use whatever the default setting happens to be. Many default settings can be set from the DAQ configuration utility.

Devices

Every DAQ VI that performs a configuration or initialization operation has a control called **device**. Device is a number that specifies the data acquisition board that you wish to access. On the Macintosh and on PCs with EISA and Micro Channel buses, it is the physical slot number of the board. On PCs with ISA buses and on the Sun, it is a user-assigned number from 1 through 16, also known as a logical slot number. The DAQ configuration utility tells you what devices are installed.

Channel Addressing

Many of the analog I/O VIs have a channel list control that you use to specify which channels to access. It is a string control with a syntax that is clearly specified in the reference manual. You can type channel selections directly into a string and hope you have entered them correctly. Or, you can write a configuration program in LabVIEW that uses Ring controls and other handy techniques to generate a syntactically correct channel string. Generation and management of such strings are discussed in Chapter 7, *Writing a Data Acquisition Program*.

Each channel you specify becomes a member of a **group**. The order of the channels in the list defines the order in which the channels are scanned during an input or output operation. To erase a group, you pass an empty channel list to the I/O configuration VI along with the group number. You can have up to 16 groups defined at any one time for a single group type. Available group types are analog input, analog output, digital I/O, and counter/timer.

The channel list is an array of strings, though it only needs to have one element, and that element can contain an arbitrarily complex list of channels. So, you can specify one channel per element of the array, specify an entire list of channels in just one array element, or use a combination of these two methods. Individual channels are specified by values separated by commas, for example, 2,3,7. To scan a sequence of channels, separate the values with a colon. For example, 2:7 would scan channels 2,3,4,5,6,7 in order. You would preferentially use the array format to specify channels when simultaneously configuring other attributes of an I/O operation (e.g., channel gains and limits) that are also specified by array inputs.

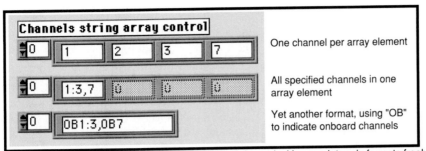

Figure 6-5. Some channel list formats for onboard channels. You can intermix formats freely in one string array.

There are three type of channels: onboard channels (literally, on the plug-in board), AMUX-64T channels, and SCXI channels. Some formats for onboard channels are shown in Figure 6-5. The keyword *OB* is optional, and indicates that the number following is an onboard channel.

Channel specifiers (and the data returned) for AMUX-64T boards are quite a bit more complicated because of the way that the board scans channels, and the fact that it can be used in either single-ended or differential mode. The key to sorting this out is that each onboard channel is multiplexed to either four, eight, or 16 physical channels depending upon whether one, two, or four AMUX boards are installed. If you have one AMUX board and your channel list just has the number zero as a parameter, the DAQ VI will return four values, corresponding to the first four physical channels on input. If you only want to read the value of one physical channel, you must specify the AMUX number in the channel specifier. Figure 6-6 shows some simple examples, and many more examples may be found in the LabVIEW DAQ manual.

SCXI systems use a channel specifier that follows the general format: onboard channel, chassis ID, module slot, module channel. Most of the time, you can omit the onboard channel, and LabVIEW assumes channel 0. Figure 6-7 shows some basic examples of SCXI channel specifiers. The channel specifier can also send special commands to manage SCXI features such as the calibration ground on an SCXI-1100, and reading temperature

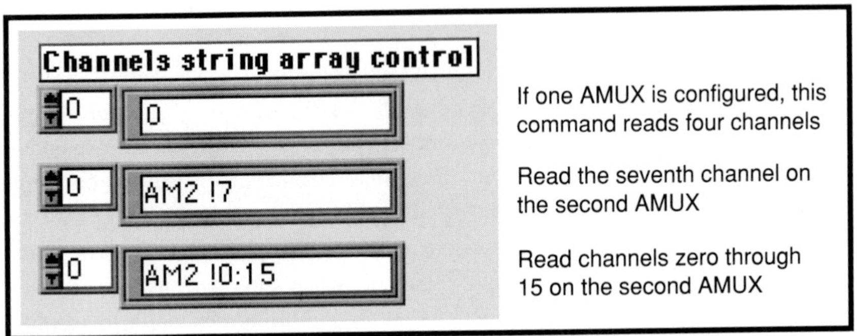

Figure 6-6. Channel list examples for systems using AMUX multiplexer boards.

references on some of the analog connector blocks. These are detailed in the LabVIEW DAQ manual.

Task ID

When you use the intermediate VIs, you will see that each VI has an input and/or output called **task ID**. The task ID is a magic number created by a group configuration VI, such as **AI Config**. Like a file refnum, it carries information about a DAQ operation between the various VIs. Information includes such items as the device, type of operation, list of channels, size of the data buffer in memory, and status of the data acquisition operation. And, like a file refnum, you should never change the value of a task ID.

You can have an arbitrary number of tasks running concurrently. For instance, you might start an analog output waveform generation task, an analog acquisition task, and a digital output task. Make sure that you don't mix up the task IDs. Task IDs can be passed to subVIs as 32-bit unsigned integers (U32 integers), so you are not forced to have all of your DAQ VIs on one diagram.

Input Limits

Many of the analog acquisition VIs have an **Input Limits** control, which is a cluster array containing upper and lower input voltage limits. Input limits are defined as *the upper and lower voltage limits for a channel*. These limits are your best estimate of the maximum and minimum voltages that you wish to measure with an analog input channel given that channel's range, polarity and gain settings. For instance, if you think your signal will range from -0.2 V to 4.4 V and you enter those values as lower and upper limits, the driver will probably adjust the hardware for a ±5 V range, the nearest practical setting. Output limits are defined as *the upper and lower voltage outputs for an analog output channel*. These limits are the maximum and minimum voltages that can be generated at an analog output channel given that channel's polarity and reference voltage. Instead of forcing you to think in terms of range, polarity, gain and reference voltage settings, LabVIEW allows to you to specify these settings more naturally as a pair of voltages—the limit settings. If you enter a value that requires a gain factor your board does not support, fear not: the driver will coerce the value to the nearest value that accommodates the requested range.

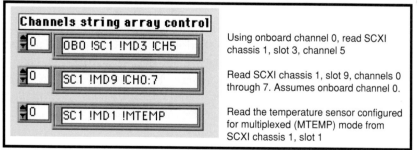

Figure 6-7.   Channel list examples for SCXI systems.

LabVIEW uses limit settings to calculate the range, polarity, gain, and reference voltage settings you can use on a board. When a board uses jumpers or dip switches to select one of these properties and you have to change a jumper setting, you must enter the correct jumper setting in the configuration utility. All of National Instruments' data acquisition boards have programmable gains (no jumpers), but some SCXI modules do not (they use jumpers or dip switches). Many of the modules have jumpered ranges and polarities. Therefore, you must enter these settings in the configuration utility. For most boards, you must also change the jumper configuration if you want to use an external analog output voltage reference.

Input limits are discussed in detail in the first chapter of the LabVIEW data acquisition VI reference manual. If you still have trouble understanding the various gain interactions, by all means run one of the example VIs and connect your I/O hardware to some known signals to see what actually happens.

Error I/O

The intermediate and advanced VIs include error I/O connections, using the standard error cluster, for your convenience. Error I/O and the task IDs are common threads that make sequential DAQ operations really simple to wire up. Your diagram will probably contain more wiring to controls and indicators than it will between DAQ VIs.

Scans, Buffering, and All That

There is a whole collection of terms that apply to acquisition and signal generation with the DAQ library. Here are the basics.

- Sample—A sample is one A/D or D/A conversion for one channel.

- Scan—A scan is a collection of one sample from each of one or more channels or ports in an analog or digital group. One sample from each of 100 channels, when taken in one operation, is a scan.

- Update—An update is an output operation that corresponds to an input scan.

- Buffer—A buffer is an area in memory that stores a series of scans for input or updates for output. The data may belong to one channel, like a single waveform, or to several channels, representing several waveforms. Contrast with a scan or update, which contains only *one* sample per channel.

The concept of a buffer is very important because that is how you store quantities of data for direct access by the hardware—and that spells performance. If your LabVIEW program always had to generate or read each individual sample, there would be little hope of sampling at accurate rates much beyond 10 Hz. Instead, the data is shoveled into and out of an area of memory, usually via DMA, through hardware-timed transfers. With these techniques, you can (theoretically, at least) acquire data and generate waveforms nearly as fast as your computer's bus can move the data.

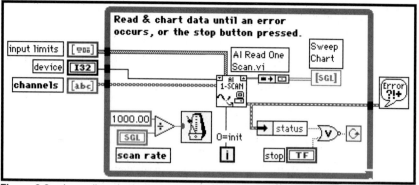

Figure 6-8. Immediate nonbuffered I/O from the example VI *Cont Acq&Chart (easy immediate).* The easy I/O VI AI Read One Scan is called at a rate determined by the value you wire to a LabVIEW timer.

Immediate Nonbuffered I/O

The simplest types of I/O operations don't use a buffer, and are suited to low-speed acquisition and signal generation. These are the **nonbuffered I/O** operations. An **immediate nonbuffered I/O** operation reads a scan from or writes an update to a group of channels when you call the appropriate DAQ VI. A group is accessed whenever you call the VI, under the control of software timing, as in the example of Figure 6-8. There is some support from hardware timing in this operation: you can control the interchannel delay for channels within a scan. You should consider immediate nonbuffered I/O for:

- Simple test programs

- Low-speed data acquisition, up to a few samples per second

- Manual actuation of output devices through Boolean controls on a panel, or low-speed, automatic sequencing

Timed Nonbuffered I/O

The next step up with regard to timing is **timed nonbuffered I/O**, also known as **hardware-timed I/O**. The DAQ VI sets up the onboard counter timers to regulate the rate at which scans or updates are performed, instead of using a software timer. Your loop runs at a reliable rate, but your program still acquires or generates one scan or update per cycle of the loop.

Depending on the amount of software overhead that you add—such as graphing of data or saving to files—a timed nonbuffered I/O loop can run reliably up to a hundred or more cycles per second. (Please note that, regardless of sample rate, you always run the risk of overburdening your system and missing some scans.) Figure 6-9 shows how you set up a simple application. Note that there are no software timers in the While Loop. The AI Single Scan VI waits until the next scan of data is available each time it is called. Applications for this DAQ technique are:

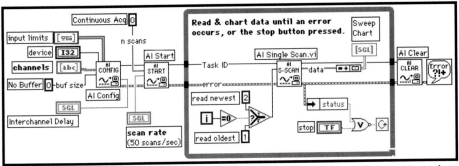

Figure 6-9. This diagram shows the intermediate VIs in a timed nonbuffered I/O arrangement, from the example VI, *Cont Acq&Chart (hw timed)*.

- Feedback control operations where an algorithm acts on a measurement and generates a corresponding result on a regular basis

- Data acquisition and signal generation at moderate rates (up to perhaps 100 Hz) where consistent sample interval is important

Timed Buffered I/O

For DAQ applications running at high speeds, you must turn to **timed buffered I/O**. With buffered I/O, precision hardware timers control the real-time flow of data between memory buffers and the ADCs and DACs. LabVIEW transfers data between the plug-in board and a buffer whenever the buffer is full (for inputs) or empty (for outputs). These operations make maximal use of hardware: the onboard counter/timers, and any DMA hardware that your system may have. Buffered operations can be triggered by hardware or software events to start the process, thus synchronizing the process with the physical world. You must use the intermediate or advanced VIs to write buffered I/O applications.

By the way, you might be wondering where the buffers reside. They are, in fact, allocated in your *system's* memory space because that is where the low-level I/O handler is installed. Increasing the memory available to LabVIEW actually *decreases* the memory available to buffered I/O operations, and any other system-related memory allocation activities as well. Be cautious when requesting very large buffers. There are three types of buffered I/O, described in the next sections.

Simple Buffered I/O

Simple buffered I/O uses a single buffer in memory big enough for all of your data. Space in memory is allocated when the data acquisition task is configured, so there are no memory management operations to slow you down during operation, unless you have turned on the **virtual memory (VM)** features that your system offers. (Virtual memory swaps blocks of memory back and forth to disk, causing brief interruptions in many operations; use it with caution in real-time applications. The same goes for some implementations of disk caching where the cache fills up and flushes to disk at unpredictable intervals.) The input or output task proceeds until the end of the buffer is

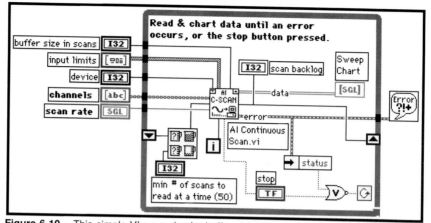

Figure 6-10. This simple VI uses circular buffered I/O to simultaneously acquire and chart data. It uses the upper-level intermediate VI, AI Continuous Scan, and it's very fast.

reached, then it stops automatically. For a simple buffered output operation, you can load the buffer all at once or a piece at a time, as long as you keep up with the output process. For input operations, you can read the data out in pieces or just wait until the operation is complete. The buffer stays intact until you call AI Clear or you reboot your system. Note that the size of the buffer is limited by available memory. Consider using simple buffered I/O for:

- Single-shot data acquisition at high speed with moderate buffer sizes
- Single-shot waveform generation at high speed

Circular Buffered I/O

If you want to continue your high-performance buffered I/O process indefinitely, or if you need to handle more data than memory will hold, use **circular buffered I/O**. A circular buffer is an area of memory that is reused sequentially. During a circular buffer input operation, you must read data from the buffer while the operation is in progress. Otherwise, old data will be overwritten when the next cycle starts. Similarly, an output operation can continue forever, but if you want the output waveform to change on-the-fly, you have to reload the buffer at an appropriate time. Figure 6-10 shows how easy it is to build a circular buffer application. For this example, I used the upper-level intermediate VI, AI Continuous Scan. If you want to see another more detailed and very flexible example, read on.

Circular buffered I/O is a powerful technique because the buffer has an apparently unlimited size, and the input or output operation proceeds *in the background with no software overhead*. The only burden on your program is that it must load or unload data from the buffer before it is overwritten. I really like circular buffered I/O because it makes the most effective use of available hardware and allows the software to process data in parallel with the acquisition activity. Use it wherever you require maximum overall performance in your program.

Multibuffered I/O

Sometimes a circular buffer fills (or empties) too quickly for your software to keep up. In that case, you must use **multibuffered I/O**, which allocates more than one memory buffer. (Another common name is double buffering, which is really a misnomer.) Each trigger event starts acquisition and fills one buffer, then acquisition stops until the next trigger. Or, you can specify continuous acquisition, in which case the buffers fill continuously and sequentially. Since there are several buffers, your program has additional time to read data out of one buffer while the hardware is writing data into another, or vice versa. You must use the intermediate or advanced VIs to implement multibuffering. Mulitbuffering is generally required when you can't reuse a simple buffer or a circular buffer. For example, you are acquiring triggered waveforms and can't read the waveform data (empty the buffer) until the next trigger occurs.

DAQ Configuration Utilities

If you want to use the DAQ library, you first have to run your system's **DAQ configuration utility** that comes with LabVIEW. On the Macintosh, it's a control panel called **NI-DAQ Utilities**. (I hear that this may change in a future version of LabVIEW.) On the PC, it's a Windows application called **wdaqconf.exe**. The Sun version will have a similar utility. They have similar capabilities, though I should mention that they are continuously evolving to incorporate more features that will make data acquisition system configuration easier. Important information that you access through these programs includes:

- Identity of installed data acquisition boards
- Data acquisition board configuration
- SCXI configuration
- List of DAQ error messages

Before you attempt to communicate with a plug-in board, you should run through the board configuration items to make sure that they match your actual system configuration. Some boards, especially the older ones, don't have as many programmable features as the new ones, so some options are disabled. Note that making a setting through the utility program is the same as making the setting through the DAQ VIs.

SCXI configurations are conveniently managed through the DAQ utility. You set the chassis information, types and positions of modules, and channel information such as gain and filtering.

Some of the setup capabilities of the configuration utilities are duplicated by calibration and configuration VIs in the advanced VI library. With these VIs you can manage hardware setups programmatically. The Get Device Information VI (and its complement, Set Device Information) reports (and sets) information about the DMA capabilities of an installed board on the PC. Other information, such as the number of AMUX boards or the input scale factors, is set by the various intermediate VIs that have such an input control. The Get SCXI

Information VI (and its complement, Set SCXI Information) permits you to read (and set) your SCXI chassis and module setup information.

About the DAQ Examples

Like all the examples that come with LabVIEW, you are encouraged to use the DAQ examples as starting points for your applications. Most of the samples presented here sprout from the examples; there's no reason to start from scratch all the time. Analog examples include all modes of buffered and nonbuffered input and output. There is a *stream to disk* library for high-speed recording of data directly to disk. Digital examples demonstrate immediate, untimed operations. Counter/timer examples show you how to generate pulse trains and measure frequency. And finally, there are examples for SCXI. Somewhere in this assemblage of over two megabytes of DAQ examples lurks a potential solution to *your* problem. Use the Readme VI that is in the Examples directory to learn about the available VIs. It reads the contents of the VI description item for each VI and displays the text for your viewing pleasure.

Analog Inputs

Analog acquisition represents about 80% of the real-world DAQ applications, so I'm going to spend a significant amount of time on the subject. The easy I/O VIs are pretty much self-explanatory, so the intermediate library will get most of our attention.

Configuration, Starting, and Stopping

The AI Config VI is the name of the game when it comes to setting up an analog input operation. From the basic task specifications—device, channel, and buffer size, and so forth—it checks the setup for errors, downloads settings to the target data acquisition board, allocates memory for any buffers, and returns a task ID number for use by subsequent DAQ VIs. Note that AI Config does not start any sampling—it only makes preparations. Perhaps the most confusing thing about DAQ configuration issues is that different plug-in board models have slightly different specifications with regard to channel ranges, input limits, and scanning order.

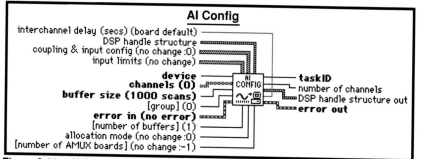

Figure 6-11. AI Config sets up conditions for analog acquisition. Of the dozen inputs, note that only four appear in boldface: those are the ones you are most likely to use.

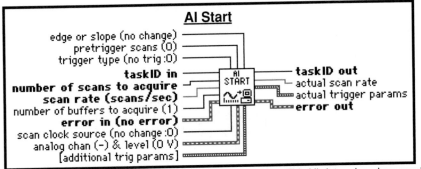

Figure 6-12. Call AI Start to start buffered data acquisition. This VI determines how much data to acquire and it sets triggering conditions.

An appendix to the LabVIEW DAQ manual summarizes these requirements. If you get something wrong, AI Config will return an error, such as invalid or inconsistent numeric parameter. These error messages are sometimes nonspecific, so it's up to you to figure out which parameter is at fault.

Once you have a task configured, you start buffered acquisition by calling the AI Start VI. Important inputs are the **number of scans to acquire** and **scan rate**. If you set **number of scans to acquire** to zero, continuous acquisition is requested. This VI is also the place where you specify triggering conditions. If your board supports it, you can choose various options such as digital or analog triggering with optional slope and level detection, much like an oscilloscope. If you have set up multibuffered acquisition using AI Config, you need to set **number of buffers to acquire** to the same value supplied to AI Config.

Unbuffered acquisition doesn't require a call to AI Start. Rather, you can use the AI Single Scan VI. It reads a single scan of data from the board and returns the data as voltage, raw binary, or both, depending on the setting of **output units**.

When you are through with all analog input operations, call the AI Clear VI to stop any in-progress acquisition and release any memory resources, such as buffers. AI Clear should be the last node in your DAQ VI chain before the error handler. It always clears the acquisition regardless of the error status. Those are the primary intermediate VIs you need to know about to get started and stopped. Next, you will want to read data.

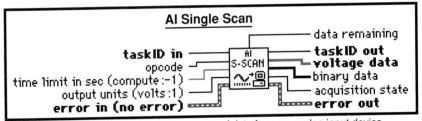

Figure 6-13. AI Single Scan fetches one scan of data from an analog input device.

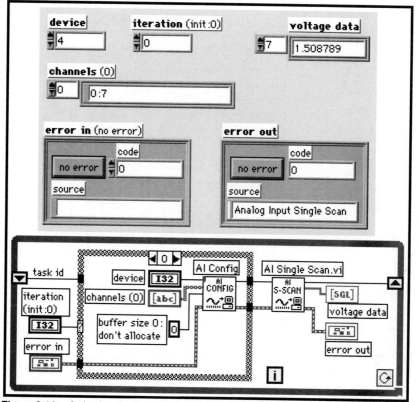

Figure 6-14. A simple subVI that reads one scan from a set of channels. It uses an uninitialized shift register to store the *task id* between calls. Case 1 has *task id* wired straight across and *error in* wired through to *error out*.

Low-Speed Acquisition

Let's say you want to read one or more channels at a modest rate, up to perhaps 10 Hz, with the sampling interval regulated by the LabVIEW timer functions. You can read one scan, or better, you can read several scans and average the samples for each channel to reduce noise. Figure 6-14 shows a driver VI that performs the simple case of acquiring one scan. It's arranged as a subVI that stores the task ID in an uninitialized shift register between calls. There is no reason to call AI Config every time, since nothing has changed. You connect the **iteration** input of this VI to the iteration terminal (I) of the calling VI, assuming that this VI is called repeatedly in the usual While Loop. On the first iteration, AI Config does its thing, but it is not called on subsequent iterations. Note that the buffer size is set to zero, so that no data buffer is allocated. Therefore, only one scan can be acquired at a time.

After the Case structure executes, the task ID and error cluster from AI Config are passed to AI Single Scan, which is the easy way to grab one sample from each channel (i.e., one scan). Since there is no buffer allocated and there is no continuous acquisition, you

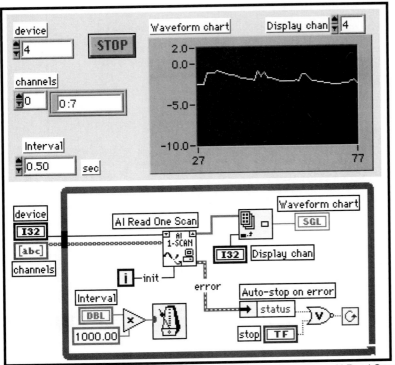

Figure 6-15. An example of a top-level VI that calls the previous driver, AI Read One Scan.

don't have to call AI Clear. Outputs of AI Single Scan are voltages for each channel and the error cluster.

This VI is a watered-down version of AI Read One Scan, an upper-level intermediate VI, that has more input parameters such as input scaling and number of AMUX boards. Like most of the examples in this chapter, I've simplified it to show only the most important controls. Controls appearing here also appear in the original AI Read One Scan in boldface. An even simpler version of this VI is available in the easy I/O library as AI Sample Channels. To summarize, you can access this same functionality at three levels, not including the advanced VIs:

- AI Sample Channels (easy I/O)
- AI Read One Scan (upper-level intermediate)
- AI Config; AI Single Scan (lower-level intermediate)

Figure 6-15 shows a simple top-level VI that calls this driver VI. A While Loop executes periodically, timed by the Wait Until Next ms Multiple function. The user can select one channel for display on the Waveform Chart. The data array returned by AI Read One Scan is indexed to extract the desired channel. The VI stops when the user clicks the Stop button, or when an I/O error is detected.

One problem occurs with the initialization technique that uses an iteration counter. If there is any possibility that the While Loop will iterate more than 2^{31} times, the iteration counter will overflow to zero and reinitialize the subVI. In such cases, create a shift register on the While Loop and wire it as shown in Figure 6-16. On the first iteration, the shift register will contain zero. On all subsequent iterations, it will contain something greater than zero.

Now, how about an enhanced operation in which you grab several samples from each channel, then average them? I started with the previous example, then added a few more intermediate VIs and some controls to come up with the VI in Figure 6-17. Looking at the diagram, AI Config is used in exactly the same way as before, except that a buffer is allocated, sized to hold the **number of scans**. Since this is a simple buffered acquisition, the AI Start VI is called next to start the acquisition clocks on the plug-in board, running at the desired **scan rate**. Next, you have to fetch the data from the buffer, a job for AI Read. The number of scans is passed to AI Read so that it reads all of the data; you could also read the data in pieces. AI Read returns a 2D array of voltages, representing each individual sample. You can use that data directly, or, for this example, pass the 2D array to Average Voltage, a utility subVI that I wrote and included on this book's diskette (see Figure 6-18). It averages all the samples for each channel and returns a 1D array that you can display and store on disk.

Since a buffer was allocated in this VI, you must call AI Clear when you are done. The **clear acquisition** Boolean should be wired to the *stop* button on the calling VI so that AI Clear is called only after the final iteration occurs. If you clear the acquisition then call this VI again (without Iteration=0), the task ID will no longer be valid and an error results.

This example, like the previous one, is quite similar to something directly available in the upper intermediate library, in this case the AI Waveform Scan VI. In turn, AI Waveform Scan is encapsulated in the easy I/O VI, AI Acquire Waveforms. It is also called by several of the DAQ examples, such as Acquire N Scans. Here is a summary of the VIs available to perform this immediate buffered I/O operation:

- Acquire N Scans (examples)

- AI Acquire Waveforms (easy I/O)

- AI Waveform Scan (upper-level intermediate)

- AI Config, AI Start, AI Read, AI Clear (lower-level intermediate)

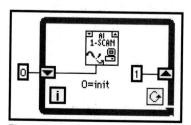

Figure 6-16.   Another way to manage the iteration terminal, with no chance of overflow.

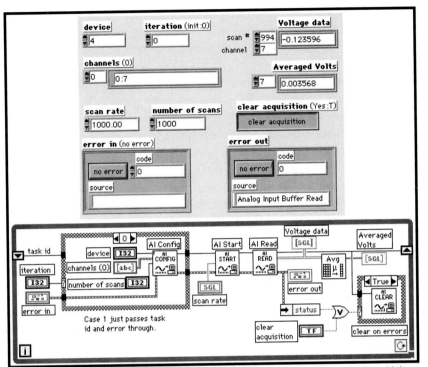

Figure 6-17. This example shows how to use the intermediate VIs to read multiple scans from multiple channels. Note the overall similarity with the driver in Figure 6-14. At the upper right is my subVI, Average DAQ Channels.

My utility VI, Average Voltage, can be added to any of the higher-level VIs where you have 2D Voltage data, including your top-level application. Speaking of which, what would a simple, top-level VI look like? Figure 6-19 shows one that calls AI Acquire Waveforms, displays one channel, and stores everything on disk in tab-delimited text format.

Sampling parameters are placed outside the While Loop so the user can't change them during the run. On the first call, the user receives a dialog for file creation, and a header is written by the file utility VI, Write Characters to File. Inside the While Loop, the averaged array of data is converted to text then appended to the file by another file utility, Write to Spreadsheet File. This example is useful for sampling rates up to about 10 Hz, beyond which the software timer is relatively imprecise. A more elaborate version of this example is discussed in the next chapter.

Medium-Speed Acquisition and Processing

Many applications demand that you sample one or more analog channels at moderate speeds, on the order of tens to thousands of samples per second, which I'll call medium-speed acquisition. At these speeds, you must have the I/O hardware do more of the time-critical work. Let's look at some of these medium-speed DAQ techniques.

Hardware-Timed Loops

Figure 6-9 shows the diagram of the example VI, Cont Acq&Chart (hw timed), which is one way of doing hardware-timed loops. It uses the intermediate VI, AI Single Scan, to fetch data from the plug-in board using nonbuffered I/O. Funny that it's called *nonbuffered*. If you think about it, there actually is a buffer out there somewhere—there has to be; otherwise some data would be lost each time AI Single Scan returns data to the calling VI, a process that takes a finite amount of time. The mystery buffer is a piece of hardware called a **first-in, first-out (FIFO)** memory that is located on the plug-in board. Samples from the ADC are temporarily stored in the FIFO pending a bus transfer to your computer's main memory, giving the software extra time to take care of other business. An important piece of information is the size of the available FIFO, which varies among models of plug-in boards. For instance, an AT-MIO-16X has 512 words (a word is 16 bits, or one sample), an AT-MIO-16F-5 has 256 words, and an NB-MIO-16 has only 16 words. If you are collecting data at 100,000 samples per second, a 16 word FIFO will fill in just 160 μs—not much time for the driver to get around to uploading the data, and no time at all for a LabVIEW loop to come around again.

So you see, these hardware timed loops, using nonbuffered I/O, are limited to moderate sampling rates. Testing the VI in Figure 6-19 on my Quadra 950 with an NB-MIO-16X (with a 16-word FIFO), I can chart one channel at up to about 200 Hz without overflowing the FIFO (DAQ error -10845, overflow error). If I make the graph smaller, change my monitor from 8-bit color to black and white, or do anything else that reduces graphics overhead, the maximum sampling rate goes up. Within these performance limits, hardware timed loops are quite useful. Control algorithms are a great application for them because the real-world output device can't wait too long for an update, and the algorithm itself is probably time-dependent to the point that it becomes unstable in the presence of a timebase with excessive jitter. So, you can run several feedback algorithms inside a hardware timed loop at 50 Hz, for instance, and display the present values, all with good timebase stability. About the only things that will mess up your timing are switching between windows,

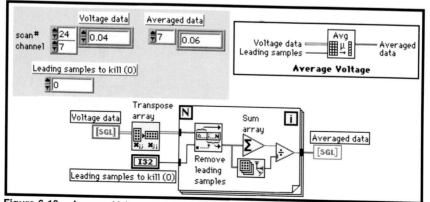

Figure 6-18.   Average Voltage averages the samples for each channel into a single value. You can also have it remove a number of leading samples in case your signal conditioning has problems with settling time.

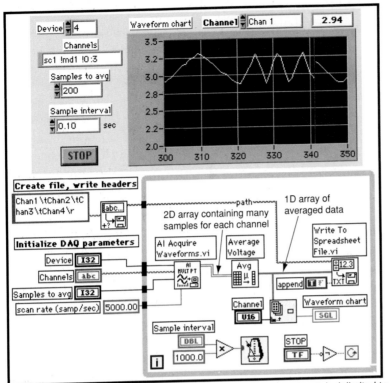

Figure 6-19. A low-speed data acquisition system with averaging, tab-delimited text storage, and a single-channel stripchart. Embellish as desired.

running too many VIs at once, or putting LabVIEW into the background in competition with another high-priority program running on your computer.

Circular Buffers and Parallel Processing

Circular buffered I/O adds a significant step in performance to your DAQ program because it can use hardware to continuously transfer data into your computer's main memory. Please note that you must have DMA hardware for this technique to work consistently beyond a few thousand samples per second.

The easiest way to set up a circular buffered acquisition is to use the AI Continuous Scan VI from the upper-level intermediate DAQ library. It has all the necessary controls for most applications, though you can copy parts from it and modify them to fit your requirements as needed. Figure 6-20 is an interesting example written by Mark Scrivener of Lawrence Livermore National Laboratory (LLNL). His objective was to monitor the current flowing in an electrochemical process and integrate that current over time to determine the total number of coulombs of ions deposited in the process. A coulomb is the amount of charge transferred by a current of 1 A flowing for 1 s. Therefore, the program must measure the current, multiply by the time since the last sample, then add the result to the previous sum. The operating equation is:

$$Q = \sum_{n=0}^{N} I_n dt$$

where Q is the charge in coulombs, I_n is the latest current measurement, and dt is the interval since the last sample was taken. This constitutes a simple rectangular integration.

This VI is set up as a kind of data server VI that communicates via global variables with several client VIs that display and store the calculated result. It runs until the global *stop* Boolean is set to True, or a DAQ error occurs. Each time around the loop, the scan backlog from AI Continuous Scan is evaluated. If there is no appreciable amount of data remaining in the circular buffer, a 5 s delay is called for. Calling any of the delay functions allows other, concurrently executing VIs to run while this VI sleeps and the hardware does the work of collecting the next buffer of data. If the backlog is very large, a small delay is requested to avoid overwriting the buffer. A large buffer size (50,000 scans) was used to give us ample time before any overwriting occurs. At 5,000 scans per second, it takes 10 seconds to fill the buffer. In that amount of time, you can do all sorts of background activity. Obviously, Mark must have lots of memory because that big buffer occupies 50,000 X 3 channels X 4 bytes per sample, for a total of 600,000 bytes. Duplication of the array elsewhere in the diagram can quickly lead to an out-of-memory condition. Keep this in mind when you start typing lots of zeroes into the **buffer size** control.

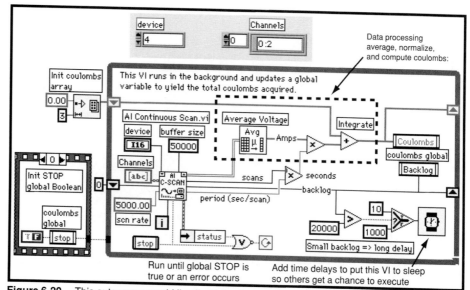

Figure 6-20. This autonomous subVI calls AI Continuous Scan to acquire several channels' worth of data using circular buffered acquisition. The data is processed and written to a global variable for use elsewhere. A delay in the loop gives other VIs a chance to execute.

In the diagram, AI Continuous Scan acquires several channels of data at a 5 kHz scan rate. This high scan rate is required because the current waveform is pulsed. The 2D data array is averaged on a channel-by-channel basis by the Average Voltage VI. Its output is an array of channels with units of amperes, courtesy of the scale factor applied during the acquisition process. Each current value is then multiplied by the actual scan period supplied by AI Continuous Scan, yielding results in units of coulombs. Summing the latest measurement with the previous total in the shift register yields an integrated value, which is written to a global variable for use elsewhere in a client VI.

With this arrangement, the acquisition server VI is asleep most of the time while the buffer is filling. When it wakes up, AI Continuous Scan will read the requested number of bytes (stored in the lower shift register). Then the data analysis happens and the VI goes back to sleep. Other VIs have plenty of time to use the collected data.

A possible enhancement to this VI would be to use the Integrate VI from the analysis library rather than performing a simple average on each buffer of data. Testing indicated

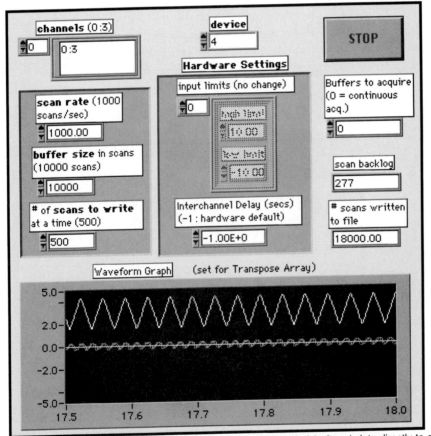

Figure 6-21. Panel for a VI that acquires data and writes scaled (voltage) data directly to disk with maximum throughput. Adapted from the example VI, Cont Acq to File (Scaled).

that the difference between the two methods was very small because the average value of a simple square pulse is equal to the integral over the same time period.

High-Speed Disk Streaming

Circular buffered I/O is the basis for **disk streaming**, recording data directly to disk at high speed. When you run your analog input hardware at near-maximum speeds in a disk streaming application, it will probably be impossible to view very much of that data in real-time because your computer will be very busy transferring data from memory to disk. On the other hand, you may be able to perform some real-time analysis, as in the previous example, that does not require extensive graphical displays. The disk streaming example in Figure 6-21 includes a waveform graph, but it could easily be deleted for higher performance. I started with the example VI, Cont Acq to File (Scaled), then added the programming for a graph that I stole from Cont Acq&Graph (Buffered). (As I always say, program by plagiarizing.)

I tested this VI on my Quadra 950 with an NB-MIO-16XH-18 and a DMA-2800, the latter of which has DMA capability, which is required for these higher sampling rates. The settings shown in Figure 6-21 are typical of maximum achievable performance of a VI that graphs four channels displayed at 1 kHz per channel, and writes the scaled data to a file. Without the graph, I could run the VI right up to the full speed of the board, which is about 55 kHz. If you have a faster A/D board, such as an NB- or EISA-A2000, that samples at rates up to 1 MHz, you will find that the limiting factor is the throughput of your disk system. One million samples per second, multiplied by four bytes per sample, is 4,000,000 bytes per second—that's a pretty fast disk system. There is a way to cut down the volume of data by a factor of two: store the data as raw (I16 integer) binary. The other stream-to-disk example, Cont Acq to File (Raw), does just that.

You will need to experiment a bit with the **scan rate**, **buffer size**, and **scans to write** controls to achieve maximum performance. As a rule, I like to make the buffer size at least twice, and preferably 10 times the scan rate to give the VI time to catch up with any scan backlog that occurs due to other activity on the machine. The **scans to write** value is a bit more nebulous. Sometimes, you can find a performance peak when the number of bytes written each time corresponds to the size of a buffer, or cache memory, in your disk system. If you are graphing data, plan to update the graph no more than about 10 times per second to avoid excessive overhead. The same rule of thumb probably applies to file I/O. I usually shoot for one or two file writes and graph updates per second.

The diagram for this VI, shown in Figure 6-22, is fairly complex. But if you examine it from left to right one VI at a time, it's not too hard to understand. There are really two parallel tasks happening in this diagram: data acquisition using the DAQ functions, and file I/O using some file utility VIs with error handling. The two tasks share error I/O as a common thread; you can see the error cluster zigzag through the diagram. The file refnum is passed from one file I/O VI to the next, while the DAQ task ID is passed between DAQ VIs. In general, the left part of the diagram is devoted to initialization, the loop contains the real-time acquisition, and the right part handles final cleanup. All of the DAQ VIs are from the lower-level intermediate library, and together they perform exactly the same function as AI Continuous Scan, which appears in the previous example. Let's go through the diagram step by step.

1. The Open/Create/Replace File VI is one of the file I/O utilities with error reporting. Here, it opens or creates a new byte stream data file.

2. The AI Config VI allocates the data acquisition buffer and sets the A/D input limits.

3. The Write File+ (SGL) VI writes the **Number of Channels** output from AI Config to the data file. A Build Array function was required because the file VI only accepts 1D and 2D arrays of data. This value represents the number of channels and is needed when an analysis program attempts to read the data file.

4. The AI Start VI starts the buffered data acquisition operation. If **Buffers to acquire** is zero, the operation will continue indefinitely. AI Start also sets the scan rate.

5. The AI Read VI waits until the requested **number of scans to write** is available from the circular buffer. It returns a 2D array containing that many scans of data, scaled to Voltage. If there is more data in the buffer, **scan backlog** will be greater than zero.

6. The utility VI, Write File+ (SGL), appends the 2D data array to the file. Internally, the VI uses the Type Cast function to convert data to a binary string before writing it to the file.

7. The icons in this area support the waveform graph. Since AI Read returns the actual scan interval, that timing information is available for scaling the x-axis in seconds. You can delete everything above the dashed line to increase the performance of this VI. Alternatively, the graph could be placed inside a Case structure so that you can turn off graphing if desired.

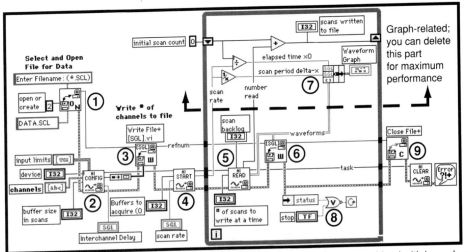

Figure 6-22. Diagram for the disk streaming example. File I/O utility VIs are combined with lower-level intermediate DAQ VIs to yield a flexible, high-performance data recording system.

8. The While Loop stops if an error occurs or the STOP button is pressed. This loop cycles at a rate determined by the amount of time that it takes to acquire **number of scans to write**.

9. Final cleanup is handled by the Close File+ and AI Clear VIs. If an error occurred, the General Error Handler VI displays a dialog.

Special Sampling

Some analog acquisition applications demand very careful control over the timing of each sample. For instance, if you are measuring the phase shift between several analog signals, you need to know precisely when each sample is taken on each channel, or use **simultaneous sampling** hardware that adds no interchannel delay. Other situations demand **triggering**, where the acquisition operation starts when a certain condition is met, such as the detection of a critical voltage level in a signal. There are many special sampling tools built into the DAQ library and various plug-in boards that make your life easier when these situations arise.

Simultaneous Sampling

When you use an ordinary MIO-series board or other analog input device that has a multiplexer, each sample arrives at a slightly different time than its neighbors. The time differential is determined by the sampling rate of the ADC. If this interchannel phase (timing skew) is important, you should consider buying hardware with multichannel, simultaneous sampling. Such hardware may have one ADC per channel like the A2150-series boards, or it may have one sample-and-hold amplifier per channel, like the A2000-series boards and the SCXI-1140 module. (A sample-and-hold takes an instantaneous "snapshot" of the input voltage and stores it with a capacitor until the ADC gets around to reading the value. That way, one expensive A/D can be shared among several channels using cheaper sample-and-holds.) Simultaneous sampling is important in many time- and phase-sensitive applications, such as vibration analysis and acoustics.

For most operations, the DAQ library attempts to scan a group of channels by running the ADC of your I/O board at top speed, thus providing the minimum timing skew. This is called **near-simultaneous sampling**. Indeed, for many applications, the 10 µs skew of a 100 kHz ADC is negligible. If you wish to override this feature, you must use the **Interchannel Delay** control on AI Config. The default value for **Interchannel Delay** is preset to the minimum value permitted by the device you are configuring, which implies near-simultaneous sampling. For example, if you were to increase the delay to 1 ms, all I/O operations would be limited to a top speed of 1,000 samples per second. Ten channels could be scanned no faster than 100 scans per second.

The good news about simultaneous sampling is that, once you buy the hardware, you don't have to do anything special with the DAQ software—the board does all the work. But if you don't have one of those fancy boards, you must correct the timing skew for each channel when you analyze the data. The best way to find out how much skew is in your data is to measure it. Connect all channels of interest to a common input signal, preferably a square wave because its rapid transitions are obvious time markers. Collect scans of data using your acquisition VI, then display the results with all channels on the same graph. The x-axis of the graph must be calibrated in seconds (see the example VIs). Use the graph cursors to measure channel-to-channel timing skew. Since the amount of skew may vary with the sampling rate and the number of channels, you may need to examine the results for several sampling conditions. The timebase correction values may then be applied to your data by adjusting the X_0 (initial time value) when graphing each channel.

Triggering

The whole subject of triggering is discussed in more detail in Chapter 9, *Physics Applications*. Here, we'll look at the options available in the DAQ world. First, there are two basic types of triggering: hardware and software. **Hardware triggering** relies on specialized hardware features included on a plug-in board. There are in turn two types of hardware triggers: analog and digital. Analog trigger circuitry generates a trigger when an input signal reaches a specified slope and level. This feature is identical to the familiar triggering controls on oscilloscopes. Analog triggering is only available on certain plug-in boards, such as the dynamic signal acquisition series (AT-A2150, AT-DSP2200, EISA-A2000, NB-A2100, and NB-A2150) from National Instruments. Digital triggers are supplied through an external connector input to the board, like the external trigger input to an oscilloscope. Digital triggers are available on all National Instruments plug-in boards. **Software triggering** uses a program (either deep inside the driver, or one written in LabVIEW) that examines continuously acquired data to see if it meets the triggering criteria. Data is only processed if it meets the criteria, thus saving CPU time and/or disk space. In summary, hardware triggering acts directly on the analog signal; software triggering acts on the digitized data.

Another aspect of triggering that you need to understand is the difference between **pretrigger** and **posttrigger** sampling. Data acquired after a trigger pulse occurs is known as posttrigger data, while data acquired before the trigger is pretrigger data. Pretrigger data is useful when you need to record some baseline data before the main signal arrives, or in situations where there is some uncertainty as to the relationship between the main event and the trigger pulse.

The upper-level intermediate VI, AI Waveform Scan, is the single most useful DAQ function for triggered acquisition. It supports all types of hardware and software triggering, and it's used in all the example VIs that demonstrate the various trigger modes. It has enough features for most applications, but if there is something missing, you can always modify it and save it under a different name. The diagram for AI Waveform Scan is complex because it allows you to transparently switch between analog hardware triggering and software triggering—similar functions with completely different implementations.

Let's look at hardware triggering first. All hardware triggering parameters are entered through AI Start. Figure 6-23 explains their basic functions, and the LabVIEW DAQ

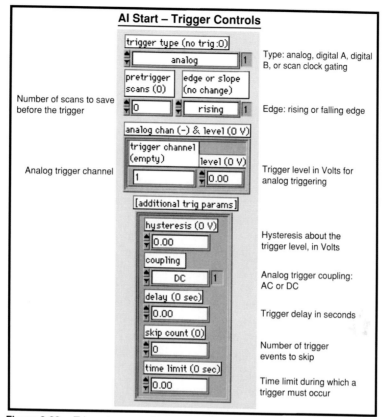

Figure 6-23. Triggering controls available on the intermediate DAQ VI, AI Start.

manual discusses them in detail. If you are using AI Waveform Scan, only a few of these controls are available on its panel.

Digital Hardware Triggering

Digital hardware triggering is easy to set up and use. You will need a TTL-compatible signal that is synchronized to the analog signal you wish to capture. On an MIO-series board, there are two digital inputs you may use for triggering a scan: STARTTRIG* and STOPTRIG. The asterisk (*) means that a TTL low level (ground) is required to assert the signal; otherwise a high level (>2.5 V) is required. So, to generate a start trigger, you need to connect a TTL signal to STARTTRIG* that is high except at the moment you want to start acquiring posttrigger data. If you are collecting pretrigger data with an MIO board, you set STOPTTRIG high at the moment when you have collected sufficient pretrigger data. On other boards, like the NB-A2100, there is only one external trigger input, and its action depends on the trigger mode set by the driver. Consult the hardware manual for details of your particular board.

For programming examples, see the Acquire N Scans-DTrig or Acquire N Scans-Multi-DTrig VIs. Both use AI Waveform Scan. A more elaborate example, Acquire&Proc N

Scans-Trig, uses the lower-level intermediate VIs and offers on-the-fly data processing. You might use this VI when you are measuring a recurrent waveform that is synchronized to a digital trigger, such as the output of a function generator. With synchronization, each acquired waveform is guaranteed to be locked in-phase with every other. Therefore, you can perform mathematical operations, such as waveform averaging or differencing, without errors due to phase mismatching.

Analog Hardware Triggering

If you have one of the fancy plug-in boards with analog triggering hardware, you have the makings of a real triggered-sweep oscilloscope (albeit somewhat limited in bandwidth). No special external connections are required because onboard analog comparators and logic sample the analog signal and generate a hardware trigger signal when the requested conditions are present. To see how this works, try one of the *ATrig* example VIs, such as Acquire N Scans-ATrig, Acquire N Scans-Multi-ATrig, or Acquire&Proc N Scans-Trig, which are the analog versions of the examples used for digital triggers.

Software Triggering

Software triggering is built into the DAQ driver and is particularly useful with I/O boards that don't offer analog triggering hardware, like the MIO series. You access software triggering through the **conditional retrieval** controls in AI Read (Figure 6-24). These controls simulate the hardware options available in AI Start, but the action of conditional retrieval is different. The I/O board actually collects data in its free-running, untriggered mode. For each buffer of data acquired, the driver searches through the buffer, looking for the first part of the data that matches the trigger conditions. If a match is found, AI Read returns the data. If no match is found, no data is returned. This saves time because it requires less copying or moving of data in memory.

For software triggering applications, you can use the features of AI Waveform Scan, which is nicely packaged in the example VI Acquire N Scans-SW Trig. Or, you can use the Acquire&Proc Scans-SW Trig VI, which uses the lower-level intermediate VIs for continuous processing. This last example continuously triggers off of data in a buffer without pausing acquisition. Furthermore, you can change the trigger parameters without stopping acquisition.

Different Sampling Rates on Different Channels

It's really easy to acquire data from several channels at the same speed, as we've already seen. But how do you set up a system that runs different sampling rates on different channels? One fundamental limitation of the DAQ VI library and the available plug-in boards is that you can only run one acquisition task on a given board at one time. That is, you can't do something simple like simultaneously calling AI Continuous Scan and AI Waveform Scan for the same board, but with different channels and sampling parameters, expecting them to run in parallel. The first one to execute will start its operation, then the second one will mess up the register settings on the board, destroying the first operation.

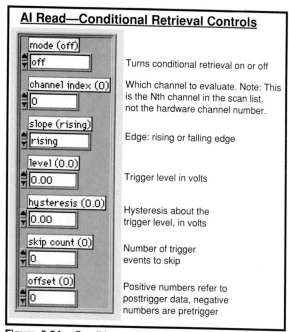

Figure 6-24. Condition retrieval controls, available from AI Read, simulate analog triggering for boards that don't have analog triggering hardware.

Instead of data, you get error messages. (Please note that you *can* run multiple tasks on a single board if they are of different types. For instance, a buffered input and a buffered output operation can run simultaneously.)

The best solution is to use a separate plug-in board for each acquisition task. The DAQ driver can manage many input tasks in parallel, so long as there is only one input task *per board*. For instance, you can run two of the continuous acquisition example VIs in parallel, with one of them scanning Board A at 10 kHz and the other scanning Board B at 1 Hz. System resources—buffer space, computations, file I/O, and overhead—are nicely allocated and scheduled, courtesy of the driver and the LabVIEW scheduler. You still have to make sure, however, that your system doesn't get overloaded to the point where it can't keep up with the aggregate data rate. The only notable drawback of this approach is the cost of the extra board(s).

If your objective is to save disk space or to avoid graphing too many data points at one time, then you have another option: sample all channels at the speed of the fastest channel, then decimate the data for the slower channels. I wrote an array manipulation VI, shown in Figure 6-25, that separates a 2D DAQ data array into two 2D arrays: one for fast channels, and one for slow. This VI works on the assumption that all of the fast channels are scanned first, then the slow ones. You specify how many fast channels there are (**N Fast**), and the ratio of sampling rates between fast and slow. Data for each fast channel is simply copied to the output array. Data for slow channels is decimated by averaging groups of samples according to the fast/slow sampling ratio. Note that the output arrays have their indices

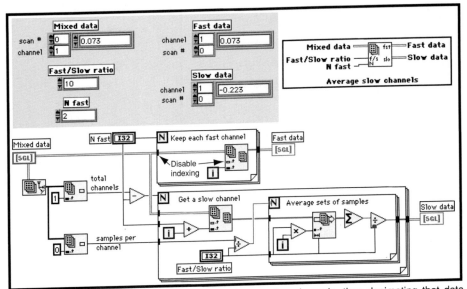

Figure 6-25. This VI averages groups of samples on *slow* channels, thus decimating that data. Separate output arrays are produced. Note the row and column swapping between input and outputs.

swapped with respect to the input arrays. Memory usage (worst-case) is when the data space is doubled, as required by the incoming array (four times, if the panel is displayed).

Figure 6-26 is an example of a continuous acquisition VI that calls the Average Slow Channels VI described above. AI Continuous Scan acquires all channels at the *fast* rate. Average Slow Channels divides the data into fast and slow arrays. You can select one channel for display from either of the arrays. Fast and slow data are appended to separate binary files by two calls to the Write File+ [SGL] VI. An error cluster propagates among the I/O VIs. If an error occurs, the While Loop stops.

Ignoring Some Data

We spend a lot of time worrying about processing every single sample of data in a continuous stream. But is that really an *absolute* requirement for your application? I worked on an electrophysiology experiment where we needed to observe the power spectrum of brain waves in real-time. I set up a VI that performs circular buffered acquisition with the data piped to a power spectrum VI, then to a graph. It quickly became apparent that my computer could not keep up with the required sampling rate because the FFT algorithms in the power spectrum were using up too much CPU time. AI Read would report a buffer overrun after only a few seconds, and the VI would give me an error dialog and stop. The important factor in this application is that I didn't really need to see all of the data samples. If I could view 50 to 75% of the data, that would be sufficient. To process any more data, I would need a much faster computer, or maybe a DSP board.

Instead of going out and buying a faster computer or slaving over the program, I simply turned off the error handler! So what if the DAQ input buffer gets overwritten? I still see

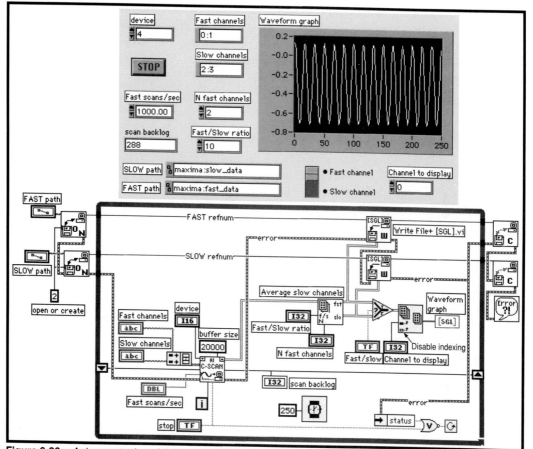

Figure 6-26. A demonstration of the Average Slow Channels VI. You can view either a fast or a slow channel from continuously acquired data.

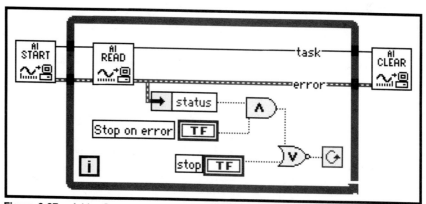

Figure 6-27. Add a *Stop on error* switch to make the loop keep running even if an error occurs.

the latest power spectrum, even though I missed some fraction of a second of data. AI Read sometimes returns an overrun error, but the While Loop keeps on running. I added a switch to the front panel that enables or disables the stopping of the main loop on errors (Figure 6-27). It's handy to have full error handling when you are setting things set up. Another solution is to add a filter for the error code you wish to ignore. If the error code is equal to the one that is permitted, keep on looping.

Analog Outputs

The analog output DAQ VIs are somewhat simpler than the input side—there aren't quite so many options on output devices. Like the input VIs, you can use the easy I/O VIs to get started, or move into the intermediate VIs for additional features. And everything you learned about inputs applies symmetrically to outputs, thanks to the consistency of the DAQ library.

Configuration and Stopping

All analog output operations begin with a call to AO Config. Like AI Config, it accepts a list of channels on a given device to which data will be written. If you set the **buffer size** to zero, no buffer is allocated, and you will only be able to perform single-value updates. A nonzero buffer length implies **waveform generation**, where multiple updates are sequentially written to one or more output channels. AO Config creates a taskID for use by other analog output VIs.

The last VI you call after stopping a buffered analog output task is AO Clear, which is similar to and just as simple as AI Clear. That's about all there is to setting up an analog output sequence, besides writing data.

Simple Updates

If you're doing low-speed updates, say 10 Hz or less, an unbuffered analog output operation should be adequate. In the easy I/O library, there is the AO Update Channel VI, which writes a single value to a single channel, and its cousin, AO Update Channels, which writes a single value to multiple channels. Both include a call to the error handler. In turn,

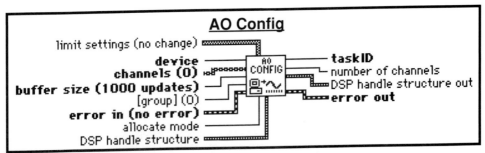

Figure 6-28. AO Config sets up conditions for analog output operations.

both of them call the AO Write One Update VI from the upper-level intermediate library. That's the VI to use for simple applications like the two-channel DC voltage source VI in Figure 6-29. AO Write One Update accepts the usual **device** and **channels** specifications, and an array of voltages containing one value per channel. The data could just as well come from a measurement, a calculation, a global variable, or a preinitialized array containing low-speed waveforms.

Like the other, upper-level intermediate VIs, AO Write One Update contains an uninitialized shift register that stores the **taskID** between calls. When the VI is called with **iteration** equal to 0, AO Config is called to create a new taskID that references the specified device and channels. For all other values of **iteration**, the taskID circulates in the shift register and is used by Analog Output Single Update, an advanced VI that actually writes data. This method saves CPU time because a new task doesn't have to be configured each time. However, you must remember that the uninitialized shift register serves as global memory. That is, if you need to invoke AO Write One Update in more than one place in your diagram, be aware that all instances will share the same taskID. Is that what you want? If you want to initialize AO Write One Update in one location, then use it to write data in several other places (to the same output channels), then the default setup is fine. But, if you want to use it to write data to different sets of channels, then you must open it, set the VI configuration to **reentrant** execution, and save the VI with a new name. Reentrant VIs create a separate set of storage locations for each instance of the VI, so the shift registers will no longer share data. This is the opposite of a global variable where you *want* the shift registers to store data between calls, regardless of who calls the subVI. To summarize, here is the hierarchy of VIs for simple analog outputs:

- AO Update Channels (easy I/O)
- AO Write One Update (upper-level intermediate)
- AO Config (lower-level intermediate)
- AO Single Update (advanced)

Analog Outputs as Digital Attenuators

Another interesting thing you can do with your analog outputs is use them as **digital attenuators**. Most of National Instruments' boards have an external reference option for each analog output. Instead of using the fixed, onboard DC reference voltage, you can supply your own external signal through the external reference input. What's interesting is that your signal can be either polarity of DC, or even an AC voltage. The output of the DAC is the product of the reference voltage (your signal) and the digital count sent to the analog output by one of the DAQ VIs. The circuit that does this is called a multiplying DAC. For unipolar setups, if you tell the D/A to go to 50% of its output range, the output signal amplitude will be 50% of the reference amplitude. For bipolar setups, a request for a negative output inverts the reference signal.

Digital attenuation is particularly useful when you need to control the amplitude of a signal that is generated by another instrument. For instance, your average MIO board isn't

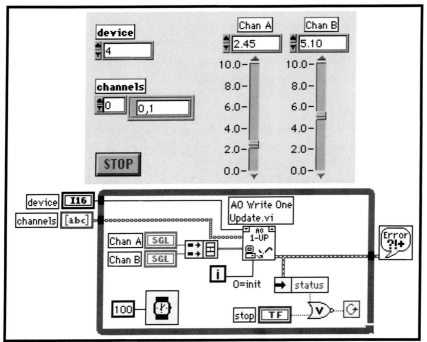

Figure 6-29. This VI calls AO Write One Update 10 times per second to create a manually operated, two-channel voltage source.

fast enough to generate a clean 50 kHz sine wave, but the multiplying D/A is more than happy to pass such a signal from an external function generator. In fact, the DC source example VI above would serve nicely as a *volume control* for a stereo audio application.

Waveform Generation

Above 10 Hz or so, you should consider using buffered waveform generation. This is much the same situation we saw with analog inputs, where software-timed loops lack the accuracy to run at higher speeds. The general steps you must perform are:

1. Create a waveform—an array of values scaled to voltage. Determine how many samples the waveform needs, and then how fast you intend to send samples (updates) to the D/A.

2. Call the AO Write VI (Figure 6-30) to load the waveform into a buffer that you previously allocated with AO Config. The buffer should be at least as long as the waveform, though you get best performance when the lengths are equal. You can also request waveform **regeneration**, where the buffer is automatically written to the D/A over and over again.

3. Call the AO Start VI (Figure 6-31) to start the actual output operation. AO Start determines the update rate and the number of **buffer iterations**. If the number of

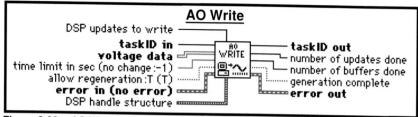

Figure 6-30. AO Write loads a waveform (an array of voltages) into a memory buffer.

buffer iterations is zero, waveform regeneration is requested. The only way to stop regeneration is to call AO Clear.

4. If you are generating a single buffer, call AO Wait before calling AO Clear. AO Wait checks to see that the whole buffer has been written to the D/A, and doesn't return until the operation is complete. If you call AO Clear too soon, you will abort the operation in midbuffer.

5. Always remember to call AO Clear when you are finished to free up memory.

There are upper-level intermediate VIs that make waveform generation easy. If you want to generate a single-shot waveform, use the AO Waveform Gen VI. It accepts an array of data (the waveform) and generates a timed, simple-buffered waveform for the given output channels at the specified update rate. It does not return until the generation is complete. Internally, it calls the expected sequence of lower-level intermediate VIs to configure, write, start, wait, and clear. The example in Figure 6-32 uses AO Waveform Gen to produce a single-shot chirp waveform. The Chirp Pattern VI from the analysis library builds an array of data that is displayed with the Waveform Graph. Since I only wanted to drive one output, I had to use a Build Array function to make a 2D array—the data type required by AO Waveform Gen. However, the rows and columns turn out to be switched (lots of channels; only one sample!), so I used the Transpose 1D Array function to swap them. The whole business of transposing DAQ arrays is discussed in detail in Chapter 1, *Getting Started with the Data Acquisition VIs*, of the LabVIEW data acquisition VI reference manual.

Somewhat more challenging is the generation of continuously repeating waveforms, especially when you wish to change the waveform on the fly. For a simple, continuous waveform, you can use the upper-level intermediate VI, AO Continuous Gen, which works

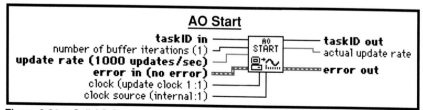

Figure 6-31. Call AO Start to initiate a buffered analog output operation.

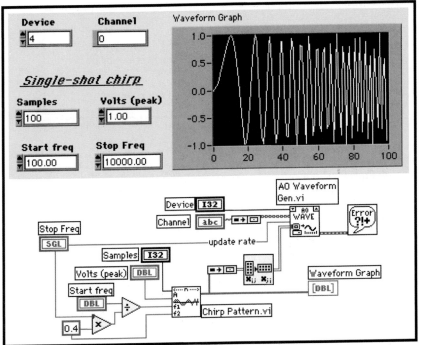

Figure 6-32. This example generates a single-shot chirp waveform with calibrated start and stop frequencies using the Chirp Pattern VI and AO Waveform Gen.

much like AO Waveform Gen. The example VI, Continuous Generation, shows you how to use it.

To change the waveform on the fly, you must turn to the lower-level intermediate VIs, as shown in Figure 6-33. For simplicity, I distilled this one from the example VI, Function Generator, which allows you to change many aspects of the waveform on the fly. The basic procedure for continuous generation is as follows:

1. Call AO Config to allocate an output buffer.

2. Create your waveform, sized to fit the output buffer. Create a 2D array (use Build Array), then use Transpose 2D Array to swap the rows and columns for compatibility with AO Write.

3. Load your waveform into the buffer with AO Write.

4. Start waveform generation with AO Start. Set the **number of iterations** to zero to force continuous generation. The buffer will be written to the output channel over and over, until you call AO Clear.

5. To change the waveform during generation, pass a new 2D waveform array to AO Write. The buffer will be overwritten, but waveform generation will not be interrupted. (Note: This is not a synchronous operation; the new waveform data will appear in the

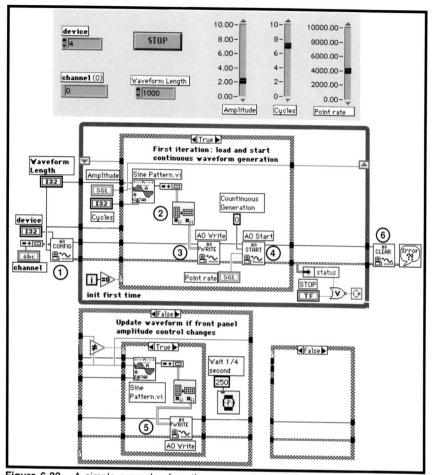

Figure 6-33. A simple example of continuous generation with on-the-fly waveform amplitude and frequency changes. This VI is taken from the example, Function Generator.

output signal as soon as the data transfer process overwrites the part of the buffer that is presently being passed to the DAC.)

6. When you're all done, call AO Clear.

In this example, the initial waveform is created and loaded, and started on the first iteration of the While Loop. After the first iteration, a Not Equal comparison function checks to see if the **Amplitude** control has changed. If so, the True frame of the inner Case structure creates a new waveform and loads it into the buffer with AO Write. The While Loop terminates when the Stop button is pressed, or when an error occurs.

You could add lots of features to this VI. For instance, there are several interacting controls (**Waveform Length**, **Cycles**, and **Point rate**) that, together, determine the frequency of the sinewave. It would make sense to write a subVI that figures out optimum settings based on a single **Frequency** control on the panel. The subVI would have to vary all three of the parameters according to some schedule that results in an acceptably clean waveform without exceeding the capabilities of the hardware.

Digital I/O

There are two types of digital I/O that you can perform with the DAQ library: digital port I/O and buffered I/O with handshaking. The **digital port I/O** VIs let you read and write one or more bits at a time from the digital interfaces available on many plug-in boards using untimed, immediate digital I/O. These simple VIs accommodate the situations in which you need to read or write a few bits at low rates. For greater performance, you must turn to **buffered digital I/O**. Boards that support handshaking, such as the DIO series, can transfer buffers of digital data at high speed. The Digital Group VIs access these features using hardware-timed, buffered digital I/O.

Simple, Bitwise I/O

Routine digital I/O operations, in which a number of bits are read or written at low speeds, are handled by the digital port VIs in the intermediate library. The easy I/O library also has some VIs that simplify these operations, but we'll look at the intermediate VIs directly because they really are quite easy to use.

Like the analog I/O libraries, digital I/O operations begin with a configuration VI, DIO Port Config. Figure 6-34 shows how it's used. You choose a **device** in the usual manner–the board's slot number. **Port** refers to the digital I/O port number. Valid entries depend on the particular board you are using—refer to the LabVIEW DAQ manual for further details. If you are using one of the SCXI digital modules, enter one of the usual SCXI specifiers, such as SC1!MD7.

The final input to DIO Port Config is the **line direction map**, an I32 control which specifies the direction of each line in the port. If a bit is 0 in the line map, the line is an input line. If a bit is 1, the line is an output line. In this example, I created a Boolean array control, then used **Boolean Array to Number** to change the array to a number. You could also use a diagram constant or an integer numeric control. If you do, pop up on the constant or control and select Show... Radix, then from the Format and Precision dialog box, set the Radix to Binary. You can then enter ones and zeros directly without trying to figure out decimal equivalents. Please note that many boards do not permit you to mix inputs and outputs within one port. In those cases, you can wire the line direction map to a zero for all inputs, or to -1 for all outputs. (Serious programmer's note: If you display the data as binary, note that -1 decimal is the equivalent of all 1s in a binary number because LabVIEW uses two's complement arithmetic.)

Once the port is configured, you can use the advanced (but easy to understand) VIs, DIO Port Read to read the bit pattern, or DIO Port Write to write a bit pattern. Input and output patterns are U32 integers that you can interpret as desired. In the example of Figure 6-35, I defined two digital port tasks: one for inputs and one for outputs. DIO Port Config is

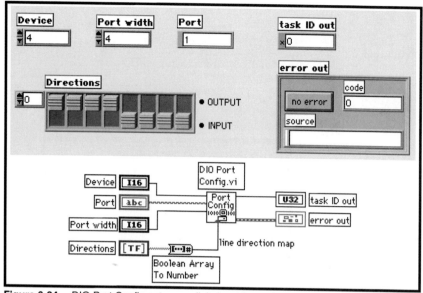

Figure 6-34. DIO Port Config sets up a digital port for untimed, immediate digital I/O.

called once for each task. Inside the While Loop, DIO Port Read reads the bit pattern from a port, then the Number to Boolean Array VI converts the pattern for display. Similarly, DIO Port Write writes data from a Boolean array control to the other port. The error cluster wiring path determines the order in which the two I/O operations occur; in this case, reading occurs before writing.

In your application, various Boolean operations such as manual controls, interlocks, and pattern generators might determine output states. Note that there is nothing preventing you from reconfiguring port directions while you're running, which yields a bidirectional port. You can also read from a port that has bits configured as outputs, permitting you to read back the port settings for confirmation.

Another way you can do untimed immediate digital I/O is to use the intermediate VI, DIO Single Read/Write. It takes care of the port configuration, then reads or writes one or more scans. It has an **iteration** input that you connect to the iteration terminal of a loop in the calling VI. When iteration equals zero, DIO Config is called. Figure 6-36 does the same job as the previous example, but this time using DIO Single Read/Write. Before running this VI, you must configure DIO Single Read/Write as reentrant because it keeps track of the task ID in an uninitialized shift register. If you don't make it reentrant, both instances of the VI will end up sharing the same task ID, which is not what you want. Note that the data inputs and outputs for DIO Single Read/Write are arrays because it can do more than one update or scan per call.

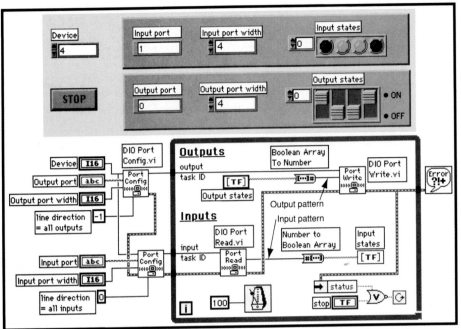

Figure 6-35. Two digital port tasks run simultaneously: one for inputs and one for outputs.

Digital I/O with Handshaking

Digital port I/O is limited to low-speed transfers because all operations occur in software-timed loops. You can transfer digital data at high speeds with precise timing and synchronization by using the **handshaking** features of certain plug-in boards (notably the DIO- and LAB-series) and the digital group I/O library. Handshaking may take one of three forms in the context of the DAQ library:

- **Internal** handshaking, where an onboard clock triggers each scan or update. Useful for fixed-rate sampling or pattern generation. (I think the rest of the world would call this *clocking* rather than handshaking...) The DIO-32F class of boards have this mode.

- **I/O connector** handshaking, where an external digital line triggers each scan or update. With this mode an external hardware device forces data synchronization. A familiar example of this type of operation is the ubiquitous Centronics-standard parallel port used on PCs for printers and other peripherals.

- **RTSI** handshaking, where the trigger is carried by an RTSI line from another plug-in board. This mode is useful when you have several I/O operations that you wish to synchronize; they can even be mixed analog and digital operations.

Handshaking in the DAQ library implies the transfer of a buffer of data, so these are in fact buffered I/O operations. Because the DAQ library is consistent in its function VI names, the buffered digital output example in Figure 6-37 should remind you of a buffered

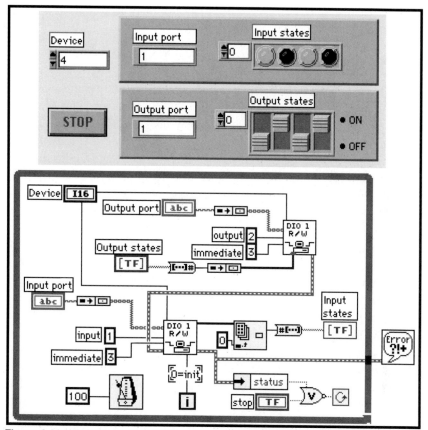

Figure 6-36. DIO Single Read/Write can simplify routine digital I/O programming. Compare this example with Figure 6-35.

analog waveform generation process. The objective here is to transfer an array of data to a digital port at a rate determined by hardware handshaking. The controls shown are set for internal handshaking with a clock frequency of 1 kHz. If you were to look at the affected output bits, you would see them update every 1.0 ms.

Here are the steps:

1. The DIO Config VI allocates a buffer and sets the port direction to output. It has many other handshaking configuration options (see the manual) that are especially useful when the handshaking source is an external signal.

2. The DIO Write VI loads the array of data into the preallocated buffer. You can also set a time limit on the I/O operation to keep your system from *hanging*. That's important when you are connected to external hardware that may or may not respond properly.

3. The handshaking mode is set, and the output operation starts when you call the DIO Start VI.

4. The DIO Wait VI puts the VI in suspense until the operation is complete.

5. The buffer is released by the DIO Clear VI. You can also abort any digital I/O operation by calling DIO Clear at any time.

Counters and Timers

While it *is* possible to count and time external events with LabVIEW software loops, these tasks are better accomplished with the counter/timer hardware included on the MIO, TIO and Lab-series plug-in boards. For instance, LabVIEW does not have the performance required to count individual external events occurring at 1 MHz, nor does it have timers that resolve anything beyond 1 ms—but the hardware does. National Instruments' hardware designers selected the Advanced Micro Devices Am9513 System Timing Controller (STC) chip—an exceptionally versatile device—for the MIO and TIO boards, and an Intel 8253 counter timer chip for the Lab-series boards. Several onboard clocks can be counted and divided to produce accurate timing intervals, or you can use an external or RTSI clock. Frequencies up to 6.9 MHz are acceptable. With the DAQ Counter/Timer VIs and a little bit of wiring, you can configure this versatile hardware for a variety of tasks, including accurately timed pulses, counting events, and measuring period and frequency.

With versatility comes complexity (which is why you might want to use software timers where appropriate; for example timing loops that run at 1 Hz or slower). These counter/timers have several modes and there are many, many ways that you can interconnect them. It helps to have some understanding of the STC itself, and that information is available from several sources. The manual for your plug-in board contains a general description of the STC, including a complete data sheet in the back of the manual. Also, the LabVIEW data acquisition VI reference manual has some introductory information associated with each model of plug-in board. By all means spend some time trying to digest this information before embarking on any unusual counting and timing adventures. It's important to note that some of the counters on an MIO board are reserved for data

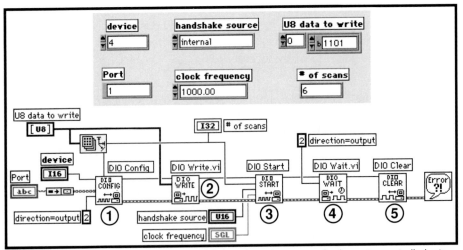

Figure 6-37.   Using the intermediate digital VIs to write out an array of values at a controlled rate.

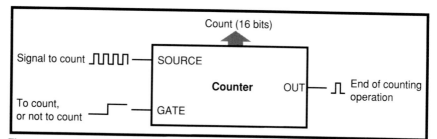

Figure 6-38. Each of the five counters in an Am9513 looks like this. Signals come from a variety of sources, including other counters.

acquisition timing (they aren't even wired to the connector), so you need to make sure that your counting application doesn't request a preassigned counter if you are also doing data acquisition at the same time. On the other hand, you can use the applications described in this chapter without too much knowledge of the hardware.

About the Am9513 System Timing Controller (STC)

Each STC contains five independent 16-bit counters and a 4-bit programmable frequency output. The part we're mainly interested in is the counter module (Figure 6-38) and its various modes of operation. Each counter has a **SOURCE** input, a **GATE** input, and an output called **OUT**. The SOURCE input is normally connected to a clock or a signal to be counted. The GATE input enables and disables counting. The output generates a pulse when a preprogrammed **terminal count (TC)** is reached. Your LabVIEW program can read the present count (a 16-bit value) and the state of the output at any time. Versatility is achieved not only through the variety of operating modes, but also through the many ways you can interconnect these signals among counters.

Here are the most useful operating modes, all of which are directly related to the function of the GATE signal. These modes are determined by the **gate parameters**, a cluster input to the CTR Mode Config VI.

- No gating—software starts and stops the counting. Marginally useful because you're at the mercy of the response time of software.

- Level gating—counting proceeds when GATE is high for high-level gating or low for low-level gating; otherwise, counting is suspended.

- Edge-triggered gating—counting starts when a GATE transition occurs. Positive or negative edge triggering is selectable.

- Terminal count gating—counting starts and/or stops when the next lower-order counter reaches its terminal count. Permits cascading of counters.

The terminal count action can also be programmed by the CTR Mode Config VI, which has two modes:

- Toggled—each time the counter reaches its terminal count, the output state is complemented (i.e., it toggles). Terminal count can be 65,535 (counting up) or zero (counting down).

- Pulsed—each time the counter reaches its terminal count, a single pulse is generated. The pulse width is equal to one cycle of the SOURCE signal and is high during that interval; it is low otherwise.

CTR Mode Config allows you to change the timebase configuration by effectively connecting the SOURCE input to one of several signals.

- Internal frequency—SOURCE connected to an on-board clock, with a choice of 100 Hz, 1 kHz, 10 kHz, 100 kHz, or 1 MHz. Can be very useful in frequency and time measurements.

- SOURCE or GATE signal of another counter—useful for sharing one input pin among several counters.

- OUT signal of counter n-1—allows cascading of counters. Especially useful when you need to count beyond 16 bits (65,535 counts).

As you can see, there are many possible interconnections and modes available. The way I set up a new application (assuming it's one that isn't in the examples) is to start with a timing diagram, a traditional tool for digital logic design. Then, I try to sketch out a schematic showing how the counters and signals should be interconnected. I make note of each counter's modes of operation, signal polarities, and clock sources. Finally, I study the options available in the configuration VIs and map my design into LabVIEW parameters. For each of the examples that follow, I'll show you a timing diagram and a simple schematic to help clarify the setup.

Event Counter

Say that your job is to count Widgets coming down a conveyor belt, logging the running total to disk every minute. One solution uses a photoelectric switch and a **totalizing counter**. Figure 6-39 shows the timing diagram and schematic for this application. The transistor in the photoelectric switch turns off when the light beam is interrupted by a passing Widget, resulting in a high level (+5 V) input at pin 41. As long as the VI is running, the counters are enabled. Two counters are cascaded (TC from the first feeds the SOURCE of the second) to permit a maximum Widget count of $2^{32}-1$, or about four billion. Every minute or so, the software should read the count and log it to disk. Interfacing for a simple transistor-output photoelectric switch is shown, along with the pin numbers for an NB-MIO-16 board.

Figure 6-40 shows the panel and diagram for the VI that performs these tasks. It's derived from the counter/timer example VI, Concatenated Counters. As usual, there's little reason to start from scratch on a problem like this when you can steal a perfectly good example VI. The diagram is fairly complex at first glance, but it's really a left-to-right

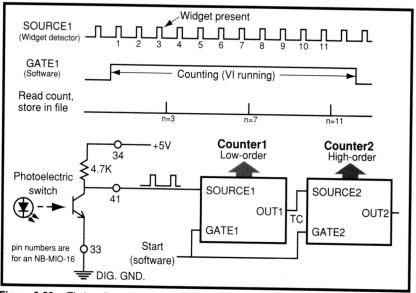

Figure 6-39. Timing diagram and block diagram for a cascaded, totalizing counter application.

sequence of intermediate DAQ VIs and a few file utilities, all linked by error clusters, DAQ task IDs, and file refnums. Let's go through it step by step. On the panel, there are just a few controls: the device, the counter numbers, and the storage interval. You must select two counters that are in sequence, e.g., 1 and 2 for *Counter 1* and *Counter 2*, respectively. If you want to use the last counter on your board (number 5 on an MIO board) as *Counter 1*, then *Counter 2* must be number 1. The VI runs until an error is detected or the *STOP* button is pressed.

1. The CTR Group Config VI allocates the desired pair of counters, and returns a task ID for use by the other DAQ functions.

2. The low-order counter is configured by the CTR Mode Config VI. It's set to count continuously (software sets the state of the GATE input to start and stop counting), and the timebase is set to the SOURCE input pin on the board's connector. The *Widget detector* is wired to that pin.

3. The CTR Mode Config VI is called again to configure the second, high-order counter. Its source is the terminal count output of counter n-1, which is the low-order counter. Thus, every time the low-order counter overflows (reaches 65,535), the high-order counter is incremented by one.

4. The data file is created by the file I/O utility VI, Open/Create/Replace File. It uses error I/O, which integrates nicely with the DAQ operations.

5. The CTR Control VI issues a start command to the group of counters, thus enabling the GATE input to the low-order counter. Widget counting begins.

6. Inside the While Loop, CTR Control reads the current count in each of the counters. It returns an array with element zero belonging to the low-order counter.

7. Values from the individual counters are combined mathematically into a value that is displayed and also formatted for saving in a text file.

8. The total count is appended to the data file by the Write File+ (String) VI, another of the file I/O utilities.

9. After the While Loop terminates (due to an error or someone pressing the STOP button), the Close File+ VI closes the data file.

10. CTR Control stops the counting operation.

11. A possible improvement to this VI would be to add timestamps to each data record.

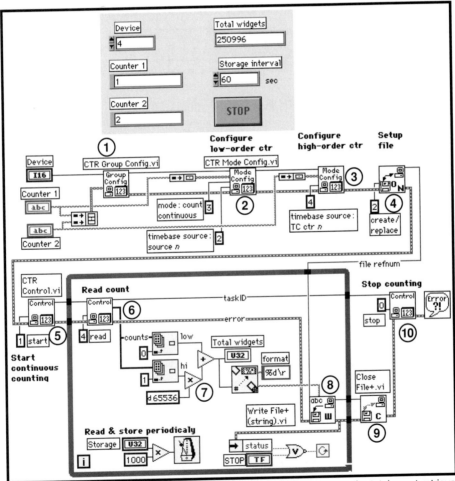

Figure 6-40. The cascaded, totalizing timer application periodically stores the total count retrieved from a cascaded pair of counters.

Interval, Duration, and Period Timers

Another measurement that you might want to make on your Widget assembly line is the **interval** between Widgets, to make sure that they don't start crashing into one another. The timing diagram and schematic are shown in Figure 6-41. An onboard clock with known frequency is applied to the SOURCE input, and the counter is configured for *period* mode. The gate mode is then configured for *low level*, so the counter accumulates clock pulses as long as the GATE signal is low. In our application, this condition is true so long as no Widgets are present. All you need to do is read the value in the counter, and multiply by the period of the clock signal to obtain the time interval between Widgets.

This same circuit also measures duration or period, in addition to interval, depending upon how the counter responds to the GATE signal. If you set the gate mode to rising or falling edge, you will measure the *period* of the GATE signal. If you set the gate mode to high level, you will measure the *duration* of the GATE signal (the time that it is high). Using these semantics, interval plus duration equals period.

The VI that implements the interval/duration/period counter is shown in Figure 6-42. Only one counter is required, though you can cascade them to count longer intervals. The input signal (Widget detector) is connected to the GATE pin of the chosen counter. **Timebase freq** must be set to one of the valid onboard clock settings (100 Hz, 1 kHz, 10 kHz, 100 kHz, or 1 MHz). Selecting too high a clock frequency will cause a counter overflow when the interval exceeds 65,535 clock periods. The **Measure mode** ring control lets you choose the mode in which the counter operates.

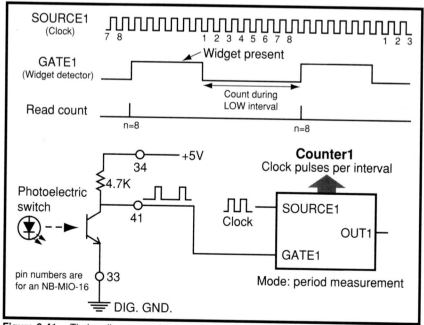

Figure 6-41.   Timing diagram and schematic for an interval/duration/period timer.

Possible values are:

> 0—High level (duration)
>
> 1—Low Level (interval)
>
> 2—Rising edge (period)
>
> 3—Falling edge (period)

These map nicely into the gate mode settings permitted by CTR Mode Config. For informational purposes, the number of **Timebase edges counted** is displayed. The measurement is scaled to seconds for the **Time** display. Here are the intricate details of this VI's operation.

1. The CTR Group Config VI allocates the counter, and returns a task ID for use by the other DAQ functions.

2. A gate parameter cluster is assembled as an input for CTR Mode Config. The **gate mode** is determined by the **Measure mode** control. Adding two to the value of the ring control puts the counter in the proper mode. **Gate action** is set to start/stop, so the counter accumulates counts only during the event specified by the **gate mode**.

3. The CTR Mode Config VI configures the counter. The counter mode is set to period measurement, and the timebase source is set to use one of the internal clock frequencies. Timebase frequency is determined by a front panel control.

4. The CTR Control VI issues a start command to the counter. Counting begins as soon as the **gate mode** condition is satisfied.

5. Inside the While Loop, CTR Control waits for the completion of one period measurement, then reads the count. It returns an array with element zero being the only available value. The While Loop cycles at a rate limited by the period of the input signal, or the maximum update rate of the graphics on the panel, if that's slower. You could put a timer in the loop to better regulate the update rate.

6. The number of clock pulses read from the counter is divided by the clock rate in hertz to yield time in seconds, the value we want.

7. After the While Loop terminates, the CTR Control VI stops the counting operation.

This is a pretty useful VI—I put it on the diskette that goes with this book. You can use it for all kinds of interval and period measurements. All you have to watch out for is counter overflow. A low-frequency signal, combined with a high-frequency clock, will eventually overflow the 16-bit counter. If that becomes a problem, you could either cascade counters or add some really tricky logic that automatically chooses the fastest usable clock speed— a kind of autoranging operation. Also note that you can make a simple frequency counter by selecting one of the edge (period) modes. Take the reciprocal of period in seconds and you have frequency in hertz. A better frequency counter is discussed later in this chapter.

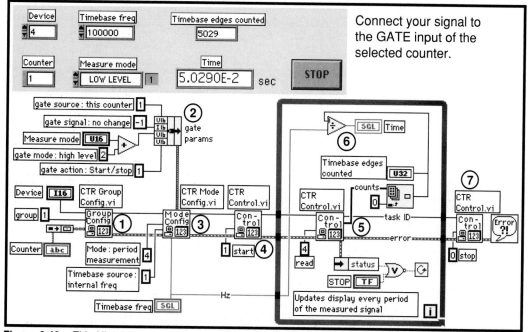

Figure 6-42. This VI measures intervals or durations, depending on the setting of the *Trigger mode* control. Resolution and range are determined by the *Timebase freq* setting. The panel shows the results obtained with a 10 Hz input signal, measuring the low-level interval, which is 50 ms.

Pulse Generation

Another mode of operation for the counter/timers is **pulse generation**. You can generate single pulses (also known as one-shot mode) or continuous pulse trains. The only additional intermediate-level VI that you need for pulse generation is CTR Pulse Config. You have direct control over duty cycle and frequency for continuous generation, or you can use the cluster of **low-level parameters** to define the pulse characteristics in more detail. If you leave all of its inputs disconnected, CTR Pulse Config simply returns all of the present settings.

Figure 6-43 is a simple pulse train generator, taken from the example VI, Pulse Generator. You preset the controls, then run the VI. A pulse train with the selected characteristics is continuously generated until the STOP button is pressed. (The complete example VI allows you to change parameters on the fly.) Here are the steps required to generate a pulse train:

1. The CTR Group Config VI allocates the counter, and returns a task ID for use by the other DAQ functions.

2. The CTR Pulse Config VI sets the duty cycle and frequency. The **pulse mode** is set to 2, continuous pulse generation.

3. The CTR Control VI starts the signal generation.

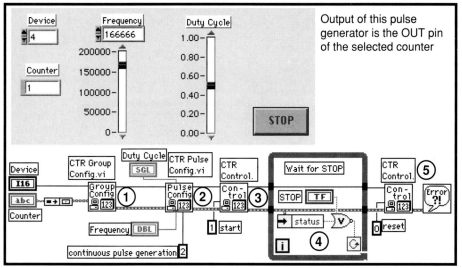

Figure 6-43.   A simple, continuous pulse generator. With my NB-MIO-16X, it generates clean pulses with a variable duty cycle up to 166 kHz.

4. The program waits in the While Loop until the STOP button is pressed. The loop terminates immediately if an incoming error occurred.

5. After the While Loop terminates, CTR Control stops the pulse generation.

If you only want to generate one pulse, you can change the pulse mode at the second step to 1, single pulse generation. There is another example VI, Single Pulse, that clearly shows this mode of operation. You can have more than one pulse generator running simultaneously as long as they use separate counters.

Frequency Counter

Frequency counting is another application area where counter/timers are effective. There are several ways to implement a frequency counter, one of which was noted in the interval/ period measurement example above. That method is very effective at low frequencies: you only have to wait for one period of the unknown signal to pass before you obtain a measurement. The disadvantage of that approach is that, as the input frequency increases towards that of the clock frequency, resolution goes to zero.

Another technique, commonly found in benchtop frequency counters, uses a fixed *gate time* (for example, 1 s) during which edges of the unknown signal are counted. The reciprocal of the count is frequency. This method works best at *high* frequencies; as frequency goes to zero, resolution goes to zero. A 10 s gate time yields 0.1 Hz resolution; a 1 s gate time yields 1.0 Hz resolution. Figure 6-44 shows the timing diagram and schematic for the high-frequency counting technique. It's really a combination of two previous examples—a pulse generator to make the gate signal, and a cascaded event counter. The unknown signal frequency can be as high as 6.9 MHz (limited by the STC

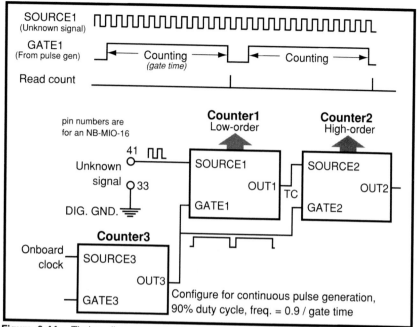

Figure 6-44. Timing diagram and schematic for a frequency counter with a fixed gate time. It requires a pulse generator for the gate and a cascaded event counter to count the unknown pulses during the gate high interval.

chip). To go faster, you must add an outboard **prescaler**, a divide-by-n counter based on digital logic ICs with sufficient speed for your application. You might also want to add signal conditioning (an amplifier and comparator) to clean up the raw signal.

The top-level VI for the frequency counter is shown in Figure 6-45. I started out by prototyping this VI with all of the code on one big diagram. That's convenient for development, but it was way too big to display here, and it was also harder to understand. Since the VI uses two other techniques that are well understood—pulse generation and event counting—I encapsulated those operations in subVIs, which are described separately. As you can see, this example is easier to understand than it would have been with all that complexity on one diagram.

Here's how it works.

1. A subVI, FCounter- Gate Gen, sets up and starts a continuous pulse generation task. The TC output of the pulse generator is the gate for the cascaded event counter.

2. A second subVI, FCounter- Setup Counters, configures a pair of cascaded counters, then starts them.

3. Inside the While Loop, CTR Control reads the current count in each of the counters. It returns an array, with element zero being the low-order counter.

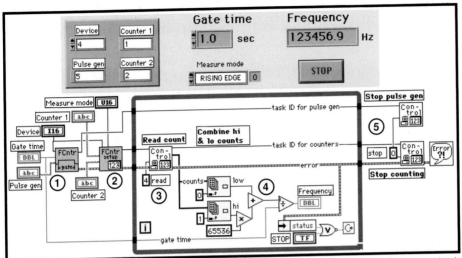

Figure 6-45. The frequency counter VI. It's based on two subVIs: a continuous pulse generator to make the gate and concatenated counters to count the incoming events.

4. Values from the individual counters are combined mathematically into a single value, the number of counts that occurred during the gate interval. Dividing this number by the gate interval yields frequency in hertz.

5. After the While Loop terminates, CTR Control stops the pulse generation and the counting operation.

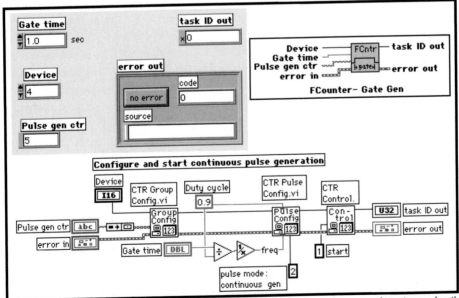

Figure 6-46. SubVI for the frequency counter that generates a continuous pulse stream for the counter's gate. The pulse waveform has a 90% duty cycle.

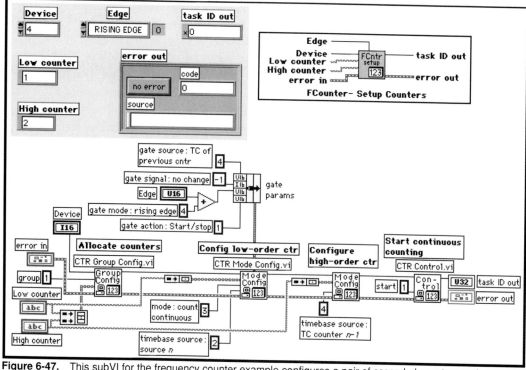

Figure 6-47. This subVI for the frequency counter example configures a pair of cascaded counters and starts the counting operation. They are gated by the TC of the previous counter, which is assumed to be the pulse generator.

Now, let's look inside the two subVIs. It should come as no surprise that their diagrams resemble the diagrams of two previous examples that we've seen. The continuous pulse generation VI is shown in Figure 6-46. Like its cousin in Figure 6-43, the counter is allocated by CTR Group Config, and then CTR Pulse Config sets the frequency and duty cycle. Finally, CTR Control starts pulse generation. The only trick here is setting up the duty cycle and frequency. A 90% duty cycle (counting incoming pulses 90% of the time) is a reasonable value, though you could probably increase it without doing any harm. The other 10% of the time is available to reset the event counters. Gate time is defined as the high duration of each cycle. Dividing by duty cycle yields period, and the reciprocal of period is frequency.

The other subVI, FCounter- Setup Counters, is shown in Figure 6-47. It is much like the setup portion of the event counter example. The only differences are in the gate and timebase sources. The low-order counter is configured with its gate coming from the TC of the previous counter, which is assumed to be the pulse generator. It's up to the user to enter a valid **Low counter** choice that pairs off correctly with that of the pulse generator. For instance, on my MIO-16, using **Low counter** = 1 requires the pulse generator to be counter number 5. Similarly, the **High counter** must be the next counter higher than the **Low counter**. You could probably write a subVI to figure out valid counter numbers to save the user from choosing invalid combinations.

Timebase source for the low-order counter is source n, which is the external input pin—the unknown signal we wish to count. The high-order counter receives its timebase from the TC output of the low-order counter, as usual, thus cascading the two. The last step in this subVI is starting the continuous counting operation.

I hope this chapter has given you insight into the diverse applications of the DAQ library. Over the years, I've found that the library is very flexible, and that it keeps getting better with each release of LabVIEW. With a couple of plug-in boards, you can handle a very large number of applications. In the next chapter, we'll look at some designs for generic data acquisition applications, some of which use the DAQ library.

Writing a Data Acquisition Program

I'm going to bet that your first LabVIEW application was (or will be) some kind of data acquisition system. I say that because data acquisition is by far the most common LabVIEW application. Every experiment or process has signals to be measured, monitored, analyzed, and logged, and each signal has its own special requirements. While it's impossible to design a universal data acquisition system to fit every situation, there are plenty of common architectures that you can use, each containing elements that you can incorporate into your own problem-solving toolkit.

As I mentioned in the preface, what you'll learn here are all the *other* things that the manuals and examples don't cover. The act of fetching data from an input device is the easy part, and it's a subject that is already well discussed. On the other hand, how do you keep track of channel assignments and other configuration information? And how does data analysis affect program design? These topics are important, yet rarely mentioned. Time to change all that.

Your data acquisition application might include some control (output) functionality as well. Most experiments have some things that need to be manipulated—some valves, a power supply setpoint, or maybe a stepper motor. That should be no problem so long as you spend some time designing your program with the expectation that you will need some control features. If your situation requires a great deal of control functionality, read Chapter 8, *Process Control Applications*, to see some methods that may work better than simply adding on to a data acquisition design.

Plan your application like any other, going through the recommended steps. I've added a few items to the procedure that emphasize special considerations for data acquisition: **data analysis, throughput**, and **configuration management** requirements. Here are the basic steps.

1. Define and understand the problem; define the signals and determine what the data analysis needs are.

2. Specify the type of I/O hardware you will need, and then determine sample rates and total throughput.

3. Prototype the user interface and decide how to manage configurations.

4. Design, and then write the program.

If your system requires extra versatility, like the ability to quickly change channel assignments or types of I/O hardware, then you will need to include features to manage the system's **configuration**. Users should be able to access a few simple controls rather than having to edit the diagram when a configuration change is needed.

Data **throughput**, the aggregate sampling rate measured in samples per second, plays a dominant role in determining the architecture of your program. High sampling rates can severely limit your ability to do real-time analysis and graphics. Even low-speed systems can be problematic when you require accurate timing. Fortunately, there are plenty of hardware and software solutions available in the LabVIEW world.

The reason for assembling a data acquisition system is to **acquire** data, and the reason for acquiring data is to **analyze** it. Surprisingly, these facts are often overlooked. Planning to include analysis features and appropriate file formats will save you (and the recipients of your data) a lot of grief.

A diagram for a simple, yet complete, data acquisition program is shown in Figure 7-1. It begins with a VI that handles I/O configuration and the opening of any data files. The rest of the program resides in a While Loop that cycles at a rate determined by the Sample Interval control. The Read Data VI communicates with hardware and returns the raw data, which is then analyzed for display and stored in files. All subVIs that can produce an error condition are linked by an error I/O cluster, and an error handler tells the user what went wrong. Simple as this diagram is, it actually works, and does some rather sophisticated processing at that. Try simplifying your next data acquisition problem to this level of detail. You can add functionality as required, but keep things modular so that it's easy to understand and modify.

Data Analysis and Storage

Data analysis has a different meaning in every application. It depends on the kind of signals you are faced with. For many applications, it means calculating simple statistics (minimum, maximum, mean, standard deviation, etc.) over some period of time. In spectroscopy and chromatography, it means peak detection, curve fitting, and integration. In acoustics and vibration studies, it means Fourier transforms, filtering, and correlation.

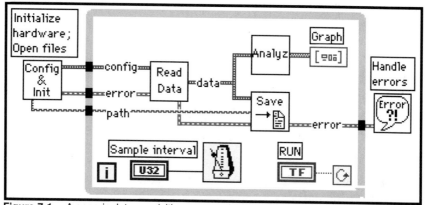

Figure 7-1. A generic data acquisition program includes the functions shown here.

Each type of analysis affects your LabVIEW program design in some way. For instance, doing a Fast-Fourier Transform (FFT) on a large array in real-time requires lots of processing power—your system could become so burdened that data collection may be disrupted. Such analysis drives the performance requirements of your VIs. And everyone worries about timing information, both for real-time analysis and when reading data from files. It's obvious that your program has to measure and store time markers reliably and in a format that is useful to the analysis programs.

What you need to avoid is *analysis by accident*. Time and again I've seen LabVIEW programs that grab data from the hardware and stuff it into a file with no thought about compatibility with the analysis program. Then the poor analyst has to grind along, parsing the file into readable pieces, trying to reconstitute important features of the data set. Sometimes, the important information isn't available on disk at all, and you *hope* that it has been written down *somewhere*. Disaster! Gastric distress also occurs when a new real-time analysis need crops up and your program is so inflexible that the new features can't be added without major surgery.

I recommend a preemptive strike. When someone proposes a new data acquisition system, make it a point to force them to describe, in detail, how the data will be analyzed. Make sure they understand the implications of storing the megabytes of data that an automated data acquisition system may collect. If there is a collective shrug of shoulders, ask them point-blank, "...then why are we collecting data at all?" *Do not write your data acquisition program until you understand the analysis requirements.*

Finally, you can get started. Divide the analysis job into real-time and post-run tasks, and determine how each aspect will affect your program.

Post-Run Analysis

You can analyze data with LabVIEW, another application, or a custom program written in some other language. Sometimes, more than one analysis program will have to read the same data file. In all cases, you need to decide on a suitable **data file format** that your data acquisition program has to write. The file type (e.g., ASCII text or binary), the structure of the data, and the inclusion of timing and configuration information are all important. If other people are involved in the analysis process, get them involved early in the design process. Write down clear file format specifications. Plan to generate sample data files and do plenty of testing. These preliminary steps will assure everyone that the real data will transfer without problems.

It's a good idea to structure your program so that a single *data saver* VI is responsible for writing a given data file type. You can easily test this data saver module as a stand-alone VI, or call it from a test program before your final application is completed. The result is a module with a clear purpose that is reliable and reusable.

You might be able to use the automatic front panel datalogging features of LabVIEW. They are very easy to use. All you have to do is click on the datalogging icon in the execution palette for a subVI that displays the data you wish to save. Every time that the subVI finishes executing (even if its front panel is not displayed), the front panel data is appended to the current log file. The first time the subVI is called, you will receive a dialog asking for a new datalog file. You can also open the subVI and change log files through the **Data Logging...** submenu in the File menu. To access logged data, you can use the file I/O functions (described below), or you can place the subVI of interest in a new diagram and choose **Enable Database Access** from its pop-up menu. You can then read the datalog records one at a time. All of the front panel controls are available—they are in a cluster that is conveniently accessed by Unbundle By Name.

LabVIEW can read and write any file format (refer to Chapter 3, *LabVIEW Programming Techniques*, in the section on Files, for a general discussion of file I/O). Which data format to use depends on the program that has to read it.

Datalog Format

If you plan to analyze data only in LabVIEW, the easiest and most compact format is the **datalog file**. A datalog file contains a sequence of binary data **records**. All records in a given file are of the same type, but a record can be a complex data structure, for instance a cluster containing strings and arrays. The record type is determined when you create the file using **New File**. You can read records one at a time in a random-access fashion, or read several at once, in which case they are returned as an array. This gives your analysis program the ability to use the data file like a simple database, searching for desired records based on one or more key fields in each record, such as a time stamp. Figure 7-2 shows a simple data saver VI that uses datalogs. It combines two arrays of data, a Boolean status input, and a timestamp into a cluster that defines the datalog format.

The disadvantage of datalog format files is that they can only be read by LabVIEW or by a custom-written program. However, you can easily write a translator in LabVIEW that reads your datalog format and writes out files with another format. Another hazard (common to all binary file formats) is that you must know the data type used when the file was written; otherwise you may never be able to decipher the file.

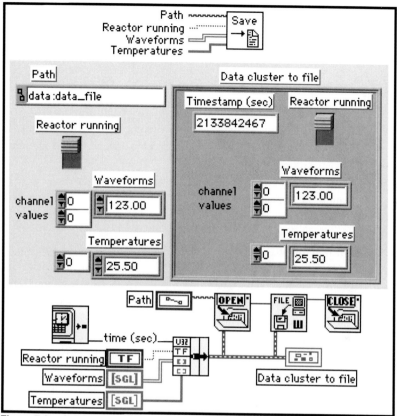

Figure 7-2. A data saver VI that writes several data items to a LabVIEW datalog file.

ASCII Text Format

Good old **ASCII text** files are your best bet for portable data files. Almost every application can load data from a text file that has simple formatting. The ubiquitous **tab-delimited text** format is a likely choice. Format your data values as strings with a tab character between each value and place a carriage return at the end of the line; then write it out. The only other thing you need to determine is the type of header information to enter. Simple graphing and spreadsheet applications are happy with column names as the first line in the file:

```
Date     Time       Channel_1    Channel_2
5-13-82  01:17:34   5.678        -13.43
5-13-82  01:17:44   5.665        -13.58
```

A spreadsheet could be programmed to interpret all kinds of header information, if you need to include more. Other applications are less versatile with respect to headers, so be sure you know who's going to be reading your file.

The disadvantages of ASCII text files are that they are bulkier than binary files, and they take much longer to read and write (often *several hundred times* longer) because each value has to be converted to and from strings of characters For high-speed data recording applications, text files are out of the question. You *might* be able to store a few thousand samples per second as text on a fast computer, but be sure to benchmark carefully before committing yourself to text files.

Custom Binary Formats

LabVIEW can write files with arbitrary binary formats to suit other applications. If you can handle the requisite programming, binary files are really worthwhile—high on performance and very compact. It's also nice to open a binary file with an analysis program and have it load without any special translation.

Binary file handlers require significant programming experience. Even if you have all the formatting information, be prepared to spend time working out the programming details. Manufacturers will generally supply you with some kind of description of their application's native binary file format if you ask the right person. Usually, you will get some kind of program listing that was lifted from their file I/O routines. If the company is interested in making their file format public, they will supply an application note and sometimes even machine-readable code. The folks at **Wavemetrics** supply all this information for **Igor** (their analysis and graphing package for the Mac) with the application. Because the information was available, the VIs to read and write Igor binary were easy to create and are now public domain. Figure 7-3 shows the panel for the VI that writes an SGL floating-point array as an Igor binary file. The diagram is very complex, so it's not shown. You can obtain these Igor support VIs from Wavemetrics, National Instruments, or the various FTP servers via Internet. By the way, Igor can also read arbitrary binary formats (simple ones, at least) directly through an external operation (XOP) called GBLoadWave. With that capability, you can write your LabVIEW data as simple binary arrays then load it right into Igor with no special programming whatsoever.

Some binary formats like the Igor format described above are unsuitable for continuous data acquisition, in which you would like to append records one at a time as the experiment proceeds. They are designed for single-shot experiments where the entire file is written at once. This is fine for single buffers of data from an oscilloscope, but less useful for a simple data logger. Buffering data in memory (in arrays) is one way to solve this problem, but if your computer should crash, that data might be lost. You could rewrite the entire file occasionally to avoid such a catastrophe if you are forced to use one of these single-shot formats. On the other hand, if you are *not* stuck with such a predefined format, it is easy and efficient to write continuously to a binary file as you can see by examining the techniques used in the DAQ disk streaming example VIs.

Time Stamps

Most data that we collect is a function of time. Therefore, timing information needs to be stored along with the data in your files. The precision or resolution of these time stamps is driven by the requirements of your experiment and the limitations of LabVIEW's timing functions. The time stamp format is determined by the application that reads the data file.

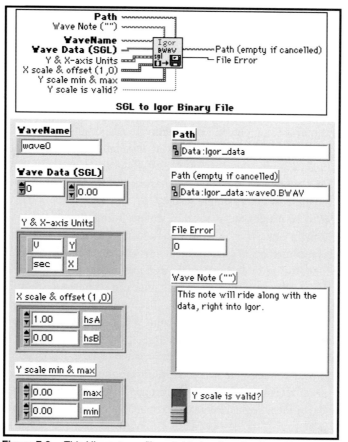

Figure 7-3. This VI creates a file suitable for direct loading with Wavemetrics' Igor.

Consider an ordinary data logging application where a few dozen channels are stored to disk as ASCII text every few seconds. A resolution of one second is probably adequate, and a source for this timing information is Get Date/Time In Seconds, or one of the other built-in timing functions. You can then format the returned value as seconds relative to 1-Jan-1904 or, as seconds relative to the start of your experiment, or divide it by 60 to obtain minutes, and so forth. Saving a simple numeric time stamp has the advantage that it is easy to interpret. If you use a spreadsheet application that can manipulate time and date formats (like mm/dd/yy hh:mm:ss), then Get Date/Time String may be appropriate.

For more resolution, you can use the Decimal Hours VI described in Chapter 4, *Building an Application*. It resolves one millisecond (limited by your computer's capability) and returns the time as a floating point value. You can get similar results by using the simple Tick Count (ms) function, which returns a relative number of milliseconds. The uncertainty of these higher-resolution timers depends on your machine and on LabVIEW's work load. You may want to do some testing if you need really accurate software-derived time stamps.

Data that is acquired at a constant rate (periodic sampling) needs a timestamp only at the beginning of the collection period because the time at any sample is easily calculated. There is no reason to store a timestamp with every sample if you already know the sample interval with acceptable precision; it would just take up extra disk space. Only data that is taken aperiodically requires such detailed timestamp information.

Sampling rates higher than about 10 Hz usually are handled by data acquisition hardware (or smart I/O subsystems) because there is too much timing uncertainty in fast LabVIEW loops on general-purpose computers. Using hardware can simplify your time-stamping requirements. Because you know that the hardware is sampling at a steady rate, there is no need to store a time stamp for every sample period. Rather, you need only save an initial time and a value for the sampling interval. The data analysis program should then be able to reconstruct the timebase from this simple scheme.

A technique used in *really* fast diagnostics is to add a timing **fiducial** pulse to one or more data channels. Also known as a *fid*, it is a pulse that occurs at some critical time during the experiment and is recorded on all systems (and maybe on all channels, as well). It's much the same as the room full of soldiers where the commander says, "Synchronize watches." For example, when testing explosives, a fiducial pulse is distributed to all of the diagnostic systems just before detonation. For analog data channels, the fiducial pulse can be coupled to each channel through a small capacitor, creating a small *glitch* in the data at the critical moment. You can even synchronize nonelectronic systems by generating a suitable stimulus, like flashing a strobe in front of a movie or video camera. Fiducials are worth considering any time you need absolute synchronization among disparate systems. One more thing. If you need accurate time-of-day information, be sure to reset the computer clock before the experiment begins. Personal computer clocks are notorious for their long-term drift.

Passing Along Configuration Information

Your analysis program may need information about the configuration of the experiment or software that generated the data. In many cases, channel names are all that are needed, and you can pass them along as the column titles in a spreadsheet file. Beyond that, you have two basic choices: use a separate **configuration file** or add a **file header** to each data file. Both methods are highly dependent upon the ability of the analysis program to read and interpret the information.

Binary files almost always have headers because the program that reads them needs information about the type and location of the data within. Here is an example of the kind of information contained in a binary file header (taken from Igor's native file format):

Wave name
Data type (single or double-precision)
Data file version (to avoid incompatibility with future versions)
Y-axis and X-axis units
Number of data points
Y-axis and X-axis scaling

Modification date

Flag to indicate whether user comments follow the data segment

As always, the format of this binary file header will be highly specified on a byte-by-byte basis. You need to make sure that each item is of the proper data type and length before writing the header out to the file. An effective way to do this is to assemble all the items into a cluster, **Type Cast** it (see Chapter 3, *LabVIEW Programming Techniques*) to a string, then write it out using bytestream mode with Write File function.

For text files, generating a header is as simple as writing out a series of strings that have been formatted to contain the desired information. Reading and *decoding* a text-format header, on the other hand, can be quite challenging for any program. If you simply want an experimental record or free-form "notepad" header for purposes of documentation, that's no problem. But parsing information out of the header for programmatic use requires careful design of the header's format. Many graphing and analysis programs can do little more than read blocks of text into a long string for display purposes; they have little or no capacity for parsing the string. Spreadsheets (and of course programming languages) can search for patterns, extract numbers from strings, and so forth, but not if the format is poorly defined. Therefore, you need to work on both ends of the data analysis problem—reading as well as writing—to make sure that things will play together.

Another solution to this header problem is to use what I call an **index file**, which is separate from the data file. The index file contains all the information necessary to successfully load the data. It can also contain configuration information. The data file can be binary or ASCII format, containing only the data values. I've used this technique on several projects, and it adds some versatility. If the index file is ASCII text, then you can print it out to see what's in the data file. Also, the data file may be more easily loaded into programs that would otherwise choke on header information. You still have the problem of loading the configuration, but at least the data can be loaded and the configuration is safely stored on disk. One caution: don't lose one of the files!

The configuration file can be formatted for direct import into a spreadsheet and used as a printable record of the experiment. This turns out to be quite useful. What I try to produce is a complete description of the hardware setup used for a given test, including module types, channel assignments, gain settings, and so forth. Here's what a simple configuration file might look like:

```
Source expt   TEST   08-SEP-1992 21:18:51.00   Maxima:TEST
File       Module ID   Slot Crate   Signal Name       Chan   Units
TEST0.T   KSC 3525     1    1       TC1               1      Deg C
TEST0.T   KSC 3525     1    1       TC2               2      Deg C
TEST0.T   KSC 3525     1    1       TC3               3      Deg C
TEST0.T   KSC 3525     1    1       Upper src temp    4      Deg C
TEST0.T   KSC 3525     1    1       Lower src temp    5      Deg C
END
```

When the experimenter has a question regarding the signal connections, I can refer to this list, which is usually clipped into the laboratory log book. We'll discuss some methods for generating configuration files later in this chapter.

Real-Time Analysis and Display

LabVIEW's extensive library of built-in analysis functions makes it easy to process and display your newly acquired data in real-time. You are limited by only two things: your system's performance and your imagination. Analysis and presentation are the things that make this whole business of virtual instrumentation useful. You can turn a voltmeter into a stripchart recorder, an oscilloscope into a spectrum analyzer, and a multifunction plug-in board into... just about anything. Here, we'll look at the general problems and approaches to real-time analysis and display. Later chapters will discuss particular applications.

Once again, we've got the old battle over the precise definition of **real-time**. It is wholly dependent upon your application. If one-minute updates for analysis and display are enough, then *one minute* is real-time. If you need millisecond updates, then *that's* real-time, too. What matters is that you understand the fundamental limitations of your computer, I/O hardware, and LabVIEW with regard to performance and response time.

For reference, Table 7-1 lists a few simple LabVIEW benchmarks that might help you decide what to include in your real-time VIs. I made these measurements on my Macintosh Quadra 950, which is of course a 33 MHz 68040, running System 7.1. Audrey Harvey of National Instruments wrote an informal report called *Benchmarking and Performance in LabVIEW Data Acquisition Applications* that goes into great detail on this subject if you're really interested

Table 7-1. LabVIEW for Macintosh Benchmarks In Order of Increasing Execution Time.

Test	Execution Time
Empty For Loop	0.393 µs
Calling an empty VI	0.7 µs
Read a numeric from a global	4.83 µs
Waveform Chart, one channel (default size)	500.0 µs
Read a DBL array global (1000 values)	527.0 µs
Update numeric indicator I32 display (default size)	1.33 ms
Standard Deviation (1000 values)	1.9 ms
Linear Fit (1000 values)	2.0 ms
Butterworth filter (1000 values)	17.0 ms
Real FFT (1024 values)	39.0 ms
Waveform graph, 1000 values (default size; autoscale)	47.0 ms
Amplitude and Phase Spectrum (1000 values)	79.0 ms
Read a string array global (1000 strings)	130.0 ms

Table 7-2. Signal Types and Analysis Examples.

Signal Type	Typical Analysis
Analog–DC	Scaling
	Statistics
	Curve Fitting
Analog–Time Domain	Scaling
	Statistics
	Filtering
	Peak Detection and Counting
	Pulse parameters
Analog–Frequency Domain	Filtering
	Windowing
	FFT/Power Spectrum
	Convolution/Deconvolution
	Joint Time-Frequency Analysis
Digital On-Off	Logic
Digital Pulse Train	Counting
	Statistics
	Time Measurement
	Frequency Measurement

The nature of your signals and the information you want to extract (Table 7-2) determine the kind of analysis you need to perform. About 150 analysis functions are available in LabVIEW's Functions menu (Figure 7-4). Other functions (and useful combinations of the regular ones) are available from the examples, the Additional Files library, and from others who support LabVIEW through the Alliance Program. If you ever need an analysis function that seems "obvious" or generally useful, be sure to contact National Instruments to find out if it's already available. They also take suggestions—user input is really what makes this analysis palette grow.

Continuous vs. Single-Shot Data Analysis

Data acquisition may involve either **continuous data** or **single-shot data**. Continuous data generally arrives one sample at a time, like readings from a voltmeter. It is usually displayed on something like a strip chart, and probably would be stored to disk as a time-dependent history. Single-shot data arrives as a big buffer, or block of samples, like a waveform from an oscilloscope. It is usually displayed on a graph, and each shot would be stored as a complete unit, possibly in its own file. Analysis techniques for these two data types may have some significant differences.

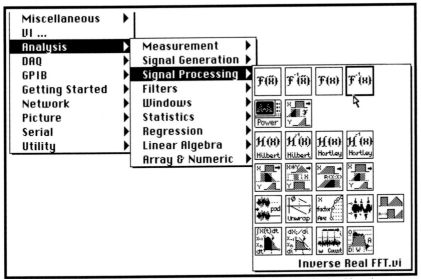

Figure 7-4. The Analysis part of the Functions menu contains hundreds of functions.

There is a special form of continuous data that I call **block-mode continuous data** where you continuously acquire measurements, but only load them into your LabVIEW program, as a block or buffer, whenever some quantity of measurements have accumulated. Multiple buffering or circular buffering can be carried out by any smart instrument. The advantage of block-mode buffered operation is reduced I/O overhead: you only need to fetch data when a buffer is half full, rather than fetching each individual sample. The disadvantage is the added latency between acquisition of the oldest data in the buffer and the transfer of that data to the program for processing. For analysis purposes, you may treat this data as either continuous or single-shot since it has some properties of both.

Here is an example of the difference between processing continuous versus single-shot data. Let's say that your main interest is finding the mean and standard deviation of a time-variant analog signal. This is really quite easy to do, you notice, because LabVIEW just happens to have a statistical VI called **S**tandard Deviation which also computes the mean. So far so good.

Single-Shot Data

A single buffer of data from the desired channel is acquired using the AI Acquire Waveform VI with a plug-in board. This subVI returns a numeric array containing a sequence of samples, a waveform, taken at a specified sample rate. To compute the statistics, wire the array to the Standard Deviation VI and display the results. Problem solved (Figure 7-5).

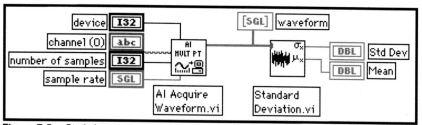

Figure 7-5. Statistics are easy to calculate using the built-in Standard Deviation function when data is acquired as a single-shot (or buffer). This example shows a case using AI Acquire Waveform from the easy-I/O DAQ library.

Continuous Data

As shown in Figure 7-6, you can collect one sample per cycle of the While Loop by calling **AI Single Scan**. If you want to use the Standard Deviation VI, you have to put all of the samples into an array and wait until the While Loop finishes running—not exactly a real-time computation. Or, you could build the array one sample at a time in a shift register and call Standard Deviation each time. That may seem OK, but the array grows without limit until the loop stops—a waste of memory at best, a major problem if LabVIEW runs out of memory altogether. The best solution is to create a different version of the mean and standard deviation algorithm, one that uses an **incremental** calculation.

I wrote a function called Running Mean & Sigma VI that recomputes the statistics each time it is called by maintaining intermediate computations in uninitialized shift registers (Figure 7-7). It is fast and efficient, storing just three numbers in the shift registers. A *Reset* switch sets the intermediate values to zero to clear the function's memory. The idea came right out of the user manual for my HP-45 calculator, proving that inspiration is wherever you find it. Algorithms for this and hundreds of other problems are available in many textbooks, and in the popular *Numerical Recipes* series [Ref. 1]. You can use the concept shown here for other continuous data analysis problems—note that it's included on the disk with this book.

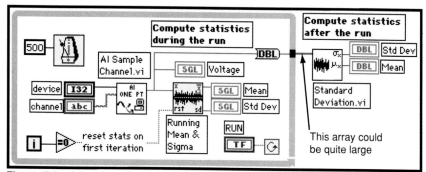

Figure 7-6. I had to write a special function, Running Mean & Sigma, that accumulated and calculated statistics during execution of a continuous data acquisition process. Building an array for post-run calculations consumes much memory.

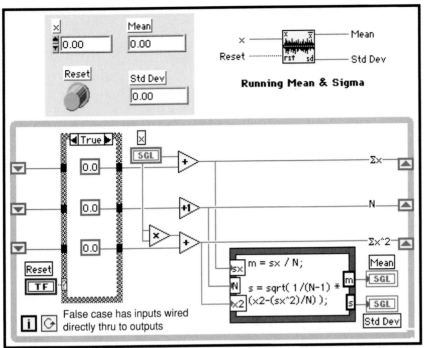

Figure 7-7. Running Mean & Sigma calculates statistics on an incremental basis by storing intermediate computations in uninitialized shift registers. The Reset switch clears the registers.

Faster Analysis and Display

Real-time analysis may involve significant amounts of mathematical computation. Digital Signal Processing (DSP) functions, such as the Fast Fourier Transform (FFT) and image processing functions, operate on large arrays of data and may require many seconds even on the fastest computers. If execution time becomes a problem, you can:

- Make sure that you are using the most efficient computation techniques.

- Figure out ways to reduce the amount of data used in the calculations.

- Do the analysis post-run instead of in real-time.

- Get a faster computer.

- Use a DSP coprocessor board.

Some of these options you may reject immediately; e.g., post-processing is of little value when you are trying to do feedback control. On the other hand, if you really *need* that 8192-point power spectrum displayed at 15 Hz, then you had better be using something faster than the average PC. Always be sure that the analysis and display activities don't interfere with acquisition and storage of data.

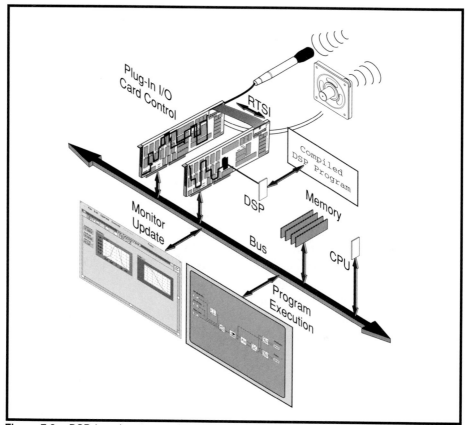

Figure 7-8. DSP boards can speed up some analysis processes. Note that all communications between the DSP board and the computer's CPU and memory (where LabVIEW runs) occur over the bus. This can limit performance.

DSP Boards

A DSP board can speed up many analysis functions, particularly those that act on arrays of data. You should *not* consider them to be general-purpose LabVIEW accelerators, however. Not, at least, until we have a version of LabVIEW that cross-compiles for downloading to and execution on a DSP board. Currently, only the boards from National Instruments and Spectral Innovations (Macintosh only) are fully supported by ready-to-use LabVIEW function libraries. Other manufacturers will probably have LabVIEW support in the future.

DSP boards normally plug into your computer's bus and function as a second bus master or as a slave processor. They have their own onboard memory, their own unique instruction set, and most of them support direct connections to some form of I/O hardware. Data has to be transferred over your computer's bus to main memory for use by LabVIEW. This can be a limiting factor in the actual performance of a DSP board because the data transfer process (even using DMA) may take more time than the actual computations. You should be cautious when it comes to DSP performance specifications. Try to borrow a board or have someone give you a demonstration using data and algorithms that are similar to your application before settling on the DSP solution.

To get the most out of a DSP board, you need to write programs in C or assembly language that execute on the board's CPU. National Instruments has some routines for these applications, called Real-time Instruments, that tie in nicely with LabVIEW. With these routines and a suitable compiler, you can program the DSP board to acquire data, do complex floating-point calculations, drive outputs, and report results to LabVIEW, all with maximum performance. If this sounds like the right solution, contact National Instruments for more information. If you can't do the programming yourself, there may be someone in your organization who can, and there are consultants who specialize in this type of work.

Reducing the Volume of Data

Execution time for most algorithms is roughly proportional to the size of the data arrays. See if you can do something to reduce the size of your arrays, especially when they are to be processed by one of the slower functions. Here are some ideas.

Sample at the minimum rate consistent with the Nyquist criteria. Many times, your data acquisition system will have to sample several channels that have widely different signal bandwidths. You may be able to rewrite the acquisition part of your program so that the low-bandwidth signals are sampled at a slower rate than the high-bandwidth signals. This may be more complex than using a single I/O function that reads all channels at once, but the reduction in array size may be worthwhile.

Process only the meaningful part of the array. Try to develop a technique to locate the interesting part of a long data record and extract only that part by using the Split Array or Array Subset function. Perhaps there is some timing information that points to the start of the important event. Or, you might be able to search for a critical level using Search 1D Array, Peak Detector, or a Histogram function. These techniques are particularly useful for sparse data, such as that received from a seismometer. In seismology, 99.9% of the data is just a noisy baseline containing no useful information. But every so often there is an interesting event that is detected, extracted, and subjected to extensive analysis. This implies a kind of triggering operation. In the DAQ library, there is a software triggering feature whereby data is transferred to the LabVIEW data space only if it passes some triggering criteria, including slope and level. This feature works for plug-in boards that don't have similar hardware triggering functionality.

Data **decimation** is another possible technique. Decimation is a process whereby the elements of an array are divided up into output arrays, like a dealer distributing cards. The Decimate 1D Array function can be sized to produce any number of output arrays. Or, you could write a program that averages every n incoming values into a smaller output array. Naturally, there is a performance price to pay with these techniques; they involve some amount of computation or memory management. Because the output array(s) are not the same size as the input array, new memory buffers must be allocated, and that takes time. But the payoff comes when you finally pass a smaller data array to those very time-consuming analysis VIs.

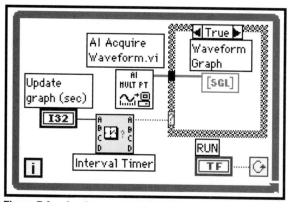

Figure 7-9. Another way to limit update rates using *modulo* arithmetic. Every *n* times, the remainder on the Quotient & Remainder function is zero, allowing the graph to update.

Improving Display Performance

All types of data displays—especially graphs and images—tend to bog down your system. Consider using smaller graphs and images, fewer displayed data points, and less-frequent updates when performance becomes a problem.

The next two figures show ways of reducing the update rates of graphics, or anything else, be it an indicator or a computation. Figure 7-9 fixes the update rate of a graph in terms of a time interval, while Figure 7-10 permits a graph to update every *n* cycles of a data acquisition loop. Yet another way to reduce display overhead is to add an *update display* button connected to the Case structure in lieu of these automatic update techniques.

The displays could also appear in independent top-level VIs that receive data from the main acquisition loop via global variables. This is the Client-Server concept from Chapter 4, *Building an Application*, and it works well here. You write the data (probably an array) to a global variable in the data acquisition loop (the server). Then, another VI

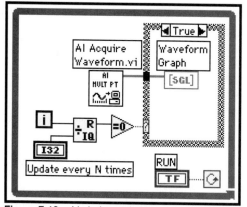

Figure 7-10. Limit the updating rates of graphics (or anything else) by using the Interval Timer VI (Chapter 4). In this case, the graph is replotted only every so many seconds, rather than each time the loop executes.

containing graphs or other displays (the client) reads data from the global variable asynchronously. Analysis can be performed in either or both VIs. The advantage is that the client can be set to execute at lower priority than the server, as well as executing at a slower rate. Also, an arbitrary number of clients can run simultaneously. You could really get carried away and use another global that indicates that the display VI wants an update, thus creating a handshaking arrangement that avoids writing to the global on every acquisition. The disadvantage of the client-server scheme is that it creates even more copies of the data, trading memory usage for speed.

Graphics accelerators are now fairly common. Both the Macintosh and PCs running Windows can use plug-in graphics coprocessor boards that may significantly reduce the overhead associated with updating the display (by as much as a factor of 50 in some cases). LabVIEW still has to figure out where the text, lines, and boxes need to go, and that takes some main CPU time. But the graphics board will do most of the low-level pixel manipulation, which is certainly an improvement. The LabVIEW Preferences item, **Smooth Updates**, makes a difference in display performance and appearance as well. Smooth updates are created through a technique called off-screen bitmaps. On the Macintosh, this is a well-known technique for speeding screen updates. However, if your Mac has an add-on graphics accelerator, smooth updates may actually cause the update time to *increase*. Experiment with this option, and see for yourself.

Sampling and Throughput

How much data do you need to acquire, analyze, display, and store in how much time? The answer to this question is a measure of system **throughput**. Every component of your data acquisition system—hardware and software—affects throughput. We've already looked at some analysis and display considerations. Next, we'll consider the input sampling requirements that determine the basic data generation rate.

Modern instrumentation can generate a veritable flood of data. There are digitizers that can sample at gigahertz rates, filling multimegabyte buffers in a fraction of a second. Even the ubiquitous, low-cost, plug-in data acquisition boards can saturate your computer's bus and disk drives when given a chance. But is that flood of data really useful? Sometimes; it depends on the signals you are sampling.

Signal Bandwidth

As we saw in Chapter 2, *Inputs and Outputs*, every signal has a minimum **bandwidth** and must be sampled at a rate at least two times this bandwidth, and preferably more, to avoid **aliasing**. Remember to include significant out-of-band signals in your determination of sampling rate.

If you can't adequately filter out high-frequency components of the signal or interference, then you will have to sample faster. A higher sampling rate may have an impact on throughput because of the larger amount of raw data that is collected. Evaluate every input to your system and determine what sampling rate is really needed to guarantee high signal fidelity.

Sometimes, you find yourself faced with an overwhelming aggregate sampling rate, like 50 channels at 180 kHz. Then it is time to start asking simple questions like, "is all this data really useful or necessary?" Quite often, you can eliminate some channels because of low priority or redundancy. Or, you may be able to significantly reduce the sampling rate for some channels by lowering the cutoff frequency of the analog lowpass filter in the signal conditioner. Just because *some* channels need to go fast doesn't mean that they *all* do...think about it.

Oversampling and Digital Filtering

Slowly varying DC analog signals give you some opportunities to improve the quality of your acquired data. At first glance, that thermocouple signal with a sub-1 Hz bandwidth and little noise could be adequately sampled at 2 or 3 Hz. But by **oversampling**—sampling at a rate several times higher than the Nyquist frequency—you can enhance resolution and noise rejection.

Noise is reduced in proportion to the square root of the number of samples that are averaged. For example, if you average 100 samples, the standard deviation of the average value will be reduced by a factor of 10 when compared to a single measurement. Another way of expressing this result is that you get a 20 dB improvement in signal-to-noise ratio when you average 10 times as many samples. This condition is true so long as the ADC has good linearity and a small amount of noise (called **dither**) is present [Ref. 2].

Resolution can also be enhanced through oversampling and averaging. Any time the input voltage is somewhere between two quantization levels of the ADC and there is some dither noise present, the least-significant bit (LSB) tends to toggle among a few codes. The duty cycle of this toggling action is exactly 50% if the voltage is exactly between the two quantization levels. Duty cycle and input voltage track each other in a nice, proportional manner (except if the ADC demonstrates some kind of nonlinear behavior). All you have to do is filter out the noise, which you can do by averaging or using other forms of digital filtering [Ref. 3].

A source of uncorrelated dither noise, about 0.5 LSB RMS or greater, is required to make this technique work. Some high-performance ADC and DAC systems include dither noise generators; digital audio systems and the National Instruments dynamic signal acquisition boards (A2100, A2150) are examples. High-resolution converters (16 bits and greater) generally have enough thermal noise present to supply the necessary dithering. Incidentally, this resolution enhancement occurs even if you don't oversample and filter; filtering simply reduces the noise level.

Digital Filtering

Once you have oversampled the incoming data, you can apply a digital lowpass filter to the raw data to remove high-frequency noise. There are a number of ways to do digital filtering in LabVIEW: by using the filter functions in the analysis library, by using the Moving

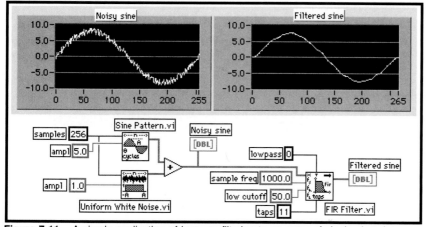

Figure 7-11. A simple application of lowpass filtering to an array of single-shot data, a noisy sine wave. Highpass filtering could also be used in this case, since we know what the minimum frequency of interest is, as well.

Averager VIs from the additional files library, or by writing something of your own. Digital filter design and application is beyond the scope of this book, but at least we can look at a few ordinary examples that might be useful in a data acquisition system.

If you are handling single-shot data, the LabVIEW filter VIs are ideal. Most of the classic analog types are available, including Butterworth, Chebyshev, Inverse Chebyshev, Elliptical, and Bessel. Also, you can specify arbitrary Finite Impulse Response (FIR) filters and Infinite Impulse Response (IIR) filters if the classical responses are unsuitable. For most filters, you just supply the sampling frequency (for calibration) and the desired filter characteristics, and the input array will be accurately filtered. Note that you can also use highpass and bandpass filters, in addition to the usual lowpass, if you know the bandwidth of interest. For examples of digital filter design and application, see the analysis examples included with LabVIEW. Figure 7-11 shows a simulated single-shot application where a noisy sine wave represents the signal. The FIR Filter VI is set up to perform a simple lowpass filter operation. An FIR filter is the correct type for single-shot data because its results are minimally contaminated by previous data, thereby reducing initialization problems. An IIR filter, in contrast, has to be initialized and is really only suitable for repetitive or continuous data.

For continuous data, the Moving Averagers are appropriate. The one demonstrated in Figure 7-12, Moving Avg Array VI operates on data from a typical multichannel data acquisition system. An array containing samples from each channel is the input, and the same array, but lowpass-filtered, is the output. Any number of samples can be included in the moving average, and the averaging can be turned on and off while running. This is a particular kind of FIR filter where all the coefficients are equal to one; it is also known as a boxcar filter. This VI is on the disk that comes with this book.

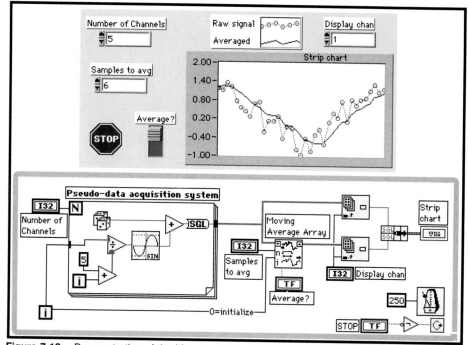

Figure 7-12.   Demonstration of the Moving Avg Array function, which applies a lowpass filter to an array of independent channels. The For loop creates several channels of data, like a data acquisition system. Each channel is filtered; then the selected channel is displayed in both raw and filtered form.

Other moving averagers are primarily for use with block-mode continuous data. They use local memory to maintain continuity between adjacent data buffers to faithfully process block-mode data as if it were a true, continuous stream.

After lowpass filtering, you can safely decimate data arrays to reduce the total amount of data. Decimation is in effect a **resampling** of the data at a lower frequency. Therefore, the resultant sampling rate must be at least twice the cutoff frequency of your digital lowpass filter. The Resample Waveform VI in Figure 7-13 does the job.

Dealing with Wide Variations in Sampling Rate

Most A/D systems are optimized for sampling or scanning all channels at the same rate. That's just fine until you need to sample some channels very fast and some very slow. There are two very good ways to deal with the situation where you have a wide mix of sampling rate requirements.

First, try dividing the fast and slow channels among different sets of I/O hardware. Group the slow channels on one input multiplexer (or board, or scanner, or whatever), and group the fast channels on another. Then you can support the various groups of channels with separate VIs that are optimized for their respective sampling rates. The program can be structured to use independent While Loops on one diagram (highest performance) or independent VIs that write data to global variables (slightly lower performance). This is the

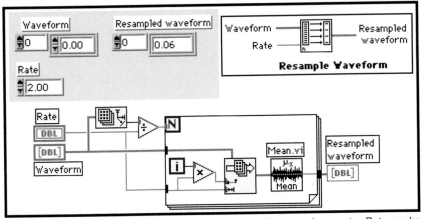

Figure 7-13. A VI that resamples, or decimates, a waveform at a lower rate. *Rate* can be any real number greater than or equal to one.

best solution because it makes optimal use of hardware and software resources and requires few compromises.

Second, you can sample all channels at the fastest rate and decimate the slower channels. As I mentioned before, this approach has certain limitations because you may be dealing with a significantly larger amount of data than necessary. The advantage of this technique is that it only requires one multichannel I/O device—the MIO-series boards, for example, using buffered acquisition, work nicely. Also, you can (at least in theory) resample each channel as required.

Timing Techniques

Using software to control the sampling rate for a data acquisition system can be a bit tricky. Because you are running LabVIEW on a general-purpose computer with lots of graphics, plus all that operating system activity going on in the background, there is bound to be some uncertainty in the timing of events, just as we discussed with regards to time stamps. Somewhere between 1 and 1000 Hz, your system will become an unreliable interval timer. For slower applications, however, a While Loop with Wait for Next ms Multiple inside works just fine for timing a data acquisition operation.

The *best* way to pace any sampling operation is with a hardware timer. Most plug-in boards, scanning voltmeters, digitizers, oscilloscopes, and many other instruments have sampling clocks with excellent stability. Use them whenever possible. Your data acquisition program will be simpler and your timing more robust.

Your worst timing nightmare occurs when you have to sample one channel at a time from a "dumb" I/O system that has no ability to scan multiple channels, no local memory, and no sampling clock. I ran into this with some old CAMAC A/D modules. They are very fast, but very dumb. Without a smart controller built into the CAMAC crate, it is simply impossible to get decent throughput to a LabVIEW system.

If the aggregate sampling rate (total channels per second) is pressing your system's reliable timing limit, be sure to do plenty of testing and/or try to back off on the rate. Otherwise, you may end up with unevenly sampled signals that can be difficult or impossible to analyze. Better to choose the right I/O system in the first place—one that solves the fast sampling problem for you.

A Low-Speed Data Acquisition Example

Life is unfair. You spend all this time reading about high-powered methods of building a data acquisition system, only to find out you need a system up and running *now*—not next week, not next month. What to do? As I've stated before, your best bet is to program by plagiarizing. Sift through the examples that come with LabVIEW and see if there's something that might do at least 50% of the job. Or, refer to some of the other resources listed in Chapter 1, *Roots*, and tap into the works of others. Eventually, you will build a personal library of VIs that you can call on to quickly assemble working applications. Following is an example that qualifies as a real solution to everyday data acquisition needs.

Here is a low-speed data acquisition VI that I've used over and over, both as a training aid and as a quick solution in many real emergencies. It's flexible enough to be the foundation of a somewhat larger package. It is intended for situations in which you need to acquire, display, and store data from a few dozen analog channels at speeds up to 10 samples per second—a very common set of requirements. The panel in Figure 7-14 has only the most rudimentary controls and indicators. Remember that this is just a starting point and you can add features as required. On the left are controls that set up the input channel assignments and sampling parameters. This example assumes the use of an MIO-series board and the DAQ VI library, but you could easily convert it to some other kind of input device with an appropriate driver VI. There are three controls for timing. **Sample**

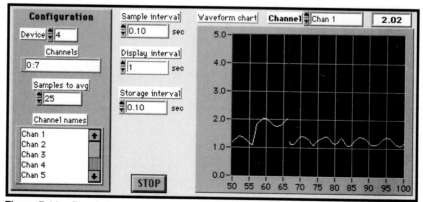

Figure 7-14. Panel of the simple low-speed data acquisition VI. It's useful for a few dozen channels at sampling rates up to about 10 Hz. This is a simple, but useful, example to which you can add features as required.

Interval determines how often the inputs are sampled. **Display Interval** controls the update speed of any indicators, such as the strip chart. **Storage Interval** determines how often data is appended to the data file, which is in tab-delimited text format.

The configuration controls at the left could be scrolled off the screen if you don't want the user to see them. **Device** and **Channels** are the usual DAQ setup items. **Samples to avg** determines how many scans will be taken for averaging. You would probably change all of these items if you used a different kind of I/O interface. **Channel names** contains a list of names for each channel separated by carriage returns (it has to contain the same number of lines that the Channels control defines). Names from this list are used as the file headers and are automatically copied into the **Channel** ring control above the Waveform Chart.

The diagram is shown in Figure 7-15 . To the left of the While Loop are the initialization operations. The String list converter (shown in Figure 7-16) converts the **Channel names** list into a tab-delimited string with a following carriage return, and to an array of strings. The tab-delimited string is used for the file header. A text file is created by using the Write Characters to File VI, which generates a file dialog and then writes the header string. The string array is written to the *Strings[]* item of an Attribute Node for the **Channels** ring control. Any input hardware initialization would also be performed outside the loop if it was required. In this case, a channel array has to be built, but that's all. The main While Loop runs at a rate determined by **Sample Interval** until the user clicks the **Stop** button.

I used the easy I/O VI, AI Acquire Waveform, to acquire data because it is simple yet versatile and meets the requirement of taking many scans. You could also use a more elaborate set of functions, or a driver for some other type of hardware. The 2D data array (scaled to voltage) is then averaged on a channel-by-channel basis by the Average Voltage subVI, detailed in Chapter 5, *Instrument Drivers*. Average Voltage also has provisions for

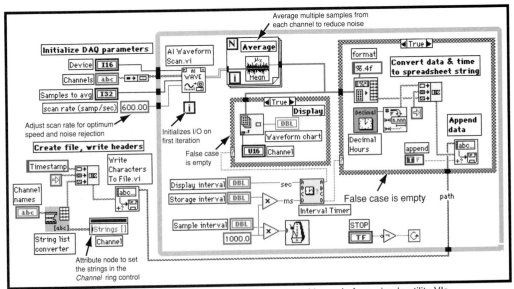

Figure 7-15. Diagram for the low-speed data acquisition system. It's made from simple utility VIs.

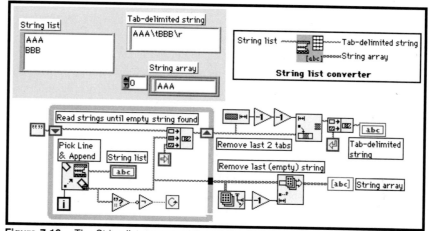

Figure 7-16. The String list converter VI accepts a list of names and changes it to a tab-delimited string (for a file header) and to a string array (for Ring control strings).

the deletion of some of the data at the start of a scan, in case your data acquisition hardware has problems with settling time.

Note that some VIs like Average Voltage perform many computations and do a good deal of memory reshuffling because of all the array accesses. There is an obvious performance penalty here that may become a limiting factor in high-speed applications. If you run into problems with marginal performance (where you *almost* meet your throughput requirements), you may want to study alternatives to such array processing. For instance, you may have to go back to taking single scans of data without averaging, and live with the higher noise level.

Reducing the frequency at which indicators are updated helps improve performance. For that reason, the strip chart (and any other indicators you might add) is placed inside a Case structure that is controlled by the Interval Timer VI subVI. Similarly, data storage is also triggered by the Interval Timer. The Array to Spreadsheet String function converts the data array to tab-delimited text, and a time stamp in decimal hours is prefixed to the string before it is written to the file. The Decimal Hours VI was discussed in Chapter 4, *Building an Application*. If you want to do more elaborate data formatting or file management, I'd recommend that you put all of the data storage services in a subVI. This example is simple enough that I decided to put those items right on the main diagram.

The one drawback to the Interval Timer method is that it induces some variability in the cycle rate of the main loop. On several iterations, you don't update the displays, and the loop can cycle at top speed. But along comes the occasional iteration where the displays *are* updated, and that cycle runs a bit long. Your average throughput has been increased, but with a penalty of having added jitter to your sampling interval. Is this a problem? In many cases it's not. If you're just recording routine 1 Hz data where having a precision timebase is irrelevant to the data analysis, then the perceived improvement in the response time (*feel*) of your system is well worth it. Hardware timed I/O may be another solution because it closely regulates loop cycle time (see Chapter 6, *Using the DAQ Library*). But ultimately, once your machine runs out of real-time computing power, you have to back off on the graphics demands.

Most of the functions in the main diagram to the left of the While Loop could be placed in an initialization subVI. You could also add many features, such as engineering units, scaling and a nicer way for the user to enter channel setups. I did put in one bit of configuration help: the String List Converter VI, shown in Figure 7-16. It permits the user to enter channel names in a list, separated by carriage returns. The outputs are a tab-delimited string for the data file header, and a string array to initialize the ring control.

I tested this example on my Quadra 950 with an MIO-16X board and eight channels defined. With the settings shown, I could sample, display, and store data as fast as 10 Hz. It takes 50 ms to acquire 25 samples at 40 kHz, and there are about 50 ms of overhead in this program due to graphics and data conversion. To improve performance, you have several options from which to choose.

First, lower the file system overhead. Don't use the open/write/close features of the Write Characters to File VI inside the While Loop because it forces the file system to access the disk each time. Instead, create and open the file before entering the loop; then use Write File inside the loop to append data, and Close File after data collection is complete (Figure 7-17A). Several LabVIEW file I/O utility VIs include error handling (Figure 7-17B). Error handling is always recommended, and you should tie your data acquisition VIs into the error I/O stream. Second, for even better performance, save the data in binary format, either as LabVIEW datalogs or as a custom binary format of your choice. The Interval Timer becomes a limiting factor, however, because of uncertainty in its timing precision, so be aware.

A third improvement you can make is to reduce the number of samples to average, which reduces the amount of time that it takes to acquire the raw data. Remember, the tradeoff is an increase in apparent noise in your measurements. Finally, you can switch to buffered, continuous acquisition by using the intermediate DAQ VIs. The easy I/O VI requires you to wait for an entire buffer of data at each call, whereas a buffered system acquires all of the data asynchronously.

As you can see, this example is simple yet functional and is easily adapted and enhanced for other applications. By using the available utility VIs, such as the Interval Timer, file support, and easy I/O, you avoid any serious programming problems. Keep this one in your hip pocket; that should be easy because it's on the disk that comes with this book.

Configuration Management

You could write a data acquisition program with no configuration management features, but do so only after considering the consequences. The only thing that's constant in a laboratory environment is *change*, so it's silly to have to edit your LabVIEW diagram each time someone wants to change a channel assignment. Make your program more flexible by including configuration management VIs that accommodate such routine changes. The rest of this chapter is devoted to this topic.

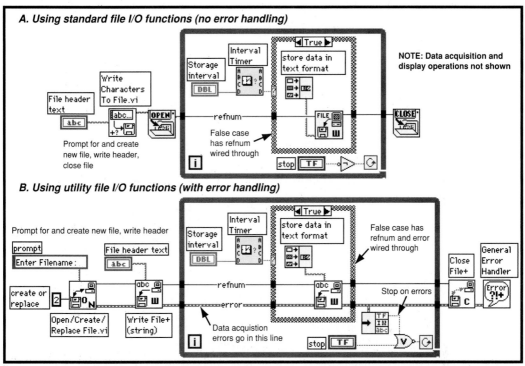

Figure 7-17. You can improve performance somewhat by rearranging the file write operations like this. It's much faster than the open/write/close operation inside the loop in the previous diagram. Example B uses the utility file I/O VIs that add error handling (recommended).

Things to Configure

Even the simplest data acquisition systems have channel names that need to be associated with their respective physical I/O channels. As the I/O hardware becomes more complex, additional setup information is required. Also, information about the experiment itself may need to be inseparably tied to the acquired data. For instance, you certainly need to know some fundamental parameters like channel names and sample intervals before you can possibly analyze the data. On the other hand, knowing the serial number of a transducer, while useful, is not mandatory for basic analysis. Here is a list of configuration-related items you might want to consider for your system:

I/O Hardware-Related

- Port number, such as GPIB board or serial port selection

- Device address

- Slot number, where multiple I/O modules or boards are used

- Module or board type

- Channel number

- Channel name

- Channel gain, scale factor, and linearization data

- Sampling rate; may be on a per-module or per-channel basis

- Filtering

- Triggering parameters—slope, level, AC/DC coupling

Experiment-Related

- Experiment identifier; short ID numbers make good foundations for data file names

- Purpose or description of the experiment

- Operator's name

- Start date and time

- Data file path(s)

- Transducer type or description for each channel

- Transducer calibration information and serial number

In a sense, all of this information comprises a **configuration database**, and any technique that applies to a database could be applied here, including inserting and deleting records, sorting, searching, and of course storing and fetching database images from disk. These are tasks for a configuration **editor**. Additionally, you need a kind of **compiler** or translator program that reads this user-supplied information, validates it, then transmits it in suitable form to the I/O hardware and the acquisition program.

The level of sophistication of such an editor or compiler is limited only by your skill as a programmer and your creative use of other applications on your computer. The simplest *editor* is just a cluster array that you type values into. The most complex editor I've seen uses a commercial database program which writes out a configuration file for LabVIEW to read and process. Just imagine: a database, such as Oracle, Fourth Dimension, or dBase, with all its processing power, as the front end to your home-grown data acquisition program. Feel adventurous?

Configuration Editors

Aside from that rather elaborate application of a commercial database, there are some reasonable ways for you to program LabVIEW as a configuration editor. There are two basic editor types: **interactive editors** and **static editors**. An interactive editor is a LabVIEW VI that runs while you enter configuration information, supplying you with immediate feedback as to the validity of your entries. A static editor is generally simpler, consisting of a VI that you run after entering information into all of its control fields. If an error occurs, you receive a dialog box and try again. With either editor, once the entries are validated, the information is passed on to a configuration compiler (which may actually be part of the editor program). If the configuration is loaded from an external file, it may pass through an editor for user updates, or go directly to the compiler for immediate use.

Static Editors for Starters

Ordinary LabVIEW controls are just fine for entering configuration information, be it numeric, string, or Boolean format. Since a typical data acquisition system has many channels, it makes sense to create a configuration entry device that is a **cluster array**. The cluster contains all the items that define a channel. Making an array of these clusters provides a compact way of defining an arbitrary number of channels (Figure 7-19).

One problem with this simple method is that it's a bit inconvenient to insert or delete items in an array control using the data selection items in the array control pop-up menu. A solution is to include an **On Scan** switch, as I did in Figure 7-19. Only when a channel is *on scan* is its configuration information passed along to the I/O driver. When a channel is off scan, the ADC or digitizer may safely ignore that channel, thus saving some I/O operations. I usually make the switch turn red when a channel is off scan to make sure that the user doesn't accidentally leave a channel turned off.

The diagram for this editor checks to see that the channel name is not empty (you could also check for invalid characters, name too long, etc.). If the name is empty, a dialog box pops up telling the user, "Channel 17 needs a name." If the name is okay, and the channel is on scan, then the name and channel number are appended to the output cluster array for

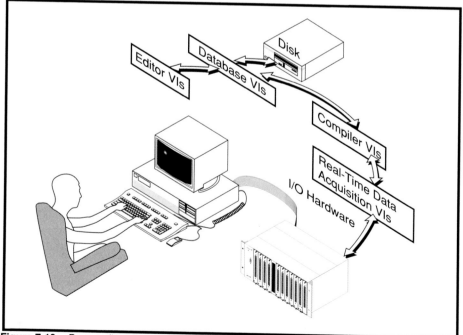

Figure 7-18. Process flow diagram for configuration management.

use later on. You can also use the empty channel name as a switch to take the channel off scan, if you like.

Obviously, you can add as many items as you need to the channel description cluster, and the amount of checking you could do will become extensive. Error checking is part of making your program robust. Even this simple example needs more checking: What if the user assigns the same channel number to two or more channels? What if the channels have the same name?

For more complex I/O systems, a nested structure of cluster arrays inside of cluster arrays may be required. Figure 7-20 configures **Opto-22** analog input modules. The outer array selects a multiplexer (MUX) number. Each multiplexer has up to 16 channels that are configured by the inner cluster array. Since there were four possible alarm responses, I grouped them inside yet another cluster, way down inside. As you can see, the data structure becomes fairly complex.

The LabVIEW **Table control** can also be used for configuration entries. Like a spreadsheet, columns can be assigned to each setup parameter with one row per channel. Tables have an advantage over cluster arrays because they have high information density;

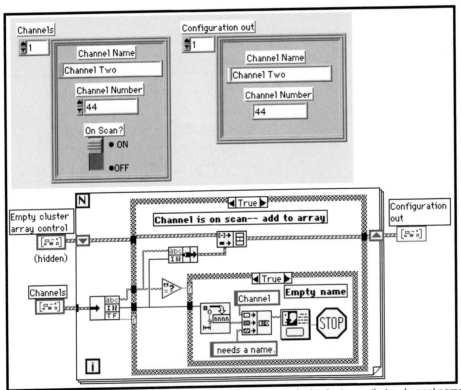

Figure 7-19. A static configuration editor using a cluster array. It checks to see that a channel name has been entered, and appends *on scan* channels to the output configuration array.

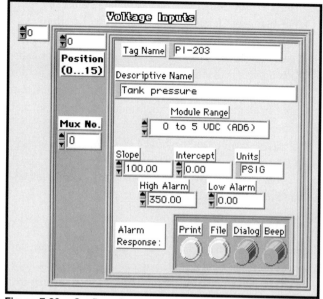

Figure 7-20. Configuration for a more complicated I/O system requires nested cluster arrays with lots of controls.

many channel definitions will fit in a small screen area. But tables have one glaring disadvantage: data validation is mandatory on each and every cell. Because a table is just a 2D string array, the user is free to type any characters into any cell. What happens when you are hoping for a numeric entry, but receive something non-numeric?

Any time you write a loop to process a Table control, you will encounter the nefarious empty row problem. It occurs when the user types something into a cell, then deletes everything. Even though the cell is empty, the 2D array now has another element that contains an empty string. If you pass this 2D array to a loop for processing, it will attempt

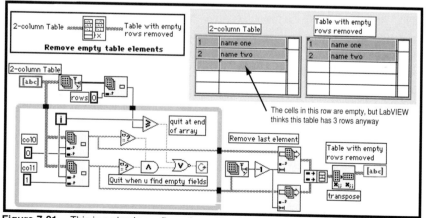

Figure 7-21. This is a simple configuration editor that interprets the contents of a Table control and converts the data into a cluster array.

to process the empty strings. You can test for empty strings later, or use the VI in Figure 7-21, Remove Empty Table Elements. It removes any number of trailing empty rows. Size the Table control so that it displays only the proper number of columns; then hide the horizontal scroll bars to keep the user from entering too many columns of data.

Figure 7-22 is a static editor that interprets the data in a Table control. It does no error checking, but that could be added right after each of the Index Array functions. As a minimum, you would have to verify that all numbers are in range and that the channel name is acceptable. Cross-checking for more complex data inconsistency gets really interesting. For instance, you might have to verify that the right number of channels are assigned dependent upon the multiplexer type.

Rumor has it that a future version of LabVIEW will include a more powerful table control that has many of these data filter features, such as numeric validation.

Interactive Editors

Interactive configuration editors are more versatile and more user-friendly than static editors because they provide instant feedback to the user. You can add pop-up windows, status displays, or even turn LabVIEW into a menu-driven system. Plan to do some extra programming if you want these extra features. Elaborate interactive editor projects are among the most challenging programming tasks I've ever tackled.

Pop-Up Editors

Say you have several different kinds of I/O modules, and they all have significantly different configuration needs. If you try to accommodate them all with one big cluster array, various controls would be invalid depending on which module was selected. You really need separate input panels for each module type if you want to keep the program simple and efficient.

One solution is to put several buttons on the panel of the main configuration VI that open customized configuration editor subVIs (Figure 7-23). Each button has its mechanical action set to **Latch When Released**, and each editor subVI is set to **Show front panel when called**. The editor subVIs do the real configuration work. Note that they don't really have to be any fancier than the static editors we already have discussed. When you create one of these pop-up subVIs, remember to disable **Allow user to close window** in the Window Options of the VI Setup dialog. Otherwise, the user may accidentally close the window of the VI while it's running and the calling VI will not be able to continue.

I threw in a handy VI, called Which Button (Figure 7-24), that makes these button-driven programs a little easier to write. To use it, build a Boolean array on your diagram containing all your buttons as shown in the previous example. The output of Which Button is zero when nothing is pressed, one for the first button, two for the second, etc. This VI is on the diskette that comes with this book.

Information may be returned by each editor subVI for further processing, or each editor can function as a stand-alone program, doing all the necessary I/O initialization, writing of global variables, and so forth. A worthy goal is for each editor to return a standard data

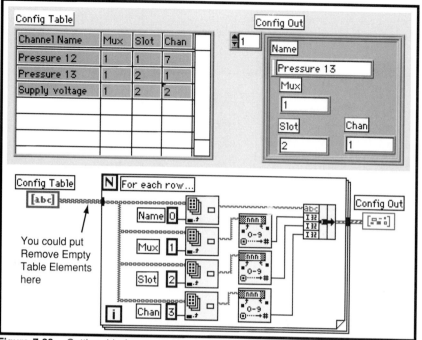

Figure 7-22. Getting rid of empty table elements. Erasing a cell completely does not remove that element of the 2D array. This VI does, though.

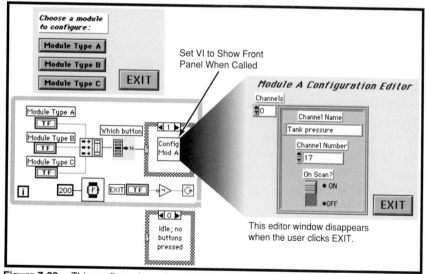

Figure 7-23. This configuration editor model uses subVIs that appear when an appropriate button is pressed. The subVI is the actual user interface (in this case, a configuration editor), and may do other processing as well. The Which Button VI (shown in Figure 7-24) chooses the right editing subVI.

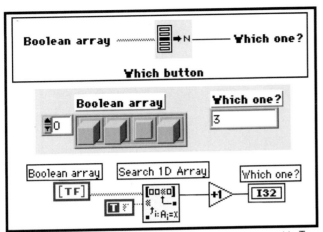

Figure 7-24. VI to tell you which Boolean in an array was set to True. Returns zero if none are True, one if the first one is True, etc.

structure (like a cluster array), regardless of the type of I/O module that it supports. This may simplify the data acquisition and analysis processes (see the *Configuration Compilers* section below).

Another way you can accommodate modules with different configuration needs is to use **Attribute nodes** to selectively hide controls when they don't apply. When the user selects module type *A*, the special controls for module *B* are hidden, and so forth. Note that you can't hide controls that are part of a cluster—you can only hide the entire cluster. This actually presents another opportunity: stack the clusters for each module on top of each other, with attribute nodes making only one visible at a time, and have a **Module Select** ring that shows the cluster for the selected module.

Here is a model for an interactive editor hierarchy that I originally built to support SCXI analog input modules. It turned out to be quite versatile, and I've used it for many other kinds of instruments. Figure 7-25 shows the VI that appears when the user clicks the **Edit SCXI Analog Inputs** button on the top-level configuration manager VI.

This program relies on a global variable, Inst Config Globals, to pass the configuration cluster array along to other parts of the data acquisition system. The configuration data is loaded from the global at startup, then circulates in a shift register until the user clicks the **EXIT** button. Two subVIs, Read/Write SCXI Config and Edit SCXI Config, act on the configuration data. Read/Write Config can either load or store an image of the cluster array in a binary file. The file path is chosen by another subVI, Change Config File, which opens like a dialog box when called. It permits the user to pick an existing file or create a new one. The real work of editing the configuration occurs inside Edit SCXI Config.

Read/Write SCXI Config is simple in principle, as you can see from Figure 7-26. The configuration file is a byte stream file and the cluster arrays are converted to strings with the mysterious Flatten To String function (from the Miscellaneous palette of the function menu). This function gathers the data in memory and converts it to a binary string that contains some clues as to the amount of data therein. For instance, if you flatten a

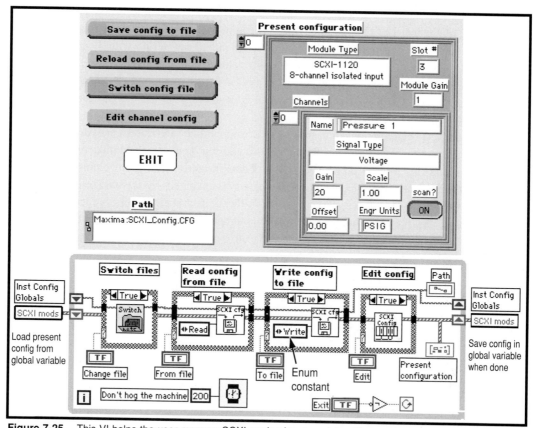

Figure 7-25. This VI helps the user manage SCXI analog input modules. The configuration is stored in a global variable for use elsewhere in the data acquisition program, and it can be loaded from and saved to files. (False frames of all the Case structures simply pass each input to its respective output.)

10-element I16 array to a string, the resulting array will begin with a four-byte integer containing the number 10, followed by 10 pairs of bytes representing the data values. The Unflatten From String function performs the reverse operation, converting the binary string back to the original data structure. However, it needs additional information to properly reconstruct the data, so it has a *type* input that is wired to a data structure of the appropriate type. Note that the flatten/unflatten functions will work with *any* data type. Therefore, this VI can be modified to accommodate other instruments by simply replacing the input and output cluster arrays. You could use datalog files instead and have the advantage of being able to archive many configurations in one file.

The tough part of this interactive editor is Edit SCXI Config. Figure 7-27 shows the front panel, which I designed purely for user comfort and efficiency with no thought whatsoever for the complexity of the underlying program. So, where's the diagram? It's *way* too complicated to show here; as a matter of fact, the diagram with its associated subVIs occupies about a half-megabyte of disk space! It's based on a state machine that looks at the present control settings, then modifies the display accordingly. For instance, if the user changes the Module # control, all the other controls are updated to reflect the present setting of channel 1 of that module. This is accomplished by reading the settings from the configuration cluster array and loading them into the controls with Local Variables. Also, the **Module Gain** and channel **Gain** controls are selectively disabled (dimmed) by using Attribute Nodes. If the user picks an SCXI-1120 module, each channel has its own gain setting, so the channel gain control is enabled while the module gain control is disabled.

This is the fanciest configuration editor that I could design in LabVIEW and it uses just about every feature of the language. The reason that this editor is so nice is that unlike the static editor with its cluster array, all of the controls update instantly without any clumsy array navigation problems. However, the programming is very involved—as it would be in any language. What I would suggest you do is stick to the simpler static editors and use some of the ideas described here until you're really confident about your programming skills. Then design a nice user interface, and have at it. If you design the overall

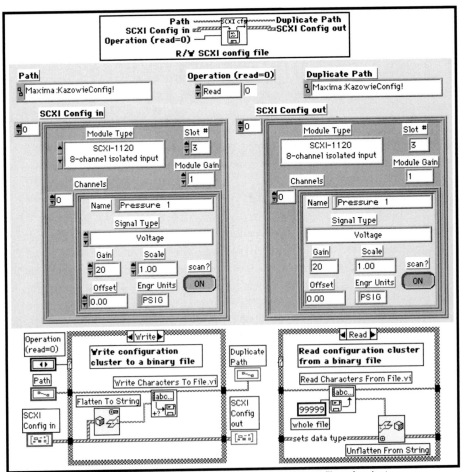

Figure 7-26.   Read/Write SCXI Config reads and writes binary image files of a cluster array.

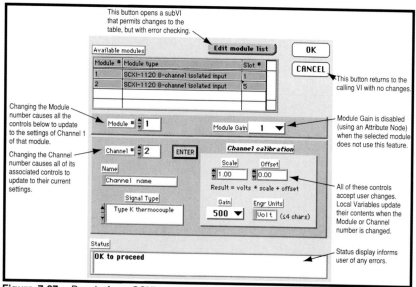

Figure 7-27. Panel of my SCXI configuration editor, showing some of the features that you can implement if you spend lots of time programming.

configuration program in a modular fashion, you can replace the simple editor with the fancy editor when it's complete.

Only you can decide if great expenditures of effort are necessary. If you only have one or two users, or they only have to deal with configuration management once a month, then it's probably not worth the effort. On the other hand, you may be able to develop an elaborate editor VI that can serve as a template for other purposes, thus leveraging your development efforts. When I wrote the SCXI configuration manager, I spent some time designing it with the intent that much of the code would be reused for other types of I/O hardware in my application. That's why the VI in Figure 7-25 has a such a clean design.

Status Displays

Since an interactive editor is a program that runs all the time, it can do things like entry validation even as the user changes settings. Give the user feedback by adding a status display that describes any errors or inconsistencies among the various settings. In Figure 7-28, for instance, you have a choice of several I/O modules, each having a certain limited range of channels. Any disagreement between module type and channel quantity needs to be rectified. A ring indicator contains predefined status messages. Item zero is "OK to continue," while item one is the error message shown. The status has to be zero before pressing the EXIT button causes termination of the While Loop.

You can also use a string indicator to display status messages, feeding it various strings contained in constants on the diagram. The string indicator can also display error messages returned from I/O operations or from an error handler VI. Some configuration situations require constant interaction with the I/O hardware to confirm the validity of the setup. For

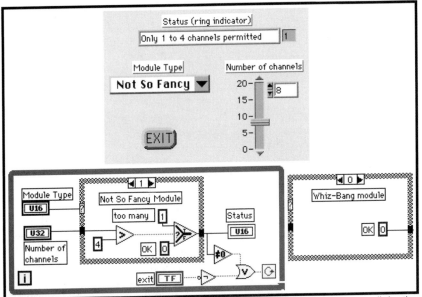

Figure 7-28. Using a Ring Indicator as a status display. The While Loop runs all the time, so the user's settings are always being evaluated. The Ring contains predefined messages—in this case, item zero is "OK to continue." Any of the real work for this configuration editor would be done inside the While Loop.

instance, if you want to configure a set of VXI modules, you might need to verify that the chosen module is installed. If the module is not found, it's nice to receive an informative message telling you about the problem right away. Such I/O checks would be placed inside the overall While Loop.

A good status message conveys information, rather than admonishing the user. You should report not only what is wrong, but how to correct the problem. "ERROR IN SETUP" is definitely *not* helpful, though that is exactly what you get from many commercial software packages. **Dialogs** can also be used for status messages, but you should reserve them for really important events, like confirming the overwriting of a file. It's annoying to have dialog boxes popping up all the time.

Menu-Driven Systems

When PCs only ran DOS, and all the world was in darkness, menu-driven systems were the standard. They really are the easiest user interfaces to write when you have minimal graphics support. The classic menu interface looks like this:

```
Choose a function:

  1:Initialize hardware
  2: Set up files
  3: Collect data
  Enter a number >__
```

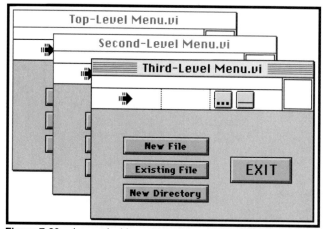

Figure 7-29.   Layout for hierarchical menu subVIs that helps users navigate. The EXIT button returns you to the previous menu.

In turn, the user's choice will generate yet another menu of selections. The good thing about these menu-driven prompting systems is that the user can be a total idiot and still run your system. On the other hand, an experienced user gets frustrated by the inability to navigate through the various submenus in an expedient manner. Also, it's hard to figure out where you are in the hierarchy of menus. Therefore, I introduce menus as a LabVIEW technique with some reluctance. It's up to you to decide where this concept is appropriate, and how far to carry it.

The keys to a successful menu-driven system are aids to navigation and the ability to back up a step (or bail out completely, returning to Step One) at any time. Using subVIs that open when called allows you to use any kind of control, prompting, status, and data entry devices that might be required.

A LabVIEW menu could be made from buttons, ring controls, or sliders. If you use anything besides buttons, there would also have to be a *do it* button. Programming would be much like the first pop-up editor's example. To make nested menus, each subVI that opens when called would in turn offer selections that would open yet another set of subVIs.

If you lay out the windows carefully, the hierarchy can be visible on the screen. The highest-level menu VI would be located toward the upper-left corner of the screen. Lower-level menus would appear offset a bit lower and to the right, as shown in Figure 7-29. This helps the user navigate through nested menus. LabVIEW remembers the exact size and location of a window when you save the VI. Don't forget that other people who use your VIs may have smaller screens.

Configuration Compilers

A **configuration compiler** translates the user's settings obtained from a configuration editor into data that is used to set up or access hardware. It may also be responsible for

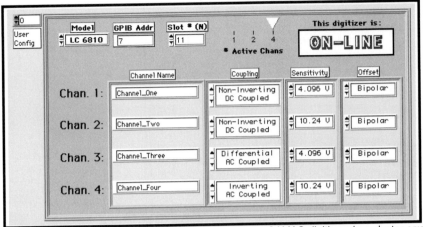

Figure 7-30. The input to this configuration compiler for CAMAC digitizers is a cluster array that a user has filled in. The four clusters (channel names, coupling, etc.) need to be checked for consistency and converted to arrays for use by the acquisition VIs.

storing and recalling old configuration records for reuse. The compiler program may or may not be an integral part of an editor VI.

The control layout on a configuration editor's panel is optimized for efficient user interaction. But those controls may not be very efficient when it comes time to send information to a real-time data acquisition driver. It would be very inefficient, for example, to have the driver interpret and sort arrays of strings that describe channel assignments every time the driver is called. Rather, you should write a compiler that interprets the strings at configuration time and creates a numeric array that lists the channel numbers to be scanned. Your objective is to write a program that does as little as possible during data acquisition and analysis phases, thus enhancing throughput.

The next three figures illustrate a simple compiler that supports some CAMAC-based digitizer modules. Each module has four channels with independent setups. Figure 7-30 is a cluster array into which the user has entered the desired setup information, perhaps through the use of an editor VI. Channel setup information is in the form of four clusters, which makes it easy for the user to see all of the setups at once. However, this is not an efficient way to package the information for use by an acquisition VI. Figure 7-31 shows a more desirable structure, where each channel is an element of an array. The compiler must make this translation. Here are the steps to be taken by this configuration compiler, whose diagram appears in Figure 7-32:

1. Convert the individual channel clusters into an array.

2. If the module is online, build the output configuration cluster and append it to the output array.

3. Check the settings for consistency (e.g., there may be limitations on sensitivity for certain coupling modes).

4. Initialize each module and download the settings.

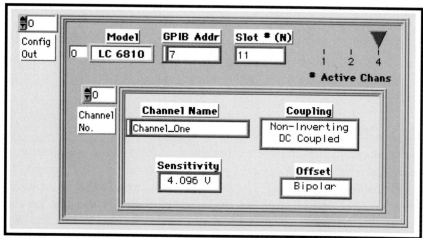

Figure 7-31. The compiler's output is a cluster array. Note that it carries all of the same information as the input cluster array did, but in a more compact form.

5. Write the output configuration cluster array to a global variable which will be read by the acquisition VI.

I left out the gory details of how the settings are validated and downloaded since that involves particular knowledge of the modules and their driver VIs. Even so, much of the diagram is taken up by bundlers and unbundlers and other conversion functions that are required to reformat the incoming data. This is typical of these compilers, and it sometimes gets rather messy because of the number of items and special conditions that you have to deal with. Where possible, encapsulate related parts of the compiler in subVIs to make the

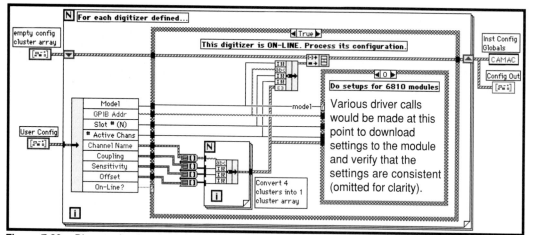

Figure 7-32. Diagram for the simple compiler. Data types are converted by the inner For Loop. Settings are checked for consistency and digitizers are initialized by the inner Case structure. If a digitizer is on-line, its configuration is added to the output array, which is passed to the acquisition VIs by a global variable.

diagram easier to understand and more compact. I would probably put all the driver functions for a given type of digitizer module in a subVI because they are logically related.

Somewhere in the edit or compile phase you should try to communicate with each I/O device to see if it responds, and report an error if it doesn't. It would be uncouth to permit the user to get all the way to the data acquisition phase before announcing that an important instrument is D.O.A.

Storing Configurations

Another useful function that the compiler can perform is the creation of a permanent record of the configuration. The record might be a spreadsheet-format text file suitable for printing, a special format for use by a data analysis program, or a LabVIEW datalog or binary file that you can read back into the configuration program for later reuse. It makes sense to put this functionality in with the editors and compilers because all of the necessary information is readily available there.

Printable Records (Spreadsheet Format)

Many systems I've worked on needed a hardcopy record of the experiment's configuration for the lab notebook. The direct approach is to generate a text file that you can load and print with something like a spreadsheet or word processor. Add tab characters between fields and carriage returns where appropriate to clean up the layout. Titles are a big help, too. Figure 7-33 is a diagram that interprets the configuration cluster array of Figure 7-31 into tab-delimited text. There is a great deal of string building to do, so don't be surprised if the diagram gets a little ugly.

Here is what this text converter VI produces, as interpreted by a word processor with suitable tab stops. As you can see, most of the settings are written in numeric form. You could add Case structures for Coupling, Sensitivity, and Offset to decode the numbers into something more descriptive.

Model	GPIB Address	Slot No.	
LC6810	1	4	
Name	Coupling	Sensitivity	Offset
Channel_One	7	2	0
Channel_Two	1	4	2
Channel_Three	0	3	1
Channel_Four	4	5	1
Model	GPIB Address	Slot No.	
LC8210	4	2	
Name	Coupling	Sensitivity	Offset
Another channel	2	5	0

Another way to print a configuration record is to lay out a suitable LabVIEW front panel and print that. You can use all the usual indicators as well as formatted strings displayed in string indicators, if that helps you get more information crammed onto one screen. You can

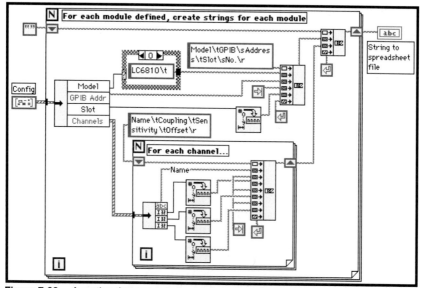

Figure 7-33.　A routine that converts the configuration cluster of Figure 7-31 into a tab-delimited text file for documentation purposes. As you can see, there is a lot of string building to do.

turn on the **Print Mode** button, ![icon], in the LabVIEW run mode palette to make the VI print automatically each time it finishes execution.

Saving and Recalling Configurations

Your configuration manager should be able to recall previous setups for reuse. Otherwise, the user would have to type in all that information each time. If you use a static editor, a simple way to save the configuration is to teach the user to set all the controls, then select **Make Current Values Default** from the Operate menu, followed by **Save** from the File

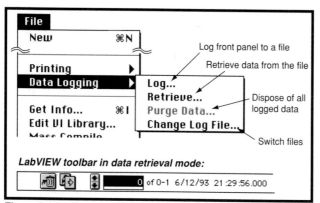

Figure 7-34.　Front-panel data logging in LabVIEW.

menu. The next time the editor VI opens, the previous settings will appear. While simple, this technique only saves one setup.

You can use the **Data Logging** functions, also in the File menu (Figure 7-34). Begin by creating a new log file (use the Log... option), or select an existing one (use the Change Log File... option). The chosen file will stay associated with the VI until you change it to something else. You can manually log a copy of the VI's panel to the file at any time by selecting the Log... option from the menu. To automatically make a log entry when the VI finishes execution, turn on the **Datalogging** button, ▶, in the run mode palette. The Data Logging functions make it easy to retrieve setups at a later time. Each record has a time and date stamp so you can see when the setup was created.

I prefer to build the configuration editor with binary file support as described above for Read/Write SCXI Config. This solution is very convenient for the user. Previous settings can be automatically loaded from a standard file each time the configuration editor is called, then the file is updated when an editing session is complete.

REFERENCES

1. *Numerical Recipes in C*, Press, William H., et al. NY: Cambridge Press, 1990.

2. E. B. Loewenstein, "Reducing the Effects of Noise by Averaging," National Instruments Applications Article, 1990.

3. E. B. Loewenstein, "Improving Accuracy with Dither," National Instruments Applications Article, 1990.

Process Control
Applications

Industrial process control has its roots in the big process industries, sometimes called the Four Ps: paper, petrochemicals, paint, and pharmaceuticals. These plants are characterized by having *thousands* of instruments measuring such variables as pressure, temperature, flow, and level, plus hundreds of control elements such as valves, pumps, and heaters. They use a great deal of automatic control, including feedback, sequencing, interlocking, and recipe-driven schemes. Modern control systems for these plants are, as you might imagine, very complex and very expensive. Most systems are designed and installed through cooperative efforts between manufacturers, system integrators, and the customer's control engineering staff. These are the *Big Boys* of process control.

Chances are that you are probably faced with a much smaller laboratory-scale system or pilot plant that needs to be monitored and controlled. Also, your system needs to be much more flexible since it is experimental in nature. Even though your needs are different, many of the concepts and control principles you will use are the same as those used in the largest plants, making it worth your while to study their techniques.

Big systems generally rely on networked minicomputers with a variety of smart I/O subsystems, all using proprietary software. Until recently, most software for these larger systems was not *open*, meaning that the end user could not add custom I/O interfaces or special software routines nor interconnect the system with other computers. Even the smaller process control packages–most of which run on PCs—have some of these lingering limitations. You, however, have an advantage—the power and flexibility of LabVIEW. It's not *just* a process control package. You can begin with a clean slate and few fundamental limitations...are you ready?

Process Control Basics

In this chapter, we'll cover the important concepts of process control and then design the pieces of a small process control system, using good LabVIEW practices. First, a plug for the ISA. In the United States, the **Instrument Society of America (ISA)** sets the standards and practices for industrial process control. I joined the ISA some years ago while working on the control system for a large experimental facility, and I've found my membership to be quite helpful. They offer a catalog of books, publications, standards documents, and practical training courses that can make your plant and your work practices safer and more efficient. Concepts and terminology presented in this chapter are straight out of the ISA publications, in an effort to keep us all speaking a common language. For information about membership or publications, contact the ISA at its Raleigh, N.C., headquarters at (919) 549-8411.

Industrial Standards

Standards set by the ISA and other organizations address the physical plant—including instruments, tanks, valves, piping, wiring, and so forth—as well as the **man-machine**

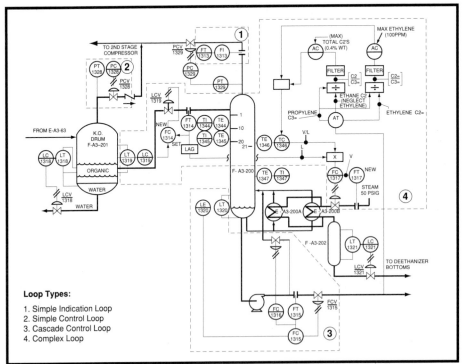

Loop Types:

1. Simple Indication Loop
2. Simple Control Loop
3. Cascade Control Loop
4. Complex Loop

Figure 8-1.   A piping and instrument diagram, the basis for a good process plant design.

interface (**MMI**) and any associated software and documentation. The classic MMI was a silkscreened control panel filled with controllers and sequencers, digital and analog display devices, chart recorders, and plenty of knobs and switches. Nowadays, we can use software-based virtual instruments to mimic these classic MMI functions. And what better way is there to create virtual instruments than LabVIEW?

Engineers communicate primarily through drawings, a simple but often-overlooked fact. In process control, drawing standards have been in place long enough that it is possible to design and build a large process plant with just a few basic types of drawings, all of which are thoroughly specified by ISA standards. By the way, ISA standards are also registered as ANSI (American National Standards Institute) standards. Some of these drawings are of particular interest to you, the control engineer. (See? I've already promoted you to a new position and you're only on the second page. Now read on, or *you're fired.*)

Piping and Instrument Diagrams and Symbols

The single most important drawing for your plant is the **piping and instrument diagram (P&ID)**. It shows the interconnections of all the vessels, pipes, valves, pumps, transducers, transmitters, and control loops. A simple P&ID is shown in Figure 8-1. From such a drawing, you should be able to understand all of the fluid flows, and the purpose of every major item in the plant. Furthermore, the identifiers, or **tag names**, of every instrument are shown and are consistent throughout all drawings and specifications for the plant. The P&ID is the key to a coherent plant design.

Tag names should follow ISA standard S5.1, a summary of which is shown in Table 8-1. The beauty of this naming system is that it is both meaningful and concise. With just a few characters, you can determine what the instrument controls or measures (e.g., P for pressure, T for temperature), as well as its function (e.g., C for controller, V for valve, T for transmitter). A numeric suffix is appended as a hierarchical serial number. Most plants use a scheme where the first digit is the zone or area, the second is the major vessel, and so forth. Tag names appear everywhere: on the P&ID, on instrument data sheets, in your control system database, and, of course, on a little metal tag riveted to the instrument. Since this is the only national standard of its type, most process engineers are familiar with this naming scheme—a good reason to consider its use.

When I write a LabVIEW program for process control, I use tag names everywhere. On the diagram, you can label wires, cluster elements, and frames of Case and Sequence structures that are dedicated to processing a certain channel. On the panel, tag names make a convenient, traceable, and unambiguous way to name various objects. Here are some examples of common tag names with explanations:

PI-203	Pressure Indicator—a mechanical pressure gauge
LT-203	Level Transmitter—electronic instrument with 4-20mA output
TIC-203	Temperature Indicating Controller—a temperature controller with readout
PSV-203	Pressure Safety Valve—a relief valve
FCV-203	Flow Control Valve—valve to adjust flow rate
ZSL-203	Position Switch, Low-Level–switch that closes when a valve is closed

Table 8-1. An abbreviated list for the generation of ISA-standard instrument tag names. Reprinted by permission. Copyright 1984, Instrument Society of America. From S-5.1—*Instrumentation Symbols and Identification.*

	First Letter Measured or initiating variable	Second Letter Readout or output function	Succeeding Letters (if required)
A	Analysis	Alarm	Alarm
B	Burner, combustion	User's choice	User's choice
C	Conductivity	Controller	Controller
D	Density/damper	Differential	
E	Voltage (elect)	Primary element	
F	Flow	Ratio/bias	Ratio/bias
G	Gauging (dimensional)	Glass (viewing device)	
H	Hand (manual)		High
I	Current (electrical)	Indicate	Indicate
J	Power	Scanner	
K	Time	Control station	
L	Level	Light	Low
M	Moisture/mass		Middle/intermediate
N	User's choice	User's choice	User's choice
O	User's choice	Orifice, restriction	
P	Pressure	Point (test) connection	
Q	Quantity	Totalize/quantity	
R	Radiation	Record	Record
S	Speed/frequency	Safety/switch	Switch
T	Temperature	Transmitter	Transmitter
U	Multipoint/variable	Multifunction	Multifunction
V	Vibration	Valve, damper, louver	Valve, damper, louver
W	Weight	Well	
X	Special	Special	Special
Y	Interlock or state	Relay/compute	Relay/compute
Z	Position, dimension	Damper or louver drive	

The little balloons all over the P&ID contain tag names for each instrument. Some balloons have lines through or boxes around them which convey information about the instrument's location and the method by which a readout may be obtained. Figure 8-2 shows some of the more common symbols. The intent is to differentiate between a field-mounted instrument (like a valve or mechanical gauge) and various remotely mounted electronic or computer displays.

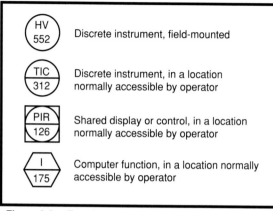

Figure 8-2. Function symbols or *balloons* used to identify instruments on the P&ID.

Every pipe, connection, valve, actuator, transducer, and function in the plant has an appropriate symbol, and these are also covered by S5.1. Figure 8-3 shows some examples that you would be likely to see on the P&ID for any major industrial plant. Your system may use specialized instruments that are not explicitly covered by the standard. In that case, you are free to improvise while keeping with the spirit of the standard. None of this is *law*, you know; it's just there to help. You can also use replicas of these symbols on some of your LabVIEW screens to make it more understandable to the technicians who build and operate the facility.

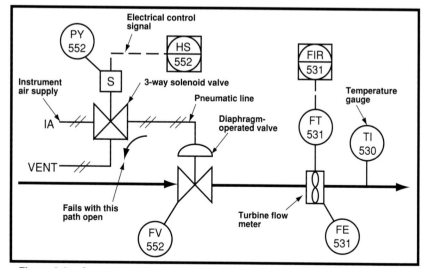

Figure 8-3. Some instrument symbols, showing valves, transmitters, and associated connections. These are right out of the standards documents; your situation may require some improvising.

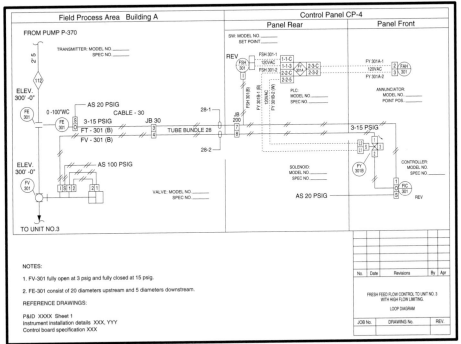

Figure 8-4. An instrument loop diagram, the control engineer's guide to wiring. Reprinted by permission. Copyright 1991, Instrument Society of America. From S-5.4—*Instrument Loop Diagrams.*

Other Drawing and Design Standards

Another of my favorite ISA standards, S5.4, addresses **instrument loop diagrams**, which are the control engineer's electrical wiring diagram. An example appears in Figure 8-4. The reasons for the format of a loop diagram become clear once you have worked in a large plant environment where a signal may pass through several junction boxes or terminal panels before finally arriving at the computer or controller input. When a field technician must install or troubleshoot such a system, having one (or only a few) channels per page in a consistent format is most appreciated.

Notice that the tag name appears prominently in the title strip, among other places. This is how the drawings are indexed, because the tag name is *the* universal identifier. The loop diagram also tells you where each item is located, which cables the signal runs through, instrument specifications, calibration values (electrical as well as engineering units), and computer database or controller setting information. I've found this concise drawing format to be useful in many laboratory installations as well. It is easy to follow and easy to maintain.Here are a few other ISA standards that can be valuable to you:

S5.5   *Graphic Symbols for Process Displays*

S51.1   *Process Instrumentation Terminology*

S50.1   *Compatibility of Analog Signals for Electronic Industrial Process Equipment*

If you are involved with the design of a major facility, many other national standards will come into play, such as the *National Electrical Code* and the *Uniform Mechanical Code*. That's why plants are designed by multidisciplinary teams with many engineers and designers who are well-versed in their respective areas of expertise. With these standards in hand and a few process control reference books, it is likely that you might well move beyond the level of the mere LabVIEW hacker and into the realm of the Certified Professional Control Engineer.

Control = Manipulating Outputs

Controlling a process implies a need for some kind of output signal from the control system. (At last! Something that uses all those analog and digital output modules that somebody sold you!) The simplest control mode, **manual control**, relies on the operator to turn a knob or throw a switch to manipulate the process through some actuator. Programming a manual control system is about as simple as things get. The other control mode, **automatic control**, requires a hardware or software machine to make the adjustments. What both modes have in common (besides output hardware) is the use of **feedback**. In manual control, the operator sees that the temperature is too high, and he turns down the heater. In automatic control, the controller makes a measurement (the **process variable**), compares it with the desired value, or **setpoint**, and then adjusts the output accordingly.

The output of the controller may be either digital or analog in nature. Digital-output controllers are also known as **on-off controllers**. An example is the thermostat on your home's furnace. On-off controllers are generally the simplest and cheapest control technique, but they may be a bit imprecise—the process variable tends to cycle above and below the setpoint. Analog controllers, on the other hand, are proportional in nature, adjusting the output in infinitesimally small steps to minimize the error. They are powerful and versatile, but generally more complex and expensive than on-off controllers.

The most common types of automatic controllers in use today rely on the well-known **proportional-integral-derivative (PID)** family of algorithms. The simplest form of the algorithm is a pure **proportional (P)** controller (Figure 8-5A). An **error** signal is derived by subtracting the process variable from the setpoint. Error is then multiplied by a proportional gain factor, and the result drives the output, or **manipulated variable**. If the process reacts by "going in the right direction," the process variable will tend toward the setpoint—the result of **negative feedback**. If the process goes the wrong direction, **positive feedback** results, followed by undesirable oscillation or saturation. By raising the proportional gain, the error magnitude can be reduced. There is a practical limit to gain, however, due to delay (**lag**) in the process that will eventually cause a destabilizing phase shift in the control loop—the loop ends up responding to old information. Therefore, some residual error is always present with a proportional controller.

One way to eliminate this error is to mathematically **integrate** or **reset** the error over time. Combining these two control techniques results in the **proportional-integral (PI)** controller (Figure 8-5B). With the PI algorithm, the error term is adjusted slowly to zero.

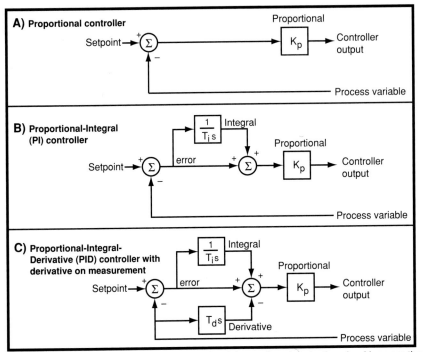

Figure 8-5. Signal flow diagrams for proportional, integral, and derivative algorithms are the basis for much of today's practical feedback control. These are just a few examples of P/PI/PID configuration; there are many more in actual use.

Like any controller, too much of a good thing may result in substandard or unstable performance. PI controllers are the most widely used in general applications.

When a process is subject to sudden upsets, the controller may not respond quickly enough. In such cases, a **derivative**, or **rate**, term may be added (Figure 8-5C). Taking the derivative of the error (a common technique) effectively increases the controller's gain during periods when the process variable is changing, forcing a quick correcting response. Unfortunately, the derivative is a kind of highpass filter that emphasizes the controller's response to noise. Therefore, the full PID algorithm can only be used when the signal has little noise, or where suitable filtering or limiting has been applied.

LabVIEW has a set of PID algorithms available in the LabVIEW PID Control Toolkit. You can use them to build all kinds of control schemes; usage will be discussed later in this chapter. PID control can also be accomplished through the use of external *smart* controllers and modules. Greg Shinskey's excellent *Process Control Systems* [Ref. 1] discusses the application, design, and tuning of industrial controllers from a practical point of view. He's my kinda guy.

There are many alternatives to the common PID algorithm so often used in industrial control. For instance, there are algorithms based on state variable analysis which rely on a fairly accurate model of the process to obtain an optimal control algorithm. Adaptive controllers, which may or may not be based on a PID algorithm, modify the actions of the controller in response to changes in the characteristics of the process. Modern **fuzzy logic** controllers are also realizable in LabVIEW. If you have experience in control theory, there are few limitations to what you can accomplish in the LabVIEW environment. I encourage you to develop advanced control VIs and make them available to the rest of us. You might even make some money!

So far we have been looking at **continuous control** concepts that apply to steady-state processes where feedback is applicable. There are other situations. **Sequential control** applies where discrete, ordered events occur over a period of time. Valves that open in a certain order, parts pickers, robots, and conveyors are processes that are sequential in nature. **Batch processes** may be sequential at startup and shutdown, but operate in steady-state throughout the middle of an operation. The difficulty with batch operations is that the continuous control algorithms need to be modified or compromised in some way to handle the transient conditions during startup and shutdown. A special form of batch process, called a **recipe operation**, uses some form of specification entry to determine the sequence of events and steady-state setpoints for each batch. Typical recipe processes are paint and fuel formulation (and making cookies!), where special blends of ingredients and processing conditions are required, depending on the final product.

Early sequential control systems used relay logic, where electromechanical switching devices were combined in such a way as to implement Boolean logic circuits. Other elements such as timers and stepper switches were added to facilitate time-dependent operations. System inputs were switch contacts (manual or machine-actuated), and outputs would drive a variety of power control devices such as contactors.

Most modern sequential control systems are based on **programmable logic controllers (PLCs)**, which are specialized industrial computers with versatile and nearly bullet-proof I/O interface hardware. Millions of PLCs are in service in all industries, worldwide, and for good reasons: they are compact, cost-effective, reliable, and easy to program. It's much easier to "rewire" a PLC's program than it is to rip out dozens of hardwired relays mounted in a rack. PLCs can be networked, and LabVIEW turns out to be a fine man-machine interface for this "rewiring."

Signals

The signals you will encounter in most process control situations are low-frequency or DC analog signals and digital on-off signals, both inputs and outputs. Table 8-2 lists some of the more common ones. In a laboratory situation, this list would be augmented with lots of special analytical instruments, making your control system heavy on data acquisition needs. Actually, most control systems end up that way because it takes lots of information to accurately control a process.

Industry likes to differentiate between **transducers** and **transmitters**. In process control jargon, the simple transducer (like a thermocouple) is called a **primary element**. The signal conditioner that connects to a primary element is called a transmitter.

In the U.S., the most common analog transmitter and controller signals are 4-20 mA current loops, followed by a variety of voltage signals including 1-5, 0-5, and 0-10 V.

Current loops are preferred because they are resistant to ground referencing problems and voltage drops. Most transmitters have a maximum bandwidth of a few hertz, and some offer an adjustable time constant which you can use to optimize high-frequency noise rejection. To interface 4-20 mA signals to an ordinary voltage-sensing input, you will generally add a 250 Ω precision resistor in parallel with the analog input. The resulting voltage is then 1-5 V. When you write your data acquisition program, remember to subtract the 1 V offset before scaling to engineering units.

Table 8-2.   Typical Process Control Signals and Their Usage.

Analog Inputs	Digital Inputs	Analog Outputs	Digital Outputs
Pressure	Pressure switch	Valve positioner	Valve open/close
Temperature	Temperature switch	Motor speed	Motor on/off
Flow rate	Flow switch	Controller setpoint	Indicator lamps
Level	Level switch	Heater power	
Power or energy	Position switch		

On-off signals are generally 24 VDC, 24 VAC, or 120 VAC. I prefer to use low-voltage signals because they are safer for personnel. In areas where potentially flammable dust or vapors may be present, the *National Electrical Code* requires you to eliminate sources of ignition. Low-voltage signals can help you meet these requirements, as well.

The world of process control is going through a major change with emerging digital **fieldbus** standards. These buses are designed to replace the 4-20 mA analog signal connections that have historically connected the field device to the distributed control systems with a digital bus that interconnects several field devices. In addition to using multidrop digital communications networks, these buses use very intelligent field devices. They are designed for device interoperability, which means that any device can understand data supplied by any other device. A control application runs across each fieldbus network with function blocks that execute a given control algorithm distributed across several field devices. For instance, one control algorithm can orchestrate a pressure transmitter, a dedicated feedback controller, and a valve actuator in a field-based control loop.

The first of these, the **HART protocol**, was created by Rosemount, Inc., and is now supported by hundreds of manufacturers. It adds a high-frequency carrier (like that used with 1200-baud modems) which rides on top of the usual 4-20 mA current loop signal. Up to 16 transmitters and/or controllers can reside on one HART bus, which is simply a twisted pair of wires. HART allows you to exchange messages with smart field devices, including data such as calibration information, and the values of multiple outputs—things that are quite impossible with ordinary analog signals. Through the use of commercially available HART modems, it should be easy for LabVIEW to talk to these instruments.

There are several new, emerging standards including the **ISP (Interoperable Systems Project)** and **World FIP (Factory Instrumentation Protocol)** that have international industry backing. The ISA is also pursuing a new standard, **SP-50**. (ISP and World FIP use the currently approved lower layers of SP-50. These other standards committees intend to use the rest of the SP-50 standard when it is finally approved.) Because the field devices on these fieldbus networks are so intelligent, and because the variables shared by devices are completely defined, the systems integration effort is greatly reduced. It is thus much more practical to implement a supervisory system with LabVIEW and one or more physical connections to the fieldbus network. You no longer need drivers for each specific field device. Instead, you can use drivers for *classes* of field devices (such as pressure transmitters or valves). National Instruments will be supporting these protocols as they progress towards final implementation and acceptance. Look for SCXI modules, plug-in boards, and LabVIEW drivers in the near future.

Control System Architectures

Hopefully, you will be designing your LabVIEW process control application along with the plant you wish to control. Choices of transducers and actuators, as well as the overall process topology, dramatically affect the possibilities for adequate control. The process control engineer is responsible for evaluating the chemistry and physics of the plant with an eye towards controllability. The best software in the world can't overcome the actions of improperly specified valves, correct unusable data from the wrong type of flowmeter, or control wildly unstable chemical reactions. You and your design team need to be on top of these issues during all phases of the project.

You will need to choose an appropriate control system architecture. There are many variables, and many personal and corporate biases that point in different directions. Industrial control journals are filled with case histories and design methodologies that represent the cumulative knowledge of thousands of plant designs. For the novice, these journals are a source of inspiration, as are consultants and of course, the major engineering firms. At the end of this section, I'll list some possible design parameters you might use to develop a checklist that leads to the right system.

Distributed Control System (DCS)

For the largest installations, distributed control systems have held the market for decades, though that position is being eroded by the improved capability of smaller, more open systems. Important characteristics of a DCS are:

- A hierarchical set of intelligent nodes, or controllers, ranging from smart I/O scanners and controllers, to man-machine interface stations, on up to corporate-level management information systems.

- Heavy reliance on local area networks (usually redundant, for reliability).

- A globally shared, real-time database scheme where all nodes can freely share information.

- Multiple levels of access security through passwords and communications restrictions.

- Integration of several different kinds of computers and I/O hardware.

- Dozens, and sometimes hundreds, of nodes.

- Thousands of I/O points.

- Very high cost, often in the millions of dollars.

Older DCSs used proprietary operating systems and custom hardware, but new designs are moving more towards *open*, or public, standards in I/O hardware and operating systems such as UNIX. All DCS vendors work closely with the customer because the system specification, configuration, and startup phases are quite complex. *Turnkey* systems (where the system vendor does the lion's share of the work) are the rule rather than the exception.

A DCS may incorporate many kinds of computers and I/O subsystems, integrated into one (hopefully) harmonious package. In principle, a DCS could be designed with multiple systems running LabVIEW, but that may be stretching things a bit. At this time, LabVIEW just isn't very well suited to this kind of massive application. Some major control system manufacturers are considering LabVIEW at this time, but only in certain subsystems as

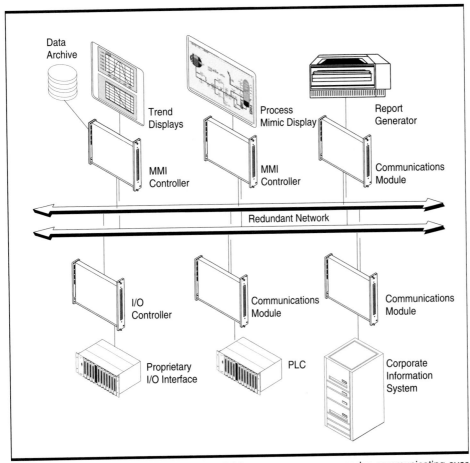

Figure 8-6. A distributed control system, or DCS, encompasses many nodes communicating over networks, and many I/O points.

part of an overall proprietary DCS. But given a few years, LabVIEW may well penetrate these high-end applications.

Enter the Personal Computer

At the other end of the scale from a DCS is the lowly personal computer, which has made an incredible impact on the world of plant automation. The DCS world has provided us with software and hardware integration techniques that have successfully migrated to desktop machines. A host of manufacturers now offer ready-to-run PC-based process control packages with most of the features of their larger cousins, but with a much lower price tag, and a level of complexity that's almost *human* in scale. LabVIEW fits into this amenable category.

A wide range of control problems can be solved by these cost-effective small systems. In the simplest cases, all you need is your PC running LabVIEW with plug-in I/O boards, or maybe some outboard I/O interface hardware. You can implement all the classical control schemes—continuous, sequential, batch, and recipe—with the functions built into LabVIEW, and have a good user interface on top of it all. Such a system is easy to maintain because there is only one programming language, and only rarely would you need the services of a consultant or systems house to complete your project.

There are some limitations with any stand-alone PC-based process control system. Because one machine is responsible for servicing real-time control algorithms as well as the user interface with all its graphics, there can be problems with real-time response. If you need millisecond response, consider using outboard smart controllers (see below). The I/O point count is another factor to consider. Piling on 3000 analog channels is likely to bring your machine to its knees; you must realistically consider some kind of distributed processing scheme.

With LabVIEW, as with the specialized process control packages, you can connect several PCs in a network, much like a DCS. You can configure your system in such a way that the real-time tasks are assumed by dedicated PCs that serve as I/O control processors, while other PCs serve as the man-machine interfaces, data recorders, etc. All the machines run LabVIEW and communicate via a local area network using supported protocols such as AppleEvents, NetDDE, or TCP/IP. The result is an expandable system with the distributed power of a DCS, but at a scale that you (and perhaps a small staff) can create and manage yourself.

PCs with Smart Controllers

Another way to accommodate medium and small-scale plants is to use your PCs with "smart" external controllers, like PLCs and single-loop PID controllers, to off-load critical real-time tasks. This approach has some advantages. Dedicated, special-purpose controllers are famous for their reliability, more so than the general-purpose computer on which you run LabVIEW. They use embedded microprocessors with small, efficient executive programs (like miniature operating systems) that run your control programs at very high speeds with no interference from file systems, graphics, and other overhead.

PLCs can be programmed to perform almost any kind of continuous or sequential control, and larger models can be configured to handle thousands of I/O points and control loops, especially when networked. However, the PLC lacks a user interface and a file system, among other amenities—just the kinds of things that your LabVIEW program can provide. LabVIEW makes an ideal man-machine interface, data recorder, alarm annunciator, and so forth. It's a really synergistic match. About the only disadvantage of this approach is that you have two programming environments to worry about: LabVIEW plus the PLC's programming package.

Single-loop controllers (SLCs) do an admirable job of PID control for industrial applications. They are generally easy to configure, very reliable, and many offer advanced features like recipe generation and automatic tuning. Like PLCs, however, they lack the ability to record data, and it may not be feasible to locate the SLC close to the operator's preferred working location. By using a communications link (usually RS-232), LabVIEW can integrate SLCs into a distributed process control system.

Choose Your System

In summary, here are some important control system design parameters that might lead you to a first-cut decision as to whether LabVIEW is a practical choice for your application.

Number of I/O points and number of network nodes—What is the overall scale of your system? Up to a few hundred I/O points, even a stand-alone PC running LabVIEW has a good chance of doing the job. With somewhat higher point counts, high speed requirements, or a need to have the I/O distributed over a wider area, PLCs offer lots of advantages, and LabVIEW could make a nice MMI. If you are tackling an entire plant, then LabVIEW might be suited to some local control applications, but a DCS or a large, integrated package may be a better choice.

Planned expansion—Continuing with the first topic, remember to include any plans for future expansion. A lab-scale pilot plant is ideal for LabVIEW, but its plant-scale implementation may be a whole 'nother story. A poorly chosen control system may result from underestimation of the overall needs. Beware.

Integration with other systems—Needs for corporate-level computing will influence your choice of control computers and networks. For instance, if you live in a UNIX/-XWindows world, then a SPARCstation running LabVIEW might be a good platform.

Requirements for handling unique, nonstandard instruments—LabVIEW has tremendous advantages over commercial process control software products when it comes to handling unusual instrument interfaces. Because you can easily write your own drivers in LabVIEW, these special situations are a nonproblem.

Ease of configuration and modification—What plans do you have for modifying your process control system? Some system architectures and software products are rather inflexible, requiring many hours of reconfiguration for seemingly simple changes. Adding a new instrument interface to a large DCS may require an Act of Congress, as many users have discovered. Meanwhile, LabVIEW remains a flexible solution, so long as you design your application with some forethought.

Overall reliability—It's hard to compare computers, operating systems, and software when it comes to reliability. Suffice it to say that simple is better, and that's why many process engineers prefer PLCs and SLCs: they are simple and robust. The MMI software is, in a sense, of secondary importance in these systems because the process can continue to operate (if desired) even while the MMI is off line. I've found that the system architecture is often more important than brand of computer or software. Using **redundant** hardware is the ultimate solution where reliability is paramount. Many PLC and DCS vendors offer redundancy. Additionally, you should consider adding fail-safe mechanisms to insure safety and prevent major hazards and losses when things go awry. Software bugs, hardware failures, and system crashes can be very costly in process control.

Existing company standards and personal biases—Everyone from the CEO to the janitor will have opinions regarding your choice of hardware and software. For the small, experimental systems that I work on, LabVIEW has many advantages over other products. As such, it has become very popular—a definite positive bias—and with good reason. However, I would *not* use it to control a new hundred-million-dollar facility, no matter how biased I (we) might be.

Cost—The bottom line is always cost. One cost factor is the need for system integration services and consultants, which is minimal with LabVIEW, but mandatory with a DCS. Another factor is the number of computers or smart controllers that you might need. A standalone PC is probably cheaper than a PC plus a PLC. Also consider the long-term costs such as operator training, software upgrades and modifications, and maintenance.

Working with Smart Controllers

Adding smart controllers to your process control system is smart engineering. PLCs, SLCs, and other programmable devices are practical solutions to your real-world control problems. They are completely optimized to perform real-time continuous and sequential control with the utmost in reliability while managing to be flexible enough to adapt to many different situations. Take advantage of them whenever possible.

Programmable Logic Controllers (PLCs)

A programmable logic controller (PLC) is an industrial computer with a CPU, nonvolatile program memory, and dedicated I/O interface hardware [Ref. 4]. Conceived by General Motors Corporation in 1968 as a replacement for hardwired relay logic, PLCs have grown dramatically in their software and hardware capabilities, and now offer incredible power and flexibility to the control engineer. Major features of a modern PLC are:

- Modular construction

- Very high reliability (redundancy available for many models)

- Versatile and robust I/O interface hardware

- Wide range of control features included, such as logic, timing, and analog control algorithms

- Fast, deterministic execution of programs—a true real-time system

- Communications supported with host computers and other PLCs

- Many programming packages available

- Low cost

You can buy PLCs with a wide range of I/O capacity, program storage capacity, and CPU speed to suit your particular project. The simplest PLCs, also called microcontrollers, replace a modest number of relays and timers, do only discrete (on-off, or Boolean) logic operations, and support up to about 32 I/O points. Mid range PLCs add analog I/O and communications features and support up to about 1024 I/O points. The largest PLCs support several thousand I/O points and use the latest microprocessors for very high performance (with a proportionally high cost, as you might expect).

You usually program a PLC with an IBM PC compatible running a special-purpose application. **Ladder logic** (Figure 8-7) is the most common "language" for programming in the U.S., though a different concept, called Grafcet, is more commonly used in Europe. Some programming applications also support BASIC, Pascal, or C, either intermixed with ladder logic or as a pure high-level language, just as you would expect to use with any computer system.

There are about 100 PLC manufacturers in the world today. Some of the major ones are Siemens, Allen-Bradley, Modicon, Telemechanique, Square-D, and General Electric. Of these, Siemens, Allen-Bradley, Modicon, and Telemechanique are currently supported by complete LabVIEW driver packages. Others are sure to follow.

ISA offers some PLC-related training you may be interested in. Course number T420, Fundamentals of Programmable Controllers, gives you a good overview of the concepts required to use PLCs. The textbook for the class, *Programmable Controllers: Theory and Implementation* [Ref. 4], is very good even if you can't attend the class. Another course,

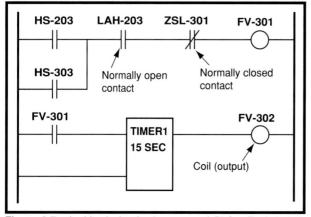

Figure 8-7. Ladder logic, the language of PLCs. Each item in the diagram corresponds to an emulated piece of hardware—contacts (switches), timers, relay coils, etc.

Figure 8-8. PLCs like this Siemens model are popular in process control. SinecVIEW is a LabVIEW driver package that communicates with Siemens PLCs via a serial interface. (Photo Coutesy of National Instruments and CITVZW Belgium.)

T425, Programmable Controller Applications, gets into practical aspects of system design, hardware selection, and programming in real situations.

Advantages of PLCs

Programmable controllers have become a favorite tool in the control industry because of their simplicity, low cost, rugged hardware, and reliable real-time performance. These are clear-cut advantages that will make them candidates for your project, as well.

Interfacing couldn't be easier. Input and output modules are available for direct connection to 240 VAC and lower AC and DC voltages, and a wide range of analog signals. Compare this with most interface systems, which require extra isolation devices or adapters, especially for high voltages and currents.

Reliability may be the main reason for choosing a PLC over other solutions. Both the hardware and the operating software in a PLC are simple in nature, making it easier to prove correctness of design and simultaneously lowering the number of possible failure points. Contrast this with a general-purpose, desktop computer. How often does your computer hang up or crash? If your process demands predictable performance, day in and day out, better consider using a PLC.

PLC Communications and Register Access

Manufacturers of PLCs have devised many communications techniques and pseudo-standard protocols. For instance, Modicon has their proprietary *Modbus* protocol, while Allen-Bradley has their *Data Highway Plus*—and the two are completely incompatible. The good news is that, through an adapter module, any computer with RS-232 capability can communicate with these various data highways, assuming that you have the right driver software. All midrange and high-end PLCs have the ability to communicate peer-to-peer, that is, between individual PLCs without host intervention. A variety of schemes exist for host computers as well, serving as masters or slaves on the network.

Once a PLC has been programmed, your LabVIEW program is free to read data from and write data to the PLC's registers. A register may represent a Boolean (either zero or one), a set of Booleans (perhaps eight or 16 in one register), an ASCII character, or an integer or floating-point number. Register access is performed at a surprisingly low level on most PLCs. Instead of sending a message like you would with a GPIB instrument ("start

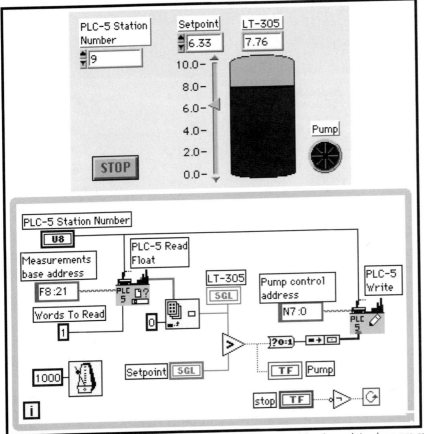

Figure 8-9. A simple example using HighwayVIEW. An array of floating point values are read from the PLC, and one is compared with a setpoint. If the tank level is too high, a pump is turned on by setting a PLC register to 1.

sequence 1"), you poke a value into a register that your ladder logic program interprets as a command. For instance, the ladder logic might be written such that a "1" in register number 10035 is interpreted as a closed contact in an interlock string that triggers a sequential operation.

There are a few things to watch out for when you program your PLC and team it with LabVIEW or any other host computer. First, watch out for conflicts when writing to registers. If the ladder logic *and* your LabVIEW program both write to a register, you have an obvious conflict. Instead, all registers should be one-way; that is, either the PLC writes to them or your LabVIEW program does. Second, you may want to implement a **watchdog** program on the PLC that responds to failures of the host computer. This is especially important when a host failure might leave the process in a dangerous condition. A watchdog is a timer that the host must "hit," or reset periodically. If the timer runs to its limit, the PLC takes a preprogrammed action. For instance, the PLC may close important valves or reset the host computer in an attempt to reawaken it from a locked-up state.

Drivers Available

Several PLC driver packages are currently available, and more are on the way. HighwayVIEW, from SEG, supports Allen-Bradley models PLC-2, PLC-3, and PLC-5. It supports all data types for both inputs and outputs. Communications are handled by a program that is installed in your computer's operating system (a Control Panel on the Macintosh; a DLL under Windows). This communications handler is particularly robust, offering automatic retries if an error occurs. Figure 8-9 shows a simple example of HighwayVIEW in action as a simple on-off limit controller application.

If you own a Siemens Simatic S5 series PLC and a Macintosh, then look into SinecVIEW from CIT in Belgium. Like HighwayVIEW, this package handles all of the

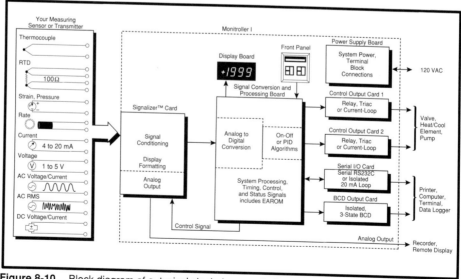

Figure 8-10. Block diagram of a typical single-loop controller. (*Courtesy Analogic.*)

available data types. It also supports two different communications protocols, Sinec L1 or 3964R, both of which adapt a network of S5 PLCs directly to a Macintosh serial port. Some models of the Siemens line that were acquired from Texas Instruments, the 500 series, are also supported by drivers available from Porter Associates. Other, newly released products are a Modicon driver from SEG and a Telmechanique driver from Saphir.

Single-Loop Controllers (SLCs)

Single-loop PID controllers are an old favorite of process engineers. Years ago, they were pneumatically operated, using springs, levers, bellows, and orifices to implement an accurate PID algorithm. To this day, there are still many installations that are entirely pneumatic, mostly where an intrinsically safe control system is required. Modern SLCs are compact, microprocessor-based units that mount in a control panel. Some models can control more than one loop. They are compatible with common input signals including thermocouples, RTDs, currents, and voltages, with various ranges. The output may be an analog voltage or current, or an on-off digital signal controlled by a relay or triac. Other features are alarms with contact closure outputs and ramp-and-soak recipe operation.

The front panel of a typical SLC consists of an array of buttons and one or more digital displays. They are fairly easy to understand and use, though some operators are frustrated by the "VCR programming syndrome" where there are too many obscure functions and too many menu choices. This is where LabVIEW can enhance the usefulness of an SLC by simplifying the presentation of controls and indicators. Low-level setup information can be hidden from the user while being properly maintained by your program.

All of the more sophisticated controllers offer communications options. Most of them use RS-232 or RS-422/485 serial, but at least one controller features GPIB (Research, Inc., with its Micristar controller). The communications protocols vary widely, generally following no standard at all. One exception is a line of controllers from Anafaze that use the Allen-Bradley Data Highway protocol, the same one used by Allen-Bradley PLCs, which is supported by AnaVIEW from SEG. A few other SLCs have LabVIEW drivers, such as the Eurotherm 808/847, which uses RS-422 communications. With a data highway, GPIB, or RS-485, a multidrop network of controllers is feasible, permitting many stations to communicate with your LabVIEW system while consuming one communications port.

The easiest way to control an SLC is with a good driver. A few controllers are in the instrument library (e.g., Eurotherm and Micristar), and a few are supported by commercial software vendors, as in the case of Anafaze. Consider the availability of drivers when choosing a controller; otherwise, you will have to write your own. A good driver package will permit you to read and write most any function in the controller.

Back in Chapter 4, *Building an Application*, I talked about the Vacuum Brazing Laboratory project, where several Eurotherm SLCs controlled furnace temperatures. LabVIEW simplified the operator's life by performing the following functions:

- Recipe entry through a table, with a graph showing time vs. temperature.
- Programmable limiting of controller outputs to prevent heater burnout.

- Automatic system startup and shutdown based on time of day or other events.
- Trending of setpoints and measured temperature.
- Audible and visual alarms.

These are typical functions that you might consider implementing. Another thing you might want to add is configuration management. The Eurotherm controllers have about 40 setup items that have to be set and verified at installation. A LabVIEW program could easily upload and download such settings to files, saving the operator a lot of button pushing with its attendant errors. Figure 8-11 shows a simple example with the Eurotherm driver VI.

In my application, LabVIEW generated the ramp-and-soak profiles by calculating and transmitting a new setpoint every second. This was easier than using the controller's built-in ramp functions because the profile could then be interrupted or modified on the fly.

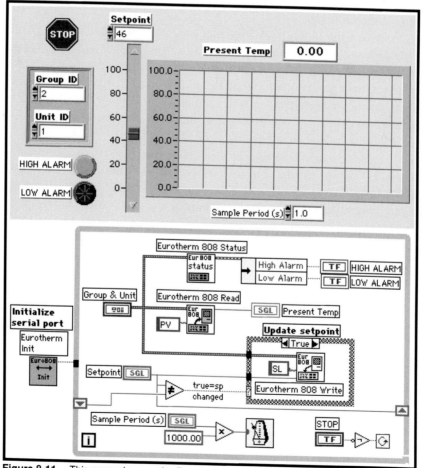

Figure 8-11. This example uses the Eurotherm 808/847 SLC driver to update the setpoint and read the process variable and alarm status.

I really recommend SLCs when you have a modest number of control loops. Their high reliability and simplicity, combined with the power and flexibility of a LabVIEW MMI, make a fine process control system.

Other Smart I/O Subsystems

There are many other effective ways to distribute the intelligence in your process control system besides using PLCs and SLCs. All you really need is an external I/O subsystem with local intelligence and communications that can either execute sequential or continuous control algorithms.

Multifunction scanners, such as the HP3852A, are more often used as simple data acquisition units, but they contain a surprising amount of control functionality as well. You can download programs to do scanning and units conversion, limit checking, and some kinds of feedback control. You have many options with the many types of interface modules available for these scanners. Check for availability of LabVIEW drivers before deciding on a particular model.

Another example is the Azonix μMAC series of controllers (formerly made by Analog Devices), particularly the μMAC-6000, for which a LabVIEW driver has been available for years. This controller is driven by an embedded microprocessor with a resident BASIC interpreter. It supports a variety of analog and digital I/O modules and communicates via RS-485 in a multidrop configuration. The driver permits you to download BASIC code (in text format) to perform scanning, conversion, and control algorithms of all kinds. It's easy to program, and the board runs autonomously much like a PLC.

An often-overlooked option is to use LabVIEW-based slave systems with little or no MMI functionality. The slave nodes communicate with the main MMI node, exchanging data in some LabVIEW formats that you decide upon. Slaves handle all the real-time data acquisition and control activity without the performance penalties of a busy graphical display or lots of user intervention. This technique is advantageous when you need sophisticated algorithms that a PLC or other simple processor can't handle. Also, since everything is written in LabVIEW, it's easier to maintain. Networking techniques are discussed later in this chapter.

One downside to using LabVIEW in the loop may be in the area of reliability, depending upon how critical your tasks are. Where I work, it is a policy never to use a general-purpose computer for safety interlocks. PLCs, on the other hand, are considered acceptable. The difference is in the simplicity of the PLC software, which simply doesn't crash, and which also has a very deterministic response time. The same cannot be said of a typical LabVIEW system running on top of a complex operating system. You will have to be the judge on this matter of safety and reliability.

Man-Machine Interfaces

When it comes to graphical man-machine interfaces, LabVIEW is among the very best products you can choose. The library of standard and customizable controls is extensive,

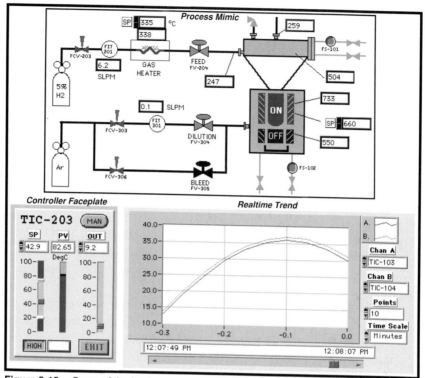

Figure 8-12. Some of the basic process displays that you can make in LabVIEW.

but more than that, the function of each control is determined by you, the crafty programmer. In the process control world, there are several commonly used displays that you will probably want to implement in one form or another (Figure 8-12).

- **Process mimic displays**, which are based on simplified P&ID diagrams. Various elements of the display are animated, tying measurements and status information directly to physical elements in the plant. Operators really like this kind of display. You can draw a representation of the system and import the picture into LabVIEW, then overlay it with various controls and indicators. Valves, heaters, and alarm indicators are usually Booleans, while various numeric controls and indicators are placed near their respective instruments.

- **Trending displays** (graphs or stripcharts), of which there are two types: historical trends and real-time trends. A real-time trend displays up-to-the-minute data, but may not go very far back in time. It relies primarily on data stored in memory. Historical trends usually read and display data from large disk files. Trending is discussed later in this chapter.

- **Controller faceplate displays**, which look and act much like the front panels of SLCs. They permit the operator to observe and control all the settings of PID and other types of analog controllers. Digital I/O or alarm status can also be presented in the form of Boolean indicators, like the example in Figure 8-13.

- **Alarm summary displays** are used to give the operator a concise overview of important status information, particularly I/O points that are out of specification in some way. You can use scrolling string indicators to list recent messages or Boolean indicators as a kind of status panel.

As an example, I decided to make a really nice controller faceplate display that makes use of some of LabVIEW's more advanced features. This one mimics some of the commercial SLC front panels, and is typical of the faceplates I've seen displayed on commercial DCS screens. (On a DCS, they usually put eight or 10 faceplates on one screen, and the faceplate is a standard indicator element.) Figure 8-13 shows the panel of the controller subVI. You would normally size the VI window such that only the faceplate part of the panel is visible; the other items are just parameters for the calling VI. This subVI is programmable in the sense that the tagname, units, and other parameters are passed from the caller. This fact permits you to use one subVI to operate many control loops. The VI must be set to Show front panel when called.

The **SP** (setpoint) slider control is customized via the various pop-up menu options and the **Control Editor**. I first added two extra sliders by popping up on the control and selecting Add Slider. They serve as high and low alarm limits. I set the Fill Options for each of these alarm sliders to Fill to Maximum (upper one) and Fill to Minimum (lower one).

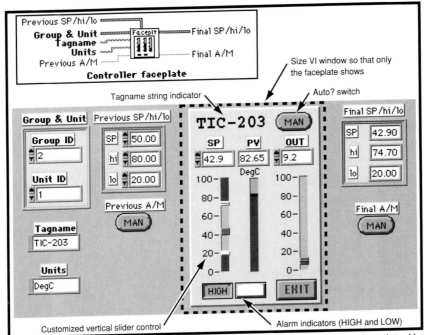

Figure 8-13. Here's the panel of a subVI that mimics a single-loop controller faceplate. You can call it from other VIs to operate many controllers since everything is programmable.

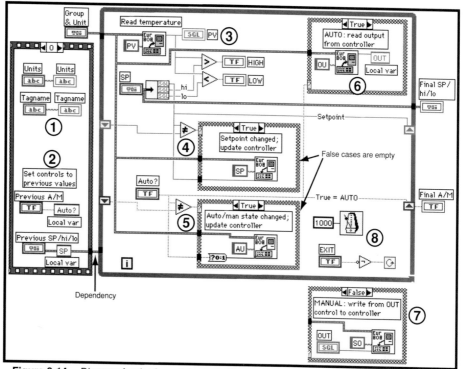

Figure 8-14. Diagram for the faceplate controller.

In the Control Editor, I effectively erased the digital indicators for the two alarm limits by setting their vertical and horizontal sizes to the smallest possible values.

The diagram in Figure 8-14 is fairly complex, so I'll go through it step by step. It illustrates the use of local variables. The I/O hardware in this example is, again, the Eurotherm 808 SLC. This VI relies on the controller to perform the PID algorithm, though you could write a set of subVIs that perform the same task with the LabVIEW PID Control Toolkit, in conjunction with any type of I/O.

1. **Tagname** and **Units** are copied from incoming parameters to indicators on the faceplate. This gives the faceplate a custom look—as if it was written just for the particular channel in use.

2. Previous settings for **Auto?** (the auto/manual switch) and **SP** (the setpoint slider) are written to the user controls on the faceplate by using local variables. This step, like Step 1, must be completed before the While Loop begins, so they are contained in a Sequence structure with a wire from one of the items to the border of the While Loop.

3. The process variable (e.g., current temperature) is read from the controller, checked against the alarm limits, and displayed.

4. The current value for the setpoint is compared against the previous value in a shift register. If the value has changed, the setpoint is sent to the controller. This saves time by avoiding retransmission of the same value over and over.

5. In a similar fashion, the **Auto?** switch is checked for change-of-state. If it has changed, the new setting is sent to the controller.

6. If the mode is automatic, the **Out** (output) control is updated by using a Local Variable. The value is read from the controller.

7. If the mode is manual, **Out** supplies a value that is sent to the controller. These two steps illustrate an acceptable use of a read-write control that avoids race conditions or other aberrant behavior.

8. The loop runs every second until the user clicks **EXIT**, after which the final values for **Auto?** and **SP/hi/lo** are returned to the calling VI for use next time this VI is called.

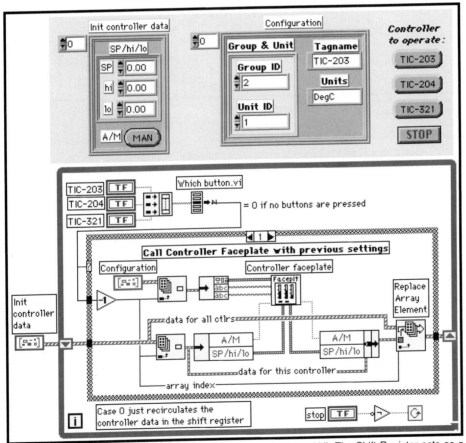

Figure 8-15. An application that uses the Faceplate Controller subVI. The Shift Register acts as a database for previous controller values.

Figure 8-15 shows how this subVI might be used in an application to support multiple controllers. The panel contains a **Configuration** array that identifies each controller, a set of buttons to call the desired controller, and an initialization array. When one of the buttons is pressed, our old friend, Which Button VI, returns a nonzero value and Case 1 is executed (Case 0 just recirculates data in the Shift Register, waiting for a button to be pressed).

Inside the Case, the **Configuration** is indexed to extract the setup information for the selected controller, which is then passed to Controller Faceplate. Similarly, the controller data array, circulating in the Shift Register, is indexed and unbundled. When Controller Faceplate finishes, the data it returns is bundled and the current element in the data array is replaced. The next time this controller is called, data from the previous call will be available from the shift register. Note the use of **Bundle by Name** and **Unbundle by Name**. These functions show the signal names so you can keep them straight.

This procedure of indexing, unbundling, bundling, and replacing an array element is a versatile database management concept that you can use in configuration management. Sometimes the data structures are very complex (arrays of clusters of arrays, etc.), but the procedure is the same, and the diagram is symmetrical when properly laid out. Little memory management is required, so the operations are reasonably fast. One final note regarding the use of global memory of this type. All database updates must be controlled by one VI to serialize the operations. If you access a global variable from many locations, sooner or later you will encounter a race condition in which two callers attempt to write data at the same time. There is no way of knowing who will get there first. Each caller got an original copy of the data at the same time, but the last guy to write the data wins. This is true for both the built-in LabVIEW globals and the ones based on shift registers that you build yourself.

Display Hierarchy

Naturally, you can mix elements from each of the various types of displays freely because LabVIEW has no particular restrictions. Many commercial software packages have preformatted displays that make setups easy, but somewhat less versatile. You could put several of these fundamental types of displays on one panel, or better, you may want to segregate them into individual panels that include only one type of display per panel. A possible hierarchy of displays is shown in Figure 8-16. Such a hierarchy relies heavily on global variables for access to information about every I/O point, and on pop-up windows (VIs that open when called).

Your displays need to be organized in a manner that is easily understood by the operator, and one that is easy to navigate. A problem that is common to large, integrated, control systems is that it takes too long to find the desired information, especially when an emergency arises. Therefore, you must work with the operators so that the display hierarchy and navigation process make sense. The organization in Figure 8-16 is closely aligned with that of the plant that it controls. Each subdisplay gives a greater level of detail about, or a different view of, a particular subsystem. This method is generally accepted by operators, and is a good starting point.

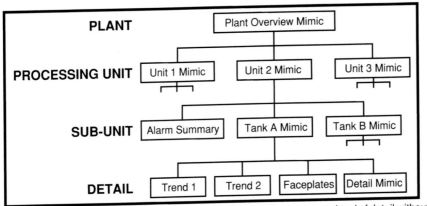

Figure 8-16. Hierarchical process displays allow the operator to see any level of detail without having overcrowded screens.

The VI hierarchy can be mapped one-for-one with the display hierarchy by using pop-up windows (subVIs set to **Show front panel when called**). Each VI contains a **dispatcher** loop similar to the one shown in Figure 8-26. Buttons on the panel are used to select which display to bring up. A Case structure contains a separate display subVI in each frame. The utility VI named Which Button multiplexes all the buttons into a number that selects the appropriate case. The dispatcher loop runs in parallel with other loops in the calling VI.

Each subVI in turn is structured the same way as the top-level VI, with a dispatcher loop calling other subVIs as desired. When it's time to exit a subVI and return to a higher level, an exit button is pressed, terminating the subVI execution, closing its panel, and returning

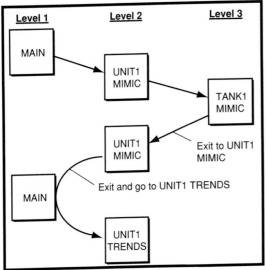

Figure 8-17. Traversing the display hierarchy. When you click an exit button on a subdisplay VI, it returns a value that tells the calling VI where to go next.

control to the caller. An extension of this exit action is to have more than one button with which to exit the subVI. A value is returned by the subVI indicating where the user wants to go next (Figure 8-17). The caller's dispatcher is then responsible for figuring out which subVI to call next.

Making the actual buttons is the fun part. The simplest ones are the built-in labeled buttons: **TREND**. Or, you can paste in a picture that is a little more descriptive. Another method is to use a transparent Boolean control on top of a graphic item on a mimic display, such as a tank or reactor. Then, all the operator has to do is click on the tank and a predefined display pops up. This is a good way to jump quickly to an associated trend, alarm, or other detail display. Remember that the operator has to *know* that the buttons are there because he can't *see* them. Therefore, you must be consistent in your use of such buttons or the operators will get confused. To make a transparent Boolean, select a simple Boolean control like the Flat Square Button, and use the Coloring tool to make both the foreground and background transparent (T).

A new option appeared just as this book went to press, tentatively called **Instrument Control VIs**. They should be available as additional files from National Instruments. The package consists of four VIs:

- Open Instrument—Loads a VI from disk, displays its panel and brings it to the front, and positions it anywhere on the screen. You specify the VI to load by its path.

- Run Instrument—Runs any loaded VI. You specify the VI by its name.

- Close Instrument—Closes any VI currently displaying its panel. You specify the VI by its name.

- Get VI State—Tells you if a specified VI is running. You specify the VI by its name.

- Call Instrument—Combines the previous four VIs, to let you Open and Run a VI, and Close the VI when it completes execution. You specify the VI by its name.

This new package offers additional opportunities for navigation among display VIs. Here is one scenario. Create a top-level VI that acts as a program loader. Its diagram

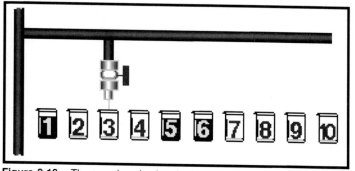

Figure 8-18. The sample valve is a horizontal slide control with the valve picture pasted in as the slider. The control has no axis labels and the housing is colored transparent. The bottles are Boolean indicators and the pipes are static pictures.

contains all of the various user interface VIs that you need, but they're only placed on that diagram so that they will be loaded into memory. Don't run this program loader VI. Instead, call Call Instrument (in response to the click of a button on some other VI) and have it run one of those user interface VIs that you previously loaded. Note that it will have to exchange all data via global variables. Now, you can freely call any user interface VI from anyplace in the hierarchy. But before running a VI, you will have to call Get VI State to see if the desired VI is already running. If it is, you'll have to wait unit it's stopped.

Similar possibilities already exist for Macintosh users—the **AppleEvents** VIs in the Networking function palette. You can use AESend Finder Open to load a VI, then AESend Run VI to run it. The scenario described above will also work using AppleEvents. Future versions of LabVIEW may include similar, but much more powerful VI calling techniques that allow you to pass parameters.

Other Interesting Display Techniques

You can customize controls and indicators by replacing the built-in pictures with custom ones from a drawing package. A useful example, submitted by Corrie Karlsen of LLNL, is shown in Figure 8-18. The system being controlled has a carousel with 10 sample bottles and a liquid sampling valve. When the operator moves the valve icon, a stepper motor moves the carousel to the appropriate bottle. The operator presses a **fill** button (not shown), and the valve is cycled open for a predetermined period of time and then closed. This LabVIEW indicator then responds by updating the full/empty status of the sample bottles, which are Boolean indicators.

You can create Boolean controls that look like valves with different open and closed states by pasting in a pair of pictures. If the operator prefers feedback regarding the status of a valve that has limit switches, you can place a **PICT ring** indicator for status on top of a transparent Boolean control for manual actuation. For a valve with high and low limit switches, the ring indicator would show open, transit, closed, and an illegal value where both limit switches are activated.

You can animate pipes, pumps, heaters, and a host of other process equipment by using picture Booleans or PICT rings. To simulate motion, create a picture such as a paddle wheel in a drawing program, then duplicate it and modify each duplicate in some way, such as rotating the wheel. Then, paste the pictures into the PICT ring in sequence. Connect the ring indicator to a number that cycles through the appropriate range of values on a periodic basis. This is the LabVIEW equivalent of those novelty movies that are drawn in the margins of books.

Perhaps the most impressive, and perhaps the most useful display is a process mimic based on a pictorial representation of your process. A simple line drawing like a P&ID showing important valves and instruments is easy to create and remarkably effective. If your plant is better represented as a photograph or other artwork, by all means use that. You can import CAD drawings, scanned images, or images from a video frame grabber to enhance a process display.

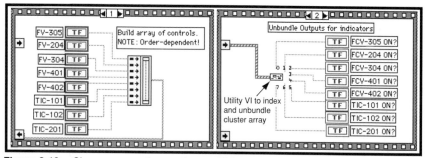

Figure 8-19. Clean up your diagram by combining controls and indicators into arrays or clusters. Other frames in this Sequence structure are the sources and sinks for data. The unbundler subVI on the right extracts Boolean values from a big cluster array. You could also use Unbundle By Name.

Handling All Those Front Panel Items

Process control panels tend to be loaded with many controls and indicators. This can make your diagram very busy and hard to understand. What you need to do is bundle related controls into arrays or clusters and pass them to subVIs for processing. Similarly, indicators are unbundled for display after being returned from source VIs (Figure 8-19). A sequence structure helps to conserve screen space. It doesn't impair the visual flow of the program too much because only a single item is passed from one frame to the next.

One hazard in this array-based scheme is that all the controls and indicators are order-dependent; that is, element three of the control array is always PV-401. Any wiring or indexing errors anywhere in your program will send the wrong value. An alternative is to use clusters and Bundle by Name and Unbundle by Name. There is still a limitation with named clusters, however; you can't arbitrarily configure channels (insert or delete them) during execution with a configuration manager. Editing of one or more diagrams will always be necessary to change the overall configuration.

Experts in human factors tell us that having too much information on one screen leads to information overload. The operator can't find what he's looking for, and the important values get lost in a sea of colored lights. If you find that your MMI display VI has a ridiculous number of controls and/or indicators, it's time to break it into multiple panels. It will then be easier for the operator to use, and easier for the programmer to design and maintain. This is just one more reason for using hierarchical displays.

Data Distribution

If you think about MMI display hierarchies, one thing you may wonder about is how the many subVIs receive current data. This is a data distribution problem, and it can be a big one. A complex process control system may have many I/O subsystems of different types, some of which are accessed over a network. If you don't use a coherent plan of attack, performance (and perhaps reliability) is sure to suffer. Global variables generally solve the problem, if used with some caution.

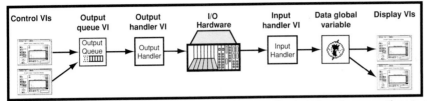

Figure 8-20. Data distribution in a process control system. Control VIs write new settings to an output queue, from which values are written to the hardware by an output handler VI. An input handler VI reads data and stores it in a global variable for use by multiple display VIs.

DCS designers use the features of a multitasking operating system to make data globally accessible in real-time. You can emulate this in your LabVIEW program. The general concept is to use centralized, asynchronous, **I/O handler** tasks to perform the actual I/O operations (translation: stand-alone VIs that talk to the I/O hardware through the use of LabVIEW drivers). Data is exchanged with the I/O handlers via one or more global variables or queues (Figure 8-20).

Input Scanners as Servers

The client-server model is very useful for the input data in process control systems. An input handler task, a server VI which I like to call a **scanner**, periodically polls all the defined input channels, applies scale factors, and writes the results to global variables. The scanner is also a logical place to check any alarm limits. Depending on your application's complexity, the scanner VI may also be responsible for some aspects of trending or data archiving as well.

Figure 8-21 is a simplified scanner VI. It is called by a top-level VI and runs periodically until a Boolean global variable called RUN is set to false. Two input handler VIs, one for

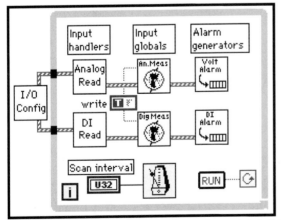

Figure 8-21. A scanner VI that handles analog and digital inputs. The I/O configuration subVI, at left, passes information to the input handlers. Data from the input handlers is written to other global variables for use by client VIs. Alarm limits are also checked and the results are written to alarm message queues.

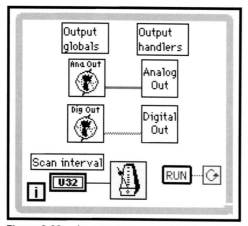

Figure 8-22. An output scanner, which is quite similar to an input scanner.

analog inputs and the other for digital, acquire raw data, filter it, and scale it to engineering units. Handler outputs are cluster arrays containing each channel's value, its name, and any other information that client tasks might need. This information is written to global variables and passed to alarm generator VIs that test each channel for alarm limit violations. Alarm flags or messages are stored in a queue (see *Alarm Handling*, below).

As you might expect, process control has many of the same configuration needs as a data acquisition system. Each input handler requires information about its associated input hardware, channel assignments, and so forth. This information comes from an I/O configuration VI, which supplies the configurations in cluster arrays. If configuration information is needed elsewhere in the hierarchy, it can be passed directly in global variables, or it can be included in the data cluster arrays produced by the input handlers.

Handling Output Data

For efficiency, it may be better to update an output only when its value changes because some devices have a fair amount of overhead associated with communications. Like the input model we've been discussing, you can use an output handler, and an output global variable that contains the values for each output channel. The global variable carries an array with each element of the array corresponding to an output channel. Any control VI can update values in the output global. The output handler checks for changes in any of the output channels, and updates the specific channels that have changed. You can combine the handler and its associated global variable into an output scanner, as in Figure 8-22, which works like an input scanner in reverse.

To test for changes of state on an array of output values, use a program similar to the one in Figure 8-23. A shift register contains the values of all channels from the last time the handler was called. Each channel's new value is compared with its previous value, and if a change has occurred, the output is written. Another shift register forces all outputs to update when the VI is loaded. You could also add a **force update** Boolean control to do the

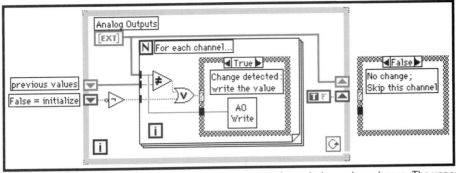

Figure 8-23. An output handler that only writes to an output channel when values change. The upper shift register stores the previous values for comparison, while the lower shift register is used for initialization. Its value is False when the VI is loaded, forcing all outputs to update. Additional initialization features may be required if the program is stopped and restarted.

same thing. Depending upon the complexity of your system, channel configuration information may be required to perform the output write operation. If it is, you can read the configuration global variable and then pass that information along to the specific subVI that writes the data.

Because the Analog Output global variable contains an *array* of values, control VIs have to *update* that array, not overwrite it. Updates are easy to do. Just read the array from the global, use **Replace Array Element** to surgically change the value of a single channel, then write the array back to the global. Please note that there is again a great probability of

DISPLAY SELECT				Goto Screen
CHARTS	MIMIC	METERS	MAIN	0

Expanded Outside Diameter (in.)

Target:	Target 0.000	Max Above 0.000	Max Below 0.000
Statistical:	UCL Setpoint 0.000	LCL Setpoint 0.000	Range UCL 0.000
Pre-Control:	Upper Limit 0.000	Lower Limit 0.000	Range Upper Limit 0.000

Longitudinal Change (%)

Target:	Desired L.C. 0.000	L.C. Setpoint 0.000	
Statistical:	UCL 0.000	LCL 0.000	Range UCL 0.000
Pre-Control:	Upper Limit 0.000	Lower Limit 0.000	Range Upper Limit 0.000

Dips per Kft

Statistical:	Process UCL 0.000	Process LCL 0.000	Spec UCL 0.000
Pre-Control:	Process U.L. 0.000	Process L.L. 0.000	Spec U.L. 0.000

Figure 8-24. Front panel of a display and control VI that is used to monitor and set operating specifications.

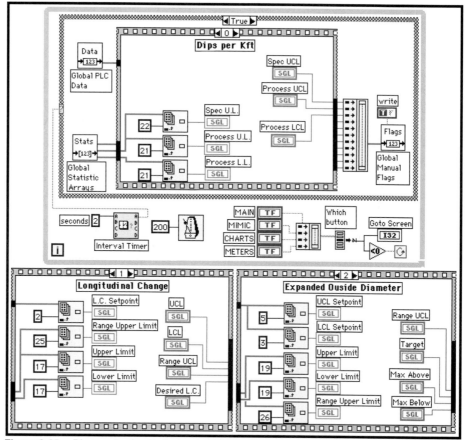

Figure 8-25. Diagram for the display/control VI. The Case structure and interval timer limit how often the displays and controls are updated. A sequence is used to logically group the controls and indicators, eliminating clutter. The VI loops until the user clicks a button to jump to another display.

a race condition arising. If the global variable is accessed by multiple callers, they will clash over "who writes last." The solution is to encapsulate all *write* operations for a global variable inside a subVI, effectively serializing access. There is, of course, no limit to the number of VIs that can simultaneously read the global data.

Display VIs as Clients

By now you should be getting the idea that global variables are key elements when designing a versatile process control system. VIs that display data are very easy to write because global variables completely solve the data distribution problem. The input scanner supplies up-to-date values for all inputs, while the configuration part of your system supplies things like channel names, units, and other general information, all available through globals. Figures 8-24 and 8-25 show how I wrote a typical display/control VI using the methods we've discussed.

Since this display example (Figure 8-24) is part of a hierarchical suite, there are buttons marked Display Select near the top. Clicking one of them terminates this VI and returns an appropriate value in Goto Screen (which would normally be positioned off-screen so the user doesn't see it). The rest of the panel is a collection of numeric controls and indicators, grouped by function, with the help of some decorations.

In the associated diagram (Figure 8-25), you can see that the Which Button subVI determines whether the VI will continue to run, based on the state of all the Display Select buttons. The While Loop runs at a fairly fast rate, on the order of every 200 ms or so, to provide rapid response to the buttons. It would be wasteful, however, to update all the display items at that rate, since the data is only updated by the scanners every couple of seconds. The Interval Timer VI controls a Case structure that contains all the really important activity. Every two seconds, the Case is True; otherwise the False case, which contains nothing, executes.

Input data comes from two global variables, Global PLC Data and Global Statistics Arrays, which are written by the input scanner VI. Output data from controls on the panel is built into an array and written to another global variable called Global Manual Flags. This is the only VI that writes to Global Manual Flags. Data in Global Manual Flags is used elsewhere to indicate system status. For clarity, I used a Sequence structure to logically group the front panel items.

If the display needs to call lower-level displays, add a second, independent While Loop as a dispatcher just like the top-level VIs have. Some buttons will then activate the lower-level displays. Other buttons that cause a return to higher-level displays are wired exactly as shown in Figure 8-25.

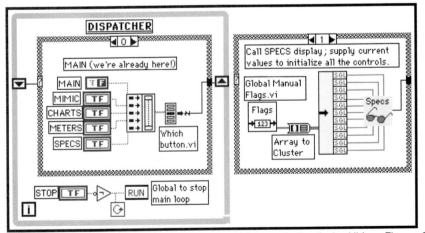

Figure 8-26. The dispatcher loop in a higher-level VI that calls the display VI from Figures 8-24 and 8-25. The display (called "Specs") controls are initialized by reading previous values from the Global Manual Flags global variable.

Initializing Controls

All controls present on your display panel have to be initialized when the VI is called. Otherwise, default values will be treated as if they were user inputs—probably not a great idea. The simplest way to initialize controls is to supply initial values from the calling VI through the connector pane. Every control will have to be wired to the connector pane, and that may be a problem: you only have 20 terminals, one of which is probably the Goto Display output. If you have more than 19 controls to initialize, some will have to be co-located in clusters. Think about your panel layout and figure out which controls might be logically grouped in this way. You can effectively hide the border of a cluster by coloring it transparent so that it disappears behind the other graphical elements of your display.

Initial values should be easy to obtain because each control's previous value was written to a global variable (Figure 8-26). In this example, Global Manual Flags contains all the control settings. Because it stores the values as an array, each value must be extracted from that array individually. For neatness, you could write a subVI that contains a bunch of array indexers (note that the index of each value has to be correct!). In this example, I used another LabVIEW conversion trick—the Array to Cluster VI. Remember to use the pop-up menu on this conversion function to set the cluster size, which is 11 elements in this case. Then, I was able to use an unbundler to obtain the individual values.

Another way you can initialize controls is to create a write-mode local variable for each control as in Figure 8-14. Put all these local variables outside the main While Loop and write the desired initial value to each control. The initial value is obtained from a global variable as before, or from some other source of your choosing. This is a safe application for local variables (no race conditions) and, unlike the connector pane method described above, you can initialize as many controls as required without limitation.

Using Network Connections

To create a distributed control system, you will need to use a network. The most versatile network connections use Ethernet and TCP/IP, which is directly supported by LabVIEW. **IP (Internet Protocol)** performs the low-level packaging of data into *datagrams* and determines a network path by which messages can reach their destination. However, it offers no handshaking and doesn't even guarantee delivery. **TCP (Transmission Control Protocol)** adds handshaking and guarantees that messages arrive in the right order, making it quite reliable. **UDP (Universal Data Protocol)** is similar to TCP, but does no handshaking, making it somewhat faster and also offering the possibility of broadcasting a message to many recipients. You establish sessions between each LabVIEW system on the network, then exchange binary data in formats of your choosing. There are several examples of TCP/IP clients and servers included in the networking examples. These example VIs could be modified to run in the background with local communications via global variables. A *Data Server* VI would then act as a tunnel for data that reappears in a *Data Client* elsewhere on the network. You can have as many connections, or *ports*, open simultaneously as you need.

On the Macintosh, you can use the lowest level of **AppleEvents**, called **Program to Program Communication (PPC)**. PPC is a high-performance, low-overhead means of transferring blocks of data between applications anywhere on a network or on the same machine. It is included, free, with System 7. As with TCP, you must choose the data format and use Type Casting or other data conversion operations to encode and decode the data. The networking examples contain some reasonably simple examples that test the speed of PPC transmission. The examples can be modified for use in a real program. Some applications support PPC, but it requires a lot of study and detailed knowledge of the data formats to successfully exchange data between LabVIEW and these other programs. You can also use AppleEvents to remotely launch applications or VIs, run, abort, or inquire about the status of a VI, or send high-level Apple Event messages to other applications on any Macintosh on the network.

Dynamic Data Exchange (DDE) is a text-based message passing scheme for Windows that is supported by many applications. It's slower than TCP/IP or PPC for transferring large quantities of data, but it is standardized to a fair extent, making it somewhat easier to use. DDE will work over a network (NetDDE) if you are running Windows for Workgroups, or a later version such as Windows NT that features networking. NetDDE works fine with the standard LabVIEW package. Applications such as spreadsheets accept DDE commands and are fairly easy to use. The example VIs show how to set up a real-time exchange with Microsoft Excel.

As you can see, these networking techniques are still, to a great degree, an advanced topic. Because of the lack of overall standardization of data formatting and high-level protocols, it's still somewhat difficult to just "drop in a networking VI" and have it act as a magic data tunnel. Many developers are hard at work, trying to make life easier for you. Keep watching for improved example VIs and third-party networking packages.

Files as Mailboxes

An old reliable way to exchange data between VIs over the network is to use files as mailboxes that any node can remotely fetch and read or write. This assumes that you have a means by which files can be transmitted under the control of LabVIEW. On the Macintosh, file sharing is built in to System 7 and is totally transparent because every Macintosh can act like a server. You specify the file path and open it in the usual manner, no matter where the volume resides. On the PC, there are many third-party networking options that permit you to mount a volume over the network, such as Novell NetWare. On the Sun (and most UNIX machines), you can use the Network File System (NFS).

For one-way transmission, files are easy to use. Just write data to a file in some predetermined format on a periodic basis; then the remote node can fetch it asynchronously, read, and decode the information. Things get tricky when you need synchronized, bidirectional communications because you must create a system of file access permission limits using flags, or some other technique.

Global Databases

If you buy a commercial DCS or PC-based industrial process control package, you will find that the entire software environment is database driven. For user interaction, there is invariably a program called the Database Builder that edits and compiles all of the configuration information. The run-time programs are then centered around this database: I/O handlers pass values in and out to hardware, alarm handlers compare measurements with limit values, and trenders display values on the screen. LabVIEW, however, is not in itself a database-driven package. In fact, it would be much less flexible if it were centered around a predefined database structure.

A particular requirement for a database used in process control is that it must be a *real-time* database, which implies that it is memory-resident and available for thousands of transactions per second. For added versatility, the database may also be distributed among various nodes in the system. This permits any node to efficiently exchange information with any other node on the network through a consistent message passing scheme. A global, real-time database requires a sophisticated client-server or peer-to-peer relationship among all nodes on the network.

Instead of a database, you can use global variables containing configuration information and data wherever appropriate. The main limitation is that you can't access the database with a key, such as: TAGNAME.FIELD. Rather, you have to use something like an array element number to pick out the desired channel. I've tried writing a proper database driver in LabVIEW, complete with string-based lookups, but system performance suffers too much. At this writing I'm waiting for some inspired third party to write a CIN-based package with a name hashing scheme that efficiently stores all the information for quick and efficient access.

Sequential Control

Every process has some need for sequential control in the form of interlocking or time-ordered events. I usually include manual inputs in this area—virtual switches and buttons that open valves, start motors, and the like. This is the great bastion of PLCs, but you can do an admirable job in LabVIEW without too much work. We've already discussed methods by which you read, write, and distribute data. The examples that follow fit between the input and output handlers.

Interlocking With Logic and Tables

LabVIEW's Boolean logic functions make ordinary interlocking simple (Figure 8-27). Boolean conditions can be derived from a variety of sources like front-panel switches, digital inputs, or comparison functions acting on analog signals. **Ladder logic**, as shown in Figure 8-27, is the most common language for PLC programming. It comes from the days of electromechanical switching, and remains a highly useful documentation technique for logical systems.

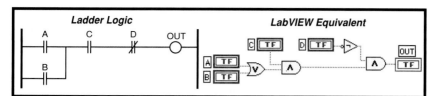

Figure 8-27.   Simple interlock logic, comparing a ladder logic network with its LabVIEW equivalent.

One way to add versatility to your logical operations is to use a **Boolean table** as shown in Figure 8-28. A table is a two-dimensional array where the columns are the mode or step number, and the elements in each row represent some state of the system, such as a permissive interlock. The **Mode** control selects the column through the use of a 2D Index Array function. The output of the Index Array is a 1D array of Booleans—a column slice from the incoming table. Another set of Index Array functions select the individual interlock permissives. If one of the input switches is true AND its corresponding permissive (from the table) is true, then the output is true. You can add whatever kind of logic is required and expand the table as necessary.

The **Mode** control could be a ring control that selects between system modes like *Startup*, *Run*, and *Maintenance*. This is an effective way to change the action of a large number of interlock chains without a great deal of wiring. Another use for the **Mode** control is to tie it to an internally generated value in your program. For instance, the mode might change in response to the time of day or the temperature in a reactor.

Tables are an efficient way to store interlock information, and they are very fast. The only bad thing about tables is that they can be hard to debug. If a table is very large and your program changes modes often, it's not always obvious what is going on. Directly wired logic is easier to understand and debug, and should be used preferentially.

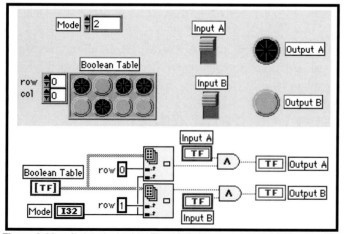

Figure 8-28.   An interlock table. The 2D Boolean array (a table) is sliced by an array indexer to deliver an interlock permissive vector, which is ANDed with a series of inputs.

State Machines

The **state machine** architecture is about the most powerful LabVIEW solution for sequential control problems. Introduced in Chapter 4, *Building an Application*, it consists of a Case structure inside of a While Loop with the Case selector being a number carried in a shift register. Each frame of the state machine's Case structure has the ability to transfer control to any other frame on the next iteration, or to cause immediate termination of the While Loop. This allows you to perform operations in any order depending on any number of conditions.

Figure 8-29 is an example of a tank filling operation. The objective is to fill the tank, stopping when an upper level is reached or when a certain time has passed. In Frame 0, you would open a valve (presumably by writing to an output device) that starts filling the tank. The starting time is saved in a shift register. The program then proceeds to Frame 1, where the elapsed time and present tank level are checked. The tank level is obtained from an analog input or from a global variable, which in turn is written by an analog input handler. If the elapsed time exceeds the specified duration, the program goes to Frame 2. If the upper limit is exceeded, jump to Frame 3. Otherwise, keep looping on Frame 1. Frames 2 and 3 may then take appropriate action to close the valve, or whatever; other operations may follow.

More activity can be managed in this same structure by looping over several frames rather than just one. The sequence could be: 1-2-3-1-2-3, etc., with the termination conditions causing a jump to Frame 4 or 5. Very complex looping is possible, though, like any scheme, it can be hard to debug if you're not careful. I usually put an indicator on the panel that shows which state it's in at the moment. Single stepping then shows the execution order. If the process has to run fast, you can accumulate a history of all the states by building an array on the boundary of the While Loop for later review.

Multiple state machines can run in parallel with each managing a different task. You could have several on one diagram with a global Boolean that requests all the loops to stop.

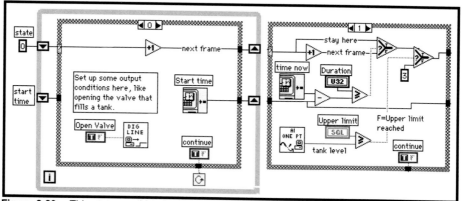

Figure 8-29. This state machine implements an operation that terminates when the tank is full or when a time limit has passed. Frame 2 of the Case (not shown) takes action if a timeout occurs. Frame 3 (also not shown) is activated when the upper limit is exceeded.

This would permit you to break your control problem down into logical, related pieces that are easy to design and debug.

Initialization Problems

Initialization is important in all control situations, and particularly so in batch processes that spend much of their time in the startup phase. When you first load your LabVIEW program, or when you restart for some reason, the program needs to know the state of each input and output to prevent a jarring process upset. For instance, the default values for all your front-panel controls may or may not be the right values to send to the output devices. A good deal of thought is necessary with regard to this initialization problem.

When your program starts, a predictable startup sequence is necessary to avoid output transients. Begin by scanning all the inputs. It's certainly a safe operation, and you probably need some input data in order to set any outputs. Then, compute and initialize any output values. If they are stored in global variables, the problem is somewhat easier because a special initialization VI may be able to write the desired settings without going through all of the control algorithms. Finally, call the output handler VI(s) to transfer the settings to the output devices.

If you use the method of initializing controls shown back in Figure 8-26, then that problem is solved because the current settings are available from global variables (the contents of which are, in turn, written to the controls). Another way to force front-panel controls into their proper state is to create a write-mode local variable for each control and write the correct settings.

Control algorithms may need initialization as well. If you use any uninitialized shift registers to store state information, you should add initialization. The method in Figure 8-30 qualifies as another Canonical VI. The technique relies on the fact that an uninitialized Boolean shift register is initially False when the VI is freshly loaded or compiled. (Remember that once the VI has been run, this is no longer the case.) The shift register is tested, and then if it's False, some initialization logic inside the Case structure is executed. A Boolean control called **Initialize** is included to permit programmatic initialization at any time, for instance, during restarts.

You could also send flags to your control algorithms via dedicated controls or global variables. Such a flag might cause the clearing of intermediate calculations, cause

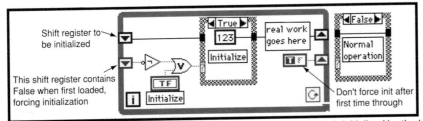

Figure 8-30. The upper shift register, used for some control algorithm, is initialized by the lower shift register at startup or by setting the Initialize control to true.

generation of empty arrays for data storage, or cause the outputs to go to a desired state. All of these items are worth considering. Be sure to test your control system thoroughly by stopping and then restarting in various states. Startup is the time where most process disasters occur. Of course, bad things never happen on my projects.

Continuous Control

Continuous control generally implies that a steady-state condition is reached in a process and that feedback stabilizes the operation over some prolonged period of time. Single-loop controllers, PLCs, and other programmable devices are well-suited to continuous control tasks, or you can program LabVIEW to perform the low-level feedback algorithms and have it orchestrate the overall control scheme. LabVIEW has some advantages, particularly in experimental systems, because it's so easy to reconfigure. Also, you can handle tricky linearizations and complex situations that are quite difficult with dedicated controllers. Not to mention the free user interface...

Most processes use some form of the PID algorithm as the basis for feedback control. I wrote the PID VIs in the LabVIEW PID Control Toolkit with the goal that they should be easy to apply and easy to modify. Every control engineer has personal preferences as to which flavor of PID algorithm should be used in any particular situation. You can easily rewrite the supplied PID functions to incorporate your favorite algorithm. Just because I programmed this particular set (which I personally trust) doesn't mean it's always the best for every application. The three algorithms in the package came right out of Shinskey's book [Ref. 1]. They are:

- **PID**: An interacting positional PID algorithm with derivative action on the process variable only.

- **PID-Error Squared**: Similar to the PID, but with a nonlinear proportional response. May exhibit superior performance with some nonlinear processes.

- **PID-External Reset Fdbk**: Similar to the PID, but with external access to the input of the reset (integral) term. For use in control schemes where a controller might be switched off line, resulting in reset windup, or saturation.

There is also a **Lead/Lag** function block that is useful for more advanced control strategies, such as feedforward control. It's also useful in simulations where you need to emulate the time-domain response of a first-order system. I won't elaborate on the contents of the whole package here. Just go ahead and order the toolkit from National Instruments and read the manual.

You can use the math and logic functions in LabVIEW to implement almost any other continuous control technique. For instance, on-off control operates much like the thermostat in your refrigerator. To program a simple on-off control scheme, all you need to do is compare the setpoint with the process variable, and drive the output accordingly. A comparison function does the trick, though you might want to add hysteresis to prevent short-cycling of the output, as I did in Figure 8-31. The programming methodology is

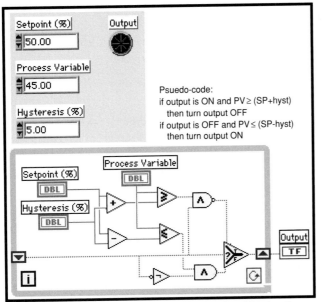

Figure 8-31. An on-off controller with hysteresis, which functions much like a thermostat. Add it to your process control library.

similar to the ones in the PID control toolkit in that it uses an uninitialized shift register to remember the previous state of the output.

Designing a Control Strategy

The first step in designing a continuous control strategy is to sketch a flowchart of your process showing control elements (for instance, valves) and measurements. Then, add feedback controllers and any other required computations, as textbooks on the subject of process control recommend. The finished product will probably look like some kind of a P&ID diagram. Your goal is to translate this diagram into a working LabVIEW system. The question is whether to have LabVIEW do the real-time feedback control loop calculations, or to have an external smart controller do the job. As we've already discussed, the choice depends on performance and reliability requirements, as well as personal preference.

If you decide to have LabVIEW do the processing, translate the flowchart into a LabVIEW block diagram using the PID control VIs with the math and logic functions of LabVIEW. An example of a translated control scheme is shown in Figure 8-32. The only elements missing from this simplified program are the loop tuning parameters and auto-/manual switching.

If you use an external controller, the program is even simpler. All you will have to do is write settings such as setpoints and tuning parameters, and read the status of various measurements from the controller. You can supplement the functionality of the external

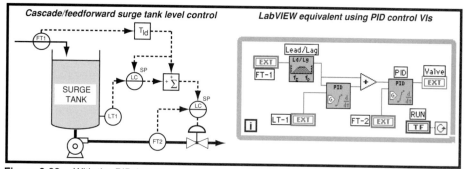

Figure 8-32. With the PID functions, you can map a control strategy from a textbook diagram to a LabVIEW diagram.

controllers with math and logic in your LabVIEW program. In all cases, there will be the usual requirements for interlocking and initialization.

Scaling Input and Output Values

All the functions in the PID control toolkit use inputs and outputs that are scaled by percentages. This makes control calculations and subVI interconnections simpler because fewer intermediate scaling calculations are required. However, you must be sure to properly scale your physical measurements and outputs between engineering units (EGU is my abbreviation) and percent. The EGU to % and % to EGU VIs can help you manage these conversions.

Here is an example. You can use an MIO-16 channel to acquire a 4-20 mA signal with a 250 Ω current sampling resistor, giving a voltage of 1 to 5 V. Assuming that the returned value has been scaled to volts, you need to subtract 1.0 then multiply by 25 to scale the signal to percentage.

When calculating controller gain (proportional band), you can easily scale your physical measurement to percentage of span. The span is defined as the difference between the maximum and minimum measurements.

Consider a temperature transmitter scaled from -100 to +1200 °C. Its span is 1300 °C. A controller proportional band of 10% means that an input error of 130 °C relative to the setpoint is just enough to drive the controller output to saturation, if you have also scaled your setpoint control in a similar manner.

Timing and Performance Limitations

Always be wary of timing limitations and system performance when you are doing continuous control. DCS manufacturers rate their I/O controllers in terms of "loops per second," referring to how many PID calculations can be performed in one second under average conditions. If the system software is well written, adding more loops will cause a gradual degradation of performance rather than an outright failure of any kind. It's much better to have a loop running 20% slow than not at all. Also, there should be no way to accidentally upset the steady operation of a continuous control algorithm. Real processes have plenty of unpredictable features without help from cantankerous software controls.

According to control theory, a sampled control system needs to run about 10 times faster than the fastest time constant in the plant under control. For instance, a temperature control loop is probably quite slow—a time constant of 60 s is common in a small system. In this case, a cycle time of about 6 s is sufficient. Faster cycling offers little or no improvement in performance. In fact, running all your control VIs too fast degrades the overall response time of your LabVIEW application. If you use the timing functions available in LabVIEW to regulate execution of a feedback algorithm, be aware of the actual precision available on your computer. On the Macintosh, 16.7 ms is the limit, while on Windows and Sun machines, it's 1 ms (don't forget that Windows has two resolution options: 1 ms and 55 ms; 55 ms is the default). Therefore, the fastest process time constants that you can control are 167 ms on the Mac and 10 ms on the PC and Sun. To go faster, you must obtain better timing information (from a hardware timer), run the algorithm on a DSP board, or use another external device with suitable performance. By the way, most industrial single-loop controllers cycle no faster than about 5 Hz (200 ms), making them suitable for processes with time constants of 2 seconds or so.

Here is an example of how timing accuracy can affect a control algorithm. A PID algorithm has two time-dependent terms, the integral and derivative responses. When the algorithm is called, the amount of time since the last execution, Δt, is used in the calculation. If Δt is in error, then the response of the algorithm may also be in error. The error magnitude depends on the tuning parameters of the PID as well as the state of the process. If the process is in steady-state, then the time-dependent terms are zero anyway, and the timing error does not matter. But during a process upset, the response to timing errors can be very hard to predict. For best results, you had better make sure that your control loops run with a steady rhythm and at a sufficiently high speed.

The PID library supports either *internal* or *external* timing. Internal timing uses LabVIEW timing functions with the resolution limits mentioned above. The advantage of this method is that the PID functions keep track of the elapsed time between each execution. External timing requires you to supply the actual cycle time (in seconds) to the PID function VI. If you are using the DAQ library, the actual scan period for an acquisition operation is returned by the Waveform Scan VI, for instance, and the value is very precise. Each PID VI has an input called **Cycle Time**. If **Cycle Time** is set to a value less than or equal to zero seconds (the default), internal timing is used. Positive values are taken as gospel by the PID algorithm.

Figure 8-33 is an example of a data acquisition operation with a PID loop on one of the input channels driving an analog output. Note how **actual scan rate**, in scans per second, is wired from the DAQ VI, AI Start, through a reciprocal function to the PID VI. The data acquisition board precisely times each data scan so you can be assured that the While Loop runs at the specified rate. This example, including the display, should run reliably and accurately at nearly 1 kHz.

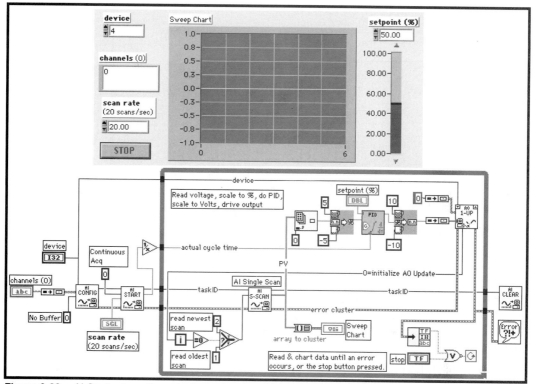

Figure 8-33. AI Start returns the actual sample rate, which can accurately regulate PID control timing. This is a working example that samples many input channels and uses one of them in a PID control loop that runs reliably at high speed.

Trending

The process control industry calls graphs and charts **trend displays**. They are further broken down into **real-time trends** and **historical trends**, depending on the timeliness of the data displayed. Exactly where the transition occurs, nobody agrees. Typically, a historical trend displays data quite a long time into the past for a process that runs continuously. A real-time trend is updated frequently and only displays a fairly recent time history. Naturally, you can blur this distinction to any degree through crafty programming. Historical trending also implies archival storage of data on disk for later review, while real-time trending is typically memory-based.

Real-Time Trends

The obvious way to display a real-time trend is to use a **strip chart** indicator or one of its cousins, the **scope chart** and the **sweep chart**. The only problem you will encounter with these chart indicators is that historical data is displayed only if the panel containing the chart is showing at all times. As soon as the panel is closed, the old data is gone. If the chart is updating slowly, it could take quite a long time before the operator sees a reasonable

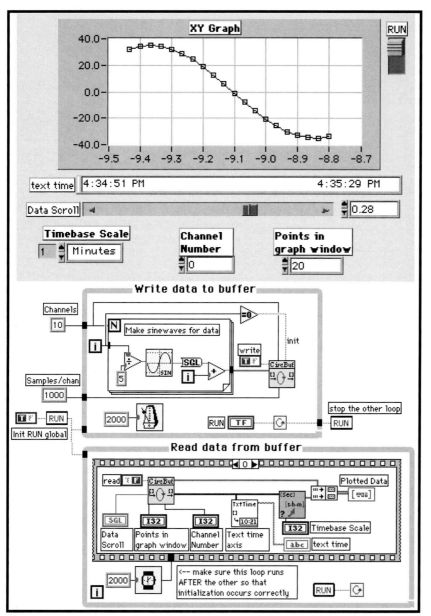

Figure 8-34. An example of the Circular Buffer real-time trending subVI in action. Parallel While Loops are used: one to write sinusoidal data for 10 channels, and the other to read a specified range from a channel for display. Note that the graphed data has been scrolled back in time.

historical record. Nevertheless, you should take advantage of strip charts whenever possible because they are simple, efficient, and require no programming on your part.

Consider using an **XY graph** or a **waveform graph** as a real-time trend display for extra versatility. You maintain arrays that contain some number of recent measurements with regular updates. Then, it's a simple matter of graphing the arrays any time a real-time trend needs to be displayed. If the arrays are stored in global variables, any VI can read and display data from any channel at any time.

An important concern with this technique is memory management. If you just keep appending samples to your trending arrays, you will ultimately run out of memory. Also, the graphs will gradually become sluggish because of the large numbers of plot points. Some kind of length-limited array or a data compression technique is required for long-term operation.

A sophisticated method of trend data management uses a **circular buffer**. A circular buffer is an array that you program to act as if it is a continuous ring of data in memory rather than a straight line of finite length. Because the array never has to change size or be relocated, no real-time memory management is required and the performance is very good. The amount of data you can store is limited only by available memory. Unfortunately, the programming is rather complex: you must keep track of where the oldest and newest data are in the buffer and figure out a way to map the (physical) linear array into a (virtual) circular one.

No problem! I did it for you, and it's included on the diskette that accompanies this book. The Circular Buffer VI has some interesting features that make it more useful than the regular strip charts. First, you preallocate all the required memory by setting the desired number of channels and samples per channel. Next, you periodically call the VI, supplying an array that contains the measurements for each channel. These are written to the next location in the circular buffer. At the same time, timestamps are recorded in a separate buffer. The timestamps are in epoch seconds, where zero is 1-Jan-1904. They are internally managed so you don't even have to supply a time measurement.

The interesting part comes when you want to read the data. The VI returns an array of data for any one channel and an array of timestamps suitable for x-y plotting. The number of samples is adjustable, as is the **start time** of the returned array. That way, you can scroll back through time, looking at a window of data rather than trying to zoom in by using the graph controls. It's much faster, too, because the graph only has to display a limited number of points. If the buffer is sized for 10,000 samples, you would be hesitant to attempt to display them all at once.

Figure 8-34 shows the panel and diagram of an example VI that uses the Circular Buffer subVI for real-time trending. Two independent While Loops are used to store and retrieve data. Because the Circular Buffer VI is a kind of global variable, you can call it in read or write mode any place, any time. The data written here is a set of sine waves, one for each of the 10 channels defined. The buffer is initialized to contain 1,000 samples per channel in this example. Every two seconds, a fresh set of values for all 10 channels are written.

Looking at the graph, you can see that the **Data Scroll** slide has been moved so that the displayed data is from nine minutes in the past. The **Points in Graph Window** control is set to display 20 data points in the window. At a rate of one sample every 2 s, that's about 40 seconds' worth of data. Underneath the graph, I've added a string indicator called **Text Time** that displays the approximate starting and ending times in hh:mm:ss format. If you scroll back many hours (or days) in time, this really helps. A subVI, Text Time Axis, does the conversion. You can also change the time scale of the graph to seconds, minutes, hours, or days.

Memory usage and performance are very good. There is a noticeably long delay when you call Circular Buffer with its initialization Boolean set to True. At that time, it allocates memory for the entire buffer, which can be quite large. The actual amount of memory used for the buffer itself is calculated from

$$bytes = (N + 1) \bullet M \bullet 8$$

where N is the number of channels and M is the number of samples per buffer. For instance, 10 channels and 10,000 samples per channel requires 880,000 bytes of memory. (The 1 in the formula accounts for the hidden timestamp buffer.) Only one duplication of the data array is required, and that is also static memory usage. When you write data, the Replace Array Element function is used, so no reallocation of memory is required. A loop reads data, and the amount of memory required there is proportional to the number of data points to be displayed, which is a number that's significantly smaller than the size of the buffer for practical usage.

Thanks go to Marty Vasey for his original work on this memory-based circular buffer concept. He designed it out of necessity: a customer was threatening bodily harm if they couldn't scroll back through their real-time data and do it *fast*. This program does the trick.

Historical Trends

Memory-resident data is fine for real-time trending where speed is your major objective. But long-term historical data needs to reside on disk both because you want a permanent record and because disks generally have more room. You should begin by making an estimate of the space required for historical data in your application. Consider the number of channels, recording rates, and how far back in time the records need to extend. Also, the data format and content will make a big difference in volume. Finally, you need to decide what means will be used to access the data. Let's look at some of your options.

All of the basic file formats discussed in Chapter 3, *LabVIEW Programming Techniques* (datalogs, ASCII text, and proprietary binary formats), are generally applicable to historical trending. **ASCII text** has a distinct speed *dis*advantage, however, and is probably not suited to high-performance trending where you want to read large blocks of data from files for periodic redisplay. Surprisingly, many commercial PC-based process control applications do exactly that, and their plotting speed suffers accordingly. Do you want to wait several minutes to read a few thousand data points? Then don't use text files.

LabVIEW datalog files are a better choice for random-access historical trending applications because they are fast, compact, and easy to program. However, you must remember that only LabVIEW can read such a format unless you write custom code for the foreign application or a LabVIEW translator program that writes a more common file format for export purposes.

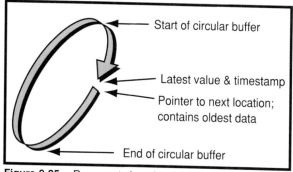

Figure 8-35. Representation of a circular buffer on disk. This buffer contains the values and time-stamps from a single channel. Other channels would be located before and after this one. The program must keep track of pointers to the start, end, and "next" locations in the file.

HIST

A custom binary file format is the optimum solution for historical trending. By using a more sophisticated storage algorithm, such as a circular buffer or linked list on disk, you can directly access data from any single channel over any time range. I wrote such a package, called **HIST**, which I sell commercially.

The HIST package is based on a simple set of VIs that set up the files, store data, and read data using circular buffers. At startup time, you determine how many channels are to be trended and how many samples are to be saved in the circular buffers on disk (Figure 8-35). Sampling rates are variable on a per-channel basis. The use of circular buffers permits "infinite" record lengths without worry of overflowing your disk. However, this also means that old data will eventually be overwritten. Through judicious choice of buffer length and sampling parameters, and through periodic dumping of data to other files, you can effectively trend forever. HIST is a disk-based analog to the memory-based Circular Buffer VI that I've discussed previously.

Data compression is another novel feature of HIST. There are two compression parameters, fencepost and deadband, for each channel (Figure 8-36). Fencepost is a guaranteed maximum update time. Deadband is the amount by which a channel's value must change before it is updated on disk. The combination of these two parameters is very flexible. If deadband is zero, then the channel will be updated each time the **Store HIST Data VI** is called (as fast as once per second). If deadband is a very large number, then the channel will be updated every time the fencepost period passes. If you choose a moderate deadband value, then transients will be stored with high fidelity while steady-state conditions will be trended with a minimum frequency to preserve buffer space. Each time you store data, you update each channel's fencepost and deadband (data compression parameters), giving real-time control over which channels are being trended at what rates.

HIST includes all the necessary file services, such as file creation, and allows you to restart historical trending with an existing set of files, picking up right where you left off. This is possible because the indexing information into the circular buffer data file is kept

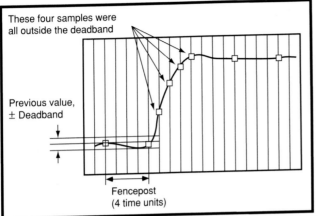

These four samples were
all outside the deadband

Previous value,
± Deadband

Fencepost
(4 time units)

Figure 8-36.   Illustration of the action of deadband-fencepost data compression. Values are stored at guaranteed intervals determined by the fencepost setting, which is four time units in this example. Also, a value is stored when it deviates from the last-stored value by greater than ±deadband (measured in engineering units).

in a separate file. Also, you can run up to four separate HIST file sets simultaneously. So you can break up your data as you see fit.

Storing and reading data with HIST is similar to the way we did it with the Circular Buffer VI example. The only difference is that Store HIST Data requires not just the data values for each channel, but a cluster of channel information, as shown in Figure 8-37. This structure permits you to change each channel's deadband, fencepost, channel name, and units on the fly. Reading data is straightforward, as you can see from Figure 8-38. You can

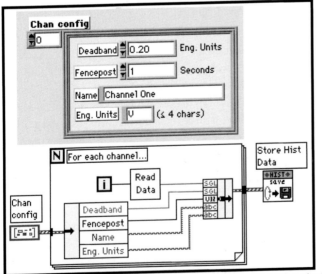

Figure 8-37.   Store HIST Data relies on a channel configuration cluster that you combine with data from each channel. You can change deadband, fencepost, channel name, and units on the fly.

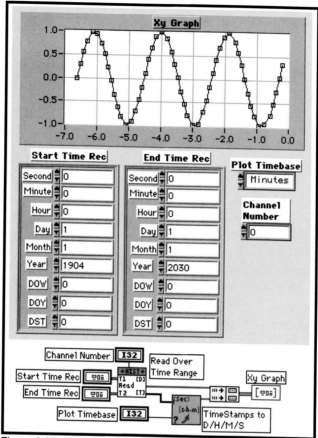

Figure 8-38.   Reading HIST data over a desired range of times.

choose from several data read functions—read the latest N samples, read data between two times, or read the entire buffer.

HIST data files are a special binary format which makes reading the data in other programs impossible without special filters. For this reason, a VI called **HIST Data to Text File** is included to do a translation to tab-delimited text within LabVIEW. You could also write your own translation VIs since the data from every channel is readily available in ordinary LabVIEW arrays.

Statistical Quality Control (SQC)

What do you do with tons of data you've collected from monitoring your process or test system? In manufacturing situations, **statistical quality control** (SQC, also known as **statistical process control**) techniques are commonly used to emphasize the range over which the process is in control and what the process is capable of producing. Once a process is in control it can be improved. Statistical techniques are used to monitor the mean and variability of a process. There is always some random variability in a process, but there may also be other nonrandom causes (i.e., systematic errors) present which must be identified and corrected.

SQC techniques aid in identifying whether or not special causes are present so that the process is corrected only when necessary. A process parameter is usually plotted against *control limits*. If the process parameter exceeds these control limits, there is a very high probability that the process is not in control, which means that there is some special cause present in the process. This special cause could be a new piece of equipment, a new untrained operator, or sundry other problems. Once a process is in control, SQC techniques can predict the yield (in parts per million for example) of the process. There are also techniques for designing experiments to improve the process capability. SQC techniques are pretty popular these days with everybody trying to meet ISO 9000 Quality Criteria.

Control charts, **Pareto charts**, **scatter diagrams**, and **histograms** are common presentation techniques for SQC. It's quite easy to create these charts, implement the SQC computations in LabVIEW, and add them to your monitoring application. Figure 8-39 shows what a control chart looks like in LabVIEW. The control limits are determined by simple statistical calculations and are overplotted with the data to emphasize the range over which the process is varying. There is a **Statistical Quality Control Library** available from National Instruments that comes with a comprehensive set of VIs and examples, and thorough documentation. Some good references for applying SQC techniques are listed at the end of this chapter [Refs. 5 and 6].

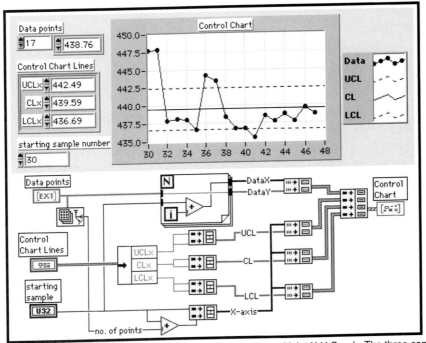

Figure 8-39. How to make a simple *control chart* using a multiplot X-Y Graph. The three control limit plots have only two data points, located at the end of each line.

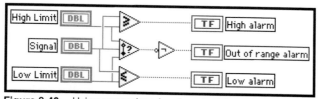

Figure 8-40. Using comparison functions to detect alarm conditions on analog signals.

Alarms

A vital function of any process control system is to alert the operator when important parameters have deviated from specified limits. Any signal can be a source of an **alarm** condition, whether it's a measurement from a transducer, a calculated value like an SQC control limit, or the status of an output. Alarms are generally classified by severity, such as informative, caution, or warning, and there are a variety of audiovisual alarm presentation methods available.

You should start by listing the signals and conditions in your process that require some form of alarm response and determining the appropriate action. For analog signals and computed values, use the **comparison** functions (Figure 8-40) to generate Boolean alarm flags. Digital signals, like contact closure inputs, are combined with the logic functions such as AND, OR, and NOT to generate flags (Figure 8-41). Naturally, you can combine these techniques as required.

Change-of-state detection is another important function that you may need for alarm generation. This enables you to react to a signal that is generally constant but occasionally undergoes a sudden deviation. To detect a change of state, the VI must remember the previous state of the signal, which implies the use of a shift register as shown in Figure 8-42.

Whenever the input changes state, the appropriate Boolean indicators will be set to True. Because the logic functions are polymorphic, you can change all of the Boolean controls and indicators to arrays of Booleans without rewiring any of these three VIs (Figures 8-41 through 8-43). This allows you to process several channels at once. If you *do* modify this example to use arrays, the initial array inside the Case must contain the desired number of elements.

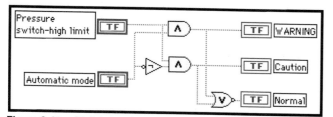

Figure 8-41. Digital signals are combined with Boolean logic to generate alarm states.

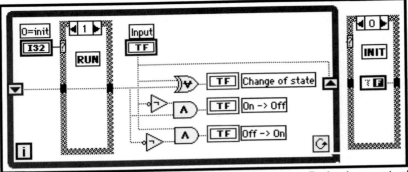

Figure 8-43. A change-of-state can be detected by comparing a Boolean's present value with its previous value stored in a shift register. Three different comparisons are shown here. This would make a reasonable subVI for general use.

An extension of this technique employs **latching**, used when you need the Boolean indicator to remain in the alarm state until a separate reset signal clears the alarm. The reset function is called *alarm acknowledge* in process control terminology. In Figure 8-43, the upper shift register detects an off-to-on change of state as in the previous example. The lower shift register is set to True when a change of state occurs, and stays that way until **Alarm Acknowledge** is True. Again, the inputs and outputs could be arrays.

Using an Alarm Handler

Detecting alarms is the easy part. But there is a potential data distribution problem just like we encountered with input and output signals. If your system is fairly complex, alarms may be generated by several VIs with a need for display elsewhere. An **alarm handler** adds a great deal of versatility to your process control system, much as the I/O handlers do for analog and digital signals.

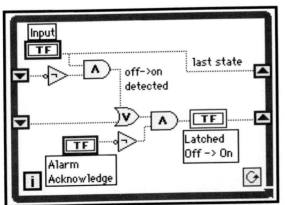

Figure 8-42. This example latches an alarm state until the Alarm Acknowledge input is set to true.

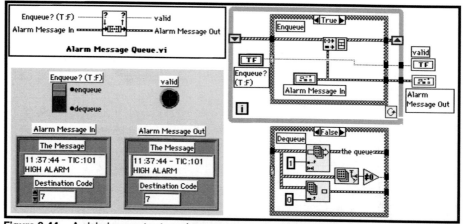

Figure 8-44.   A global queue to store alarm messages. A message consists of a cluster containing a string and a numeric. In Enqueue mode, elements are appended to the array carried in the shift register. In Dequeue mode, elements are removed one at a time.

Global Alarm Queue VI

One way to handle distributed alarm generation is to store alarm messages in a **global queue**. A queue is a first-in, first-out storage device that works like people waiting in line. In LabVIEW, it's a special case of a global variable VI that contains some data management. Multiple VIs can deposit alarm messages in the queue for later retrieval by the alarm handler. A queue guarantees that the oldest messages are handled first and that there is no chance that a message will be missed because of a timing error. The alarm message queue in Figure 8-44 was lifted directly from the Global Queue utility VI that was supplied with older versions of LabVIEW. All I did was change the original numeric inputs and outputs to clusters. The clusters contain a message string and a numeric that tells the alarm handler what to do with the message. You could add other items as necessary. This is an unbounded queue which grows without limits.

Alarms can be generated anywhere in your VI hierarchy, but the I/O handlers may be the best places to do so because they have full access to most of the signals that you would want to alarm. You can combine the output of an alarm detector with information from your configuration database to produce a suitable alarm message based on the alarm condition. For instance, one channel may only need a high-limit alarm while another needs both high- and low-limit alarms. And the contents of the message will probably be different for each case. All of these dependencies can be carried along in the configuration. Once you have formatted the message, deposit it in the global alarm queue.

Alarm Handler VI

Once the alarm messages are queued up, an alarm handler can dequeue them asynchronously then report or distribute them as required. The alarm handler in Figure 8-45 performs two such actions: First, it reports each alarm by one of four means

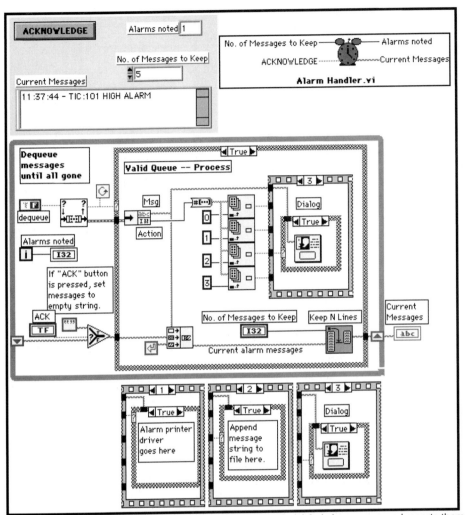

Figure 8-45. An alarm handler VI. It reads messages from the global alarm queue and reports them according to the bits set in the **Destination** code. Messages are appended to the *Current Messages* string. The subVI, Keep N Lines, keeps several of the latest messages and throws away the older ones to conserve space in the indicator for current messages.

as determined by the bits set in the *Destination Code* number that's part of the message cluster. Second, it appends message strings to a string indicator, *Current Messages*, for direct display. This alarm handler would be called periodically by a high-level VI that contains the alarm message display.

There are other operations that an alarm handler might perform. If many other VIs need to display alarm messages or status information, you could have the alarm handler copy messages to a global variable for reading and display elsewhere. The handler could also call subVIs or set special global flags that cause some control operations to occur.

Another way to manage alarms is to use a global database as a repository for all your data. Each I/O point is represented by a cluster of information, and part of that information is a set of flags that represent alarm limits and alarm status flags. Alarm generators (probably part of the I/O handlers) set the alarm status flags based on the current value and the desired limits. Since the database is globally accessible, any VI can read the status of any alarm and take appropriate action. All of this is limited by the real-time performance of the database, so you should approach with caution.

Techniques for Operator Notification

The fun part of this whole alarm business is notifying the operator. You can use all kinds of LabVIEW indicators, log messages to files, make sounds, or use external annunciator hardware. Human factors specialists report that a consistent and well-thought-out approach to alarm presentation is vital to the safe operation of modern control systems. Everything from the choice of color to the wording of messages to the physical location of the alarm readouts deserves your attention early in the design phase. When automatic controls fail to respond properly, it's up to the operator to take over, and he or she needs to be alerted in a reliable fashion.

Boolean indicators are simple and effective alarm annunciators. Besides the built-in versions, you can paste in graphics for the True and/or False cases for any of the Boolean indicators. Attention-getting colors or shapes, icons, and descriptive text are all valuable ideas for alarm presentation.

You can log alarm messages to a file to provide a permanent record. Each time an alarm is generated, the alarm handler can call a subVI that adds the time and date to the message then appends that string to a preexisting text file. Useful information to place in the message includes the tag name, the present value, the nature of the alarm, and whether the alarm has just occurred or has been cleared. This same file can also be used to log other operational data and important system events, such as cycle start/stop times, mode changes, and so forth.

The same information that goes to a file can also be sent directly to a printer. This is a really good use for all those old dot matrix serial printers you have lying around. Since the printer is just a serial instrument, it's a simple matter to use **Serial Port Write** to send it an ASCII string. If you want to get fancy, look in your printer's manual and find out about the special escape codes that control the style of the output. You could write a driver VI that formats each line to emphasize certain parts of the message. As a bonus, dot matrix printers also serve as an audible alarm annunciator if located near the operator's station. When the control room printer starts making lots of noise, you know you're in for some excitement.

Audible alarms can be helpful or an outright nuisance. Traditional control rooms and DCSs had a snotty-sounding buzzer for some alarms, and maybe a big bell or klaxon for real emergencies. If the system engineer programs too many alarms to trigger the buzzer, it quickly becomes a sore point with the operators. However, sound does have its place, especially in situations where the operator can't see the display. You could hook up a buzzer or something to a digital output device, or make use of the more advanced sound recording and playback capabilities of your computer. LabVIEW has a utility VI, Beep, that works on all platforms and serves as a simple annunciator. The Macintosh has always had sound capability built in and there are some example VIs available.

Commercial **alarm annunciator panels** are popular in industry because they are easy to understand and use, and are modestly priced. You can configure these units with a variety of colored indicators that include highly visible labels. They are rugged and meant for use on the factory floor. Hathaway/Beta Corp. makes several models, ranging from a simple collection of lamps to digitally programmed units.

That covers sight and sound; what about our other senses? Use your imagination. LabVIEW has the ability to control most any actuator. Maybe you could spray some odoriferous compound into the air, or dribble something incredibly interesting into the supervisor's coffee.

REFERENCES

1. Shinskey, F. G., *Process Control Systems*. New York: McGraw-Hill, 1988. ISBN 0-07-056903-7.

2. Corripio, Armondo B., *Tuning of Industrial Control Systems*. Raleigh, NC: ISA, 1990. ISBN 1-55617-233-8.

3. Hughes, Thomas A., *Measurement and Control Basics*. Raleigh, NC: ISA, 1988. ISBN 1-55617-098-1

4. Bryan, Luis A. and Bryan, E.A., *Programmable Controllers: Theory and Implementation*. Chicago: Industrial Text Co., 1988. ISBN 0-944107-30-3

5. Montgomery, Douglas C., *Introduction to Statistical Quality Control*. New York: Wiley.

6. Breyfogle, Forrest W., III, *Statistical Methods for Testing, Development, and Manufacturing*. New York: Wiley.

Physics Applications

Physics is Phun, they told me in Physics 101 and, by golly, they were right! Once I got started at LLNL, where there are plenty of physics experiments going on, I found out how interesting the business of instrumenting such an experiment can be. One problem I discovered is just how little material is available in the way of instructional guides for the budding diagnostic engineer. Unfortunately, there isn't enough space for me to do a complete brain dump in this chapter. What I will pass along are a few references [Refs 1,2]. Look for application notes from the makers of specialized instruments [Ref 3]. Like National Instruments, they're in the business of selling equipment, and the more they educate their customers, the more equipment they are likely to sell. So start by collecting catalogs and look for goodies like sample applications inside. Then, get to know your local sales representatives, and ask them how to use their products. Having an experienced experimental physicist or engineer on your project is a big help, too.

I'm going to treat the subject of physics in its broadest sense for the purpose of discussing LabVIEW programming techniques. The common threads among these unusual applications are that they use sensors, signal conditioning, and data acquisition equipment that are all unconventional, and often involve very large data sets. Even if you're not involved in physics research, you are sure to find some interesting ideas in this chapter. Remember that the whole reason for investing in automated data acquisition and control is to improve the quality of the experiment. You can do this by improving the quality of the recorded data, and by improving the operating conditions of the experiment. Calibrating transducers, instruments, and recording devices, as well as monitoring and stabilizing the physical parameters of the experiment, all lead to better results. Having a flexible tool like LabVIEW makes these goals much easier to achieve than in the past. Twenty years ago, we had computers, but they were so cumbersome to configure that the researcher needed a large staff just to support simple data acquisition. That meant less money and time available for improving the experiment and examining the data.

Special Hardware

In stark contrast to ordinary industrial situations, physics experiments by their nature involve exotic measurement techniques and apparatus. I feel lucky to come across a plain old low-frequency pressure transducer or thermocouple. More often, I'm asked to measure microamps of current at high frequencies, riding on a 35 kV DC potential. Needless to say, some fairly exotic signal conditioning is required. Also, some specialized data acquisition hardware, much of which is rarely seen outside of the physics lab, must become part of the researcher's repertoire. Thankfully, LabVIEW is flexible enough to accommodate these unusual instrumentation needs.

Signal Conditioning

High voltage, high current, and high frequency measurements require specialized signal conditioning and acquisition equipment. The sources of the signals, though wide and varied, are important only as far as their electrical characteristics are concerned. Interfacing the instrument to the data acquisition equipment is a critical design step. Special amplifiers, attenuators, delay generators, matching networks, and overload protection are important parts of the physics diagnostician's arsenal.

High Voltage Measurements

To measure high voltage signals, you will need to reduce the magnitude of the signal to something that your A/D converter can safely and accurately accommodate. For most signals, resistive voltage dividers are the easiest to use. You can buy commercial high voltage probes of several types. Special oscilloscope probes are available with divider ratios of 10, 100, and 1000-to-1, and are useful up to 40 kV, frequencies up to 500 MHz, and with input impedance of 10 to 100 MΩ. All you have to do is match the output impedance (and capacitance, for high frequencies) to that of your data acquisition equipment, perhaps by using a suitable amplifier. A 'scope probe with a 1 MΩ resistor for termination works fine with a plug-in data acquisition board.

For measurements up to hundreds of kilovolts, you can buy high-voltage probes from Ross Engineering and others. These probes are compact (considering their voltage ratings) and are intended for permanent installation. As with 'scope probes, you have to match the output impedance for highest accuracy (Figure 9-1).

Pulsed high voltages can be challenging because of their extra high-frequency content. Resistive probes incorporate frequency compensation capacitors to flatten frequency

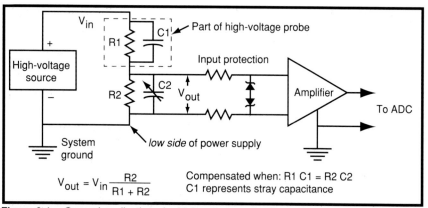

$$V_{out} = V_{in} \frac{R2}{R1 + R2}$$

Compensated when: R1 C1 = R2 C2
C1 represents stray capacitance

Figure 9-1. General application of a high-voltage probe. Frequency compensation is needed only for AC measurements. Always make sure that your amplifier doesn't load down the voltage divider.

response. Proper matching at the output is paramount. Capacitive dividers and custom-made pulse transformers may be a better choice in certain cases.

If the measurement you are making is part of a floating system (that is, it is not referenced to ground), you also need an **isolation amplifier**. Commercial isolation amplifiers operate only at relatively low voltages, so you must insert them after the voltage divider. Sometimes, you can float an entire measurement including the sensor and signal conditioning system at high voltage. This requires an isolated power supply for the electronics, and typically incorporates a fiber optic link for communications. Many accelerator experiments have been constructed around such systems.

Safety is your number one concern in high-voltage system design. First, protect the personnel, then protect the equipment, then protect the data. Floating systems are probably the most dangerous because they tempt you to reach in and turn a knob—a sure way to an early grave. Cover all high-voltage conductors with adequate insulation and mark all enclosures with warning labels. Enclosures should be interlocked with a safety devices that shut down and *crowbar* (short circuit) the source of high-voltage. Cables emerging from high-voltage equipment must be properly grounded to prevent accidental energization. At the input to your signal conditioning equipment, add over-voltage protection devices such as current limiting resistors, zener diodes, Transorbs, varistors, and so forth. Protect *all* inputs, because improper connections and transients can and will zap your expensive equipment... and it always happens two minutes before a scheduled experiment.

Current Measurements

It seems that I spend more time measuring electrical currents than almost anything else in the physics lab. Whether it's high or low current, AC or DC, the measurement is always more complex than expected.

AC and pulse currents are often the easiest to measure because you can use a **current transformer**. Simple, robust devices, current transformers rely on a dynamic magnetic field to couple a fraction of the measured current flowing in the primary winding into the

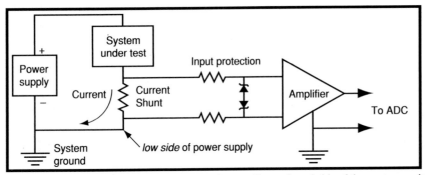

Figure 9-2. Signal conditioning for a current shunt on the preferred side of the system under test.

secondary winding. Pearson Electronics makes a wide variety of current transformers, usable up to tens of thousands of amps and 20 MHz. All models have an output impedance of 50 Ω, so they match well with wideband amplifiers and digitizer inputs. There are two limitations to current transformers. First, DC current tends to prematurely saturate the core, resulting in distortion and other amplitude errors. Second, these transformers are naturally AC-coupled, so you have to be aware of the low-frequency response limit of your transformer. Specifically, DC and low-frequency AC information will be lost. On the other hand, don't worry about contact with high DC voltages because of the isolation.

Hall Effect devices are used to make clamp-on DC-coupled current probes. These solid-state devices respond to the instantaneous magnetic field intensity surrounding a conductor, producing a proportional output. One commercial Hall Effect current probe is the Tektronix AM503S. With it, you can measure AC or DC currents from milliamps to 500 A at frequencies up to 50 MHz, and to do this you merely clamp the probe around the conductor. Though expensive, they are real problem solvers.

Current shunts are the simplest, and often cheapest, current transducers, consisting of a resistor placed in series with the source of current. The resulting voltage drop follows Ohm's Law, where the voltage is equal to the current multiplied by the resistance. You can make your own shunt for low currents by inserting a low-value resistor in the circuit. For high currents, up to thousands of amps, there are commercially made shunts available. Standard outputs are usually 50 or 100 mV at full current, so you may need an amplifier if your A/D converter system can't handle low-level signals. Try to connect the shunt on the *low side*, or ground return, of the power source to eliminate common mode voltage (Figure 9-2). If you must wire the shunt in series with the positive side of the power supply, you need an isolation amplifier (Figure 9-3). Unfortunately, isolation amplifiers are expensive, don't have very wide bandwidths, and may have a low input impedance, though the last disadvantage shouldn't exist with current shunts.

High-Frequency Measurements

Many experiments involve the detection of pulsed phenomena, such as nuclear particle interactions, lasers, and explosions. The detector may sense ion currents or some electrical event in a direct manner, or it may use a multistep process, such as the conversion of

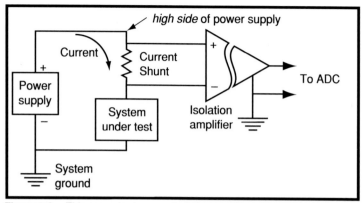

Figure 9-3. This example shows an isolation amplifier with a "high side" current shunt. The common-mode voltage is that which appears across the system under test, and may exceed the capability of nonisolated amplifiers.

particle energy to light, then light to an electrical signal through the use of a photomultiplier or photodiode. Making quantitative measurements on fast, dynamic phenomena is quite challenging, even with the latest equipment, because there are so many second-order effects that you must consider. High-frequency losses and phase shifts due to stray capacitance and reflections from improperly matched transmission lines can severely distort a critical waveform. It's a rather complex subject. If you're not well-versed in the area of pulsed diagnostics, your best bet is to find someone who is.

There are a number of instruments and ancillary devices that you will often see in high-frequency systems. For data acquisition, you have a choice of acquiring the entire waveform or measuring some particular characteristic in real-time. Waveform acquisition implies the use of a fast **transient digitizer** or digitizing oscilloscope, for which you can no doubt find a LabVIEW driver to upload the data. Later in this chapter, we'll look at waveform acquisition in detail. Some experiments, like those involving particle drift chambers, require only time interval or pulse coincidence measurements. Then, you can use a time interval meter, or **time-to-digital converter**, a device that directly measures the time between events. Another specialized instrument is the **boxcar averager**, or **gated integrator**. This is an analog instrument that averages the signal over a short gate interval, then averages the measurements from many gates. For periodic signals, you can use a boxcar averager with a low-speed ADC to reconstruct very high-frequency waveforms.

CAMAC

CAMAC (Computer Automated Measurement and Control) is an old, reliable standard for data acquisition in the world of high-energy physics research. Way back in 1964, the European Standard of Nuclear Electronics (ESONE) committees decided that a genuine data acquisition standard was necessary. It's fortunate that nuclear physics researchers have traditionally cooperated on a worldwide basis; CAMAC was established as both a European standard (IEC 516) in 1975 and as a U.S. standard (IEEE 583) in 1967. These standards guarantee interoperability between the many brands of controllers and modules. Though the standard is quite old, it retains a very important role in research labs all over the world. LabVIEW has instrument drivers available for use with a variety of CAMAC instruments and controllers.

CAMAC Basics

Modules in a CAMAC system plug into a CAMAC crate, which contains a power supply and a passive backplane, or dataway, with up to 25 slots. Slot 25 is reserved for the crate controller, which is responsible for initiating and timing all command and data transfers over the dataway. The dataway consists of 24 read/write data (R) lines, 24 station address (N) lines, five function code (F) lines, four subaddress (A) lines, and nine control and timing lines. One of the control lines is called the Look-at-Me (LAM) line and serves as a method by which a module can asynchronously request service from the crate controller (i.e., an interrupt). LAMs are frequently used to indicate that an operation is complete. The 32 available function codes are generally allocated to read, write, control, and test classes. Subaddress codes are used to access different channels or memory areas in a module, or as a kind of subfunction code. A dataway operation takes exactly 1 μs, which implies a maximum 1 MHz cycle rate. Eight, 16, or 24-bit transfers may occur in each cycle.

There are several types of crate controllers available. Parallel crate controllers connect directly to your host computer via a ribbon cable and plug-in adapter board. These offer the highest performance. An example is the Kinetic Systems 3922 with either the 2926 bus

Figure 9-4.   CAMAC equipment in action with a LabVIEW system.

adapter for the PC or the 2932 bus adapter for the Macintosh II. A LabVIEW driver for the 2932 is available from Kinetic Systems. Serial crate controllers permit the remote operation of a CAMAC crate over coaxial or fiber-optic links. Both parallel and serial controllers support multiple crates. GPIB crate controllers are the easiest way to connect CAMAC to LabVIEW-based systems, and that is what I'll discuss here. In all cases, the crate controller accepts simple commands to address the desired module (N-F-A codes), then proceeds to read or write data as requested. When a LAM occurs, serial or parallel controllers cause an interrupt on the host computer, while GPIB controllers can generate a service request (SRQ).

Another type of crate controller uses an embedded processor. Traditionally, LSI-11 microprocessors were the processor of choice for this application, but 80X86 processors are now used as well—an example is the Kinetic Systems 3966. Embedded processors offer the advantage of local intelligence tightly coupled to the I/O subsystem, off loading much real-time work from the host system and the communications link. The end result is much like a VXI system with an embedded controller. With sufficient processing power, it is very reasonable to set up a Windows-based LabVIEW system, right in the crate.

If you want to learn more about CAMAC, contact any of the manufacturers and request one of their introductory guides. You could also get a copy of the IEEE standard, but it's not what you would call user friendly. If you really get stuck, call me. I wrote several of the CAMAC drivers in the LabVIEW library, and have built lots of modules over the years.

Here's a bit of history. Back in 1987, when LabVIEW version 1.2 was around, Jack MacCrisken, one of LabVIEW's inventors, came to LLNL to ask us what instruments LabVIEW needed to support. I said "CAMAC." Jack said, "What's that?" So, I sent him a CAMAC crate, a GPIB crate controller, and some modules for which to write drivers. And so the CAMAC library was born. Then, in late 1989, a beta copy of LabVIEW 2.0 appeared on my desk. I was desperate to replace our old LSI-11/CAMAC-based data acquisition system, and the new features in 2.0 (particularly the fact that it was compiled) made LabVIEW the logical choice. So, Hank Andreski and I set about writing a general-purpose package, which was eventually christened **MacDALE** (Macintosh Data Acquisition for Laboratory Environments). MacDALE provides all the services you expect—configuration management, support for lots of instruments (even non-CAMAC equipment), logging of user comments, file management, etc. I even went through the pain and suffering of a formal software release, so it's available (for a price) to anyone who wants a copy. Unfortunately, it's written in LabVIEW 2.1 for the Macintosh, so it may be a bit of an adventure to convert to 3.0, or later versions.

Limitations and Performance of CAMAC

Though popular, CAMAC has a number of limitations that you should understand. First, its transfer rate is *only* 1 MHz, which translates to 2 megabytes per second for 16-bit transfers. If you are using a GPIB crate controller, this is of little concern because GPIB is limited to about 800 kilobytes per second. Parallel controllers and embedded processors run at the full speed of CAMAC. Second, it has a rather small (24-bit) address space, which limits your options regarding large memory modules. Third, the standard is rather old and sometimes perceived as obsolete. But judging by the number of new modules entering the market, CAMAC has a long life ahead.

Another limitation not unique to CAMAC is its extensive dependency on the host computer. Most CAMAC modules and crate controllers are *really dumb*. Many of the older ADC modules, for instance, can't even scan a list of channels or do multiple acquisitions. Instead, you have to send a command to read each sample, resulting in enormous overhead. Because LabVIEW runs on top of rather complex operating systems, each I/O operation is rather expensive in terms of execution time. On a fast Mac or PC using a GPIB crate controller, for instance, you can perform about 200 CAMAC writes or 100 reads per second. That's all. The good news is that each read or write operation can transfer a very large buffer of data using DMA, so the situation is not so bad for modules like transient digitizers with large memories. What you need to avoid is the situation where you need to do lots of single-channel operations in a short period of time. That was acceptable on the old LSI-11 systems, but must be avoided now.

When you read data from digitizers with large memories, throughput will rarely be limited by the performance of CAMAC, GPIB, or the overhead of I/O calls because a single block read operation, with DMA support, is used. Limitations are more likely to come from your use of graphics, and disk performance. Intelligent use of parallel programming techniques in LabVIEW can moderate this situation. Here are a couple of benchmarks, taken on a Macintosh IIfx:

- Twelve Joerger TR digitizers (1 K samples, 12 bits), scaled to voltage, graphing data for one channel, and saving all 12 channels to binary files: 6.7 seconds

- One LeCroy 6810 digitizer (16 K samples, 12 bits), scaled to voltage, no graphing, and saved in a binary file: 1.5 seconds

Manufacturers and Modules

Don't let anyone tell you CAMAC is obsolete and dead! There are still quite a few manufacturers of CAMAC equipment in the world today making hundreds of modules and releasing new ones all the time. Some of the major players are Kinetic Systems Corporation (KSC), LeCroy, DSP Technology, AEON, and Joerger Enterprises.

The general functions available are ADCs, DACs, transient digitizers, time-to-digital converters, trigger generators, clock generators, delays, and signal conditioners. Modules are available with state-of-the-art GHz data recording rates. Consult the current instrument library listing to see what modules are supported with LabVIEW drivers.

My favorite crate controller is the Kinetic Systems 3988-G3A GPIB Crate Controller, with the LeCroy 8901A GPIB Crate Controller coming in second. The 3988 is the easiest to program, especially if you have to write or modify a driver, and it supports all of the CAMAC data transfer modes.

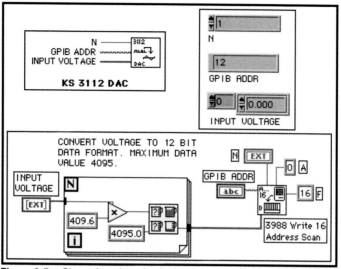

Figure 9-5. Shown here is a simple driver for the Kinetic Systems 3112 DAC, using their 3988 GPIB crate controller.

CAMAC Drivers

The LabVIEW instrument library contains many CAMAC instrument drivers, most of which are based on the two most popular GPIB crate controllers, the KSC 3988 and the LeCroy 8901A. If you are lucky enough to use a module that's already supported, it should be easy to start your application. If you need to write your own driver or add a function that is not already supported, study the 3988 or 8901A support libraries for tips and techniques.

All of the driver VIs have a common method of addressing modules, using N-F-A codes. N is the slot number (1–25), F is the function code (0–31), and A is the subaddress (0–15). Consult your module manual to see what F and A codes are required for each operation. You can read or write data in 8, 16, or 24-bit words; be sure to use the right word length, because some modules return garbage in the unused bits. There are several data transfer modes to choose from. Single-word transfers are the simplest, and do just what you would expect. Block mode transfers are very efficient when you need to move a large buffer of data to or from a module's memory. Only one subVI call is required for a block mode transfer. A simple driver for a DAC is shown in Figure 9-5. It uses the 3988 crate controller driver in address scan mode, which writes an array of values to the eight outputs on a Kinetic Systems 3112 DAC. Here are some tricks I've learned by suffering through the development of some big CAMAC drivers:

• Like many driver development efforts, it's easiest to start by sending simple commands with the utility VI, LV-to-CAMAC (Figure 9-6). Start out by talking to a simple module, like a digital output register, that doesn't require complex programming to get results. Also, you should spend plenty of time looking over drivers for similar modules to get an idea of how things should be done.

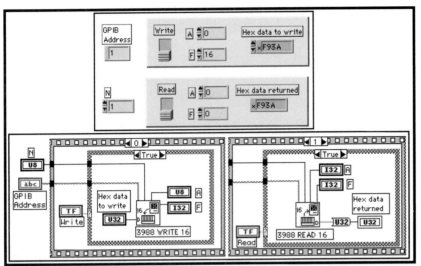

Figure 9-6. LV-to-CAMAC, a helpful program when you are developing a CAMAC driver. This one is based on the Kinetic Systems 3988 GPIB crate controller. It optionally sends, then optionally reads back a 16-bit word of data. The False states of both Case structures are empty.

- Command ordering is important. Various registers need to be set in the right order, and LAMs must be enabled and disabled at the right time. Owing to the *dumbness* of some modules, failure to get the ordering right may result in a locked up module.

- LAMs within one crate are hard to sort out. The problem is that, unlike the SRQ function in GPIB where each instrument has one address, a CAMAC crate gives you just one LAM for any module that needs attention. You have to send a special command to the crate controller to find out which module raised the LAM.

- Data byte ordering is selectable on the LeCroy 8901A, and is sometimes other than what you expect on many modules. If you Type Cast a binary string from a digitizer into, say, an array of floating-point numbers (Figure 9-7), don't be surprised if you have to swap bytes or words first. Misordered data bytes make no sense when type cast.

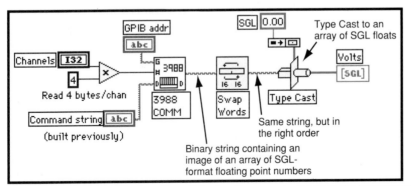

Figure 9-7. The Swap Words or Swap Bytes functions are needed when the instrument returns data bytes out of order.

Controller SubVIs for the KSC 3988

For the Kinetic Systems 3988, there are 12 read and 12 write VIs, divided into 8 bit, 16 bit, and 24 bit folders. Each folder contains four read and four write operations that support the single, address scan, Q-Stop scan, and Q-Repeat transfer modes. Each subVI requires N, A, F, and the GPIB address. The read VIs have an additional binary input that selects between signed and unsigned data formats. The connector pane is standardized for all the read VIs. The document that comes with the 3988 driver is quite helpful in getting started.

Controller SubVIs for the LeCroy 8901A

For the LeCroy 8901A, there are six read and one write VIs. Read operations are divided into 8 bit, 16 bit, and 24 bit folders, each containing two read operations that support the single or block mode transfers. The write VI writes a single word, up to 24 bits. There is no block mode transfer for write operations. Each subVI requires N, A, F, and the GPIB address. The read VIs have an additional binary input that selects between signed and unsigned data formats. The connector pane is standardized for all the read VIs. The 8901A also comes with a helpful document.

Other I/O Hardware

Though CAMAC is still popular, there are some other I/O and signal conditioning standards that you may run into in the world of physics research. And of course, there really is no limit on what you can use; it's just that there are some specialized functions that have been implemented over the years that aren't always commonly available.

FASTBUS

FASTBUS (ANSI/IEEE 960-1986) represents the fastest, highest-density data acquisition hardware available today. It is a modular standard featuring a 32-bit address and data bus, an asynchronous ECL backplane capable of 80 MHz operation (now that's *fast)*, and the ability to use multiple masters or controllers. It's in fairly wide use in high-energy physics at such institutions as CERN in Switzerland. It's a sophisticated I/O system, but it's not for the casual user or those with miniature budgets. If you work in a high-energy physics laboratory, you may well see FASTBUS equipment. Currently, you can interface it to a LabVIEW system by using CAMAC as an intermediary, or with a PC bus interface, either of which are perfectly acceptable.

VXI

I think VXI is a great candidate for the future title of workhorse data acquisition interface for physics applications. It's a new standard, well-planned, supported by dozens of major manufacturers, and offers many of the basic functions you need. And of course, there is excellent LabVIEW support. Drivers are available for many instruments. PCs and Macs can be installed right in the crate and Sun Microsystems, Tektronix, and National Instruments are collaborating to support the SPARCstation. An application written by Los

Alamos National Laboratory that is described later in this chapter makes extensive use of VXI equipment.

NIM

Another older standard still in use in the physics community is the **NIM (Nuclear Instrumentation Manufacturers)** module format, originally established in 1964. It's not an I/O subsystem standard like CAMAC or VXI; instead it's a modular signal conditioning standard. Modules are either full or half-height and plug into a powered NIM bin, a backplane with limited interconnections. Because the CAMAC format was derived from the earlier NIM standard, NIM modules can plug into a CAMAC crate with the use of a simple adapter.

Many modern instruments are still based on NIM modules, particularly nuclear particle detectors, pulse height analyzers, and boxcar averagers like the Stanford Research SR250. I still use them in the lab because there are so many nice functions available in this compact format, such as amplifiers, trigger discriminators, trigger fanouts, and clock generators.

Field and Plasma Diagnostics

Among the low-speed applications of LabVIEW in physics are those that deal with **field mapping** and DC **plasma** diagnostics. These applications combine data acquisition with motion control for field mapping, and the generation of ramped potentials for plasma diagnostics. These experiments have many variations. I'll cover a few simple applications that will give you some insight as to how LabVIEW might help out in your lab.

Step-and-Measure Experiments

When you have a system that generates a static field or a steady-state beam, you probably will want to map its intensity in one, two, or three dimensions, and maybe over time as well. I call these step-and-measure experiments because they generally involve a cyclic procedure that moves a sensor to a known position, makes a measurement, moves, measures, and so forth, until the region of interest is entirely mapped. You need some type of **motion control** hardware to move a probe or sensor designed to detect the phenomenon of interest.

Motion Control Options

There are many actuators that you can use to move things around under computer control—the actuators that make robotics and numerically controlled machines possible.

For simple two-position operations, a pneumatic cylinder can be controlled by a solenoid valve that you turn on and off from a digital output port. Its piston moves at a velocity determined by the driving air pressure and the load. Electromagnetic solenoids can also move small objects back and forth through a limited range.

But more important for your step-and-measure experiments is the ability to move from one location to another with high precision. Two kinds of motors are commonly used in these applications, **stepper motors** and **servo motors**. Think of a stepper motor as a kind of digital motor. It uses an array of permanent magnets and coils arranged in such a way that the armature (the part the moves) tends to snap from one location to the other in response to changes in the polarity of the DC current that is applied to each coil. Stepper motors are available with anywhere from four to 200 steps per revolution. Linear stepper motors are also available. Steppers have the advantage of simplicity and reasonable precision. Their main disadvantages are that you can't position them with infinite resolution and their speed is somewhat limited, typically 1000 to 2000 steps per second. There is one option for increasing resolution, called microstepping. With microstepping, the effective steps per revolution can be increased 10 times, and sometimes more. This requires special control hardware and sometimes compromises the performance of the motor with regard to torque.

Servo motors are similar to ordinary motors except that they are intended for variable speed operation, down to and including stalled, for indefinite periods. Both AC and DC servo motors are in wide use. A servo system also includes a positional or velocity feedback device, such as a shaft encoder or tachometer, to precisely control the motion of the shaft. With the use of feedback, servo motor systems offer extremely high precision and the ability to run at high speed. Their disadvantage is the requirement for somewhat complex control circuitry.

With any motor, you also need an electronics package to drive the coils of the motor in an appropriate fashion and to interface the motor to your computer. Motor controls are available as packaged systems controlled via RS-232 or GPIB from companies like Newport and Compumotor, or as plug-in boards for the PC and Mac from nuLogic and Compumotor. Motor controllers are also available in various modular formats such as CAMAC and VXI. LabVIEW drivers are available for many of these devices. Figure 9-8 shows the connector pane and front panel for a Kinetic Systems 3361 Stepper Motor Controller CAMAC module. It's an old and very simple single-channel stepper motor translator module that requires an external DC power supply. As you can see, operating a

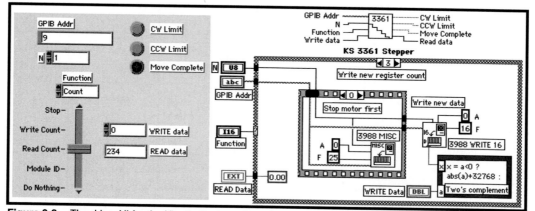

Figure 9-8. The driver VI for the Kinetic Systems 3361 Stepper Motor Controller module. This is about as simple as motion control gets.

motor with a VI like this is child's play, though it is very limited in terms of automation—for instance, you can't enter an acceleration profile.

For sophisticated control of stepper motors or servo motors, the products from **nuLogic** are outstanding. They offer plug-in boards for the PC (pcControl and pcStep) and for the Macintosh (nuControl and nuStep). The nuControl and pcControl series of boards are three-axis DC servo motor controllers that support quadrature encoders for position and velocity feedback. The nuStep and pcStep boards are three-axis stepper motor controllers. A unique feature of the stepper control boards is the ability to tailor the acceleration profile to match the torque vs. speed characteristics of your stepper motor. This minimizes the time spent in acceleration and deceleration phases of a point-to-point move. All of these boards have extensive on-board intelligence, supporting indexing, velocity profiling, limit switches, and home switches. Program the boards with a low-level communications packet protocol (if you are masochistic), or use nuLogic's Motion VIs with LabVIEW.

The nuLogic VI libraries are divided into support for servos and steppers, and demonstration VIs are included to help you get started. The nuControl servo support is impressive, with interactive PID control tuning and Bode (gain and phase) analysis, trajectory control (acceleration and velocity), and limit switch functions. The nuStep library is similar, except that stepper motors don't require many feedback control features.

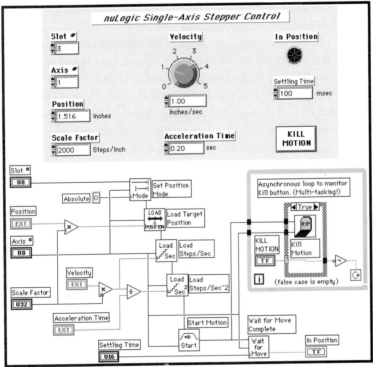

Figure 9-9. A single-axis stepper motor control example using the nuStep VIs. It calibrates the motor's position, and provides control over acceleration, velocity, and target position. The common thread running between function VIs is the slot number of the nuStep interface board.

The example in Figure 9-9 is a VI for controlling a single axis stepper motor using the nuStep library. Inputs are **Slot No.**, **Axis No.**, **Position**, **Velocity**, **Acceleration Time**, **Scale Factor** (in Steps/Inch), and a control for specifying the settling time. The **In Position** Boolean output signals that the move is complete and that the axis is in position. You don't have to wait for the move to complete. A While Loop monitors the **Kill Motion** button, allowing you to abort the move at any time. The diagram is quite easy to follow because all of the nuLogic functions use the **Slot Number** input as a common thread to ease dataflow programming.

Ion Beam Intensity Mapper

One lab that I worked in had a commercially made ion beam gun that we used to test the sputter rate of various materials. We had evidence that the beam had a nonuniform intensity cross section (the X-Y plane), and that the beam diverged (along the Z axis) in some unpredictable fashion. To obtain quality data from our specimens, we needed to characterize the beam intensity in X, Y, and Z. One way to do this is to place sample coupons (thin sheets of metal or glass) at various locations in the beam and weigh them before and after a timed exposure to obtain relative intensity values. However, this is a tedious and time-consuming process that yields only low-resolution spatial data. Preliminary tests indicated that the beam was steady and repeatable, so high-speed motion and data acquisition was not a requirement.

Our solution was to use a plate covered with 61 electrically isolated metal targets (Figure 9-10). The plate moves along the Z-axis, powered by a stepper motor that drives a fine-pitch lead screw. The stepper motor is powered by a Kinetic Systems 3361 Stepper Motor Controller CAMAC module. Since the targets are arranged in an X-Y grid, we can obtain the desired X-Y-Z mapping by moving the plate and taking data at each location. Each target is connected to a negative bias supply through a 100 Ω current sensing resistor, so the voltage across each resistor is 100 mV/mA of beam current. Current flows because the targets are at a potential that is negative with respect to the ion gun, which is grounded. A National Instruments AMUX-64T samples and multiplexes the resulting voltages into an NB-MIO-16 multifunction board. This limited the amount of bias voltage to less than 10 V because that's the common-mode voltage limit of the board. We would have liked to increase that to perhaps 30–50 V to collect more ions, but that would mean buying 61 isolation amplifiers.

The front panel for this experiment is shown in Figure 9-11. Two modes of scanning are supported: unidirectional or bidirectional (out-and-back), selectable by a Boolean control (**Scan Mode**) with pictures pasted in that represent these motions. A horizontal fill indicator shows the probe position as the scan progresses to cover the desired limits.

Examine the diagram of the main VI in Figure 9-12. An overall While Loop keeps track of the probe location in a shift register, which starts at zero, increases stepwise to a limit set by **Total Range**, then steps back to zero if a bidirectional scan is selected. The VI stops when the scan is finished, then returns the probe to its starting location. Arithmetic in the upper half of the loop generates this stepped ramp.

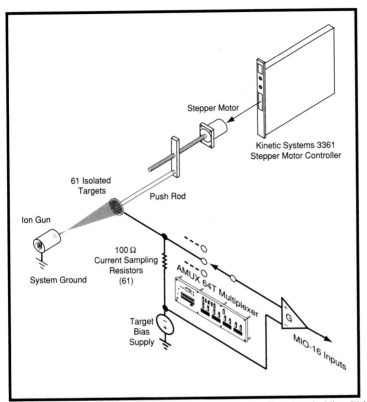

Figure 9-10. The ion beam intensity mapper hardware. The plate holding 61 isolated probes moves along the axis of the ion beam. Current at each probe is measured at various positions to reconstruct a 3D picture of the beam intensity.

The Sequence structure inside the main loop has three frames. Frame zero commands the motor controller to move to the new position. Frame one polls the motor controller, waiting for it to set the DONE flag. If the VI encounters a limit switch, it tells the user with a dialog box and stops execution. Frame two acquires data by calling a subVI that scans the 64 input channels at high speed and averages the number of scans determined by a front-panel control. Finally, the time, position, and the data are appended to a data file in tab-delimited text format for later analysis. As always, the format of the data is determined beforehand to assure compatibility with the analysis software.

Preliminary plotting of the data was performed in another Macintosh application, Delta Graph, because it has 3D graphics capability and is very easy to use. Serious analysis and model simulations were performed on mainframe computers. This application was written several years ago, before Metric Systems created **SurfaceView**, a LabVIEW add-on package that permits live 3D plotting. SurfaceView could easily be integrated into this program, giving the experimenter a progressive real-time picture of the beam's intensity. SurfaceView is discussed in Chapter 10, *Data Visualization and Image Processing*.

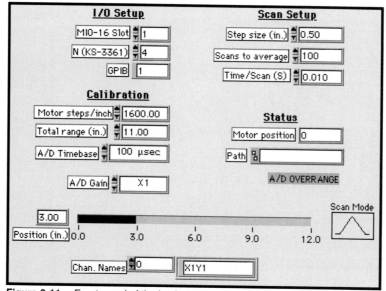

Figure 9-11. Front panel of the ion beam intensity scan VI. The user runs the VI after setting all the parameters of the scan. A horizontal fill indicator shows the probe position.

Plasma Potential Experiments

The plasma we're talking about here doesn't flow in your veins. This plasma is the so-called fourth state of matter, where almost all of the atoms are ionized. Plasmas are formed by depositing sufficient energy into a substance (usually a gas) to rip away one or more electrons from the atoms, leaving them positively charged. The ionizing energy may come from an electrical discharge (an electron bombardment) or some form of ionizing radiation, such as light, gamma rays, or nuclear particles. The ions and electrons in a plasma love to recombine and react with other materials, so most plasma experiments use a vacuum chamber with a controlled atmosphere containing only the desired gaseous species.

Some parameters that we like to determine in plasma experiments are the plasma space potential, electron temperature, floating potential, and ion and electron densities. A very simple plasma diagnostic technique, the **Langmuir probe**, simplifies most of these measurements. The method involves the measurement of ion and/or electron current flowing in a small metal probe that is positioned in contact with the plasma. By varying the voltage (potential) applied to the probe and measuring the current, a curve called the probe characteristic is acquired. All you need is a variable voltage source, a sensitive current monitor, and a recording mechanism (anyone for LabVIEW?). Figure 9-13 shows how a simple Langmuir probe experiment might be connected.

Electrically, the most important piece of equipment is the voltage source that drives the probe. Depending on the experiment, you may need a source that can produce anywhere from ±10 V at 10 mA up to ±50 V at 100 mA, or greater. Ordinary DACs, like those built into a typical plug-in board, can only reach ±10 V and a few mA, which is still sufficient

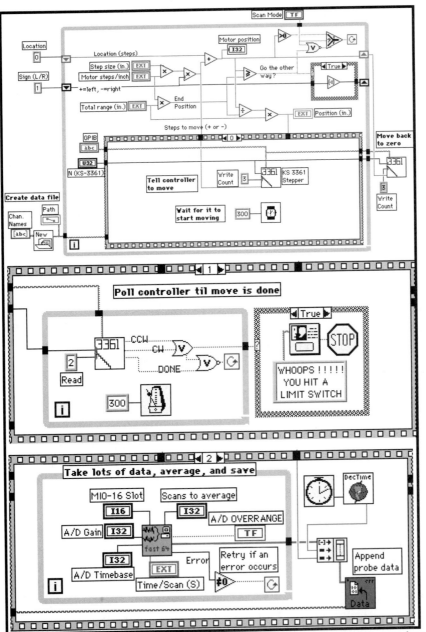

Figure 9-12.   Diagram of the ion beam intensity scan VI. The While Loop executes once for each step of the positional ramp. The sequence moves the probe and acquires data.

for many laboratory experiments. For low-speed DC experiments, I like to use a laboratory power supply with an external analog input driven by a DAC. The output of such a supply is isolated from ground and is nearly bullet-proof. For experiments in which you need a

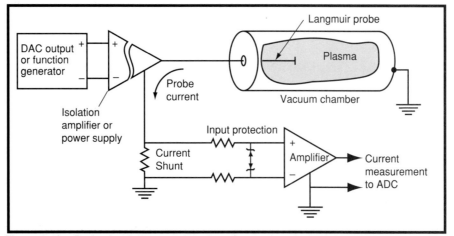

Figure 9-13. Basic electrical connections for a Langmuir probe experiment. The probe voltage is supplied by an isolation amplifier, programmable power supply, or function generator with a large output voltage swing.

high-speed ramp waveform or pulse, you need a function generator and a high-performance amplifier. As for the current sensing function, pick a shunt resistor that only drops a fraction of a volt at the expected probe current ($R = V/I$), and follow it with the usual differential amplifier. Input protection in the form of voltage limiting devices is a good idea because the plasma source generally has a high-voltage source. Accidental contact between the probe and any high-voltage elements (or arcing) will very likely destroy the amplifier.

To obtain the Langmuir probe characteristic response, your LabVIEW program has to generate a ramp waveform. Steady-state plasma experiments can be performed at low speeds over a period of seconds or minutes. Therefore, it's practical for your program to calculate the desired voltage and drive an output device. Figure 9-14 shows a simple V-I scan experiment that uses a precalculated array of values, representing a ramp waveform, that are sent to a DAC repeatedly. You can use any conceivable waveform to initialize the data array. Nested For Loops step through the values. After each step, a measurement is taken from the system (for instance, the current from a Langmuir probe). Inside the inner For Loop the new voltage is written to the output, and the resulting probe current is measured. The voltage value is carried through the Dac Out subVI and into the Read Probe subVI so that they execute in the proper order. If extra settling time is required before the measurement, add a suitable delay between the Dac Out and the Read Probe subVIs.

The X vs. Y graph (**Current vs. Voltage**) acts like a real-time XY recorder. Since LabVIEW doesn't have a built-in XY strip chart, you can simulate one by updating the graph each time the inner For Loop executes. A shift register carries the accumulated array of clusters, in which each cluster contains X (voltage) and Y (current) data. An empty graph data structure, shown on the front panel, initializes the shift register. Normally, you would select **Hide Front Panel Control** from the pop-up menu on the diagram to hide this empty

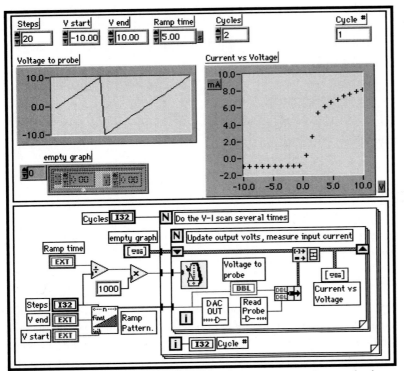

Figure 9-14. A simple V-I scan experiment. This is another way of generating low-speed, recurrent ramps, using a precalculated array of output voltages. Values are sent to a DAC repeatedly, and the response of the system under test is measured and recorded after each output update. The current vs. voltage graph acts like a real-time XY Chart recorder.

array. If you don't care to see the graph update for every sample point, put it outside the inner For Loop and let the cluster array build itself on the border of the loop (Figure 9-15). This is much faster and more efficient, too.

Read Probe acquires and scales the current measurement. If you want to store the data on disk, that subVI is a logical place to write the data to a file. Outside the For Loops, you would open a suitable file, and probably write some kind of header information. Remember to close the file when the VI is through. The File I/O Utility VIs make this simple.

In faster experiments LabVIEW may not have enough time to directly control the stimulus and response sequence. In that case, you can use a couple of different approaches, based on plug-in data acquisition boards or external, programmable equipment.

The data acquisition library supports buffered waveform generation as well as buffered waveform acquisition on plug-in boards with DMA. Essentially, you create an array of data representing the waveform, then tell the DMA controller to write the array to the DAC, one sample at a time, at a predetermined rate. Meanwhile, you can run a data acquisition operation also using DMA that is synchronized with the waveform generation. The VI in Figure 9-16 is such a program. The controls allow you to specify the ramp waveform's start and stop voltages, number of points, and the D/A update rate. Multiple cycles can be

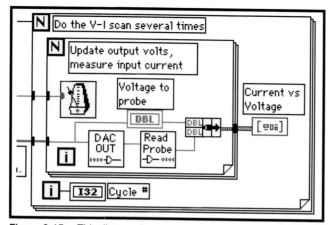

Figure 9-15. This diagram fragment is from a slightly different version of the VI scan experiment that uses the XY Graph in multiplot mode. This version displays the results of an entire scan when the scan is complete, rather than updating the plot for each sample point.

generated, and each cycle is plotted independently. For the analog inputs, you can acquire data from one or more channels with adjustable scan rate and adjustable number of points to acquire. Only one channel is plotted in this example, but data from all scanned channels is available on the diagram.

This example, written by Audrey Harvey of National Instruments, makes effective use of the intermediate-level data acquisition functions. Two tasks are defined, one for input and one for output. Error in/error out is used to control the execution sequence and of course, handle errors. Synchronization of the input and output operations is determined by the D/A update clock, which is externally wired to an input which clocks each scan of the A/D. Each time a new step value in the ramp is generated, the A/D collects one value from each defined input channel (i.e., one scan). Referring to the diagram, here are the details of the program's steps:

1. Ramp Pattern (from the Signal Generation VIs in the Analysis library) creates an array of values corresponding to a ramp waveform. You could use other functions if you needed a different waveform.

2. AI Config sets up the analog input hardware on the board for the desired number of channels and allocates a data acquisition buffer that's sized for the number of scans to be acquired.

3. AI Start begins the buffered acquisition process that was defined by AI Config. The Trigger Type is set to 2, which tells the board to use an external scan clock.

4. AO Config sets up the analog output hardware on the board and allocates a data buffer sized for the number of points to be generated.

5. AO Write puts the ramp waveform into the output buffer to prepare for the upcoming waveform generation.

6. AO Start begins the buffer waveform generation process that was defined by AO Config. The number of buffer iterations is set by the **Number of Cycles** control, meaning that the waveform will be produced several times.

7. AI Read fetches the acquired data from the buffer and makes it available to the XY Graph, where the measured voltage is plotted versus the calculated scan ramp. AI Read makes an estimate (based on the number of points to acquire and the sample rate) of how long to wait for data before timing out, so your program won't get stuck if there is a hardware failure.

8. The While Loop will continue executing the AI Read until an error occurs or the user clicks the **Stop** button.

9. Always clean up your mess. The AI Clear and AO Clear VIs terminate any I/O in progress and release their respective memory buffers. No error checking is done here because these functions can do no harm, even if no AI or AO operations are in progress. The Simple Error Handler checks for and reports any data acquisition errors.

Another way to solve this problem is to use a function generator for the stimulus waveform and a plug-in board or external digitizing instrument for the measurement. A great way to synchronize the stimulus and measurement operations is to use a timebase

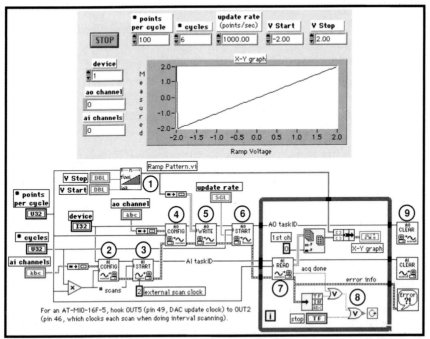

Figure 9-16. Using the Data Acquisition library and an MIO-16 series board, this VI simultaneously generates a ramp waveform and acquires data from one or more analog inputs. Only one external jumper connection is required; and note that the pin number and signal name vary slightly between models of MIO-16 boards.

clock. If you can get your hands on a modern **arbitrary waveform generator**, you will find that it has a clock output. Each time the instrument updates the DAC output, a pulse is delivered to the clock output. This clock can then be applied to the external clock input of your data acquisition board or digitizer. If the signal generator is programmed to produce 1,024 clocks in one cycle of the waveform, your digitizer is guaranteed to acquire exactly 1,024 ADC samples. Nice and neat, and always in-phase.

If you can't use a clock, then there may be some way to use a trigger signal. Even simple analog function generators have a trigger output that occurs when the waveform starts. Use that to start a data acquisition operation or trigger a digital oscilloscope (see **triggering**, below). All you have to do is make sure that the period of the waveform is a little longer than the DAQ operation. Also, as with any external signal generation, you may want to dedicate a second ADC channel to monitoring the stimulus waveform, just to be sure that the amplitude is what you think it is.

Handling Fast Pulses

Pulse and transient phenomena abound in the world of physics research. As I mentioned before, there is a host of specialized instrumentation to accompany the various detectors that produce transient waveforms. In this section, we'll look at some of those instruments, the LabVIEW programs that support them, and some of the programming tricks that may be of general use.

Waveform Digitizers

A whole class of instruments, called **waveform digitizers** (or **transient recorders**), have been developed over the years to accommodate pulsed signals. They are essentially high-speed ADCs with memory and triggering subsystems and are often sold in modular form, such as CAMAC and VXI. Transient recorders are a bit like digital oscilloscopes without the display, saving you money when you need more than just a few channels. In fact, the digital oscilloscope as we know it today is somewhat of a latecomer. There were modular (i.e., CAMAC) digitizers, supported by computers for displays, back in the 1960s. Before that, we used analog oscilloscopes with Polaroid cameras, and digitizing tablets to convert the image to ones and zeros. Anyone pine for the "good ol' days?" The fact is, digitizers make lots of sense today because we have virtual instruments, courtesy of LabVIEW. The digitizer is just so much hardware, but VIs make it into an oscilloscope, or a spectrum analyzer, or the world's fastest strip chart recorder.

Table 9-1 lists some of the transient recorders that are currently supported by LabVIEW. The driver for a typical digitizer consists of some setup VIs to set sampling rates, scale factors, and so forth, VIs to arm and trigger the digitizer, and a VI to read the data. The data is generally returned as a floating-point array scaled to voltage. Figure 9-17 shows the panel and connector pane for a typical transient recorder, the LeCroy 6810.

Table 9-1. Representative Transient Recorders for Which There Are LabVIEW Drivers.

Manufacturer	Model	Channels per Modules	Speed sample/sec	Bits	Memory Samples	Format
Tektronix	VX4250	2	100 M	8	16 K	VXI
Tektronix	VX4240	1	10 M	12	1 M	VXI
Tektronix	RTD720A	4	2 G	8	4 M	Rackmount
Analytek	2000	16	2 G	12	8 K	VME
DSP	2012	1	20 M	12	8 K	CAMAC
LeCroy	6810	4	5 M	12	8 M	CAMAC

Input Characteristics

High-speed models generally have a 50 Ω input impedance, low-speed models are high-impedance, and many offer switchable input impedance. AC or DC coupling is also available on most models, but you can always add your own coupling capacitor if the input is DC-coupled only. Another useful feature is an input offset adjustment. Because many of the high-speed digitizers only have 8-bit resolution, you should offset the actual range of the ADC to match that of your signal, thus optimizing the dynamic range. All modern digitizers have input amplifiers and/or attenuators to adjust the scale factor. Old CAMAC digitizers were fixed at one range, like 2 V. You have to supply your own wideband amplifiers and attenuators with those.

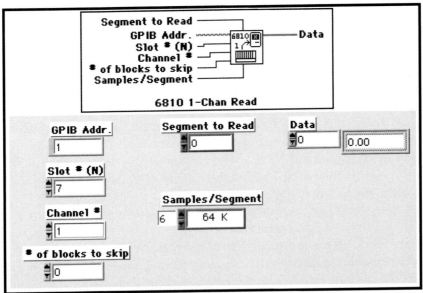

Figure 9-17.   The front panel and connector pane for a typical digitizer, the LeCroy 6810. This one lets you read data in small chunks (using the **blocks to skip** control), which really helps when you have a full 8 megasamples of memory!

Triggering

Most digitizers rely on a TTL or ECL-level external trigger to start or stop acquisition. Most models have some form of internal, level- or edge-sensitive triggering, much like an oscilloscope. Through software commands, you begin acquisition by arming the digitizer, after which you either poll the digitizer to see if it has received a trigger event or, in the case of most GPIB instruments, wait for an SRQ telling you that it's time to read the data.

Like digital oscilloscopes, you can store pretrigger and posttrigger data. Once the digitizer is armed, its ADC samples at the desired rate and stores data in high-speed memory, which is arranged as a circular buffer. When the trigger occurs, the current memory location is saved, and sampling continues until the desired number of posttrigger samples are acquired. Because data was being stored before the trigger, you can retrieve pretrigger data as well. This is very useful because there may well be important information that arrives before the trigger event in many experiments. The data acquisition library, supporting plug-in boards, does a similar trick (though the speed is somewhat limited when compared to high-speed digitizers).

Data Storage and Sampling

An important choice you have to make when picking a transient recorder is how much memory you will need, and how that memory should be organized. Single-shot transient events with a well-characterized waveshape are pretty easy to handle. Just multiply the expected recording time by the required number of samples per second. With any luck, someone makes a digitizer with enough memory to do the job.

Far more interesting is the observation of a long tail pulse, such as fluorescence decay. In this case, the intensity appears very suddenly, perhaps in tens of nanoseconds, decays rapidly for a few microseconds, then settles into a quasi-exponential decay that tails out for the better part of a second. If you want to see the detail of the initial pulse, you need to sample at many MHz. But maintaining this rate over a full second implies the storage of millions of samples, with much greater temporal resolution than is really necessary. For this reason, the designers have come up with digitizers that offer **multiple timebases**. While taking data, the digitizer can vary the sampling rate according to a programmed schedule. For instance, you could use a LeCroy 6810 (which has dual timebases) to sample at 5 MHz for 100 μs, then have it switch to 50 kHz for the remainder of the data record. This conserves memory and disk space and speeds analysis.

Another common experiment involves the recording of many rapid-fire pulses. For instance, the shot-to-shot variation in the output of a pulsed laser might tell you something significant about the uniformity of performance of the laser's power supplies, flash lamps, and so forth. If the pulse rate is too high, you probably won't have time to upload the data to your computer and recycle the digitizer between pulses. Instead, you can use a digitizer that has **segmented memory**. The Tektronix RTD720A is such a beast. It can store up to 1,024 events separated by as little as 5 μs, limited only by the amount of memory installed. After the rapid-fire measurement sequence has ended, you can upload the data at your leisure via GPIB. Other instruments with segmented memory capability are the HP54510

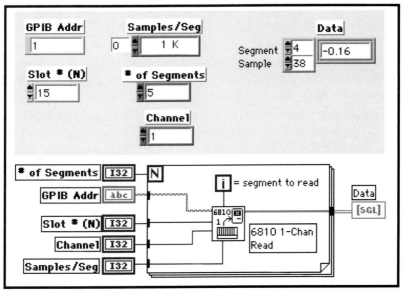

Figure 9-18. Reading segmented memories from a LeCroy 6810 digitizer. It's easy; the driver does all the work.

digital oscilloscope, and the LeCroy 6810. Figure 9-18 shows how it's done with a 6810. The instrument returns the waveform from any memory segment you choose. In this example, sequential segments are returned in a 2D array.

This is a perfect example of letting specialized hardware do the work where it is most appropriate. I get lots of calls asking me why LabVIEW can't deliver this type of machine-gun performance on waveform acquisition. Sorry, but general-purpose computers with plug-in boards just don't offer that kind of speed; such a problem is best solved with hardware, not software, at least until we have computers with gigahertz clock speeds. Conceptually, PC-based virtual instruments can replace real instruments, but that is true only to a point, limited by practical matters such as size, heat, and cost effectiveness. LabVIEW-based VIs can control and augment high-performance, special-purpose instruments, but not replace them.

Calibration

As a practical precaution, I never trust a digitizer when it comes to amplitude calibration. While the timebases are generally quite accurate, the same cannot be said for high-speed ADC scale factors. I like to warm up the rack of digitizers, apply known calibration signals, like a series of precision DC voltages, and store the measured values. If you want to get fancy, add an input switching system that directs all the input channels to a calibration source. Then, LabVIEW can do an automatic calibration before and after each experiment. You can either store the calibration data and apply it to the data later, or apply the prerun calibration corrections on the fly. One precaution: if you have several digitizers with 50 Ω inputs, make sure they don't overload the output of your calibrator. It's an embarrassing, but common, mistake.

Digital Oscilloscopes

For the physics researcher, the **digital storage oscilloscope (DSO)** has several uses—for troubleshooting and initial setup of experimental apparatus, for convenient display of live waveforms during an experiment, and as a waveform digitizer when combined with a LabVIEW system.

As a utility instrument, the oscilloscope (either analog or digital) is unsurpassed. As much as I would like to think that a digitizer and a LabVIEW display can duplicate an oscilloscope, it never really pans out in the practical world. The reasons are partly aesthetic, partly portability, but mostly... I like *real knobs*. Some of the digital 'scopes aren't very good in this respect, either. All covered with buttons and nary a knob in sight. For general-purpose test and measurement, I'll take a real 'scope with knobs any day.

For real-time waveform display, LabVIEW sometimes approaches the common DSO in terms of display update speed. If you have a modest record length like 512 samples, and a fast computer, a GPIB or VXI digitizer can do a credible job of mimicking a real-time display. You can also throw lots of traces on one screen, which is something that most DSOs can't do. Nevertheless, every lab I've ever worked in has had every available oscilloscope fired up, displaying the live waveforms.

Most DSOs have a GPIB interface and a LabVIEW driver. Therefore, you can use them to make permanent records of transient events. The only limitation I've seen is in some really old models that were incredibly slow at accepting commands and transferring data.

Timing and Triggering

The key to your success in pulsed experiments is setting up timing and triggering of all the diagnostic instruments and recording equipment. Just having a rack full of digitizers that all go off at the same time may, or may not, solve your problems. All of your pulsed diagnostics must trigger at the proper time, and you have to know exactly when that important trigger event occurred.

What's All This Triggering Stuff, Anyhow?

The experiment itself may be the source of the main trigger event, or the trigger may be externally generated. As an example of an externally triggered experiment, you might trigger a high-voltage pulse generator to produce a plasma. Experiments that run on an internally generated timebase and experiments that produce random events, such as nuclear decay, generally are the source of the trigger event. The instruments must be armed and ready to acquire the data when the next event occurs. All of these situations generate what we might classify as a first-level, or primary, trigger.

First-level triggers are distributed to all of your pulsed diagnostic instruments to promote accurate synchronization. Some utility hardware has been devised over the years to make the job easier. First, you probably need a **trigger fanout**, which has a single input and multiple outputs to distribute a single trigger pulse to several instruments, such as a bank of digitizers. A fanout module may offer selectable gating (enabling) and inverting of each output. A commercial trigger fanout CAMAC module is the LeCroy 4418 with 16 channels. Second, you often need **trigger delays**. Many times, you need to generate a rapid sequence of events to accomplish an experiment. Modern digital delays are very easy to use. Just supply a TTL or ECL-level trigger pulse, and after a programmed delay, an output pulse of programmable width and polarity occurs. Examples of commercial trigger delays are the Stanford Research DG535 and the LeCroy 4222. Third, you may need a **trigger discriminator** to clean up the *raw* trigger pulse from your experimental apparatus. It works much like the trigger controls on an oscilloscope, permitting you to select a desired slope and level on the incoming waveform.

A fine point regarding triggering is timing uncertainty, variously known as trigger skew or jitter. Sometimes you need to be certain as to the exact timing relationship between the trigger event and the sampling clock of the ADC. A situation where this is important is waveform averaging. If the captured waveforms shift excessively in time, then the averaged result will not accurately represent the true wave shape. Most transient digitizers have a sampling clock that runs all the time. When an external trigger occurs, the current sample number is noted by the digitizer's hardware. Note that the trigger event could fall somewhere in between the actual sampling events that are driven by the clock. One way to force synchronization is to use a master clock for your experiment that drives all the digitizers. Then, derive the trigger signal from the clock so that triggering always occurs at the same time relative to the clock. Unfortunately, this trick can't be used when the trigger event is random or uncontrollable in nature. In those cases, you must make sure that the trigger generator is stable and repeatable and that the sampling rate is high enough that a timing offset of plus or minus one sample will do no harm.

Figure 9-19 illustrates an application of several of these trigger processing devices with a pulsed laser as the source of the primary trigger event. In this case, the laser excites some plasma phenomenon in a target chamber. Then, a high-voltage pulse generator is triggered to collect ions in the plasma. Finally, the digitizers are triggered to observe the ion current. A trigger delay helps adjust the "zero time" for the digitizers to center the recorded data with respect to the physical event. Note that a delay generator cannot produce an output that occurs *before* the input. (I can't count the number of times I needed such a device!) If you want your instruments to acquire data before the trigger, you will need digitizers with pretrigger sampling capability.

Second-level triggers are another useful tool in physics diagnostics. Some experiments require a bit more intelligence to decide when to trigger the data acquisition hardware. For instance, the coincidence of two pulses or digital words (a logical operation) is commonly used to detect high-energy particles. Coincidence detection helps to filter out undesired, anomalous events. In such cases, you can use commercial triggering logic systems, like those made by LeCroy. Or, if the problem is simple, just put together some analog and/or digital logic yourself.

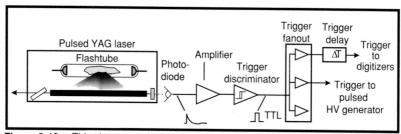

Figure 9-19. This shows a typical application of a trigger discriminator, fanout, and delays used in a pulsed laser experiment.

Third-level triggers represent an even higher level of sophistication in trigger event detection. In some experiments, there may be enough noise or other false events that the first-level and even the second-level trigger causes you to record many nonevents. If this occurs very often, you end up with a disk full of empty baselines and just a few records of good data. That's okay, except for experiments where each event consists of 85 megabytes of data. The poor fellow analyzing the data (you?) is stuck plowing through all this utterly useless information.

The solution is to use a hardware or software-based third-level trigger that examines some part of the data before storage. For instance, if you have 150 digitizers, you might want to write a subVI that loads the data from one or two of them and checks for the presence of some critical feature—perhaps a critical voltage level or pulse shape. Then, you can decide whether to load and store all the data or just clear the digitizer memories and rearm.

If there is sufficient time between events, the operator might be able to accept or reject the data through visual inspection. By all means, try to automate the process. However, there is often barely time to do any checking at all. The evaluation plus recycle time may cause you to miss an actual event. If there is insufficient time for a software pattern recognition program to work, you can either store all the data (good and bad), or come up with a hardware solution, or perhaps a solution that uses fast, dedicated microprocessors to do the pattern recognition.

Managing Trigger Setups

Traditionally, triggering equipment consists of rack after rack of timing and delay modules, fanouts, buffers, and patch panels. If that's your case, you "manage" triggering by keeping careful track of which signal goes where and what all the knobs are set to. No short cuts there. But, if you have moved into the New Age of data acquisition and control, you can use programmable modules to do much of this work. In that case, a good LabVIEW program can simplify the management and setup of your experiment's timing and triggering system.

Here is a good example. The radio frequency (RF) Controls and Signal Processing section of the RF Technology group of Los Alamos National Laboratory (LANL) designed, built, and delivered a low-level RF control system for the University of Twente's Free

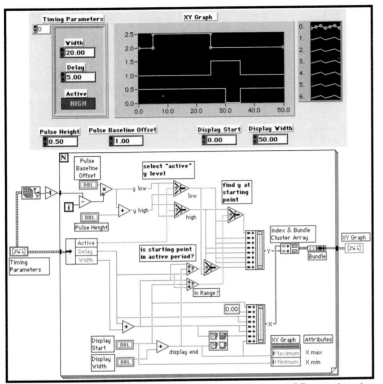

Figure 9-20. Timing setup display from the LANL low-level RF control package. This is a really intuitive way of displaying timing and triggering information. The diagram is complex; I did the best I could to label important parts.

Electron Laser in Holland [Ref. 5]. The purpose of the RF system in such a particle accelerator is to create a controlled high-power RF field in the accelerator cavity which enables the bunching and acceleration of a charged-particle beam. The purpose of the low-level RF control system is to maintain the amplitude and phase of the cavity's RF field within specifications. Measurement and control of amplitude, phase, and timing are crucial, because the system is quite complex; automatic controls are a must.

LANL decided to use a VXI-based LabVIEW control system to meet these requirements. The controller is a National Instruments VXIpc-030, which is an embedded Macintosh SE-30, with a MXIbus interface to support two VXI chassis. A total of 14 modules were used, and many of them were custom-designed for the experiment. The LabVIEW program monitors and controls the RF equipment, maintains resonance conditions in an RF cavity through PID feedback control, and then will display alarm and status indications.

A particular subVI of interest, shown in Figure 9-20, controls a custom timing distribution module with programmable delays and pulse widths. The graph displays a nice timing diagram that makes the timing relationships among the many channels very clear. You could easily adapt this type of display to your own timing control system.

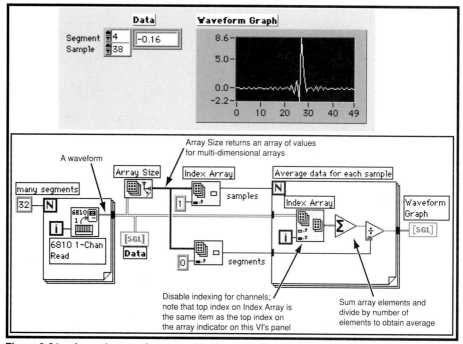

Figure 9-21. Averaging waveforms acquired from a digitizer that has segmented memories. Be really careful with array indexing; this example shows that LabVIEW has a consistent pattern with regard to indexes. The first index is always "on top," both on the panel and on the diagram.

Each of the waveforms is constructed through the use of a Build Array function. High and low Y-axis values for a given waveform are selected based on the For Loop's index and the polarity of the waveform (active "high" means a more positive level occurs after the delay time). The user can adjust the height and spacing of the displayed waveforms through the **Pulse Height** and **Pulse Baseline Offset** controls. **Width** and **delay** parameters determine which of these (high or low) values are to appear at which location on the graph. An X-axis array has to be built for each waveform because each waveform has different transition points. To show where the transitions occur, I made the upper trace in the graph display points as little circles.

The user can adjust the time scale of the graph by changing **Display Start** and **Display Width**. Those values affect the generation of points to be displayed and are also applied to an Attribute Node for the graph to set the X-axis minimum and maximum. That's easier than forcing the user to manually scale the graph.

Credit where credit is due: Lynda Gruggett of G Systems (Dallas, TX) did much of the programming on this project, which amounted to about 150 VIs. And thanks to Amy Regan of LANL for supplying the VIs and the technical description of the project.

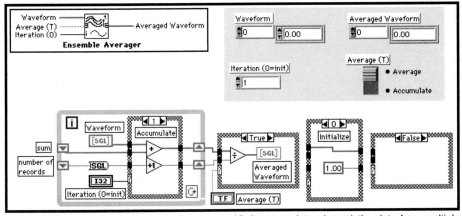

Figure 9-22. This shows an ensemble averager VI. It accumulates (sums) the data from multiple waveforms, then calculates the average on command. It uses uninitialized shift registers to store the data between calls.

Capturing Many Pulses

Many pulsed experiments produce rapid streams of pulses that you need to grab without missing any events. Assuming that you have all the right detectors and wideband amplifiers, you need to select the right acquisition hardware.

There are two ways to treat multipulse data—capture each pulse individually, or average the pulses as they occur. Averaging has the distinct advantage of improving the signal-to-noise ratio on the order of $\sqrt{N}$, where N is the number of pulses averaged. Of course, if you are able to capture and store all of the pulses, you can always average them afterward. Figure 9-21 is a VI that uses a digitizer with segmented memories to acquire many waveforms. It shows some of the array indexing tricks required to average the waveforms.

This VI is memory intensive because it assembles multiple waveforms (1D arrays) into a large 2D array. At first, it may seem that there is no other solution because you need to have all of the waveforms available before you can perform averaging. There is another solution: use an **ensemble averager** subVI like the one in Figure 9-22. Each time this VI is called, it sums the incoming data with the previous data on a sample-by-sample basis. When called with **Average** set to true, the sum is divided by the number of samples. The **Iteration** control is used to initialize the two uninitialized shift registers. At initialization time, the incoming waveform determines the length of the array.

Now you can rewrite the data averaging VI in a way that saves memory. The improved version is shown in Figure 9-23, and it produces the same result but with much less memory usage. To further improve performance, averaging is turned off until the last iteration of the For Loop. This step saves many floating point division operations. If you want to see the averaging operation evolve in real-time, you could move the waveform graph inside the For Loop and turn averaging on all the time. Each time a new segment of data is read, the graph will be updated with a newly computed average.

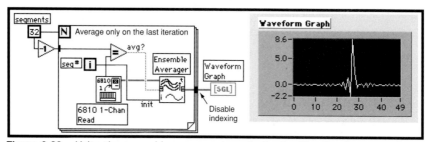

Figure 9-23. Using the ensemble averager dramatically simplifies the diagram and cuts memory usage while yielding the same results as before.

Individual pulses need to be stored when the information contained in each pulse is significant. The big issues (as far as LabVIEW is concerned) are how often the pulses occur and how fast your data transfer rate and throughput are. If the pulses only occur every second or so, there is no problem. Any simple acquisition loop that you write with a good external digitizer will probably work. But sometimes you will want to capture pulses at much higher rates, perhaps tens or hundreds of pulses per second. That calls for digitizers with segmented memories, as previously mentioned.

If the running average value of many pulses is interesting, then you can use some other instruments. Most DSOs offer built-in signal averaging. Assuming that you can trigger the DSO reliably, this is a really easy way to obtain averaged waveforms over GPIB. For a more modular approach, DSP Technology makes a line of averaging memories for use with their CAMAC digitizers. They use high-speed memory and an adder to accumulate data from synchronized waveforms. After the desired number of events (N), you read out the memory and divide the data by N. Future VXI modules will no doubt support this kind of waveform acquisition and processing, as well.

You can also use a **boxcar averager** to acquire averaged pulse waveforms. The basic timing diagram for a boxcar averager is shown in Figure 9-24. The gate interval is a short period of time during which the analog signal voltage is sampled and its amplitude stored as charge on a capacitor. The output of the boxcar is the average of many such gate events over a selected period of time. If the gate is fixed at one location in time, relative to the recurrent analog waveform, then the boxcar output represents the average value of the waveform at that time—just like putting cursors on the graph of the waveform. Now we can vary the gate delay with an analog voltage, thus scanning the gate's sampling location over the entire width of the pulse. By scanning the gate slowly, the boxcar output accurately reconstructs the analog waveform. With this technique, a simple X-Y chart recorder or slow data acquisition system can record the shape of *nanosecond* waveforms.

One boxcar system, the Stanford Research Systems SR250, offers a GPIB interface module (for which we have a LabVIEW driver) that directly supports gate scanning and also measures the boxcar output. Even without this special support, you can use a ramp generator VI like the one described in Plasma Potential Experiments to scan the gate and make the output measurements. On the SR250, the gate delay signal is a 0–10 V input (drive it directly from your MIO-16 output), and the gate delay ranges from 1 ns to 10 ms,

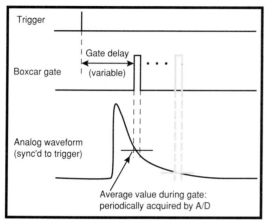

Figure 9-24. Basic timing diagram for a boxcar averager. The output of the boxcar is the average of many measurements that are acquired during many gate events. By slowly varying the gate delay, the boxcar output reconstructs the shape of the analog waveform.

so you can cover a very wide range of pulse widths. The boxcar output ranges up to ±2 V and is well-filtered, making accurate measurements a snap.

Handling HUGE Data Sets

Experiments have a way of getting out of hand with respect to the quantity of data generated. At the NASA Ames Research Center's Hypervelocity Free-Flight Aerodynamic Facility (HFFAF) [Ref. 4], they use about 180 channels of transient digitizers with anywhere from 8 K to 256 K samples per channel—about 16 MB per shot, typical. (The good news is that they can only do a couple of shots per week.) In another common situation, seismology, they need to digitize and record data at hundreds of samples per second from many channels... forever. Forever implies a *really big* disk drive. Obviously, there must be some practical solutions to memory and disk limitations, and that's what we'll look at next.

Reducing the Amount of Data

The concept of third-level triggers can certainly reduce the amount of data to be handled. Or, you can do some kind of preliminary data reduction to compact the raw data before storing it on disk.

In seismology, an algorithm called a "P-picker" continuously processes the incoming data stream, searching for features that indicate the presence of a P wave (a high-frequency, perpendicular shock wave), which indicates that an interesting seismic event has occurred. If a P wave is detected, then a specified range of recent and future data is streamed to disk for later, more detailed, analysis. Saving all of the raw data would be impractical, though they sometimes set up large circular buffer schemes just in case a really important event (*The Big One*) occurs. That permits a moderate time history to remain in memory and/or on disk for immediate access. But in the long run, the P-picker is key.

If your data is of a contiguous but sparse nature, like that of a seismic data recording system, consider writing a continuous algorithm to detect and keep interesting events. Because the detection algorithm may require significant execution time, it probably needs to run asynchronously with the data acquisition task. If you are using a plug-in board, you can use buffered DMA. Some kinds of smart data acquisition units also support buffering of data. Either way, the hardware continues collecting and storing data to a new buffer even while the computer is busy analyzing the previous buffer. If you can't use one of these hardware-based, double-buffering schemes, you might be able to write one yourself.

Figure 9-25 shows a simplified data acquisition program that relies on parallel While Loops. The left loop acquires data from some source and stores it in one of two global variable buffers, alternating between the two each time. Whenever a buffer is written, an associated Boolean flag (B1 for Buf1, B2 for Buf2) is set to true. The right-hand loop waits for one of the flags to become true, at which time the associated buffer is read and processed, and the flag is reset to False. A subVI is called to analyze the data, looking for something interesting. If that something is found, then the buffer is written to disk. This software double buffer shares one limitation with its hardware counterpart: if the analysis part takes too long, you could miss the next buffer. Perhaps a DSP board or other coprocessor scheme can be used to accelerate the analysis if you run into trouble. (As for me, I always lust after a SPARCstation when my Mac runs out of suds!)

If you can't afford to throw away any of your data, then data reduction on the fly might help reduce the amount of disk space required. It will also save time in the postexperiment data reduction phase. Is your data of a simple, statistical nature? Then maybe all you really

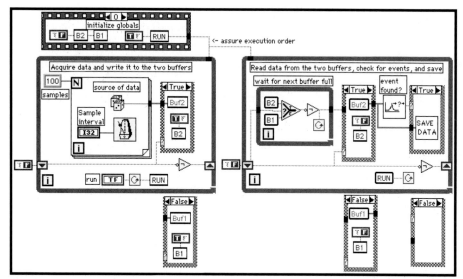

Figure 9-25. A homemade double-buffered data acquisition VI with an event detector that determines whether the latest buffer should be saved. The left loop acquires data and stores it in the two buffers. The right loop asynchronously reads the data, checks for the trigger event, and stores data on disk.

need to save are those few statistical values, rather than the entire data arrays. Maybe there are other characteristics—pulse parameters, amplitude at a specific frequency, or whatever—that you can save in lieu of raw data. Can many buffers of data be averaged? That reduces the stored volume in proportion to the number averaged. If nothing else, you might get away with storing the reduced data for every waveform, plus the raw data for every Nth waveform. As you can see, it's worth putting some thought into real-time analysis. Again, there may be performance limitations that put some constraints on how much real-time work you can do. Be sure to test and benchmark before committing yourself to a certain processing scheme.

Optimizing VIs for Memory Usage

Large data sets tend to consume vast quantities of memory. Some experiments require digitizers that can internally store millions of samples, because there simply isn't time during the run to stream the data to your computer. When the run is over, it's time to upload, analyze, and save all those samples. If your computer has only, say, 8 MB of RAM, then it's unlikely that you will be able to load more than a few hundred thousand samples of data in one chunk. You have two choices: buy more memory, or write a smarter program.

Expanding the memory capacity of your machine is certainly worthwhile. LabVIEW is a big memory user, no doubt about it. And modern operating systems aren't getting any smaller. Even **virtual memory**, now available on all of LabVIEW's platforms, may not save you because there are significant real-time performance penalties due to the disk swapping that VM causes. For best performance, and simplicity in programming, nothing beats having extra memory. Of course it costs money, but memory is cheap.

So you find yourself a little short on memory, a little short on cash, and a little down in the mouth because LabVIEW dies every time you try to load those megasamples of data. It's time to optimize, and perhaps rewrite, your program. By the way, I guarantee that you will see an increase in the *performance* of your program when you optimize memory usage. Anything you do to reduce the activity of our old friend the memory manager will speed things up considerably. Here are the basic optimizing techniques that every one should know.

Use Cyclic Processing Rather Than Trying to Load All Channels at Once

Once you see this concept, it becomes obvious. Below is a trivial example of the way you can restructure a data acquisition program. In Figure 9-26A, 10 waveforms are acquired in a For Loop, which builds a 10-by-N 2D numeric array. After collection, the 2D array is passed to a subVI for storage on disk. The 2D array is likely to be a memory burner. Figure 9-26B shows a simple, but effective, change. By putting the data storage subVI in the loop, only one 1D array of data needs to be created, and its data space in memory is reused by each waveform. An instant factor of 10 reduction in memory usage.

Of course, you can't always use cyclic processing. If you need to perform an operation on two or more of the waveforms, they obviously have to be concurrently memory-

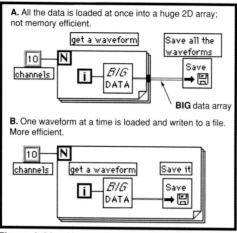

Figure 9-26. Use cyclic processing of data (B) to avoid storing all of your data in memory at the same time, as in A.

resident. But keep trying. If you only need to have *two* waveforms in memory, then just keep *two*, and not the whole bunch.

Break the Data Into Smaller Chunks

Just because the data source contains a zillion bytes of data, you don't necessarily have to load it all at once. Many instruments permit you to read selected portions of memory, so you can sequence through it in smaller chunks that are easier to handle. The LeCroy 6810 CAMAC digitizer has such a feature, which is supported by the LabVIEW driver. It's relatively simple to write a looping program that loads these subdivided buffers and appends them to a binary file one at a time.

Use the Smallest Practical Numeric Types

Remember that LabVIEW supports many numeric types, from a single-byte integer on up to a 12-byte extended-precision float. The amount of memory that your data will consume is the number of samples multiplied by the size of the numeric type, in bytes. Lots of digitizers have eight-bit resolution, which fits perfectly into a single-byte integer, either signed (I8) or unsigned (U8). That's a case of maximum efficiency. Many times, however, you will want to scale the raw binary data to engineering units, which require a floating-point representation. For most cases, try to use the single-precision float (SGL), which is four bytes long and offers seven significant figures of precision. In the rare case where you need greater precision, use double-precision (DBL), which uses eight bytes.

Avoid Coercion and Conversion When Handling Arrays

Minimizing data space requires constant vigilance. Begin by looking at any driver VIs, or whatever your data sources may be. Make sure that the data is *born* in the smallest practical type. Drivers that were created way back in version 1.2 of LabVIEW are notorious for

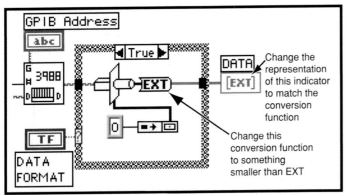

Figure 9-27. This old driver (from the Kinetic Systems 3988 library) converts 16-bit binary data to EXT floating-point numbers, which wastes much memory. Change the indicated conversion function to something smaller, like SGL. Save big! And get the Ginsu Knife!!

supplying all data in EXT format (the only numeric type then available). Figure 9-27 shows one such example, an old CAMAC driver VI. You might even create your own versions of driver VIs, optimized for your memory-intensive application.

The analysis VIs in the LabVIEW library, like all VIs, are not polymorphic and handle only double-precision (DBL) floating point data. Double-precision floats are used because they provide the best mix of good precision and fast computation time. Most math coprocessors support only DBL, so passing data in this format yields the best performance because it doesn't need to be converted by the math coprocessor. Using one of the analysis VIs on your more compact SGL data results in a doubling of memory usage. There are several things you can do if you need to conserve memory. First, call National Instruments and complain that you want polymorphic analysis VIs. Second, if it's not too complex, try writing your own equivalent function subVI in LabVIEW, one that uses only your chosen (smaller) data type. Realize that your routine may run a bit slower than the optimized, CIN-based, analysis function. Third, you can perform the analysis at a time when less data is resident in memory.

Keep a sharp eye open for coercion dots at terminals that handle large arrays. Anywhere you see one, the data type is being changed and that means that reallocation of memory is required. This takes time and, especially if the new data type is larger, results in the consumption of even more memory. If the coercion dot appears on a subVI, open the subVI and try to change all of the related controls, indicators, and functions to the same data type as your source. Sometimes this is impossible, as with the analysis VIs, or with any VI that contains a CIN. By the way, *NEVER* change the data type that feeds data into a CIN! A crash will surely ensue because the CIN expects a specific data type; it has to be recompiled to change the data type. Maybe one day we'll have polymorphic CINs, too. Finally, don't convert between data types unnecessarily. For instance, changing a numeric array to a string for display purposes is costly in terms of memory and performance. If you must display data, try to use an indicator in the native format of that data.

Avoid Data Duplication

Technical Note 012, *Minimizing the Number of Data Buffers* [Ref. 6], goes into some detail on the subject of efficient use of memory. Here are some of the most important rules to keep in mind.

- *An output of a function reuses an input buffer if the output and the input have the same data type, representation, and—for arrays, strings, and clusters—the same structure and number of elements.* This category includes all of the Trig & Log functions; most of the Arithmetic functions, including those that operate on Boolean data; a few string functions like To Upper Case; the Transpose Array function; and the Bundle function to the extent that the cluster input and output can use the same buffer. Most other functions do not meet this criteria; among them are the Build Array and Concatenate String functions.

- *In general, only one destination can use the buffer of the data source.* More specifically, where the source of a data path branches to two or more destinations that change the input data, the source buffer can be used by only one. A way to conserve memory is to do processing in a serial fashion—one subVI after another—rather than wiring the subVIs in parallel.

- *If there are multiple destinations that read data but do not change it, they may use the same source buffer.* Also, under certain circumstances, when a node that alters data and one or more nodes that merely read data have the same source, LabVIEW can determine that the readers execute before the node that changes the data so that the source buffer can be reused.

- *If the source is a terminal of a control that is not assigned to a connector terminal or receives no data from the calling VI, the source data is stored in a separate buffer.* Without an external source to supply data when the subVI executes, the data is locally supplied. This means you can save memory by not displaying it.

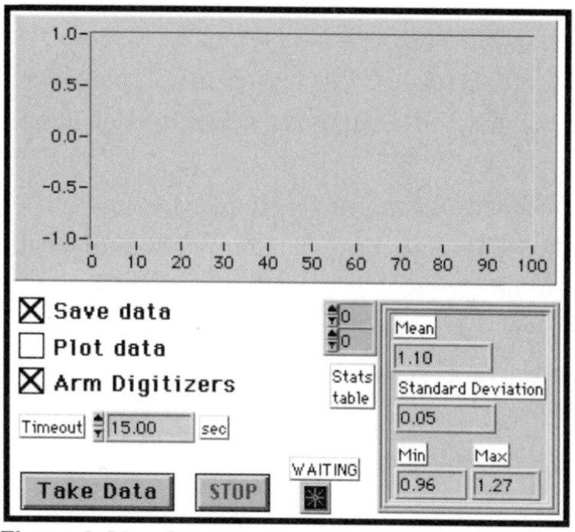

Figure 9-28. Simplified front panel for the NASA digitizer experiment.

- *If a buffer can be reused by an input and output of a structure or subVI, the buffer can be used by other nodes wired to that node.* Thus, in a multilevel program, a buffer can be reused from the top level VI to the lowest subVI and back up to the top. Don't be afraid to use subVIs, so long as they do not duplicate arrays internally.

- *Data allocated to a top-level VI cannot be deallocated during execution;* data allocated to a subVI can be.

If your application uses much more memory than you think it should, it's probably because of array duplication. Try to sift through these rules (study the technical note for more) and figure out where you might modify your program to conserve memory.

Case Study: NASA Digitizer Acquisition

At the NASA Ames Research Center, they are studying the aerodynamics of hypersonic aerospace vehicles by using a 16-inch, combustion-driven shock tunnel. Projectiles, simulating spacecraft structures, are accelerated to high velocity then fly through an observation chamber where they meet a counter-propagating shock wave. This simulates flight at Mach 20-25 under high-altitude conditions. Diagnostics include photography, laser holography, pressures, temperatures, calorimeters, currents, and voltages. Data from all but the optical instruments, a total of 180 channels, is acquired by CAMAC digitizers preceded by custom-designed wideband instrumentation amplifiers. LeCroy 6810 and 8210 digitizers, both of which are four-channel units, are installed in several CAMAC crates with LeCroy 8901A GPIB crate controllers. LabVIEW is installed on a Macintosh Quadra 950 with 64 megabytes of RAM, and erasable optical disks are used for archiving data. Primary analysis is performed with Igor on the Macintosh, and final analysis and model verification is performed on Silicon Graphics workstations and other computers.

This is a single-shot experiment, so there are no particular constraints on data transfer rates, other than impatience on the part of the experimenters, who are often desperate to see some results! The challenge is that some digitizer channels may have as many as 256 K 12-bit samples, and that takes a long time to load and display. Most of the channels are set to 16 K on a typical experiment, resulting in about four million data points. Because the data needs to be scaled to engineering units in SGL format, this represents 16 megabytes of data. Even with four times this amount of memory installed, it is evident that the danger zone is not too far away.

The program I wrote for this NASA experiment is structured around a configuration editor VI and a separate acquisition VI, with configuration information passed through a global variable. A highly simplified version of the acquisition VI is shown in Figures 9-28 and 9-29. The For Loops shown in this frame of the Sequence read data from the various digitizers, calculate statistics, store, and graph data. Preceding this part of the code in the Sequence structure are three other operations:

1. Initialize each digitizer

2. Arm each digitizer

3. Check for the LAM bit on each digitizer, which indicates that the trigger has occurred and data is ready.

Steps one through three can optionally be skipped to permit immediate rereading of data that resides in the digitizers. This is a safety feature. If the computer should crash, or the program fail for some reason, the experimenter can restart the program and reread the data without initializing the digitizers, which would erase the data. These three steps are explained in Figures 9-32, 9-33, and 9-34.

Why send the configuration information via a global variable? To save memory. The configuration manager VI is completely independent of the acquisition VI; the only thing they share is the configuration global. This allows the configuration manager to be loaded, run, then thrown out of memory while leaving behind only the setup information. When I first wrote this application, memory was tight because we couldn't access more than eight megabytes of RAM and even the few hundred kilobytes occupied by the configuration manager was critical.

Another way this can be accomplished automatically (at least on a Macintosh) is to use one of the high-level **Apple Event** VIs, AESend Open, Run, Close VI (see Figure 9-30). This is a VI included with the **Network** functions. You supply the path to the VI you wish

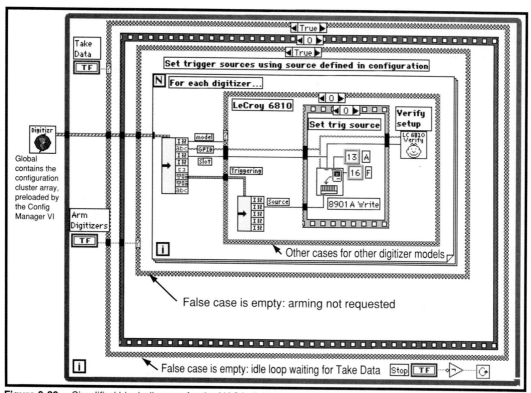

Figure 9-29. Simplified block diagram for the NASA digitizer experiment.

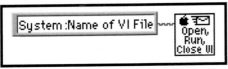

Figure 9-30.   It's simple to use AppleEvents, like AESend Open, Run, Close VI, to cause a VI to load and run, then go away.

to open. LabVIEW opens the VI and runs it as if the user had manually opened the VI and clicked the Run arrow. When execution is completed, the VI closes automatically, freeing up memory. Currently, the rumor is that Apple Events are migrating to the Sun and PC; keep watching.

One problem with this approach is that AESend Open, Run, Close VI, once called, will not complete execution until the VI that it opens has finally closed. That means the calling program has to wait, and you need to be careful how your diagram is laid out if you want other things to happen in parallel. An alternative is to break the open-run-close sequence into two pieces. In Figure 9-31 is a VI that does the open and run part by calling the Apple Event functions, AESend Open Document and AESend Run VIs. These same functions are part of AESend Open, Run, Close VI, so it's easy to steal the required parts of the program. To close the VI, you can have the user manually close the window or configure the VI to **Close front panel when finished**, from the Execution menu of the VI Setup dialog box.

In the last frame of the Sequence structure, data is read from each of the digitizer channels one channel at a time, thus eliminating the need for more than 256K-samples worth of memory. Since the digitizers are 12-bit instruments, SGL floats are sufficient. The basic LeCroy 8901 driver (which supports high-speed GPIB data transfers for all digitizers) supplied EXT floats, so I had to modify it as previously discussed.

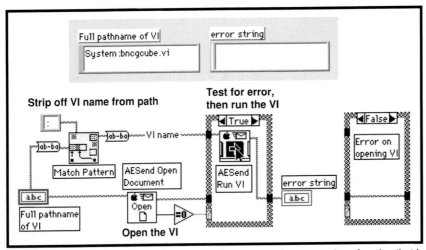

Figure 9-31.   I stole some code from AESend Open, Run, Close to make a function that just opens and runs a VI, leaving the user to close it later.

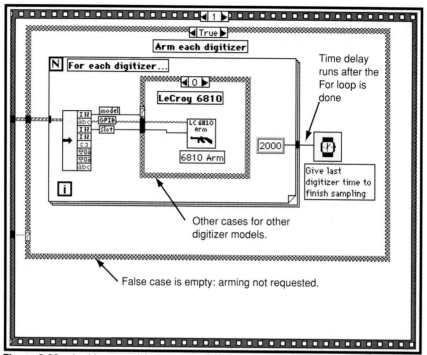

Figure 9-32. In this second frame of the sequence, each digitizer is armed to prepare it for an impending trigger.

Graphing data on the front panel requires a duplication of the data array, so I put the graph's terminal in a Case structure so that the user could decide whether to make plots. The user is forewarned that plotting is not recommended if any digitizers are set for very large data buffers because of speed and memory limitations. When this VI was originally written in LabVIEW 2.2, the representation of the graph had to be manually set to SGL. Version 3.0 took care of that—the **waveform graph** is polymorphic.

Next, the data can optionally be stored on disk in a special binary format that is readable in Igor. The Store Digitizer Data subVI has to unbundle the input cluster that contains the data, so that counts for one duplication of the array. Then, it passes the input cluster to another subVI (Append Index Data), which in turn does more manipulation and accounts for three duplications. Finally, formatting the data and writing the file requires two duplications. The total is a rather atrocious six duplications of the data array. No wonder we tend to run out of memory! Because it takes time (and memory) to write out the data, the user is permitted to turn off data storage for test purposes.

Finally, statistics are calculated on the acquired waveforms. Because the analysis VIs use DBL floats, I chose to create my own SGL-format statistics calculations to prevent coercion. The Stats subVI does several computations that require one duplication of the data array, and that's as good as it gets.

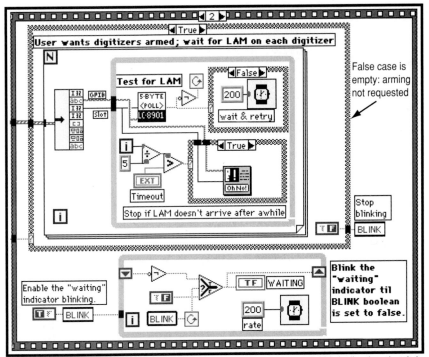

Figure 9-33. This third frame waits for each digitizer to report a LAM, indicating that it has been triggered. If a trigger is not received in time, a warning dialog is displayed. The little While Loop at the bottom blinks a "waiting" sign to tell the user that the VI is waiting for a trigger.

By the way, after looking closely at this whole NASA application, I decided that two array duplications could have been saved in Store Digitizer Data. However, it would have required me to rip the guts out of that Append Index Data subVI down inside, and then place all of its code on the diagram of Store Digitizer Data. Here, I draw the line on this business of memory miserliness. In the interest of readable, maintainable code, I'm not going to suggest that this change be made because the resulting diagram would be a mess. It's a trade-off that you too will encounter. Where efficiency and modularity conflict, you must decide which prevails.

How do you find out how much memory a subVI actually uses? Test it for yourself. There is a VI called **Free Memory** that can monitor the amount of memory that is free in the LabVIEW heap (the place where all data is allocated). Open the subVI under test, and run it with an empty array (or one with only one or two data points), then run Free Memory to measure the available RAM. Then, set the input array's index to, say, 9999, and poke in a value. Now the array has 10,000 values. Run the VI, then find out how much free memory is available. If no array duplications or other major events occur, the memory consumed will be 10,000 times the number of bytes in the numeric representation.

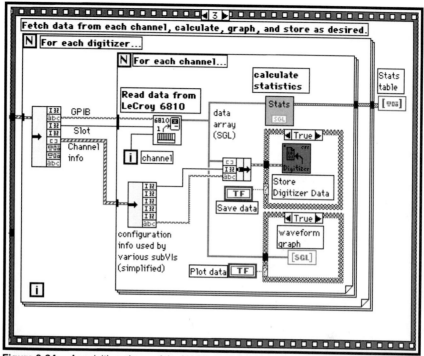

Figure 9-34. Acquisition phase of the NASA digitizer experiment (simplified for clarity). Digitizer data is read out from one instrument at a time and then, (optionally) saved to disk and/or graphed. Memory optimization is important here due to the large data array.

REFERENCES

1. *Data Acquisition in High-Energy Physics,* G. Bologna, and M. I. Vincelli, eds. Proc. International School of Physics. Amsterdam: North Holland, 1983. ISBN 0-444-86520-9

2. *Plasma Diagnostic Techniques,* H.S.W. Mass and Keith A. Brueckner, eds. New York: Academic Press, 1965.

3. *1992 LeCroy Research Instrumentation Catalog,* LeCroy Corporation, New York (914) 578-5984.

4. Reactivation and Upgrade of the NASA Ames 16 Inch Shock Tunnel: Status Report, D. W. Bogdanoff et. al. American Inst. of Aeronautics and Astronautics 92-0327.

5. *Low-Level RF LabVIEW Control Software User's Manual,* Accelerator Technology Div. AT-5, Los Alamos National Laboratory, LA-12409-M. Available from: National Technical Information Service, Springfield, VA.

6. National Instruments LabVIEW Technical Note 012, *Minimizing the Number of Data Buffers* (part number 340202-01).

Chapter 10

Data Visualization and Image Processing

With today's sophisticated computer systems, you can collect and observe information in ways that used to be impractical or impossible. Once the bastion of the High Priests of Graphic Arts, the ability to produce multidimensional color plots, acquire and manipulate images, and even make movies of your data is directly available (live!) through LabVIEW. All you need to do is configure your system appropriately and, for some features, buy some third-party LabVIEW applications that offer these advanced capabilities. This chapter tells you how.

We humans have a marvelous ability to absorb visual information, but only when it is presented in optimum form. A well-designed graph or image conveys a great deal of information and gives us unexpected insight into hidden relationships buried in our data. You have to invest some programming effort, time, money, and thought to create the right visualization instrument, but the results are both valuable and impressive.

Keep in mind that **imaging** is just another data analysis technique. That's a fact that is overlooked when you haven't seen it in action. Images can be born of cameras and live scenes—the usual pictures—or they can arise from other forms of numerical data. Images are more than pretty pictures; they can be quantitative as well, spatially and in intensity. Further, you can make those images into movies and even combine them with sound by using the new concepts embodied in **multimedia**. LabVIEW does all of these things.

There are dozens—perhaps hundreds—of data visualization (graphing, imaging, and presentation) programs available on various computer platforms these days. But LabVIEW has one big advantage over most of them: it can tie in data visualization with other operations in your real-world laboratory. For example, you can direct a robot arm, measure temperatures, control an electron beam welder, acquire images of the weld, process and display those images, store data on disk... and do it *all in real-time, right there in LabVIEW.* This is an exceptional capability! Only a few years ago, you had to use several different programs (probably not simultaneously, either) or write a zillion lines of custom code to perform all of these tasks. Sometimes, the processing you wish to perform isn't practical in LabVIEW. In that case, you can still exchange data files with other specialized programs on various computers.

This chapter covers data graphing and image acquisition and processing. LabVIEW has built-in graphs that are adequate for both real-time and post-test data presentation of ordinary two-dimensional data. It also has the capability to display images in color or grayscale. With the addition of third-party products discussed here, you can also acquire and analyze video images and make multidimensional plots, QuickTime movies, and other advanced displays.

System Requirements

Basic graphing and simple image processing tasks are handled easily by any of the common LabVIEW-compatible computers, even the older, lower-performance Macs and PCs. But serious, real-time display and analysis call for more CPU power, more memory, and more disk space. And of course, video input and output adds requirements for specialized interface hardware not normally part of your average computer.

Computer Configuration

When it comes to computer configuration, don't worry yourself too much if your data is presented in the form of simple x-y graphs because the LabVIEW charts and graphs are fast and efficient. Problems may arise, however, if you routinely plot tens of thousands of data points at a shot. Some quick benchmarking in LabVIEW will tell you if an older, low-power PC is up to the task. If not, plan on reducing the amount of data displayed or upgrading your system.

If it's images you're dealing with, then it's time to get serious about hardware. Image processing and display are absolutely, positively, the most CPU- and memory-intensive tasks you can run on your computer. Images contain enormous quantities of data. Many algorithms perform millions of calculations, even for apparently simple operations. And storing high-resolution images requires a disk drive with enormous capacity. You can never afford the ideal computer that's really fast enough, or has enough memory or big enough disks. But practical cost-performance tradeoffs can lead you to a reasonable choice of hardware for your configuration.

For real-time image processing (typically 30 frames per second), you will probably have to add specialized DSP hardware, often in conjunction with a frame grabber board. The fastest general-purpose computers available today come *close* to handling full-speed video, but be really cautious of manufacturers' claims. If you run custom-written applications with direct access to the I/O hardware, real-time video is possible on these faster machines. But if you expect LabVIEW to do lots of other things at the same time—like running an experiment—there will be performance problems. As with high-speed data acquisition, buy and use specialized hardware to offload these burdensome processing tasks and you will be much happier with the performance of your system.

Video I/O Devices

Unless your computer already has built-in video support (and LabVIEW support for *that*), you will need to install a **frame grabber** to acquire images from cameras, video recorders, and other video sources.

Frame Grabbers

A frame grabber is a high-speed ADC with memory that is synchronized to an incoming video signal. Almost all frame grabbers have eight-bit resolution, which is adequate for most sources. It turns out that cameras aren't always the quietest signal sources, so any extra bits of A/D resolution may not be worth the extra cost. Preceding the ADC, you will generally find an amplifier with programmable gain (*contrast*) and offset (*brightness*). These adjustments help match the available dynamic range to that of the signal. For the North American NTSC standard video signal, 640 by 480 pixels of resolution is common. For the European PAL standard, up to 768 by 512 pixels may be available, if you buy the right grabber. Keep in mind that the resolution of the acquisition system (the frame grabber) may exceed that of the video source, especially if the source is video *tape*.

Frame grabbers have been around for many years, previously as large, expensive, outboard video digitizers, and more recently in the form of plug-in boards for desktop computers. With the birth of multimedia, frame grabbers have become cheaper and even more capable. The trick is to choose a board that LabVIEW can control through the use of suitable driver software. Graftek, a French company, is the supplier of the one major image acquisition and analysis packages available for LabVIEW: **Concept VI**. (It's discussed in detail later in this chapter.) When you buy Concept VI, you can select from several frame grabber drivers. If you're interested in using other boards, contact Graftek and discuss the possibility of having a special driver developed. Frame grabbers discussed here are the ones that are supported by Concept VI (at the time of publication), with exceptions noted.

Macintosh: For the Mac, there are many choices. (Refer to manufacturers' addresses in Appendix C, *Sources*.)

- Data Translation's model DT2255 QuickCapture board. It is a four-channel board that supports NTSC and PAL with an input lookup table. Color acquisition from RGB cameras is also supported. A TTL-level trigger is available for synchronization with external events.

- Neotech's Image Grabber NuBus. This was the first board supported by Concept VI. It is a single-channel board that supports NTSC and PAL, monochrome or color, with an input lookup table, and programmable gain and offset. A high-quality, basic grabber board at a reasonable price, it's also available through NuLogic and GTFS.

- Perceptics' PixelTools family of image grabbers and processing boards. The Perceptics line is among the most sophisticated image acquisition and processing hardware available this side of the VME-based Datacube equipment. With the PixelPipeline, you can continuously acquire and display processed images to the Mac's screen at 30 frames per second. Processing includes averaging, addition, subtraction, multiplication, and logical operations. (A few additional products are detailed below.)

- Hammamatsu makes NuBus boards for digital cameras (the IQ-D100), as well as ordinary video cameras (the IQV50/55). Both offer an onboard arithmetic logic unit (ALU) for real-time processing.

- A relatively low-cost board, primarily designed for multimedia work, is the ColorSnap32 from Computer Friends. It offers one channel with 24-bit color.

PC: Because Concept VI was only recently ported to the PC, only a limited number of boards are supported as of this writing. Expect many other popular frame grabbers to be supported in the near future.

- The model MFG from Imaging Technology is an ISA-bus board with four channels that supports 24-bit color and has a line scan mode.

- Scentech makes a line of ISA-bus boards (the ImageVGA and ImageVGA Plus) that support 16 or 24 bit color with resolutions up to 1024 by 512.

Real-Time Image Processors

Acquiring, processing, and storing live video requires gobs of processor power and bus bandwidth—capability that your computer may not have. One workaround is to record the video on tape and play it back frame by frame later, though this is not an option for real-time situations. Instead, you will have to consider buying an image grabber system that includes a large image memory and maybe a DSP processor. Extra memory adds the ability to store rapid bursts of frames, or perhaps the chance to devise an exotic buffering scheme to overlap acquisition and disk storage. Adding DSP support opens the door to *real* real-time image processing. Remember, though, that you must write your own special programs using the DSP manufacturer's C compiler or assembly language.

There are a couple of practical solutions I'm aware of on the Mac. Perceptics offers two products for the Mac that qualify for the real-time realm. To acquire and store many frames in a short period of time, you can add the PixelStore board with up to 16 megabytes of video RAM. This hardware solution eliminates the disk throughput limitations of live video capture. An extension of the PixelStore, the SmartStore, adds an onboard DSP processor, a TMS320C30 running at 32 MHz, and up to 32 megabytes of video RAM. The C language support includes an image processing library, which might make the programming job... bearable.

Another Macintosh board, made by Scion Corporation, is the LG/3. It has four inputs, hardware triggering, and space for memory expansion that permits storage of up to 128 frames of real-time video (that's 4.27 s at 30 frames per second). The LG/3 driver is available with Concept VI and also as part of the **Video VI** package by Stellar Solutions, a simple and affordable package of video acquisition VIs that is an alternative to the more expensive and sophisticated Concept VI.

Now that you've got an image, how are you going to show it to someone? For live display you can use your computer's monitor from within LabVIEW or another application, or you might be able to use an external monitor. Hardcopy or desktop-published documents are always in demand. And recording to tape with a VCR makes a lot of sense, though there are some tricks you need to be aware of.

Recorders, Monitors, and Other Video Equipment

The good folks at Sony make the coolest little VCRs for computer video applications, the **CVD-1000 Vdeck**, and its big brother, the EVO-9650 (My friend Paul Daley calls it a "Vdeck on steroids"). The most important feature of the Vdeck line is the use of VISCA serial communications protocol (the 9650 also supports a direct serial interface). Developed by Sony, VISCA supports a variety of video devices such as tape machines, switchers, and effects generators. That means your LabVIEW program can directly control the VCR for recording or playback, nicely synchronized with your experiment. The Vdecks use the Hi8 (8 mm) video tape format with time code and frame search, produce *clean* still images, and have digital stereo audio. They're my first choice in video recording for LabVIEW systems.

A driver for the EVO-9650 is available from Graftek of France (GTFS in the U.S.). The driver uses a serial port protocol and supports Graftek's Image Concept VI for image acquisition. With the basic driver, you can do frame-by-frame editing, and it's a relatively simple matter to add other commands.

If you have need to control professional video tape machines, switchers, and effects units, there is a sophisticated solution available from Pyxis Corporation in the form of their **Multimedia VIs**. This VI suite is a collection of VIs that implement a professional-quality video and audio tape editing system in LabVIEW. They use VideoMedia Corporation's VLAN device control transmitters and receivers to control hundreds of professional video and audio recording devices. Figure 10-2 shows the panel of the Pyxis BV-90 videotape editor, which provides more functionality than the commercially available Sony BVE-9000, an editing system that costs more than $20,000. This is a very elaborate system and is generally customized for your specific application by VideoMedia and Pyxis.

One catch in the business of video output from your computer is the fact that high-resolution computer displays use a signal format, RGB (red-green-blue) component video, that is much different than the regular baseband NTSC-standard format required by VCRs. There are several solutions (again, multimedia demands easy and cheap solutions, so expect to see some better ways of doing this). First, you can buy special converter boxes that accept various RGB video signals and convert them to NTSC. An example is

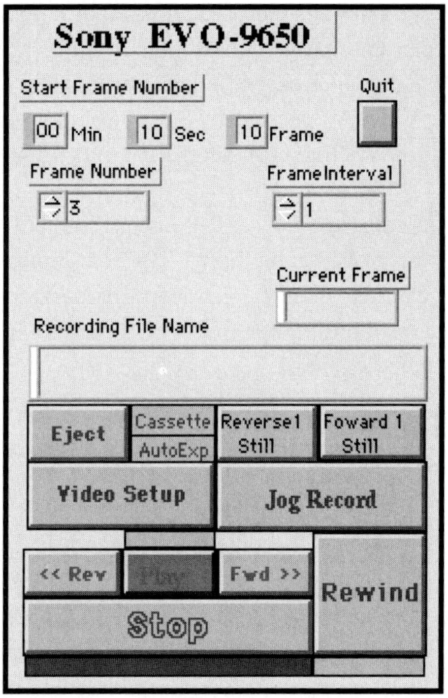

Figure 10-1. The driver for the Sony EVO-9650 video tape recorder, available from Graftek, uses the serial port for remote control.

TelevEyes from Digital Vision, which converts the signals from many 640-by-480 pixel resolution RGB color displays to NTSC or S-video (the still video standard).

A better solution is to use a frame grabber board with video output capability, such as the Neotech board. You can write processed images to its output buffer and it runs the data through a DAC to create a standard video signal. You can also use computer display boards that generate NTSC outputs. On the newer Macintosh models, for instance, the built-in video circuits support NTSC video, as do many third-party boards such as those from Raster Ops and Radius. This scheme is really tidy because all you're doing is plugging in a second monitor (sorry, PC and Sun folks, you can't do it so easily).

Hardcopy

For publications, you will need to print images one frame at a time. Desktop publishing applications and modern printers make this relatively easy (but a little expensive). The first step is to save your images in a standard file format such as TIFF (Tagged Image Format File) which is readily accepted by many applications on all of LabVIEW's platforms. Concept VI and Video VI can read and write TIFF files, among others. Next, open the file with an image editing application such as Adobe Photoshop (which is about the best product of its kind). You can then manipulate the image if required, doing things like cropping, adding annotations, adjusting color balance, or converting color to greyscale. Finally, you can send the image to a suitable printer. Ordinary 300 DPI laser printers are

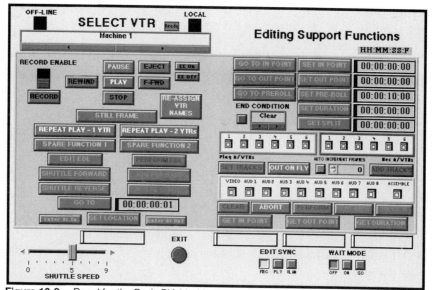

Figure 10-2. Panel for the Pyxis BV-90 videotape editor, which uses MultiMedia's VLAN hardware to control multiple video tape recording devices. The functionality in this package gives you the ability to do serious audio/video production work from LabVIEW. This panel sets some kind of record for the number of buttons on one screen!

sometimes adequate, but you usually want higher resolution, and you may well want to print colors. If the cost of the printer is prohibitive, consider using a local desktop publishing service bureau. Just make sure you know what file formats they can handle.

Graphing

The simplest way to display lots of data is in the form of a graph. We've been drawing graphs for about 200 years with pens and paper, but LabVIEW makes graphs faster, and more accurate. Most importantly, they become an integral part of your data acquisition and analysis system.

Part of your responsibility as a programmer and data analyst is remembering that a well-designed graph is intuitive in its meaning and concise in its presentation. In his book, *The Visual Display of Quantitative Information* [Ref. 1], Edward Tufte explains the fundamentals of graphical excellence and integrity, and preaches the avoidance of graphical excess that tends to hide the data. Personally, I've been appalled by the way modern presentation packages push glitzy graphics for their own sake. Have you ever looked at one of those 256-color three-dimensional vibrating charts and tried to *actually see the information?*

Here are your major objectives in plotting data in graphical format [paraphrased from Ref. 1, page 13]:

- Induce the viewer to think about the substance rather than the methodology, graphic design, the technology of graphic production, or something else.

- Avoid distorting what the data have to say (for instance, by truncating the scales, or plotting linear data on logarithmic scales).

- Try to present many numbers in a small space, as opposed to diffusing just a few data points over a vast area. This makes trends in the data stand out.

- Make large data sets more understandable by preprocessing.

- Encourage the eye to compare different pieces of data.

- Reveal the data at several levels of detail, from a broad overview to the fine structure. You can do this by making more than one plot with different scales or by allowing the user to rescale a graph—a standard LabVIEW feature.

- Design the graph in such a way that it serves a clear purpose with respect to the data— for description, exploration, or tabulation.

- The graph should be closely integrated with other descriptions of the data. For example, a graph should be synergistic with numeric displays of statistics derived from the same database.

- Above all, make sure that the graph *shows the data.*

The worst thing you can do is overdecorate a graph with what Tufte calls *Chartjunk.* Chartjunk is graphical elements that may catch the eye but tend to hide the data. You don't want to end up with a graphical puzzle. Though this is more of a problem in presentation applications, there are some things to avoid when you set up LabVIEW graphs:

- High-density grid lines—they cause excessive clutter.

- Oversized symbols for data points, particularly when the symbols tend to overlap.

- Colors for lines and symbols that contrast poorly with the background.

- Color combinations that a colorblind user can't interpret. (Know thy users!)

- Too many curves on one graph.

- Insufficient numeric resolution on axis scales. Sometimes scientific or engineering notation helps (but sometimes it hinders—the number 10 is easier to read than 1.0E1).

Waveform and Cartesian Data

Most data that you'll acquire is a function of time or some other variable and is described by y = f(x), where x is the independent variable (e.g., time) and y is the dependent variable (e.g., voltage). This is generalized **Cartesian** (x-y) data. The x-values are most often based on time. Time-series, or **waveform**, data is effectively displayed on an ordinary graph or in the case of real-time data, on a stripchart. Graphs and charts are standard LabVIEW indicators with many programmable features. Read through the graphing chapter of the LabVIEW user manual to see how all those features are used.

Figure 10-3 shows the simplest way to use the **Waveform Graph**. Like many LabVIEW indicators, it's polymorphic, so you can wire several data types directly to it.

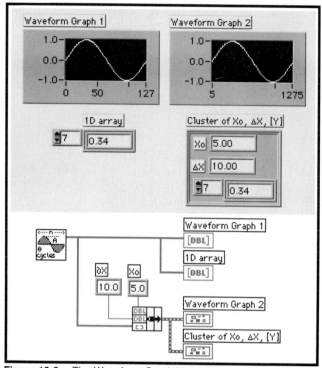

Figure 10-3. The Waveform Graph is polymorphic. This example shows the two basic data types that it accepts for the making of single-variable plots.

Numeric arrays (any numeric representation) can be wired directly and are displayed with the x-axis scaled with values beginning with zero ($x_0 = 0$) and increasing by one ($\Delta x = 1$) for each data point in the array. You can also control x_0 and Δx by bundling your data into a cluster as shown in Figure 10-3. Any time your data has evenly spaced x values, use the waveform graph. Compared with an XY graph, it takes less memory, is faster, and is certainly the easiest to set up.

Polymorphism makes the waveform graph more versatile because the graph directly accepts five data types. Above, you saw that a single variable could be plotted with or without x-axis scaling. Figure 10-4 shows how to make a multiplot graph where each signal has the same number of points. You scale the x-axis in a manner consistent with the previous example.

What if the signals don't have the same number of points? Two-dimensional arrays require that each row of data have the same number of points, so that approach won't work. Your first guess might be to make an array of arrays. Sorry, can't do that in LabVIEW. Instead, make an array that contains a cluster with an array inside it (Figure 10-5). There are two ways to build this data structure. One uses a Bundler function for each array followed by Build Array. The other way uses the Build Cluster Array function, which saves some wiring. The index of the outer array is the plot number and the index of the inner array is the sample number.

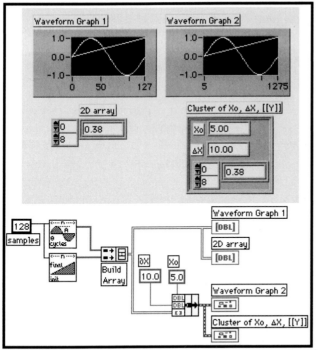

Figure 10-4. Two ways of making multiple plots with a Waveform Graph when the number of data points in each plot is equal. Note that the Build Array function can have any number of inputs. Also, the 2D array could be created by nested loops.

A slightly different approach, shown in Figure 10-6, is required if you want to make multiple plots with different numbers of points *and* you want to scale the x axis. For this example, I plotted a sine wave and a line representing its mean value (which might be useful for a control chart in statistical process control). The mean value is used as both elements of a two-element array, which is the y-axis data for the second plot. The trick is to use some math to force those two data points to come out at the left and right edges of the plot.

So far, we've been looking at graphs with simple, linear x axes which are nice for most time-based applications, but not acceptable for **parametric plots** where one variable is plotted as a function of another. For that, use the **XY Graph**. Figure 10-7 shows a way of building one of the data structures that defines a multiplot XY Graph. A plot is defined as an array of clusters that contain x and y data point pairs. In this example, I turned on all the display options on the graph, including the legend, palette, and cursor display. These are also available on the Waveform Graph.

Figure 10-8 shows how to use the other available data structure for an XY Graph. Here, a plot is defined as a cluster of x and y data arrays. Why would you use this format in place of the previous one? That depends on how your data is acquired or created. If you collect single data point pairs, for instance with a low-speed data recorder, then the previous

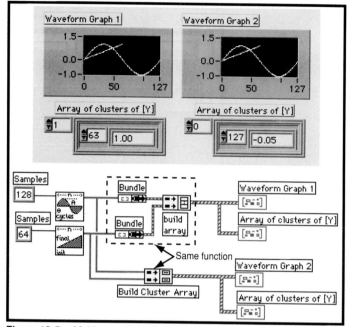

Figure 10-5. Making multiple plots where each plot has a different number of samples. Build Cluster Array performs the same function as the combination in the dashed rectangle.

format is probably best. For data that arrives in complete arrays for each plot, use the format in Figure 10-8.

Bivariate Data

Beyond the ordinary Cartesian data we are so familiar with, there is also **bivariate** data, which is described by a function of two variables, such as $z = f(x,y)$. Here are some examples of bivariate data that you might encounter:

- A photographic image is an example of bivariate data because the intensity (z) changes as you move about the (x,y) area of the picture.

- Topographic data of a surface, such as the Earth, contains elevations (z) that are a function of latitude and longitude (x,y).

- A series of waveforms can be treated as bivariate data. For instance, the z axis can be amplitude, the x axis time, and y the sequence number. This series of waveforms is also called a **waterfall plot**.

Bivariate data may be displayed in many formats. **Surface plots** have a three-dimensional (3D) look to them and are the most computationally intensive displays to generate. Surface plots may be solid models (sometimes including shading) or wireframes with or without hidden lines removed. These plots can be very dramatic and give the reader insight into the general nature of the data, if properly displayed. The disadvantage of

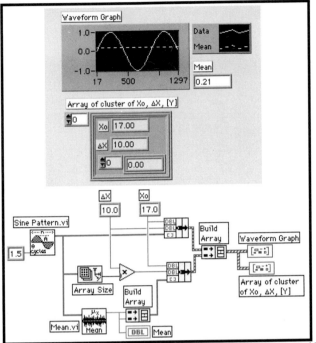

Figure 10-6. Yet another data structure for multiple plots accepted by the Waveform Graph. In this example, the sine wave is plotted with a line representing the mean value. This second plot has only two data points.

surface plots is that it is often difficult to use them quantitatively. Even with calibrated axes and the application of color, it's still hard to read out the value of a particular point as you would do on a simple x-y graph. We'll look at a practical way of obtaining three-dimensional plots in LabVIEW in the next section.

Adding color to a surface plot effectively adds another dimension to the display, though it can be more confusing than helpful unless the data is well-behaved. An example of effective use of color would be to display the topography of a mountain range and color the surface according to the temperature at each location. In general, temperature decreases with elevation, so a smooth progression of colors (or grays) will result. On the other hand, if you used color to encode wind speed at each location, you would probably end up with every pixel being a different color because of the rather uncorrelated and chaotic nature of wind speed variations over large areas. Don't be afraid to try coloring your plots—just be sure that it adds *information* not just glitz.

Bivariate data can also be displayed as an image. The **Intensity Graph** is a LabVIEW indicator that displays the value at each (x,y) location as an appropriate color. You choose the mapping of values to colors through a Color Array control, which is part of the Intensity Graph. This type of display is very effective for data such as temperatures measured over an area, and of course for actual images. Further explanation of the use of the Intensity Graph appears later in this chapter.

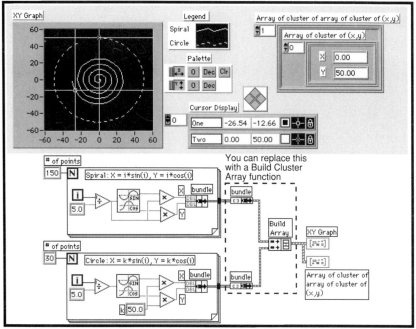

Figure 10-7.   One of the data structures for an XY Graph is shown here. It probably makes sense to use this structure when you gather (x,y) data point pairs one at a time. This is the way it had to be done in LabVIEW 2.2.

Yet another way to display bivariate data is to use a **contour plot**. A contour plot consists of a series of isometric lines that represent constant values in the data set. Familiar examples are topographical maps, maps of the ocean's depth, and isobars on a weather chart showing constant barometric pressure. LabVIEW does not offer a contour plotting capability at this time, but Metric Systems is coming out with a new package, **Contour View**, that may do the trick. Many other data analysis and graphing packages already offer contour plotting, so you might plan on exporting your data. I might mention that contour plots are not as easy to generate as it might seem. The big problem is interpolation of the raw data. For instance, even though your measurements are acquired on a nice x-y grid, how should the program interpolate between actual data points? Is it linear, logarithmic, or something else? Is it the same in all directions? Worse yet, how do you handle missing data points or measurement locations that are not on an even grid? I watched an analyst friend of mine struggle for *years* on such a problem in atmospheric dispersion. Every change to the interpolation algorithm produced dramatically different displays. You generally need some other display or analysis techniques to validate any contour plot.

Multivariate Data

Beyond bivariate data is the world of **multivariate data**. Statisticians often work in a veritable sea of data that is challenging to present because they can rarely separate just one

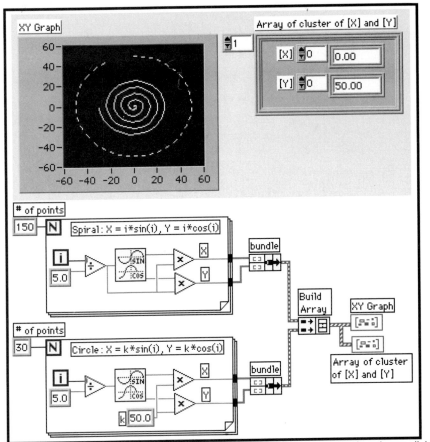

Figure 10-8. Similar to the last XY Graph example (Figure 10-7), but using the other available data structure. This one is convenient when you have complete arrays of x and y data.

or two variables for display. For instance, a simple demographic study may have several variables: *location, age, marital status*, and *alcohol usage*. All of the variables are important, yet it is very difficult to display them all at once in an effective manner.

The first thing you should try to do with multivariate data is analyze your data before attempting a formal graphical presentation. In the demographic study example, maybe the *location* variable turns out to be irrelevant; it can be discarded without loss of information (though you would certainly want to tell the reader that *location* was evaluated). Graphics can help you in the analysis process, perhaps by making quick plots of one or two variables at a time to find the important relationships.

Some interesting multivariate display techniques have been devised [Ref. 2]. One method that you see all the time is a **map**. Maps can be colored, shaded, distorted, and annotated to show the distribution of almost anything over an area. Can you draw a map in LabVIEW? If you have a map digitized as x-y coordinates, then the map is just an x-y plot. Or, you can paste a predrawn map into your LabVIEW panel and overlay it with a graph

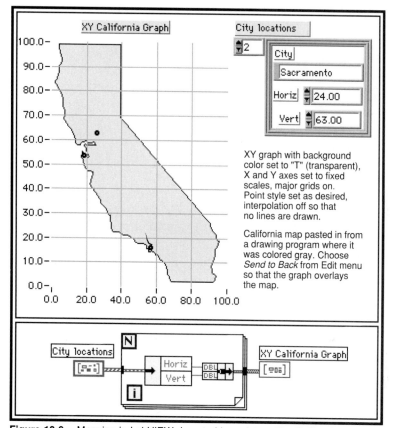

Figure 10-9. Mapping in LabVIEW. I pasted in a picture (the California state map) from a drawing program, then overlaid it with an XY Graph to display city locations.

as I did in Figure 10-9. In this example, I created a cluster array containing the names and locations of three cities in California with coordinates that corresponded to the map. When the VI runs, the horizontal and vertical coordinates create a scatter plot. This might be useful for indicating some specific activity in a city (like an earthquake). Or, you could add cursors to read out locations, then write a program that searches through the array to find the nearest city. Note that a map need not represent the Earth; it could just as well represent the layout of a sensor array or the surface of a specimen. The hardest part of this example was aligning the graph with the map. The map that I pasted into LabVIEW was already scaled to a reasonable size. I placed the XY Graph on top of it and carefully sized the graph so that the axes were nicely aligned with the edges of the map. Through trial and error, I typed horizontal and vertical coordinates into the cluster, running the VI after each change to observe the actual city location.

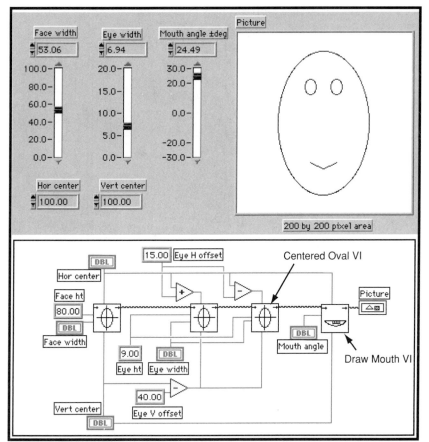

Figure 10-10. A simplified Chernoff Face VI, with only three variables: face width, eye width, and mouth angle. This VI calls two subVIs that I wrote to draw some simple objects using the Picture Control Toolkit.

The Picture VI Library

The most interesting multivariate data display technique I've heard of is the **Chernoff Face** [Ref. 2]. The technique was invented by Herman Chernoff at Stanford University in 1971 for the purpose of simultaneously displaying up to 18 variables in the form of a simplified human face. His idea works because we are quite sensitive to subtle changes in facial expressions. Some applications where the Chernoff face has been successful are showing relative living quality in various metropolitan areas, displaying psychological profiles, and my favorite, showing the state of Soviet foreign policy over the years. The trick is to map your variables into the proper elements of the face with appropriate sensitivity, and of course, to draw the face in a controllable manner. I spent some time with the VIs in the **Picture Control Toolkit**, and managed to build a crude face (Figure 10-10) with three variables: face width, eye width, and mouth shape. The Picture Control Toolkit is a LabVIEW option that you can purchase separately from National Instruments.

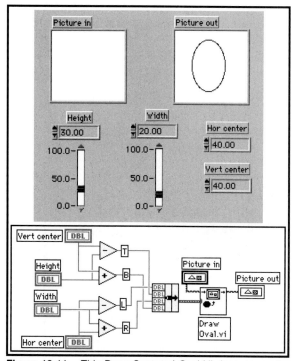

Figure 10-11. This Draw Centered Oval VI does some simple calculations to locate an oval on a desired center point, then calls the Draw Oval picture function. Note the consistent use of Picture in-Picture out to maintain dataflow.

Because the Picture functions are all very low-level operations, you will generally have to write your own subVIs that perform a practical operation. In this example, I wrote one that draws a centered oval (for the face outline and the eyes), and another that draws a simple mouth. All of the Picture functions use *Picture in–Picture out* to support dataflow programming, so the diagram doesn't need any Sequence structures. Each VI draws additional items into the incoming picture—much like string concatenation. Don't be surprised if your higher-level subVIs become very complicated. Drawing arbitrary objects is not simple. In fact, this exercise took me back to the bad old days when computer graphics (on a mainframe) were performed at this level, using Fortran, no less. The first time I saw a Macintosh in action, my jaw dropped because I knew what those programmers had gone through at the lowest levels to create such wonderful graphics. Picture Control Toolkit now has high-level VIs!

You could proceed with this train of development and implement a good portion of the actual Chernoff Face specification, or you could take a different tack. Using the flexibility of the Picture functions, you could create some other objects, such as polygons, and vary their morphologies, positions, colors, or quantities in response to your multivariate data parameters. Be creative, and have some fun.

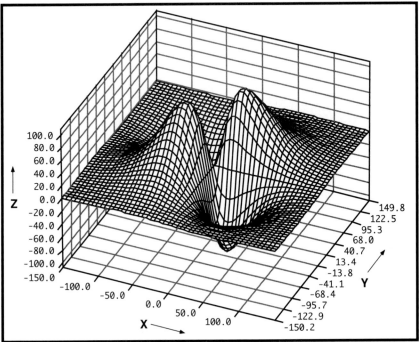

Figure 10-12.   Output from SurfaceView. Note the inclusion of grids and axis calibration. Plotted data changes color as a function of its z axis (vertical) value. You should see it in color!

Special Graphing and Display Products

Besides the Intensity Graph and Picture Control that are part of LabVIEW, there are some third-party packages that you can use to create sophisticated data displays from within your LabVIEW programs.

SurfaceView

SurfaceView is a package of VIs for plotting of bivariate data as a 3D wireframe surface. It was written by Jeff Parker of Metric Systems—you can order it directly from him. Jeff was a member of the first LabVIEW development team way back in 1985, and he's among the most capable programmers I've ever met. Just the kind of guy who would write a 3D plotting package, which is a really challenging programming project. Figure 10-12 shows a typical SurfaceView plot.

SurfaceView uses the concept of a **CIN window**: a window that is not a regular LabVIEW panel or control. The CIN window concept was invented some years ago to give programmers a way to create arbitrary displays (including interactive ones) without having to ask National Instruments to customize LabVIEW. SurfaceView's CIN window behaves the same as any other window on your computer, but its contents and actions are controlled by CINs inside VIs that you call from a diagram.

The package contains many VIs arranged in layers of increasing complexity. You can start off with one of the demonstration VIs, which illustrate how to integrate SurfaceView into your application by calling some of the low-level functions. I prefer to work at this level—keeps the old brain from boiling over. At the next level are dialog panels that open when called to present a nice palette of choices to manipulate the plot characteristics. For instance, you can easily change axis scaling, colors, and styles from these VIs. Next, there are some utility VIs that provide services like data conversion. At the lowest level are the SurfaceView primitives, most of which are implemented as CINs. These primitives act directly on the surface plot in the CIN window. By working with the primitive functions, you can create highly customized SurfaceView applications.

Managing SurfaceView Windows

It is instructive to explore how SurfaceView stores the information associated with a plot window in a data structure in memory, because many other LabVIEW third-party packages (and LabVIEW itself) use many of these same techniques. A VI called SurfaceView New allocates a block of memory and assigns a reference number (refnum) to it, much the way the LabVIEW file system uses refnums to keep track of files. This refnum is actually a **handle** to the window.

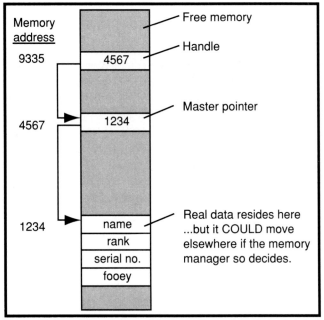

Figure 10-13. A *handle* is a pointer to another pointer that points to the data you are trying to access. If that seems confusing, just be glad you're using LabVIEW and not C, where you have to deal with it all the time. The scheme was designed for the convenience of the Memory Manager, not you.

Figure 10-13 explains the concept of a handle, a mechanism used by the memory manager scheme in LabVIEW and many operating systems. Essentially, a handle is a pointer to a pointer, which gives you the location in memory at which your data (in this case, a SurfaceView plot) resides. Handles are a means by which our modern computer systems dynamically manage memory. Every time LabVIEW or any other program needs to store information, it calls the Memory Manager and requests some space. If there isn't enough contiguous space, other pieces of data need to be moved. This double-dereferencing scheme, as it is sometimes known, permits the Memory Manager to keep track of thousands of different blocks of memory. You really don't need to know much about handles unless you are writing CINs or other programs outside of LabVIEW, where they are very important.

Once SurfaceView New has been called to create a new window and its associated refnum, you pass the refnum along to the other SurfaceView functions to manipulate the contents of that window. Note that you can have more than one window active at a time, and that SurfaceView New is the only way to create a new window. When you are finished with the window, you should call SurfaceView Dispose to destroy the window and release the memory used by its data structures. Failure to do so will keep the memory unavailable for other uses until you quit and restart LabVIEW.

Other window operations are **SurfaceView Open** and **SurfaceView Close**, which show or hide an existing window, **SurfaceView Open?**, which checks to see if the window is visible, and **SurfaceView Update**, which redraws the window. The Update VI saves time because you can call many SurfaceView VIs that change the plot without actually drawing any graphics, then call Update to redraw.

Formatting Data

SurfaceView requires that the z=f(x,y) data lie on a grid where there is one and only one z value for each (x,y) location. Depending on your source of data, you may need to use one of the SurfaceView utility VIs, and perhaps some ingenuity, to format the data properly. Figure 10-14 shows two conversion routes and the required cluster containing x, y, and z arrays. The SurfaceView utility that makes the vital conversion is the "Convert Data (Mins&Deltas)" VI. Once the data cluster is ready, create a new SurfaceView window and pass the data to one of the display functions.

Here is an example I put together that handles the kind of data you might collect with a two-axis motion control system that collects measurements over an even grid. Assume that the data from your program is stored in a spreadsheet-format text file.

Here's the sample data:

0.152	0.258	0.261	0.294	0.180
0.370	0.671	0.976	0.735	0.333
0.526	1.305	2.104	1.292	0.247
0.328	0.912	1.892	0.829	0.303
0.256	0.381	0.214	0.261	0.108

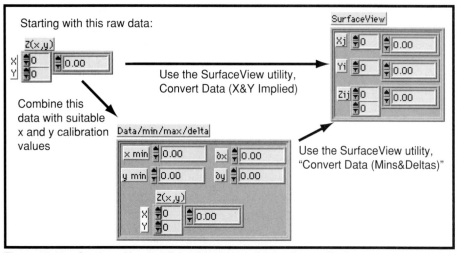

Figure 10-14. Starting with a two-dimensional array of data where z=f(x,y), you can use one of two SurfaceView utilities to convert the array into the proper format.

The program in Figure 10-15 loads this file, displays it in an Intensity Graph, converts it to SurfaceView format, and displays it as a 3D wireframe. Never work too hard when loading spreadsheet data. The utility VI, Read From Spreadsheet File, makes it easy. It has lots of options, but I only needed to access two of them to achieve the desired results—set the **number of rows** to a large number to assure that all the data is read, and set the **transpose** Boolean to true so that the rows and columns mapped correctly.

An array indicator displays the loaded data numerically and the intensity graph displays it as a coarse, greyscale image. I had to use the **color array** option on the intensity graph to adjust the range of colors. Next, the 2D array is passed to "Convert Data (Mins&Deltas)" with suitable scale factors. I set xMin and yMin to zero and the incremental values to one. To display the data, call **SurfaceView New** and pass the refnum to **Update Data, Title, Scales,** which is one of the high-level SurfaceView functions that serves to plot the data and name the window. Just like the file utilities, I prefer to use the highest-level functions I can to save programming. If the utility VI doesn't do exactly what I want, I modify it and save it with a different name. After this VI runs, the user clicks QUIT, the plot window disappears, and its memory is released by **SurfaceView Dispose**.

FastDraw

FastDraw is another third-party product that uses the CIN window to provide special graphing capability. FastDraw is produced by ASTER of France, and is distributed in the U.S. by Dixon DSP Design. It plots 1D data as line plots, histograms, 3D flat spectrograms, 3D sonograms, and 3D spectrograms, at very high speeds. The window has a set of controls to scroll, zoom, and scale the plot, plus cursors. One of the cursor options that I really like is called a harmonic cursor. You place the cursor at a location corresponding to a

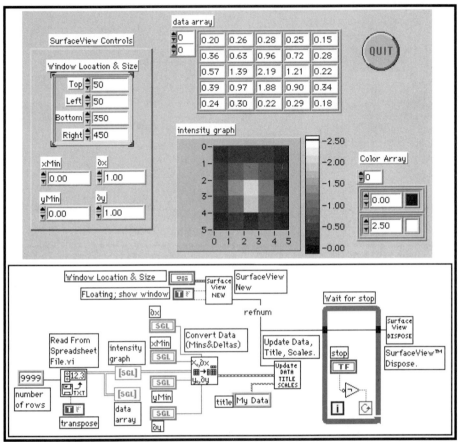

Figure 10-15. An example that loads x-y data from a spreadsheet file and displays it as an Intensity Graph and as a SurfaceView wireframe.

fundamental frequency in a spectrogram, and several other cursors automatically appear at the related harmonics.

FastDraw uses just one VI to access all of its many programmable features. You feed it an SGL numeric array which it then analyzes by performing a spectrogram or histogram operation, and then displays. Currently, FastDraw is only available for the Macintosh, but should soon be ported to the PC and Sun as well.

QuickTime Movies

Apple Computer invented **QuickTime** to fill a perceived need in multimedia—the need to conveniently and efficiently display movies with synchronized sound in *any* computer document. It turned out to be an enabling technology for data visualization as well because you can now *play* your data as a live, fluid entity, rather than just a stack of plots or pictures. Subtle interframe differences otherwise missed are readily apparent.

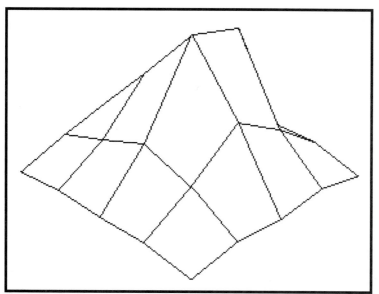

Figure 10-16.   Screen shot of the SurfaceView plot produced by the above example. Yeah, I know it's not all that dramatic, but this was a simple data set and I didn't call any of the fancy formatting VIs in the package.

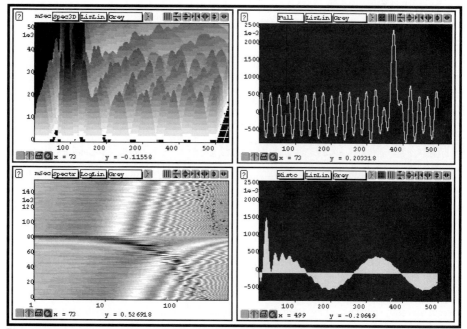

Figure 10-17.   Plots that you can make with FastDraw. Clockwise from upper left: 3D spectrogram, waveform plot, flat spectrogram, and histogram.

The first time I saw the use for movies in data analysis was when a physicist I worked with at LLNL, Ed Ng, pasted a series of plots into a HyperCard stack, one at a time. The plots represented a recurrent pulsed waveform that varied little from frame to frame. But when played in a movie...obvious differences appeared. We immediately observed mutations in the pulse shape, and gained a qualitative insight into the magnitude of the changes. This kind of observation points us in unexpected directions—exactly the reason we use data visualization.

Created for the Macintosh, QuickTime is now available for Windows and the Sun as well. There are many multimedia applications available that you can use to manually load images or graphics files into QuickTime movies, and there are LabVIEW extensions. Graftek's Concept VI can create, modify, and play QuickTime movies. Since Concept VI accepts 2D arrays of data as well as captured or stored images, you can display a variety of data types. On the Macintosh, you can use the sophisticated data visualization package, Spyglass Transform, or Wavemetrics' Igor, to load binary or text data, plot it, and directly generate a QuickTime movie containing a sequence of plots.

FastDraw can also create QuickTime movies. Each time the window is updated with fresh data, another movie frame is generated. You can start and stop the recording of a movie programmatically or through a button in the plot window.

The Intensity Chart

Another interesting indicator, the **Intensity Chart**, adds a third dimension to the ordinary strip chart. In Figure 10-18, the Intensity Chart gives you another way to look at a rather conventional display, a power spectrum. In this example, you can see how the power spectrum has changed over a period of time. The horizontal axis is time, the vertical axis is frequency (corresponding to the same frequency range as the Spectrum Plot), and the gray scale value corresponds to the amplitude of the signal. You use the Color Array item (part of the Intensity Chart) to set the range of colors or grays that you wish to display. Here, I adjusted the values to correspond to the 0 to -120 dB range of the spectrum.

Image Acquisition and Processing

Your LabVIEW system can be a powerful imaging tool if you add the right combination of hardware and software products. You will likely need hardware, in the form of a frame grabber and perhaps some video output devices, and software, in the form of image acquisition and processing VIs. The important thing to remember is that images are just another kind of data, and once you're working in LabVIEW, that data is going to be easy to handle. In fact, it's no harder to acquire, analyze, and display images than it is to acquire, analyze, and display analog waveforms. Good news, indeed.

The basic data format for an image is a two-dimensional (2D) matrix, where the value of each element (a **pixel**) is the intensity at a physical location. **Image acquisition** involves the use of a frame grabber for live video signals, or the use of mathematical transforms applied to other forms of data to convert it into a suitable 2D format. Standard image

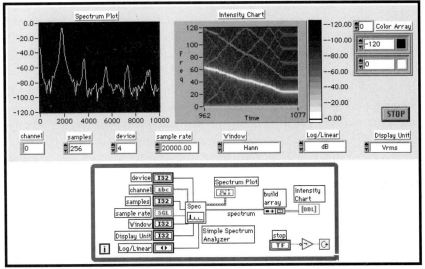

Figure 10-18.   The Intensity Chart in action displaying a power spectrum. White regions on the chart represent high amplitudes. Frequency was swept from high to low while this VI was running. The chart scrolls to the left in real-time.

processing algorithms operate only on this normally formatted image data. **Image processing** algorithms can be broadly grouped into five areas:

- **Image enhancement:** Processing an image so that the result is of greater value than the original image for some specific purpose. Examples: adjusting contrast and brightness, removing noise, and applying false color.

- **Image restoration:** A process in which you attempt to reconstruct or recover a corrupted image (which is obviously easier when you know what messed up the image in the first place). Examples: deblurring, removal of interference patterns, and correcting geometric distortion. The Hubbell Space Telescope benefited from these restoration techniques.

- **Image encoding:** Processing images to reduce the amount of data needed to represent them. In other words, data compression and decompression algorithms. These methods are very important when images must be transmitted or stored.

- **Image segmentation:** Dividing an image into relevant parts, objects, or particles. These algorithms allow a machine to extract important features from an image for further processing to recognize or otherwise measure those specific features.

- **Object representation and description:** Once an image has been segmented, the objects need to be described in some coherent and standardized fashion. Examples of these descriptive parameters are area, perimeter, major axis, center of mass, and comparisons with other known objects.

Like signal processing, image processing is at once enticing and foreboding: there are so many nifty algorithms to choose from, but which ones are really needed for your particular application? When I first decided to tackle an imaging problem, I ran across the hall to visit a fellow EE and asked for a book. What I came back with was, *Digital Image Processing* by Gonzales and Wintz [Ref. 4], which is the favorite of many short courses in image processing. It's also *my* favorite. What you really need to do is study a textbook such as that one and get to know the world of image processing—the theory and applications—before you stumble blindly into a VI library of nifty algorithms. Also, having example programs, and perhaps a mentor, is of great value to the beginner.

Aside from all the commercial imaging applications, only two packages are really relevant to LabVIEW work. First is **NIH Image**, a Macintosh application with modular Pascal source code written by the National Institutes of Health. It's available (free!) via the Internet, telephone bulletin board, or for $100 from the National Technical Information Service (see the supplier list for details). In principle, you can encapsulate the NIH routines in CINs of your own design, thus integrating them into LabVIEW on any computer. The package is very popular in academia because of its low (zero) cost, and is highly respected for its performance. Its processing algorithms are machine-independent, even though the full NIH Image application is written for the Mac.

But the most important imaging software for LabVIEW is Graftek's **Concept VI**. Graftek, a French company, has assembled a highly modular package of CIN-based VIs that supports image acquisition and processing with interactive displays, file I/O, and a generally free exchange of data with the rest of LabVIEW. Putting together an imaging application with Concept VI really is as easy as writing a data acquisition program.

Concept VI has two family members offering different levels of image processing capability. The **Image Concept VI** library includes fundamental functions for image acquisition and file management, display and sizing utilities, histogram computation, and image-to-array conversions. It also has the ability to create and edit 8- and 24-bit color QuickTime movies with sound. The **Ultimage Concept VI** library includes image processing and analysis functions, lookup table transformations, and spatial filters which allow for contrast and brightness adjustment, extraction of continuous and directional edges, noise removal, detail attenuation, texture enhancement, and so forth. It also includes frequency processing operations, arithmetic and logic operators, as well as object manipulations such as thresholding, erosion, dilation, opening, closing, labeling, hole filling, and particle detection.

Either of these products is available with drivers for a variety of frame grabber boards. Contact GTFS (Santa Rosa, CA) for more information.

Using Concept VI

Concept VI is very well designed and the included example programs make it pretty clear how you put together an image acquisition and processing application. Also, their manual is quite thorough. What I'll show you here are the really important things I've discovered,

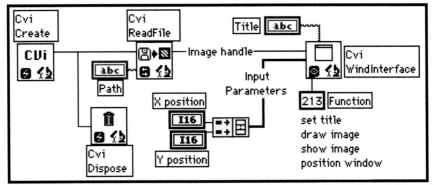

Figure 10-19.   A simple Concept VI application that reads an image from a file and displays it.

and some real-world applications. The first thing you need to understand is just how images are managed.

Image Handles

Concept VI carries information about an image (name, size, resolution, data, and so forth) in a data structure that is accessible by each function in the Concept VI library but hidden from LabVIEW. To indicate which image you are working with, you use an I32 numeric value called an **image handle** which is much like the window refnums used by SurfaceView. Image handles are created by the Cvi Create and Cvi Duplicate VIs and marked for destruction by the Cvi Dispose VI. You must never fiddle with the value of an image handle, or the program will cease to function (or *worse*). A new image handle must be created for every independent image. Like all data in LabVIEW, images (and their handles) are no longer accessible once the calling VI finishes execution. Suffice it to say the image handle is the means by which you keep track of images.

One advantage to this image handle scheme is that you have explicit control of image creation and destruction, unlike the situation with LabVIEW's data types. If you create an image handle, load an image, then submit the handle to 10 different image processing functions from the Concept VI library, rest assured that there will be no duplication of the data array (image). In contrast, a LabVIEW array, if passed in parallel fashion to several different DSP functions, will require duplications of the array for nearly every function. You *might* be able to chain some functions in series, if you're careful, thus eliminating much duplication.

Managing the Image Window

Images are displayed in a CIN window (as in SurfaceView) that is separate from your LabVIEW front panel. It is a normal, well-behaved window over which you and your program have full control. Figure 10-19 shows the diagram for a simple Concept VI application that reads and displays an image from a file.

Notice that the diagram begins at the left with an image handle that is created and marked for disposal—the canonical Concept VI opening move. Next, the Cvi ReadFile VI loads a suitably formatted image file, one that was probably saved by Concept VI or by another imaging program. Finally, the Cvi WindInterface VI creates and positions the window, draws the image, and sets the window's title. The *Function* input determines what operation(s) will be performed. See Table 10-1 for a list of function codes, which you select and sum up to yield an integer that is wired to the VI's input. Input parameters, in this case x and y locations of the window, are supplied as an array. If Cvi WindInterface is being used to read something from the window, an array of output parameters are also available.

Table 10-1. Function Codes for Cvi WindInterface

0 Get Last Event	200 Position Window
1 Set Title	300 Set Pensize
2 Draw Image	400 Set Grid Size
10 Show Window	1000 Disable Draw & Click
20 Hide Window	2000 Enable only Click
30 Select Window	3000 Enable Draw Line
40 Reserved	4000 Enable Draw Rect
50 Tolerant Palette	5000 Enable Draw Oval
60 Exact Palette	6000 Enable Centered Rect
100 Set Rectangle	7000 Enable Centered Oval

If the user clicks and/or drags in the image window, and one of the drawing options has been enabled, the selected object, such as a rectangle, is drawn in the window and the coordinates of the new object are returned in an array. This allows you to interactively select a **region of interest (ROI)** for later processing (not to mention play *Etch-A-Sketch*). The concept of an ROI (sometimes pronounced *roy*) is widely used in image processing to refer to an area, normally rectangular, in which an interesting feature resides.

Here are some other simple tools for drawing: the Cvi InsertText VI allows you to annotate an image by drawing a string of any font, style, or size at any position, in black or white. The Cvi Draw VI programmatically draws lines, ovals, rectangles, rounded rectangles, and arcs, with optional fill patterns. Lines, rectangles, and ovals can also be drawn interactively with the Cvi WindInterface VI. With these and other Concept VI tools, you can build a fully interactive image display in LabVIEW. Refer to the example VIs for more interesting demonstrations.

Acquiring an Image

Acquiring an image is really easy. Just create an image handle, call the appropriate acquisition subVI for your particular board, call Cvi WindInterface to display the image, and finally dispose of the handle. Just that easy; just that quick.

Here is a useful example I call Grab Movie VI. I needed a VI that would capture a sequence of frames as fast as the program would allow, display the captured frames in a continuous loop, then store them sequentially to disk if desired. The panel is shown in Figure 10-20. An ordinary CCD video camera feeds its signal to a Neotech Image Grabber board, in this case installed in an old Macintosh IIx with barely enough memory to do the

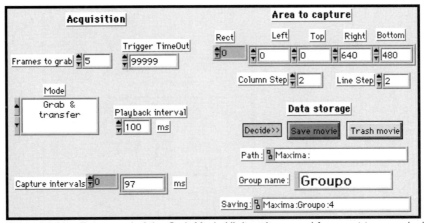

Figure 10-20. Front panel of the Grab Movie VI. It grabs several frames at top speed, plays them back as a loop, then permits storage of the images in files.

job. I was observing the effects of a pulsed laser, which had to fire in sync with the video signal (the laser's pulse is short enough that it could occur during vertical retrace, the time when the camera *isn't looking*). For proper synchronization, I connected the vertical sync output of the camera (a 60 Hz pulse train) to the laser's trigger input, and also to the trigger input of the frame grabber board. For some experiments, a digital delay generator was needed to get everything precisely phased.

On the panel, the controls under *Acquisition* set the number of frames to acquire, the trigger mode for the frame grabber, and the trigger timeout. **Playback interval** adds an optional delay between frames when the movie begins to play. Controls under *Area to capture* limit the amount of data acquired by windowing and decimating the raw image. This improves the capture speed by reducing the amount of data transferred from the board to main memory. **Capture intervals** is an array indicator that shows how much time actually elapsed between each frame, just for information.

Once the capture sequence is completed and the movie loop starts to play, the **Decide** indicator blinks, prompting the user to either save the movie frames as a series of TIFF images on disk, or just trash the movie and stop the VI. If the files will be saved, a new directory is created with the **Group name**, then the files are written with names based on the **Group name** and a sequence number. I did it that way to make automated data analysis easier. Another LabVIEW/Concept VI program reads the files sequentially for analysis, and a simple naming scheme makes it very easy to load those files.

The diagram in Figure 10-21 covers a fair amount of territory, but it's really easy to understand—no hidden sequences or anything. Starting at the lower left, the image grabber board settings are loaded from a set of controls that are off-screen. These controls set the gain, offset, vertical image position (VIP), and several other hardware options. In the first For Loop, an array of image handles are created for immediate use in the next For Loop, where the Cvi NeotechGrab VI does the acquisition. Each time the loop executes, the time

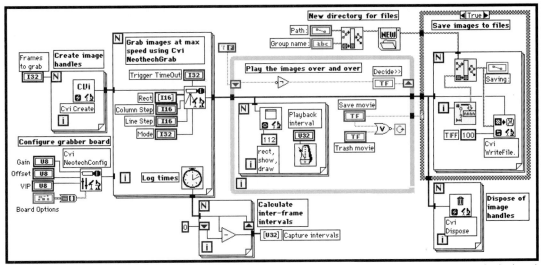

Figure 10-21.   Dataflow programming in action for the Grab Movie VI. From left to right, frames are acquired, played as a movie loop, and stored in files if desired.

in milliseconds is appended to an array. When the loop is done, the interframe intervals are calculated so that you can see just how incredibly fast your imaging system really is.

A While Loop in the middle of the diagram cycles once for each playing of the movie. The **Decide** indicator toggles on and off for each loop, and the loop stops when the user clicks **Save movie** or **Trash movie**. A For Loop calls the Cvi WindInterface VI to draw each frame sequentially.

If the *Save* button is selected, the final Case structure (True case) is executed and Cvi WriteFile is called once for each frame to write a TIFF-format file. The file name is based on the **Group name**, the same name used to create the directory. Finally, the image handles are disposed, releasing memory for other hungry customers.

Performance is limited by the data transfer rate between the image grabber board and the main memory of the computer, plus some LabVIEW overhead. If you need to go faster, you will have to use a frame grabber with a large amount of onboard memory, such as the Scion board for the Mac. You program the board to capture a specified number of frames in real-time, then download the frame to LabVIEW after the movie has been captured.

Transforming Data

An important feature of Concept VI is the ability to convert images to and from LabVIEW 2D arrays. This opens a world of possibilities in data transformations and computations because you aren't stuck with just the functions that come with the package. Figure 10-22 is a simple example VI that inverts an image. Cvi ImageToArray fetches the image identified by the incoming image handle and returns it as a 2D array of unsigned bytes (U8). The Not function (also called invert, or complement) changes the state of each bit in each element in the array. For instance, the value 255 (all ones) is changed to zero (all

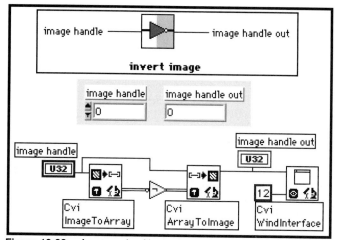

Figure 10-22. An example of image to array conversion. This VI inverts the image.

zeros). Then, the Cvi ArrayToImage VI writes the array back into the location of the original image, and the image is displayed. The indicator, *image handle out*, makes it easy to use this as a subVI in a nice dataflow program.

When performance is critical, you should remember that Cvi ImageToArray has to create a new (large) array to store the converted image. This will cost you some time in memory management, especially the first time the VI is called. However, this function *is* useful; any time that you create data mathematically or transform data from other sources into a 2D array, you can display it as an image and use the advanced processing features of Concept VI. One thing to remember is that you have to limit all values to a range of zero (typically black) to 255 (typically white). Values outside this range are folded back in with unexpected results. For instance, converting the integer -1 to the requisite unsigned byte format results in a value of 255—a real surprise if you expected -1 to be very *black* and it comes out very *white*.

Image Files

While we're on the subject of transforming data, file I/O should be mentioned because it's really another kind of transformation. To export and import data, you need to write an image out to disk and/or read it back in again with predictable results. Concept VI includes functions to read and write standard image-format files, notably TIFF. TIFF is one of the most useful formats because many other applications, such as image processing, desktop publishing, and drawing programs, can all read it. The format supports various resolutions and pixel depths (from 8 to 32 bits per pixel), as well as color. It is portable between all of LabVIEW's platforms.

You can also write the data to files of your own format. Convert the image to a 2D array, then pass it to Write File, which writes the data as straight binary or as LabVIEW datalogs. If there are serious data interchange problems, you could also convert each value to a two-digit hexadecimal ASCII value (00-FF) and write the string out as text. The disadvantage is that this format takes exactly twice as much disk space. However, text files are the closest thing we have to a universal data language.

What If I Don't Have Concept VI?

Surely, this isn't a one-product imaging market! While Concept VI is the most comprehensive imaging package for LabVIEW, there are alternatives. The other product you might consider, especially on a budget, is **Video VI** by Stellar Solutions. At this writing, it runs only in LabVIEW 2.2 for the Macintosh, but will be ported to LabVIEW 3 soon. Video VI supports several frame grabber boards, reads and writes TIFF files, performs rudimentary analysis, and manages its display window. All data is returned as LabVIEW 2D arrays, so you can easily write your own VIs for image processing. It's also a good bargain.

You can certainly put your own system together from scratch, especially if you're a skilled programmer. You can find image processing algorithms in various books and publications and implement them as G programs or write some C code and encapsulate them in CINs. Or, you can import the NIH Image routines into CINs, which is a very realistic alternative. If all else fails, you have to fall back on a commercial image processing application outside of LabVIEW.

Acquiring images from a frame grabber requires an accessible driver for your board. This is likely to be a rather involved process, even if the manufacturer supplies a driver for the operating system you are using. You will almost certainly have to write CINs to call the low-level hardware driver, then build the CINs into a usable LabVIEW driver. Contact the manufacturer of the frame grabber and discuss your options before plunging in head-first.

Reading and writing image files can also be an adventure. Raw images, in binary format, are easy to read and write in LabVIEW, but less so in other applications. You might be able to locate special file format specifications, such as TIFF, and implement that yourself. Most of the image file standards consist of a header describing the data to follow, then the data in a specific format. Reading and writing TIFF files is a good enough reason for buying Video VI, if you ask me.

This still leaves you with a display problem. Fortunately, LabVIEW has a means by which you can display images right on the front panel: the **Intensity Graph**. The Intensity Graph accepts several data types, among them a 2D array corresponding to an image. I wrote a simple VI (Figures 10-23 and 10-24) to load a raw binary image from a file and format the data for display in an Intensity Graph. Because a raw binary file contains no header to describe the dimensions of the image, the user has to supply that information. The control called **Rows** supplies this key information. If you enter the wrong number, then the image will be hopelessly scrambled.

Looking at the diagram, the file is read as a string which is then converted to an array of U8 using **String to Byte Array**. A For Loop breaks the long array of values into rows, which are then placed in a 2D array for display. An **Attribute Node** for the Intensity Graph sets the Y and X axis scales to fit the actual number of rows and columns in the image. Note

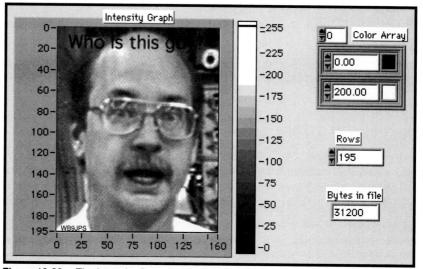

Figure 10-23. The Intensity Graph displaying an image from a binary file. The user has to know the size of the image, particularly the number of rows.

that the Y axis has zero at the top, rather than its usual place at the bottom. That makes the image come out right-side up. You also have to select **Transpose Array** from the pop-up menu on the Intensity Graph to swap the x and y axis data.

I used the Color Array control (part of the Intensity Graph) to set the data range to 0-200, corresponding to a pleasing greyscale ranging from black to white. For fun, you can pick various colors, or put in palette breakpoints by adding elements to the color array. This is a means of generating a color lookup table (CLUT) for greyscale or color correction.

A limitation of the Intensity Graph in this application is that the physical size of the graph can't be changed programmatically. The result is that an image is not guaranteed to

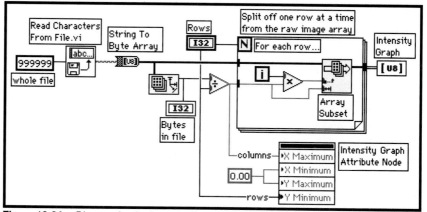

Figure 10-24. Diagram for the Intensity Graph image display. The raw data string is converted to an array, which is then transformed into a 2D array suitable for display.

map one pixel of data to one physical screen pixel, so the image may be slightly blurred and/or distorted. I fiddled with the size of the graph in this case to make the image look acceptable. If the images are always the same size, this isn't much of a problem. If there are relatively few sizes, you can create several indicators, each with its size optimized for a particular image. Place the indicators one on top of the other and use Attribute Nodes to hide those not in use.

Imaging Example: Laser Beam Analysis

An image processing package like Concept VI makes it feasible to analyze the spatial energy distribution of a laser beam at low cost and with the option to customize the analysis as you desire. An add-on to Concept VI, the **Beam Analysis VI** package (sold by GTFS), includes a suite of customized VIs that are modeled after commercial beam analyzers. The package automatically computes a host of beam profile characteristics, as you can see from the screen shot in Figure 10-25. The Cursor Window uses the interactive features of Concept VI. You click on a desired center reference location, and the vertical and horizontal profile computations are made instantly. For live video input, multiple frames can be averaged. A Gaussian fit (shown as a heavy gray line in the figure) is also computed. This is appropriate when a conventional TEM-00 mode beam, like the Helium-Neon beam in this example, is being observed.

An ordinary CCD camera and a frame grabber is all it takes to obtain profiles of visible and near-infrared lasers. More exotic cameras, like charge integrating device (CID) cameras, offer lower blooming (bleeding between pixels) and an extended spectral range that covers near-ultraviolet to mid-infrared. Some vidicon-based cameras are sensitive to various wavelengths outside the visible, especially infrared, though they tend to bleed and smear a lot.

Remember to prepare the laser beam. If the beam diameter is already fairly large, you can point it right into the CCD array (no lens required). Or, you can add a beam expander so that the beam covers a greater area of the array, which yields better spatial resolution. Always be sure to attenuate the beam to very low power levels; there are plenty of stories about cameras returned to the manufacturer with the detector reduced to a smoking ruin. Neutral density filters, beam splitters, and low-transmission windows all work well. If the beam is pulsed, the frame grabber must be synchronized to the laser (or the laser must be synchronized to the frame grabber).

Analyzing the Beam

Most of the statistics about an acquired beam are calculated by the 2D Analysis VI (Figure 10-26). It uses several Concept VIs in combination with some LabVIEW programming and makes a good example of image analysis. The image to be analyzed can be masked by another image, a common operation in image processing in which you want to confine processing to a particular area or object of interest. Values returned by the 2D Analysis VI are the area of the beam that is above a specified threshold intensity, and

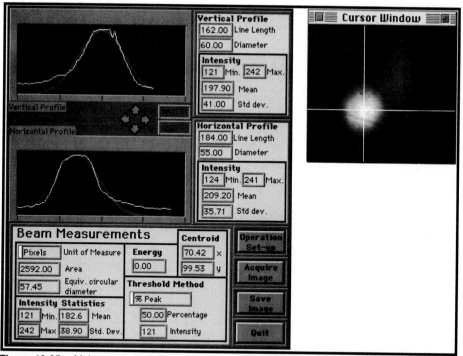

Figure 10-25. Main panel of the Beam Analysis VI package, with a cursor window open displaying the image of a He:Ne laser. Like many of the figures in this book, this one is a screen shot from my Mac. What you see here is exactly what you get on a real LabVIEW system.

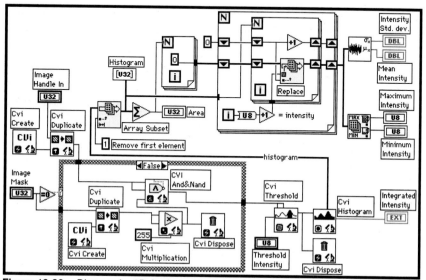

Figure 10-26. Diagram for 2D Analysis. The beam image is optionally masked; then a histogram is computed and used to compute statistics.

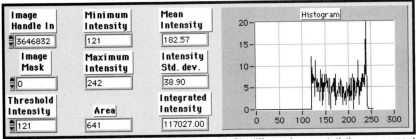

Figure 10-27. Front panel for the 2D Analysis VI. Six different image statistics are computed.

statistics about the beam's intensity, including minimum, maximum, mean, standard deviation, and integrated intensity.

The image for analysis is duplicated to preserve the original; the same is done with the image mask (Figure 10-27). If you don't use the Cvi Duplicate VI, then the original image is overwritten. If the image mask's handle is not zero, then the masking operation is performed. Inside the Case structure, the mask is multiplied by 255 using the Cvi Multiplication VI. Because all image values are unsigned bytes, this operation converts all nonzero values to 255, or white. Any zero values remain zero, so the mask is effectively *binarized*, or turned to pure black and white, which is required for logical masking operations. The binarized mask is then ANDed with the beam image by the Cvi And&Nand VI. Anywhere the mask is zero, the resulting image is also zero.

Next, the Cvi Threshold VI eliminates low-level noise in the image below a specified threshold intensity. Cvi Histogram, a very important image processing routine, produces a histogram of the image in the form of a LabVIEW numeric array. The Array Subset function removes the first element of the histogram, which represents the number of values in the image that are zero: a very large number when thresholding and masking are performed, and therefore meaningless. Image area is obtained by summing the values in the histogram array.

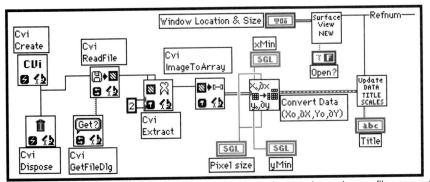

Figure 10-28. Here's the major part of the program that reads an image file, converts it to SurfaceView format, and displays the surface plot.

The nested For Loops create a one-dimensional array of intensity values. The number of array elements at a given intensity is determined by the value of the histogram. This conversion permits the use of the LabVIEW statistical function, Standard Deviation, the Array function, and Array Min & Max.

Displaying the Beam with SurfaceView

Another part of the beam analysis package uses SurfaceView to display a 3D wireframe representation of beam intensity as shown in Figure 10-28. This is a really intuitive way of displaying the laser's beam profile. As usual, you can access all the features of SurfaceView, including viewpoint, scaling, colors, and so forth. The X and Y scales can be calibrated in actual units of distance if you know the pixel spacing for your camera. (Look in the manual for the camera. The manufacturer usually supplies the CCD array size and number of pixels, so you can figure out the spacing.)

What's amazing is how easy it is to generate this plot. Figure 10-29 shows most of the diagram. After reading an image from a file, the Cvi Extract VI decimates the image by a factor of two (it skips every other row and column), which reduces the amount of data to be plotted. This is a practical measure to speed up the display process. Next, the image is

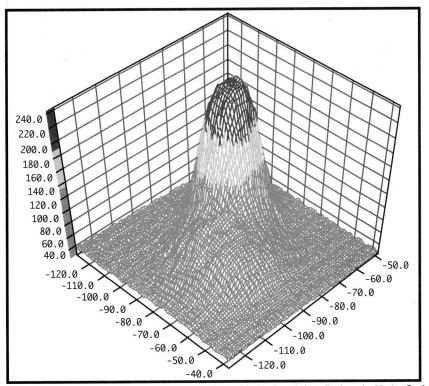

Figure 10-29. Same data as in Figure 10-25 (the He:Ne laser), but displayed with the SurfaceView part of the Beam Analysis package. Vertical scale is beam intensity; x and y scales can be calibrated in actual units of distance.

converted to a LabVIEW 2D array, as before. To format the data for display, the SurfaceView utility VI, "Convert Data (Mins&Deltas)", is called with the calibration factors for the camera that acquired the image. Finally, a new SurfaceView window is created and the plot is drawn. The Refnum of the new image can be passed to additional SurfaceView functions to support all those cool display options.

This program uses a large amount of memory. Besides the image loaded from disk, a LabVIEW array is created in unsigned byte (U8) format. Because SurfaceVIEW requires single-precision floating-point values, the array is promoted to SGL, quadrupling the memory usage. The plot itself requires at least one byte per pixel if your system supports eight-bit greyscale or color. Note that once the plot is drawn, memory usage will no longer increase because SurfaceVIEW will continue to reuse the existing display buffer. Redrawing the plot is purely dependent on the speed of your computer, particularly the graphics performance.

REFERENCES

1. Tufte, Edward R., 1983, *The Visual Display of Quantitative Information*. Cheshire, CT: Graphics Press.

2. Wang, Peter C. C., 1978, *Graphical Representation of Multivariate Data*. NY: Academic Press, ISBN 0-12-734750-X.

3. Cleveland, William S., 1985, *The Elements of Graphing Data*. Monterey, CA: Wadsworth, ISBN 0-534-03729-1.

4. Gonzalez, Rafael C. and Paul Wintz, 1987, *Digital Image Processing*. Reading, MA: Addison-Wesley, ISBN 0-201-11026-1.

11

Automated Test Applications

Automated testing generally applies to manufacturing and production test applications. Automated testing removes the *human factor* from performance testing, thus increasing data consistency, and enhancing throughput—the number of items tested in a period of time. Most automated test equipment (ATE) setups are intended for use by semiskilled operators. Therefore, the equipment and software must be simple, robust, and easy to use. The more automation and built-in intelligence, the better. Finally, a general goal of ATE system design is to maintain a high degree of flexibility so that one system can be easily reconfigured to test different products.

A major development leading to more frequent use of LabVIEW in the ATE world is VXI, which has its roots in the automated test systems used by the United States military. Military testing applications have always placed a high premium on modular, reliable automated test systems. The military branches each developed separate specifications for their own standardized modular test systems, and even their own ATE languages. The goal of these standards was to compact the large racks of instrumentation and standardize the test software. This standardization, in conjunction with instrument manufacturers' efforts to meet military needs and to produce high-speed, small footprint test systems, led to the creation of the VXI Consortium and ultimately the VXI specification.

VXI instruments have no front panels. You need a computer for the user interface. Enter LabVIEW, whose combination of graphical front panels and programming paradigm makes it an obvious match with VXI. And, because VXI is used extensively in ATE applications, LabVIEW has become popular in ATE.

LabVIEW is a natural tool for bridging the testing requirements of design and production. The methods you use for developing test VIs are pretty much the same in the lab as in automated production testing. In fact, a big bonus in using LabVIEW in production testing is that you can use the VIs you developed in the design phase. The many examples in this book about developing VIs, especially those involving instrument drivers, are all applicable to automated testing.

Unlike laboratory research, where the developer and operator of an experiment are often the same person, an ATE system requires a very clear distinction between capabilities available to the *developer* of test programs and capabilities available to the *operator* of test programs. The test developer can simulate tests and devices, interactively control instruments from front panels, and will see improved programming efficiency in LabVIEW's block diagram programming approach. The test operator, however, is not a LabVIEW developer. In fact, the operator has no reason to know or care how a test was developed. He has no knowledge of block diagrams, instrument drivers, VXI, or any of the myriad details that concern a test developer. An operator does exactly what the title implies—he operates a test program.

It is this distinction between developer and operator that most distinguishes ATE from the laboratory. There are numerous ways to use LabVIEW to satisfy the different requirements for the developer and the operator. This chapter focuses primarily on using LabVIEW as a centralized platform for automated testing. A number of third parties also use LabVIEW for automated testing by invoking LabVIEW VIs from an external application. This external application implements the operator environment. These types of applications are also discussed in this chapter. Note that this chapter does not discuss specific types of testing, such as analog or digital testing, or types of measurements.

Here are a few ATE-specific terms that we'll be using. A device being tested is called the unit under test (UUT). The term test refers to a routine or procedure that determines a specific characteristic of a UUT. In LabVIEW terms, the software module that performs the operations of a test is a VI. A test may consist of any operation that you can create a VI to perform, including instrument configuration, measurement, and numeric calculation. A test program is a collection of tests that, taken as a whole, verifies all of the characteristics of the UUT needed to determine that the UUT performs acceptably. A UUT passes if it meets all of the parameters characterized by a test program and fails if it does not meet those requirements.

Before proceeding with specific LabVIEW programming details, let's consider some of the standard approaches used in ATE. In many cases, the test is called **Go/No-Go**. In Go/No-Go testing, the operator runs a test program simply to see if the UUT passes or fails. If the UUT passes, it's placed in the *good pile* and if it fails, it's placed in the *bad pile*. In Go/No-Go testing, the operator does not try to figure out why the UUT failed. He or she simply moves on to the next UUT. The test program produces a test report that documents the reason that the UUT failed. This report will be used later to repair the UUT. In Go/No-Go

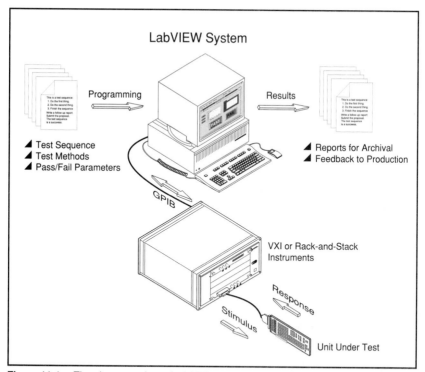

Figure 11-1. The elements of a typical ATE system include a computer, some I/O hardware, and the unit under test.

testing, you can generally use a run-time copy of LabVIEW (or generate a standalone application using the Application Builder) because the operator needs no low-level access to your VI suite.

In some test systems, the operator may actually be expected to diagnose the UUT failure or make some adjustment, such as a manual calibration. To perform diagnostics, the operator must have some flexibility beyond simply running a test program from start to finish. He may need to execute individual tests, change input parameters to a given test, or even write a new test to measure a characteristic of the UUT in a different way. The operator may need to view the front panels of individual VIs and run interactively. In such cases, a development copy of LabVIEW is needed, and the operator will of course need extra training.

Test Executive

The most distinguishing feature of the automated test environment is the **test executive**. The test executive is an application that sequences the execution of tests, so it's also called a **test sequencer**. While this definition sounds simple, there are many possible ways to implement a test executive, and the development process can be quite lengthy.

A test executive performs the following basic operations:

• Schedules tests based upon pass/fail status

• Interfaces the operator to the testing process

• Organizes and logs test results

You don't have to write your own test executive from scratch (though we will go through the basic design concepts you will need to know). Instead, you can order the LabVIEW Test Executive Toolkit from National Instruments, or one of the third-party packages listed in the National Instruments *Solutions* guide. TESTniques has such a package, *Test Executive for LabVIEW*, with about all the features you could ask for. Most of this chapter describes the concepts behind the test executive toolkit.

Execution Control

The most fundamental job of the test executive is to run a set of test VIs in a prescribed order. Many people get the idea that you can simply drop a set of VIs onto a block diagram in a line across the screen, and LabVIEW will just run the VIs in order. As anyone familiar with data flow programming knows, this scenario does not result in LabVIEW simply running the VIs *in order*. You must have a block diagram structure that enforces sequential execution of a set of VIs, with the execution order spelled out in some way. There are several ways to make VIs execute in order. One way is to use the LabVIEW Sequence structure. If you have a fixed number of test VIs, you can create a simple test sequencer by dropping the VIs in a Sequence structure. Or, you can use a common thread such as error I/O to link your test VIs in order across the diagram. If your application always runs from start to finish, waiting until the last test finishes before determining if the UUT passed, such a linear, sequential approach may be sufficient. In most cases, however, you will want more flexibility in defining the order in which test VIs run.

Returning Test Data

Before you can develop a test executive, you must decide how you will return the results from each test. (Imagine that! Doing some design work before writing your program...) The simplest approach is for each test VI to contain a Boolean indicator on its front panel and connector pane. This Boolean indicator serves as the Pass/Fail flag for the test. The VI performs the complete test, determines if the test passes, and sets the Pass/Fail flag to True if the test passed and to False if it failed. The test executive block diagram, in which the test VIs reside, inspects this Boolean value to see if the test passed. This approach places the burden of determining the test result on the VI itself. The drawback here is that you must write the test VI for a specific test scenario. Suppose you have a common type of test, such as output power of an amplifier, that differs from UUT to UUT only in the desired measured value that is considered passing. You could expand upon the Boolean flag approach and make your test VI more generic by passing in the comparison limit as a

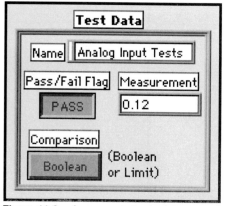

Figure 11-2. A proposed standard data type for test results. Test VIs return either a *Measurement* or the Boolean *Pass/Fail Flag* indicating pass/fail status.

control for the VI. This approach still places the logic for making the pass/fail comparison inside the VI.

Consider an approach in which the VI does not actually make the comparison itself, but merely returns results. The cluster shown in Figure 11-2 contains several pieces of information. The results may be returned as either a Boolean **Pass/fail flag** or a numeric value, **Measurement**. The **Comparison** Boolean determines which of the result types are valid. The name of the test VI is also returned for use in report generation. In the general case, the test VI is simply a measurement routine that returns its measured value using the *Measurement* indicator. The test executive determines if the test passed by comparing the measurement with limits specified elsewhere. If the measurement for a test requires more than one value, you can still perform the comparison in the VI itself and set the Pass/Fail flag. Alternatively, you could include an array as a standard output. In either case, a separate test program specification tells the test executive how to determine if the test passed. This arrangement achieves a separation between the test executive and test VIs, which helps you reuse test VIs. A later section discusses the data logging responsibility of the test executive. A common data output for all VIs provides a standard mechanism for test VIs to pass their measurement data to the test executive.

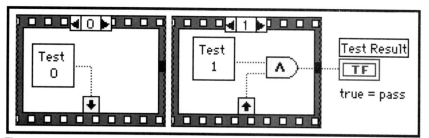

Figure 11-3. A simple test sequence where test results are combined into a final pass/fail flag.

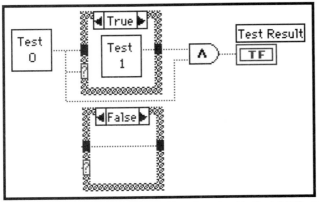

Figure 11-4. The second frame adds a Case to skip Test 1 if Test 0 has failed, thus saving some time. This technique quickly becomes cumbersome and inflexible for complex sequences.

An Architecture for Test Sequencing

Once you have a mechanism for returning the result of a test, you can decide on the sequencing capabilities you require and how best to implement them in LabVIEW. A simple way to sequence test programs is to use a Sequence structure. Suppose that you are using a Boolean flag to indicate if a test passes. Figure 11-3 shows how frames 0 and 1 might look for a test program with two tests, assuming that the test VIs return a simple pass/fail flag. The Sequence structure forces Test 0 to execute before Test 1. Note that you could eliminate the Sequence and wire the two test VIs directly to the And function if the order of execution is unimportant.

Figure 11-4 shows how the diagram might look if you wanted Test 1 to execute only if Test 0 passed. It is apparent that extending this approach for many tests will quickly become unmanageable, with many Case structures. And suppose you wish to execute only one test or even execute the tests in a different order than they are originally placed? Either of these alternatives requires that you modify the block diagram to get the desired behavior. These simple Sequence and Case structure combinations are most appropriate for a short, fixed sequence of VIs that always execute from start to finish.

A more flexible sequencing method is shown in Figure 11-5. This approach places all of the test VIs in a Case structure, one VI per case. The string constant at the left of the loop lists which cases to execute. The Extract Numbers VI converts the list of case numbers into a numeric array (it's on the diskette with this book). Using autoindexing, the For Loop executes once for each element in the array of test numbers. For each iteration, the test number selects the VI to execute. This block diagram replicates the functionality of the simple Sequence structure but allows you to specify any order of VI execution by changing the specification in the string constant. Results from each test are accumulated in a Boolean array. A logical AND operation is performed on all of the results by **AND Array Elements**. The final result is true only if all of the individual results are true.

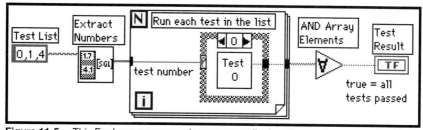

Figure 11-5. This For Loop sequencer is more versatile than the previous examples. Numbers in the Test List string correspond to frame numbers in the Case structure.

If you want to stop the tests when one fails, use a While Loop as shown in Figure 11-6. In this example, front panel controls specify the list of case numbers and whether or not to stop on a failure. The list of case numbers is still converted to a numeric array to index the case structure containing the test VIs. You must include the logic to stop the loop when all of the tests are done.

The architecture illustrated in Figure 11-6 forms the basis for a test executive with many capabilities. This architecture is used by many third party test executives as well as by the LabVIEW Test Executive Toolkit. An important feature of this approach is that, for a given set of VIs, you can create different sequences of tests without modifying the block diagram of the test executive. Even adding a new VI is a simple matter of adding one case to the case structure. You can encapsulate the case structure itself in a subVI (called a **test container** in the Test Executive Toolkit). A person writing test VIs could thus add them to the test executive in a well-defined location (the subVI) without having to modify (and possibly mess up) the block diagram of the test executive itself.

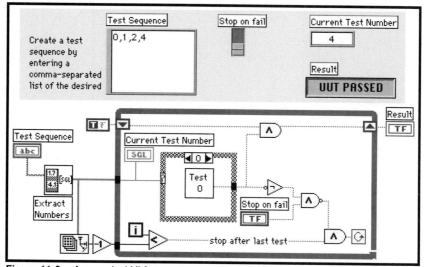

Figure 11-6. A canonical VI for a test executive. This sequencer steps through tests in an arbitrary order, and can stop after any test fails.

One other possible architecture for test executives should be mentioned: **state machines**. As we've discovered through many examples in this book, a state machine permits you to jump from one test to another depending on the results encountered at each step. This can be of great value in situations where a subsequence of tests must be repeated because of a failure or readjustment that was performed at an earlier time. However, the state machine requires a much greater degree of programming skill and care during configuration; it is unlikely that the casual user would be very successful in rewiring such a complex VI. Therefore, you should consider state machines only for applications where:

- The state machine is embedded in a test VI that nobody will need to modify.

- Your test executive will be maintained only by expert programmers.

- There is no other alternative to the state machine architecture.

Operator Interface

The second major task of the test executive is to present an effective user interface for the testing process. When creating the user interface, you must keep in mind the skills of the operator, which may be far different from your own. The complexity of the front panel depends upon the capabilities you wish to give to the operator. In many applications, the test executive's user interface consists of a single front panel that contains every control and indicator of interest to the operator. The simplest front panel may have a single button

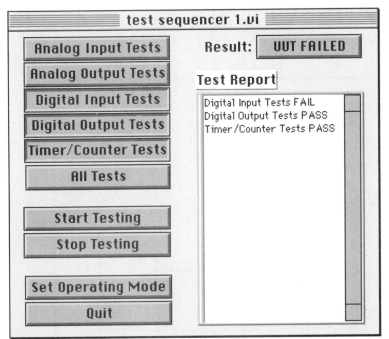

Figure 11-7. This panel for a typical test executive is simple yet effective. Its only disadvantage is that you must edit the front panel to change the list of tests.

labeled GO. The operator presses this button to run a given test. After the testing is completed, a message tells the operator to move onto the next UUT and press GO when he's ready. For a versatile test executive, you will probably have a front panel that is not quite this simple-minded. If you want the operator to be able to run an individual test, for example, you'll need a mechanism for selecting individual tests. And, if you want the same test executive to work for both simple and sophisticated operators, you'll want to selectively hide or display options based on a password or flag of some kind.

Figure 11-7 shows the front panel for a test executive that allows the operator to test the entire UUT or just run specific tests; it is similar to the one found in the test executive toolkit. At startup, the buttons for individual tests are disabled through the use of Attribute Nodes, which are visible at the left side of the diagram shown in Figure 11-8. The button called **Set Operating Mode** opens a dialog box asking for a password. If the password is correct, the other test buttons are enabled, allowing the operator to select an arbitrary set of tests. A test report, summarizing the results of each test, is displayed in a string indictor. Because this front panel has buttons to select the test(s) to run, adding a new test requires that you add a new button to the front panel as well as add the logic to the diagram required to integrate the new test VI.

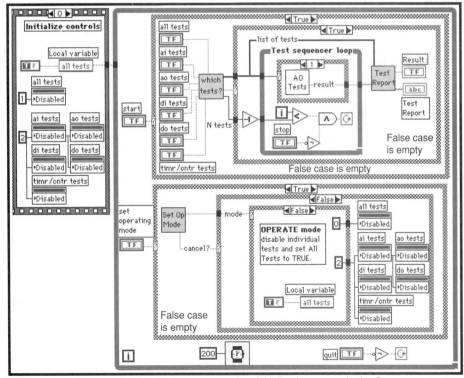

Figure 11-8.   Diagram for the simple test executive. Initialization occurs in the Sequence structure, followed by continuous execution of the While Loop. The upper Case contains the real testing work, and the lower Case manages mode changes.

The diagram for this test executive has several major zones: control initialization in a Sequence structure, and two major Case structures inside the main While Loop. At startup, buttons for test selection are enabled and disabled with Attribute Nodes. A local variable sets the **All Tests** button to true, the default test selection. These initialization items are grouped inside a Sequence structure with one wire tunneling out to the While Loop, thus guaranteeing that initialization occurs first.

After initialization, the loop runs until the user presses the Quit button. When he presses the Start Testing button, the upper Case structure starts the test sequencer loop—a loop similar to the kind we've already seen. Rather than reading the list of tests as a string, this VI reads the front panel push buttons to determine which tests to run and executes the Which Tests VI to create the array of case numbers. Outputs from Which Tests are an array containing the test numbers, a Boolean that is true if any tests are selected, and the number of tests requested. Each test VI returns a Boolean value to indicate if the test passed. The Boolean values from each test are accumulated into an array. After testing completes, the array of test results and the original sequence array are passed to the Create Test Report VI, which formats the test report for display on the front panel.

The lower Case structure allows the operator to change operating modes from *All Tests* (the default) to an arbitrary selection of tests. The Set Operating Mode VI opens when called and requests the password. If the password is correct, the innermost Case structure sends values to a set of Attribute Nodes to enable and disable the appropriate controls.

The Set Operating Mode VI is shown in Figure 11-9. The VI clears the **Password** control using a Local Variable, sets the Key Focus on the Password control using an Attribute Node, then waits for the operator to select **OK** or **Cancel**. **Set Operating Mode**

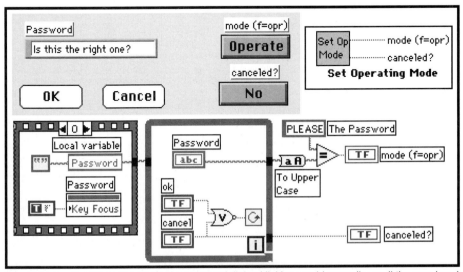

Figure 11-9. Set Operating mode is a password dialog VI. You would normally scroll the panel such that the mode and canceled? buttons are not visible, then use VI Setup to configure the window like a dialog box.

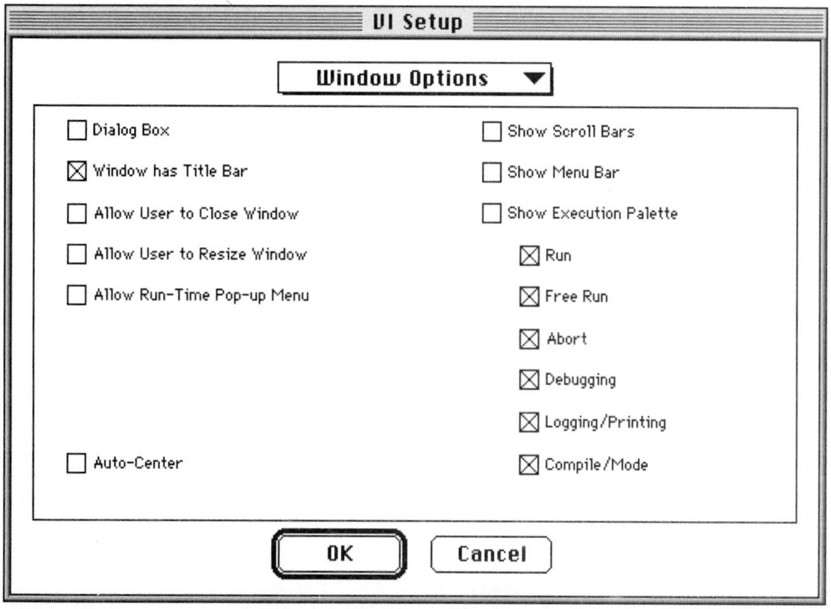

Figure 11-10. Window Options in the VI Setup dialog. Spend some time trying out various combinations of features to improve your user interface.

uses a single password for changing the operating mode of the test executive. If the operator enters the word "please," then the VI returns True for the mode of operation. The VI also returns a value to indicate if the operator selected **Cancel**. Note that the indicator for **mode** and **canceled** would not normally be visible on the front panel; you should scroll them off to the side and resize the VI's window to hide them. This is obviously not a sophisticated password mechanism, but it does illustrate how you can use attribute nodes and local variables to selectively enable or disable front panel controls.

This test executive also illustrates the use of **VI Setup...** options to customize the user interface. In Figure 11-7, note that the front panel does not display scroll bars, LabVIEW menus or execution palette, or window options such as the close box. You configure these options using the **Window Options** section of VI Setup options. Figure 11-10 shows the Window options for this test executive.

Figure 11-11 shows the front panel from another LabVIEW test executive, the one you get with the LabVIEW Test Executive Toolkit. This test executive uses a table control to show the list of available tests rather than a set of buttons. This approach allows you to display different lists of tests without adding new buttons like the previous example. It uses the basic Case-structure-in-a-While-Loop architecture described previously, with a *lot* of additions. With it, you can store and recall multiple test sequences from disk, and generate reports. And it has a test sequence editor that is quite impressive. Configuration (inserting your test VIs) is easy—they are all contained within one *test container* subVI. All you do is add them to individual frames of a Case structure, and type the names of each test VI into a string constant that acts like a database of available tests. From then on, the upper-

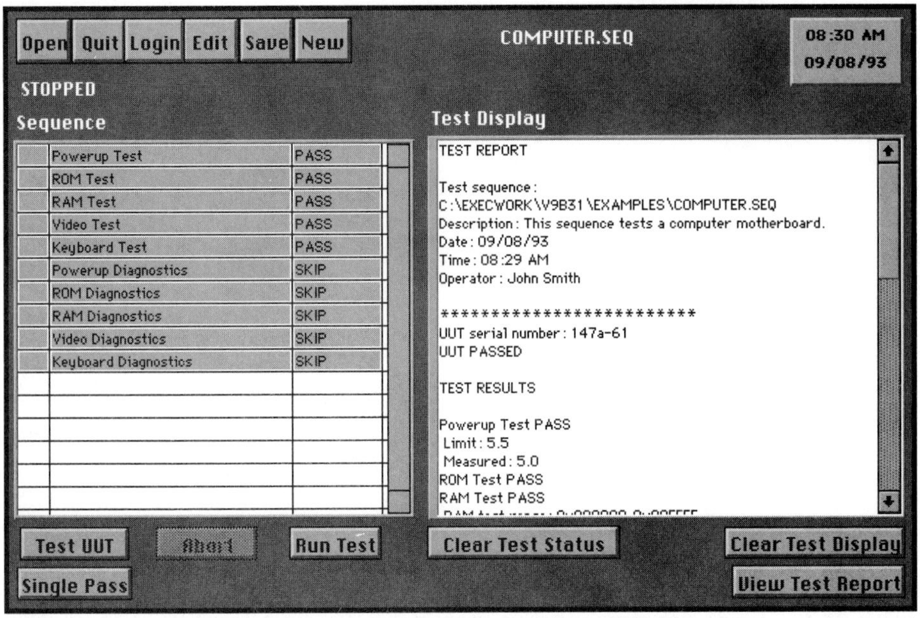

Figure 11-11. A serious test executive panel from the toolkit. I modified the appearance of some of the controls for clarity; you may use color and contrast to enhance operator efficiency.

level sequencing is a simple matter of entering the desired test names. If you want to learn all the details, by all means order the whole package. It's a large, comprehensive, flexible framework with a nice user manual.

One interesting feature of this test executive is its use of a table control to show the test names and test results. The table labeled *Sequence* shows the list of tests to execute. When a test is running, the word RUNNING appears next to the name of the test in the Sequence table. After the test executes, the word PASS appears if the test passed, FAIL if the test failed, and SKIP if the operator has deselected the test. Figure 11-12 shows a VI that illustrates how this display is created. It's a highly simplified version of the main test executive VI. The key is to use local variables to overwrite the *Seq Table* control from multiple locations on the diagram, thus providing a real-time status display.

The front panel shows how the display looks when a test is currently executing. Note several things about the diagram of this VI. First, because the tests are identified in the sequence table by names instead of by case numbers, you must have some type of cross-reference that relates a test name to a case number. For this example, the test names are in a string array control; you could also read the list from a file or global variable. The left For Loop uses the Search 1D Array function to determine the index of each test in the sequence. Since the data type for a table control is a 2D string array, you pull out the 0th element for each line in the table to get the test name. You'd probably want some logic here to post an error message if one of the tests is not found in the array of allowable test names. The left For Loop also creates a 2D string array that has element 1 of each line in the table (the

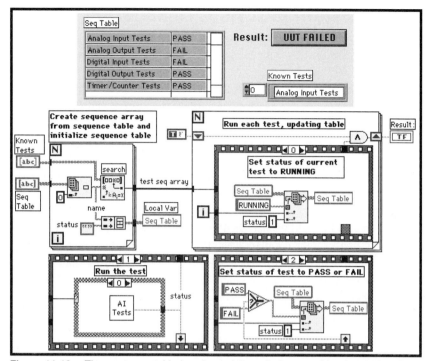

Figure 11-12. The sequence table is animated through the use of local variables. The status field (second column in the table) is updated as the VI runs.

status column) empty. This 2D array is written to the **Seq Table** using a local variable (between the two loops), thus erasing any previous results in the table.

The actual test sequencing is once again built around a Case structure, but this time inside a For Loop—the number of tests in the sequence is known ahead of time. This example also has some extra programming to animate the **Seq Table**. In the first sequence frame, the 2-D string array is read from the table using a local variable, element 1 of the current test's row is set to the word RUNNING, and the array is written back to the table, again using a local variable. Notice that you must write the entire 2-D array to a table; you cannot "poke" individual cells in the table. The Case structure containing the test is in Frame 1. In Frame 2, element 1 of the test's row is set to either PASS or FAIL, depending upon the result of the test, using the same method as in frame 0. This is a "safe" application of local variables because the order in which reading and writing occur is strictly defined. The only other source of interference might be the user editing the table contents while the VI runs. You could add an Attribute Node for the table that disables the control at the appropriate times.

Now you can see how LabVIEW allows you to control the user interface and tune it for the particular operator who will be executing tests. These examples show only a few of the capabilities available using attribute nodes, local variables, and VI Setup options.

Data Organization and Report Generation

The third major responsibility of a test executive is to organize and log test data, and to generate test reports. While the test sequencing mechanisms and user interfaces tend to be common across many ATE applications, test data logging and reporting formats vary greatly. The best data log or test report format depends on how you intend to use the data. If it's to be printed and stored in file cabinets, then the main concern is requirements for formatting the test report. Many companies have quality guidelines and standard forms that dictate how to present the test data. Military and government applications have very specific documentation standards. You may wish to use another application, such as a spreadsheet or word processor, to actually prepare the document. In this case, you can write the data to a file or use an interapplication communication mechanism to send the report directly to the other application.

If you plan to process the data further, then you have to consider what form of data storage is most appropriate for the recipient data processing application. You may want to write the data to the corporate data base. There may be strict rules for time stamping data and ensuring the integrity and security of the data. Most of these issues may be handled by the recipient application, so your LabVIEW application only has to present the data in the correct data format (proper location of tab characters, newline characters, numeric formatting, etc).

Earlier in this chapter, we discussed the use of a common data structure (a cluster) for passing data from a test VI to the test executive. The data structure you've chosen goes a

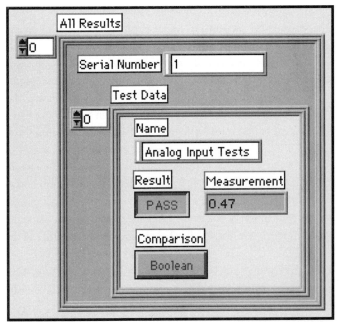

Figure 11-13.   Likely data structure for returning results from a sequence of tests on many UUTs.

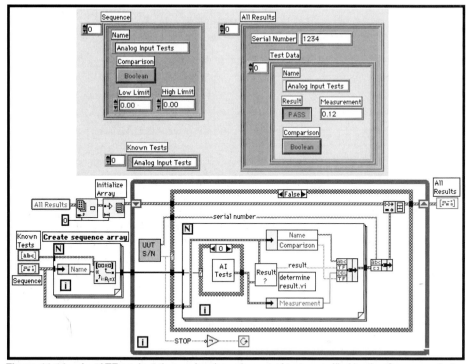

Figure 11-14. An "ATE engine" that cycles through a set of tests specified by the *Sequence* cluster array. Results are accumulated into the *All Results* cluster array for later reporting.

long way towards defining the best structure in LabVIEW for accumulating the results of multiple tests for a UUT. Figure 11-13 shows a data structure that you could use for accumulating test results for multiple UUTs.

The basic data structure is an array of clusters. The cluster in the outer array contains the serial number and the test data for one UUT. The **Test Data** array contains the results of each test for the UUT. Each element of the **Test Data** array is a cluster containing the name of the test, the results (PASS or FAIL), the measured value, and the type of comparison made to determine if the test passed. Use of this four-element cluster assumes that your test executive has a way to specify whether pass/fail determination for a specific test is done by looking at the Boolean Pass/Fail flag or by comparing the numeric measurement to some limits. The **Comparison** Boolean indicates whether the comparison was Boolean or numeric, thus determining if the value in **Measurement** is relevant for this test. You may also wish to include the actual test limits in the **Test Data** array.

Figure 11-14 shows a VI that creates the data structure discussed above. The input to the VI (**Sequence**) is an array of clusters containing a list of tests to run, comparison types, and acceptance limits. This VI again references tests by names. After creating the test array, the outer While Loop runs once for each UUT to be tested. The first thing that happens in the loop is a prompt for the UUT serial number, performed by the UUT S/N Prompt VI. This VI is configured, through its VI Setup options, to pop up like a dialog box (details are

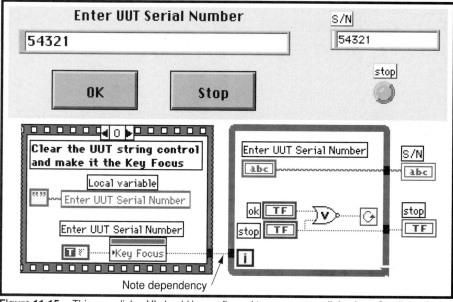

Figure 11-15. This user dialog VI should be configured to appear as a dialog box. Scroll the *S/N* and *stop* indicators out of the window. A Local Variable and an Attribute Node initialize the UUT Serial Number string control.

shown in Figure 11-15). When testing is complete, the operator clicks the **Stop** button on the panel of UUT S/N Prompt, which stops the main VI.

The For Loop cycles through each requested test in order. The test result, along with the name and comparison type of the test and the measurement value from the test, are bundled together into a cluster. These clusters are accumulated into an array using autoindexing on the For Loop. After the test sequence completes, the UUT serial number and array of results clusters are bundled into a cluster. This cluster is appended to the array of results contained in the shift register of the outer While Loop. When the user decides to stop testing, the True case of the Case structure executes. That case simply recycles data in the shift register. If you chose instead to accumulate results by autoindexing on the border of the While Loop, the final cycle of the While Loop would produce an empty array element that you would have to remove.

Figure 11-15 shows how the UUT S/N Prompt VI works. The UUT Serial Number string control is initialized to an empty string with a local variable. Then, an Attribute Node makes it the Key Focus so that the user doesn't have to click in the field before entering characters. You should use the VI Setup options to make this look like a regular dialog box. Also, the **S/N** and **stop** indicators should be scrolled out of view.

In the main VI, the Determine Result subVI (Figure 11-16) accepts the Test Data cluster and the current test description, and returns a Boolean value to indicate whether the test passed. Depending on the comparison mode, the test result is computed by comparing the

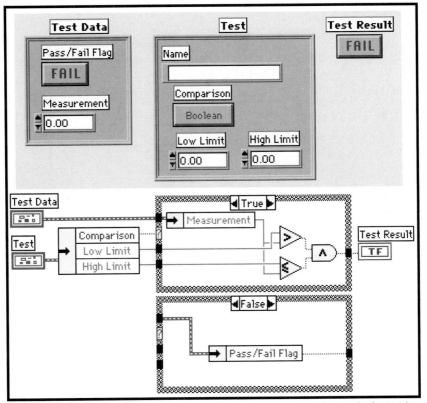

Figure 11-16.   In this example, the Determine Result VI computes the result of a test based on the comparison mode.

measurement with its high limit and low limit, or, in Boolean mode, the pass/fail flag is simply duplicated.

Storing Data In a LabVIEW Datalog File

If you plan to process the data in LabVIEW, using the analysis VIs or statistical process control (SPC) routines, you will want to maintain the data in a native LabVIEW format in a datalog file. You can perform automatic data logging directly from the front panel of your test VIs. Do this by enabling data logging for the VIs when you place them in your test executive. The input and output data for each VI are logged automatically after the VI executes. A drawback to this approach is that you cannot easily disable data logging for all test VIs from the test executive. If you are interactively running tests, you may not want all of the intermediate data going into your data log file. To turn off data logging, you must open each VI's front panel and turn off data logging.

A solution that gives you more flexibility for data logging is to log the combined test results accumulated into the cluster array previously shown in Figure 11-13. You can write the test results to a data log file by placing that cluster array on the front panel of a VI,

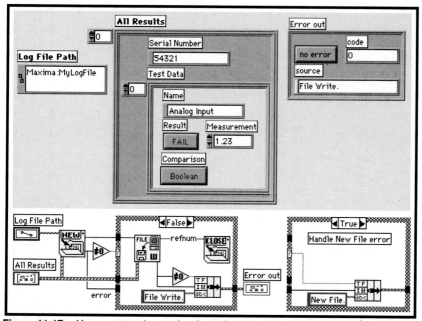

Figure 11-17. You can store the results of a series of tests in a LabVIEW datalog file with a simple VI like this. It creates a new file each time it's called; you could change New File to Open File, thus appending results to an existing file.

making the array an input on the VI's connector pane, and executing the VI. This VI does not need a diagram because you simply want to execute it to force data logging. To enable or disable data logging, you only need to access this one VI.

You could alternatively write a VI that saves the data programmatically, as shown in Figure 11-17. The block diagram method gives you the ability to change the name of the target data log file without having to open the front panel of the data log VI and setting the file name manually. This example creates a new datalog file, writes an image of the **All Results** cluster array to it, then closes the file. You could replace the New File function with Open File, which would permit you to append results to an ever-growing datalog file.

ASCII Test Report

To save test results for processing by other applications, such as a data base or spreadsheet, you'll probably want to save the data in ASCII text format. Once you've accumulated your test results into a structure as shown in Figure 11-13, it is easy to develop a VI that formats the data into an ASCII string. The VI in Figure 11-18 does the trick.

The report contains the serial number and test results for each UUT. This VI first creates a test report header with the date and time of testing. The outer For Loop executes once for each UUT tested (the outer array in the **All Results** cluster array). It creates a header for each UUT, showing the serial number. The inner For Loop processes each element in the inner cluster array of **All Results**, corresponding to each test performed on the UUT. A

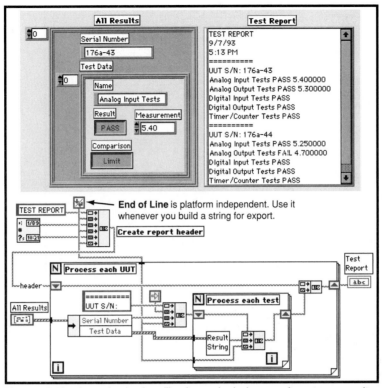

Figure 11-18. Lots of string handling is required when you format your results as ASCII text. The Test Report string would probably be written to a file for use in another application.

subVI, Format Result String, creates one line in the string for each test, with a carriage return/line feed separating lines. Figure 11-19 shows the front panel and block diagram of Format Result String. Note how the **All Results** data structure maps nicely into this report generation VI. Results were collected by a test executive that had a similar loop-within-a-loop construct. This demonstrates the close coupling between algorithms and data structures. The Format Result String produces each line in the test report with the following format:

<test name><TAB><result><TAB><measurement>

Notice that if the comparison type is Boolean, the ASCII test report does not include the measurement. The calling VI appends an appropriate end-of-line character. Under Windows, you should use carriage return/line feed. For the Macintosh, use a carriage return. For Sun, use a line feed. To simplify this portability problem, you can use the End of Line constant that automatically inserts the proper character(s).

This VI formats the test report into an ASCII string. Within the test executive, you can use this string to display the test results to the operator using a front panel string indicator. You can also write the string to a file so that other applications can load the test results for generating reports. This format, using carriage return/line feed to separate lines, and tabs

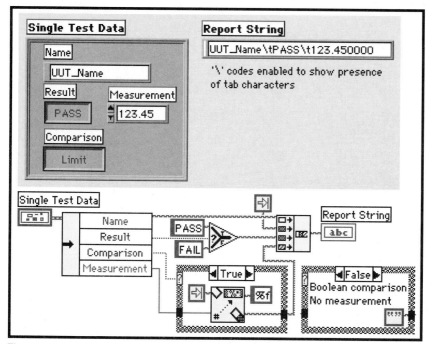

Figure 11-19. Format Result String is typical of subVIs that you might write to translate a cluster of information into one line of a text-format report.

to separate fields on a single line, can be imported by many applications, including spreadsheets, data bases, and word processors.

Using Interapplication Communication for Report Generation

LabVIEW has many functions for passing data directly to another application without writing the data to a file. For example, you can use **Dynamic Data Exchange (DDE)** on Microsoft Windows to send the ASCII test report to Microsoft Excel. On the Macintosh, you can use **AppleEvents** and the lower level protocol, **Program-to-Program Communication (PPC)**. All of these interapplication communication (IAC) techniques are included with LabVIEW in the Network submenu of the Functions menu and are documented in the *LabVIEW Networking Reference Manual*. Be aware that you need detailed knowledge of the data formats required by other applications. I might mentions that, as of this writing, software manufacturers rarely publish much information about their IAC interfaces. You may have to make some phone calls and request additional information, and be sure to have the latest version of the application.

DDE is a popular, text-based protocol that is easy to use, so let's study how test results may be sent from LabVIEW to an Excel spreadsheet using DDE. It's a true client-server protocol (as opposed to the internal data distribution model using global variables that we've used throughout this book) where LabVIEW and other applications exchange data and commands. To use DDE, both applications must be running and both must register

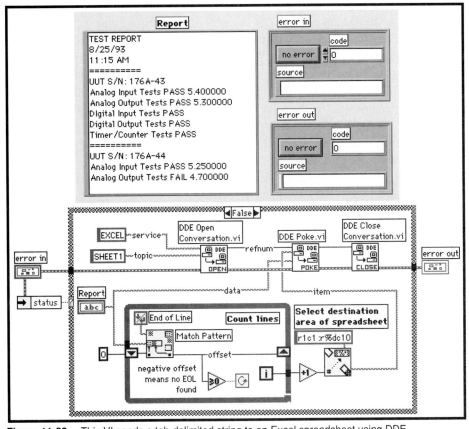

Figure 11-20.   This VI sends a tab-delimited string to an Excel spreadsheet using DDE.

with Windows—an operation that is normally performed automatically when you launch an application. Next, the client (in this case, LabVIEW) establishes a **conversation** with a server, referred to as the **service**. Associated with each service is a topic, which normally refers to the current file. If you have an application like Excel running, you could have more than one topic active by having more than one spreadsheet open.

Once a conversation is established using the DDE Open Conversation VI, you can send data with the DDE Poke VI, send commands with the DDE Execute VI, or obtain data with the DDE Request VI. All of these operations transmit single messages. For a bit less overhead, you can use the DDE Advise Start VI to establish an ongoing link with the server. The server will send LabVIEW a message each time new data is available. Your VI has to periodically call the DDE Advise Check VI to see if new data is ready. If it is, data is returned as a string.

The VI shown in Figure 11-20 uses DDE to send the ASCII test report to an Excel spreadsheet. On the diagram, *service* identifies the server application—Excel. The *topic* identifies the server's data container, which is a worksheet file in Excel called Sheet1. The

DDE Open Conversation VI accepts strings for the service and topic with which you wish to communicate and returns a refnum for use with other DDE functions.

Before sending the report to Excel, the VI determines the number of lines in the report by counting the number of line feeds. You need to know the length of the report because Excel requires you to specify the range of cells in which to place the data. The VI assumes that the first cell is *r1c1*, the cell in the upper left-hand corner of the spreadsheet, and that the report is no more than 10 cells wide. Using Format & Append, the VI creates the range specification. The DDE Poke VI sends the data to Excel. You must specify the *item* that is to receive the test report. This item is the range of cells in the worksheet. After sending the test report, the VI executes DDE Close Conversation to disconnect from Excel. Notice that the DDE VIs in LabVIEW use the error cluster for passing error information, greatly simplifying the diagram of this example.

Figure 11-21 shows how the test report shown on the front panel in Figure 11-20 appears in the Excel spreadsheet.

Controlling LabVIEW With DDE

In some automated test applications, the test executive is not actually a LabVIEW application. Some other application presents the high level operator interface and list of tests to run, and sends messages to LabVIEW via an interapplication communication mechanism. The basic structure of the LabVIEW portion of this application is the same as

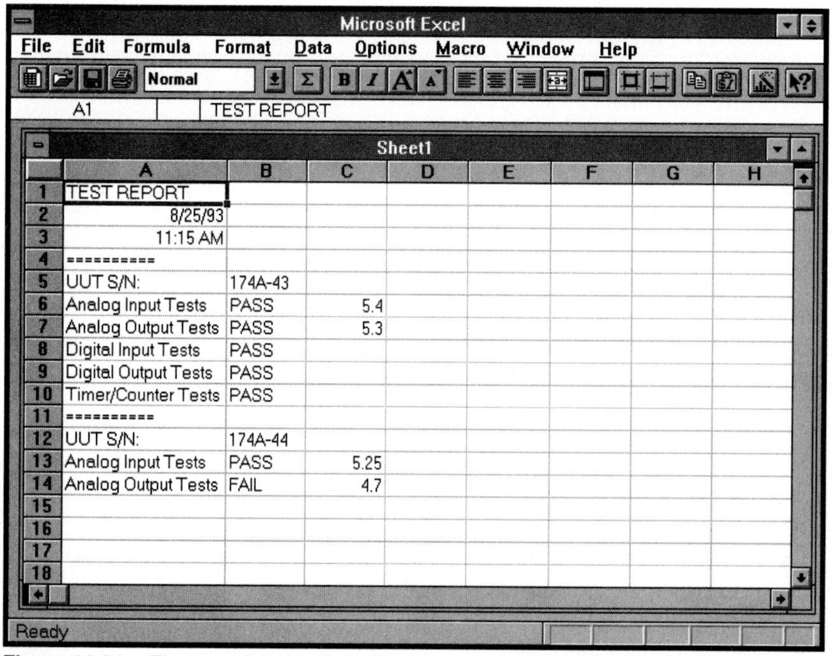

Figure 11-21. The spreadsheet, filled with data from the LabVIEW VI described above.

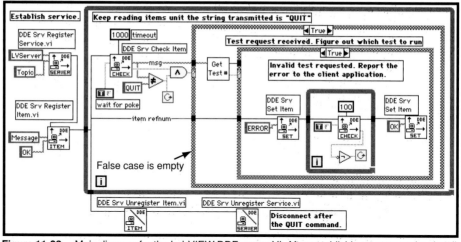

Figure 11-22. Main diagram for the LabVIEW DDE server VI. After establishing a new service, it polls for messages from a client, expecting a string that specifies which test to run. Results of the test are reported back to the client.

described for the test executive built entirely in LabVIEW, namely a test executive engine built around a case structure. The main difference is that the list of tests to execute now resides outside of LabVIEW and the case selection for choosing the test to run is passed into the test executive engine through an interapplication communication mechanism.

Figure 11-22 shows a VI that implements a simple DDE server in LabVIEW. This VI does not have any front panel controls because all input comes from a DDE connection and all results are returned by the same path. Unlike the previous example, where Excel was the server, this VI creates a server to which other applications can connect. The server is created by calling the DDE Srv Register Service VI. This VI registers a DDE service and topic with the Windows operating system. This server has the name *LVServer* and a topic named *Topic*. The DDE Srv Register Item VI adds an item to the server registered by DDE Srv Register Server. This server has just one item, named *Message*, associated with the topic named *Topic*. After creating the item, the VI enters a loop that continuously monitors the topic for incoming messages using the DDE Srv Check Item VI. DDE Srv Check Item has a Boolean output that is set to True if a client has written data to the topic it is monitoring. If no message arrives within the timeout period (1 s), the loop cycles again.

If the server receives the message *QUIT*, it stops looping and unregisters the topic, item, and service by executing the DDE Srv Unregister Item VI and the DDE Srv Unregister Service VI, located below the While Loop on the diagram. If the message is not *QUIT*, the message is passed to a subVI, Get Test Number. This example accepts the name of a test to run and uses a list of known names to determine the correct case number to execute. If the name is not recognized, Get Test Number sets its error indicator to True; otherwise, the error indicator is set to False and the test number is passed into the inner Case structure. In Figure 11-22, the inner Case shows the state where an invalid test was requested.

The following steps take place:

1. Set *Message* to ERROR.

2. Wait for the client to acknowledge the error by writing any value back to *Message*.

3. Set *Message* to OK and wait for another command.

If the Boolean error output from Get Test Number is False, indicating no error, the following steps take place:

1. Set *Message* to *BUSY*, so the client knows that you've accepted the command.

2. Execute the test in the case number passed out from **Get Test Number**.

3. Set *Message* to either *PASS* or *FAIL*, depending on the output from the test. The client application knows the test is done when *Message* changes from *BUSY* to either *PASS* or *FAIL*.

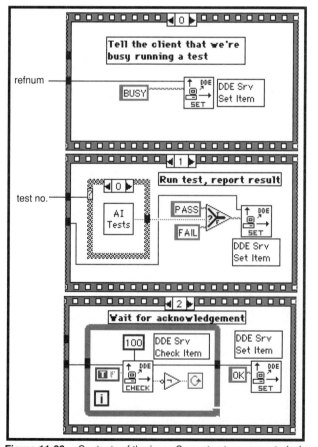

Figure 11-23. Contents of the inner Case structure, executed when a valid test is requested.

4. Wait for the client to acknowledge receipt of the test result by writing any value back to *Message*.

5. Set *Message* to *OK* and wait for another command.

Figure 11-23 shows the contents of the Sequence structure that resides in the False frame of the inner Case structure.

Some Closing Words

Appropriately, we end where we began–with LabVIEW assisting in the automation of a measurement process. I hope that each chapter has been enjoyable, enlightening, and relevant to your particular situation. In the two years that it has taken to write this book, I've talked to a lot of people just like you, studying their problems, asking and answering questions, and learning more with every encounter. So my advice to you is, take a class, join a user group, hang out on the email circuit, talk to your neighbor—and *learn*.

Guide to LabVIEW Platform Dependency

LabVIEW version 3.0 is a portable application, which means that versions of the program are available that run on several different computer platforms. VIs created with LabVIEW 3.0 are portable among LabVIEW for Windows, LabVIEW for Sun, and LabVIEW for Macintosh. When making LabVIEW a portable application, National Instruments tried to ensure that your job as a developer is as easy as possible. You still need to follow a few guidelines, which I've assembled here. Please note that while these guidelines will help you move the VIs from one system to another, there is no guarantee regarding performance. For instance, a complex, real-time VI that runs fast and trouble-free on a Sun workstation may have problems on a 386/20 MHz.

Portable VIs

VIs created using LabVIEW for Windows, LabVIEW for Sun, and LabVIEW for Macintosh have identical file formats. They use a proprietary binary format that does not use a resource fork on the Macintosh. You can transfer VIs from Windows, Sun, or Macintosh to another system running Windows, Sun, or Macintosh either by disk or over a network. Once the file is on the new system, you can open the VI from within LabVIEW on that platform. LabVIEW detects that the VI is from another platform and recompiles the VI to use the correct instructions for the local processor.

To simplify the act of moving a set of VIs from one platform to another, consider placing most of your VIs in VI libraries. Libraries remove many of the constraints on VI names (see below), they reduce the number of files you have to carry around, and they offer some compression to save disk space.

The closest thing to a universal media for portable VIs is the high-density (1.4 MB) floppy, in DOS format. On the Macintosh, use Apple File Exchange or one of the many system extensions, such as PC Exchange, that enable you to directly access DOS-format diskettes. On the Sun, under SunOS 4.1.2 and 4.1.3, as superuser, issue the command, "mount /pcfs". This will mount the floppy to the /pcfs directory. On the Solaris 2.x, as superuser, cd to the directory "/etc/init.d" and type "./volmgt stop". Insert the floppy, then type "/usr/sbin/mount -F pcfs/ dev/diskette /floppy".

VIs That Are NOT Portable

- VIs distributed in the vi.lib directory. Each distribution of LabVIEW contains its own vi.lib, so do not move VIs in vi.lib across platforms.

- Some compatibility VIs. For instance, if you are a converting an older LabVIEW 2.2 Macintosh program with the older-style DAQ or file I/O VIs, you should replace these with version 3.0 functions or VIs before porting. This step will also ensure compatibility with future versions of LabVIEW.

- VIs containing CINs. If you write your CIN source code in a platform independent manner, you can recompile it on another platform and relink it to a ported VI. Otherwise, you will get an "object code not found" error if the CIN is from a different platform. See the LabVIEW Code Interface Node manual for information on CIN portability.

- VIs in the Function:Utility:System menu are platform-dependent and may not be available on all machines. Examples are the LabVIEW for Windows Input and Output Utility VIs and the LabVIEW for Macintosh Peek and Poke Utility VIs.

- Macintosh LabVIEW 2.2 (or earlier) VIs. These VIs must be converted to LabVIEW 3.0 on a Macintosh computer. Then, you must remove the compatibility VIs in them before you can port the VIs to another platform. This is necessary with an application using File I/O functions and data acquisition VIs, which have changed extensively between versions 2.2 and 3.0.

Strings

All three platforms use different end-of-line (EOL) markers. A platform-independent constant, EOL, is available in the Structures and Constants palette that automatically generates the proper character when ported. The proper characters are:

- Macintosh: carriage return (\r)

- PC: carriage return, then line feed (\r\n)

- Sun: line feed (\n)

A really interesting problem crops up with string controls when the user types a carriage return into the string: LabVIEW always inserts a linefeed, regardless of platform.

Timing

Resolution of LabVIEW timing functions is system dependent. Applicable functions are Tick Count (ms), Wait (ms), Wait Until Next ms Multiple:

- Macintosh: 1/60th second (16.66 ms)
- PC: 55 ms (default) or 1 ms if you modify labview.ini (see your LabVIEW Release Notes for instructions)
- Sun: 1 ms

Networking and Interapplication Communication

All platforms support the TCP/IP VIs. Other protocols are platform specific:

- Macintosh: AppleEvents and Interapplication Communication (IAC)
- PC: Dynamic Data Exchange (DDE)

Files and File Names

Path naming standards are system dependent. The LabVIEW path control is fairly intelligent in that it understands and translates the various delimiter characters.

- Macintosh: Volume:folder:folder:file
- PC: disk:directory\directory\file.ext
- Sun: directory/directory/file.ext

New Directory and New File functions:

- The Permissions and Group inputs only apply to Sun
- Type and Creator VI only applies to Macintosh

When you enter text into the file name box of a file dialog, you either specify a file or directory name or you specify a new pattern to apply to the file list box. If the text that you type contains either pattern matching character, (*) or (?), then the text is treated as a pattern, otherwise the text is treated as a file or directory name. If you want to enter the characters * or ? as part of a name, you need to precede it with an escape character. On Macintosh and UNIX systems, the escape character is (\ ). On Windows systems, the escape character is (`) to avoid conflicting with the path separator character (\ ).

If you are developing a VI for use on multiple platforms, you should not use any of the platform-specific path separator characters in your file names; that is, avoid (\ ), (/), and (:) in file names. The escape character will not prevent a path separator from being treated as a path separator. Therefore, any file name that contains a path separator for a given platform cannot be specified using file dialogs on that platform. In general, avoid using special characters in VI names and file names.

Naming Your VIs

Filenames are limited to eight characters plus an optional three-character extension following a period, typically .vi under DOS/Windows. LabVIEW for Macintosh filenames can have 31 characters. LabVIEW for Sun filenames can have 255 characters, including the .vi extension. To avoid complications, you should either save VIs with short names, or better yet, save them in a VI library. A VI library is a single file that can contain multiple VIs. A library name must conform to platform limits, but VIs in libraries can have names up to 255 characters, regardless of platform. Thus, VI libraries are the most convenient format for transferring VIs, because libraries eliminate most file system dependencies. See Chapter 1, Introduction to LabVIEW, of the LabVIEW for Sun/Macintosh/Windows User Manual for more information on creating VI libraries.

Fonts and Cosmetics

Another portability issue concerns differences in resolution and fonts. Fonts can vary from platform to platform, so after porting a VI, you may have to choose new fonts to get an appealing display. When designing VIs, three fonts map the best between platforms: the Application Font, the System Font, and the Dialog Font. If you use these fonts, you will encounter fewer problems.

When you move a VI to a new platform, controls and labels may change size, depending on whether the fonts are smaller or larger. On front panels, LabVIEW avoids making labels overlap their owners by moving them away from the owning control. Also, every label and constant (on the front panel or diagram) has a default attribute called Size to Text. When you first create a label or constant, this attribute is set, so the bounds of the object resize as necessary to display all of the enclosed text. If you ever manually resize the object, LabVIEW turns off this attribute (the item in the pop-up menu is no longer checked). With Size to Text turned off, the bounds of the object stay constant, and LabVIEW clips the enclosed text as necessary. If you do not want LabVIEW to clip text when you move between systems or platforms, you should leave this attribute on for labels and constants.

Most Sun monitors are much larger and have a higher resolution than PC monitors. Thus, Sun users should not make their front panels very large if they want them to port well. The same holds true for Mac and PC users with large, high-resolution displays. A good compromise is 640 by 480 pixels for portable VIs. I put pencil marks on my monitor at the locations representing those dimensions, then size every VI to fit before saving.

Index to VIs on the Accompanying Diskette

This is an index to the VIs on the diskette that accompanies this book. Where a VI has one or more subVIs in the same library, I've made a note "Run this VI" to indicate which one is the main, or top-level, VI that you should open and run. There are four LabVIEW archives, or libraries, on the diskette:

- UTILITY.LLB—miscellaneous utility VIs

- CIRCBUF.LLB—circular buffer real-time stripchart VI

- SIMPLDAS.LLB—simple data acquisition system VI

- VI_LIST.LLB—extracts Get Info comments from VIs

The diskette is a high-density (1.4 MB) floppy, in DOS format. On the Macintosh, use Apple File Exchange or one of the many system extensions, such as PC Exchange, that enable you to directly access DOS-format diskettes. On the Sun, under SunOS 4.1.2 and later, there is a simple option on the mount command that enables you to directly access DOS-format diskettes. Issue the command "mount /pcfs" (as root) to mount the DOS floppy, then access the files as /pcfs/*.*.

And now a word from the lawyers:

> Permission is hereby granted to licensed users of LabVIEW, without written agreement and without license or royalty fees, to use, copy, and

modify the software that accompanies this book. Permission is further granted to licensed users of LabVIEW, without written agreement and without license or royalty fees, to freely distribute the software to other licensed users of LabVIEW.

UTILITY.LLB: Utility Functions

This library contains a set of useful utility VIs that were discussed throughout the book.

Average Voltage (from Chapter 6)

Accepts raw 2D voltage array from a DAQ scan function and averages each channel's data into a single value. Deletes selected number of samples to get rid of settling time problems. Applies offset and scale calibration information from the configuration to produce results in engineering units. Output is an array with one value per channel, all SGL format.

DAQ Interval/Period Timer (from Chapter 6)

A general-purpose interval/period measurement VI. Requires a plug-in board with an available counter-timer. An input signal is connected to the GATE input pin of the chosen counter. Select a **measurement mode** from this list:

    0—High level (duration)
    1—Low Level (interval)
    2—Rising edge (period)
    3—Falling edge (period)

The TIME indicator scales the result to seconds. The signal being measured is actually used as a gating signal while the counter counts edges produced by an internal timebase signal. The faster the internal timebase, the more edges counted and the better the time resolution. If your signal is slow enough (15 Hz or less using the 1 MHz timebase), the counter will overflow (events counted will be 1 or 2) and you will need to pick a slower timebase. You may select one of the following values for **internal timebase**:

    1000000.0, 100000.0, 10000.0, 1000.0, and 100.0

Decimal Hours (from Chapter 3)

This VI returns the decimal hour equivalent of the current time. For instance, if it is now 3:45 PM, **Decimal Hours** equals 15.75. Resolution is 1 ms, or whatever the limitation of this implementation of LabVIEW might be. Time overflows after 2^{32} ms, which equals 50 days.

Extract Numbers (from Chapter 11)

Finds all numbers in the input string and puts them into an array as single-precision (SGL) floating point numbers. All of the following formats are recognized:

123   1.23   1.23E2

No spaces or other characters may appear within the number, but any characters may appear before or after the number.

Fix String Length (from Chapter 4)

Forces the input string to be a fixed length. If it's too long, truncate it. If it's too short, append **Padding Chars** as required.

Interval Timer (from Chapter 3)

Interval timer for four independent events. Resolution is one second, except for D, which is one ms. Intervals are entered in seconds (for **A** and **B**), minutes (for **C**), or ms (for **D**). When the desired time has passed, the associated **Event** Boolean is set to true. **Iteration** initializes the state logic and synchronizes all the timers when set to zero. The default for **iteration** is 1. This VI is reentrant, so it can be called from multiple locations without experiencing interference.

Moving Average Array (from Chapter 7)

This VI is designed as a subVI to perform an equal weighted moving average on the data in X[]. A moving averager is a type of low pass finite impulse response (FIR) filter, and it is also known as a smoothing filter. This type of moving averager is also called a boxcar filter, because the weighting window is rectangular. For example, all of the coefficients in the averaging window are equal. **No. of Coefficients** is the size of the window, and should be an odd number 3 or larger.

X[] is an array containing one or more separate channels of data, perhaps coming from a multiple-channel A/D converter. Each channel is filtered independently.

The VI remembers the most recent n elements of **X[]** for use on the next call, in order to smooth segmented data without transients. **X[]** may contain as few as one element. The VI is reentrant, so that each subVI node of this VI has its own data space. Initial conditions are reset when **iteration**=0.

Range Finder (from Chapter 4)

Searches the numeric array to locate the number to find. If the value is less than the maximum value in the array, then **Range Found** is set to true. The nearest value found is also returned, as is the index into the numeric array. This VI is useful for picking control settings on instruments.

Running Mean & Sigma (from Chapter 7)

Compute the mean and standard deviation of **x** on an incremental basis. Each time this subVI is called, the new value of x is added into the calculation. If **Reset** is True, the stats are set to zero and only the newest **x** is used in the computation. This VI is set for reentrant execution; you can call it from multiple locations without interference.

Which Button (from Chapter 7)

This VI searches through the Boolean array and finds the first element that is set to true. It returns the ordinal number of that element, where 1 is the first element. It returns zero if none are true.

CIRCBUF.LLB: Circular Buffer VI

The circular buffer VI was discussed in Chapter 9, *Process Control Applications*. It provides real-time stripchart services that are otherwise unobtainable in LabVIEW. Examine the Circular buffer example VI to learn how it's applied.

Circular Buffer Example (Run This VI)

Demonstration of the Circular Buffer realtime trending routine. This VI writes fake data (sinusoids) to the circular buffer in one loop, then reads the desired range of data back from the buffer in another loop. This parallel While Loop scheme permits you to acquire and display data at different rates. The graph timebase can be changed from seconds to hours, minutes, or days. Also, the start and end times of the graph are displayed in hh:mm:ss format for convenience.

See the description of the Circular Buffer VI below for details on how all the underlying functions work.

Circular Buffer

A memory-based circular buffer for realtime trending. This VI is a *smart* global variable that stores many channels of data in a circular buffer with high efficiency. You can read back any range of data (varying the number of samples and starting point) from the buffer. Timestamps in epoch seconds are stored and retrieved automatically, so this VI can be called at irregular intervals.

- Setting **Initialize** to True allocates a circular buffer to hold the desired number of channels and samples/chan. During the initialization process, the inputs **Channels** and **Samples/chan** determine the buffer size. They are not used at any other time. *Note—* This step can take a fairly long time if a large buffer has to be created, but it only has to be done once. After that, this VI is very fast.

- Set **Write?** to True to write data from the **Data to Write** array into the buffer. The VI uses Replace Array Element to prevent reallocation of memory. When **Write?** is set to False, one channel's worth of data, plus the associated timestamps, are returned.

- **Channel to read** determines which channel to read. Range: 0 to Channels-1.

- **Data Scroll** determines where in the buffer the data shall come from when reading. It has a range of zero to 1.0. Zero returns the latest data, while 1.0 returns the oldest. This permits you to scroll through a long history.

- The **Points in graph window** control determines how many values will be returned, starting at the location set by **Data Scroll**.

- **Values** is an array containing the channel's data. All data are in SGL floating point format for memory conservation purposes. **Timestamps** is an associated array of [U32] epoch seconds (since 1-Jan-1904). You can do an x-y plot of **Values** vs. **Timestamps**, with **Timestamps** scaled as desired.

- Memory usage: For N channels and M samples, this example requires (N+1) * M * 8 bytes of memory. For instance, 10 channels and 10,000 samples consumes 880,000 bytes of memory. This does not include memory required for any graphs, other indicators, or sources of data.

- Read from circ buffer. Low-level VI to read a segment of data from a circular buffer.

- Text time axis. Interprets first and last elements of **Timebase** array as time in hh:mm:ss. Adds desired number of spaces in between, for use as a graph x-axis label. For use with graphs generated by the Circular Buffer VI.

- TimeStamps to D/H/M/S. Subtracts the current clock time from an array of times (in seconds), then scales to seconds, hours, minutes, or days. For use with data generated by the Circular Buffer VI.

SIMPLDAS.LLB: Simple Data Acquisition System (for DAQ)

This library contains the simple data acquisition system discussed in Chapter 7, *Writing a Data Acquisition Program*. It acquires data from a plug-in DAQ board, displays data, and logs it to a tab-delimited text file.

- **Simple Data Acq System** (Run this VI). Simple data acquisition and display VI that makes use of handy subVIs. Acquires data through a DAQ board (with optional multiplexers or SCXI modules) and scales data to volts.

- To cut down on overhead, the subVI Interval Timer controls how often the stripchart is updated and how often data is appended to the data file. You can add more displays to the Case structure that contains the stripchart if you like.

- Data is saved in tab-delimited text format. Headers are written first. The first column is a time stamp formatted in decimal hours, where 3:15PM would be 15.250 hours, with a resolution of 1 ms, or whatever the current version of LabVIEW supplies.

- Performance—Making the display interval very long speeds things up by reducing graphics overhead. The averaging is a somewhat limiting factor, as is the conversion of numeric data to strings and the open-write-close VI. Therefore, this VI is really at its best for sampling rates of less than about 5 Hz.

- String list converter. Converts a list of items in a string (separated by carriage returns) into a tab-delimited string followed by a carriage return, and to an array of strings. For use with the Simple Data Acq System VI.

VI_LIST.LLB: VI Comment Extractor

VI List extracts the information from the Get Info dialog boxes for a directory full of VIs and stores all of the text in a plain text file. It is useful for generating documents, as described in Chapter 4, *Building an Application*.

- **VI List** (Run this VI). Recursively searches a directory or VI library, extracts the Get Info descriptions from all VIs and controls, extracts the contents of any text files (.txt) that may describe VI directories or libraries, then writes the material to a user-specified file. You can use this VI to document your VI set.

  Note—This VI uses the *getinfo* VI from the LabVIEW Examples/rdsubvis directory. It contains a platform-dependent CIN and therefore is not distributed on the diskette with this book. The first time you open this VI, LabVIEW will not be able to find "getinfo.vi", so you will have to manually locate it in the Examples/rdsubvis directory.

- Comment Queue. A global variable subVI designed as a first-in, first-out queue of strings. The queue is step-wise unbounded—its initial size is 16 elements, and it doubles automatically when it fills up. Access is very fast except when the queue is expanding. Empty the queue before using to ensure it is initialized, and after using to deallocate its buffers; do not write or read when emptying. This VI is non-reentrant and callable from multiple locations.

- Directory Stack. A global variable subVI designed as a last-in, first-out stack of strings. The stack is step-wise unbounded—its initial size is 16 elements, and it doubles automatically if it fills up. Access is very fast except when the stack is expanding. Empty the stack before using to ensure it is initialized and after using to deallocate its buffers; do not push or pop when emptying. This VI is non-reentrant and callable from multiple locations.

- Get & Write Descriptions. Recursively searches a directory or VI library and creates a file of the contents along with Get Info descriptions of VIs or controls, and with contents of text files (.txt) that may describe directories or VI libraries.

- Get Lists & Descriptions. Extracts VI descriptions from the Get Info boxes of each file in the present path. Then it passes along an array of directory names that are also present in this path.

Sources

Chapter 1 Sources

LTR Publishing
5614 Anita
Dallas, TX 75206
(214) 827-9931 FAX (214) 827-9932

Chapter 3 Sources

Bancomm, a division of Datum, Inc.
6541 Via Del Oro
San Jose, CA 95119
(408) 578-4161 FAX (408) 578-4165

TrueTime Corp.
3243 Santa Rosa Ave.
Santa Rosa, CA 95407
(707) 528-1230 FAX (707) 527-6640

Chapter 5 Sources

Black Box Corp. (communications interface equipment)
P.O. Box 12800
Pittsburgh, PA 15241
(412) 746-5500

IOTech (GPIB equipment)
25971 Cannon Road
Cleveland, OH 44146
(216) 439-4091 FAX (216) 439-4093

Chapter 7 Sources

Wavemetrics (Igor)
P.O. Box 2088
Lake Oswego, OR 97035
(503) 620-3001 FAX (503) 620-6754
wavemetrics@applelink.apple.com

Spectral Innovations
1885 Lundy Avenue
Suite 208
San Jose, CA 95131
(408) 955-0366 FAX (408) 955-0370
applelink/macdsp

Chapter 8 Sources

Software Engineering Group (SEG) (HighwayVIEW; AnaVIEW)
1 Dana St.
Cambridge, MA 02138
(617) 492-6664 FAX (617) 661-6483

Allen-Bradley (PLCs)
1201 South Second St.
Milwaukee, WI 53204
(414) 382-2000 FAX (414) 382-2400

Anafaze (Single-loop controllers)
1041 17th Ave.
Santa Cruz, CA 95062
(408) 479-0415 FAX (408) 479-0526

Research, Inc. (Micristar controllers)
P.O. Box 24064
Minneapolis, MN 55424
(612) 941-3000 FAX (612) 941-3628

Hathaway/Beta (Alarm annunciators)
2029 McKenzie #150
Carrollton, TX 75011
(800)537-2181 FAX (214) 241-6752

SAPHIR (Telemechanique PLC driver; imaging products)
L' Epinette
F-38 530 Chapareillan, France
011-33-76-45-21-21
FAX 011-33-76-45-20-78

Chapter 9 Sources

Pearson Electronics
1860 Embarcadero Rd.
Palo Alto, CA 94303
(415) 494-6716
FAX (415) 494-6716

Ross Engineering
540 Westchester Dr,
Campbell, CA 95008
(408) 377-4621
FAX (408) 377-5182

LeCroy USA
700 Chestnut Ridge Rd.
Chestnut, NY 10977
(914) 578-6013
FAX (914) 578-5984

Joerger Enterprises
166 Laurel Rd.
East Northport, NY 11731
(516) 757-6201
FAX (516) 757-6201

Chapter 10 Sources

ASTER (see Dixon DSP Design)

Neotech (frame grabbers)
distributed in the US by GTFS and nuLogic
120 Winchester Road
Chandlers Ford
Hampshire SO5 2QD, UK
(44) 703 270 200

Metric Systems (SurfaceView)
1506 Taron Dr.
Round Rock, TX 78681
(512) 388-4458 FAX (512) 244-7203

Perceptics Corp. (frame grabbers)
725 Pellissippi Parkway
Knoxville, TN 37933
(615) 966-9200

nuLogic, Inc. (motion control equipment)
475 Hillside Ave.
Neeham, MA 02194
(617) 444-7680

Sony Corp. of America (video equipment)
Computer Peripherals Products Co.
655 River Oaks Parkway
San Jose, CA 95134
(800) 352-7669

GTFS (Graftek products)
2455 Bennett Valley Rd., Suite 100C
Santa Rosa, CA 95404
(707) 579-1733 FAX (707) 578-3195

Computer Friends (frame grabbers)
14250 NW Science Park Dr.
Portland, OR 97229
(503) 626-2291

Dixon DSP Design (ASTER products)
2515 Hollow Bend
Mesquite, TX 75150
(800) 967-0708 FAX (214) 681-1502
wdixon@applelink.apple.com

Data Translation (frame grabbers)
100 Locke Drive
Marlboro, MA 01752
(508) 481-3700

Digital Vision, Inc. (video converters)
270 Bridge St.
Dedham, MA 02026
(617) 329-5400

Hammamatsu (frame grabbers and cameras)
360 Foothill Rd.
Bridgewater, NJ 08807
(908) 231-1116

Imaging Technology
55 Middlesex Turnpike
Bedford, MA 01730
(617) 275-2700

Pyxis Corporation
Scott E. Hamilton
5577 Ann Peake Drive
Fairfax, VA 22032-2132
Voice/Fax: (703) 978-0534

Scentech (frame grabbers)
800 West Cummings Park
Woburn, MA 01801
(617) 935-1770

Scion Corp.
152 W. Ptarick St.
Frederick, MD 21701
(301) 695-7870

Stellar Solutions (Video VI)
735 Hickey Blvd, Suite 301
Pacifica, CA 94044
Voice/Fax: (415) 738-1139

VideoMedia Corporation
Roland Levin
175 Lewis Rd.
San Jose, CA 95111
Phone (408) 227-9977, Fax (408) 227-6707

NIH Image is available to Internet users via anonymous ftp from zippy.nimh.nih.gov. Those without Internet access can get updates from many Macintosh bulletin boards and user group libraries. A reasonably current version, including Pascal source code and example images, should be available from one of the following:

1. From a friend. The Image program, including source code and documentation, is public domain and may be freely copied, distributed, and modified. However, if you modify Image, please update the about box before distributing your version of the program.

2. Via anonymous FTP from zippy.nimh.nih.gov[128.231.98.32]. Enter "anonymous" as the user name and your email address as the password. The /pub/image directory contains the latest version of Image(image145.hqx), a version of Image that runs on Macs without a floating-point coprocessor (image145NonFPU.hqx), documentation in Word format(image145_manual.hqx), and complete Think Pascal source code(image145_source.hqx). The directory /pub/image/images contains sample TIFF and PICT images. The directory /pub/image/image_spinoffs contains versions of Image extended to do FFTs, to do fractal analysis, to capture and analyze color images, and to support quantitative evaluation of cerebral blood flow, glucose metabolism, and protein synthesis. Most of the same files are also available from zippy.nimh.nih.gov in the directory /pub/image. There is a README file(0README.txt) with information on the file formats used.

3. Library 9(Graphics Tools) of the MACAPP forum on CompuServe.

4. Twilight Clone BBS in Silver Spring, MD. The Clone has 16 lines on sequential rollover, starting with 301-946-8677. To guarantee a V.32 connection, call 946-5034. Image is currently available at no charge from the Twilight Clone.

5. NTIS(National Technical Information Service), 5285 Port Royal Road, Springfield, VA 22161, phone 703-487-4650, order number PB90-500687 ($100 check, VISA, or Mastercard). Both the zippy.nimh.nih.gov FTP site and the Twilight Clone BBS are likely to have newer versions of Image than NTIS.

The author of Image, Wayne Rasband, can be reached at the following electronic mail addresses:

Internet, BitNet:	wayne@helix.nih.gov
AppleLink:	wayne@helix.nih.gov@internet#
CompuServe:	>INTERNET: wayne@helix.nih.gov

Chapter 11 Sources

TESTniques (Test Executive for LabVIEW)
P.O. Box 27401
Minneapolis, MN 55427
(612) 533-4107
FAX (612) 241-9972

Index

Numerics

4-20 mA current loops, 327
800 IEEE 488, 40

A

Acquire N Scans - ATrig, 248
Acquire N Scans - DTrig, 247
Acquire N Scans - Multi-ATrig, 248
Acquire N Scans - Multi-DTrig, 247
Acquire N Scans - SW Trig, 248
Acquire N Scans, 237
Acquire&Proc N Scans - Trig, 247–248
Acquire&Proc Scans - SW Trig, 248
Acquiring the Signal, 63
active filter, 65
actuators, 46, 325
Advanced LabVIEW class, 77
AESend Finder Open, 348
AESend Open, Run, Close VI, 419
AESend Run VI, 348
AI Acquire Waveform, 286, 298
AI Acquire Waveforms, 237, 238
AI Clear, 231, 234, 245, 252, 400
AI Config, 227, 233, 244, 245, 252, 399
AI Continuous Scan, 231, 240, 244, 250
AI Read One Scan, 236
AI Read, 237, 244, 248, 400
AI Sample Channels, 236
AI Single Channel, 91
AI Single Scan, 229, 234–235, 239, 287

AI Start, 234, 237, 244, 246, 399
AI Waveform Scan, 237, 246
alarms
    alarm annunciator panels, 378
    Alarm Handler VI, 375
    alarm handler, 374
    alarm summary displays, 342
    in process control, 373
algorithm, 152
aliasing, 64, 292
Alliance Program—Consultants, 40
Allow user to close window, 306
amplifiers, 58, 73
Analog Devices 5B series, 59, 62, 218
Analog Output Single Update, 253
analog signals, 47, 63
analog to digital converter (ADC), 45,
    63, 67, 73
analysis
    concepts, 276
    file formats, 278
    improving performance, 288
    VI library, 284, 416
Analyze the User's Needs, 134
AND Array Elements, 468
anti-aliasing, 58
    filter, 65
AO Clear, 252, 257, 400
AO Config, 252, 256, 399
AO Continuous Gen, 255
AO Start, 254, 256, 400

About the Author

Gary W. Johnson is an instrumentation engineer in the Chemical and Materials Science Department at the Lawrence Livermore National Laboratory. He is also a part-time consulting engineer, specializing in instrumentation and control, and works very closely with National Instruments, creating add-on features for the LabVIEW product. His professional interests include data acquisition/process control system design, instrumentation and transducers, analog circuit design, and Macintosh/LabVIEW programming.